July 1989

relevant to thesis on RS -
p117. orofacial dyskinesias

NEURAL MECHANISMS IN
DISORDERS OF MOVEMENT

Editors

A.R. Crossman

*Experimental Neurology Group,
Department of Cell and Structural Biology,
University of Manchester, Manchester M13 9RJ*

M.A. Sambrook

*Department of Neurology, University Hospital of
South Manchester, and Experimental
Neurology Group, University of Manchester,
Manchester M13 9PJ*

Cover illustration courtesy of Drs Crossman and Sambrook.
Pseudocolour transformation of an autoradiograph showing
the regional uptake of tritiated 2-deoxyglucose in hemiballism.

NEURAL MECHANISMS IN DISORDERS OF MOVEMENT

Edited by
A.R. CROSSMAN
and
M.A. SAMBROOK

British Library Cataloguing in Publication Data

Neural mechanisms in disorders of
   movement.—(Current problems in
   neurology, ISSN 0268-6252; V.9).
   1. Man. Movement disorders
I.   Crossman, A.R.   II. Sambrook, M.A.
   616.7'4

   ISBN 0-86196-916-4

First published in 1989 by
John Libbey & Company Ltd
13 Smiths Yard, Summerley St, London SW18 4HR, UK. (01) 947 2777
John Libbey Eurotext Ltd
6 rue Blanche, 92120 Montrouge, France. (1) 47 35 85 52

© John Libbey & Company Ltd. 1989 All rights reserved
Unauthorized duplication contravenes applicable laws

Typeset by Activity Ltd, Salisbury, Wiltshire.
Printed in Great Britain by Whitstable Litho Ltd, Whitstable, Kent

PREFACE

The term 'disorders of movement' is used here to include abnormalities of movement arising from disorders affecting the basal ganglia such as Parkinson's disease, chorea, ballism, dystonia and myoclonus. While generally they remain poorly understood, developments over the last two decades have introduced new insights into their aetiology, neuropharmacology and treatment. Techniques now available for the first time have presented opportunities for a rapid expansion in research both experimentally and in man. Computed tomography and magnetic resonance imaging have greatly enhanced non-invasive visualization of the basal ganglia while positron emission tomography has facilitated *in vivo* studies of brain neurochemistry. Dynamic studies of the structure and function of the basal ganglia from the first appearance of disease are now possible, in contrast to our previous reliance upon post mortem examination of the terminal changes of the disease process.

Serendipity has played an important role in our understanding of the basal ganglia and the disorders affecting them. The accidental self-administration of a synthetic pethidine analogue, 1-methyl-4-phenyl-1,2,3,6-tetrahydropyridine (MPTP) by a number of drug abusers led to the discovery of a form of parkinsonism which, on closer examination, bears increasing resemblance to idiopathic Parkinson's disease. This has stimulated a complete re-examination of the aetiology of Parkinson's disease and simultaneously provided the chance to develop a realistic experimental model of the condition in the monkey. It has also presented the opportunity of applying research methods not previously possible, such as studies of cerebral metabolism, neuronal activity and neurotransmitter receptor binding and the effects of drug administration under strictly controlled conditions. The wealth of scientific data on MPTP-induced parkinsonism that has appeared and its extrapolation to Parkinson's disease is testimony to the valuable potential of this chance discovery.

In parallel with these developments, experimental models of chorea, ballism and dystonia have become available. For the first time, the opportunity has presented itself of examining and comparing the pharmacology and the physiology of the basal ganglia under normal conditions and in disease states. This volume attempts to combine the information arising from these various scientific disciplines and to form a cohesive approach to the neural mechanisms which mediate normal and abnormal movements. The contributions arise from an international conference held in Manchester in April 1988, entitled 'Neural Mechanisms in Disorders of Movement', which was designed to bring together clinicians and basic scientists. The enthusiasm both of the delegates and of the many contributors is evidence of the ever increasing importance of this aspect of clinical neurology.

Finally, we wish to record our thanks to Merck, Sharp and Dohme Limited for their technical assistance and generous financial support towards the organisation of this conference.

Manchester
1988

M. A. Sambrook
A. R. Crossman

CONTENTS

Preface
M. A. Sambrook and A. R. Crossman — v

I. Anatomical, physiological and pharmacological studies

1. Dopaminergic and cholinergic systems in the striatum — 3
   A. M. Graybiel

2. Neuropharmacology of basal ganglia functions: relationship to pathophysiology of movement disorders — 17
   A. B. Young, R. L. Albin and J. B. Penney

3. The subthalamic nucleus in primates. A neuroanatomical and immunohistochemical study — 29
   A. Parent, L.-N. Hazrati and Y. Smith

4. The rat subthalamic nucleus: electrophysiological and behavioural data — 37
   J. Féger, I. Vezole, N. Renwart and P. Robledo

5. The compartmental organization of the ventral striatum in the rat — 45
   H. J. Groenewegen, G. E. Meredith, H. W. Berendse, P. Voorn and J. G. Wolters

6. Coding in spatial rather than joint coordinates of putamen and motor cortex preparatory activity preceding planned limb movements — 55
   G. E. Alexander and M. D. Crutcher

7. Neuronal activity in the primate caudate nucleus and ventral striatum reflects association between stimuli determining behaviour — 63
   G. V. Williams

8. The afterhyperpolarization in striatal cells — 75
   M. Garcia-Munoz, G. W. Arbuthnott and A. Rutherford

9. Dopamine uptake in the basal ganglia studied in real time with fast cyclic voltammetry: evidence for a low affinity, high capacity dopamine uptake system — 81
   J. A. Stamford, Z. L. Kruk and J. Millar

10. The role of 'non-specific' thalamic nuclei in the control of dopaminergic function in the basal ganglia of the rat — 89
    J. Cornwall, M. W. Jones, I. C. Kilpatrick and O. T. Phillipson

11. The pontine tegmentum as a functional interface between the basal ganglia and the spinal cord — 97
    E. Scarnati, S. Di Loreto and T. Florio

12. The primate nigro-striato-pallido-nigral system. Not a mere loop — 103
    G. Percheron, C. François, J. Yelnik and G. Fénelon

13. Heterogeneous role of neostriatal and mesostriatal pathology in disorders of movement: a review and new facts 111
    A. R. Cools, W. Spooren, E. Cuypers, R. Bezemer and R. Jaspers

II. Experimental models of movement disorders

14. The basal ganglia mechanisms mediating primate models of movement disorders 123
    M. A. Sambrook, A. R. Crossman, I. Mitchell, R. G. Robertson, C. E. Clarke and S. Boyce

15. Neural mechanisms in the basal ganglia related to the initiation of movements 145
    W. Schultz, R. Romo, E. Scarnati, A. Studer, G. Jonsson and E. Sundström

16. Excessive and unselective responses of medial pallidal neurones to both passive movement and striatal stimulation in monkeys with MPTP-induced parkinsonism 157
    M. Filion, L. Tremblay and P. J. Bédard

17. GABA/benzodiazepine receptors in the primate basal ganglia following treatment with MPTP: evidence for the differential regulation of striatal output by dopamine? 165
    R. G. Robertson, C. E. Clarke, S. Boyce, M. A. Sambrook and A. R. Crossman

18. The supplementary motor cortex and internally directed movement 175
    D. E. Thaler and R. E. Passingham

19. Anatomical, behavioural and positron emission tomography studies of unilateral excitotoxic lesions of the baboon caudate-putamen as a primate model of Huntington's disease 183
    Ph. Hantraye, D. Riche, M. Maziere, B. Maziere, C. Loc'h and O. Isacson

20. Striatal output pathways involved in mechanisms of rotation in rats 195
    J. S. McKenzie, A. D. Shafton and C. A. Stewart

21. Ipsilateral turning after local application of (-)sulpiride into the dorsal, but not the ventral, striatum of the rat 207
    S. Ahlenius, V. Hillegaart, C. J. Fowler and O. Magnusson

22. Sustained release 4-propyl-9-hydroxynaphthoxazine in the treatment of MPTP-induced parkinsonism in the primate 213
    C. E. Clarke, S. Boyce, M. A. Sambrook, A. R. Crossman and S. M. Stahl

23. A behavioural model for studying dopaminergic grafts in the marmoset 217
    L. E. Annett, S. B. Dunnett, D. C. Rogers, R. M. Ridley, H. F. Baker, P. Jenner and C. D. Marsden

24. Combined levodopa and bromocriptine therapy for Parkinson's disease: evidence suggesting that levodopa acts at sites in the substantia nigra pars reticulata 223
    H. A. Robertson and G. S. Robertson

25. 3-PPP enantiomers suppress neuroleptic-induced persistent abnormal movements in *Cebus apella* monkeys 229
    D. Clark, P. LeWitt and B. Kovacic

26. Alterations in the binding of the muscarinic ligand [3H]-quinuclidinyl benzilate (QNB) in brains from patients with Parkinson's disease and in hemi-parkinsonian monkeys 237
S. Boyce, P. Griffiths, C. C. Clarke, M. A. Sambrook and A. R. Crossman

III. Clinical aspects

27. The medical treatment of movement disorders 249
S. Fahn

Parkinson's disease

28. Current topics of interest in Parkinson's disease 271
E. Ch. Wolters and D. B. Calne

29. The relationship between parkinsonian rigidity and long-latency stretch reflex activity studied in individual patients 277
R. J. Meara and F. W. J. Cody

30. Cortical Lewy body disease: a pathological substrate for dementia in Parkinson's disease 287
G. Lennox, J. Lowe, J. Byrne, G. Reynolds and R. Godwin-Austen

31. Iron levels and transferrin binding sites in the post-mortem brains of parkinsonian patients and age-matched controls 291
P. D. Griffiths, M. A. Sambrook and A. R. Crossman

32. A 9 month follow-up study of cognitive impairment in idiopathic Parkinson's disease 297
J. L. Hulley, R. J. Smith, C. A. Cruickshank, F. Harrop, R. H. S. Mindham and A. G. Oswald

33. The bereitschaftspotential in Parkinson's disease 301
J. P. R. Dick, J. C. Rothwell, B. L. Day, R. Cantello, O. Buruma, M. Gioux, R. Benecke, A. Berardelli, P. D. Thompson and C. D. Marsden

34. Vibration-induced illusions of movement are normal in Parkinson's disease: implications for the mechanism of the movement disorder 307
A. P. Moore

35. The saccadic dysmetria in Parkinson's disease is stimulus-dependent 313
T. J. Crawford, L. Henderson and C. Kennard

36. Role of gait analysis in the assessment of parkinsonism in old age 319
A. L. Leeman, J. Hughes, S. G. Bowes, C. J. A. O'Neill, C. Weller, P. Clark, A. A. Deshmukh, P. W. Nicholson, S. M. Dobbs and R. J. Dobbs

Chorea, dystonia and myoclonus

37. Receptor autoradiographic studies in neurodegenerative disorders of the basal ganglia 327
J. N. Joyce, N. Lexow, B. Neal, H. Hurtig, J. Q. Trojanowski and A. Winokur

38. Increase in diazepam binding inhibitor (51-70) in Huntington's disease 337
J. A. Ball, P. W. J. Burnet and S. R. Bloom

39. Tryptophan metabolism and quinolinic acid in the brain in Huntington's disease — 343
   S. J. Pearson and G. P. Reynolds

40. Chorea-acanthocytosis (the Levine–Critchley syndrome): an update — 347
   E. M. R. Critchley

41. Reflex responses and movement velocity induced by head rotation in spasmodic torticollis — 351
   N. Bathien, P. Rondont, D. Bazalgette and M. Zattara

42. Orofacial dyskinesia: D-1/D-2 dopamine receptors in rodents, and familial/obstetric correlates of tardive dyskinesia in schizophrenia — 359
   J. L. Waddington, A. M. Murray, E. O'Callaghan and C. Larkin

43. Dopa-responsive dystonia: the spectrum of clinical manifestations in a well-studied family — 367
   T. G. Nygaard, D. Gardner-Medwin and C. D. Marsden

44. An effect of unilateral frontoparietal lesions on ipsilateral finger stability in man — 371
   J. D. Cole, H. I. Philip and E. M. Sedgwick

45. Clinical and electrophysiological observations in post-anoxic myoclonus — 375
   P. D. Thompson, A. Maertens de Noordhout, B. L. Day, J. C. Rothwell, W. Van der Kamp and C. D. Marsden

Surgical treatment

46. Lessons from surgical treatment of movement disorders — 385
   H. Narabayashi

47. Physiologically identified, selective ventrointermedius thalamotomy ameliorates various kinds of tremor and other disorders of movement related to tremor — 393
   T. Shibazaki, T. Hirai, M. Hirato, Y. Kawashima, M. Matsumura and C. Ohye

48. CT-guided thalamotomy in the treatment of movement disorders — 403
   T. Z. Aziz and M. J. Torrens

49. Chronic VIM-thalamic stimulation in movement disorders — 413
   A. L. Benabid, P. Pollak, A. Louveau, M. Hommel, J. Perret and J. de Rougemont

Imaging studies

50. The integrity of the dopaminergic system in multiple system atrophy and pure autonomic failure studied with PET — 419
   D. J. Brooks, E. P. Salmon, R Bannister, C. Mathias and R. S. J. Frackowiak

51. Single photon emission tomography (SPET) in progressive supranuclear palsy: a comparison with cortical dementias — 427
   P. J. Goulding, D. Neary, J. S. Snowden, B. Northen, A. W. I. Burjan, R. A. Shields, M. C. Prescott and H. J. Testa

52. A magnetic resonance imaging evaluation of movement disorders — 433
   Ph. Lebrun-Grandié, P. Kien, F. Tison, P. Henry, J. M. Caillé and B. Bioulac

53. Cerebral glucose metabolism in Parkinson's disease and the PD complex of Guam 445
R. F. Peppard, W. R. W. Martin, M. Guttman, E. Grochowski, J. Okada, P. L. McGeer, G. D. Carr, A. G. Phillips, J. C. Steele, J. K. C. Tsui and D. B. Calne

Index 453

I

ANATOMICAL, PHYSIOLOGICAL AND PHARMACOLOGICAL STUDIES

1

DOPAMINERGIC AND CHOLINERGIC SYSTEMS

IN THE STRIATUM

Ann M. Graybiel

*Department of Brain and Cognitive Sciences,
Massachusetts Institute of Technology,
45 Carleton Street, E25–618,
Cambridge, Massachusetts 02139, USA*

Summary

Both the cholinergic and the dopaminergic systems in the striatum are represented differently in its striosome and matrix subdivisions. This essay reviews the nature of these differences, some of the implications of this compartmentation for pharmacological targeting of specific subsystems in the basal ganglia, and new evidence that this compartmentation may be important in understanding the pathophysiology of certain extrapyramidal disorders.

Introduction

The signs and symptoms of basal ganglia disease are among the most baffling of those associated with disorders of the motor system. On the one hand, involuntary movements occur that disrupt normal motor sequences and the resting state. On the other hand, disorders occur in which the act of making a movement becomes difficult or even impossible. In certain classes of basal ganglia disease, these sensorimotor disorders may be accompanied by disturbances of affect, personality and cognition. These non-motor manifestations, no less than the hypokinetic and hyperkinetic extremes of disordered movement, challenge scientists trying to understand the organization of the basal ganglia and allied nuclei, including the dopamine-containing cell groups of the midbrain. Clinical evidence strongly implicates the dopaminergic and cholinergic mechanisms of the basal ganglia in the aetiology of these disorders. This brief review considers new findings related to these classic modulatory systems of the basal ganglia and to their status in extrapyramidal disease.

The cholinergic mechanism of the basal ganglia is principally, but not exclusively, represented by neurons intrinsic to the striatum—that is, intrinsic to the caudate nucleus, the putamen and the associated ventrally adjoining striatal tissues, including the nucleus accumbens septi and olfactory tubercle. The cholinergic interneurons of the striatum exert their influence locally on the pathways that lead into and out of the striatum. By contrast, dopaminergic influences on striatal function are exerted almost exclusively by an external control system originating in the substantia nigra pars compacta and associated parts of the A8-A9-A10 cell complex of the midbrain. There are other major catecholamine-containing cell groups in the brain, for example, the locus coeruleus, which may influence processing in the basal ganglia directly and indirectly. The serotonin-containing raphé nuclei also project directly to several parts of the basal ganglia and allied nuclei. Finally, other cholinergic systems, including those originating in the midbrain and in the basal forebrain, may influence the striatal mechanism indirectly; for example, they may interact with the dopamine-containing neurons that lie in the substantia nigra. Little is yet known about how these other modulatory systems affect the striatum. Within the striatum itself, however, the terminal arbors of cholinergic interneurons[1] and of dopamine-containing mesostriatal afferents[2] are in positions to exert controlling influences on trans-striatal circuits, and both are organized in relation to a highly differentiated functional architecture.

At the time these cholinergic and dopaminergic modulating systems were first studied, the architectural heterogeneity of the striatum was still unknown. Most of the early work on the biochemical anatomy of the striatum was done in the rat, a species in which the striatum is less differentiated than in the human. It is now firmly established, however, that there are two main tissue compartments in the striatum of all mammalian species studied, and that these compartments can be related to pharmacologically and anatomically distinct subsets of cholinergic and dopaminergic neurons. These compartments are: (1) the striosomes ('striatal bodies') which *in toto* account for about 20 per cent of the tissue of the caudate nucleus and putamen, and (2) the extrastriosomal matrix.[3] The striosomes are branched three-dimensional labyrinths running through the larger matrix. In cross-sections (Fig. 1), they appear as discs, ellipses and irregularly shaped forms with diameters comparable to those of cortical columns.[4,5] The central point of focus here is that both the cholinergic and the dopaminergic mechanisms of the striatum are represented differently within striosomes and extrastriosomal matrix. The potential clinical significance of this differential distribution rests on evidence that the striosomes and matrix represent functionally distinct subsystems in the striatum.

Functional subsystems in the basal ganglia

The most convincing evidence that the striosome and matrix subdivisions are functionally specialised is that the input-output connectivity of the striatum is organized in relation to these compartments[4,5] (Fig. 2). Every known major input connection of the striatum observes striosomal boundaries. Afferents from the sensory and motor cortex, from much of the parietal-temporal-occipital association cortex, and from the intralaminar thalamus project to the extrastriosomal matrix. By contrast, afferents from much of the frontal cortex, from the insula, from the temporal pole and from the basolateral amygdala and midline thalamus, project to striosomes.[6-9]

These findings seem to implicate the matrix in functions related to sensorimotor processing and the striosomal system in functions more closely related to the conditional and affective components of behaviour. However, although inputs to the striosomal system from sensory, sensory association, and motor areas of the neocortex seem to be negligible, the distinction between the respective inputs to the striosomal and matrical compartments is not adequately captured by a simple subdivision between sensorimotor and limbic system

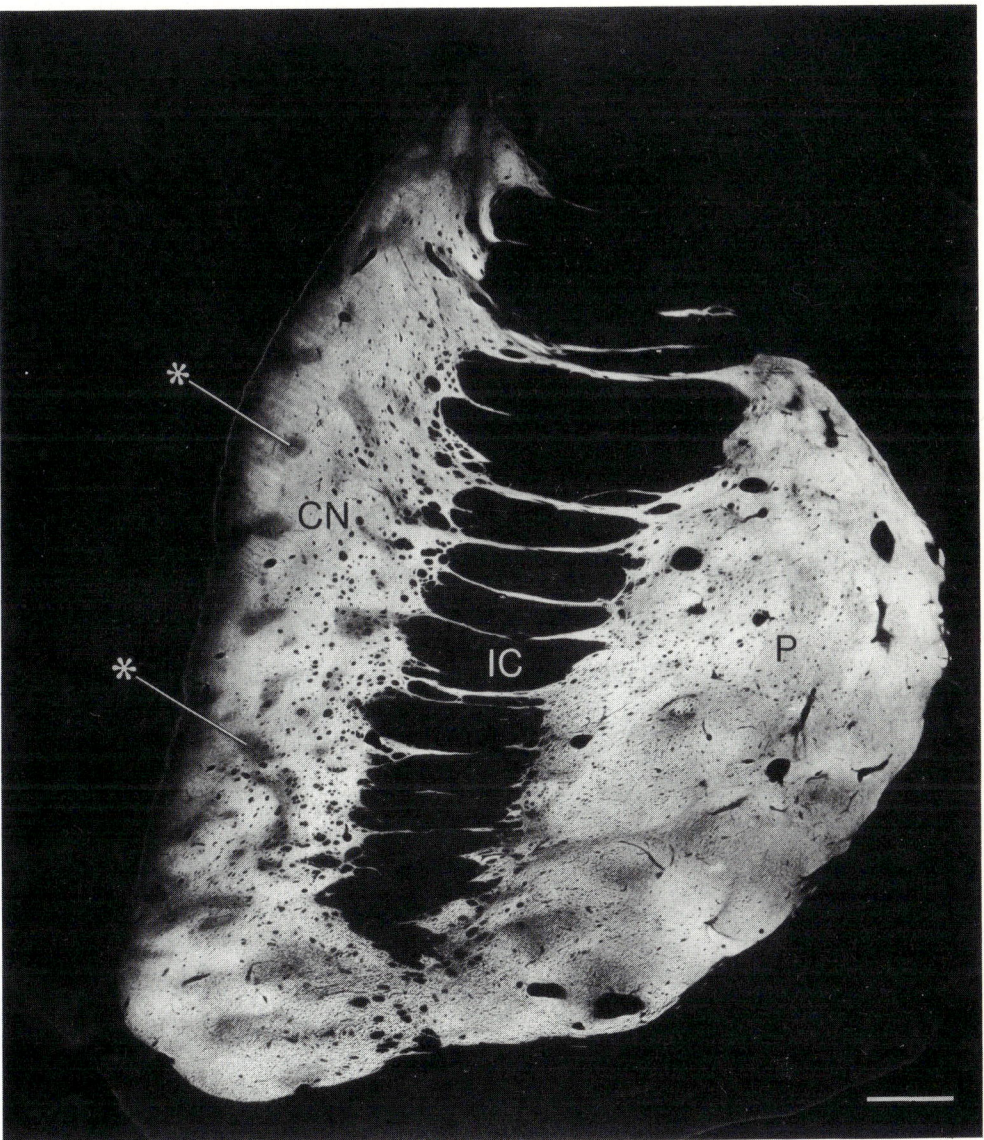

Fig. 1. *Photomicrograph illustrating striosomal distribution of acetylcholinesterase (AChE) activity in the human striatum*. The AChE staining appears white in the reverse-contrast image. The section is from a brain categorized as Huntington's disease stage 2. The AChE-poor striosomes (examples at asterisks) are still clearly visible in the caudate nucleus (CN) despite the loss of tissue. The patterning of the AChE staining in the putamen (P) is not as sharply defined as in the caudate nucleus; this is true also in the normal human striatum. The zone of diminished staining along the ventricular aspect of the caudate nucleus is probably a fixation artifact. IC – internal capsule. Scale bar = 2 mm. Based on [59] and [61].

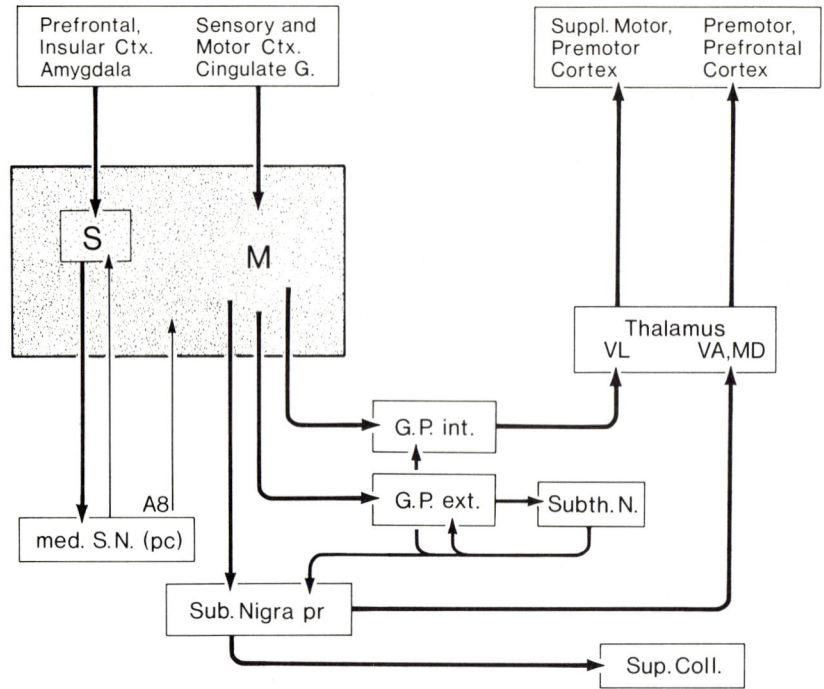

Fig. 2. *Schematic illustration of some of the main input-output connections of the striosome (S) and matrix (M) compartments of the striatum (stippled rectangle).* The density of stippling indicates the density of cholinergic neuropil in the striatum as seen in stains for choline acetyltransferase in the monkey[22] and human[22a]. The diagram shows that the striosomal system receives predominant cortical inputs from prefrontal and insular cortex, inputs from the (basolateral) amygdala, and inputs from a specialized medial part of the substantia nigra pars compacta (med. S.N.(pc)). The main outputs of the striosomal system are directed to the medial substantia nigra and may be directed to the substantia nigra pars compacta. The matrix system has quite different connections. Its cortical inputs are from sensory and motor cortex and the cingulate gyrus. Three output channels from the matrix are known: (1) to the substantia nigra pars reticulata (Sub. Nigra pr); (2) to the external segment of the globus pallidus (G.P. ext.); and (3) to the internal segment of the globus pallidus (G.P. int.) These three regions, in turn, participate in different connections leading, respectively, to the superior colliculus (Sup. Coll.) and the VA-MD nuclei of the thalamus; to the subthalamic nucleus (Subth. N.); and to the VL nucleus of the thalamus. Note that, together, the nigral and pallidal paths leading to the thalamus affect different regions of the frontal cortex. Note also that the external pallidum, by way of its subthalamic connections, can influence not only both segments of the pallidum but also the substantia nigra pars reticulata.

representations. First, there are components of the limbic system that preferentially project to the matrix—including one of the classic cortical territories of the Papez circuit, the cingulate gyrus.[8,9] Second, not all parts of the striosomal system share the same inputs[6] (and Ragsdale & Graybiel, unpublished data). Third, a heterogeneous organization of inputs to the matrix itself has been discovered.[10] This phenomenon has not yet been as thoroughly studied as the striosome/matrix compartmentalization but already several examples of patchy terminal distributions in the matrix have been identified.[6,7,10]

The efferent connections of the striosomal and matrix systems are also sharply different (Fig.2). The main outputs of the matrix are distributed within the pallidum and the substantia nigra pars reticulata.[11-13] The internal segment of the globus pallidus and the substantia nigra pars reticulata are the broadcast mechanisms of the basal ganglia: they give rise to the main pathways leading to the thalamus and to pre-motor centres of the brainstem. The nigro-collicular connection[14] is the most thoroughly studied of these pathways. It has been shown unequivocally to participate in controlling the production of saccadic eye movements.[15] Like the striato-pallido-thalamic pathway, this connection involves 'double inhibition' of the substantia nigra by the striatum, and of the superior colliculus by the substantia nigra. Accordingly, the net effect of excitation of the striatum, for example by a cortical input, is excitation (release of inhibition) of the superior colliculus.[16,17]

The external segment of the globus pallidus, which also receives its principal input from the extrastriosomal matrix, is a specialized part of the pallidum projecting to the subthalamic nucleus. The subthalamic nucleus projects back to the pallidum (and to the substantia nigra pars reticulata) in loop circuits now thought to excite the pallidum and substantia nigra. Thus neurons of the striatal matrix, by projecting to each segment of the pallidum, can apparently excite as well as inhibit the pallidum and substantia nigra pars reticulata.

Experiments in the cat[18] and most recently in the monkey[13] strongly suggest that the fibre projections to each of the two segments of the pallidum and to the substantia nigra pars reticulata arise from different neurons in the matrix. Conceivably, then, each of these pathways may be regulated separately. In fact, clinicopathological findings (see below) suggest that such independent regulation may be critical to understanding extrapyramidal dyskinesias. It is still uncertain whether this division of projection neurons in the matrix is related to the heterogeneity of inputs to the matrix mentioned above, but patchy constellations of striatal projection neurons have been observed both in the cat (Jimenez-Castellanos, J. and Graybiel, A.M., unpublished data; Glowinski et al., personal communication) and in the monkey.[13]

The striosomal system does not appear to contribute strongly, if at all, to these pathways to the globus pallidus and substantia nigra pars reticulata.[11-13,19] The striosomes do, however, project to the medial part of the substantia nigra (Fig. 2), possibly to the dopamine-containing pars compacta of the substantia nigra.[12,19,20] The striosomal system may therefore play a major role in controlling dopaminergic input to the striatum. Evidence in the cat suggests that a target of this striatonigral projection from striosomes lies in the immediate vicinity of the striosome-projecting part of the substantia nigra itself[20] (see below). If so, striosomes may participate in a nigro-striato-nigral modulatory loop of the type long postulated on physiological and pharmacological grounds.[21]

Cholinergic subsystems in the striatum

Striosomes were first noticed in sections stained for the enzyme acetylcholinesterase (AChE).[3] This is, of course, the degradative enzyme for acetylcholine, but AChE may have other functions as well. Accordingly, the lower AChE activity in the striosomes is not necessarily evidence for a lower density of cholinergic neuropil in the striosomes than the extrastriosomal matrix. This is precisely the conclusion, however, that more recent studies support.[22]

Maps of the cholinergic neurons and neuropil of the striatum (stained for the accepted marker-enzyme for cholinergic neurons, choline acetyltransferase) have now been made for the human[22a] as well as in the monkey and cat.[22] In each of these species, the processes of the intrinsic cholinergic neurons of the striatum are more concentrated in the matrix than in the striosomes. The neuropil of the striosomal system is also more weakly stained than that of the matrix. There are important regional differences in density of cholinergic neuropil as well. In the primate, the highest intensites of choline acetyltransferase immunoreactivity are in the putamen. The caudate nucleus has more clearly visible choline acetyltransferase-poor striosomes than the putamen, and apparently has altogether weaker staining in the matrix. Interestingly, some cholinergic neurons actually have their cell bodies inside striosomes, and cholinergic neurons lying near striosomal borders send some of their processes across the borders.[23] It is as though the cholinergic neurons participate in interactions between the two compartments.

A second type of evidence for augmented cholinergic function in the extrastriosomal matrix is the finding by Lowenstein and coworkers[24] that sodium-dependent high affinity uptake sites for acetylcholine, marked with the compound [^{3}H]hemicholinium, are more highly concentrated in the matrix than in striosomes. Thus, markers associated with the synthesis, degradation, and uptake of acetylcholine predominate in the part of the striatum that lies outside the striosomal system.

Cholinergic function in the striatum is not only quantitatively different inside and outside the striosomal system, but is also qualitatively different: cholinergic receptor-related ligand binding characteristics of the two compartments differ.[25,26] Most of the cholinergic receptors in the striatum are thought to be muscarinic, not nicotinic. Within the muscarinic family, common current nomenclature distinguishes two major classes, M1 and M2 types, though there may be a number of subtypes given that at least four genes control muscarinic receptor synthesis. Ligand binding studies carried out under conditions selective for the muscarinic M1 and M2 subtypes have shown that M1 muscarinic binding sites are the main class represented in the striatum but that M1 binding is higher inside striosomes than in the matrix.[25] By contrast, M2 muscarinic binding is nearly uniformly distributed across the two compartments.[25] The heightened M1 binding in striosomes has been observed in the human as well as in non-human primate and in cat; as with other receptor-binding distributions, in each species there are regional differences in the binding in the dorsal and in the ventral striatum (see[25,26]).

These patterns suggest that the influence of the cholinergic interneurons may predominate in the matrix because there is more cholinergic neuropil there, but that some cholinergic receptors (so far identified as the M1-subtype) are more concentrated in the striosomal system than in the matrix. The enhanced M1 binding in striosomes could serve to offset the lower density of cholinergic neuropil in the striosomes. One interesting possibility is that the augmentation might be selective for a particular set of intrastriosomal neural interactions between cholinergic neurons and other elements. For example, interactions might be with a subset of dopamine-containing fibres (see[25] and below).

Dopaminergic subsystems in the midbrain and in the striatum

There is now compelling evidence that dopamine-containing neurons in the midbrain are organized into groups projecting preferentially to striosomes and groups projecting preferentially to the extrastriosomal matrix.

The first experimental evidence for this arrangement was obtained in the cat and in the rat,[12,20,27,28] but such subdivisions have now also been demonstrated in the monkey (see[29]). The groupings apparently partly correspond to those of the original scheme of Dahlström & Fuxe[30] who distinguished (in the rat) *cell group A8* (the retrorubral region), *cell group A9* (the substantia nigra pars compacta and pars lateralis) and *cell group A10* (the ventral tegmental area). Cell group A8, which is made up of dopamine-containing neurons in the tegmentum, projects strongly to the extrastriosomal matrix (Fig. 2). Cell group A10, which is the cell group associated with the 'mesolimbic dopamine system', does project most strongly to the ventral striatum (nucleus accumbens-olfactory tubercle), but some of its fibres reach dorsally, where they appear to innervate tissue of the matrix. This A10-matrix connection, though weak, is another example of a limbic-related innervation of the extrastriosomal matrix.

Within the substantia nigra pars compacta itself, a particular zone, called the densocellular zone because of the close packing of its cells, has been identified in the cat as the origin of a strong nigrostriatal pathway to striosomes (Fig. 2).[27] Other parts of the substantia nigra pars compacta seem either to project both to striosomes and to matrix, or to project mainly to matrix;[27] but this is a difficult point to establish with certainty. Experiments on the monkey[29] have so far shown (a) that the region of cell group A8 projects to the extrastriosomal matrix, and (b) that there is a zone within the substantia nigra pars compacta that sends a massive and apparently selective projection to striosomes. The limits of the striosome-projecting zone have not yet been determined.

One of the most interesting recent findings in relation to these projection systems is that the striosome-projecting densocellular zone (as identified in the cat) has especially dense concentrations of haloperidol-sensitive non-dopaminergic 'sigma' sites.[31,32] Thus, drugs such as haloperidol may lead to highly selective effects in the dopamine-containing cell groups of the substantia nigra through an action not only at dopamine receptors but also at sigma sites, and may lead to different activity in the striosomal as opposed to the matrix-projecting systems of the dopamine-containing midbrain. There are also heterogeneous distributions of dopamine D1- and D2- selective ligands in the substantia nigra. Evidence to date suggests that the zones of dense D1 (ie, ^{3}HSCH23390) and sigma binding are at least partly complementary, whereas the sigma and D2 site distributions partly overlap.[32,33]

Within the striatum, markers for enzymes and receptor binding sites related to dopaminergic function also tend to follow striosomal ordering. The distributions of dopamine receptor binding sites are different for D1 and D2 subtypes. Especially in parts of the caudate nucleus, the striosomes are sites of preferential D1 binding[33] whereas binding sites for D2 receptor-ligands are more concentrated in the extracellular matrix and have heterogeneous distributions there.[34–37] The D2 sites, apparently negatively coupled to adenylate cyclase, have been the focus of considerable pharmacological and pharmaceutic interest for a number of years. The D1 sites, positively coupled to adenylate cyclase, have only recently become the subject of intense study because ligands suitable for relatively specific functional binding to these receptors have only recently become available. Evidence now suggests that the D1- and the D2-mediated effects of dopamine interact and that, in addition, some stereotypic behaviours are particularly related to activation of D1 sites.[38–39]

Immunostaining for the catecholamine synthesizing enzyme tyrosine hydroxylase is more strongly represented in the matrix than in striosomes. This is particularly clear in the caudate nucleus, but patterning of the immunoreactivity is apparent also in the putamen. These observations, first made in the human brain,[40,41] suggest at least three possibilities: (a) that there are more dopamine-containing terminals in the matrix than in the striosomes; (b) that the transport of tyrosine hydroxylase to nigrostriatal terminals is different for fibres innervating the two striatal compartments; or (c) that the rate of turnover of dopamine is different for fibres in and out of striosomes. Observations by Fuxe and his coworkers[42] favour the third possibility. Recent evidence that there are different mRNAs encoding tyrosine hydroxylase in the brain[43] points to a fourth alternative: that the expression of tyrosine hydroxylase is different in neurons innervating striosomes and matrix.

Pharmacological targeting of neurotransmitter-specific subsystems in the striatum

The immunohistochemical and ligand binding studies described suggest that there may be marked differences in the dopamine-related and acetylcholine-related activities in the striosomal and matrix systems. The differences are at the level of type of innervation as well as at the level of different representation of receptor subtypes. A major implication of these findings is that it should be possible to target drugs specifically to functionally specified dopaminergic or cholinergic subsystems. Eventually it may also be possible to elicit specific cholinergic and dopaminergic effects with neurons introduced into the striatum by grafting techniques.

What different behavioural effects would one expect to see from selective activation of striosomes or matrix? Our guides here must still be mainly from the anatomy because there is as yet no known physiological or behavioural correlate of the striosomal system. From the evidence just reviewed, however, there seems little reason to doubt that functional distinctions will be found between neurons in striosomes and matrix, and among different parts of the striosomal and matrical systems as well. Consequently, we can anticipate that the classic 'cholinergic-dopaminergic balance' of the clinical and pharmacological literature[44] will be found to subsume a variety of systems.

The distribution of cholinergic and dopaminergic neurons and receptors that may influence extrapyramidal functions extends beyond the confines of the striatal territories discussed above. Drug therapies must be designed to take these extrastriatal targets into account. Within the basal ganglia, important new findings include (a) the differential concentration in the primate of D1 binding sites in the internal pallidum[33,45] and D2 sites in the external pallidum;[34,45] (b) evidence for innervation of the primate pallidum by TH-containing (catecholaminergic) fibres;[33,46] (c) evidence suggesting extensive (D1) dopaminergic innervation of the cerebral cortex;[47,48] and (d) the presence of a widespread distribution of cholinergic fibres in subcortical regions probably including the substantia nigra.[49,50]

Finally, much new evidence suggests that dopamine receptor-selective ligands regulate the expression of neuropeptides in the striatum,[51-57] so that the very pharmaco-anatomic substrate of striatal function may undergo modification as a result of activation or blockade of dopaminergic transmission. As reviewed elsewhere[58] the neuropeptides expressed by striosomal and matrix neurons differ, and there is, in addition, heterogeneity in neuropeptide expression by neurons of the matrix. Compartmentalization of dopaminergic activity therefore could be of direct relevance to the regulation of peptides in these striatal neurons and in the striatopallidal and striatonigral pathways.

Disease states of the basal ganglia

The elaborate chemo-architecture just summarized provides a new context for studying the symptoms and the cell biology of basal ganglia diseases.

Huntington's disease

Striosomes survive in the Huntington's striatum into late stages of the disease[59-61] and may even be differentially spared[60] (see Fig. 1). Hence striosomal functions might be emphasized disproportionately in such brains. At the same time, two classes of neurons in the matrix, the somatostatin-containing interneurons and the cholinergic interneurons, are selectively spared despite profound loss of medium-sized neurons.[59,62-64] Young and her colleagues[65] have found a large loss of enkephalin-like immunoreactivity in the external segment of the pallidum with sparing of substance P in the internal pallidum in adult-onset Huntington's disease. This suggests that the matrix neurons projecting to the external segment reduce peptide synthesis or transport, or die early, or become otherwise dysfunctional in the disease. Such changes would primarily affect the subthalamic loop, possibly leading to involuntary movements by increasing thalamocortical discharge (see Young, this volume, p17). It must be emphasized, however, that such changes in activity of the subthalamic loop would occur in the context of a radically altered balance of neuronal activity in the striatum, possibly including heightened cholinergic function in the extrastriosomal matrix. As this matrix tissue gives rise to the striatopallidal and striatonigral 'broadcast systems' as well as to the pallidosubthalamic connection, changes in thalamocortical discharge could have more than one aetiology.

Gilles de la Tourette disease

A loss of dynorphin-like immunoreactivity from the internal pallidal segment has been reported in a single case of Gilles de la Tourette disease.[66] The function of dynorphin in the striatopallidal pathway is not known. Dynorphin B is thought to coexist with substance P in virtually all substance P-positive neurons in the striatum.[67,68] The finding in the Tourette's brain, if confirmed, would suggest a decline in modulation by dynorphin of the direct striatopallido-thalamic mechanism due to dysfunction of a specific subset of dynorphinimmunoreactive neurons in the striatum, presumably neurons of the matrix. Whether there is also down-regulation or loss of dynorphin from striosomes is not yet known. This would be of great interest given the association of striosomes with the amygdala and frontotemporal cortex (see above).

Parkinson's disease and related parkinsonian disorders

New evidence suggests that there may be selective vulnerability of subsets of neurons in the dopamine-containing cell complex of the midbrain in Parkinson's disease.[69] In Parkinson's brains, the degree of cell loss in the different dopaminergic cell groups of the midbrain is directly correlated with the percentage of neuromelanin-pigmented neurons present in these cell groups in normal brains. Interestingly, the different cell groups vary sharply in their content of visibly pigmented neurons. The close analysis of such neuronal loss should be of great help in distinguishing pathways related to different symptom complexes, because these cell groups have different projections to the striatum (and to non-striatal regions as well). For example, the A8 cell group, which projects strongly to the matrix, is less affected than the substantia nigra pars compacta. The ventral tegmental area and related median and paramedian cell formations are also less affected in the disease; these are the regions that project most strongly into the limbic parts of the striatum, and probably contribute fibres to the frontal lobes as well. The severe loss of noradrenergic neurons in Parkinson's disease, and the loss of cholinergic neurons in the pedunculopontine nucleus,[70] must also be reflected in the symptom complexes.

The possibility that MPTP-induced parkinsonism is related to selective death of melanized neurons is favoured by the finding that MPTP and its toxic metabolite, MPP$^+$, bind to neuromelanin.[71] Selective sparing of certain subpopulations of neurons in MPTP-treated monkeys has been reported.[72,73] Unfortunately, the onset of the effects of MPTP has not been followed systematically, but there now is evidence in the dog that at short survival times after MPTP treatment there is selective degeneration of fibres innervating the extrastriosomal matrix (see[74]; and personal communication).

Acknowledgements—Supported by The Seaver Institute and The McKnight Foundation. I thank Mr. Glenn Holm and Ms. Elizabeth Connors for their help in manuscript preparation, Miss Alice Flaherty and Mr. Fu-Chin Liu for reading the manuscript, and Mr. Henry Hall for help with the illustrations.

References

1. Izzo, P. N. & Bolam, J. P. (1988): Cholinergic synaptic input to different parts of spiny striatonigral neurons in the rat. *J. Comp. Neurol.* **269**, 219–234.
2. Fruend, T. F., Powell, J. F. & Smith, A. D. (1984): Tyrosine hydroxylase immunoreactive synaptic boutons in contact with identified striatonigral neurons, with particular reference to dendritic spines. *Neuroscience* **13**, 1189–1215.
3. Graybiel, A. M. & Ragsdale, C. W. (1978): Histochemically distinct compartments in the striatum of human, monkey, and cat demonstrated by acetylthiocholinesterase staining. *Proc. Natl. Acad. Sci. USA* **75**, 5723–5726.
4. Graybiel, A. M. (1983): Compartmental organization of the mammalian striatum. In *Molecular and cellular interactions underlying higher brain function*, eds J.-P. Changeux, J. Glowinski, M. Imbert & F. E. Bloom, pp 247–256. Amsterdam: Elsevier.
5. Graybiel, A. M. & Ragsdale, C. W. (1983): Biochemical anatomy of the striatum. In *Chemical neuroanatomy*, ed P. C. Emson, pp 427–504. New York: Raven Press.
6. Ragsdale, C. W. & Graybiel, A. M. (1988): Fibers from the basolateral nucleus of the amygdala selectively innervate striosomes in the caudate nucleus of the cat. *J. Comp. Neurol.* **269**, 506–522.
7. Ragsdale, C. W. & Graybiel, A. M. (1988): Multiple patterns of thalamostriatal innervation in the cat. In *Cellular thalamic mechanisms*, eds M. Bentivoglio & R. Spreafico, pp 261–267. Amsterdam: Elsevier.
8. Donoghue, J. P. & Herkenham, M. (1986): Neostriatal projections from individual cortical fields conform to histochemically distinct striatal compartments in the rat. *Brain Res.* **365**, 367–403.
9. Ragsdale, C. W. & Graybiel, A. M. (1984): Further observations on the striosomal organization of frontostriatal projections in cats and monkeys. *Soc. Neurosci. Abstr.* **10**, 514.
10. Malach, R. & Graybiel, A. M. (1986): Mosaic architecture of the somatic sensory-recipient sector of the cat's striatum. *J. Neurosci.* **6**, 3436–3458.
11. Graybiel, A. M., Ragsdale, C. W. & Moon Edley, S. (1979): Compartments in the striatum of the cat observed by retrograde cell-labelling. *Exp. Brain Res.* **34**, 189–195.
12. Gerfen, C. R. (1985): The neostriatal mosaic. I. Compartmental organization of projections from the striatum to the substantia nigra in the rat. *J. Comp. Neurol.* **236**, 454–476.
13. Gimenez-Amaya, J. M. & Graybiel, A. M. (1988): Compartmental origins of the striatopallidal projection in the primate. *Soc. Neurosci. Abstr.* **14**, 156.
14. Graybiel, A. M. (1984): Neurochemically specified subsystems in the basal ganglia. In *Functions of the basal ganglia*. Ciba Foundation Symposium 107, eds D. Evered & M. O'Connor, pp 114–143. London: Pitman Press.
15. Hikosaka, O. & Wurtz, R. H. (1983): Visual and oculomotor functions of monkey (Macaca mulatta) substantia nigra pars reticulata. 4. Relation of substantia nigra to superior colliculus. *J. Neurophysiol.* **49**, 1285–1301.
16. Hikosaka, O. & Wurtz, R. H. (1985): Modification of saccadic eye movements by gamma aminobutyric-acid-related substances. 2. Effects of muscimol in monkey (Macaca mulatta) substantia nigra pars reticulata. *J. Neurophysiol.* **53**, 292–308.
17. Deniau, J. W. & Chevalier, G. (1984): Synaptic organization of output pathways of the basal ganglia: an electroanatomical approach in the rat. In *Functions of the basal ganglia*. Ciba Foundation Symposium 107, eds D. Evered & M. O'Connor, pp 48–58. London: Pitman Press.
18. Beckstead, R. M. & Cruz, C. J. (1986): Striatal axons to the globus pallidus, entopeduncular nucleus and substantia nigra come mainly from separate cell populations in cat. *Neuroscience* **19**, 147–158.
19. Smith, Y. & Parent, A. (1986): Differential connections of caudate nucleus and putamen in the squirrel monkey (Saimiri sciureus). *Neuroscience* **18**, 347–371.
20. Jimenez-Castellanos, J. & Graybiel, A. M. (1985): The dopamine-containing innervation of striosomes: nigral subsystems and their striatal correspondents. *Soc. Neurosci. Abstr.* **11**, 1249.
21. Grace, A. A. & Bunney, B. S. (1985): Opposing effects of striatonigral feedback pathways on midbrain dopaminergic cell activity. *Brain Res.* **333**, 271–284.
22. Graybiel, A. M., Baughman, R. W. & Eckenstein, F. (1986): Cholinergic neuropil of the striatum observes striosomal boundaries. *Nature* **323**, 625–627.

22a Hirsch, E. C., Graybiel, A. M., Hersh, L. B., Duyckaerts, C. & Agid, Y. (1988): Striosomes and extrastriosomal matrix contain different amounts of immunoreactive-choline acetyltransferase in the human striatum. *Neurosci. Lett.* (In Press).
23 Penney, G. R., Wilson, C. J. & Kitai, S. T. (1988): Relationship of the axonal and dendritic geometry of spiny projection neurons to the compartmental organization of the striatum. *J. Comp. Neurol.* **269**, 275–289.
24 Lowenstein, P. R., Slesinger, P. A., Singer, H. S., Walker, L. C., Casanova, M. F., Price, D. L. & Coyle, J. T. (1987): An autoradiographic study of the development of [3H] hemicholinium-3 binding sites in human and baboon basal ganglia: a marker for the sodium-dependent high-affinity choline uptake system. *Devel. Brain Res.* **34**, 291–297.
25 Nastuk, M. A. & Graybiel, A. M. (1988): Autoradiographic localization and biochemical characteristics of M1 and M2 muscarinic binding sites in the striatum of the cat, monkey, and human. *J. Neurosci.* **8**, 1052–1062.
26 Nastuk, M. A. & Graybiel, A. M. (1985): Patterns of muscarinic cholinergic binding in the striatum and their relation to dopamine islands and striosomes. *J. Comp. Neurol.* **237**, 176–194.
27 Jimenez-Castellanos, J. & Graybiel, A. M. (1987): Subdivisions of the dopamine-containing A8-A9-A10 complex identified by their differential mesostriatal innervation of striosomes and extrastriosomal matrix. *Neuroscience* **21**, 223–242.
28 Moon Edley, S. & Herkenham, M. (1984): Heterogeneous dopaminergic projections to the neostriatum of the rat: nuclei of origin dictate relationship to opiate receptor patches. *Anat. Rec.* **208**, 120A.
29 Feigenbaum, L. A. & Graybiel, A. M. (1988): Heterogeneous striatal afferent connections from distinct regions of the dopamine-containing midbrain of the primate. *Soc. Neurosci. Abstr.* **14**, 156.
30 Dahlström, A. & Fuxe, K. (1964): Evidence for the existence of monoamine containing neurons in the central nervous system. I. Demonstration of monoamines in the cell bodies of brainstem neurons. *Acta Physiol. Scand.* **62**, 1–55.
31 Graybiel, A. M., Weber, E., Besson, M.-J. & Karuzis, K. (1986): Haloperidol-sensitive sigma receptors in the substantia nigra pars compacta: autoradiographic evidence for specific anatomical localization of [3H] DTG binding sites. *Soc. Neurosci. Abstr.* **13**, 28.
32 Graybiel, A. M., Besson, M.-J. & Weber, E. (1988): Neuroleptic-sensitive binding sites in the nigrostriatal system: evidence for a differential distribution of sigma sites in the substantia nigra, pars compacta of the cat. *J. Neurosci.* (In Press).
33 Besson, M.-J., Graybiel, A. M. & Nastuk, M. A. (1988): [3H]-SCH23390 binding to D1 dopamine receptors in the basal ganglia of the cat and primate: delineation of striosomal compartments and pallidal and nigral subdivisions. *Neuroscience* **26**, 101–119.
34 Richfield, E. K., Young, A. B. & Penney, J. B. (1987): Comparative distribution of dopamine D-1 and D-2 receptors in the basal ganglia of turtles, pigeons, rats, cats, and monkeys. *J. Comp. Neurol.* **262**, 446–463.
35 Joyce, J. N., Sapp, D. W. & Marshall, J. F. (1986): Human striatal dopamine receptors are organized in compartments. *Proc. Natl. Acad. Sci. USA* **83**, 8002–8006.
36 Beckstead, R. M., Wooten, G. F. & Trugman, J. M. (1988): Distribution of D1 and D2 dopamine receptors in the basal ganglia of the cat determined by quantitative autoradiography. *J. Comp. Neurol.* **268**, 131–145.
37 Loopuijt, L. D., Sebens, J. B. & Korf, J. (1981): A mosaic-like distribution of opiate receptors, parafascicular projections, and acetylcholinesterase in rat striatum. *Nature* **291**, 415–418.
38 Molloy, A. G. & Waddington, J. L. (1985): Sniffing, rearing and the locomotor response to the dopamine agonist R-SKF 38393 and to apomorphine: differential interactions with the selective D1 and D2 agonists SCH23390 and metoclopramide. *Eur. J. Pharm.* **108**, 305–308.
39 Rosengarten, H., Schweitzer, J. W. & Friedhoff, A. J. (1983): Introduction of oral dyskinesias in naive rats by D1 stimulation. *Life Sci.* **33**, 2479–2482.
40 Graybiel, A. M., Hirsch, E. C. & Agid, Y. A. (1987): Differences in tyrosine hydroxylase-like immunoreactivity characterize the mesostriatal innervation of striosomes and extrastriosomal matrix at maturity. *Proc. Natl. Acad. Sci. USA* **84**, 303–307.

41 Ferrante, R. J. & Kowall, N. W. (1987): Tyrosine hydroxylase-like immunoreactivity is distributed in the matrix compartment of normal human and Huntington's disease striatum. *Brain Res.* **416**, 141–146.
42 Fuxe, K., Andersson, K., Schwarcz, R., Agnati, L. F., Pérez de la Mora, M., Hökfelt, T., Goldstein, M., Ferland, L., Possani, L. & Tapia, R. (1979): Studies on different types of dopamine nerve terminals in the forebrain and their possible interaction with neurons containing GABA, glutamate, and opioid peptides. In *Advances in neurology*, Vol. 24, eds L. J. Poirier, T. L. Sourkes & P. J. Richard, pp 199–215. New York: Raven Press.
43 Grima, B., Lamouroux, A., Boni, C., Julien, J.-F., Javoy-Agid, F. & Mallet J. (1987): A single human gene encoding multiple tyrosine hydroxylases with different predicted functional characteristics. *Nature* **326**, 707–711.
44 Lehmann, J. & Langer, S. Z. (1983): The striatal cholinergic interneuron: synaptic target of dopaminergic terminals? *Neuroscience* **10**, 1105–1120.
45 Graham, W. C. & Crossman, A. R. (1987): Autoradiographic localization of dopamine D1 binding sites in areas receiving striatal input. *Eur. J. Pharm.* **142**, 479–481.
46 Parent, A. & Smith, Y (1987). Differential dopaminergic innervation of the two pallidal segments in the squirrel monkey (Saimiri sciureus). *Brain Res.* **426**, 397–400.
47 Boyson, S. J., McGonigle, P. & Molinoff, P. B. (1986): Quantitative localization of the D1 and D2 subtypes of dopamine receptors in rat brain. *J. Neurosci.* **6**, 3177–3188.
48 Reader, T. A., Brieve, R., Gottberg, E., Diop, L. & Grondin, L. (1988): Specific [3H]SCH23390 binding to dopamine D1 receptors in cerebral cortex and neostriatum: evidence for heterogeneities in affinity states and cortical distribution. *J. Neurochem.* **50**, 451–463.
49 Beninato, M. & Spencer, R. (1987): A cholinergic projection from the pedunculopontine tegmental nucleus to the substantia nigra in the rat: a light and electron microscopic immunohistochemical study. *Soc. Neurosci. Abstr.* **13**, 28.
50 Henderson, Z. & Greenfield, S. A. (1987): Does the substantia nigra have a cholinergic innervation? *Neurosci. Lett.* **73**, 109–113.
51 Young, W. S., Bonner, T. I. & Brann, M. R. (1986): Mesencephalic dopamine neurons regulate the expression of neuropeptide mRNAs in the rat forebrain. *Proc. Natl. Acad. Sci. USA* **83**, 9827–9831.
52 Sabol, S. L., Yoshikawa, K. & Hong, J. S. (1983): Regulation of met-enkephalin precursor mRNA in rat striatum by haloperidol and lithium. *Biochem. Biophys. Res. Commun.* **113**, 391–399.
53 Tang, F., Costa, E. & Schwartz, J. P. (1983): Increase of proenkephalin mRNA and enkephalin content of the rat striatum after daily injection of haloperidol for 2 to 3 weeks. *Proc. Natl. Acad. Sci. USA* **80**, 3841–3844.
54 Romano, G. J., Shivers, B. D., Harlan, R. E., Howells, R. D. & Pfaff, D. W. (1987): Haloperidol increases proenkephalin mRNA levels in the caudate-putamen of the rat: a quantitative study at the cellular level using in situ hybridisation. *Mol. Brain. Res.* **2**, 33–41.
55 Angulo, J. A., Davis, L. G., Burkhart, B. A. & Christoph, G. R. (1986): Reduction of striatal dopaminergic neurotransmission elevates striatal proenkephalin mRNA. *Eur. J. Pharmacol.* **130**, 343–344.
56 Morris, B. J., Herz, A. & Höllt, V. (1988): Localisation of striatal opioid gene expression, and its modulation by the mesostriatal dopamine pathway: an in-situ hybridisation study. *Molec. Neurosci.* (In Press).
57 Morris, B. J., Höllt, V. & Herz, A. (1988): Dopaminergic regulation of striatal proenkephalin mRNA and prodynorphin mRNA: contrasting effects of D1 and D2 antagonists. *Neuroscience* **25**, 525–532.
58 Graybiel, A. M. (1986): Neuropeptides in the basal ganglia. In *Neuropeptides in neurologic and psychiatric disease*, eds J. B. Martin & J. D. Barchas, pp 135–161. New York: Raven Press.
59 Feigenbaum, L. A. Graybiel, A. M. Vonsattel, J. P., Richardson, E. P. & Bird, E. D. (1986): Striosomal markers in the striatum in Huntington's disease. *Soc. Neurosci. Abstr.* **12**, 1328.
60 Ferrante, R. J., Kowall, N. W., Beal, M. F., Martin, J. B., Bird, E. D. & Richardson, E. P. (1987): Morphologic and histochemical characteristics of a spared subset of striatal neurons in Huntington's disease. *J. Neuropathol. Exp. Neurol.* **46**, 12–27.

61 Graybiel, A. M. (1983): In *Peptides in neurology*, ed. M. Rosser *et al.* Sandoz conference, Cambridge, England.
62 Ferrante, R. J., Kowall, N. W., Beal, M. F., Richardson, E. P., Bird, E. D. & Martin, J. B. (1985): Selective sparing of a class of striatal neurons in Huntington's disease. *Science* **230**, 561–563.
63 Ferrante, R. J., Beal, M. F., Kowall, N. W., Richardson, E. P. & Martin, J. B. (1987): Sparing of acetylcholinesterase-containing striatal neurons in Huntington's disease. *Brain Res.* **411**, 162–166.
64 Dawbarn, D., De Quidt, M. E. & Emson, P. C. (1985): Survival of basal ganglia neuropeptide Y-somatostatin neurons in Huntington's disease. *Brain Res.* **340**, 251–260.
65 Albin, R. L., Reiner, A., Anderson, K. D., D'Amato, C. J., Penney, J. B. & Young, A. B. (1987): Differential loss of substance P-containing and enkephalin-containing striatofugal projections in adult-onset and juvenile-onset Huntington's disease. *Soc. Neurosci. Abstr.* **13**, 1361.
66 Haber, S. N., Kowall, N. W., Vonsattel, J. P., Bird, E. D. & Richardson, E. P. (1986): Gilles de la Tourette's Syndrome: A postmortem neuropathological and immunohistochemical study. *J. Neurol. Sci.* **75**, 225–241.
67 Besson, M.-J., Graybiel, A. M. & Quinn, B. (1986): Coexistence of dynorphin B-like and substance P-like immunoreactivity in striatal neurons in the cat. *Soc. Neurosci. Abstr.* **12**, 876.
68 Besson, M.-J., Graybiel, A. M. & Quinn, B. (1988): Patterns of coexistence of neuropeptides and glutamic acid decarboxylase in neurons in the feline striatum. *Soc. Neurosci. Abstr.* **14**, 156.
69 Hirsch, E., Graybiel, A. M. & Agid, Y. A. (1988): Melanized dopaminergic neurons are differentially susceptible to degeneration in Parkinson' disease. *Nature* (In Press).
70 Hirsch, E. C., Graybiel, A. M., Duyckaerts, C. & Javoy-Agid, F. (1987): Neuronal loss in the pedunculopontine tegmental nucleus in Parkinson disease and in progressive supranuclear palsy. *Proc. Natl. Acad. Sci. USA* **84**, 5976–5980.
71 D'Amato, R. J., Lipman, Z. P. & Snyder, S. H. (1986): Selectivity of the parkinsonian neurotoxin MPTP: toxic metabolite MPP$^+$ binds to neuromelanin. *Science* **231**, 987–989.
72 Deutch, A. Y., Elsworth, J. D., Goldstein, M., Fuxe, K., Redmond, E. D., Sladek, J. R. & Roth, R. H. (1986): Preferential vulnerability of A8 dopamine neurons in the primate to the neurotoxin 1-methyl-4-phenyl-1,2,3,6-tetrahydropyradine. *Neurosci. Lett.* **68**, 51–56.
73 German, D. C., Dubach, M., Askari, S., Speciale, S. G. & Bowden, D. M. (1988): 1-methyl-4-phenyl-1,2,3,6-tetrahydropyridine-induced parkinsonian syndrome in Macaca fascicularis: which midbrain dopaminergic neurons are lost? *Neuroscience* **24**, 161–174.
74 Wilson, J. S., Turner, B. H., Morrow, G. D. & Hartman, P. J. (1987): MPTP produces a mosaic-like pattern of terminal degeneration in the caudate nucleus of the dog. *Brain Res.* **423**, 329–332.

2

NEUROPHARMACOLOGY OF BASAL GANGLIA FUNCTIONS: RELATIONSHIP TO PATHOPHYSIOLOGY OF MOVEMENT DISORDERS

Anne B. Young, Roger L. Albin and John B. Penney

Department of Neurology, University of Michigan, Ann Arbor, Michigan 48104-1687, USA

Summary

Disorders of basal ganglia function give rise to a variety of motor symptoms ranging from the excessive and adventitious movements of Huntington's disease (HD) to the restriction of movements seen in Parkinson's disease (PD). We present a model based on a synthesis of animal experimental and human postmortem data that accounts for both the hyperkinesis of HD and the hypokinesis of PD. In this model, chorea results from selective dysfunction of striatal neurons projecting to the lateral globus pallidus. In PD, the loss of dopaminergic input to the striatum results in complex changes in striatal projection neuron function with resulting disinhibition of the medial globus pallidus and substantia nigra pars reticulata. The differential activity and dysfunction of different subpopulations of striatal neurons underlies some of the varied motor manifestations of basal ganglia disease.

Introduction

One of the challenges for scientists studying the anatomy and biochemistry of the basal ganglia is to explain the multitude of clinical symptoms that can arise from pathology in this region of the human brain. On the one hand, disorders such as Parkinson's disease and progressive supranuclear palsy can cause slowness of movement, rigidity and, in certain instances, tremor. Conversely, Huntington's disease is characterized by chorea and dystonia. Wilson's disease can manifest any or all of the above clinical signs. Until

---

Correspondence may be sent: Anne B. Young, M.D., Ph.D., Neuroscience Laboratory Bldg., 1103 E Huron, Ann Arbor, MI 48104-1687.

recently, it has been difficult to reproduce in primates the clinical symptoms observed in human basal ganglia disorders. Rodents are sufficiently different from primates for it to be almost impossible to mimic human clinical disorders in animals such as rats and mice. In the past decade, substantial information from animals and human postmortem samples has accumulated concerning the biochemistry and functional anatomy of the basal ganglia and it is now possible to speculate on how pathology in specific pathways may give rise to certain clinical signs.[1,2] In this chapter we shall review recent investigations which suggest that specific neuronal subpopulations in the striatum are differentially affected in Parkinson's and Huntington's diseases. The consequences of differential pathology in these neuronal subpopulations will be discussed in the context of our current understanding of striatal inputs and outputs.

Early models of striatal function

For many years, the caudate nucleus and putamen were thought to process information received from various cortical regions in a uniform fashion.[1,3,4] Striatal inputs from subcortical nuclei such as the substantia nigra and raphé nucleus were thought to modify striatal neuron function, again, in a uniform manner. Cortical inputs were thought to excite striatal neurons whereas dopamine inputs from substantia nigra pars compacta were considered inhibitory to striatal cholinergic interneurons which in turn excited striatal medium-sized spiny GABAergic output neurons (Fig. 1).[1,5,6] This scheme could be used to explain the symptoms of Parkinson's and Huntington's diseases. These two prototypic basal ganglia disorders were considered clinical opposites. In Parkinson's disease patients develop slowness of movement, lack of spontaneous movement, impaired fine motor coordination, tremor and rigidity.[7,8] In contrast, in Huntington's disease, individuals manifest excessive movements characterized by brief random involuntary movements of the limbs, trunk or face (chorea) which cannot be completely suppressed voluntarily. In addition, they develop abnormal rapid eye movements (saccades) and slow and irregular fine motor coordination.[9]

Patients with the two diseases differ in their response to drugs. Persons with Parkinson's disease treated with excess levodopa develop involuntary movements that are virtually indistinguishable from the chorea seen in Huntington's disease, while dopamine D-2 receptor blockers, the butyrophenones and phenothiazines, make their rigidity, bradykinesia and tremor worse. Persons with Huntington's disease, however, treated with D-2 blockers have a diminution in their involuntary movements and can develop rigidity, tremor and bradykinesia, similar to that seen in Parkinson's disease, while levodopa can make their chorea worse. Another feature that distinguishes the two diseases is their response to cholinergic medications. Parkinsonian patients benefit from anticholinergic medication whereas the same agents often worsen the involuntary movements in Huntington's disease. Cholinergic agonists aggravate symptomatology in Parkinson's disease yet improve the signs of Huntington's disease.[6] Thus, in terms of manipulation of the dopamine and acetylcholine systems, these two diseases appear as clinical opposites. In Parkinson's disease, there is insufficient dopamine and excess acetylcholine whereas in Huntington's disease, dopamine predominates and acetylcholine is deficient.

Test of the model

The simple scheme described above was supported by pharmacological and neuropathological data in Huntington's disease demonstrating that cholinergic interneurons were depleted and dopaminergic afferents to the striatum were relatively concentrated

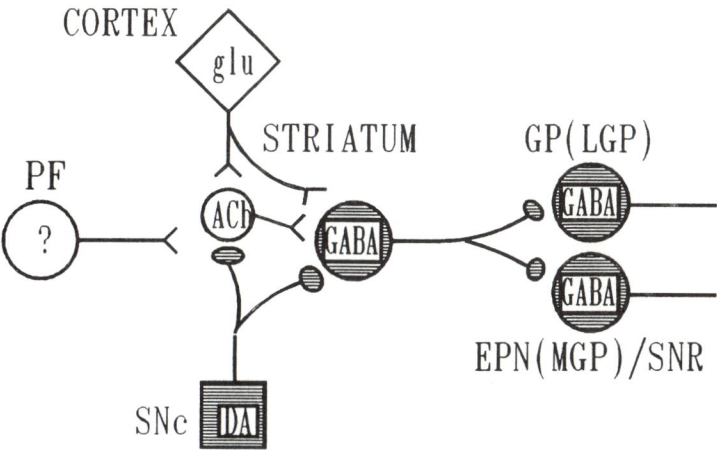

Fig. 1. *Simplified diagram of basal ganglia circuitry based on initial concepts of striatal functional anatomy.* The primary inputs to striatum were considered to be from the cerebral cortex (excitatory and glutamatergic), the parafascicular nucleus of thalamus (PF) (excitatory but transmitter unknown) and the substantia nigra pars compacta (SNC) (dopaminergic and presumably inhibitory). Filled symbols are inhibitory and open symbols are excitatory. After striatal lesions, a local decrease in GABA/benzodiazepine receptors and an increase in globus pallidus (GP) (or lateral globus pallidus, LGP, in primates), entopeduncular (EPN) (or medial globus pallidus, MGP, in primates) and substantia nigra pars reticulata (SNR) is expected. In animals with lesions of the SNC, a decrease in striatal and GP, EPN and SNR receptors is expected because of the removal of a presumed inhibitory input and the subsequent overactivity of these striatal GABAergic neurons. See text for amplification on this model and the results of experiments testing it.

secondary to the loss of intrinsic striatal neurons.[10,11] In Parkinson's disease there was a loss of the striatal dopamine afferents from substantia nigra and preservation of cholinergic striatal interneurons.[12,13] In Parkinson's disease, then, there would appear to be an excess of striatal outflow because of the loss of dopaminergic inhibition and in Huntington's disease there would be deficient striatal GABAergic activity because of loss of the intrinsic striatal neurons. Since the primary projection areas of the striatum, the lateral and medial globus pallidus and the substantia nigra pars reticulata, are also GABAergic and project to the brainstem and thalamus, the consequences of striatal neuron loss would be disinhibition of the projection areas and excess inhibition of thalamus.[1,14]

In studies of GABA and benzodiazepine receptors in rat models of Huntington's disease, GABA and benzodiazepine receptors were upregulated in all three primary striatal projection areas after striatal lesions, while GABA receptors were significantly decreased in the thalamus consistent with the loss of inhibition of a GABAergic, inhibitory projection to the thalamus.[15] Electrophysiological data by Deniau and colleagues likewise supported this concept that the striatum normally functions to disinhibit thalamocortical systems.[16,17]

If Parkinson's disease is in fact the opposite of Huntington's disease, one would predict that interruption of the nigrostriatal dopamine pathway would result in the opposite receptor changes, ie downregulation of striatal and pallidal GABA receptors and upregulation of thalamic GABA receptors. Such studies in rodents, however, produced a decrease in striatal and globus pallidus GABA receptors after the nigral lesion, in keeping with our hypothesis, though they also produced a marked increase in substantia nigra pars reticulata (SNR) and entopeduncular nucleus (EPN) GABA and benzodiazepine receptors, contrary to our hypothesis.[18] The increase in EPN and SNR GABA receptors were of the same or even higher magnitude than the changes that occurred after striatal lesions themselves. These data suggested that dopamine was functionally inhibitory to GABAergic striatal neurons projecting to globus pallidus but was functionally excitatory to GABAergic striatal neurons projecting to EPN and SNR.[2,18–20] Whether these differential effects were produced locally in the striatum or via direct dopamine projections to EPN and SNR is not known.

On the other hand, in the past five years it has become clear that subpopulations of striatal neurons are not only distinguished on the basis of their differential projections to the basal ganglia outflow regions but also on the basis of peptide neuromodulators that are co-contained in the GABAergic neurons.[21–28] GABAergic neurons projecting to globus pallidus contain high concentrations of enkephalin, whereas those projecting to entopeduncular nucleus and substantia nigra pars reticulata contain high concentrations of substance P and dynorphin. Studies examining the levels of striatal substance P and enkephalin messenger RNA after 6-hydroxydopamine lesions demonstrate findings in keeping with the differential effects of dopamine on the striatal-globus pallidus *versus* striatal-entopeduncular nucleus and substantia nigra pars reticulata neurons. In rats, after 6-hydroxydopamine lesions, the message level for enkephalin increases dramatically, whereas the message for substance P decreases in the same animals.[29–31] In primates, similar changes in enkephalin mRNA have been observed in MPTP-treated animals.[32]

Striatal inhomogeneities

In isolation, these data seem complex and difficult to explain in terms of the simple circuitry of the basal ganglia discussed so far in this chapter. However, a wealth of additional data has become available based on the elegant studies of Graybiel and her colleagues as well as others to show that far from being an homogeneous structure, the striatum is characterized by marked heterogeneities.[21,33–36] In general, the striatum can be described as having two major compartments, the striosomes and the matrix. These two compartments are defined by the density of acetylcholinesterase staining observed in adult and infant cat, primate and human. They are also characterized by their unique inputs and outputs.[36,37] The striosomes receive inputs from the prefrontal cortex, amygdala, hippocampus and medial substantia nigra pars compacta, whereas the matrix receives input from primary motorsensory cortex as well as frontal, parietal and occipital association cortices.[36–39] The matrix also receives dopaminergic input from the lateral substantia nigra and the ventral tegmental area.[40] The medium-sized spiny GABAergic matrix neurons provide the main projections to lateral and medial globus pallidus and substantia nigra pars reticulata, whereas the striosomes project primarily to substantia nigra pars compacta.[36,38,41]

Within the matrix, there are also subpopulations of neurons. Discrete neuronal populations in the matrix project to lateral globus pallidus and others to medial globus pallidus; another population projects to substantia nigra pars reticulata.[42,43] Parent *et al.* have shown that in primates there is very little collateralization of striatal neurons to these projection regions.[43]

What then are the consequences of these differential striatal matrix projections? It has also been puzzling that it has not been possible to induce chorea in primates with striatal lesions.[4] The only region of primate brain where lesions will produce these involuntary movements is the subthalamic nucleus.[4] The subthalamic nucleus (see Parent *et al.*, this volume, p29) receives input from the cerebral cortex and the lateral globus pallidus.[44] The subthalamic nucleus itself projects back to the lateral globus pallidus, striatum and also the medial globus pallidus and substantia nigra pars reticulata. The input from the cerebral cortex to the subthalamic nucleus is excitatory and is probably glutamatergic and mediated through quisqualate receptors.[45] The input to the subthalamic nucleus from the lateral globus pallidus is inhibitory and GABAergic.[36] The subthalamic nucleus itself is probably glutamatergic and excitatory, based on immunocytochemical and electrophysiological studies.[44,46,47]

A revised model of striatal function

Figure 2a illustrates what is known now about the detailed circuitry of differential striatal matrix outflow and its pathway through the globus pallidus, subthalamic nucleus, medial globus pallidus and substantia nigra pars reticulata. One can see that, depending on the subpopulation of striatal neurons that are affected, quite different patterns of final basal ganglia output may be generated. In studying the inputs and outputs of the subthalamic nucleus, in fact one would hypothesize that if only the GABA/enkephalin striatal output to lateral globus pallidus was affected in a disease (Fig. 2b), one would remove inhibition of the lateral pallidum only. The lateral pallidum is inhibitory and is the major projection through the basal ganglia to the subthalamic nucleus. If inhibition from striatum to the lateral pallidum is removed, the lateral pallidum will become excessively active and overinhibit the subthalamic nucleus. The consequences of such a lesion would be similar to an actual lesion of the subthalamic nucleus itself, ie chorea.[2] However, if all striatal output neurons were affected, the final output through the medial pallidum and substantia nigra pars reticulata would be quite differently affected.[19,48] Thus electrolytic and non-selective neurotoxic lesions to the striatum would be unlikely to cause chorea because they would affect most striatal output neurons equally. If, however, selective toxins could be found that only affected subpopulations of these matrix neurons, then perhaps an animal model of Huntington's disease could be created.

One possible model would be the use of selective N-methyl-D-aspartate (NMDA) agonists such as NMDA itself or the endogenous neurotoxin, quinolinate. These agents have been shown to spare the somatostatin/neuropeptide Y/NADPH-diaphorase positive interneurons in rodents; these neurons are also spared in Huntington's disease.[49–51] Whether GABA/enkephalin matrix neurons are particularly vulnerable to NMDA agonists has yet to be shown. We have formed the hypothesis that the first neurons to be affected in Huntington's disease might in fact be these GABA/enkephalin neurons,[2] and we examined this possibility in a series of postmortem brains from patients who died with Huntington's disease.[52,53]

Seventeen Huntington's brains, ranging from early grade 2 to late grade 4 pathology, were studied blindly along with a set of age and postmortem delay-matched controls.[52,53] The intensity of substance P and enkephalin immunoreactivity in the three striatal projection areas, substantia nigra, medial globus pallidus and lateral globus pallidus was assessed in serial sections. In grade 2 (early) Huntington's cases, there was striking loss of enkephalin immunoreactivity in the lateral globus pallidus and of substance P immunoreactivity in substantia nigra pars reticulata. In these same brains, there was good preservation of substance P immunoreactive fibre staining in the medial globus pallidus and in the substantia nigra pars compacta. In grade 3 (later) cases, these differential effects were also observed. However, there was some limited loss of substance P immunoreactivity in medial globus pallidus as compared to control, but there remained a striking contrast between the near complete loss of enkephalin-like immunoreactivity in the lateral globus

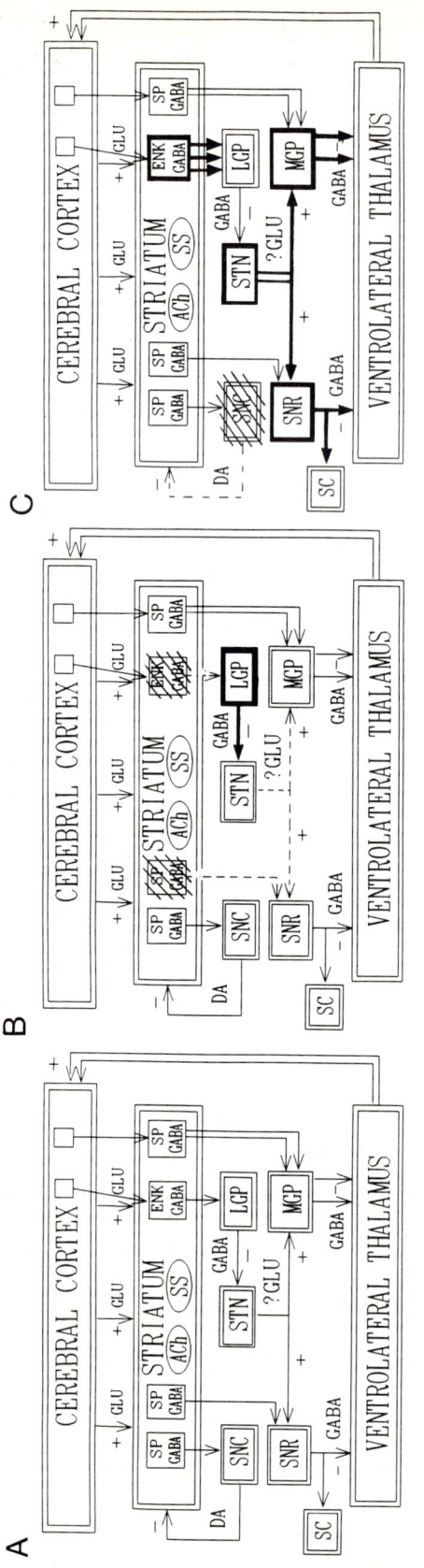

Fig. 2. *Revised model of basal ganglia circuitry based on more recent data.* The normal circuitry is shown in A. In B, the situation for early Huntington's disease is summarized. The GABA/SP pathway to SNR and GABA/ENK pathway to LGP are lost early, thus disinhibiting LGP which in turn overinhibits STN. In C, the situation in Parkinson's disease is summarized. There is loss of dopamine input from SNC resulting in loss of inhibition of striatal GABA/ENK neurons and loss of excitation of GABA/SP neurons. The cumulative effects of these losses are to increase STN and MGP/SNR neuronal activity but to decrease LGP neuronal activity.
Abbreviations: LGP = lateral globus pallidus; MGP = medial globus pallidus; SNR = substantia nigra pars reticulata; SNC = substantia nigra pars compacta; STN = subthalamic nucleus; SC = superior colliculus; GLU = glutamic acid; ACh = acetylcholine; SS = somatostatin; DA = dopamine.

pallidus as compared to relative preservation of substance P-like immunoreactivity in the medial globus pallidus. In grade 4 (very late) cases, immunoreactivity for both peptides was diminished in all the striatal output regions examined. These findings are of interest for two reasons. First, our initial hypothesis that matrix neurons were differentially affected in Huntington's disease was confirmed (Fig. 2b). In addition, this differential effect did not seem to be specific to any single neurotransmitter system since GABA/substance P neurons projecting to substantia nigra pars reticulata were affected very early, as well as GABA/enkephalin projections to the lateral globus pallidus. These findings are in keeping with the clinical observations seen in Huntington's disease that demonstrate abnormal eye movements developing early in the course of the disease in concert with the development of choreiform movements and poor fine motor coordination.[9] Later in the disease, other neurological symptoms (parkinsonian features and dystonia) become manifest, but these later symptoms progress at a different rate than the abnormalities of eye movement and chorea.[9]

A major pathway for the control of voluntary saccades is the projection from the frontal eye fields to the caudate nucleus and thence to the substantia nigra pars reticulata and superior colliculus.[54-56] Abnormalities in voluntary saccades are observed very early in Huntington's disease and pathology in this pathway is likely to explain the early development of the symptoms.

Previous data actually support the findings discussed above. A review of Spokes' biochemical studies in Huntington's disease revealed that GAD levels are significantly decreased in lateral globus pallidus of Huntington's brains when medial globus pallidus and substantia nigra pars reticulata GAD levels are not reduced, in comparison with a set of controls who died after a protracted illness.[57] Receptor data showed that GABA receptors increase in the substantia nigra and lateral globus pallidus of Huntington's brains but not in medial globus pallidus.[58] This latter finding would be consistent with the development of GABA receptor supersensitivity in lateral globus pallidus and substantia nigra pars reticulata, which are deafferented early in the disease, as opposed to medial globus pallidus which is involved only later. Finally, as discussed by Crossman,[59,60] microinjection studies in primate revealed that chorea can be produced directly by suppressing subthalamic nucleus activity or indirectly by injections of bicuculline into the lateral globus pallidus. Such bicuculline injections would block striatal GABA/enkephalin inputs and result in excess lateral pallidal activity and decreased subthalamic activity. In choreic animals given these injections, deoxyglucose studies demonstrated changes consistent with such an effect on pallidum, subthalamic nucleus and subsequently thalamus.

In Parkinson's disease (Fig. 2c), a contrasting set of events occurs. Loss of nigrostriatal inputs results in disinhibition of striatal-lateral globus pallidus projections which inhibit the lateral globus pallidus and thereby disinhibit the subthalamic nucleus. The same loss of nigrostriatal neurons results in loss of excitation to striatal-medial globus pallidus and striatal-substantia nigra pars reticulata pathways.[59,61] The result is a loss of striatal inhibition of medial globus pallidus and substantia nigra pars reticulata and an increase in subthalamic nucleus excitation of these same regions. The ultimate effect is increased output from these regions to thalamus. The above scheme is supported by electrophysiological and deoxyglucose studies of monkeys made parkinsonian by MPTP treatment.[59,61-63] Studies by Miller & DeLong and Filion et al. demonstrate an increase in medial globus pallidus activity in primates after MPTP treatment.[61] The activity of lateral globus pallidus neurons in contrast is diminished in these parkinsonian monkeys. Deoxyglucose studies in MPTP-treated monkeys show an increase in deoxyglucose uptake in lateral globus pallidus, presumably reflecting the disinhibition of the GABA/enkephalin striatal projection to lateral globus pallidus.[59,62,63] Deoxyglucose activity in medial globus pallidus and substantia nigra pars reticulata is relatively unchanged in the MPTP-treated monkeys, presumably reflecting a balance of increased terminal activity from the subthalamic nucleus inputs and decreased terminal activity in neurons coming from striatum. Deoxyglucose uptake in the subthalamic nucleus is depressed in the parkinsonian monkeys.

The scheme described here for explaining the pathophysiology of Parkinson's disease and Huntington's disease is supported by data from a variety of disciplines. However, a number of observations are still difficult to explain based on our current knowledge of the functional anatomy of the basal ganglia. If increased medial globus pallidus and substantia nigra pars reticulata activity is seen in primate models of Parkinson's disease, then what is the explanation for parkinsonian symptoms observed in persons with progressive supranuclear palsy who have prominent cell loss in the medial globus pallidus and substantia nigra pars reticulata? In addition, what is the explanation for dystonic symptoms that are seen spontaneously in both Parkinson's disease and Huntington's disease? In patients with idiopathic torsion dystonia, there is no overt pathology seen in the basal ganglia. Presumably, biochemical abnormalities are responsible for the marked clinical symptomatology seen in these disorders. Perhaps dystonia is not due to a particular pathology in any one of these pathways but rather due to improper spatial and temporal sequencing of striatal inputs and outputs. One prediction from the model described here is that patients with juvenile onset Huntington's disease who manifest predominant rigidity and dystonia rather than chorea will show a loss of striatal-medial globus pallidus pathways concomitant with the loss of striatal-lateral globus pallidus pathways, rather than the selective loss of the latter as seen in adult Huntington's disease.

Despite our inability to explain all the features of basal ganglia disorders based on this model, at least it provides a framework whereby specific hypotheses can be tested experimentally so that the model can be improved and modified appropriately. In the past decade, our understanding of the functional anatomy of the basal ganglia has improved dramatically and hopefully even more will be learned in the next decade.

Acknowledgements—Supported by USPHS grants NS 15655 and 19613.

References

1 Penney, J. B. & Young, A. B. (1983): Speculations on the functional anatomy of basal ganglia disorders. *Annu. Rev. Neurosci.* **6**, 73–94.
2 Penney, J. B. & Young, A. B. (1986): Striatal inhomogeneities and basal ganglia function. *Movement disorders* **1**, 3–15.
3 Kemp, J. M. & Powell, T. P. S. (1971): The connections of the striatum and globus pallidus: synthesis and speculation. *Philos. Trans. R. Soc. Lond. Ser. B* **262**, 441–457.
4 DeLong, M. R. & Georgopoulos, A. B. (1981): Motor functions of the basal ganglia. In *Handbook of physiology: The nervous system II*, Vol. 1, ed V. B. Brooks, pp 1017–1061. Washington DC: American Physiological Society.
5 McGeer, P. L. & McGeer, E. G. (1976): The GABA system and function of the basal ganglia: Huntington's disease. In *GABA in nervous system function*, eds E. Roberts, T. N. Chase & D. B. Tower, pp 487–495. New York: Raven.
6 Barbeau, A., Mars, H., Gillo-Joffrey, L. (1971): Adverse clinical side effects of levodopa therapy. In *Recent advances in Parkinson's disease*, eds F. H. MacDowell & C. H. Markham, pp 203–208. Philadelphia: Davis.
7 Fahn, S. (1986): Parkinson's disease and other basal ganglion disorders. In *Diseases of the nervous system*, eds A. K. Asbury, G. M. McKhann & W. I. McDonald, pp 1217–1228. Philadelphia: W. B. Saunders.
8 Marsden, C. D. (1984): The pathophysiology of movement disorders. *Neurol. Clin.* **2**, 435–459.
9 Young, A. B., Shoulson, I., Penney, J. B., Starosta-Rubinstein, Gomez, F., Travers, H., Ramos-Arroyo, M. A., Snodgrass, S. R., Bonilla, E., Moreno, H. & Wexler, N. S. (1986):

Huntington's disease in Venezuela: Neurologic features and functional decline. *Neurology* **36**, 244–249.
10 Martin, J. B. & Gusella, J. F. (1986): Huntington's disease: Pathogenesis and management. *New Engl. J. Med.* **315**, 1267–1276.
11 Martin, J. B. (1984): Huntington's disease: new approaches to an old problem. *Neurology* **34**, 1059–1072.
12 Hornykiewicz, O. (1977): Biogenic amines in the central nervous system. In *Handbook of clinical neurology*, vol. 29 (eds P. J. Vinken & G. W. Bruyn): *Metabolic and deficiency diseases of the nervous system*, Part III, ed H. L. Klawans, pp 459–483. Amsterdam: North Holland.
13 Hornykiewicz, O. (1982): Brain neurotransmitter changes in Parkinson's disease. In *Movement disorders*, eds C. D. Marsden & S. Fahn, pp 41–58. London: Butterworth Scientific.
14 Young, A. B. & Penney, J. B. (1984): Neurochemical anatomy of movement disorders. *Neurol. Clin.* **2**, 417–433.
15 Pan, H. S., Frey, K. A., Young, A. B. & Penney, J. B. (1983): Changes in [^{3}H]muscimol binding in substantia nigra, entopeduncular nucleus, globus pallidus and thalamus after striatal lesions as demonstrated by quantitative autoradiography. *J. Neurosci.* **3**, 1189–1198.
16 Chevalier, G., Vacher, S., Deniau, J. M. & Desban, M. (1985): Disinhibition as a basic process in the expression of striatal functions. I. The striato-nigral influence on tecto-spinal/tecto-diencephalic neurons. *Brain Res.* **334**, 215–226.
17 Deniau, J. M. & Chevalier, G. (1985): Disinhibition as a basic process in the expression of striatal functions. II. The striato-nigral influence on thalamocortical cells of the ventromedial thalamic nucleus. *Brain Res.* **334**, 227–233.
18 Pan, H. S., Penney, J. B. & Young, A. B. (1985): GABA and benzodiazepine receptor changes induced by unilateral 6-hydroxydopamine lesions of the medial forebrain bundle. *J. Neurochem.* **45**, 1396–1404.
19 Scheel-Kruger, J. (1986): Dopamine-GABA interactions: evidence that GABA transmits, modulates and mediates dopaminergic functions in the basal ganglia and limbic system. *Acta Neurol. Scand.* **73**, suppl. 107.
20 Wooten, G. F. & Collins, R. C. (1983): Effects of dopaminergic stimulation on functional brain metabolism in rats with unilateral substantia nigra lesions. *Brain Res.* **263**, 267–275.
21 Graybiel, A. M. (1984): Neurochemically specified subsystems in the basal ganglia. In *Functions of the basal ganglia. CIBA Foundation Symposium 107*, eds D. Evered and M. O'Connor, pp 114–144. London: Pitman.
22 Oertel, W. H., Riethmuler, G., Mugnaini, E., Schmechel, D. E., Weindl, A., Gramsch, C. & Herz, A. (1983): Opioid peptide-like immunoreactivity localized in GABAergic neurons of rat neostriatum and central amygdaloid nucleus. *Life Sci.* **33**, 73–76.
23 Afsharpour, S., Penny, G. R. & Kitai, S. T. (1984): Glutamic acid decarboxylase, leucine-enkephalin and substance-P immunoreactive neurons in the neostriatum of the rat and cat. *Soc. Neurosci. Abstr.* **14**, 702–702.
24 Aronin, N., DiFiglia, M., Graveland, G. A., Schwartz, W. J. & Wu, J.-Y. (1984): Localization of immunoreactive enkephalins in GABA synthesizing neuron of the rat striatum. *Brain Res.* **300**, 376–380.
25 Watson, S. J., Khachaturian, H., Akil, H., Coy, D. H. & Goldstein, A. (1982): Comparison of the distribution of dynorphin systems and enkephalin systems in brain. *Science* **218**, 1134–1136.
26 Haber, S. N. & Elde, R. P. (1981): Correlation between met-enkephalin and substance P immunoreactivity in the primate globus pallidus. *Neuroscience* **6**, 1291–1297.
27 Haber, S. N. & Watson, S. J. (1985): The comparative distribution on enkephalin, dynorphin and substance P in the human globus and basal forebrain. *Neuroscience* **14**, 1011–1024.
28 Graybiel, A. M., Hirsch, E. T. & Agid, Y. A. (1987): Differences in tyrosine hydroxylase-like immunoreactivity characterize the mesostriatal innervation of striosomes and extrastriosomal matrix at maturity. *Proc. Natl. Acad. Sci. (USA)* **84**, 303–307.
29 Young, W. S., III, Bonner, T. I. & Brann, M. R. (1986): Mesencephalic dopamine neurons regulate the expression of neuropeptide mRNAs in the rat forebrain. *Proc. Natl. Acad. Sci. (USA)* **83**, 9827–9831.

30 Bannon, M. J., Elliott, P. J. & Bunney, E. B. (1987): Striatal tachykinin biosynthesis: regulation of mRNA and peptide levels by dopamine agonists and antagonists. *Mol. Brain Res.* **3**, 31–37.
31 Normand, E., Popovici, T., Onteniente, B., Fellmann, D., Piatier-Tonneau, D., Auffray, C. & Bloch, B. (1988): Dopaminergic neurons of the substantia nigra modulate preproenkephalin A gene expression in rat striatal neurons. *Brain Res.* **439**, 39–46.
32 Augood, S. J., Emson, P. C. & Crossman, A. R. (1988): Transmitter hybridisation and histochemistry: application to movement disorders. *Neural mechanisms in disorders of movement*, Abstract poster 35, Manchester, England, April, 1988.
33 Graybiel, A. M. & Ragsdale, C. W. (1978): Histochemically distinct compartments in the striatum of human, monkey and cat demonstrated by acetylcholinesterase staining. *Proc. Natl. Acad. Sci. (USA)* **75**, 7523–7526.
34 Graybiel, A. M., Chesselet, M.-F., Wu, J.-Y., Eckenstein, F. & Joh, T. E. (1983): The relation of striosomes in the caudate nucleus of the cat to the organization of early-developing dopamine fibers, GAD-positive neuropil, and CAT-positive neurons. *Soc. Neurosci. Abstr.* **9**, 14–14.
35 Graybiel, A. M. & Hickey, T. L. (1982): Chemospecificity of ontogenic units in the striatum: demonstration of combining [3H]thymidine neuronography and histochemical staining. *Proc. Natl. Acad. Sci. (USA)* **79**, 198–202.
36 Graybiel, A. M. & Ragsdale, C. W. (1983): Biochemical anatomy of the striatum. In *Chemical neuroanatomy*, ed P. C. Emson, pp 427–504. New York: Raven Press.
37 Ragsdale, C. W. & Graybiel, A. M. (1981): The fronto-striatal projection in the cat and monkey and its relationship to inhomogeneities established by acetylcholinesterase histochemistry. *Brain Res.* **208**, 259–266.
38 Gerfen, C. R. (1985): The neostriatal mosaic. I. Compartmental organization of projections from the striatum to the substantia nigra in the rat. *J. Comp. Neurol.* **236**, 454–476.
39 Selemon, L. D. & Goldman-Rakic, P. S. (1985): Longitudinal topography and interdigitation of corticostriatal projections in the rhesus monkey. *J. Neurosci.* **5**, 776–794.
40 Jimenez-Castellanos, J. & Graybiel, A. M. (1985): The dopamine-containing innervation of striosomes: nigral subsystems and their striatal correspondents. *Soc. Neurosci. Abstr.* **11**, 1249–1249.
41 Gerfen, C. R. (1984): The neostriatal mosaic: compartmentalization of corticostriatal input and striatonigral output systems. *Nature* **311**, 461–464.
42 Beckstead, R. M. & Cruz, C. J. (1986): Striatal axons to the globus pallidus, entopeduncular nucleus and substantia nigra come mainly from separate cell populations in the cat. *Neuroscience* **19**, 147–158.
43 Parent, A., Bouchard, C. & Smith, Y. (1984): The striatopallidal and striatonigral projections: two distinct fiber systems in primate. *Brain Res.* **303**, 385–390.
44 Parent, A. & Smith, Y. (1988): The organization of the subthalamic nucleus in primates: A study of efferent projections and transmitter localization. In *Neural mechanisms in disorders of movement*, eds A. R. Crossman & M. A. Sambrook. London: John Libbey.
45 Rouzaire-Dubois, B. & Scarnati, E. (1987): Pharmacological study of the cortical-induced excitation of subthalamic nucleus neurons in the rat: evidence for amino acids as putative neurotransmitters. *Neuroscience.* **21**, 429–440.
46 Nakanishi, H., Kita, H. & Kitai, S. T. (1987): Intracellular study of rat substantia nigra pars reticulata neurons in an *in vitro* slice preparation: electrical membrane properties and response characteristics to subthalamic stimulation. *Brain Res.* **437**, 45–55.
47 Kitai, S. T. (1981): Electrophysiology of the corpus striatum and brainstem integrating systems. In *Handbook of physiology: the nervous system II*, Vol. 1, ed V. B. Brooks, pp 997–1015. Washington DC: American Physiological Society.
48 Klockgether, T., Schwarz, M., Turski, L., Ikonomidou-Turski, C., Ossowska, K., Heim, C., Turski, W., Wullner, U. & Sontag, K.-H. (1987): Neurotransmitters in the basal ganglia and motor thalamus: Their role for the regulation of muscle tone. In *The Basal Ganglia II*, eds M. B. Carpenter & A. Jayaraman, pp 185–202. New York: Plenum.
49 Beal, M. F., Kowall, N. W., Ellison, D. W., Mazurek, M. F., Swartz, K. J. & Martin, J. B. (1986): Replication of the neurochemical characteristics of Huntington's disease by quinolinic acid. *Nature* **321**, 168–171.

50 Dawbarn, D., Dequidt, M. E. & Emson, P. C. (1985): Survival of basal ganglia neuropeptide Y-somatostatin neurones in Huntington's disease. *Brain Res.* **340**, 251–260.
51 Beal, M. F., Bird, E. D., Langlais, P. J. & Martin, J. B. (1984): Somatostatin is increased in the nucleus accumbens in Huntington's disease. *Neurology* **34**, 663–666.
52 Albin, R. L., Reiner, A., Anderson, K. D., D'Amato, C. J., Penney, J. B. & Young, A. B. (1987): Differential loss of substance P-containing and enkephalin-containing striatofugal projections in adult-onset and juvenile-onset Huntington's disease. *Soc. Neurosci. Abstr.* **13**, 1361.
53 Reiner, A., Albin, R. L., Anderson, K. D., D'Amato, C. J., Penney, J. B. & Young, A. B. (1988): Differential loss of striatal projection neurons in Huntington's disease *Proc. Natl. Acad. Sci. (USA).* **85**, 5733–5737.
54 Hikosaka, O. & Wurtz, R. H. (1985): Modification of saccadic eye movements by GABA-related substances. I. Effect of muscimol and bicuculline in monkey superior colliculus. *J. Neurophysiol.* **53**, 266–291.
55 Lasker, A. G., Zee, D. S., Hain, T. C., Folstein, S. E. & Singer, H. S. (1987): Saccades in Huntington's disease: Initiation defects and distractibility. *Neurology* **37**, 364–370.
56 Lasker, A. G., Zee, D. S., Hain, T. C., Folstein, S. E. & Singer, H. S. (1988): Saccades in Huntington's disease: Slowing and dysmetria. *Neurology* **38**, 427–431.
57 Spokes, E. G. S. (1980): Neurochemical alterations in Huntington's disease. *Brain* **103**, 179–210.
58 Walker, F. O., Young, A. B., Penney, J. B., Dorovini-Zis, K. & Shoulson, I. (1984): Benzodiazepine receptors in early Huntington's disease. *Neurology* **34**, 1237–1240.
59 Crossman, A. R., Mitchell, I. J. & Sambrook, M. A. (1985): Regional brain uptake of 2-deoxyglucose in N-methyl-4-phenyl-1,2,3,6-tetrahydropydrine (MPTP)-induced parkinsonism in the macaque monkey. *Neuropharmacology* **24**, 587–591.
60 Crossman, A. R. (1987): Primate models of dyskinesia: The experimental approach to the study of basal ganglia-related involuntary movement disorders. *Neuroscience* **21**, 1–40.
61 Filion, M., Tremblay, L., Bedard, P. J.: The responses of pallidal neurons to passive limb movement and to striatal stimulation are abnormally large and unselective in monkeys with MPTP-induced parkinsonism. This volume, p. 197.
62 Mitchell, I. J., Cross, A. J., Sambrook, M. A. & Crossman, A. R. (1986): Neural mechanisms mediating 1-methyl-4-phenyl-1,2,3,6-tetrahydropyridine-induced parkinsonism in the monkey: Relative contributions of the striatopallidal and striatonigral pathways as suggested by 2-deoxyglucose uptake. *Neurosci. Lett.* **63**, 61–65.
63 Porrino, L. J., Burns, R. S., Crane, A., Palombo, E., Kopin, I. J. & Sokoloff, L. (1987): Changes in local cerebral glucose utilization associated with Parkinson's syndrome induced by 1-methyl-4-phenyl-1,2,3,6-tetrahydropyridine (MPTP) in the primate. *Life Sci.* **40**, 1657–1664.

3

THE SUBTHALAMIC NUCLEUS IN PRIMATES. A NEUROANATOMICAL AND IMMUNOHISTOCHEMICAL STUDY

A. Parent, L.-N. Hazrati and Y. Smith

*Centre de recherche en neurobiologie,
Université Laval et Hôpital de l'Enfant-Jésus,
Québec, Qué., Canada*

Summary

The organization of the subthalamic nucleus in the squirrel monkey (*Saimiri sciureus*) was studied using retrograde and anterograde tracing methods for analyzing efferent projections and immunohistochemical procedures for localizing neurotransmitters. Studies with retrograde tracers (WGA-HRP and fluorescent dyes) revealed that the subthalamic nucleus in primates is organized according to a complex pattern comprising: (a) a large dorsal 'sensorimotor' zone where most neurons project to the lenticular nucleus and terminate either in pallidum and/or putamen; (b) a small ventral 'associative' zone whose neurons give rise to either ascending projections to caudate nucleus or descending projections to the substantia nigra; and (c) a smaller overlapping zone whose neurons send axon collaterals to both the lenticular nucleus and substantia nigra. The anterograde (PHA-L) labelling experiments showed that subthalamic nucleus axons invading the globus pallidus emit numerous collaterals forming up to four distinct bands lying parallel to the medullary laminae. In contrast, the axons continuing their route to striatum were extremely long, linear, and did not branch frequently. The most medial portion of the subthalamic nucleus projected exclusively to the rostral portion of globus pallidus and ventral pallidum and could thus represent a 'limbic' zone in the subthalamic nucleus. A small contingent of fibres also descended along the ventromedial aspect of the cerebral peduncle to arborize within the substantia nigra pars reticulata. The immunohistochemical experiments revealed that, in contrast to a long held belief, subthalamic nucleus neurons in primates utilize the excitatory transmitter glutamate instead of the inhibitory transmitter GABA for neuronal communication.

Introduction

The subthalamic nucleus is known to play a crucial role in the control of motor function as demonstrated by clinicopathological investigations in humans[1] and experimental studies in animals.[2] Thus, the subthalamic nucleus has been the subject of numerous neuroanatomical investigations where the results have often been difficult to interpret because this relatively small structure is closely surrounded by several complex fibre systems. Furthermore, preliminary data indicate that significant species differences may exist between rodents and primates in regard to the connections of the subthalamic nucleus.[3] We therefore thought it of interest to investigate in detail the organization of the efferent projections of the subthalamic nucleus in the squirrel monkey (*Saimiri sciureus*) with retrograde and anterograde neuronal tracing methods. We also used the immunohistochemical approach to study the localization of GABA and glutamate at the level of the subthalamic nucleus in the same species.

Methods

Retrograde tracer experiments

In a first series of experiments, wheat germ agglutinin-horseradish peroxidase conjugate (WGA-HRP) was injected in similar quantities in the left putamen and the right caudate nucleus in five squirrel monkeys. After a survival period of 48 hours, the animals were sacrificed and their brains dissected out and sectioned on a freezing microtome. The sections were processed for the visualization of HRP according to the tetramethyl benzidine (TMB) method, as described in detail elsewhere.[4] In a second series of experiments, the fluorescent tracers Fast blue and Nuclear yellow were injected on the same side of the brain and in various combinations into the putamen, caudate nucleus, substantia nigra, and globus pallidus. Nuclear yellow was injected into putamen and Fast blue into substantia nigra in three monkeys; Nuclear yellow was delivered into caudate nucleus and Fast blue into substantia nigra in two monkeys; and Nuclear yellow was injected into globus pallidus and Fast blue into the substantia nigra in two other monkeys. After appropriate survival periods, which were 18 hours after the injection of Nuclear yellow and 48 hours after Fast blue, the animals were sacrificed and their brains prepared for the simultaneous demonstration of the two fluorescent tracers as described previously.[3,4]

Anterograde tracer experiments

In this series of experiments, the lectin *Phaseolus vulgaris*—leucoagglutinin (PHA-L) was injected micro-iontophoretically into various portions of the subthalamic nucleus in four monkeys. The animals were sacrificed 10 days after the injection and the anterograde transport of the lectin was visualized by using a PHA-L antibody and the avidin-biotin complex (ABC) immunohistochemical method.[5]

Immunohistochemical experiments

An antibody raised against GABA-glutaraldehyde-lysyl-protein complex[6] was used to study the distribution of GABA-immunoreactivity in subthalamic nucleus in two monkeys. The peroxidase antiperoxidase (PAP) method was employed to visualize

GABA-immunoreactive profiles following a procedure described in detail elsewhere.[5] In another animal, a monoclonal antibody specific for carbodiiamide-fixed glutamate[7] served for the visualization of glutamate-immunoreactivity in the subthalamic nucleus. This immunoreactivity was demonstrated by the ABC immunohistochemical method.

Results and discussion

Retrograde tracer experiments

After WGA-HRP injection into the putamen, numerous retrogradely labelled cells were found, principally in the dorsolateral two-thirds of the subthalamic nucleus (Fig. 1A). In contrast, WGA-HRP injection into the caudate nucleus resulted in a much smaller number of retrogradely labelled cells, mostly confined to the ventromedial third of the subthalamic nucleus (Fig. 1B). Although present along the entire rostrocaudal extent of the nucleus, these positive neurons were clearly more abundant and closely packed in the rostral two-thirds than in the caudal third. These results indicate that the subthalamostriatal projection is particularly massive and topographically organized in primates. By comparison, only a small number of subthalamostriatal neurons have been detected in the cat,[8] and such neurons appear absent in the rat.[9]

The results obtained with retrograde fluorescent tracers may be summarized as follows. After injections into putamen and substantia nigra, subthalamic cells containing the tracer injected into the putamen, which represented approximately 75–80 per cent of all retrogradely labelled neurons, occurred in the dorsolateral two-thirds of the subthalamic nucleus. The cells containing the tracer injected into the substantia nigra amounted to about 20–25 per cent of all retrogradely labelled neurons and were confined to the ventromedial third of the subthalamic nucleus. Only 5–10 per cent of all positive neurons were double-labelled after these injections. Following caudate nucleus/substantia nigra injections, cells containing the tracer injected into the two sites occurred in about equal number and were closely intermingled in the ventromedial third of the subthalamic nucleus. Less than 10 per cent of all positive subthalamic neurons were double-labelled after these injections. In cases of globus pallidus/substantia nigra injections, cells containing the tracer delivered into globus pallidus were approximately four times more numerous than those labelled with the tracer injected into substantia nigra, and about 10–20 per cent of all positive subthalamic neurons were double-labelled after these injections.

These results suggest that in regard to its efferent projections, the subthalamic nucleus in primates is organized according to a complex pattern that consists of: (a) a large dorsal 'sensorimotor' zone, occupying approximately 80 per cent of the volume of the nucleus, from which neurons project to the lenticular nucleus and terminate in globus pallidus and/or putamen; (b) a small ventral 'associative' zone, comprising 20 per cent of the volume, from which neurons give rise to either ascending projections to caudate nucleus or descending projections to substantia nigra, and (c) an even smaller overlapping zone, occupying approximately 10 per cent of the volume, from which neurons send axon collaterals to both the lenticular nucleus and substantia nigra (Fig. 2). The small percentage of double-labelled neurons disclosed in the subthalamic nucleus after globus pallidus/substantia nigra injections in the squirrel monkey contrasts strikingly with the results obtained in the rat, which indicate that the vast majority of subthalamic neurons in rodents send axon collaterals to both globus pallidus and substantia nigra.[10] We believe that more studies are needed to unravel the full significance of such a marked

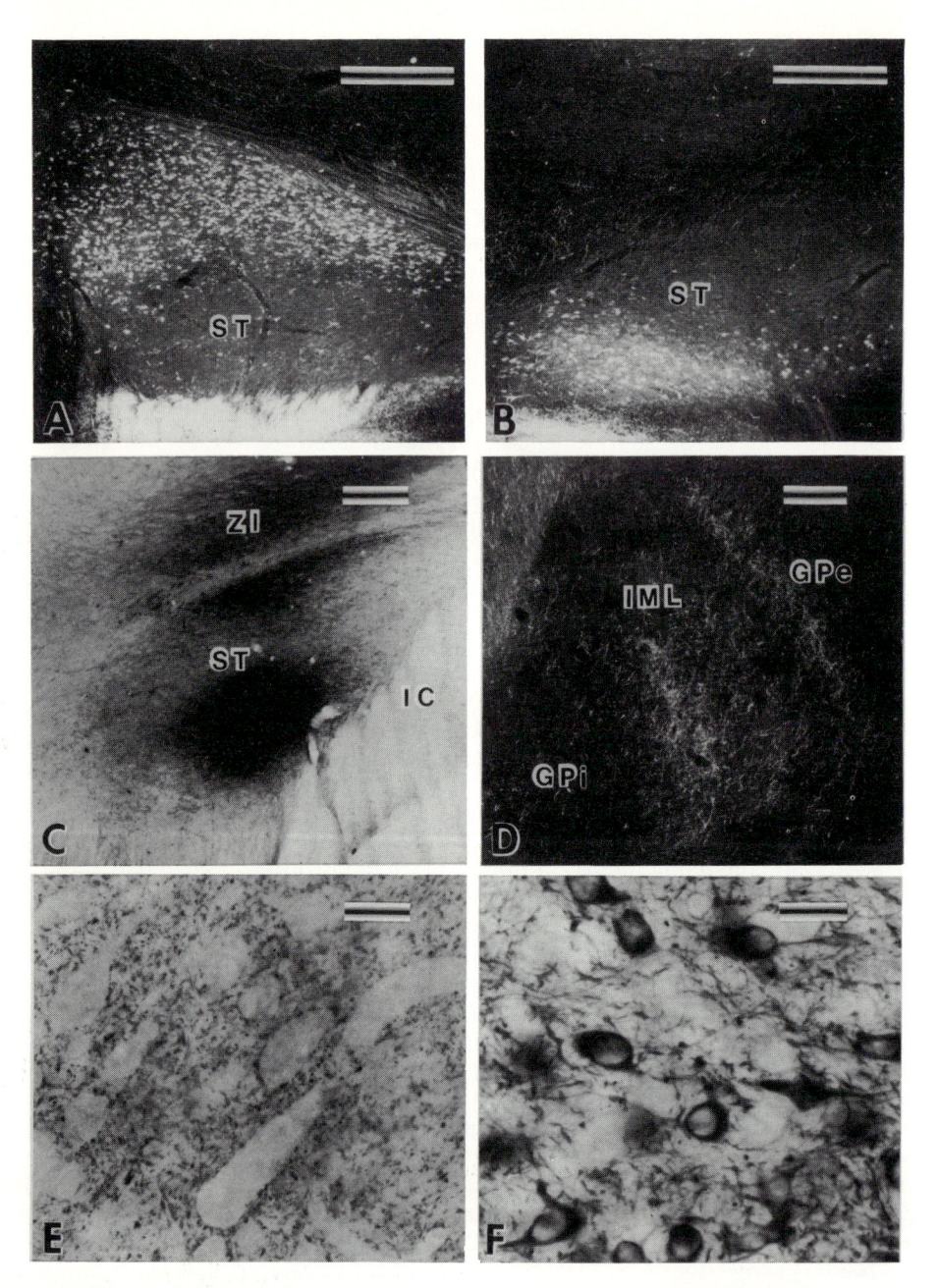

Fig. 1. A,B: *Dark field photomicrographs showing the large numbers of retrogradely labelled cells observed in the dorsolateral portion of the subthalamic nucleus after WGA-HRP injection into the left putamen (A) compared to a much smaller number of labelled cells in the ventromedial portion of the nucleus after injection into the right caudate nucleus (B). C,D: Examples of a PHA-L injection site in the core of the subthalamic nucleus (C) and of the type of anterograde fibre labelling it produced in the pallidum (D). E,F: Samples of the immunohistochemical staining for GABA (E) and for glutamate (F) in the subthalamic nucleus. Scale bars: 500 μm (A–C), 50 μm (D) and 30 μm (E,F).*

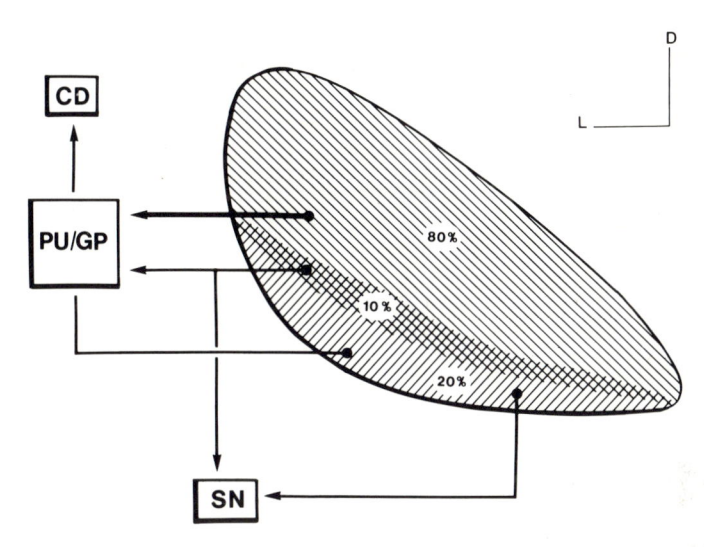

Fig. 2. Diagram summarizing the major organizational features of the subthalamic nucleus in primates as revealed after study of its major efferent projections by means of retrograde double-labelling methods.

species difference if one hopes to reach a more global understanding of the functional organization of the basal ganglia in mammals.

Anterograde tracer experiments

After small injections of PHA-L into the core of the subthalamic nucleus (Fig. 1C), labelled axons were seen invading both segments of the globus pallidus (Fig. 1D), where they branched into numerous collaterals forming up to four distinct bands aligned parallel to the medullary laminae (Fig. 3). Usually, one band lay along the external medullary lamina, two bands occurred on each side of the internal medullary lamina, whereas another group of fibres lay within the core of the internal segment of the globus pallidus in relation with the accessory medullary lamina. These bands were composed of a multitude of short axon collaterals forming dense meshworks closely surrounding pallidal neurons, including their long dendrites. Other labelled axons were visualized in smaller numbers in the putamen and caudate nucleus. However, the axons continuing their route into the striatum were extremely long, followed a linear course, and did not emit numerous collaterals. A small contingent of fibres also descended along the ventromedial aspect of the cerebral peduncle and swept dorsolaterally to arborize principally within the pars reticulata of the substantia nigra. They formed small and diffuse plexuses at the base of the substantia nigra, but some fibres also ascended along the typical cell columns of the pars compacta that impinge deeply within the pars reticulata of the substantia nigra (Fig. 3). In cases in which only the medial tip of the subthalamic nucleus was injected, the labelled fibres were mostly confined to the rostral pole of the globus pallidus and ventral pallidum. At these levels the fibres formed diffuse plexuses rather than well-defined bands. Thus, the pattern of labelling in the globus pallidus varied markedly according to the location and extent of subthalamic nucleus injection sites. The fact that neurons in the medial tip of the subthalamic nucleus project only to rostroventral portions of globus pallidus indicates that this region could represent a 'limbic' zone within the nucleus.

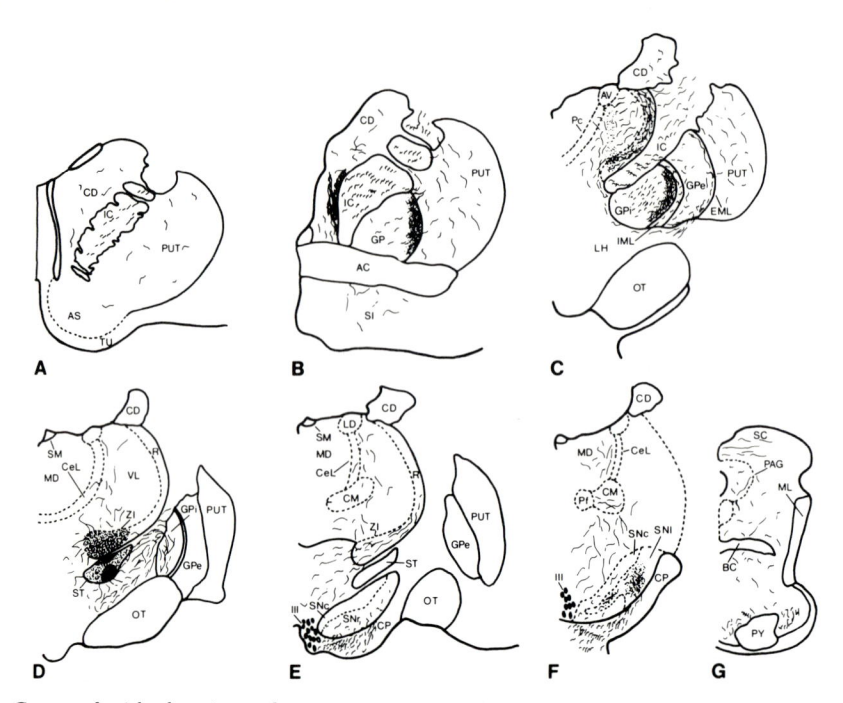

Fig. 3. Camera lucida drawings of transverse sections through the basal forebrain (A–C) and upper brainstem (D–G) of the squirrel monkey to illustrate a typical PHA-L injection site into the core of the subthalamic nucleus (D) and the distribution of anterogradely labelled fibres (sinuous lines) and terminals (dots) resulting from this injection. AC, anterior commissure; AS, nucleus accumbens; AV, anterior ventral nucleus; BC, brachium conjunctivum; CeL, central lateral nucleus; CD, caudate nucleus; CM, centre median nucleus; CP, cerebral peduncle; EML, external medullary lamina; GP, globus pallidus; GPe, external segment of GP; GPi, internal segment of GP; IC, internal capsule; IML, internal medullary lamina; LD, laterodorsal nucleus; LH, lateral hypothalamus; MD, mediodorsal nucleus; ML, medial lemniscus; OT, optic tract; PAG, periaqueductal grey matter; Pc, paracentral nucleus; Pf, parafascicular nucleus; PUT, putamen; PY, pyramids; R, reticular nucleus; SC, superior colliculus; SM, stria medullaris; SNc, substantia nigra pars compacta; SNl, substantia nigra pars lateralis; SNr, substantia nigra pars reticulata; SI, substantia innominata; ST, subthalamic nucleus; TU, olfactory tubercle; VL, ventral lateral nucleus; ZI, zona incerta; III, oculomotor nerve root fibres.

Earlier autoradiographic studies showed that subthalamopallidal fibres formed a band-like pattern in the globus pallidus in both cats and monkeys.[11,12] Since striatopallidal fibres have also a tendency to terminate in bands in the globus pallidus,[13] we believe that subthalamic and striatal inputs are organized according to a highly specific pattern, the complexity of which will be unravelled only after careful, anterograde, double-labelling investigations.

Immunohistochemical experiments

When examined with a polyclonal antibody raised against GABA-glutaraldehyde-lysyl-protein complex,[6] the cell bodies of the subthalamic nucleus did not display any immunoreactivity, although they were surrounded by numerous GABA-immunoreactive axon terminals (Fig. 1E), indicating that they receive a massive GABAergic innervation.

In contrast, virtually all cell bodies showed a strong immunoreactivity after incubation with a monoclonal antibody directed against carbodiimide-fixed glutamate[7] (Fig. 1F). These immunohistochemical results reveal that, in contrast to a long held belief, subthalamic neurons in primates utilize the excitatory transmitter glutamate instead of the inhibitory transmitter GABA for neuronal communication. These findings are at variance with previous electrophysiological studies of the subthalamic nucleus in the rat suggesting that this structure exerts a potent inhibitory influence upon globus pallidus cells, mediated through GABA.[14] However, they are congruent with recent electrophysiological studies demonstrating that subthalamic neurons in rodents do not inhibit the globus pallidus, but excite it, along with cells of the substantia nigra.[15]

Acknowledgement—This work was supported by grants from the MRC, FRSQ and FCAR.

References

1 Dereux-Mortier, S. A., Dereux, J. F. & Galois, P. H. (1985): Hémiballisme par métastase du corps de Luys. *Revue Neurol. (Paris)* **141**, 819–821.
2 Crossman, A. R., Sambrook, M. A. & Jackson, A. (1985): Experimental hemichorea/hemiballism in the monkey: studies on the intracerebral site of action in a drug-induced dyskinesia. *Brain* **107**, 579–596.
3 Parent, A., Bouchard, C. & Smith, Y. (1984): The striatopallidal and striatonigral projections: two distinct fiber systems in primate. *Brain Res.* **245**, 201–213.
4 Parent, A. & Smith, Y. (1987): Organization of efferent projections of the subthalamic nucleus in the squirrel monkey as revealed by retrograde labelling methods. *Brain Res.* **436**, 296–310.
5 Smith, Y. & Parent, A. (1988): Neurons of the subthalamic nucleus in primates display glutamate but not GABA immunoreactivity. *Brain Res.* **453**, 353–356.
6 Ségéla, P., Geffard, M., Buijs, R. M. & LeMoal, M. (1984): Antibodies against γ-aminobutyric acid: specificity studies and immunohistochemical results. *Proc. Natl. Acad. Sci. (U.S.A.)* **81**, 3883–3892.
7 Madl, J. E., Larson, A. A. & Beitz, A. J. (1986): Monoclonal antibody specific for carbodiimide-fixed glutamate: immunocytochemical localization in the rat CNS. *J. Histochem. Cytochem.* **34**, 317–326.
8 Beckstead, R. M. (1983): A reciprocal connection between the subthalamic nucleus and the neostriatum. *Brain Res.* **275**, 137–142.
9 Jackson, A. & Crossman, A. R. (1981): Subthalamic nucleus efferent projection to the cerebral cortex. *Neuroscience* **6**, 2367–2377.
10 Van der Kooy, D. & Hattori, T. (1980): Single subthalamic nucleus neurons project to both the globus pallidus and substantia nigra in rat. *Brain Res.* **192**, 751–768.
11 Nauta, H. J. W. & Cole, M. (1978): Efferent projections of the subthalamic nucleus: an autoradiographic study in monkey and cat. *J. Comp. Neurol.* **180**, 1–16.
12 Carpenter, M. B., Batton III, R. B., Carleton, S. C. & Keller, J. T. (1981): Interconnections and organization of pallidal and subthalamic nucleus neurons in the monkey. *J. Comp. Neurol.* **197**, 579–603.
13 Smith, Y. & Parent, A. (1986): Differential connections of caudate nucleus and putamen in the squirrel monkey (*Saimiri sciureus*). *Neuroscience* **18**, 347–371.
14 Rouzaire-Dubois, B., Scarnati, E., Hammond, C., Crossman, A. R. & Shibazaki, T. (1983): Microiontophoretic studies on the nature of the neurotransmitter in the subthalamo-entopeduncular pathway in the rat. *Brain Res.* **271**, 11–20.
15 Kitai, S. T. & Kita, H. (1987): Anatomy and physiology of the subthalamic nucleus: a driving force of the basal ganglia. In *The basal ganglia II-structure and function: Current concepts*, eds M. B. Carpenter & A. Jayaraman, pp 357–373. New York: Plenum Press.

4

THE RAT SUBTHALAMIC NUCLEUS:

ELECTROPHYSIOLOGICAL AND BEHAVIOURAL DATA

J. Féger, I. Vezole, N. Renwart and P. Robledo

Laboratoire de Pharmacologie, Faculté des Sciences Pharmaceutiques et Biologiques, 4 Avenue de l'Observatoire, 75006 Paris, France

Summary

This paper comprises behavioural and electrophysiological data concerning the effect of chemical stimulation of the subthalamic nucleus in the rat. The electrophysiological results presented here put forward the excitatory nature of the subthalamic control on other structures of the basal ganglia. Results are discussed in relation to behavioural experiments carried out in the monkey under similar conditions.

Introduction

In order to determine the role of a defined brain structure on behaviour it is worthwhile using chemical stimulation which avoids the uncontrolled and inescapable activation of passing fibres occurring with electrical stimulation. This procedure has previously been used in various parts of the basal ganglia in rats,[1-5] cats,[6,7] and monkeys.[8-11] However, the net effect of such pharmacological stimulation on neuronal activity was rarely verified at the level of the injection site or of related structures receiving primary projections from this area.

We applied this method in the case of the subthalamic nucleus for the following reasons. first, microinjections of bicuculline into the subthalamic nucleus of the monkey produce hemiballismus.[8-11] In the rat, different effects have been observed after picrotoxin or bicuculline injection into the subthalamic nucleus: an initial catalepsy, sedation followed by dyskinesia,[4,5] or contralateral spasmodic dyskinesia occurring immediately after unilateral microinjection.[2,3] Thus it seems interesting to re-examine the type of dyskinetic movements observed in the rat and the changes in local neuronal activity after chemical stimulation of the subthalamic nucleus. Second, this method will afford results related only to the involvement of neurons localized within the site of injection, without activation of the fibres running through or close to the subthalamic nucleus.

In the near future, these experiments will be complemented by metabolic studies using the 2-deoxyglucose technique. The rat provides a useful model for combining behavioural observations, electrophysiological recordings and metabolic activity studies within the same set of structures related to the subthalamic nucleus.

Materials and methods

Briefly, for behavioural studies all experiments were performed on male Wistar rats. Bilateral microinjections (0.5 µl) into the subthalamic nucleus were performed in awake animals bearing two cannula guides. Behaviour was observed over a 30 min period. Owing to the need to record various motor activities, the total number of events was counted every five min over a period of thirty min using the following scale: 0: for a frequency less than two per 5 min and an event duration less than 5 sec; 1: frequency between three and nine and duration between 6 and 15 sec; 2: frequency between 10 and 25 and duration between 16 and 40 sec; 3: frequency between 25 and 50 and duration between 41 and 80 sec; 4: frequency greater than 50 and duration more than 80 sec. The different types of movements observed were distributed between: (a) forelimb movement and (b) trunk or whole-body movement. According to the type of movement, different variables were analysed: duration only for (a) and frequency only for (b). Each animal received three microinjections separated by an interval of at least three days.

In electrophysiological experiments two injection procedures were used. The first consisted in the use of an assembly of two micropipettes in order to perform an injection and simultaneously to record unit activity in the subthalamic nucleus. A broken micropipette (tip diameter 50 µm) for microinjection was glued laterally to the micropipette used for recording, with a mean distance of 200 µm between each tip. In other cases, an injection tube and a micropipette were lowered independently into the subthalamic nucleus. After amplification, unit discharge was counted by a rate meter giving the number of spikes per 10 sec. The average firing rate for a period of 200 sec before the bicuculline injection was determined and considered to be the base line activity before treatment. After injection, when the increased activity reached a plateau, the mean rate for another period of 200 sec was determined. At the end of the experiments, the position of the recorded cell was marked by iontophoretic deposit of pontamine blue.

Brains were removed, frozen and cut with a freezing microtome. Sections of 50 µm were microscopically checked after staining with cresyl violet. Only results from rats with injections close to the subthalamic nucleus were retained in this study. Evaluation of statistical significance was performed by means of a paired, one-tailed Student's test for electrophysiological data and ANOVA analysis of variance followed by Dunnett t test for behavioural data.

Results

Behavioural data

In no case was immobility or catalepsy observed during the period of latency between the microinjection and the beginning of dyskinetic motor activities. With the lowest concentration (0.18 µg/µl) used in these experiments, bicuculline induced only various simple repetitive head and forelimb movements. The head movements observed were mostly side-to-side and upward-downward displacements. The forelimb movements consisted of successive alternate flexion and extension. A larger concentration

(0.37 μg/μl) induced a decrease in orofacial movements (chewing and sniffing), and an increase in forelimb movements and rearing. The forelimb movements included alternate flexion and extension with rubbing of the extremities on the floor. During rearing, the forelimb movements had a wider and circular appearance, and sometimes repetitive striking together of both forelimbs, like clapping, could be observed during these periods. Larger doses (0.75 μg/μl) led to violent movements of the trunk with rearing, jumping and torsion, frequently followed by tumbling, all of which were in competition with the forelimb movements. A larger concentration of 1.25 μg/μl was tried in four animals. There was again an increase in jumping, trunk torsion and falls. The limb movements were disorganized, apparently due to the occurrence of myoclonus. Moreover, in these animals, chewing was almost continuous, with abundant salivation. All these activities evoked a convulsive state. The behavioural data are shown in the Table.

Table. *Activity scores (mean ± S.E.M.) counted over a period of 30 minutes.*

	Saline	Bicuculline			
	0.9%	0.18 μg/μl	0.37 μg/μl	0.75 μg/μl	1.25 μg/μl
Forelimb movements:					
flex/extension	0.2 ± 0.2	3.2 ± 2.5	14.8 ± 2.3**	6.4 ± 3.2*	18.7 ± 2.2**
clapping	0	1.8 ± 1.5	5.3 ± 2.1	5.2 ± 3.4	0.7 ± 0.7
Trunk/body movements:					
torsion	0	1.4 ± 1.4	1.1 ± 1.1	7 ± 3.6*	8.75 ± 3.4*
jump	0	1.6 ± 1.6	3.2 ± 1.5	6.2 ± 1.9*	11.7 ± 1.8**

*$P < 0.05$, **$P < 0.01$ *versus* control.

In order to verify whether or not the behaviour observed was specific to subthalamic stimulation, a microinjection of bicuculline (concentration of 0.18 μg/μl) was performed just below the thalamus in the zona incerta. The motor behaviour of these animals was not importantly different from controls receiving saline into the subthalamic nucleus, which exhibited only the usual exploratory and grooming behaviour.

Electrophysiological data

Microinjection of bicuculline (0.2 μl) at 0.18 and 0.37μg/μl always induced a significant increase in the rate of spontaneous neuronal discharge. The maximal increase ranged from 140 to 451 per cent (mean 315 per cent) for 0.18 μg/μl, and from 140 to 600 per cent (mean 449 per cent) for a concentration of 0.37 μg/μl. The neuronal activity remained at a high rate throughout the recording (mean observation time: 20 min after the beginning of increase, maximal duration: 45 min). Microinjection of bicuculline at a concentration of 0.75 μg/μl induced an intense increase in activity with shorter latency than that of the low doses. In three cells out of four, this increase was followed by an alteration of spike aspect, reduction in amplitude and important fluctuations of baseline activity. Finally, a long arrest of spike discharge was observed in these cells. All these features evoked spike disappearance due to a block of depolarization. With larger quantities of bicuculline (0.2–0.3 μl), due to an increase in volume or concentration, 50% of the cells studied (n=24) showed a block of depolarization and the other 50% showed important sustained increases in neuronal activity. Using a concentration of 1.25 µg/µl, strong excitation followed by an arrest of discharge was observed in all cells (4/4). In control experiments performed with microinjection of saline, no significant variation was observed.

In a second set of electrophysiological experiments, we were interested in the study of changes in neuronal activity within the structures receiving subthalamic efferents, ie, the substantia nigra and the pallidal complex. In this part of the study the volume injected into the subthalamic nucleus was reduced to 0.2 µl of a solution containing bicuculline (0.2 µg/µl) and eosine (1 per cent). This dye allows control of the injection site and provides an indication of the diffusion range. The injection was carried out in 30 sec. The following results were obtained (Figure):

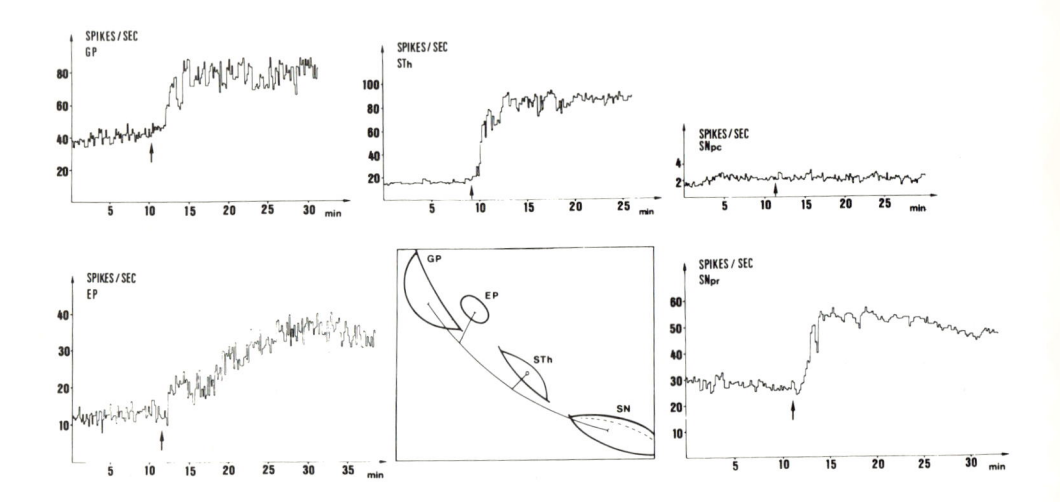

Figure. *Changes in discharge rate of neurons recorded either in the subthalamic nucleus (STh), in the substantia nigra with differentiation of dopaminergic (SNpc) or non-dopaminergic neurons (SNpr), in the entopeduncular nucleus (Ep) and in the globus pallidus (GP) after microinjection of bicuculline (0.04 µg in 0.2 µl over 30 sec [arrow]) into the subthalamic nucleus* (reproduced from[12], courtesy of Gauthier-Villars, Paris).

(1) In the substantia nigra, dopaminergic and non-dopaminergic units were differentiated according to the usual criteria (frequency of discharge, width and shape of recorded spike). In the first group a slight but significant ($P < 0.01$) increase or decrease was observed: in eight neurons the change in frequency was from 4 ± 0.5 per sec to 5.6 ± 0.4 and in 12 others the rate of discharge was reduced from 6.4 ± 0.8 to 4.8 ± 0.7; in the case of neurons identified as non-dopaminergic and localized more ventrally in the pars reticulata, an increase in activity was usually seen with a mean value of 74.3 per cent in 20 neurons out of 22 (baseline mean frequency: 32.4 ± 1.6; maximal increase: 55.8 ± 3.8, $P < 0.001$).

(2) In the pallidal complex, 13 neurons were recorded in the entopeduncular nucleus and 14 in the globus pallidus. In the first structure, 12 units exhibited a mean increase of 139 per cent (change in frequency from 20 ± 3 to 43.5 ± 6.7, $P < 0.001$). In the second, the activity of 11 neurons was increased by 82.5 per cent (31.6 ± 5.8 to 57.8 ± 8.8, $P < 0.01$).

Control injections of saline into the subthalamic nucleus did not modify the neuronal discharge of cells tested in the subthalamic nucleus itself, the substantia nigra or the pallidal complex. Bicuculline injected into the surrounding zona incerta was also unable to modify the discharge rate of non-dopaminergic neurons.

Discussion

The results presented in this chapter and summarized below are largely discussed in two reports ([12] and Renwart et al. [submitted to Exp. Neurol.]). However, it seems of interest to stress their main points and to enlarge the present discussion to include some controversial aspects. First, a microinjection of bicuculline into the subthalamic nucleus induces several forms of dyskinesia with particular movements of the forelimbs. Second, the same quantities of this GABA antagonist produce an increase in neuronal discharge recorded in the subthalamic nucleus followed by a prolonged arrest of spike formation. Third, an increase in neuronal activity at pallidal and nigral level was observed in relation to the pharmacological excitation of subthalamic neurons induced by microinjection of 40 ng bicuculline.

According to this last result, the electrophysiological demonstration of an excitatory effect of the subthalamic projections to the substantia nigra and the pallidal complex is in good agreement with ultrastructural and immunohistochemical data reported in other parts of this volume (Parent et al., this volume, p.35). These data were obtained in the primate and in the rat; thus, it could be assumed that in these different species the subthalamic nucleus provides an excitatory control on the two basal ganglia outputs, ie, the internal part of the globus pallidus and the pars reticulata of the substantia nigra. This assumption is in opposition to the inhibitory function, mainly on the globus pallidus, commonly attributed to the subthalamic nucleus.[13]

Since a long-lasting increase in firing rate was observed in globus pallidus after microinjection of bicuculline into the subthalamic nucleus, and since this structure provides an inhibitory control on the entopeduncular nucleus, changes in neuronal activity observed at entopeduncular level are the summation of direct activation and indirectly driven inhibition. The integration of these opposite actions is important in regard to the pallidal influence on the thalamus, lateral habenula and pedunculopontine nucleus. The question arises whether the situation is comparable in rodents and primates, in relation to the differences in organization of the subthalamic output: independent relationship in the primate (see Parent et al., this volume, p.31), and in the rat, axons highly collateralized with an independent projection to the pedunculopontine nucleus.[14]

Different descriptions of changes in motor behaviour after microinjection of GABA antagonists like picrotoxin or bicuculline into the subthalamic nucleus have been published previously.[2–5,15] In some reports,[4,5] these changes are characterized by a biphasic evolution, involving an initial period of catalepsy or immobility and a second phase of motor activation. The dose-related changes in neuronal activity observed in the present study, namely an increase at a low dose and a cessation of activity at a high dose, might explain the different behavioural effects reported after microinjection of various doses of picrotoxin.[4] On the other hand, our observations are closely related to those describing an immediate activation with spasmodic dyskinesia of the forelimbs.[2,3] But the pattern of forelimb motor activity that we observed appears more organized. This feature is especially obvious when the rat is standing up, a posture which releases the forelimbs as in primates and cannot be confused with spasmodic clonus. This difference in observed movements is likely to be related to the fact that in our experiments we used smaller doses, thereby avoiding larger movements of the entire body. However, there is a consensus as to the involvement of the forelimbs in this dyskinesia which seems characteristically related to the microinjections performed only within the subthalamic nucleus itself.

On the basis of electrophysiological records obtained in conditions as closely as possible resembling behavioural experiments, these dyskinetic movements seem to be related to a block in neuronal activity within the subthalamic nucleus. In primates, behavioural experiments combined with 2-deoxyglucose methods[11,16] have indicated a similar explanation: the microinjection of bicuculline ($2\,\mu l$ of a solution containing $15\,\mu g/\mu l$) should induce a depolarizing block, involving almost all of the neurons and mimicking a reversible lesion of the subthalamic nucleus. It is difficult to extrapolate to primates from our electrophysiological data recorded in rats. However, by comparison with the size of the nucleus in each species and the concentration and volume used, it is likely that the microinjection of bicuculline induces a blocking depolarization within the entire subthalamic nucleus of the primate, as was hypothesized. The appearance of hemiballismus is thus related to a reduction of neuronal activity in the subthalamic nucleus. This hypothesis agrees with reports on experimental hemiballismus obtained by electrolytic[17,18] and kainic acid[19] lesions.

In conclusion, these results bring a new insight on the functions of the subthalamic nucleus. First, it is obviously demonstrated that this nucleus exerts an excitatory control on other basal ganglia structures. Thus, it is necessary to enlarge the concept of a structure devoted only to the production of an excitatory input to counterbalance the inhibitory control exerted by the striatum and the external globus pallidus. Since there are similarities in the basal ganglia organization between the striatum and the subthalamic nucleus which both receive cortical,[20,21] thalamic[22] and nigral dopaminergic[23] inputs, and send efferents to all the other structures, it could be suggested that the subthalamic nucleus has a complementary function in relation to the striatum, enhancing the level of excitability in these different structures in opposition to the main inhibitory striatal control. Second, it could be assumed that the basic neural mechanisms are the same in both rodents and primates. However, their integration may be different, reflecting the specificity of the anatomical organization.

Acknowledgement—This research was supported by grants from INSERM (CRE 846008 and 876010) and from Fondation pour la Recherche Médicale.

References

1 Arnt, J. & Scheel-Kruger, J. (1980): Intranigral GABA antagonists produce dopamine independent biting in rats. *Eur. J. Pharmacol.* **62**, 51–61.
2 Crossman, A. R., Latham, A., Longman, D. A., Patel, S. & Slater, P. (1983): Motor dysfunction induced by application of GABA antagonists to the subthalamic nucleus of rat brain. *J. Physiol. (Lond.)* **334**, 85P.
3 Crossman, A. R., Latham, A., Longman, D. A., Patel, S. & Slater, P. (1983): The role of the entopeduncular nucleus in the motor dysfunction induced by application of a GABA antagonist to the subthalamic nucleus of rat brain. *J. Physiol. (Lond.)* **342**, 61–62p.
4 Scheel-Kruger, J. & Magelund, G. (1981): GABA in the entopeduncular nucleus and the subthalamic nucleus participates in mediating dopaminergic striatal output function. *Life Sci.* **29**, 1555–1562.
5 Scheel-Kruger, J. (1986): Dopamine-GABA interactions: evidence that GABA transmits, modulates and mediates dopaminergic functions in the basal ganglia and the limbic system. *Acta Neurol. Scand.* **73**, suppl. 107, 1–54.
6 Sontag, K. H., Heim, Schwarz, M., Jaspers, R., Cools, A. R. & Wand, P. (1984): Consequences of disturbed gabaergic transmission in substantia nigra pars reticulata in freely moving cats and their motor behaviour and in anaesthetized cats on their spinal motor elements. In *The basal ganglia, structure and function*, eds J. S. MacKenzie, R. E. Kemm & L. N. Wilcock, pp 495–512. New York and London: Plenum Press.

7. Wolfarth, S., Kolasiewicz, W. & Sontag, K. H. (1981): The effects of muscimol and picrotoxin injections into the cat substantia nigra. *Naunyn-Schmiedberg's Arch. Pharmacol.* **317**, 54–60.
8. Crossman, A. R., Sambrook, M. A. & Jackson, A. (1980): Experimental hemiballismus in the baboon produced by injection of a gamma-amino-butyric acid antagonist into the basal ganglia. *Neurosci. Lett.* **20**, 369–372.
9. Crossman, A. R., Sambrook, M. A. & Jackson, A. (1984): Experimental hemichorea/hemiballismus in the monkey: studies on the intracerebral site of action in a drug-induced dyskinesia. *Brain* **107**, 579–596.
10. Crossman, A. R. (1987): Primates models of dyskinesia: the experimental approach to the study of basal ganglia-related involuntary movements disorders. *Neuroscience* **21**, 1–40.
11. Mitchell, I. J., Jackson, A., Sambrook, M. A. & Crossman, A. R. (1985): Common neural mechanisms in experimental chorea and hemiballismus in the monkey. Evidence from 2-deoxyglucose autoradiography. *Brain Res.* **339**, 346–350.
12. Robledo, P., Vezole, I. & Féger, J. (1988): Mise en évidence d'un effet excitateur des efferences subthalamo-nigrales et subthalamo-pallidales chez le rat. *C.R. Acad. Sci. ser. III. Paris* **307**, 133–138.
13. DeLong, M. R. & Georgopoulos, A. P. (1981): Motor functions of the basal ganglia. In *Handbook of physiology, the nervous system*, vol. II, part 2, ed J. M. Brookhart & V. B. Mountcastle, pp 1017, 1061. Bethesda: American Physiology Society.
14. Takada, M., Nishinama, M. L. & Hattori, T. (1988): Two separate neuronal populations of the rat subthalamic nucleus project to the basal ganglia and pedunculopontine tegmental region. *Brain Res.* **442**, 72–80.
15. Di Chiara, G., Morelli, M., Porceddu, M. L. & Gessa, G. L. (1978): Evidence that nigral GABA mediates behavioural responses elicited by striatal dopamine receptor stimulation. *Life Sci.* **23**, 2045–2052.
16. Mitchell, I. J., Sambrook, M. A. & Crossman, A. R. (1985): Subcortical changes in the regional uptake of (3H)-2-deoxyglucose in the brain of the monkey during experimental choreiform dyskinesia elicited by injection of a gamma-aminobutyric acid antagonist into the subthalamic nucleus *Brain* **108**, 405–422.
17. Carpenter, M. B., Whittier, J. R. & Mettler, F. A. (1950): Analysis of choroid hyperkinesia in the rhesus monkey. Surgical and pharmacological analysis of hyperkinesia resulting from lesions in the subthalamic nucleus of Luys. *J. Comp. Neurol.* **92**, 293–331.
18. Whittier, J. R. (1947): Ballism and the subthalamic nucleus (nucleus hypothalamicus: corpus luysi). *Arch. Neurol. Psychiat.* **58**, 672–692.
19. Hammond, C., Féger, J., Bioulac, B. & Souteyrand, J. P. (1979): Experimental hemiballism in the monkey produced by unilateral kainic acid lesion in corpus luysi. *Brain Res.* **171**, 577–580.
20. Hartmann-Von Monakow, K., Akert, K. & Kûnzle, H. (1978): Projections of the precentral motor cortex and other cortical areas of the frontal lobe to the subthalamic nucleus in the monkey. *Exp. Brain Res.* **33**, 395–403.
21. Rouzaire-Dubois, B. & Scarnati, E. (1985): Bilateral corticosubthalamic nucleus projections: an electrophysiological study in rats with chronic cerebral lesions. *Neuroscience* **15**, 69, 79.
22. Sugimoto, T., Hattori, T., Mizuno, N., Itoh, K. & Sato, M. (1983): Direct projections from the centre median-parafascicular complex to the subthalamic nucleus in the cat and rat. *J. Comp. Neurol.* **214**, 209–216.
23. Meibach, R. C. & Katzman, R. (1979): Catecholaminergic innervation of the subthalamic nucleus: evidence for a rostral continuation of A9 (substantia nigra) dopaminergic group. *Brain Res.* **173**, 364–368.

5

THE COMPARTMENTAL ORGANIZATION OF THE VENTRAL STRIATUM IN THE RAT

H. J. Groenewegen, G. E. Meredith, H. W. Berendse,
P. Voorn and J. G. Wolters

*Department of Anatomy and Embryology, Vrije Universiteit,
Amsterdam, The Netherlands*

Summary

The purpose of this communication is to review briefly the present ideas about the compartmental organization of the ventral, limbic-related part of the striatum, with main emphasis on the nucleus accumbens. The immunohistochemical and connectional characteristics of various compartments are described, emphasizing the differences between rostral and caudal compartments and between 'shell' and 'core' regions of the nucleus.

Introduction

It is generally accepted that the striatum is very inhomogeneous both anatomically and functionally.

First, a distinction in motor, associational and limbic sectors can be made on the basis of the organization of corticostriatal connections.[1-3] This crude tri-partition is reflected to some extent in the distribution patterns of neuroactive substances.[4,5] Moreover, the results of pharmaco-behavioural studies have demonstrated that different, on some occasions even opposing, effects can be elicited from different striatal regions.[6-9]

Second, a fine-grained compartmental patch/matrix system appears to exist within each of the larger, functionally different sectors. This compartmental organization is defined on the basis of the distribution patterns of various neuroactive substances, the differential disposition of receptors, and the organization of afferent and efferent connections.[4,10] One of the main questions to be answered is whether and how these compartments communicate to integrate various inputs and outputs. Communication between different compartments could take place through local axon collaterals of the medium-sized spiny projection neurons, or through the projections of the aspiny interneurons. Recently, it has been shown that in the rat both the dendrites and axon collaterals of the projection neurons are confined by compartmental boundaries[11] (however see also[12]), whereas the dendrites of the interneurons tend to ignore these boundaries.[11–14]

Methods

The distribution patterns in the ventral striatum of dopamine (DA)-immunoreactivity (IR), enkephalin (ENK)-IR, substance P (SP)-IR, calcium binding protein (CaBP; calbinding-D_{28kDA})-IR and choline-acetyltransferase (ChAT)-IR were visualized using immunohistochemical procedures that are described in detail elsewhere.[15–18] Injections of the anterograde tracer *Phaseolus vulgaris*-leucoagglutinin (PHA-L) were placed in the subiculum of the hippocampal formation, the basolateral amygdaloid nucleus and the midline and intralaminar thalamic nuclei to determine the organization of these projections to the ventral striatum.[19,20] PHA-L was also injected in the ventral striatum in order to study its output, and these data were supplemented with the results of retrograde tracing experiments in which the tracer Fluorogold was injected in the region of the substantia nigra. In a number of experiments, double-labelling was employed, eg, ENK-immunostaining with tract-tracing or both ENK- and ChAT-immunostaining in the same tissue section.[18,19,21]

Results and discussion

Distribution of neuroactive substances

On the basis of several criteria, nucleus accumbens can be subdivided into 'shell' and 'core' regions.[22] Cytoarchitectonically, the outer shell contains relatively cell-poor regions and the neurons are loosely arranged. Cell clusters line dorsal and lateral borders and are dispersed ventrally and medially within the shell.[23,24] In the central core, neurons are more closely packed and more homogeneously distributed than in the shell. However, inhomogeneities in the distribution of various neuroactive substances are distinct in the central part of the nucleus. Since ENK-IR provides a reproducible pattern that can be demonstrated with various fixation procedures, we have used the distribution of this peptide as a reference in the description of the distribution of other neuroactive substances and of afferent and efferent connections.

Enkephalin. Enkephalin-IR in nucleus accumbens shows roughly three different intensities. Rostrolaterally, patches of strong immunoreactivity, closely associated with the anterior commissure, stand out against a moderately stained matrix of uneven intensity (Fig. 3C). These dark patches form a complex, interconnected three-dimensional network (see also[25]). The dimensions of the patches are greatest rostrally where 'fingers' of ENK-IR extend medially into nucleus accumbens and dorsally into the caudate-putamen complex. More caudally, these dark ENK-IR patches are reduced in size (Fig. 4).

Caudomedially, at the level of the major island of Calleja, regions virtually non-immunoreactive for ENK stand out against a cone-shaped area of moderate staining intensity (Fig. 1A). This cone-shaped region in the shell of nucleus accumbens extends into the ventral and lateral parts of the nucleus, but is less clearly demarcated there. In the caudomedial region, there is a clear relationship between the cytoarchitecture and the distribution of ENK-IR. Virtually all cell clusters are in perfect register with regions

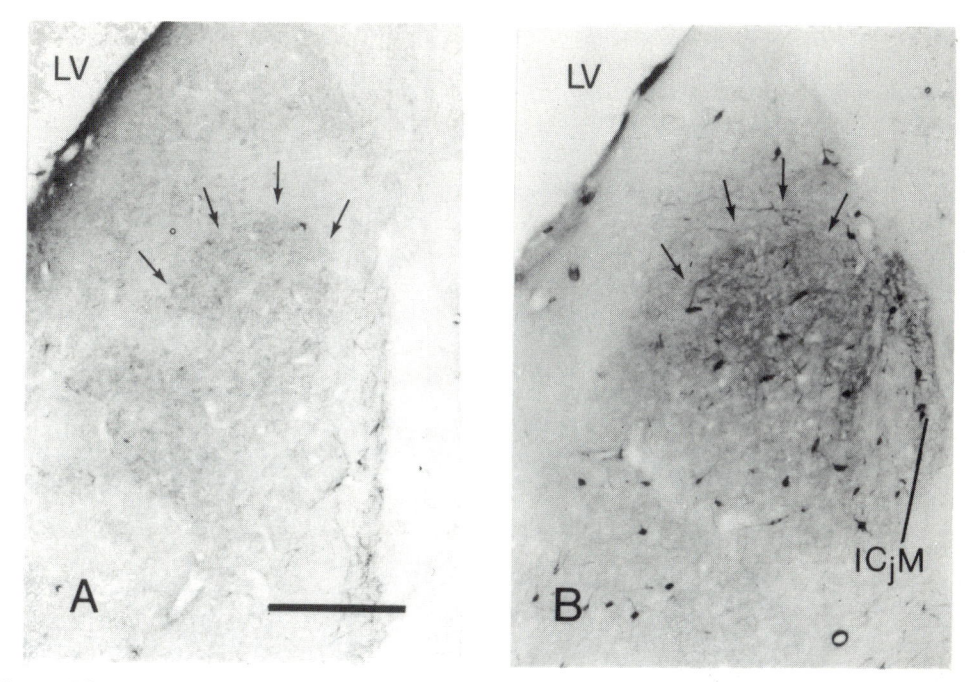

Fig. 1. *Photomicrographs of adjacent sections which have been immunostained for ENK (A) and ChAT (B). These micrographs illustrate the match between the moderate ENK-IR and dense ChAT-IR in the cone-shaped portion (marked with arrows) of the outer shell of nucleus accumbens. Scale bar 250 μm. ICjM, major island of Calleja; LV, lateral ventricle*

of low ENK-IR, whereas the moderate ENK-IR overlies relatively cell poor regions (Fig. 4).

Dopamine, substance P and calcium binding protein. Antisera to DA and SP labelled only fibre structures, and that to CaBP labelled both cell bodies and fibres. Rostrolaterally in nucleus accumbens, patches of intense ENK-IR overlie similarly shaped areas of weak DA- and SP-IR and strong CaBP-IR. The moderate ENK matrix is coincident with moderate DA-, SP- and CaBP-IR. In the caudomedial shell, the cone-shaped area of ENK-IR matches densely DA- and SP-labelled areas. In this same region CaBP-IR is virtually absent. The relatively small, dark ENK-positive patches along the border region between the caudate-putamen complex and nucleus accumbens overlie similarly shaped areas of high SP-IR and low DA- and CaBP-IR (Fig. 4).

Choline acetyltransferase. Distinct inhomogeneities are present in the distribution of ChAT-positive perikarya and ChAT-immunoreactive neuropil.[26] Densest ChAT-IR is evident in the shell of nucleus accumbens. Rostrally, a dense ChAT-IR region is apparent ventral to the anterior commissure. Further caudally, this region expands first ventrally and then medially. Caudomedially, at the level of the major island of Calleja, the intensely stained zone (Fig. 1B) coincides with the cone-shaped area seen in the ENK- (Fig. 1A), DA- and SP-immunoreacted sections. In the central core, ChAT-poor areas overlie the dark ENK patches. In the matrix ChAT-IR is moderate (Fig. 4).

The heterogeneous pattern of ChAT-labelled fibres correlates well with the distribution of ChAT-positive perikarya, such that most neuronal cell bodies and their dendrites are retained within darkly or moderately stained zones. In sections double-labelled for ChAT

47

and ENK, it appears that, with some exceptions, ChAT-immunoreactive neurons lie outside dark ENK-positive patches. The few ChAT-labelled neurons which align the borders of these patches have dendrites that either follow the edge of the patch or occasionally cross over into the patch.

Organization of afferent and efferent fibres

The degree to which afferent systems comply with the compartmental structure of the ventral striatum depends on the source of the fibres. Injections of PHA-L in the thalamic paraventricular nucleus result in a strong projection to the cone-shaped area in the

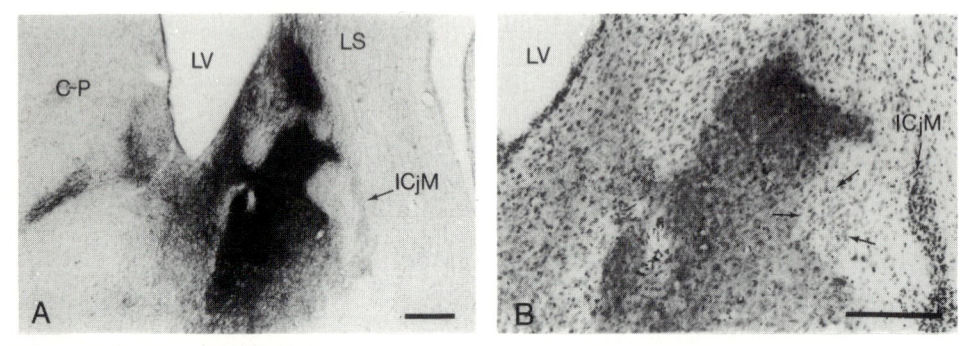

A, B. Distribution of labelled fibres in the caudomedial part of nucleus accumbens following a PHA-L injection in the paraventricular nucleus of the thalamus. Note that the densest innervation occurs in the cone-shaped area in the shell of nucleus accumbens, but that more laterally in the border region of nucleus accumbens and caudate-putamen, patches of labelling are also present. Arrows in (B) denote a cell cluster directly lateral to the major island of Calleja, that remains free of labelling (see also Fig. 2F).

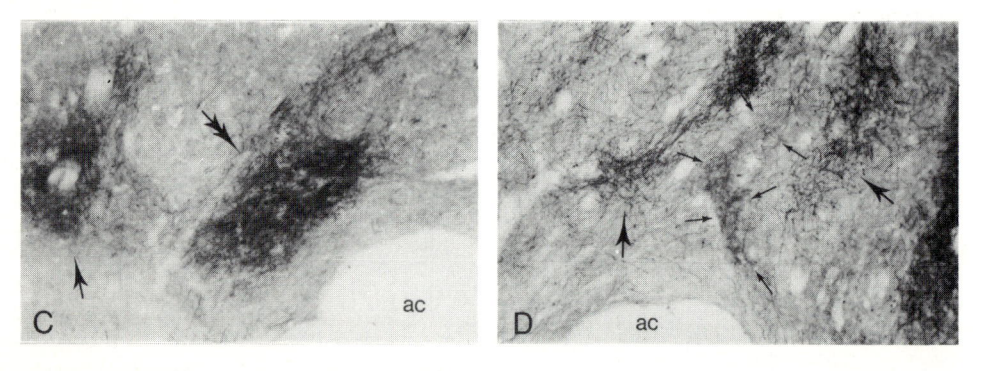

C, D. Double labelled sections for ENK-IR and PHA-L labelled fibres following injections of the tracer in the thalamus. In (C) the injection was placed in the paraventricular nucleus. The single arrow points to an ENK patch which remains relatively free of PHA-L labelling, whereas the double arrow points to an ENK patch which contains a high density of PHA-L labelled fibres. The surrounding moderate ENK matrix is relatively free of PHA-L labelling. In (D) the PHA-L injection was placed in the central medial thalamic nucleus. In this case the PHA-L labelling (indicated with large arrows) avoids the ENK patches (indicated with smaller arrows). Note the difference in texture of the PHA-L- and the ENK-labelling, respectively black and brown in the double stained sections: PHA-L labelled fibres have a crisp appearance, whereas the ENK-staining is more diffuse. Note also that there is a halo surrounding the ENK patch which is relatively free of PHA-L labelling.

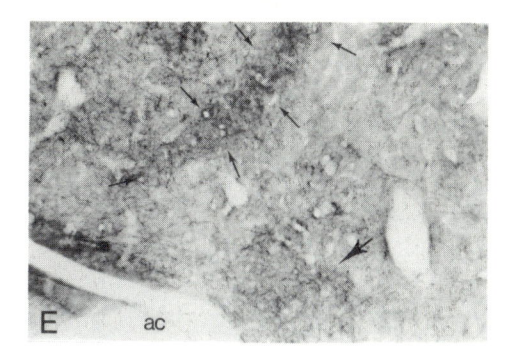

E. Double labelled section of nucleus accumbens following a PHA-L injection in the dorsal part of the subiculum. Small arrows denote an ENK patch, the large arrow a cluster of PHA-L labelled fibres. Note that the PHA-L labelled fibres are present both in the matrix and in the patch compartments.

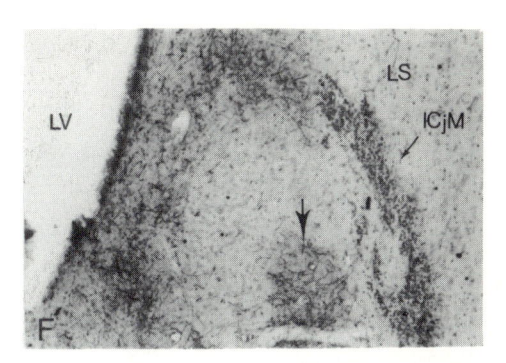

F. Distribution of PHA-L labelled fibres in the caudomedial portion of nucleus accumbens following an injection in the basolateral nucleus of the amygdala. The section is counterstained with Cresyl Violet to show the cytoarchitecture. Note that labelled fibres are present in the cell cluster lateral to the island of Calleja (large arrow) and in the cell dense areas surrounding the cone-shaped area (compare also Fig. 2B).

Fig. 2. *Photomicrographs illustrating some aspects of the compartmental organization of a number of afferents of nucleus accumbens.*

Scale bar in A 200 μm, in B 250 μm (applies also to C–F). ac, anterior commissure; C-P, caudate-putamen; ICjM, major island of Calleja; LS, lateral septal nucleus; LV, lateral ventricle.

caudomedial part of nucleus accumbens (Fig. 2A, B), leaving the areas of low ENK-IR free of labelling. In the more central and rostral regions of nucleus accumbens, paraventricular thalamic fibres preferentially terminate in the darkly stained ENK patches (Fig. 2C). In contrast, fibres from the intralaminar central medial and paracentral thalamic nuclei, which terminate predominantly in the central core and rostral parts of the nucleus, appear to avoid the ENK-immunoreactive patches (Fig. 2D; and[19]). In accordance with Herkenham *et al.*,[24] we found that thalamic fibres avoid cell clusters (Figs 2B, 4).

Hippocampal inputs, originating primarily in the subiculum, are topographically organized such that the ventral subiculum projects to the caudomedial shell, whereas successively more dorsal regions project to progressively more rostral and lateral parts of nucleus accumbens.[20] Caudomedially, ventral subicular fibres terminate predominantly in the cell-poor cone-shaped area, avoiding the cell clusters. The main terminal field of dorsal subicular fibres overlies the strong ChAT-IR in the ventral part of the shell. In addition, fibres terminate rostrolaterally in the nucleus, dorsal to the anterior commissure. In sections double-labelled for PHA-L and ENK, dorsal subicular afferents terminate both inside and outside the intense ENK patches (Figs 2E, 4).

In preliminary experiments with PHA-L injections in the caudal part of the basolateral amygdaloid nucleus, projections were observed to the caudomedial part of nucleus accumbens. These fibres terminate around the cone-shaped area and appear to show preference for the cell clusters (Figs 2F, 4).

Small injections of PHA-L in nucleus accumbens result in one of two different projection patterns in the mesencephalon. In a number of cases terminations were found

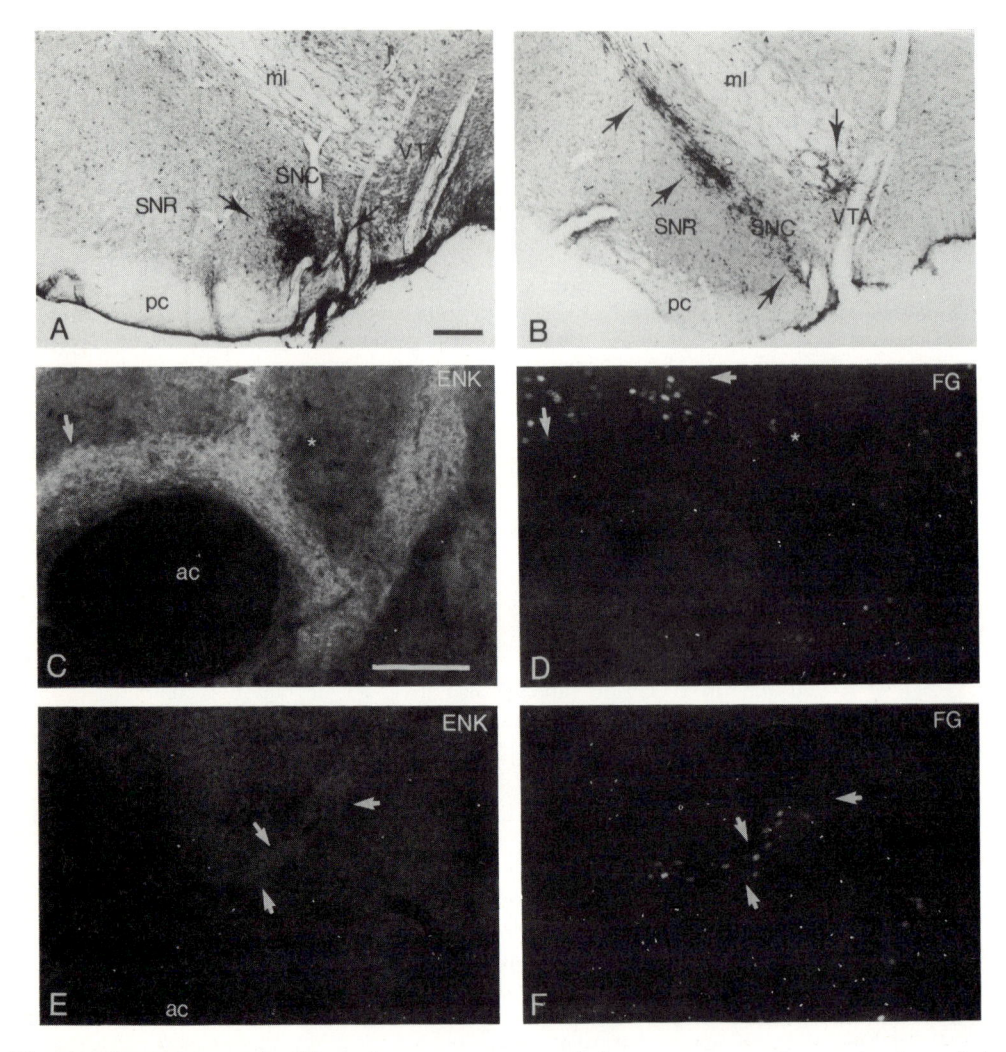

Fig. 3. *Photomicrographs illustrating some aspects of the compartmental organization of the efferents of nucleus accumbens.*
A, B. Anterograde PHA-L labelling in the medial part of the pars reticulata of the substantia nigra (A), and in the pars compacta (A9) and the ventral tegmental area (A10) following PHA-L injections in two different locations in nucleus accumbens (B). Scale bar represents 200 μm.
C-F. Two pairs of fluorescence micrographs showing the lack of neurons retrogradely labelled with Fluorogold (FG) in Encephalin (ENK) patches in the rostrolateral part of nucleus accumbens (C,D), and the overlap of a cluster of Fluorogold labelled cells and an ENK patch in the border region of nucleus accumbens and the caudate-putamen (E,F). The injection of Fluorogold was placed in the ventral tegmental area. Arrows and starlets indicate the same spots in the two pairs of photomicrographs. Scale bar represents 250 μm. ac, anterior commissure; ml, medial lemniscus; pc, cerebral peduncle; SNC, pars compacta of substantia nigra; SNR, pars reticulata of substantia nigra; VTA, ventral tegmental area.

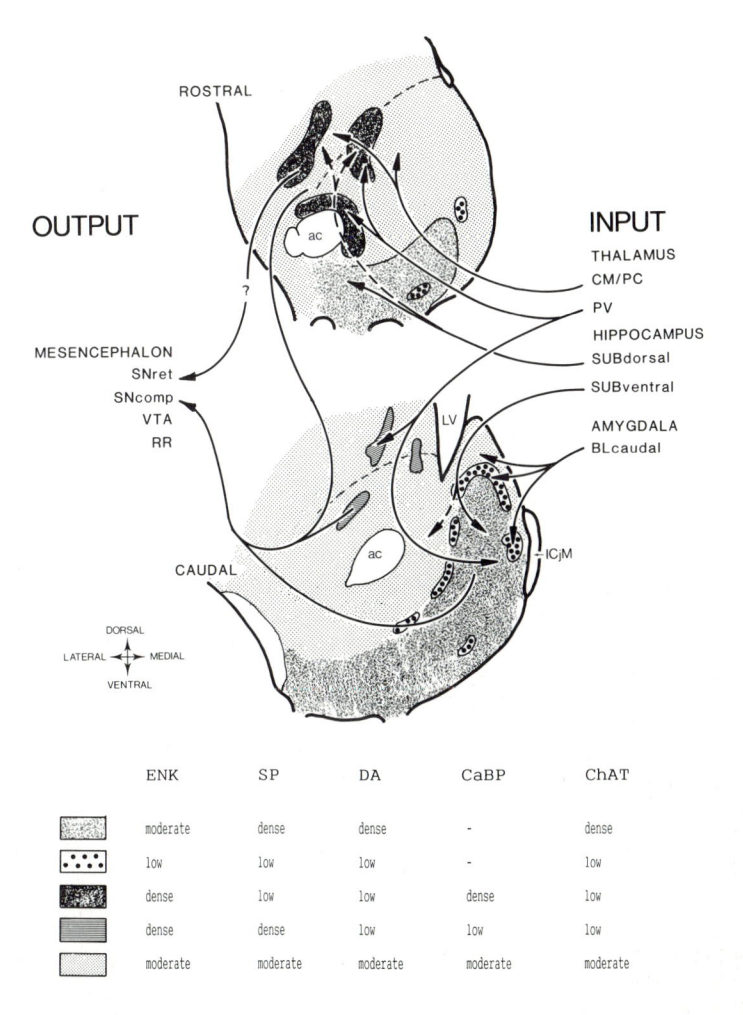

Fig. 4. *Diagram of two levels of nucleus accumbens showing the compartmental distribution of various neuroactive substances and the relation of some afferent and efferent fibre systems with this compartmental structure.* Note the difference between the outer shell and the inner core of the nucleus. Cell clusters are indicated with large dots.
ac, anterior commissure; BL, basolateral nucleus; CM, central medial nucleus; ICjM, major island of Calleja; LV, lateral ventricle; PC paracentral nucleus; PV, paraventricular nucleus; SN, substantia nigra (pars compacta and pars reticulata); SUB, subiculum; RR, retrorubral area; VTA, ventral tegmental area.

predominantly in the dorsomedial part of the pars reticulata of the substantia nigra (Figs. 3A, 4), with relatively little labelling in the adjacent dopaminergic cell group A9. Another set of PHA-L injections resulted in extensive terminal labelling in the ventral tegmental area (A10), the substantia nigra pars compacta (A9), and the retrorubral cell group (A8) (Figs 3B, 4). Thus, whereas the total distribution of ventral striatal projections in the mesencephalon matches the pattern described by Nauta *et al.*,[27] the results of the present experiments suggest that there exist two neuronal populations in the ventral striatum, each with their own mesencephalic terminal field. This conclusion is supported by the results of retrograde tracing experiments. Injections of the fluorescent tracer Fluorogold that included both the pars reticulata and the pars compacta resulted in a rather diffuse distribution of retrogradely-labelled neurons in nucleus accumbens. In constrast, following injections in the ventral tegmental area, clusters of retrogradely-labelled neurons are present throughout the nucleus. Employing immunofluorescent staining for ENK-IR, it was found that, caudomedially, the Fluorogold-positive cells are located within the cone-shaped area, whereas more laterally, in the border region between the caudate-putamen and nucleus accumbens, retrograde labelling overlaps dark ENK patches (Figs 3E,F, 4). Rostrally, the fluorescent cells lie outside the ENK patches (Figs 3C,D, 4).

Concluding remarks

Nucleus accumbens is a structure characterized by inhomogeneities in cyto- and chemo-architecture. The central core contains a complex patch/matrix type of organization, and the more loosely organized outer shell is formed into compartments which bear little resemblance to those in the core. Moreover, correspondence of various chemical markers with ENK patches in the core is highly dependent upon the rostrocaudal level. In the shell the neurochemical matches are more subtle and seem dependent upon gradients in ENK-immunoreactive staining. Furthermore, the input/output relations of the different compartments of the ventral striatum are quite specific. For example, although the cone-shaped area in the shell and the rostrolateral ENK-positive patches both receive thalamic inputs from the paraventricular nucleus, the outputs of these two regions to the mesencephalon are quite separate.

We speculate, therefore, that in contrast to the bicompartmental organization reported for the dorsal striatum (patch/matrix in rat[14,28]; striosome/matrix in cat[4,5]), nucleus accumbens in the ventral striatum comprises at least five different compartments (Fig. 4). Regarding the possible role of cholinergic neurons in intercompartmental communication, our immunohistochemical findings indicate that very few dendrites of these neurons cross borders between compartments. This suggests that their role in communicating between compartments in the ventral striatum is limited.

Acknowledgement—Supported by Medigon/NWO Program-Grant No. 900–550–093. Our thanks to Dr. M. P. Witter for reading the manuscript, Drs. F. P. Eckenstein and B. C. Wainer for the ChAT antisera, and Dr. C. R. Gerfen for the CaBP antiserum.

References

1 Kelley, A. E., Domesick, V. B. & Nauta, W. J. H. (1982): The amygdalo-striatal projection in the rat – an anatomical study by anterograde and retrograde tracing methods. *Neuroscience* **7**, 615–630.
2 Parent, A. (1986): *Comparative neurobiology of the basal ganglia*. New York: John Wiley & Sons, Inc.
3 Selemon, L. D. & Goldman-Rakic, P. S. (1985): Longitudinal topography and interdigitation of corticostriatal projections in the Rhesus Monkey. *J. Neurosci.* **5**, 776–794.
4 Graybiel, A. M. (1984): Neurochemically specified subsystems in the basal ganglia. In *Functions of the basal ganglia*, eds D. Evered & M. O'Connor, pp 114–149. London: Pitman.
5 Graybiel, A. M. & Ragsdale, C. (1983): Biochemical anatomy of the striatum. In *Chemical neuroanatomy*, ed P. Emson, pp 427–504. New York: Raven Press.
6 Cools, A. R. (1986): Mesolimbic dopamine and its control of locomotor activity in rats: differences in pharmacology and light/dark periodicity between the olfactory tubercle and the nucleus accumbens. *Psychopharmacology* **88**, 1–9.
7 Cools, A. R. & Van Rossum, J. M. (1980): Multiple receptors for brain dopamine in behavioural

regulation: concept of dopamine-e and dopamine-i receptors. *Life Sci.* **27**, 1237–1253.

8 Scheel-Krüger, J. (1986): Dopamine-GABA interactions: evidence that GABA transmits, modulates and mediates dopaminergic functions in the basal ganglia and the limbic system. *Acta Neurol. Scand.* Suppl. **107**, 1–54.

9 Scheel-Krüger, J. & Arnt, J. (1985): New aspects on the role of dopamine, acetylcholine, and GABA in the development of tardive dyskinesia. In *Psychopharmacology supplementum 2*, eds D. Casey, T. Chase, A. V. Christensen & J. Gerlag, pp 46–57. Berlin, Heidelberg: Springer–Verlag.

10 Gerfen, C. R. (1987): The neostriatal mosaic: the reiterated processing unit. In *Neurotransmitter interactions in the basal ganglia*, ed M. Sandler, C. Feuerstein & B. Scatton, pp 19–46. New York: Raven Press.

11 Penny, G. R., Wilson, C. J. & Kitai, S. T. (1988): Relationship of the axonal and dendritic geometry of spiny projection neurons to the compartmental organization of the neostriatum. *J. Comp. Neurol.* **269**, 275–289.

12 Bolam, J. P., Izzo, P. N. & Graybiel, A. M. (1988): Cellular substrate of the histochemically defined striosome/matrix system of the caudate nucleus: a combined Golgi and immunocytochemical study in cat and ferret. *Neuroscience* **24**, 853–875.

13 Chesselet, M. F. & Graybiel, A. M. (1986): Striatal neurons expressing somatostatin-like immunoreactivity: evidence for a peptidergic interneuronal system in the cat. *Neuroscience* **17**, 547–571.

14 Gerfen, C. R. (1985): The neostriatal mosaic. I. Compartmental organization of projections from the striatum to the substantia nigra in the rat. *J. Comp. Neurol.* **236**, 454–476.

15 Gerfen, C. R., Baimbridge, J. & Miller, J. J. (1985): The neostriatal mosaic: Compartmental distribution of calcium-binding protein and parvalbumin in the basal ganglia of the rat and monkey. *Proc. Natl. Acad. Sci. U.S.A*, **82**, 8780–8784.

16 Voorn, P., Jorritsma-Byham, B., Van Dijk, Ch. & Buijs, R. M. (1986): The dopaminergic innervation of the ventral striatum of the rat: a light-and electron microscopic study, using antibodies against dopamine. *J. Comp. Neurol.* **251**, 84–99.

17 Voorn, P., Gerfen, C. R. & Groenewegen, H. J. (1988): The compartmentalized organization of the ventral striatum of the rat: immunohistochemical distribution of enkephalin, substance P, dopamine, and calcium-binding protein. *J. Comp. Neurol.*, (in Press).

18 Wouterlood, F. G. (1988): Anterograde neuroanatomical tracing with *Phaseolus vulgaris*-leucoagglutinin combined with immunocytochemistry of gamma-amino butyric acid, choline acetyltransferase or serotonin. *Histochemistry* **89**, 421–428.

19 Berendse, H. W., Voorn, P., te Kortschot, A. & Groenewegen, H. J. (1988): Nuclear origin of thalamic afferents of the ventral striatum determines their relation to patch/matrix configurations in enkephalin-immunoreactivity in the rat. *J. Chem. Neuroanat.* **1**, 3–10.

20 Groenewegen, H. J., Vermeulen-Van der Zee, E., te Kortschot, A. & Witter, M. P. (1987): Organization of the projections from the subiculum to the ventral striatum in the rat. A study using anterograde transport of *Phaseolus vulgaris*-leucoagglutinin (PHA-L). *Neuroscience.* **23**, 103–120.

21 Wouterlood, F. G., Bol, J. G. J. M. & Steinbusch, H. W. M. (1987): Double-label immunocytochemistry: combination of anterograde neuroanatomical tracing with *Phaseolus vulgaris*–leucoagglutinin and enzyme immunocytochemistry of target neurons. *J. Histochem. Cytochem.* **35**, 817–823.

22 Zaborsky, L., Alheid, G. F., Beinfeld, M. C. Eiden, L. E., Heimer, L. & Palkovits, M. (1985): Cholecystokinin innervation of the ventral striatum: a morphological and radioimmunological study. *Neuroscience,* **14**, 427–453.

23 Domesick, V. B. (1981): Further observations on the anatomy of nucleus accumbens and caudatoputamen in the rat: similarities and contrasts. In *The neurobiology of the nucleus accumbens*, eds R. B. Chronister & J. F. DeFrance, pp 7–41. Brunswick, Maine: Hear Institute.

24 Herkenham, M., Moon Edley, S. & Stuart, J. (1984): Cell clusters in the nucleus accumbens of the rat, and the mosaic relationship of opiate receptors, acetylcholinesterase and subcortical afferent terminations. *Neuroscience* **11**, 562–593.

25 Groves, P. M., Martone, M., Young, S. J. & Armstrong, D. M. (1988): Three-dimensional pattern of enkephalin-like immunoreactivity in the caudate nucleus of the cat. *J. Neurosci.* **8**,

892–900.
26 Phelps, P. E. & Vaughn, J. E. (1986): Immunocytochemical localization of choline acetyltransferase in rat ventral striatum: a light and electron microscopic study. *J. Neurocytol.* **15**, 595–617.
27 Nauta, W. J. H., Smith, G. P., Faull, R. L. N. & Domesick V. B. (1978): Efferent connections and nigral afferents of the nucleus accumbens septi in the rat. *Neuroscience* **3**, 385–401.
28 Gerfen, C. R., Herkenham, M. & Thibault, J. (1987): The neostriatal mosaic. II. Compartmental organization of mesostriatal dopaminergic and non-dopaminergic systems. *J. Neurosci.* **7**, 3915–3934.

6

CODING IN SPATIAL RATHER THAN JOINT COORDINATES OF PUTAMEN AND MOTOR CORTEX PREPARATORY ACTIVITY PRECEDING PLANNED LIMB MOVEMENTS

G. E. Alexander and M. D. Crutcher

Department of Neurology, Johns Hopkins University School of Medicine, Baltimore, Maryland 21205, USA

Summary

Single cell studies in behaving monkeys have revealed that the putamen and various precentral motor areas, including primary motor cortex, contain neurons that show sustained changes in discharge rate following presentation of an instructional stimulus that specifies the required direction of a forthcoming, stimulus-triggered limb movement. Such preparatory activity has appeared to be related to the intended direction of limb movements, but in studies involving the preparation for visually guided reaching or tracking movements the directions of the limb movements have covaried systematically with the locations of the spatial targets. Thus, to determine whether this type of preparatory activity is linked to the intended direction of limb movement or to the spatial location of the target, we devised a set of motor preparation tasks that dissociated these two variables. In monkeys performing this set of tasks, neuronal activity was recorded from the arm areas of the putamen and primary motor cortex. In the putamen, the directional preparatory activity of 15 of 30 neurons was found to depend upon the expected location of the forthcoming target, rather than the intended direction of the limb movement required to acquire the target. This was also the case for 25 of 40 motor cortex neurons with directional preparatory activity. These results indicate that in both the putamen and primary motor cortex much of the preparatory neuronal activity related to target-directed limb movements may be coded in terms of the spatial coordinates of the target, rather than limb coordinates.

Introduction

Single cell recordings in monkeys making limb movements to track visual targets have shown that several precentral motor fields, including the primary motor cortex, premotor cortex and the supplementary motor area, contain not only movement-related neurons but also neurons that discharge selectively during the preparation for limb movements.[1-4] Recently, we have also found evidence of such preparatory activity in the putamen,[5] which receives topographic inputs from each of these precentral motor fields.[6-9]

Preparatory activity in all four of these motor areas is manifested by a sustained change in neuronal discharge rate preceding a stimulus-triggered limb movement for which the target has been specified in advance. When directionally selective, this type of preparatory activity is generally assumed to reflect the direction of the intended limb movement and thus to represent a neural correlate of 'motor set'.[2,10] However, in previous studies in which the location of a target served as the instructional stimulus for a reaching or tracking movement, the direction of the required limb movement was systematically related to target location. Thus, to determine whether directionally selective preparatory activity in primate motor areas was actually linked to the intended direction of limb movement, rather than the spatial location of the target, we devised a set of motor preparation tasks that dissociated these two variables. The results reported here are focused on preparatory activity in the putamen and primary motor cortex.

Methods

Three rhesus monkeys were each trained to perform two visuomotor delayed step-tracking tasks in which elbow movements were made both with and without prior knowledge of the direction of the forthcoming movement. The basic features common to both tasks are illustrated in Fig. 1. The angular displacement of the working forearm, which rested on a torqueable handle ('manipulandum'), was reflected by the position of a cursor (1 mm spot of light) that moved horizontally across the centre of the display in correspondence with flexion and extension movements of the elbow. The cursor would move one degree of visual angle (5.3 mm) for every one degree of elbow movement. The monkey was required to make such movements in order to align the cursor with a set of computer-controlled targets (0.5 × 7.5 mm vertical lines) presented sequentially on the display screen. Three targets were used in this paradigm, each defined by its location on the display screen: a 'centre' target was presented in the centre of the screen, a 'right' lateral target was presented 4 cm (7.5 degrees of visual angle) to the right of the centre position, and a 'left' lateral target 4 cm to the left of centre.

At the start of the trial, the centre target appeared and the monkey 'captured' it by making the appropriate arm movement to align the cursor with the target. During the 'pre-instruction' period, the monkey held the cursor stationary over the centre target for 1.5–3 sec. During this time the monkey could not predict the location of the upcoming target or the required direction of the next limb movement. When the centre target 'jumped' to one of the two (randomly selected) lateral locations, the monkey was required to capture this new target by moving his forearm in the appropriate lateral direction. After the first lateral target had been captured (and the cursor held in alignment with it for 500 msec), it jumped back to the centre position and the monkey was required to track the apparent target movement by returning the cursor to the centre position. During the ensuing 1.5–3.0 sec 'post-instruction' period, the monkey knew the direction of the upcoming (second) lateral movement of the trial because it was required

PRE-INSTRUCTION
(IMPENDING TARGET UNKNOWN)

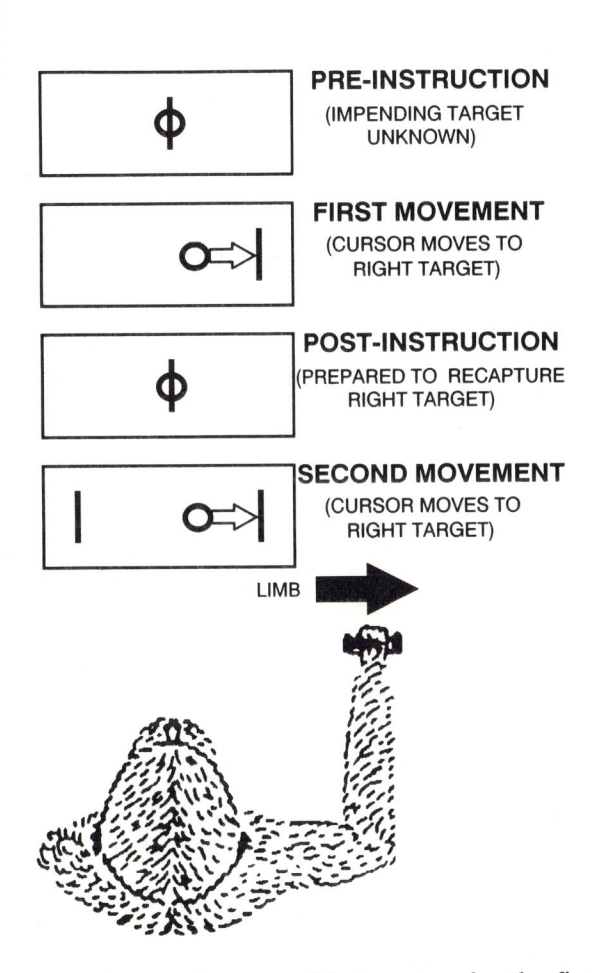

FIRST MOVEMENT
(CURSOR MOVES TO RIGHT TARGET)

POST-INSTRUCTION
(PREPARED TO RECAPTURE RIGHT TARGET)

SECOND MOVEMENT
(CURSOR MOVES TO RIGHT TARGET)

LIMB

Fig. 1. *Basic delayed step-tracking trial*. The four rectangles show the CRT display screen in front of the monkey at four different times in a single trial. Targets are represented by vertical bars, and the cursor by an open circle. See text for details.

to recapture the same side target as for the first lateral movement. The simultaneous appearance of both lateral targets was the cue for the monkey to make the second lateral movement.

The basic behavioural paradigm required the subject to remember the location of the first lateral target, which was extinguished throughout the post-instruction period, in order to be able to make the second lateral movement to the correct target when both lateral targets appeared. This feature of the task was designed to insure that the sensory conditions during the pre- and post-instruction periods were identical, and to guarantee the development of a directional motor set during the post-instruction period.

In order for the direction of the intended limb movement and the expected location of the correct side target to be dissociated during the post-instruction period, two types of delayed step-tracking tasks were used. The differences between the two tasks are illustrated in Fig. 2. For the 'standard' task, the directions of movement of the manipulandum and the cursor were directly related, so that the forelimb and cursor moved in the same direction. Thus on the standard task the monkey would move his forearm in the same relative direction as the target had moved in order to capture it with the cursor. For the 'visuomotor inversion' task, however, the directions of movement of the manipulandum and cursor were inversely related, so that the monkey was required to move the forelimb in the direction opposite to that in which the target had moved in order to capture it with the cursor. Except for the fact that on standard trials the target (and

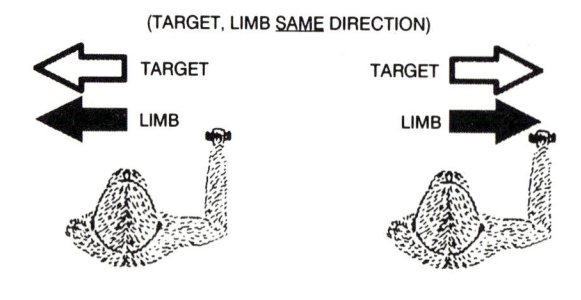

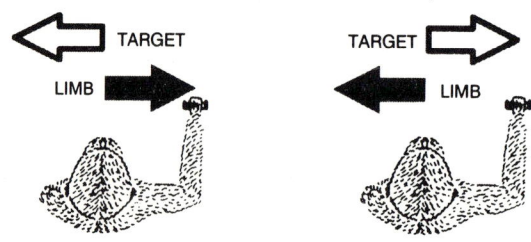

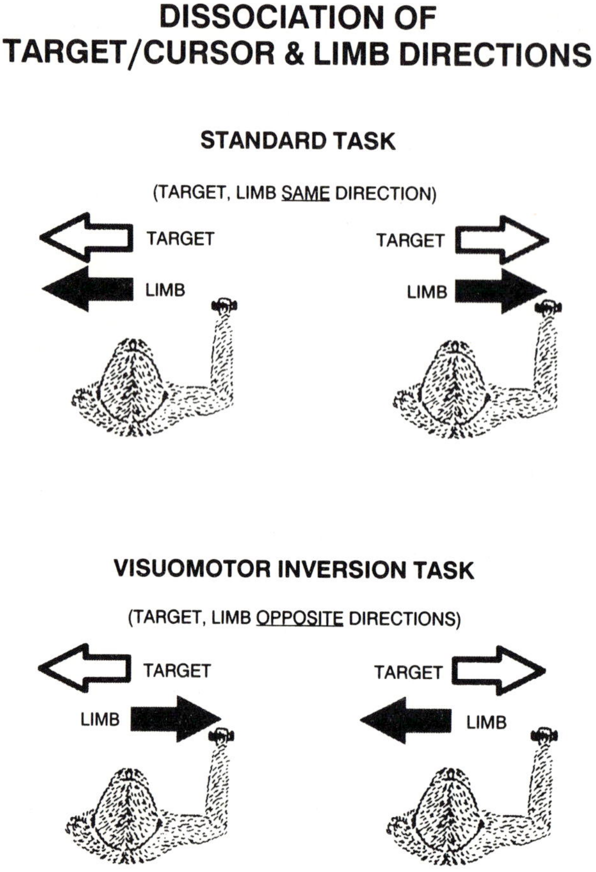

DISSOCIATION OF TARGET/CURSOR & LIMB DIRECTIONS

STANDARD TASK

(TARGET, LIMB SAME DIRECTION)

VISUOMOTOR INVERSION TASK

(TARGET, LIMB OPPOSITE DIRECTIONS)

Fig. 2. *Schematic illustration of the two tasks used to dissociate expected target location and direction of intended limb movement.* See text for details.

cursor) and the forelimb/manipulandum moved in the same direction, while on visuomotor inversion trials they moved in opposite directions, the two tasks were identical. The two tasks were administered in separate blocks of trials, making it unnecessary to provide an explicit cue as to which of the two tasks was being administered.

While the monkeys performed both types of delayed step-tracking tasks, neuronal activity was recorded either from the arm area of the putamen or from the arm area of primary motor cortex. Data collection and administration of the behavioural paradigms were controlled by an LSI-11/73 computer. Action potentials were discriminated and digitized using conventional techniques, and the resulting impulse trains, along with analog data including limb velocity, EMG activity and eye position (measured with the scleral search coil technique[11]), were collected on disk. Neuronal activity was analysed off-line in relation to the events (target shifts, movement onsets, movement offsets) and controlled variables (direction of limb movement, target location, instructional status) of the behavioural paradigms.

Results

Neurons with directional preparatory activity showed sustained increases or decreases in discharge rate throughout the post-instruction period (in comparison with the pre-instruction period) as well as significant differences between the preparatory activity that preceded movements to capture right- vs. left-sided targets. From three hemispheres of three monkeys, a total of 30 neurons in the arm area of the putamen and 40 neurons in the arm area of the primary motor cortex neurons showed directional preparatory activity and were tested with both the standard task and the visuomotor inversion task. For each of these cells, a comparison was made between the preparatory activity associated with the two different tasks, to determine whether such activity was dependent upon the direction of the forthcoming limb movement or the location of the next target to be captured.

Putamen

For 15 of 30 putamen neurons, the directional preparatory activity was found to depend upon the location of the next target to be captured, and not upon the direction of the limb movement needed to make the capture. The preparatory (post-instruction period) activity of one of these cells is illustrated in Fig. 3. This cell showed a sustained increase in discharge rate throughout the post-instruction period (relative to the pre-instruction firing rate) on trials in which the monkey had been instructed that the target to be captured at the end of this period would be located on the right side of the display. This was true both for standard trials and for visuomotor inversion trials. While it might have appeared from an analysis of only the standard trials, in which the limb and cursor moved in the same

TARGET-DEPENDENT PREPARATORY ACTIVITY IN PUTAMEN

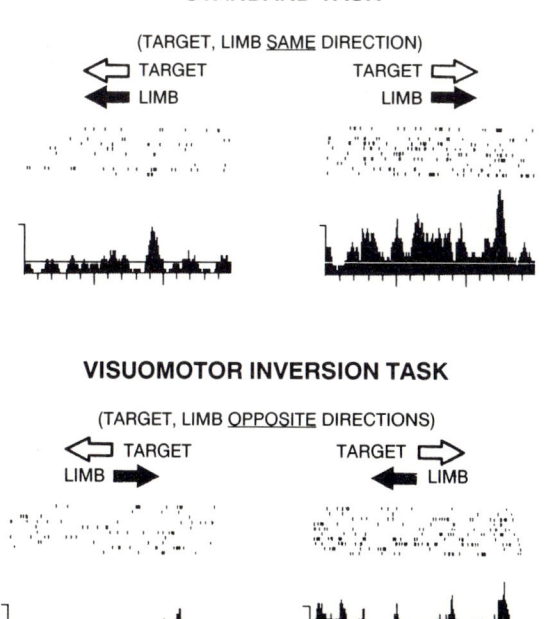

Fig. 3. *Example of target-dependent preparatory activity in the putamen.* Rasters and histograms illustrate the activity of a single neuron during the last 1500 ms of the post-instruction period of both the standard and the visuomotor inversion tasks. The tics on the x-scale at the bottom of each histogram are placed at 100 msec intervals, and the tic on the vertical scale at the left of each histogram represents 20 impulses/sec. The horizontal line through each histogram represents the 'baseline' firing rate during the pre-instruction period.

direction, that this type of preparatory activity was related to a forthcoming elbow extension movement that would move the forearm to the right, such an interpretation is precluded by the results observed on the visuomotor inversion trials. For on these trials the preparatory activity continued to be related to the expectation of capturing the right target at the conclusion of the post-instruction period, even though the monkey was now required to make an elbow flexion movement (that would move the forearm to the left) to achieve the same end.

While such 'target-dependent' preparatory activity was found to depend upon the location of the next target to be captured, scleral search coil recordings showed that it was not dependent upon eye position. Throughout the post-instruction periods of both standard trials and visuomotor inversion trials, each monkey would focus its gaze predominantly on the centre target, but would make frequent saccades to *both* side targets, regardless of the previously instructed location of the next target to be captured.

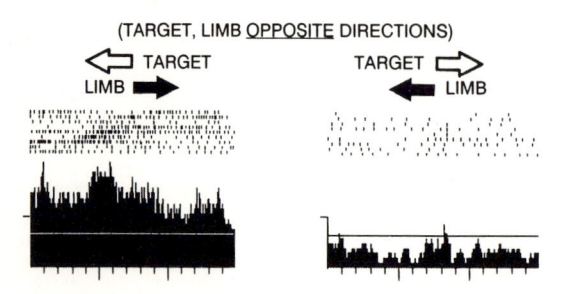

Seven putamen neurons showed directional preparatory activity that was found to depend upon the intended direction of limb movement, rather than the location of the next target to be captured. Extensive surveys of EMG activity from neck, trunk and limb muscles during task performance (including 20–30 muscle groups from each subject) failed to reveal any task-related patterns of muscular activity that corresponded to either the 'target-dependent' or 'limb-dependent' directional preparatory activity.

TARGET-DEPENDENT PREPARATORY ACTIVITY IN MOTOR CORTEX

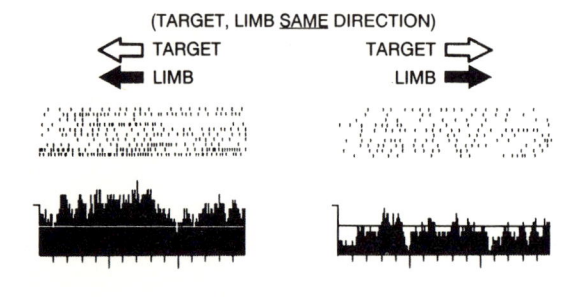

Fig. 4. *Example of target-dependent preparatory activity of a single neuron in the motor cortex.* Conventions are the same as Fig. 3.

Eight putamen neurons that showed directional preparatory activity on the standard task manifested preparatory activity on the visuomotor inversion task that was non-directional. These cells were classified as having preparatory activity that was 'indeterminate' in terms of possible target- or limb-dependence.

Motor cortex

Directional preparatory activity was found to be target-dependent in 25 of the 40 motor cortex neurons. The post-instruction activity of one such cell is illustrated in Fig. 4. This neuron showed selective activation throughout the post-instruction period (relative to the pre-instruction period) of both standard and visuomotor inversion trials in which the monkey had been instructed that the next target to be captured would be on the left side of the display, regardless of whether this would require him to move his forearm to the left (as on the standard trials) or to the right (as on the visuomotor inversion trials). Microstimulation at the recording site evoked elbow flexion at a threshold of 30 microamps.

Two motor cortex neurons showed directional preparatory activity that was limb-dependent, and the remaining 13 were classified as indeterminate.

Discussion

The present study of neuronal activity in the putamen and primary motor cortex was designed to determine whether directionally-selective preparatory activity that precedes planned, target-directed limb movements is actually related to the intended direction of limb movement or reflects, instead, the expected location of the target. The principal finding was that in both structures this type of activity is largely target-dependent, although a few cells showed limb-dependent activity. We consider both types of preparatory activity to be involved in the planning of movements. A number of alternative interpretations of the target-dependent and limb-dependent preparatory activity observed in this study have been considered and rejected, for various reasons. The possibility that such responses might be attributable either to tonic muscular activity or to fixations of gaze during the post-instruction period has been ruled out by concurrent EMG and scleral search coil recordings during task performance. Such general factors as arousal, motivation or task-related sensory conditions would seem to be excluded by the directional nature of the preparatory activity.

For motor structures such as the putamen and primary motor cortex, it seemed natural to expect that directionally selective preparatory activity was more likely to be related to the direction of the movement itself than to the spatial location of the instructional stimulus, even when that stimulus would serve as the target or goal of the movement. Previous reports of directionally-selective preparatory activity have suggested that such activity represented a neural correlate of motor set, and that the directional nature of the response reflected the intended direction of limb movement.[1,3,5] Those cells with limb-dependent preparatory activity observed in the present study do support such an interpretation. However, the target-dependent preparatory activity observed in this study is clearly incompatible with such an interpretation, as it appears to be coded in terms of the expected location of the spatial target, irrespective of the intended direction of limb movement required to capture the target. The demonstration of such target-dependent preparatory activity in the putamen and motor cortex suggests that it may be necessary to reassess the role of these structures in the control of movement.

It is well recognized that certain types of movements, including target-directed limb movements, must be planned at the 'highest' level in terms of the goal or object of the movement, even though at some (presumably 'lower') level of motor processing the execution of such movements will require translation of object level specifications into the appropriate patterns of muscle activations.[12,13] What remains unclear, of course, is how and where these top-down transformations are implemented in the nervous system. Largely on the basis of their connections with other motor structures, the putamen and primary motor cortex are generally considered to participate in the 'middle' levels of motor processing. The prevalence of target-dependent preparatory activity in these two structures suggests, however, that while both have been strongly implicated in the direct control of movement execution, they may also play a role in some of the highest levels of motor planning. This is not to suggest that the putamen and motor cortex should now be considered 'high-level' motor structures, or that the motor system does not include hierarchical features, but to emphasize that even the 'middle' levels of the motor system may be concerned with the target or goal of a movement, and not simply with the joint movements and muscle activations needed to achieve that goal.

Acknowledgement—This study was supported by NIH grant NS-17678 from the United States Public Health Service.

References

1. Tanji, J. & Evarts, E. V. (1976): Anticipatory activity of motor cortex neurons in relation to direction of an intended movement. *J. Neurophysiol.* **39**, 1062–1068.
2. Thach, W. T. (1978): Correlation of neuronal discharge with pattern and force of muscular activity, joint position and direction of intended next movement in motor cortex and cerebellum. *J. Neurophysiol.* **41**, 654–676.
3. Weinrich, M. & Wise, S. P. (1982): The premotor cortex of the monkey. *J. Neurosci.* **2**, 1329–1345.
4. Tanji, J., Taniguchi, K. & Saga, T. (1980): Supplementary motor area: neuronal response to motor instructions. *J. Neurophysiol.* **43**, 60–68.
5. Alexander, G. E. (1987): Selective neuronal discharge in monkey putamen reflects intended direction of planned limb movements. *Exp. Brain Res.* **67**, 623–634.
6. Kunzle, H. (1975): Bilateral projections from precentral motor cortex to the putamen and other parts of the basal ganglia. An autoradiographic study in Macaca fascicularis. *Brain Res.* **88**, 195–209.
7. Liles, S. L. (1975): Cortico-striatal evoked potentials in the monkey (Macaca mulatta). *Electroencephalogr. Clin. Neurophysiol.* **38**, 121–129.
8. Kunzle, H. (1978): An autoradiographic analysis of the efferent connections from premotor and adjacent prefrontal regions (area 6 and 9) in Macaca fascicularis. *Brain Behav. Evol.* **15**, 185–234.
9. Selemon, L. D. & Goldman-Rakic, P. S. (1985): Longitudinal topography and interdigitation of cortico-striatal projections in the rhesus monkey. *J. Neurosci.* **5**, 776–794.
10. Wise, S. P. & Mauritz, K. H. (1985): Set-related neuronal activity in the premotor cortex of rhesus monkeys: effects of changes in motor set. *Proc. R. Soc. Lond.* **233**, 331–354.
11. Robinson, D. A. (1963): A method of measuring eye movement using a scleral search coil in a magnetic field. *IEEE Trans. Biomed. Electron.* **10**, 137–145.
12. Bernstein, N. (1984): The problem of the interrelation of co-ordination and localization. In: *Human motor actions. Bernstein reassessed*, ed H. T. A. Whiting, pp 77–119. Amsterdam: North-Holland.
13. Hollerbach, J. M. (1982): Computers, brains and the control of movement. *Trends Neurosci.* **5**, 189–192.

7

NEURONAL ACTIVITY IN THE PRIMATE CAUDATE NUCLEUS AND VENTRAL STRIATUM REFLECTS ASSOCIATION BETWEEN STIMULI DETERMINING BEHAVIOUR

Graham V. Williams

Department of Experimental Psychology, University of Oxford, South Parks Road, Oxford OX1 3UD, UK.

Summary

Extracellular recordings were made from more than 1000 cells in both the ventral striatum and supra-adjacent caudate nucleus of three cynomologus monkeys. Neuronal responses were examined in a number of different tasks and to a wide range of stimuli.

Nearly 20 per cent of striatal cells responded to stimuli used as cues in a visual discrimination task. Many of these neurons responded to cues used in other tasks and to other visual stimuli. A smaller group of cells (124), not exclusive from those above, responded to the S+ stimulus (= lick to obtain fruit juice) presented in visual discrimination task. Cells responding to both S+ and the sight of food (42) were usually found in the caudate nucleus, while most cells responding to the sight of food but not to S+ (74) were located in ventral striatum (86 per cent). All cells responding to aversive stimuli (34), and the large majority (50/62) of cells responding to novel or familiar stimuli, were located in the ventral striatum.

A large convergence of inputs from different stimuli was found on single cells. Many such stimuli had the ability to signal reward availability, and the neuronal responses appeared to be dependent on this condition whether or not a behavioural response was required.

These neuronal responses indicate an association between stimuli which is regulated by a discriminative feedback and not necessarily determined by a behavioural response.

Introduction

Since the original description of parkinsonism and Huntington's chorea, research in basal ganglia function and motor disorders has sought to elucidate the abnormal mechanisms involved. Lesions of striatum or substantia nigra do not readily provide a clear relationship between their function and the production of movements, but do suggest their involvement in the control of behaviour generally.[1,2]

The striatum itself consists of certain regions defined by their morphology, histochemistry and telencephalic afferents. The head of the caudate is primarily innervated by prefrontal cortex,[3] the putamen is innervated by somatomotor cortex[4] (areas 1, 2, 3, 4, & 6) and ventral striatum receives inputs from the limbic system, including hippocampus and amygdala, as well as inferotemporal, entorhinal and anterior cingulate cortex.[5]

Lesions in particular parts of striatum produce deficits which closely resemble those found after lesions of the particular cortical areas which are the main afferents to those parts.[6] It appears that the striatum provides an important route for the modulation of behaviour by sensory events.[7] This is exemplified by the deficit seen in parkinsonism of the somatosensory guidance of movements in the absence of visual feedback.[8] As well as the observable movement disorders, people with parkinsonism also show cognitive deficits[9] and a high incidence of depression has been reported. Thus parkinsonism is a complex disorder, not just affecting movement but probably a number of internal correlates of behaviour in the wider sense.

Recordings from single cells in the striatum make it possible to study the information processing which occurs at this site. It is likely that the vast majority of these recordings are from output cells, as some 96 per cent of striatal neurons have efferent axons and it is these cells that appear to be typically recorded from.

Consistent with its known cortical afferents, the putamen displays neuronal responses which are somatotopically organized, with responses which appear to be focussed around the movement of joints and body parts.[10,11] These responses appear to be both somatosensory and movement-related. However, this activity does not appear to code for the parameters of movements *per se* but rather for the anticipated target (see Alexander & Crutcher, this volume, p.60).

Neuronal activity in the caudate nucleus appears from a number of studies to be related to the conditional nature of stimuli, particularly those that signal for the preparation for or initiation of movements.[12–14]

In preliminary reports of neuronal responses recorded in ventral striatum,[15,16] a similarity was seen with caudate nucleus, but in addition a number of cells displayed responses to stimuli of emotional or motivational significance.

This report is of certain findings from a large-scale study (see Williams[17]) of neuronal activity in caudate nucleus and ventral striatum which illustrate a particular aspect of striatal function—the correlation between neuronal responses to a stimulus and the ability of that stimulus to make the animal anticipate, expect, or predict the occurrence of following stimuli or events. This will be examined in relationship to behaviour, particularly in terms of feedback control.

Methods

Recordings were taken from the extracellular impulses of 1002 neurons in caudate nucleus and 1112 neurons in ventral striatum using glass-coated tungsten microelectrodes. Daily recording tracks were made in different positions in the striatum so that in three male cynomologus monkeys most areas of ventral striatum and the supra-adjacent caudate nucleus were surveyed. Once accustomed to the laboratory and the behavioural tasks each monkey was fitted with an implant under thiopentone sodium anaesthesia. This implant consisted of a well upon which a miniature stereotaxic electrode positioner could be placed, a number of reference electrodes, and silver/silver chloride electrodes for recording eye movements.

After 1 or 2 weeks recovery the animals were reintroduced to the laboratory and recordings began once they were proficient in the tasks. At the start of each day the positioner as well as the arm of an hydraulic microdrive were fitted over the implant. The electrode was attached to the microdrive and ran through a small guide tube (used to puncture the dura under local anaesthesia) which could be moved through the positioner. Recordings were made on the majority of tracks from the top of caudate nucleus to the base of ventral striatum, using a six degree medial tilt.

The monkeys were trained in a number of situations. In a visual discrimination task (VST) each trial began with the simultaneous presentation of a light and tone for 500 msec. These stimuli provided cues to the animal that a visual discriminative stimulus would follow immediately. One discriminative stimulus was a white circle, termed S+, which indicated that the monkey could lick a tube just in front of the mouth to obtain fruit juice on reward trials. The other stimulus was a white square which indicated that the monkey should not lick in order to avoid receiving hypertonic saline on passive avoidance trials. The S+ and S− trials were presented in semi-random order, usually for 2 sec. The VDT is shown schematically at the top of Fig. 1. As well as being presented on a monitor, the S+ and S− stimuli could be presented behind a shutter.

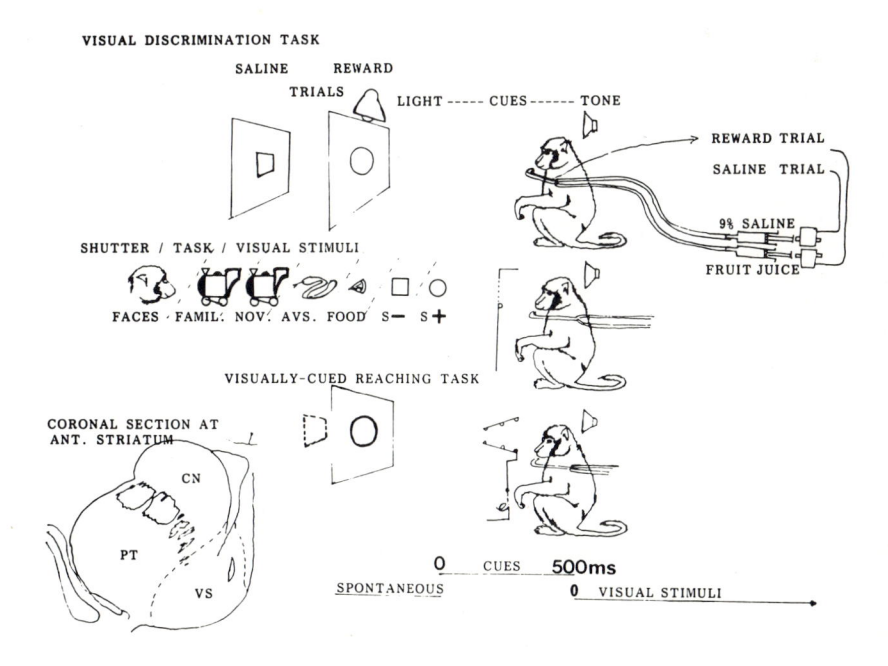

Fig. 1 *Schematic illustration of the visual discrimination task (VDT), the shutter presentation of visual stimuli and the visually-cued reaching task (VCRT). Bottom left: coronal section of striatum showing arbitrary demarcations of caudate nucleus (CN) and ventral striatum (VS). Bottom right: typical recording period.*

As shown in Fig. 1, the use of the electromagnetic shutter (15 msec opening time, 6 cm diameter) allowed the presentation of a number of different categories of visual stimuli. These categories included foods, as small pieces (eg, peanuts), which were given to the monkey to eat after a short delay following presentation. Aversive stimuli included toy snakes and other objects which the monkey would seek to avoid and was generally somewhat fearful of. These stimuli were presented only as necessary and were interspersed with food and S+ trials. A large selection of junk objects were used to present novel stimuli (seen for the first time for that day) and then the same stimuli shown once again as familiar objects after 0–100 intervening stimuli had been presented.

Stimuli in these categories were presented for typically 2 sec. By interspersing S+ and S− trials among these stimuli the monkey was kept alert and ready to respond. Only very rarely were any licks made (by accident) on presentation of any stimulus but the S+. Food trials were automatically reinforced *without any required response from the animal*. Aversive trials were only occasionally reinforced by bringing the object close to the animal. Control trials were often made with no stimulus present or with the shutter obscured.

In a visually-cued reaching task (VCRT), illuminating an LED indicated that the monkey had 1 sec to reach to a hidden compartment to obtain foods (usually peanuts). The VCRT was often used in conjunction with VDT so as to interrupt that task. The VCRT is illustrated in Fig 1 beneath the shutter paradigm. A similar auditory-cued task was used (not shown) in which a loud click indicated that the monkey could lick *ad libitum* to obtain juice.

Finally, each cell was tested directly for responses related to feeding. Cells were also studied for any somatosensory, auditory, and movement-related responses.

The data were logged on computer as peristimulus time rastergrams or histograms, ie, the number of spikes (impulses) occurring per bin (a unit of time which could be varied from 10 msec to 100 msec). Spikes were recorded over the whole trial, as shown in the bottom right of Fig. 1, or in more detail over part of the trial. Thus accurate response latencies could be obtained, as well as the mean response to a particular stimulus.

Recording sites were reconstructed to an accuracy within 0.5 mm from X-ray photographs taken at the end of each track, microdrive readings, and numerous reference sites, Perfusion was performed after a lethal dose of anaesthetic. Brain sections were stained with cresyl violet or silver stained for nissl or myelin, from which an arbitrary boundary of ventral striatum was estimated. This is shown for one coronal plane at the bottom left of Fig. 1. Recordings were made from 3 mm anterior to 2 mm posterior to this plane.

Results

It was found that 6.6 per cent of cells in caudate nucleus and 4.3 per cent in ventral striatum showed differential responses to the S+ and S−, ie, between reward and passive avoidance trials. These were mainly excitatory responses to S+ and were closely related to stimulus onset. The latencies of these responses varied from 100 to 230 msec, with a median of 160 msec in ventral striatum and 180 msec in caudate nucleus. Another 2 per cent of cells in caudate nucleus and 1.8 per cent in ventral striatum responded to both S+ and the sight of foods. This is shown for one cell in Fig. 2. This is a rastergram recording the neuronal activity during presentation of visual stimuli. Little or no activity occurs during presentation of the cues but an excitatory response is evident from about 190 msec to the sight of foods or S+, but not to aversives or S−, The monkey obtained the foods after the end of each trial without having to make any conditioned response. On S+ trials

Stimulus-induced neuronal activity in the primate striatum

the monkey had to lick, as shown by the tall bars, to obtain juice. This is evidence of the convergence of information on two different conditioned stimuli on the same neuron for a small population of striatal units. One requiring a conditioned response for reinforcement but the other simply predicting reinforcement.

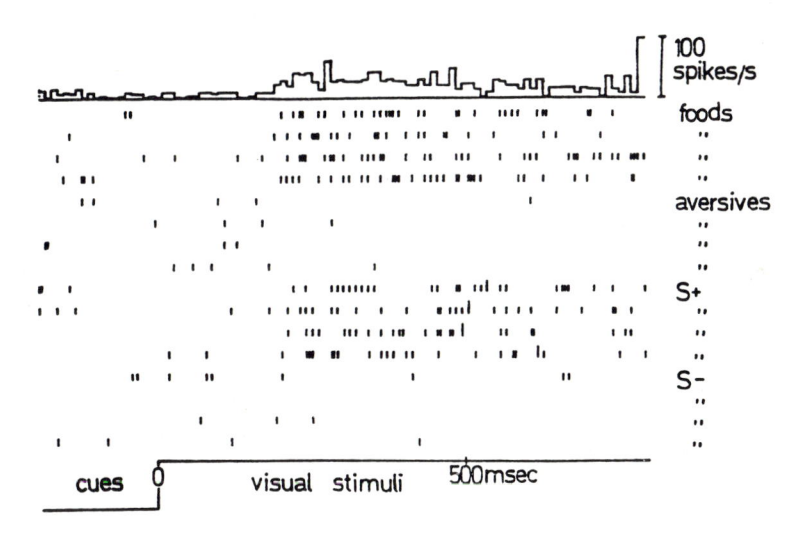

Fig. 2. *Rastergram showing activity as the presence of a count in 10 msec bins for one neuron during presentation of four types of visual stimulus. Long bar: lick response on S+ trials. Top: peristimulus-time histogram (sum of counts over all trials).*

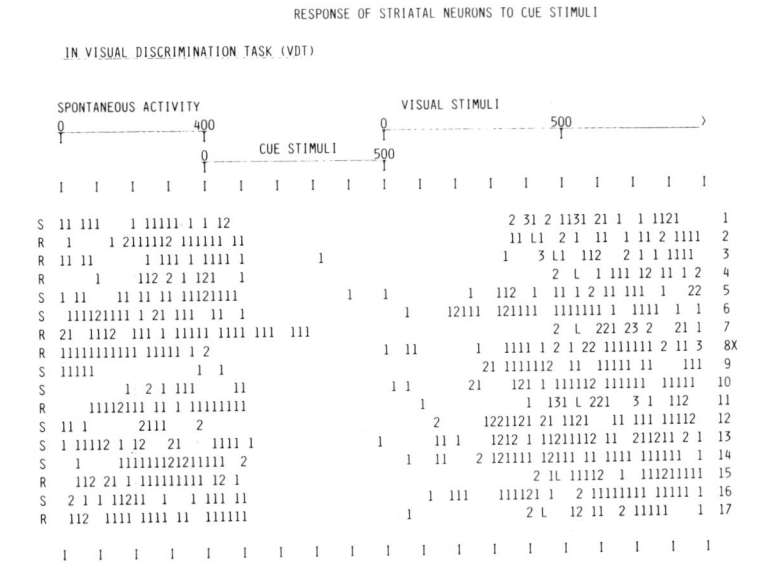

Fig. 3. *Rastergram of activity of one cell as counts/20 msec bins during visual discrimination task. S: S− trial. R: S+ trial. X (trial 8): error.*

Responses to the task cues were a common feature of striatal cells, being found in 23 per cent of cells in the caudate nucleus and 17.5 per cent of those in ventral striatum. Some 34 per cent of these responses were inhibitory as can be seen in the rastergram of the response of one cell in Fig. 3. Note that the activity remains low for longer on reward (R) trials except where the monkey omits making a response on trial 8 (X). The opposite was seen for many cells with an excitatory response to the cues which continued on presentation of the S+ but halted on S− trials. These are described as enabling responses. More than 50 per cent of units discriminating in response between S+ and S− also responded to the task cues. This shows a convergence of responses to a conditioned stimulus which signals for the preparation of making or withholding lick movements and the conditioned stimulus which indicates which action is appropriate.

Besides this convergence to two related stimuli in the visual discrimination task many cells which responded to the task cues also responded to the audio cue for *ad libitum* licking, and/or the LED cue in the visual reaching task, as well as other environmental cues such as the sight of the investigator's arm reaching over to a place where food was kept. The breadth of this convergence is illustrated by the responses of one cell to a range of stimuli as shown in Fig. 4. This is a bar chart showing firing rates of the cell with the spontaneous (resting) activity as the baseline. Both the task cues and S+ produced a robust excitatory response, while S− had no effect. An even greater response was found to the auditory cue for *ad libitum* licking when the monkey was receiving fruit juice, but this deteriorated rapidly over the next few trials (shown averaged in one bar) when saline was received instead. In prefeeding, mouth movements and probably salivation were initiated but no neuronal response was evoked. Finally, when the juice was actually delivered a clear response is evoked: this was found for 15 cells responding to S+ in the VDT, 14 of which showed clear post-lick responses in the task. This response is much greater than that to less preferred liquids such as 20 per cent glucose or water. General arousal evoked by sudden noises or touching the tail did not activate this or other such cells. These cells show a convergence of information on conditioned stimuli indicating reward is available and the stimulus indicating the reward itself.

Investigations were made to examine the nature of the responses to conditioned stimuli. It was found that cells responding to the original S+ could develop a similar response to an entirely new S+ stimulus. This is shown for one cell in Fig. 5. When the monkey learned the task using the new stimulus the neuron developed a similar response to this stimulus. In a separate test the fruit juice was withheld on reward trials and the cell response, like that of others tested, showed an extinction which matched the extinction of the behavioural lick response. Likewise, the cell also responded to the auditory cue for *ad-libitum* licking, but not if the juice was withheld. Priming the monkey to lick again, by a squirt of juice from the tube, also activated the cell. Mouth movements evoked no activity, but this cell, like 21 others tested, responded when the monkey reached for food but not for non-food objects outside of any task. Thus a sub-population of striatal cells show conditional or context-dependent activity. These cells respond in a number of different situations which have the availability of reward in common but not necessarily a common behavioural response.

In a similar fashion neurons responding to the sight of food, 33 in the caudate nucleus and 82 in the ventral striatum, could also respond (in 38 cases) to the taste of different foods. This is illustrated by the responses of one cell shown in Fig. 6a. As well as responding to the sight of different foods this cell, like many others, responded to the taste of different foods. Note the conditional response to the auditory cue for *ad libitum* licking which was abolished when reward was withheld. In further tests the cell can be seen to respond differentially to the taste of different foods: maximally to raisin, the most preferred food all the time, and not at all to water. This convergence of the sight and

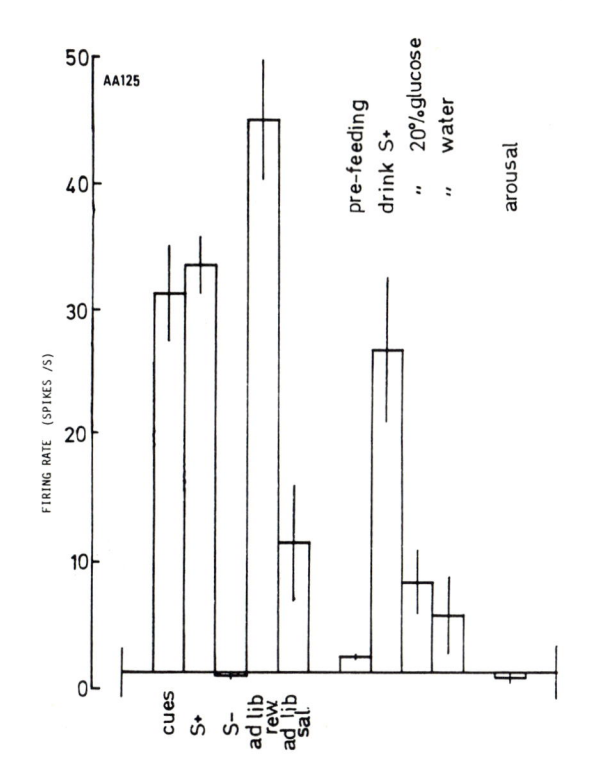

Fig. 4. Bar chart showing mean responses of one cell to different stimuli in various situations. Baseline: spontaneous activity.

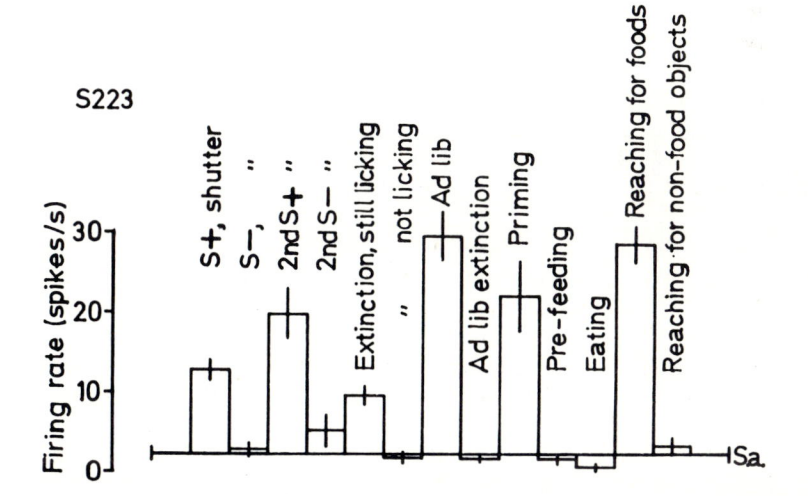

Fig. 5. Bar chart showing mean responses of one cell to a number of conditional stimuli presented in various situations. Sa: spontaneous activity.

taste of foods influencing the same cells may reflect an association between stimuli dependent upon a discriminatory feedback. Many of these cells, when tested, showed differential responses to the sight and taste of different foods which reflected the animal's preference for those foods.

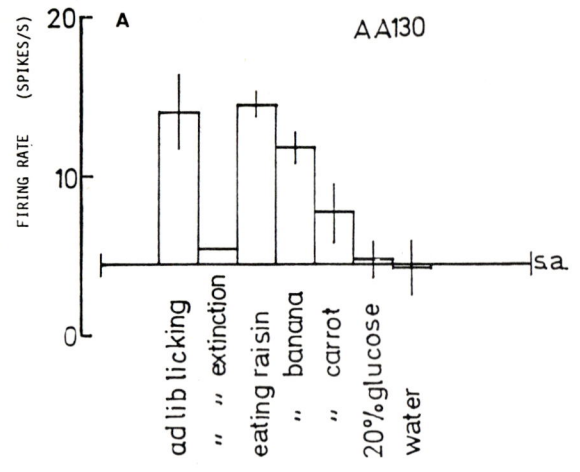

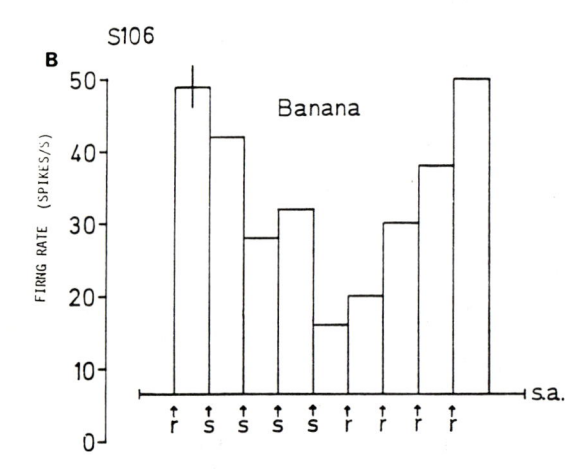

Fig. 6. *A: Bar chart showing mean responses of one cell during drinking or eating different foods.* This neuron was one of the group responding to the sight of foods. *B: responses of another cell to sight of banana after normal reinforcement (r) or aversive reinforcement (s). Sa: spontaneous activity.*

The importance of the reinforcement for neuronal responses evoked by the sight of food is illustrated in Fig. 6b. This cell initially shows a large response to the sight of banana when this is reinforced by the normal food (r) but after reinforcement with aversive salted banana (s) this response attenuates rapidly over successive trials. Once normal reinforcement is returned the response also recovers rapidly. In general, for these neuronal responses, showing foods without reinforcement led to habituation over three to five trials. Thus an association between the conditioned stimulus (ie, sight of food) and the reinforcer (ie, taste of food) may be regulated by reward or incentive feedback. One key difference in neuronal activity between caudate nucleus and ventral striatum was that 2.3 per cent of cells in ventral striatum showed responses to aversive stimuli whereas this response was never found in caudate nucleus. This is shown in Fig. 7. A clear excitatory response can be seen on aversive trials, but an inhibition occurs on food trials. In addition, many neurons in the ventral striatum responded to foods only and not to S+. A total of 20 cells in this region showed responses in opposite directions to the sight of foods and aversives.

Another important difference was seen in neuronal responses to novel and familiar stimuli. These responses are illustrated for five different cells in Fig. 8. In VS, 4.5 per cent

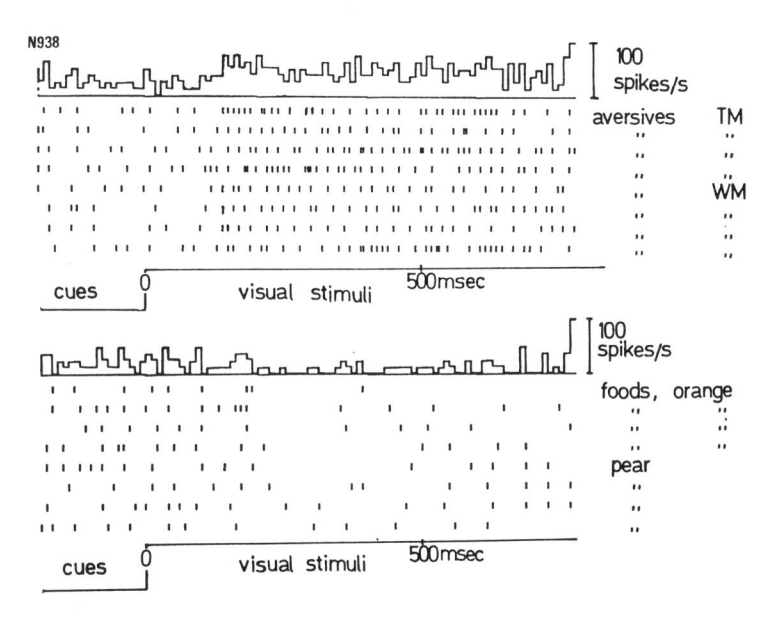

Fig. 7. *Rastergrams of neuronal activity of one cell (10 msec bins), with peristimulus-time histograms shown above.* Top: aversive trials; TM; toy monkey, WM, white mask. Bottom: food trials with two different stimuli.

of neurons yielded one or other of these responses, many showing inhibition to novel stimuli or opposite responses to novel and familiar stimuli. Only 1.4 per cent of cells in caudate nucleus gave responses to the stimuli, and then usually a simple excitatory response to novel objects. It was found that 45 of these units in ventral striatum also responded to the sight of foods and/or S+, or to aversive stimuli. This is evidence for a convergence of recognition and association memory on single cells in VS.

Discussion

The data presented here suggest that association between stimuli that are significant to behaviour is important in striatal function. It has been shown that information from many different stimuli can converge on single striatal units. Most of these stimuli have in common the ability to signal availability of reward although the behavioural responses to obtain these rewards may differ. This suggests that the outputs of single striatal units are not sequestered to influencing any particular movement. However, different populations may have such an influence. The neuronal responses reported here appear to be very dependent on discriminatory feedback. Thus, if several events are occurring more or less simultaneously, the stimulus which is associated with the strongest reinforcement is liable to influence striatal transmission more than other stimuli present. Such stimuli may influence whole arrays of striatal cells and may thus influence movement. However, it was found that striatal neurons, especially those in ventral striatum, could respond to stimuli which signalled forthcoming reward without any required response. This finding, as well as the abundance of cue-related responses, suggests an important role for the striatum not just in directing attention or behavioural orientation towards a particular stimulus but also in holding attention on that stimulus.

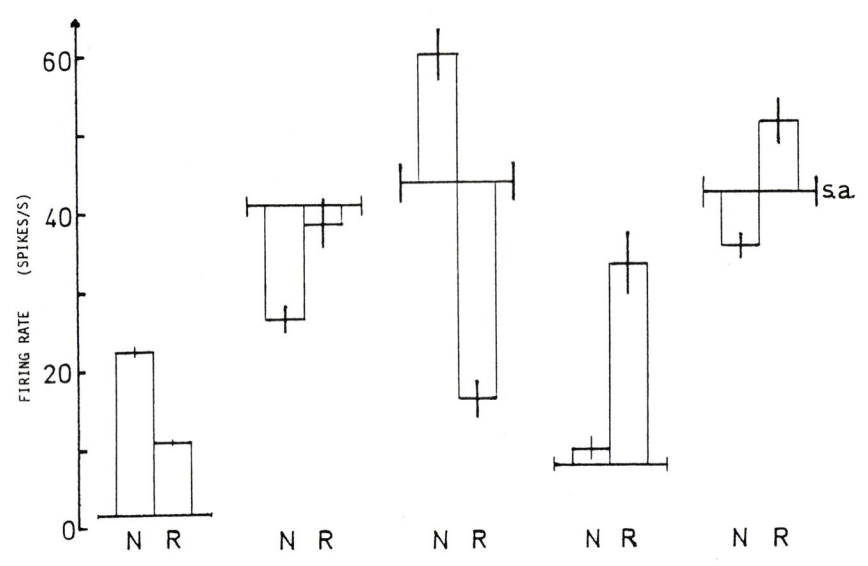

Fig. 8. *Bar chart showing mean responses of five different cells to novel (N) and familiar (R) stimuli, each cell exhibiting one of the response types found for these stimuli.*

The striatum has many loops of afferent and efferent connections with other brain structures through which association between stimuli may be modified by feedback. One obvious loop is that formed with substantia nigra pars compacta.[18] Schultz[19] has obtained data from recordings of dopaminergic neurons in awake primates which show a remarkable similarity between the general responses of those neurons and many of the neuronal responses reported here. However, dopaminergic neurons appear to be activated by similar stimuli at clearly earlier latencies. Thus dopaminergic inputs may modulate striatal responses, and striatal outputs may then feedback on to the cells providing those inputs. Another important loop is created by the influence of the caudate nucleus on premotor cortex, which in turn projects directly to the putamen. It is conceivable that activation of an array of caudate neurons could lead to an enabling of an array of putamen cells. The topography of this linkage may be highly dependent on associative mechanisms in the caudate nucleus and might reflect some of the spatial parameters of the stimulus.

In conclusion, caudate nucleus appears to process stimuli which depend on the context for their significance, part of which is an association with another sensory stimulus (or reinforcement) which may in turn depend on a behavioural response. A similar processing may be occurring in ventral striatum but on information in a more general context, being related to emotion, motivation and memory. The abundance and variation of cue-related activity in both regions is consistent with suggested functions of selective attention and behavioural switching based on the competing significance of environmental events and the general context in which they occur.

Acknowledgements—This work was undertaken in collaboration with a number of colleagues at various times, particularly Edmund Rolls, Tiana Leonard and Chantal Stern, with whom it is hoped to publish this work in full. The author was supported by an S.E.R.C. CASE studentship in conjunction with Janssen Pharmaceuticals.

References

1. Villablanca, J. R. & Olmstead, C. E. (1982): The striatum: A fine tuner of the brain. *Acta Neurobiol. Exp.* **42**, 227–299.
2. Iversen, S. D. (1984): Behavioural effects of manipulations of basal ganglia neurotransmitters. In *Functions of the basal ganglia*, Ciba Symposium 107, pp 183–195. London: Pitman.
3. Goldman, P. S. & Nauta, W. J. H. (1977): An intricately patterned prefrontocaudate projection. *J. Comp. Neurol.* **171**, 369–386.
4. Jones, E. G., Coulter, J. D., Burton, H. & Porter, R. (1977): Cells of origin and terminal distribution of corticostriatal fibres arising in sensorymotor cortex of monkeys. *J. Comp. Neurol.* **181**, 53–80.
5. Hemphill, M., Holm, G., Crutcher, M., DeLong, M. & Hedreen, J. (1981): Afferent connections of the nucleus accumbens in the monkey. In *The neurobiology of the nucleus accumbems*, eds R. B. Chronister & J. F. DeFrance, pp 75–81. Brunswick, NJ: Haer Institute.
6. Iversen, S. D. (1979): Behaviour after neostriatal lesions in animals. In *The neostriatum*, eds I. Divac & R. E. G. Oberg, pp 195–210. Oxford: Pergamon.
7. Lidsky, T. I., Manetto, C. & Schneider, J. S. (1985): A consideration of sensory factors involved in motor functions of the basal ganglia. *Brain Res. Rev.* **9**, 133–146.
8. Cooke, J. D., Brown, J. D. & Brooks, V. B. (1978): Increased dependence on visual information for movement control in patients with Parkinson's disease. *Can. J. Neurol. Sci.* **5**, 413–415.
9. Canavan, A. G. M. & Passingham, R. E. (1985): The basal ganglia and cognition. *Neurosci. Lett.,* Suppl **21**, S24.
10. Crutcher, M. D. & DeLong, M. R. (1984): Single cell studies of the primate putamen. I: Functional organization. *Exp. Brain Res.* **53**, 233–243.
11. Crutcher, M. D. & DeLong, M. R. (1984): Single cell studies of the primate putamen. II: Relations to directions of movements and pattern of muscular activity. *Exp. Brain. Res.* **53**, 244–258.
12. Rolls, E. T., Thorpe, S. J. & Maddison, J. (1983): Responses of striatal neurons of the behaving monkey. 1. Head of the caudate nucleus. *Behav. Brain Res.* **7**, 179–210.
13. Lidsky, T. I., & Manetto, C. (1987): Context dependent activity in the striatum of behaving cats. In *Basal ganglia and behaviour: Sensory aspects of motor functioning*, eds J. S. Schneider & T. I. Lidsky, pp 123–133. Toronto: Haer Institute, Hans Huber.
14. West, M. O., Michael, A. J., Knowles, S. E., Chapin, J. K. & Woodward, D. J. (1987): Striatal unit activity and the linkage between sensory and motor events. In *Basal ganglia and behaviour: sensory aspects of motor functioning*, eds J. S. Schneider & T. I. Lidsky, pp 27–35. Toronto: Haer Institute, Hans Huber.
15. Rolls, E. T., Ashton, J., Williams, G. V., Thorpe, S. J., Mogenson, G. J., Colpaert, F. & Phillips, A. G. (1982): Neuronal activity in the ventral striatum of the behaving monkey. *Soc. Neurosci. Abstr.* **8**, 169.
16. Rolls, E. T. & Williams, G. V. (1987): Sensory and movement-related activity in different regions of the primate striatum. In *Basal ganglia and behaviour: sensory aspects of motor functioning*, eds J. S. Schneider & T. I. Lidsky, pp 37–59. Toronto: Haer Institute, Hans Huber.
17. Williams, G. V. (1986): *Neurophysiological investigations of striatal function.* Doctoral Thesis, University of Oxford.
18. Nauta, W. J. H. & Domesick, V. B. (1984): Afferent and efferent relationships of the basal ganglia., In *Functions of the basal ganglia*, pp 3–29. Ciba Foundation Symposium 107. London: Pitman.
19. Schultz, W. (1986): Responses of midbrain dopamine neurons to behavioural trigger stimuli in the monkey. *J. Neurophysiol.* **56**, 1439–1461.

8

THE AFTERHYPERPOLARIZATION IN STRIATAL CELLS

M. Garcia-Munoz*, G. W. Arbuthnott[†] and A. Rutherford[†]

*Department of Psychiatry, School of Medicine, UCSD, M–003, La Jolla, CA 92093, and [†]MRC Brain Metabolism Unit, 1 George Square, Edinburgh EH8 9JZ, UK

Summary

One of the actions of dopamine applied to slices of rat neostriatum *in vitro* was to decrease the afterhyperpolarization (AHP) which follows trains of action potentials evoked in striatal neurons. In a normal medium the AHP was absent at resting potentials but became obvious at depolarized potentials. Its reversal potential was about 95 mV. When the K^+ concentration of the medium was varied the reversal potential of the AHP followed the equilibrium potential for K^+. When the Ca^{++} in the bathing fluid was replaced with Mg^{++} the AHP was no longer obvious.

It seems likely that the AHP, which is the substrate for dopamine action, is the result of a K^+-dependent, voltage-dependent, and Ca^{++}-dependent current similar to that which underlies afterhyperpolarizations in other cells of the central nervous system.

Introduction

The site of action of dopamine which is relevant to movement disorders is likely to be the neostriatum. Nevertheless, the actions of dopamine at the level of the cell membrane seem to have been little studied. Detailed biophysical descriptions of possible dopamine actions in the hippocampus[1] are available, but only recently has it been possible to attempt such a description in the striatum.[2,3] The development of a slice preparation with the corticostriatal pathway at least partly intact[4,5] makes possible the study of the action of dopamine on this major synaptic input to striatal neurons. Since 90 per cent of neurons in the striatum of the rat are of the medium-sized densely spiny type it is likely that the *in vitro* recordings come from this type of cell. The dopamine synaptic contacts seen on them on electron microscopy are predominantly on the necks of spines which receive, on their heads, corticostriatal afferent contacts.[6] We therefore studied the action of applied dopamine both on corticostriatal excitation and on the firing properties of the striatal neurons maintained *in vitro*.

Methods

Young adult male albino Wistar rats were humanely killed and decapitated. The brain was dissected from the skull as quickly and carefully as possible. Blocks were cut from hemisected forebrain at an angle of 15 degrees to the horizontal, and glued to the cutting block of a 'Vibroslice' (Camden Instruments Ltd). The 350 μm slices were cut along the plane of the incoming corticostriatal fibres and maintained at the interface of oxygenated Krebs solution (composition in mM; NaCl 124, KCl 3.28, $CaCl_2$ 2.48, $MgSO_4$ 2.39, [or $MgCl_2$ 1.3] $NaHCO_3$ 25.7, KH_2PO_4 1.25, glucose 9.99). Glass microelectrodes filled with potassium acetate (2M), or potassium chloride (2M), had a resistance of 70–140 Mohm (with potassium acetate). When the extracellular fluid was altered to lower K^+ concentration, Na^+ was exchanged for K^+. K^+ gluconate was added to increase K^+ concentration. In one experiment, Ca^{++} was replaced by Mg^{++}, while in a further two, tetrodotoxin (1 μM) was applied in normal perfusion medium.

Records were made with an axoclamp 2A which was carefully balanced for electrode capacity and resistance. The switching frequency was usually 3 kHz but was adjusted in every case to ensure that the voltage settled to baseline by the end of each sampling cycle.

Dopamine was applied by iontophoresis (25–50 nA through a 0.5 M solution for 3–5 min) from a double-barrelled pipette placed as close as possible to the recording pipette. Sodium chloride (1M) was used in the 'balance' barrel and a retaining current of 10 nA was maintained between applications.

Results

In normal medium intracellular impalements were stable for at least 30 min, had resting membrane potentials of less than −70 mV (mean 83 ± SD 6.4 mV) and all were silent. They were activated either by a stimulus in the adjacent subcortical white matter, or by intracellular current pulses applied through the recording electrode. In both cases dopamine applied by iontophoresis reduced the likelihood of action potentials. In the cases when we were able to measure it systematically the voltage threshold for action potential initiation was raised by dopamine as well as the current required to reach threshold (Fig. 1). No change in resting membrane potential, or in input resistance (measured from the slope of a plot of voltage response against current pulse applied, at resting membrane potential), was ever seen after dopamine application.

If the cell was depolarized to above −65 mV, action potentials were usually followed by a pronounced afterhyperpolarization. When trains of spikes followed suprathreshold stimulation these could be seen to sum to a larger, prolonged AHP following the train. The reversal potential of the AHP was about 90 mV in normal medium and when the K^+ concentration of the medium was changed the reversal changed in the direction predicted by the Nernst equation (Fig. 2). When the medium contained only 1.5 mM K^+, action potential trains were followed by a series of potentials which complicated the measurements, but they have not been analysed in further detail here. The AHP had identical properties when the electrodes were filled with KCl.

Dopamine application clearly reduced the size of the AHP. The action did not seem to depend on the resting potential of the cell from which the AHP was elicited (Fig. 3). On the 45 occasions when the AHP followed equivalent stimuli at the same resting potentials on the same cell before and after dopamine application the reduction seen was highly significant (paired t-test $P < 0.001$).

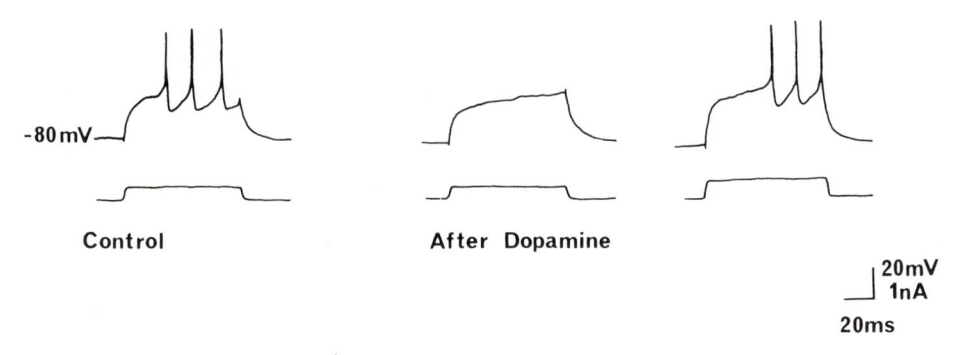

Fig. 1. *Recordings from striatal cells in 'current clamp' mode.* Current pulses are represented under the voltage records. After dopamine iontophoresis action potential threshold is elevated but normal responses are still driven by slightly larger stimuli.

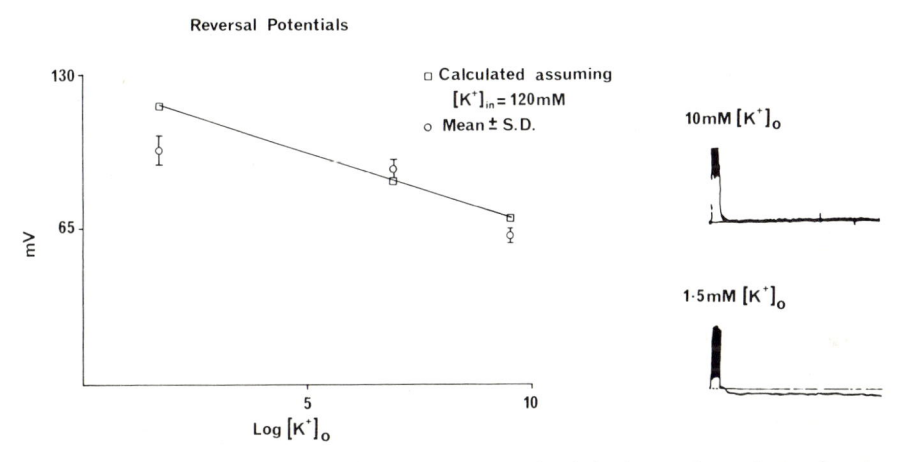

Fig. 2. *Estimates of reversal potentials.* The plot on the left shows the values of estimates of reversal potential for the AHP at three external K^+ concentrations. The solid line was calculated from the Nernst equation assuming an internal K^+ of 120 mM. On the right are representative traces showing AHP in 1.5 mM and 10 mM K^+. The complex afterpotentials in 1.5 mM at -70 mV resting membrane potential illustrate the difficulty of estimating reversal potential in these conditions.

Removing Ca^{++} from medium, or adding tetrodotoxin (TTX), both abolished the AHP, although the stimuli used in TTX were insufficient to initiate Ca^{++} spikes.

Discussion

Except in so far as we have activated the cells from cortical stimuli instead of by local stimulation our results agree with those of Calabresi *et al.*[3] but they went further by showing that the increased threshold was associated with activation of dopamine D1 receptors. They do not report on AHP in striatal neurones.

One possible explanation for the AHP is that the cells from which we recorded received recurrent inhibition,[7] which is likely to have been mediated by GABA. Since GABA

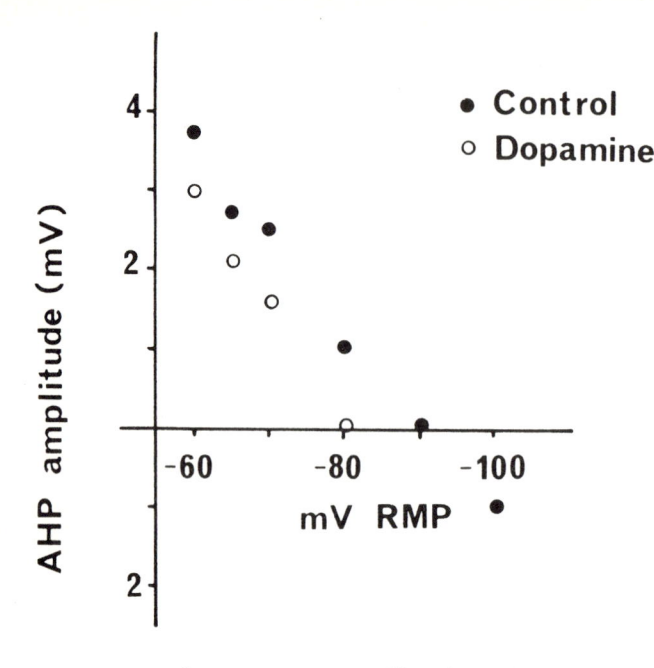

Fig. 3. Measurements of AHP amplitude at different resting membrane potentials plotted from one neuron before (●) and after (○) dopamine application. Dopamine seems not to change the voltage sensitivity of the AHP but reduces it at all levels of membrane polarization.

receptors are known to act on Cl⁻ channels on the postsynaptic membrane, recurrent inhibitory postsynaptic potentials would be reduced or reversed by increasing intracellular Cl⁻. We saw no sign of such an action. The AHP, however, was sensitive to the extracellular concentration of K^+ in such a way as to suggest that it was mediated by K^+ channels.

Although we have few experiments, the inhibition of the AHP in zero Ca^{++} medium suggests that this AHP, like the one described in hippocampal cells, is the result of Ca^{++} activation of a K^+ channel. The sensitivity of the AHP to TTX suggests that it depends on normal Ca^{++} entry during action potentials. Although striatal neurons do show Ca^{++} action potentials,[8] we did not activate these at the level of current stimulation reached.

We think that these intracellular records suggest an explanation for some of the confusion in the literature about the action of dopamine on striatal cells. In work in which the *threshold* of the cells was measured before and after dopamine then its *inhibitory* action would be noticeable. On the other hand when the action of dopamine was assessed upon prolonged excitatory stimuli (glutamate iontophoresis, for example) then the *reduction of the AHP* would allow neurons to fire more rapidly, an effect which would be reported as an *excitation*. Thus the action of dopamine might depend on the characteristics of the stimuli used to study it.

Acknowledgements—M.G-M. was supported by the Wellcome Trust, for work in the Department of Physiology, University of Edinburgh. A.R. was supported by an MRC Research Training Award.

References

1 Malenka, R. C. & Nicoll, R. A. (1986): Dopamine decreases the calcium-activated afterhyperpolarization in hippocampal CA1 pyramidal cells. *Brain Res.* **370**, 210–215.
2 Akaike, A., Ohne, Y., Sasa, M. & Takaori, S. (1987): Excitatory and inhibitory effects of dopamine on neuronal activity of the caudate nucleus neurons *in vitro*. *Brain Res.* **418**, 262–272.
3 Calabresi, P., Mercuri, N., Stanzione, P., Stefani, A. & Bernardi, G. (1987): Intracellular studies

on dopamine-induced firing inhibition of neostriatal neurons *in vitro*: evidence for D_1 receptor involvement. *Neuroscience* **20**, 757–771.
4 Miller, J. J. (1981): Characteristics of neuronal activity in striatal and limbic forebrain regions maintained *in vitro*. In *Electrophysiology of isolated mammalian CNS preparations*, eds G. A. Kerkut & H. V. Wheal, pp 309–336. London: Academic Press.
5 Arbuthnott, G. W., MacLeod, N. K. & Rutherford, A. (1985): The rat cortico-striatal pathway *in vitro*. *J. Physiol.* **367**, 102P.
6 Freund, T. F., Powell, J. F. & Smith, A. D. (1984): Tyrosine hydroxylase immunoreactive boutons in synaptic contact with identified striatonigral neurons, with particular reference to dendritic spines. *Neuroscience* **13**, 1189–1215.
7 Park, M. R., Lighthall, J. W. & Kitai, S. T. (1980): Recurrent inhibition in the rat neostriatum. *Brain Res.* **194**, 359–369.
8 Cherubini, E. & Lanfumey, L. (1987): An inward calcium current underlying regenerative calcium potentials in rat striatal neurons *in vitro* enhanced by BAY K 8644. *Neuroscience* **21**, 997–1005.

9

DOPAMINE UPTAKE IN THE BASAL GANGLIA STUDIED IN REAL TIME WITH FAST CYCLIC VOLTAMMETRY: EVIDENCE FOR A LOW AFFINITY, HIGH CAPACITY DOPAMINE UPTAKE SYSTEM

Jonathan A. Stamford*, Zygmunt L. Kruk* and Julian Millar[†]

Departments of *Pharmacology and* [†]*Physiology,*
The London Hospital Medical College, Turner Street, London E1 2AD, UK

Summary

Dopamine uptake was monitored in real time using fast cyclic voltammetry *in vivo*. Electrical stimulation was used to evoke endogenous dopamine release in the rat caudate-putamen. Upon cessation of stimulation, the dopamine concentration in the extracellular fluid declined in a biphasic manner, showing zero- and first-order components. The V_{max} of the system, calculated using literature values for extracellular space, was 43–61 nmol/min per g tissue, exceeding the reported V_{max} of neuronal dopamine uptake by at least an order of magnitude. It was possible to block this uptake system with nomifensine, amphetamine and high doses of methylphenidate. Amfonelic acid and benztropine had no effect, while mazindol potentiated uptake. The data were interpreted as evidence for a low affinity, high capacity dopamine uptake in the caudate-putamen, separate from the neuronal uptake system. The localization and physiological role of this uptake system are not yet established, but it may prove to be a useful site of pharmacological intervention in the treatment of parkinsonism.

Introduction

Studies of dopamine uptake in the basal ganglia have usually been conducted using *in vitro* preparations.[1-3] *In vivo* studies of dopamine uptake are generally unable to provide detailed quantitative information.[4,5] However, recently the application of high resolution voltammetric techniques[6,7] has allowed detailed measurement of dopamine uptake to be performed in real time *in vivo*.[8,9] This paper describes experiments carried out to characterize the processes involved in uptake of endogenous dopamine *in vivo* in the rat caudate-putamen.

Methods

All experiments were conducted in male Sprague-Dawley rats (250–350 g) anaesthetized with chloral hydrate. The head of the rat was positioned in a stereotaxic frame in the cranial orientation of Pellegrino et al.[10] A carbon fibre voltammetric electrode[11] was positioned into the caudate-putamen (CPu). The reference (Ag/AgCl) and auxiliary electrodes were located on the skull and in the neck muscle respectively. A bipolar stimulating electrode was located in the region of the median forebrain bundle (MFB) in order to stimulate the axons of the nigrostriatal and mesolimbic pathways.[12] Figure 1A shows a schematic representation of the electrode placements.

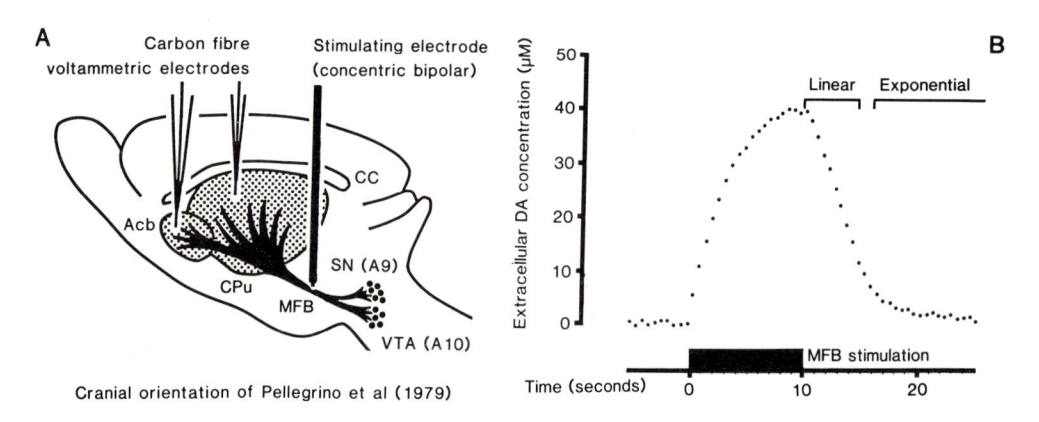

Fig. 1. *Schematic descriptions of experimental protocol.* A: Schematic representation of the rat brain showing voltammetric recording electrodes in caudate-putamen (CPu) and nucleus accumbens (Acb). (The results described here relate to CPu only.) The stimulating electrode is positioned in the median forebrain bundle (MFB). B: Effect of MFB stimulation on dopamine (DA) release in CPu. During stimulation DA overflows into the extracellular fluid (ECF). Following cessation of stimulation, the ECF DA concentration falls in a biphasic manner. Initially the decline is linear, followed by an exponential fall to background values.

The MFB was stimulated using trains of 10 sec duration (50 Hz sinusoidal waveform, 80–100 μA r.m.s.) at intervals of 20 min. Endogenous DA, released into the extracellular fluid (ECF), was measured in the caudate-putamen using fast cyclic voltammetry (FCV)[13] with a 300 V/s scan rate sweeping from −1.0 to +1.0 V vs Ag/AgCl. Each scan lasted only 20 msec and was applied twice per second, giving a temporal resolution of 500 msec. In one set of experiments, 1.0 sec stimulus trains were used and the voltammetric waveform was applied 40 times per second, giving 25 msec time resolution. A sample-and-hold circuit was set to monitor faradaic current at +600 mV vs Ag/AgCl (the dopamine oxidation peak potential).[13] The output from this circuit was displayed upon an oscilloscope or chart recorder. This means of data presentation provided, in effect, a continuous readout of the ECF dopamine concentration.

Results and discussion

Upon stimulation of the median forebrain bundle (10 s train) there was a rapid release of dopamine in the caudate-putamen (see Fig. 1B). The peak ECF dopamine concentration reached 31.8 ± SEM 1.2 µM (n = 76). Upon cessation of stimulation the ECF dopamine concentration declined, falling below the detection limit of FCV (about 0.1 µM) in 10–20 sec. Close examination of the time course of dopamine decline revealed it to be biphasic, with an initial linear component followed by an exponential decline (Fig. 1B).

The presence of a zero-order component followed by a first-order phase made it unlikely that the decline in dopamine concentration was due to diffusion and was consistent with a model of a saturable dopamine removal system. At high dopamine levels (immediately after the stimulation) the rate of uptake was no longer proportional to the dopamine concentration. Thus the initial linear region of decline represented the maximum rate (V_{max}) of the uptake process.

In order to confirm that the dopamine removal was by an uptake system, a number of recognized blockers of dopamine uptake[2,4,14–17] were investigated. These yielded initially confusing results, shown in Fig. 2. In all cases relatively high doses of the drugs were tested. The uptake system was blocked (seen as a prolongation of the dopamine decline phase and a decrease in the slope) by nomifensine and amphetamine. Methylphenidate only caused blockade at very high doses and mazindol, paradoxically, seemed to facilitate this uptake. Benztropine and amfonelic acid had no effect. Since some of the drugs also elevated dopamine release, levodopa was used as a positive control. Levodopa elevated release by about 100 per cent yet it had no effect on the linear rate of decline, thus confirming that effects upon uptake were not artefacts of elevated dopamine release.

The fact that only some of the drugs inhibited uptake, despite all being recognized uptake blockers, led us to conclude that either those drugs devoid of effect (benztropine, amfonelic acid) had been given at inappropriate doses, or the uptake process we were measuring was not the classical neuronal dopamine uptake system.

In order to test these possibilities, shorter stimulations were used. Whereas the 10 sec stimulation led to peak ECF dopamine concentrations of more than 30 µM, it was found that a 1.0 sec stimulation caused a peak ECF dopamine concentration of only 0.45 ± SEM 0.06 µM (n = 5), a value similar to the Michaelis constant (K_m) for neuronal dopamine uptake of around 0.4 µM.[1] Under these conditions, benztropine showed the predicted effect, elevating dopamine release and slowing uptake (Fig. 3). Thus the inactivity of benztropine at high dopamine concentrations could not be explained by the dose being inadequate. Clearly the dose was sufficient to block neuronal dopamine uptake.

These observations supported the notion that the uptake system measured following 10 sec stimulations was different from high-affinity neuronal dopamine uptake. Support for such a proposal was obtained from calculations of the V_{max} values. The rate of the zero-order phase corresponded to a decline in dopamine concentration of 5.1 ± SEM 0.2 µM/s (n = 76). In order to compare this value with the literature it was necessary to convert it to more familiar *in vitro* units. By taking a value of 14–20 per cent for the extracellular space[18,19] the V_{max} of the uptake system became 43–61 nmol/min per g tissue. This value was far greater than those reported in the literature for high-affinity dopamine uptake in slices (4–5 nmol/min per g[20] and 0.096 nmol/min per g[21]) and supported its identification as a separate low-affinity, high capacity uptake system.

In vitro data from other laboratories have also provided evidence for a low-affinity, high capacity uptake system in addition to neuronal uptake. The V_{max} values of 15.3–17.4 nmol/min per g[20] and 22.4 nmol/min per g,[21] although lower, are within range of the value seen *in vivo*. The fact that the *in vivo* values are higher may reflect the absence of a diffusional barrier *in vivo*.

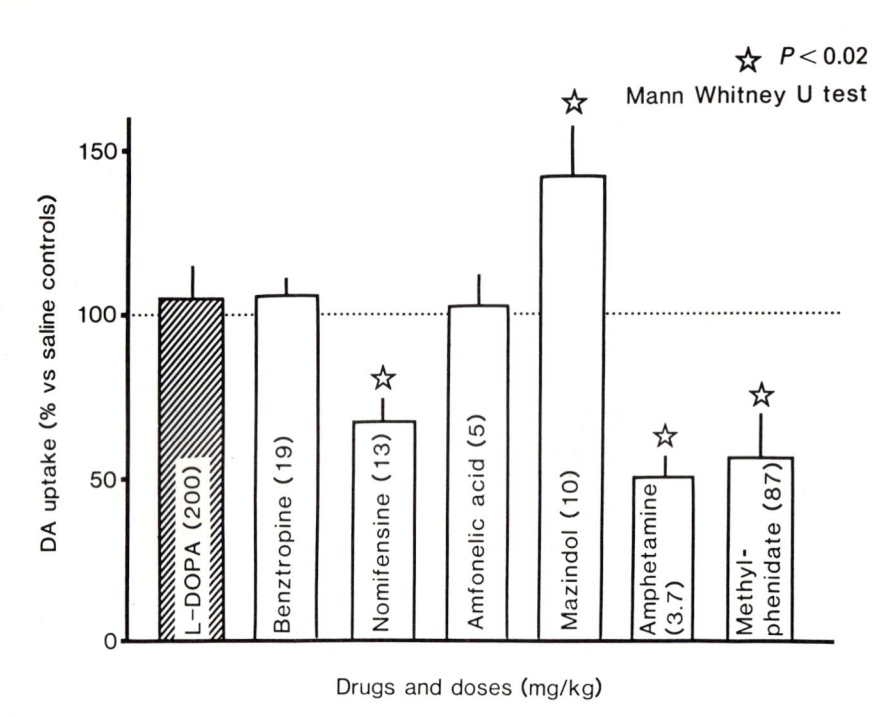

Fig. 2. *Effects of uptake blockers on dopamine uptake in caudate-putamen.* The initial rate of dopamine uptake (following cessation of stimulation) after intraperitoneal administration of levodopa (L-DOPA, 200 mg/kg) or various uptake inhibitors: benztropine 19 mg/kg (t = 20 min post-administration); nomifensine 13 mg/kg (t = 60 min); amfonelic acid 5 mg/kg (t = 40 min); mazindol 10 mg/kg (t = 20 min); amphetamine 3.7 mg/kg (t = 40 min); methylphenidate 87 mg/kg (t = 20 min). All values are means ± SEM (n = 4/5) expressed as a percentage of appropriate saline controls. *P < 0.02 *vs* saline controls (Mann Whitney U test). All drug doses are expressed as base (t = time, in minutes, after drug administration).

In a detailed study over a wide range of dopamine concentrations, Mireylees' group have compared the importance of high- and low-affinity dopamine uptakes.[21] Figure 4 (reproduced with the kind permission of the authors) shows the relative contributions. High-affinity, low capacity neuronal uptake (Uptake 1) dominates at submicromolar dopamine concentrations, whereas the low-affinity, high capacity system (Uptake 2) is mainly effective between 1.0 and 100 μM. The source of the first-order component is not clear. It may be due to the mode of tissue preparation and in any case does not seem to be observed *in vivo*.

These *in vitro* data[21] match our results *in vivo*. Benztropine, for instance, showed clear uptake blockade *in vivo* at a dopamine concentration of about 0.5 μM (Fig. 3) where Uptake 1 is the dominant system (Fig. 4). However, at ECF dopamine concentrations of around 30 μM, benztropine was inactive since Uptake 2 is the main contributor in this range.

The presence of a second low-affinity, high capacity dopamine uptake system poses several questions, particularly concerning its localization and physiological role. The anatomical localization of the system is unclear. Desipramine and chlorimipramine have no effect upon low-affinity uptake (J. A. Stamford—unpublished data) indicating that the system is not localized upon noradrenergic or serotonergic nerves. Most probably, the low affinity high capacity dopamine uptake system is located on glia or vascular endothelia, both of which have been shown *in vitro* to possess catecholamine uptake systems.[22-24]

Dopamine uptake in the basal ganglia

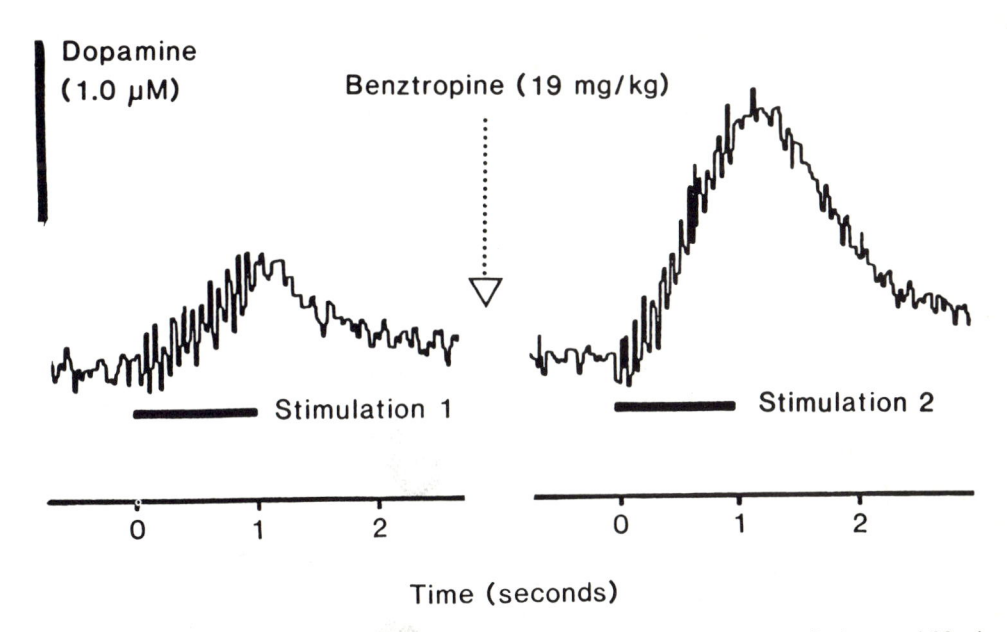

Fig. 3. *Effect of benztropine upon uptake on short stimulations.* Typical traces (before and 20 min after benztropine 19 mg/kg intraperitoneally), showing the effect upon dopamine (DA) uptake at low ($< 1\,\mu M$) DA concentrations. The effect of benztropine upon overflow and uptake was significant ($P < 0.01$, Students t-test).

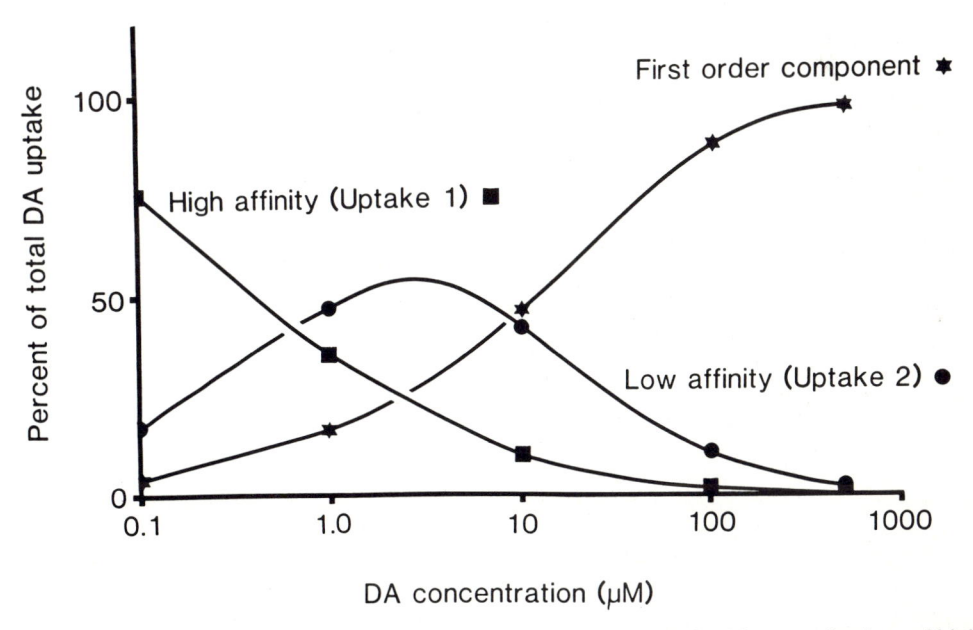

Fig. 4. *Contributions of various uptake systems to total dopamine uptake.* The contributions of high affinity (Uptake 1), low-affinity (Uptake 2) and first order components to the total uptake of tritiated dopamine (DA) by dispersed striatal cells (neural somata, axon fragments and glial cells) in Krebs buffer at 37°C over a wide range of dopamine concentrations. Data reproduced, with permission, from Mireylees et al.[21]

The physiological role of low-affinity, high capacity dopamine uptake (Uptake 2) clearly depends upon its anatomical localization. A system situated upon perisynaptic elements will have a very different effect from one located more distantly from the synapse. Until the localization is established it is difficult to assess the physiological relevance of this uptake. Perhaps the system constitutes an emergency mechanism to restrict ECF dopamine levels to the submicromolar concentrations typically seen *in vivo*.[25] It is possible that Uptake 2 may be operational in circumstances where neuronal uptake is blocked or overloaded by high neuronal activity. If it is a functional physiological mechanism under normal circumstances, it would be a potentially useful site of pharmacological intervention in parkinsonism or other diseases involving malfunction of dopaminergic mechanisms.

In conclusion, the voltammetric data present evidence for a low-affinity, high capacity dopamine uptake system in rat caudate-putamen. The system could be blocked by nomifensine, amphetamine and methylphenidate at high doses. Benztropine and amfonelic acid had no effect. The capacity of the uptake system exceeds that of neuronal dopamine uptake, making it likely that the system has a different role. Preliminary results[26] indicate that the system also exists in the nucleus accumbens.

Acknowledgements—This research was funded, in part, by the Wellcome Trust.

References

1. Snyder, S. M. & Coyle, J. T. (1969): Regional differences in ^{3}H-norepinephrine and ^{3}H-dopamine uptake into rat brain homogenates. *J. Pharmacol. Exp. Ther.* **165**, 78–85.
2. Heikkila, R. E., Orlansky, H. & Cohen, G. (1975): Studies on the distinction between uptake inhibition and release of [^{3}H] dopamine in rat brain tissues slices. *Biochem. Pharmacol.* **24**, 847–52.
3. Bonnet, J. J., Lemasson, M. H. & Costentin, J. (1984): Simultaneous evaluation by a double labelling method of drug-induced uptake inhibition and release of dopamine in synaptosome preparation of rat striatum. *Biochem. Pharmacol.* **33**, 2129–35.
4. Cooper, B. R., Hester, T. J. & Maxwell, R. A. (1980): Behavioural and biochemical effects of the antidepressant bupropion (Wellbutrin): evidence for selective blockade of dopamine uptake in vivo. *J. Pharmacol. Exp. Ther.* **215**, 127–34.
5. Sirinathsinghji, D. J. S., Heavens, R. P. & Sikdar, S. K. (1988): In vivo studies on the dopamine re-uptake mechanism in the striatum of the rat: effects of benztropine, sodium and ouabain. *Brain Res.* **438**, 399–403.
6. Stamford, J. A., Kruk, Z. L. & Millar, J. (1986): Sub-second striatal dopamine release measured by in vivo voltammetry. *Brain Res.* **381**, 351–5.
7. Kuhr, W. G. & Wightman, R. M. (1986): Real-time measurement of dopamine release in rat brain. *Brain Res.* **381**, 168–71.
8. Stamford, J. A., Kruk, Z. L., Millar, J. & Wightman, R. M. (1984): Striatal dopamine uptake in the rat: in vivo analysis by fast cyclic voltammetry. *Neurosci. Lett.* **51**, 133–8.
9. Stamford, J. A., Kruk, Z. L. & Millar, J. (1986): In vivo voltammetric characterisation of low affinity striatal dopamine uptake: drug inhibition profile and relation to dopaminergic innervation density. *Brain Res.* **373**, 85–91.
10. Pellegrino, L. J., Pellegrino, A. S. & Cushman, A. J. (1979): *A stereotaxic atlas of the rat brain.* New York: Appleton-Century-Crofts.
11. Armstrong-James, M. & Millar, J. (1979): Carbon fibre microelectrodes, *J. Neurosci. Meth.* **1**, 279–87.
12. Ewing, A. G., Bigelow, J. C. & Wightman, R. M. (1983): Direct in vivo monitoring of dopamine released from two striatal compartments. *Science* **221**, 169–171.
13. Millar, J., Stamford, J. A., Kruk, Z. L. & Wightman, R. M. (1985): Electrochemical, pharmacological and electrophysiological evidence of rapid dopamine release and removal in the rat caudate nucleus following electrical stimulation of the median forebrain bundle. *Eur. J.*

Pharmac. **109**, 341-8.
14 Randrup, A. & Braestrup, C. (1977): Uptake inhibition of biogenic amines by newer antidepressant drugs: relevance to the dopamine hypothesis of depression. *Psychopharmacology* **53**, 309-14.
15 Dubocovich, M. L. & Zahniser, N. R. (1985): Binding characteristics of the dopamine uptake inhibitor [^{3}H] nomifensine to striatal membranes. *Biochem. Pharmacol.* **34**, 1137-44.
16 Heikkila, R. E. & Manzino, L. (1984): Behavioural properties of GBR 12909, GBR 13069 and GBR 13098: specific inhibitors of dopamine uptake. *Eur. J. Pharmacol.* **103**, 241-8.
17 Koe, B. K. (1976): Molecular geometry of inhibitors of the uptake of catecholamines and serotonin in synaptosomal preparations of rat brain. *J. Pharmacol. Exp. Ther.* **199**, 649-61.
18 Woodward, D. L., Reed, D. J. & Woodbury, D. M. (1967): Extracellular space of rat cerebral cortex. *Am. J. Physiol.* **212**, 367-70.
19 Nicholson, C. & Rice, M. E. (1987): The migration of substances in the neuronal microenvironment. *Ann. N.Y. Acad. Sci.* **481**, 55-68.
20 Shaskan, E. G. & Snyder, S. H. (1970): Kinetics of serotonin accumulation into slices from rat brain: relationship to catecholamine uptake. *J. Pharmacol. Exp. Ther.* **175**, 404-18.
21 Mireylees, S. E., Brammer, N. T. & Buckley, G. A. (1986): A kinetic study of the in vitro uptake of [^{3}H] dopamine over a wide range of concentrations by rat striatal preparations. *Biochem. Pharmacol.* **35**, 4065-71.
22 Leisi, P., Paetau, A., Rechardt, L. & Dahl, D. (1981): Glial uptake of monoamines in primary cultures of rat median raphe nucleus and cerebellum. *Histochemistry* **73**, 239-50.
23 Pelton, E. W., Kimelberg, H. K., Shipherd, S. V. & Bourke, R. S. (1981): Dopamine and norepinephrine uptake and metabolism by astroglial cells in culture. *Life Sci.* **28**, 1655-63.
24 Hardebo, J. E. & Owman, C. (1980): Characterisation of the in vitro uptake of monoamines into brain microvessels. *Acta. Physiol. Scand.* **108**, 223-9.
25 Zetterstrom, T., Sharp, T., Marsden, C. A. & Ungerstedt, U. (1983): In vivo measurement of dopamine and its metabolites by intracerebral dialysis: changes after d-amphetamine. *J. Neurochem.* **41**, 1769-73.
26 Stamford, J. A., Kruk, Z. L., Palij, P. & Millar, J. (1988): Diffusion and uptake of dopamine in rat caudate and nucleus accumbens compared using fast cyclic voltammetry. *Brain Res.* **448**, 381-5.

10

THE ROLE OF 'NON-SPECIFIC' THALAMIC NUCLEI IN THE CONTROL OF DOPAMINERGIC FUNCTION IN THE BASAL GANGLIA OF THE RAT

J. Cornwall, M. W. Jones, I. C. Kilpatrick and O. T. Phillipson

Departments of Anatomy and Pharmacology, Medical School, University of Bristol, Bristol BS8 1TD, UK

Summary

The organization of thalamic inputs to caudate-putamen (CP) and nucleus accumbens (NA) has been examined and the functional role of these pathways in the regulation of transmitter release from dopaminergic terminals is studied *ex vivo* by high performance liquid chromatography (HPLC) with electrochemical detection. The anatomical results indicate topographic thalamic inputs from parafascicular-intralaminar and midline nuclei to CP and NA respectively. These pathways appear to have a comparable influence on transmitter function following electrical or chemical stimulation of each projection. Analysis of thalamic afferent projections to parafascicular and midline nuclei also shows a distinct anatomical topography of inputs. Those to the parafascicular nucleus arise mainly from motor and reticular-related channels, while those to midline nuclei arise mainly from limbic, hypothalamic and reticular channels.

These results show that the concept of a differentiation between dorsal and ventral striatum is also reflected by (1) inputs to these striatal regions from different groups of thalamic nuclei, and (2) inputs to the same thalamic nuclei. Furthermore, the reticular activating system, by providing major inputs to the thalamus, appears to play an important role in the regulation of dopamine function in the basal ganglia.

Introduction

Our understanding of the principles of neuroanatomical organization in the basal ganglia complex has been strongly influenced by the concept of two 'parallel' systems associated with the dorsal and ventral striatum.[1] This idea has arisen from an analysis of the structure, histochemistry, transmitter content, and connections of the basal ganglia, which demonstrates that the ventromedial extension of the caudate-putamen (CP), the nucleus accumbens and olfactory tubercle may be viewed as a ventral striatum by comparison with the CP (dorsal striatum). Dorsal striatum has links with the motor cortex, globus pallidus and both pars compacta and reticulata of the substantia nigra, while outflow pathways relay in part via globus pallidus to the ventral thalamus and thereby to the supplementary motor cortex. Ventral striatum, on the other hand, has links with limbic cortex, ventral pallidum and ventral tegmental area, while the corresponding outflow pathways relay instead via ventral pallidum to the mediodorsal thalamic nucleus and thereby to the prefrontal cortex. Recent work has added further information about additional thalamic links in the context of this circuitry, and has shed some light on the control of dopaminergic functions in both dorsal and ventral striatum by these connections.[2-10]

Thalamic projections to dorsal and ventral striatum

It is well known that a massive, direct unilateral projection to dorsal striatum arises from the parafascicular-intralaminar (PF-IL) complex in several species.[11,12] Studies in the rat have shown that a parallel, chiefly midline, thalamic projection to ventral striatum arises from cells in the paraventricular, central medial, reuniens, and rostral paracentral nuclei and in a region lying medial to the fasciculus retroflexus.[2] Additional isolated islands of thalamic cells lateral to the habenula in the dorsal centrolateral nucleus also provide ventral striatal inputs. This distribution indicates a topographic extension of thalamic inputs to those described for dorsal striatum (Fig. 1). Similar results have been reported in the cat.[13,14] Even within the ventral striatum, it appears that there is a degree of topographic organization in these thalamic inputs, and in particular, the posteromedial nucleus accumbens appears to receive a distinct set of thalamic (and other) inputs compared to other subregions of accumbens.[2] Thus, in contrast to traditional concepts about the 'diffuse' nature of 'non-specific' thalamic nuclei which project to the cerebral cortex, their projections to the dorsal and ventral striatum appear to be rather specifically organized.

The anatomical evidence, therefore, suggests a parallel role for the PF-IL and midline thalamic nuclei in the control of basal ganglia function. Recent neurochemical evidence supports this possibility since these pathways appear to play a similar role in regulating transmitter release from the dopaminergic terminals arising from the substantia nigra and ventral tegmental area respectively. For example, electrical stimulation of the parafascicular nucleus, followed by HPLC analysis of dopamine (DA) and its principal metabolites, 3,4-dihydroxyphenylacetic acid (DOPAC) and homovanillic acid (HVA), results in an increase in the metabolite:amine ratios in the CP for both DOPAC- and HVA-based calculations.[3] Since it is thought that HVA can only be formed extraneuronally (while DOPAC is primarily formed inside the synaptic terminal), the most likely interpretation is that dopamine release is increased following parafascicular stimulation. In contrast, no changes are found in nucleus accumbens, or substantia nigra, and opposite changes are found in the prefrontal cortex. Furthermore, no response in dorsal striatum is obtained following electrical stimulation of the neighbouring pretectum or the overlying cortex. Stimulation of the parafascicular nucleus with the excitatory amino acid ibotenic acid (Fig. 2) results in similar responses to those obtained with electrical stimulation.[4] In addition to these acute effects, chronic treatments of the parafascicular nucleus also appear to influence dorsal striatal dopaminergic functions. Thus radiofrequency or ibotenic acid lesions of the parafascicular thalamic nucleus result in an increased Bmax for D2 dopamine receptor binding and increased high affinity dopamine uptake.[5] Similar

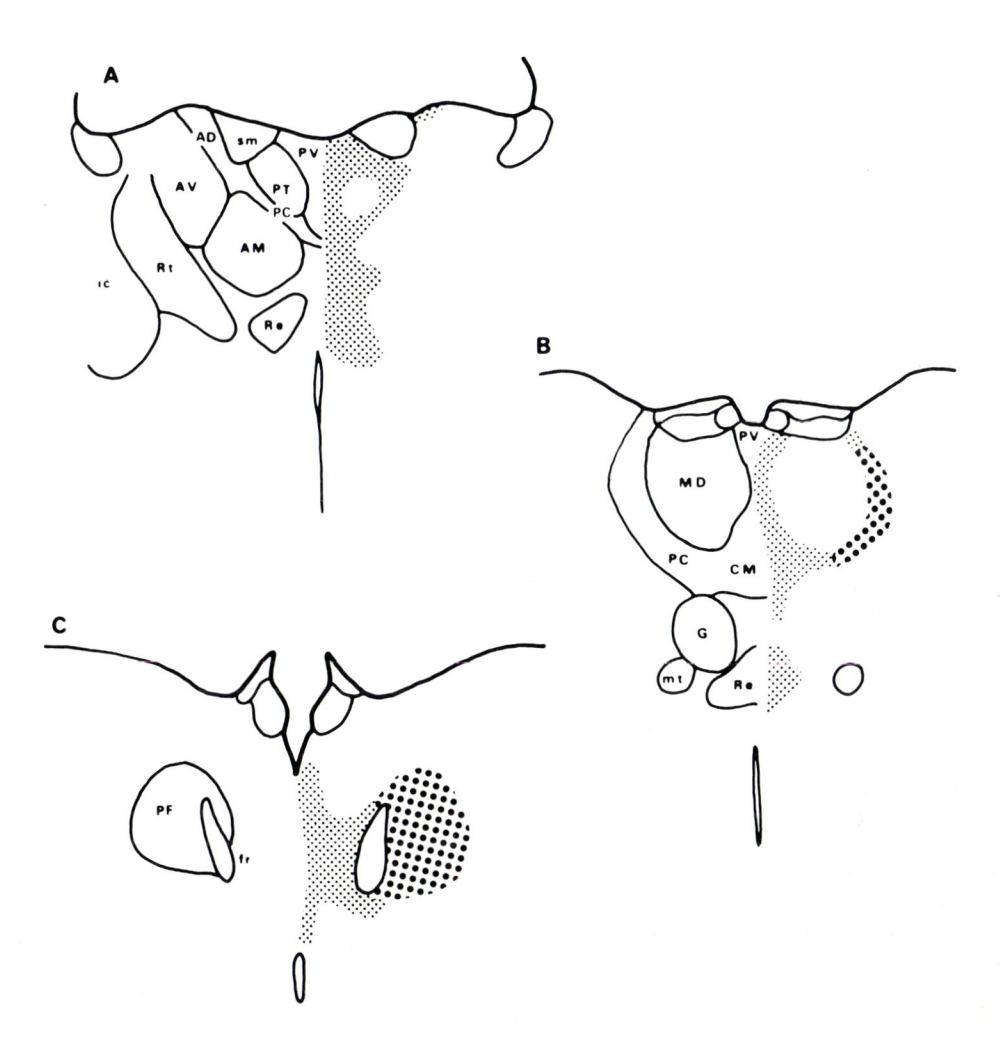

Fig. 1. *Location of cells providing the thalamic projections to dorsal and ventral striatum.* Three levels are shown: A, rostral; B, mid, and C, caudal thalamus. Inputs to dorsal striatum (coarse stipple); inputs to ventral striatum (fine stipple). Abbreviations: AD, anterodorsal thalamic nucleus; AM, anteromedial thalamic nucleus; AV, anteroventral thalamic nucleus; CM, central medial thalamic nucleus; fr, fasciculus retroflexus; G, gelatinosus nucleus of thalamus; ic, internal capsule; MD, mediodorsal thalamic nucleus; mt, mammillothalamic tract; PC, paracentral thalamic nucleus; PF, parafascicular thalamic nucleus; PT, paratenial thalamic nucleus; PV, paraventricular thalamic nucleus; Re, reuniens thalamic nucleus; Rt, reticular thalamic nucleus; sm, stria medullaris.

experiments in the ventral striatum, in which acute manipulations of the midline thalamic nuclei have been carried out, show that either electrical stimulation or microinjections of low concentrations of the excitant amino acid, quisqualic acid, result in an increased apparent release of dopamine in the nucleus accumbens, following stimulation of the midline thalamus either at rostral or caudal levels (Fig. 2).[10]

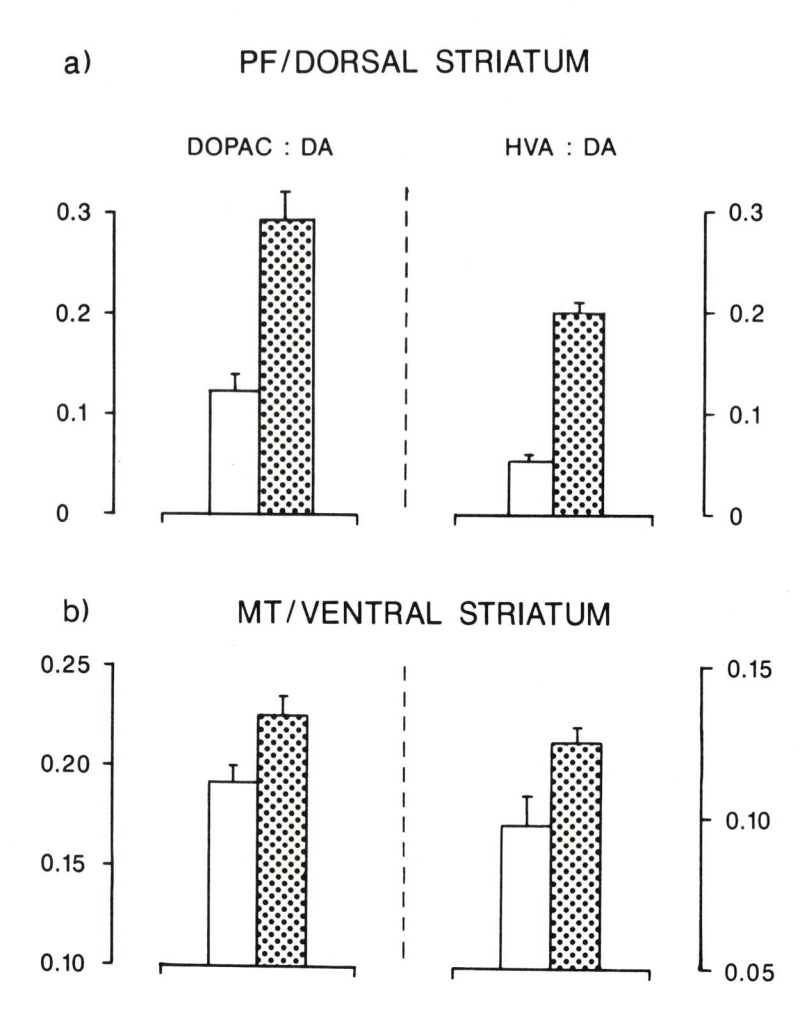

Fig. 2. *The effects of excitant amino acid application to (a) the parafascicular (PF), and (b) midline thalamic nuclei (MT) on metabolite:amine ratios in dorsal and ventral striatum respectively in halothane-anaesthetized (1.5% v/v in O_2) rats.* In (a) animals were killed 4 h following injection of 10 nmol ibotenic acid in 200 nl saline. In (b) animals were killed immediately following injection of 1 pmol quisqualic acid in 200 nl saline. Vehicle-injected animals served as controls (open bars). All ratio changes were the result of metabolite changes only, and are significant at least to the $P < 0.05$ level.

Nature of inputs to the two thalamic cell groups

The conclusion appears to be that parallel thalamic input channels to dorsal and ventral striatum exert similar functional effects in the dopamine terminal fields to which they project. The question then naturally arises as to the nature of inputs to the two thalamic cell groups that are responsible for controlling their outputs. Recent evidence with anatomical tracing techniques show that these inputs are completely separate.[6,7] Afferents to parafascicular thalamus arise from motor, reticular, postural and visual structures; while by contrast afferents to midline thalamus arise from limbic, hypothalamic, reticular,

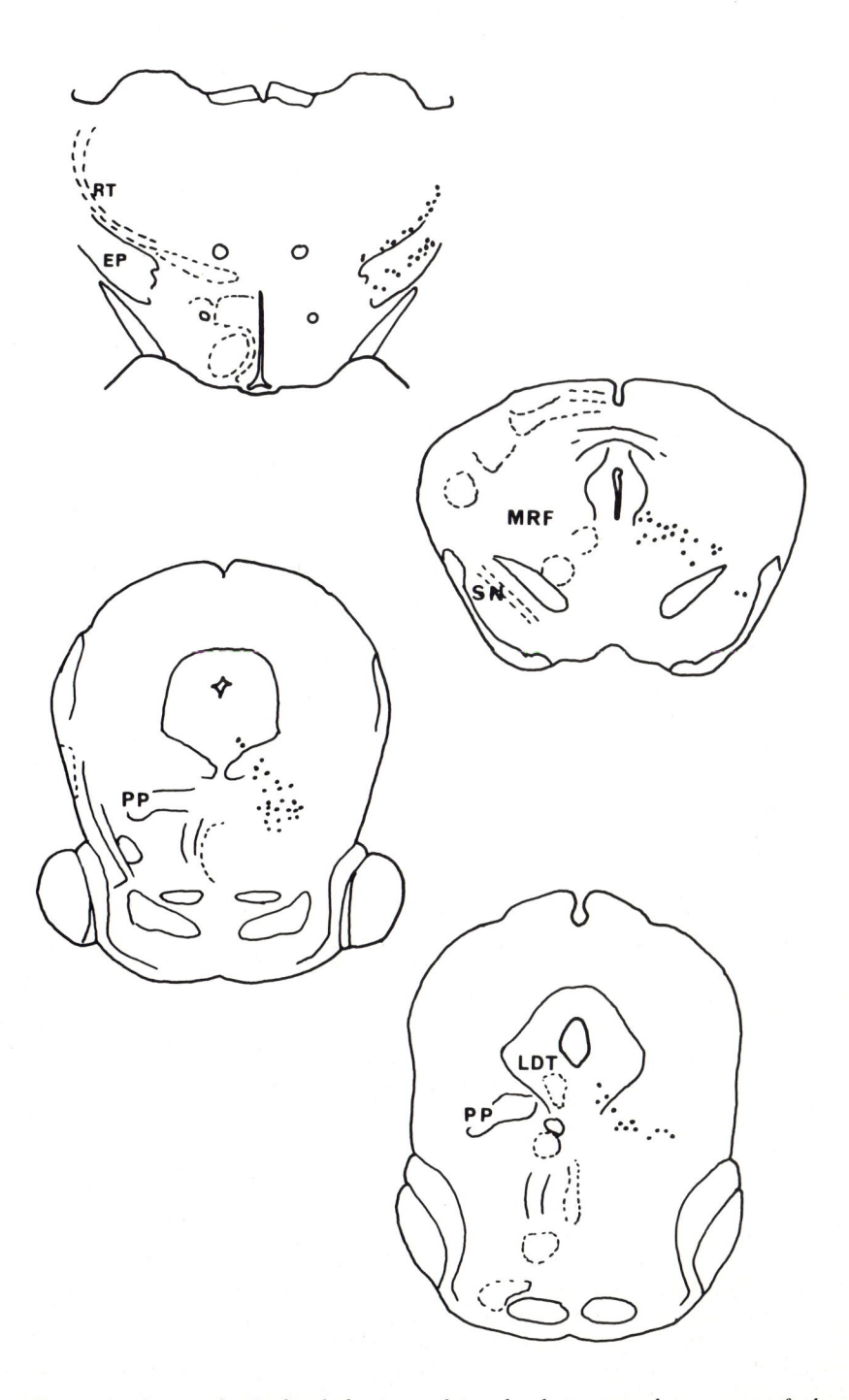

Fig. 3. *Afferents to the parafascicular thalamus as shown by the retrograde transport of wheatgerm agglutinin.* Abbreviations: EP, entopeduncular nucleus; LDT, laterodorsal tegmental nucleus; MRF, mesencephalic reticular formation; PP, pedunculopontine tegmental nucleus; SN, substantia nigra.

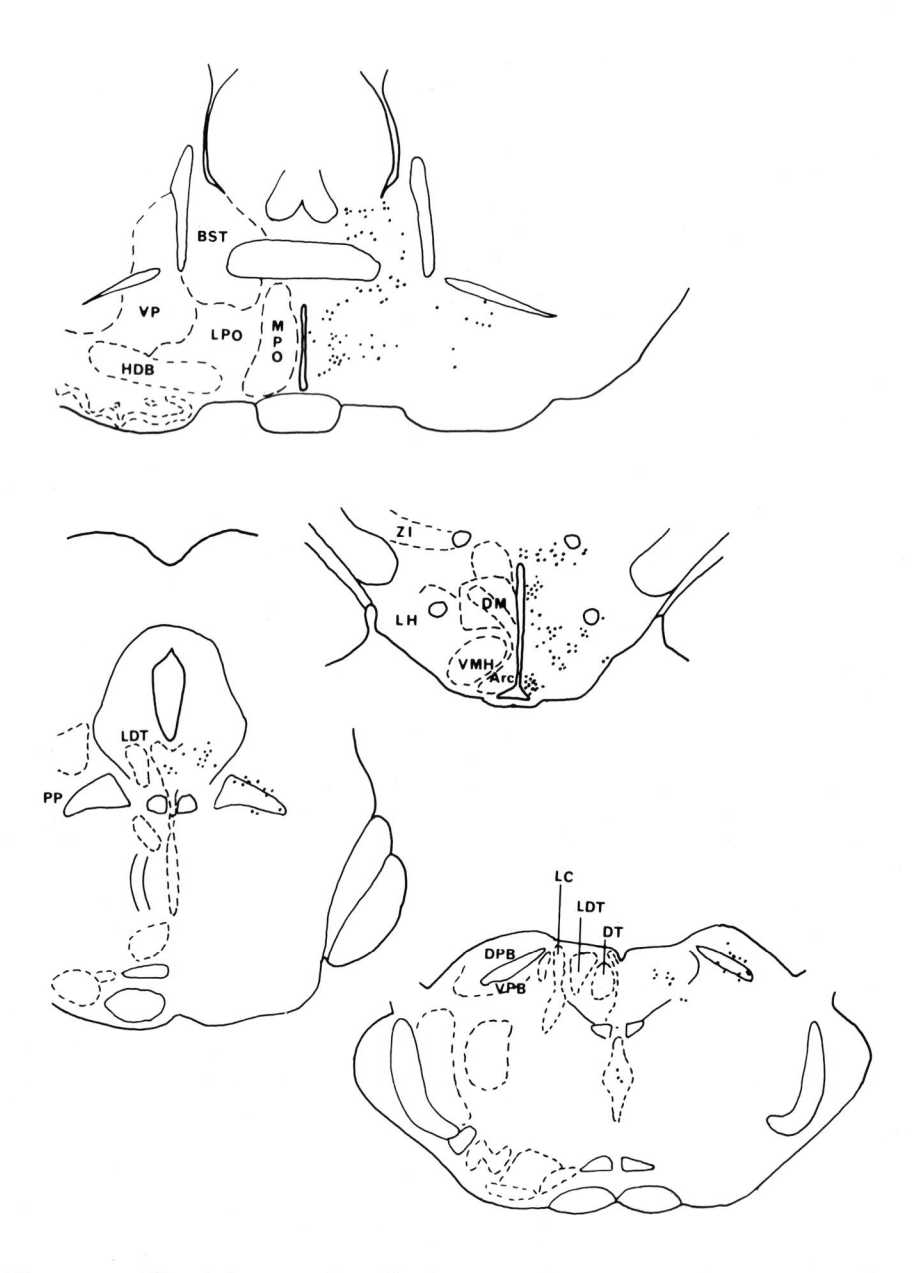

Fig. 4. *Afferents to midline thalamus as shown by the retrograde transport of wheatgerm agglutinin.* Abbreviations: Arc, arcuate nucleus; BST, bed nucleus of stria terminalis; DM, dorsomedial hypothalamic nucleus; DPB, dorsal parabrachial nucleus; DT, dorsal tegmental nucleus; HDB, horizontal limb of diagonal band; LC locus coeruleus; LDT, laterodorsal tegmental nucleus; LH, lateral hypothalamus; LPO, lateral preoptic area; MPO, medial preoptic area; PP, pedunculopontine tegmental nucleus; VMH, ventromedial hypothalamic nucleus; VP, ventral pallidum; VPB, ventral parabrachial nucleus; ZI, zona incerta.

autonomic, visceral and gustatory centres. Figs 3 and 4 illustrate some of these structures in detail. Motor structures projecting to parafascicular thalamus are found in lamina V and VI of the primary motor cortex, entopeduncular nucleus and to a lesser extent in substantia nigra reticulata, caudate-putamen and all three subdivisions of the deep cerebellar nuclei. Afferent projections from the reticular activating system are found in the thalamic reticular nucleus, mesencephalic reticular formation, and both large and small cells in the region of the pedunculopontine tegmental nucleus. Minor contributions are found from vestibular and pretectal nuclei.[6] Inputs to midline thalamus, on the other hand, arise from subiculum and perirhinal cortex; limbic inputs arise from septum, diagonal band, bed nucleus of stria terminalis and medial preoptic area. All the main nuclei of the medial hypothalamus including the arcuate and suprachiasmatic nucleus and supramamillary area, but excluding the paraventricular hypothalamic nucleus, also provide inputs. In the reticular activating system, a specific region of thalamic reticular nucleus and its medial extension (the zona incerta), central grey, and the laterodorsal tegmental nucleus all provide inputs; while in the brainstem, parabrachial nuclei and nucleus of the tractus solitarius provide minor inputs.[7] Spinal projections were not examined in these experiments.

Indications of the relative importance of each of these projections can be obtained from the numbers and intensity of staining of input pathways. For the parafascicular thalamus, the dominant afferent pathways would appear to be those from thalamic reticular nucleus, entopeduncular nucleus, mesencephalic reticular formation and motor cortex. In contrast, the dominant afferent pathways for the midline nuclei appear to be from thalamic reticular nucleus, medial hypothalamic nuclei and laterodorsal tegmental nucleus.

These inputs seem to mark out the thalamic nuclei, which provide projections to the dorsal and ventral striatum, as significant relay stations for processing information from the reticular activating system, although from topographically distinct regions of that system. Thus thalamic reticular inputs to midline thalamus arise from cells rostral and medial to those in that part of the thalamic reticular nucleus which projects to PF. Similarly in the brainstem, reticular inputs to thalamus are topographically distinct. Those from pedunculopontine tegmental nucleus and laterodorsal tegmental nucleus are probably cholinergic, at least in part, indicating that the parallel anatomical topography is mirrored by parallel transmitter chemistry.

One of the implications of these anatomical and functional findings is that the dopamine terminal fields in both dorsal and ventral striatum are under a strong influence from thalamic and brainstem components of the reticular activating system via the parafascicular and midline thalamic nuclei. In other words, it seems that parts of the reticular activating system should be seen to function as integral components of basal ganglia circuitry.

Implications for future research

Future experimental efforts to understand more fully some parkinsonian symptoms and the effectiveness of treatment may also be usefully directed at some of these pathways in dorsal striatal circuits. For example, it is known that the outflow pathway of the internal segment of globus pallidus (the homologue of the rat entopeduncular nucleus) is excessively active in Parkinson's disease and experimental MPTP-induced parkinsonism in monkeys (see Filion *et al.*, this volume, p. 159). It is also known that for many patients some symptoms may be relieved by surgical treatment of the internal segment of the globus pallidus (see Narabayashi, this volume, p. 387). The pallido-thalamic pathway is apparently inhibitory.[15] Thus this surgical procedure, in addition to its effects on outflow pathways to the ventral thalamus, may also have a further beneficial effect by removing excessive inhibitory tone acting on the PF, thereby enhancing residual dopamine function in the dorsal striatum.

Acknowledgement—Supported by the Wellcome Trust.

References

1. Heimer, L. & Wilson, R. D. (1975): The subcortical projections of allocortex; similarities in the neural associations of the hippocampus, the pyriform cortex and the neocortex. In *Golgi Centennial Symposium* ed M. Santini, pp 177–193. New York: Raven Press.
2. Phillipson, O. T. & Griffiths, A. C. (1985): The topographic order of inputs to nucleus accumbens in the rat. *Neuroscience* **16**, 275–296.
3. Kilpatrick, I. C. & Phillipson, O. T. (1986): Thalamic control of dopaminergic functions in the caudate-putamen of the rat. I. The influence of electrical stimulation of the parafascicular nucleus on dopamine utilisation. *Neuroscience* **19**, 965–978.
4. Kilpatrick, I. C., Jones, M. W., Johnson, B. J., Cornwall, J. & Phillipson, O. T. (1986): Thalamic control of dopaminergic functions in the caudate-putamen of the rat. II Studies using ibotenic acid injection of the parafascicular-intralaminar nuclei. *Neuroscience* **19**, 979–990.
5. Kilpatrick, I. C., Jones, M. W., Pycock, C. J., Riches, I. & Phillipson, O. T. (1986): Thalamic control of dopaminergic functions in the caudate-putamen of the rat. III. The effects of lesions in the parafascicular-intralaminar nuclei on D2 dopamine receptors and high affinity dopamine uptake. *Neuroscience* **19**, 991–1005.
6. Cornwall, J. & Phillipson, O. T. (1988): Afferent projections to the parafascicular thalamic nucleus of the rat, as shown by the retrograde transport of wheat germ agglutinin. *Brain Res. Bull.* **20**, 139–150.
7. Cornwall, J. &. Phillipson, O. T. (1988): Afferent projections to the dorsal thalamus of the rat as shown by retrograde lectin transport. II. The midline nuclei. *Brain Res. Bull.* **21**, 147–161.
8. Cornwall, J. & Phillipson, O. T. (1988): Afferent projections to the dorsal thalamus of the rat as shown by retrograde lectin transport. I. The mediodorsal nucleus. *Neuroscience* **24**, 1035–1049.
9. Jones, M. W., Kilpatrick, I. C. & Phillipson, O. T. (1987): Regulation of dopamine function in the prefrontal cortex of the rat by the thalamic mediodorsal nucleus. *Brain Res. Bull.* **19**, 9–17.
10. Jones, M. W., Kilpatrick, I. C. & Phillipson, O. T. (1988): Regulation of dopamine function in the nucleus accumbens by midline thalamic nuclei in the rat. *J. Physiol.* **401**, 73P
11. Jones, E. G. & Leavitt, R. Y. (1974): Retrograde axonal transport and the demonstration of non-specific projections to the cerebral cortex and striatum from thalamic intralaminar nuclei in the rat, cat and monkey. *J. Comp. Neurol.* **154**, 349–378.
12. Royce, G. J. & Mourey, R. J. (1985): Efferent connections of the centromedian and parafascicular thalamic nuclei: an autoradiographic investigation in the cat. *J. Comp. Neurol.* **235**, 277–300.
13. Groenewegen, H. J., Becker, M. E. H. M. & Lohman, A. H. M. (1980): Subcortical afferents of the nucleus accumbens septi in the cat, studied with retrograde axonal transport of horseradish peroxidase and bisbenzimid. *Neuroscience* **5**, 1903–1916.
14. Jayaraman, A. (1985): Organisation of thalamic projections in the nucleus accumbens and the caudate nucleus in cats and its relation with hippocampal and other subcortical afferents. *J. Comp. Neurol.* **231**, 346–420.
15. Pycock, C. J. & Phillipson, O. T. (1984): A neuroanatomical and neuropharmacological analysis of basal ganglia output. In *Handbook of psychopharmacology,* Vol. 18, eds L. L. Iversen, S. D. Iversen & S. H. Snyder, pp 191–278. New York and London: Plenum Press.

11

THE PONTINE TEGMENTUM AS A FUNCTIONAL INTERFACE BETWEEN THE BASAL GANGLIA AND THE SPINAL CORD

E. Scarnati, S. Di Loreto and T. Florio

*Department of Biomedical Technology and Biometry,
Laboratory of Human Physiology, School of Medicine,
University of L'Aquila, 67100 L'Aquila, Italy*

Summary

Electrophysiological investigations have been carried out in order to elucidate the relationships of the pedunculopontine nucleus (PPN) with major basal ganglia nuclei and reticulospinal neurons. The PPN appears to exert a predominantly activatory influence on its targets while receiving inhibitory signals from the substantia nigra. The data are discussed according to the possible functional purpose of the PPN.

Introduction

Descending basal ganglia efferents in mammals innervate a specific group of cells located in the pontine tegmentum just caudal to the decussation of the brachium conjunctivum. These cells, many of which are cholinergic,[1] have been identified by several authors as corresponding to the nucleus tegmenti pedunculopontinus (PPN) of the human brainstem. During the past few years, considerable attention has been directed to these cells owing to their peculiar input-output relationships with several motor-related structures. Indeed, reciprocating connections of the PPN with the substantia nigra as well as the subthalamic and entopeduncular nuclei have been described in neuroanatomical studies.[2,3] In addition to the basal ganglia the PPN is linked to the spinal cord both through fibres directed to nuclei of origin of reticulospinal pathways[3] and through certain cells projecting to the spinal cord.[2,4]

The location of the PPN at the interface between the basal ganglia and the lower motor systems implies an intriguing role of this nucleus in motor control. In this context we have also to take into account the reciprocating connection that the PPN establishes with the motor cortex, as well as the input from the limbic system mediated by the peripallidal region. In keeping with a possible motor involvement of the PPN two crucial findings have been recently provided. One is that stimulation of the PPN region induces locomotion in animals.[5] The other is that a depopulation of PPN neurons occurs in Parkinson's disease and in the parkinsonian syndrome of supranuclear palsy.[6] Comprehension of the action of PPN cells on their targets would help to elucidate their role in the physiology of the basal ganglia. Over the past years we have investigated the electrophysiology of the PPN-substantia nigra pathway. As a further step in analysing the major outputs of the PPN to motor-related structures we have examined the influence of the PPN on entopeduncular and reticulospinal neurons. This article will review the most striking data obtained in these studies and propose hypotheses on the functions of the PPN.

Methods

The experiments were carried out on male Sprague-Dawley rats weighing 280–320 g, anaesthetized with urethane or ketamine. Surgery, stimulating and recording techniques, lesion procedures and histology were as reported elsewhere.[7,8]

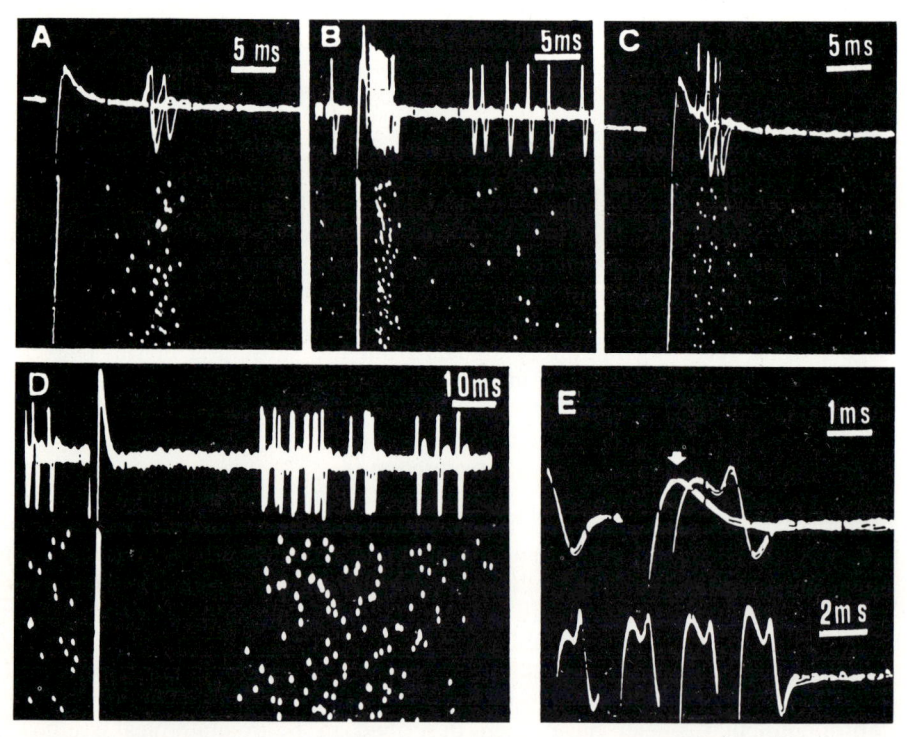

Fig 1. *Examples of short-latency activation consistently evoked by PPN stimulation.* (A) neurons of substantia nigra (SN) pars compacta; (B) neurons of entopeduncular nucleus; (C) neurones of reticular formation. Stimulation of the SN evoked mainly an immediate suppression of activity of PPN cells (D). (Dot displays from 128 consecutive stimulations and 4–5 superimposed sweeps). A PPN cell antidromically activated by stimulating the SN is shown in E. Positivity of the collision test (arrow) and high frequency following are illustrated.

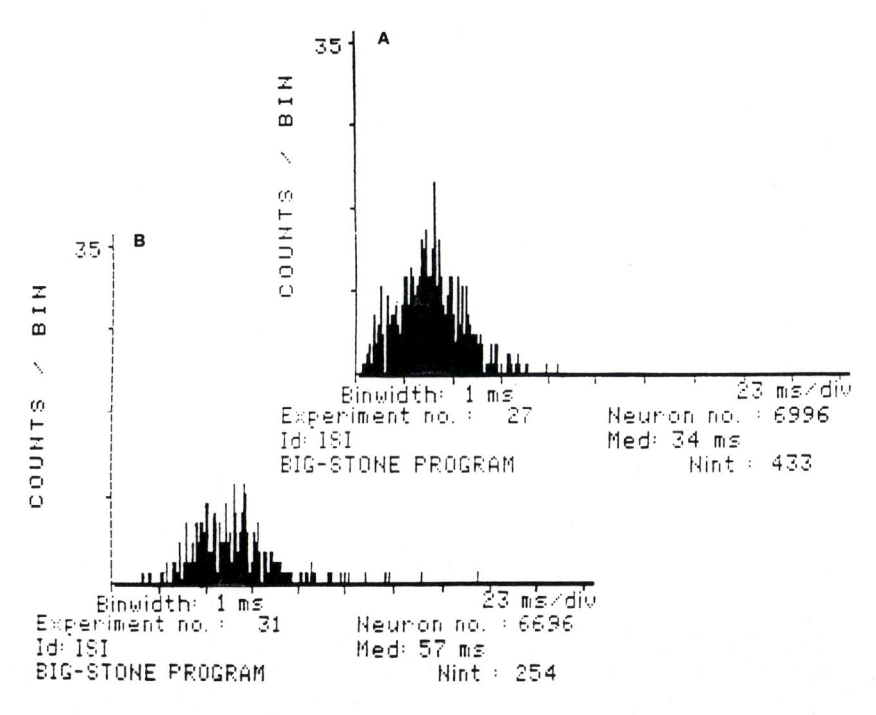

Fig. 2. *Representative examples of computerized distribution of interspike intervals collected during 15 sec in normal rats (A) and in rats receiving 0.2 µg of kainic acid into the PPN 10–12 days before recording.*

Results

Neurones from substantia nigra, entopeduncular nucleus and reticular formation were identified by antidromic activation from their targets and/or histological localization of recording sites. Electrical stimulation of the PPN evoked mainly a brief (2–10 msec) short-latency (2–5 msec) activation of both substantia nigra (26/77, 33.7 %) and entopeduncular cells (24/104, 23.1 %). This orthodromic activation was still present when structures which could give fibres *en passage* in the PPN region as well as polysynaptic pathways (cerebellum, subthalamic nucleus, cerebral cortex) were destroyed. A short-latency (2 msec) activation was the only response found in cells of the reticular formation (nuclei reticularis pontis oralis and caudalis, nucleus gigantocellularis) (21/51, 41.2 %) (Fig. 1). Some of these reticular formation neurons (21.6 %) were identified as reticulospinal neurons since they were antidromically activated from C2-C3. In addition, we found cells of the reticular formation which were antidromically activated from the PPN, while only a few PPN cells (3/36, 8.3 %) were found to be antidromically invaded following stimulation of the spinal cord at C2–C3.

Electrical stimulation of the substantia nigra evoked an immediate suppression of impulse activity of PPN neurons (96/363, 26.3 %) lasting up to 50 msec. Activatory responses were found in 43 out of the 363 neurons recorded (11.8 %) but their occurrence greatly decreased (3/104, 2.9 %) when a large bilateral decortication was carried out 10–12 days before recording.

The mean impulse frequency of entopeduncular neurons in intact rats was 27.5 ± 5.5 per sec (n = 106) and the overall mean interspike interval (ISI) was 36.8 ± 7.1 ms. A discrete kainate lesion of the PPN slowed the impulse frequency in 50 out of 80 neurons recorded (62.5%) to 14.3 ± 6.3 msec. The distribution of ISIs in these deregulated neurons was greatly disrupted compared to normal cells, the mean ISI being 68.2 ± 20.1 msec (Fig. 2).

Discussion

The present data point out a peculiar activatory role of the PPN on its main motor-related rostral and caudal targets. This input appears to be tonic since the impulse activity of a large number of entopeduncular cells was greatly slowed and disrupted when PPN cell bodies were destroyed by kainic acid. The nature of this input is a matter of controversy. Despite the abundance of cholinergic cells in the PPN region[1] data denying involvement of acetylcholine in basal ganglia-related PPN fibres have been provided.[8,9]

As far as the nature of basal ganglia inputs to the PPN is concerned we limited our study to the nigral input since in the rat substantia nigra fibres reaching the PPN are far more numerous than those coming from the entopeduncular and subthalamic nuclei. The nigral input to the PPN appears to exert an inhibitory role on the PPN. This matches well with the GABAergic nature of pars reticulata neurons of the substantia nigra, from which this input largely arises. If one considers the influence of the PPN on reticulospinal neurons, then one can propose a role for the PPN in integrating and modulating basal ganglia signals directed to the lower centres. This role would be more complex than that of a simple relay structure. The neuronal loop with the cerebral cortex, which has not yet been investigated with electrophysiological techniques, adds further complexity to the functional meaning of the PPN.

The possibility that basal ganglia signals reach the spinal cord through the PPN challenges the classical concept of the basal ganglia as a neuronal system acting on motor function exclusively by means of the thalamocortical route. According to this view modulation of spinal cord mechanisms mediated via the PPN would be expected. Actually, preliminary data from our current experiments seem to show that a facilitation of the H-reflex can be obtained in the rat by stimulating the PPN region.

At present the precise role of the PPN in motor control is unknown. The finding that degeneration of PPN cells occurs in Parkinson's disease raises the question whether certain symptoms of this motor disorder are related to cell death in the PPN. Although an early hypothesis involved the PPN in the genesis of parkinsonian tremor,[3] the location of the PPN in the mesencephalic locomotor area, as well as its connections with the SN, argue also in favour of an involvement in deficits of starting and stopping movements which are typical of Parkinson's disease.

Acknowledgement—This research was supported by grants from Consiglio Nazionale delle Ricerche.

References

1 Woolf, M. J. & Butcher, L. L. (1986): Cholinergic systems in the rat brain: III. Projections from the pontomesencephalic tegmentum to the thalamus, tectum, basal ganglia, and basal forebrain. *Brain Res. Bull.* **16**, 603–637.
2 Jackson, A. & Crossman, A. R. (1983): Nucleus tegmenti pedunculopontinus: efferent connections with special reference to the basal ganglia, studied in the rat by anterograde and retrograde transport of horseradish peroxidase. *Neuroscience* **10**, 725–765.
3 Moon-Edley, S. & Graybiel, A. M. (1983): The afferent and efferent connections of the feline nucleus tegmenti pedunculopontinus pars compacta. *J. Comp. Neurol.* **217**, 187–215.
4 Newman, D. B. (1985): Distinguishing rat brainstem reticulospinal nuclei by their morphology. II. Pontine and mesencephalic nuclei. *J. Hirnforsch.* **26**, 385–418.

5 Garcia-Rill, E. (1986): The basal ganglia and the locomotor region. *Brain Res. Rev.* **11**, 47–63.
6 Hirsch, E. C., Graybiel, A. M., Duyckaerts, C. & Javoy-Agid, F. (1987): Neuronal loss in the pedunculopontine tegmental nucleus in Parkinson disease and in progressive supranuclear palsy. *Proc. Nat. Acad. Sci.* **84**, 5976–5980.
7 Scarnati, E., Di Loreto, S., Proia, A. & Gallié, G. (1988): The functional role of the pedunculopontine nucleus in the regulation of the electrical activity of entopeduncular nucleus in the rat. *Arch. Ital. Biol.* **126**, 145–163.
8 Scarnati, E., Proia, A., Campana, E. & Pacitti, C. (1986): A microiontophoretic study on the nature of the putative neurotransmitter involved in the pedunculopontine-substantia nigra pars compacta excitatory pathway of the rat. *Exp. Brain. Res.* **62**, 470–478.
9 Rye, D. B., Saper, C. B., Lee, H. J. & Wainer, B. H. (1987): Pedunculopontine tegmental nucleus of the rat: cytoarchitecture, cytochemistry, and some extrapyramidal connections of the mesopontine tegmentum. *J. Comp. Neurol.* **259**, 483–528.

12

THE PRIMATE NIGRO-STRIATO-PALLIDO-NIGRAL SYSTEM. NOT A MERE LOOP

G. Percheron, C. François, J. Yelnik and G. Fénelon

Inserm Unité 3, Hôpital de la Salpêtrière, Pavillon Claude Bernard, 47 Boulevard de l'Hôpital, 75651 Paris Cedex 13, France

Summary

Quantitative morphological data measured in monkeys show that the striato-pallido-nigral system is not a mere loop but a system compressing or expanding nervous information: the nigro-striatal communication is extensively divergent, the striato-nigral communication is extremely convergent.

Introduction

Most past studies devoted to basal ganglia and to their role in movement disorders mainly focused on the dopaminergic nigro-striatal system. The striato-pallido-nigral bundle was reduced to a mere feed-back and the ensemble to a loop. We recently submitted that the striatum, its main efferent bundle and its direct targets, pallidum and substantia nigra, constitute the core of the basal ganglia where the type of information processing can explain the fundamental properties of the system.[1-3] The present paper extends the analysis to the primate nigro-striato-pallido-nigral system.

Methods

Stereotaxy and cartography were based on a stable system of ventricular coordinates, the CA-CP system.[4,5] The stereotactic method used millimetric orthogonal teleradiography. Three *Macaca irus* and one *Macaca mulatta* received intranigral injections of

[³H]leucine and proline for autoradiography. Three monkeys received intra-striatal injections. Cartography was done on brains that all were sectioned at the same angle in relation to the system of coordinates. All sections were drawn using a precisely calibrated XY plotter, transformed into maps by locating them in relation to the three planes of the ventricular system and by adjusting their metric scale. The contours of basal ganglia were introduced into a computer. Plane bi-dimensional data were transformed into volumes. Neuronal densities used to determine numbers of neurons were measured by means of camera lucida drawings of the contours of neuronal somata. Abercrombie's correction[6] was made. Golgi material was also used.

Results and discussion

Nigro-striatal axons essentially originate from the pars compacta. Not all are dopaminergic, and not all dopaminergic neurons projecting to the striatum are in the pars compacta; some are also in the nucleus paranigralis and scattered in the pars mixta and in the mesencephalic reticular formation.[7,8] Previous descriptions[9-11] did not present the complete cartography of nigro-striatal axons. Figure 1 shows regularly interspaced transverse sections after an injection in the anterior substantia nigra in a *Macaca mulatta*. Axons first gather dorso-medially, follow the H_2 field above the subthalamic nucleus and cross the capsule in the most dorsal part of or dorsally to Edinger's comb system. While some of them course through the two pallidal nuclei, which indeed are known to contain dopamine[12] and dopaminergic receptors,[13] most nigral axons follow the interpallidal and pallido-putaminal laminae. They cross through groups of cholinergic neurons of the basalis complex, with which they could synapse (Fig. 1). Inside the striatum the nigral projection was first described as homogeneous.[9] The observation of patches was observed later and only in the caudate nucleus of non-primates.[14,15] The topography of the nigral territory inside primate striatum is not yet firmly established.

The striato-pallido-nigral bundle, known for years to be very dense,[16] was in fact neglected. The striatal neuronal species from which it originates was not even known. It is now established that spiny neurons constitute the bulk of projection neurons of the striatum. Their axons are thin, weakly myelinated or unmyelinated and tightly apposed one with the other. Atlases of the striato-pallido-nigral bundle have already been published.[2,17] Striatal axons first gather into intra-striatal fascicles and are successively perpendicular to the lateral stria medullaris, to the medial interpallidal stria and to the postero-medial border of the medial pallidal nucleus. Inside the pallidum, they constitute an extremely dense and very peculiar axonal stream.[2] In the internal capsule they are the main component of the so-called comb system which leads them to the antero-lateral border of the substantia nigra in which they end. It has been recently demonstrated[18,19] that axons of individual spiny neurons end either in the lateral or the medial nucleus of the pallidum or in the pars lateralis or pars reticulata of the substantia nigra. Spiny neurons are the constituent of the two striatal compartments: striosomes and matrix.[20] These have not been shown to be the origin of distinctive targets in primates. On the contrary, the observation of separate distributions of spiny neurons projecting to different pallidal or nigral targets[19] leads to the consideration of another level of striatal organization, the opposition between sensorimotor and associative territories. Atlases plotting the intra-striatal distributions of cortico-striate endings[1-3] have already shown that this subdivision is preferable to the classical anatomical opposition between caudate nucleus and putamen. The parallel course of striatal axons induces sensorimotor and associative territories inside

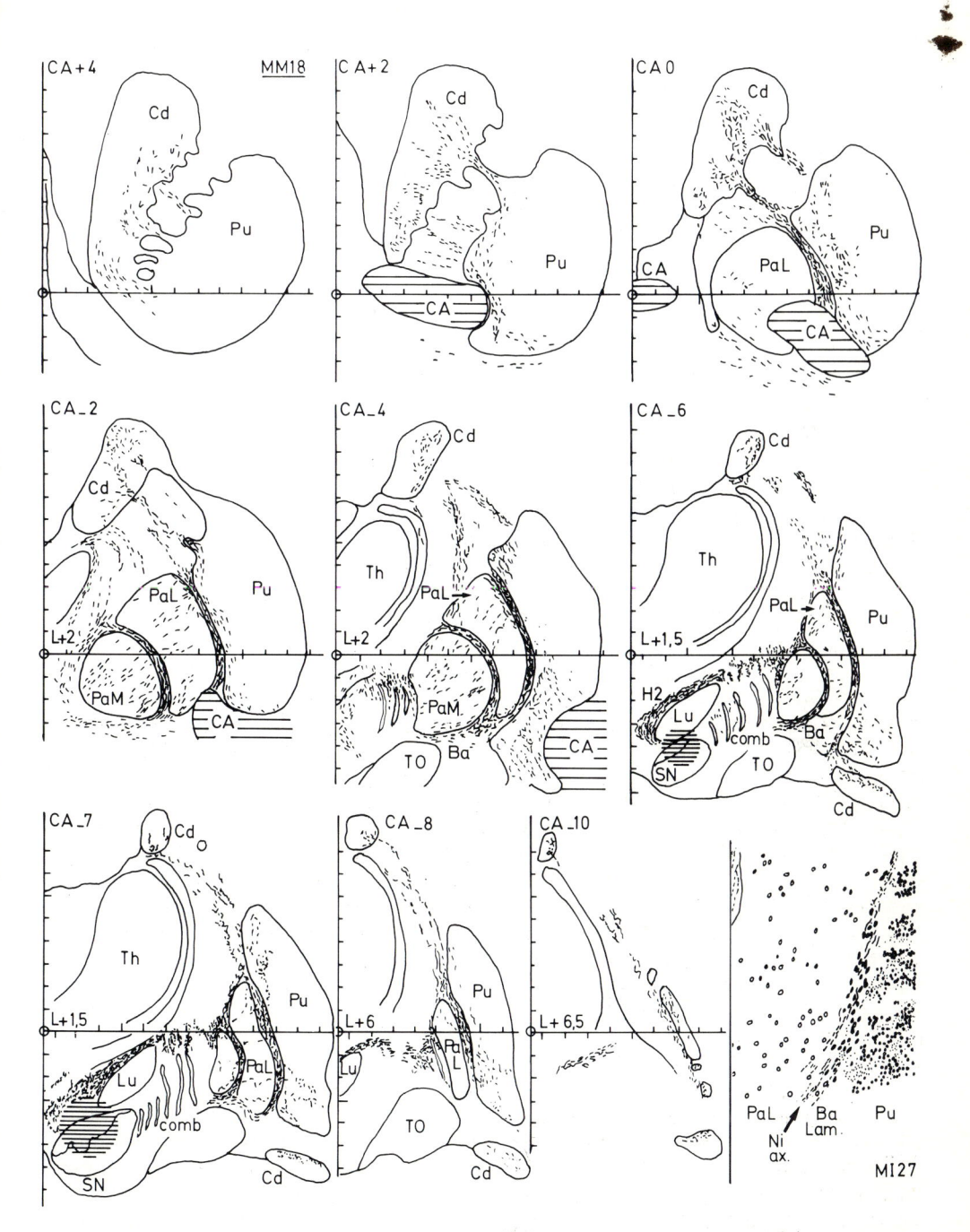

Fig. 1. *Course of nigro-pallido-striatal axons (dashed lines) after an injection of tritiated aminoacids in the anterior substantia nigra of a* Macaca mulatta. *Transverse sections are located in relation to the CA-CP ventricular system. Bottom right: The course of nigral axons through the external lamina. The small dots in the lamina and in the striatum are probable endings. Cholinergic neurons are blackened.*

the two pallidal nuclei and substantia nigra. In the pallidum the sensorimotor territory is more posterior and inferior than the associative territory. In the substantia nigra, the pars lateralis which receives axons from the sensorimotor territory projects to the tectum.[21] The pars reticulata which contains the ventral dendrites of pars compacta neurons mainly receives axons from the associative territory.[3] The nigro-striato-nigral loop is likely to be a real one since nigral neurons projecting to a given striatal place receive striatal axons from the same place.[22]

The comparison between the distributions of striato-nigral and nigro-striatal axons shows noticeable topographic differences. In the internal capsule, nigro-striatal axons are clearly more dorsal and more posterior than striato-nigral axons. While every striatal axon enters the pallidum through its lateral border, nigro-striatal axons tend to go round the pallidum and to merely follow its borders. Most nigro-striatal axons in fact do not enter the pallidum. Nigro-striatal axons make bridges between the putamen and the caudate nucleus which is never the case for striato-pallido-nigral axons.

The proof of the existence of a connection is not sufficient for an understanding of how two different neuronal species communicate and how they process information. Numbers of neurons must be considered (Fig. 2). There are many more cortico-striatal axonal endings than nigro-striatal ones.[23] The loop is predominantly fed with cortical information. If every neuron of the pars compacta sends an axon to the striatum, there could be about 160 000 nigro-striatal axons in macaques (Fig. 2). If every spiny neuron of the striatum sends an axon to one of the two pallidal nuclei or to the substantia nigra, there would be 31 million striato-pallido-nigral axons. Although the exact number of the sole striato-nigral neurons is not yet known, the most important bundle, quantitatively, is not the nigro-striatal but the striato-pallido-nigral bundle.

The numbers of neurons are not sufficient to analyse validly the amount of divergence or convergence, or the number of possible items of information of neuronal systems.[1,3] Three-dimensional analyses of the domain of communication (the three-dimensional swarm of synapses involved in the communication), of dendritic dwellings (the average space in which dendritic arborizations expand) (Fig. 2), and of the cladonal parcels (the average space in which terminal axonal arborizations expand) have to be done.[1,3] The average shape of the dendritic dwellings of spiny neurons is spherical and its average diameter is 350 μm, which is very small in comparison to the volume of the striatum. This is a finely grained cerebral region where an important number of possible items of information can be distributed. Unfortunately, there are no data available concerning the size of the axonal arborizations of the dopaminergic neurons in the striatum. The arborization shown in Fig. 2 is similar to that presented[23] as a nigro-striatal ending. It looks very small but it is probably the mere distal part of a much larger arborization. The only comparison that can be made is between the number of nigral axons, which is relatively low, and the volume of their striatal territory which contains a very large number of spiny neurons. This is typical of neuromodulator neuronal systems. The nigro-striatal communication is probably extensively divergent.

The striato-nigral communication is the reverse. The ventral dendrites of pars compacta neurons are very long (up to 1000 μm[24]). The domain of communication, mostly limited to pars reticulata, seems to be compressed dorsally by the somata of the pars compacta neurons. Posteriorly, it is narrow enough to correspond to the size of a single dendritic arborization. Striatal axons have only short (less than 50 μm) and very rare collaterals. Their cladonal parcels are thus almost linear (Fig. 2), but they are very numerous and grossly perpendicular to the dendrites of nigral neurons.[25] The striato-nigral communication is extremely convergent.

The so-called nigro-striato-nigral loop is thus not a simple loop but an extraordinary system producing extreme divergence and extreme convergence of information.

The primate nigro-striato-pallido-nigral system. Not a mere loop

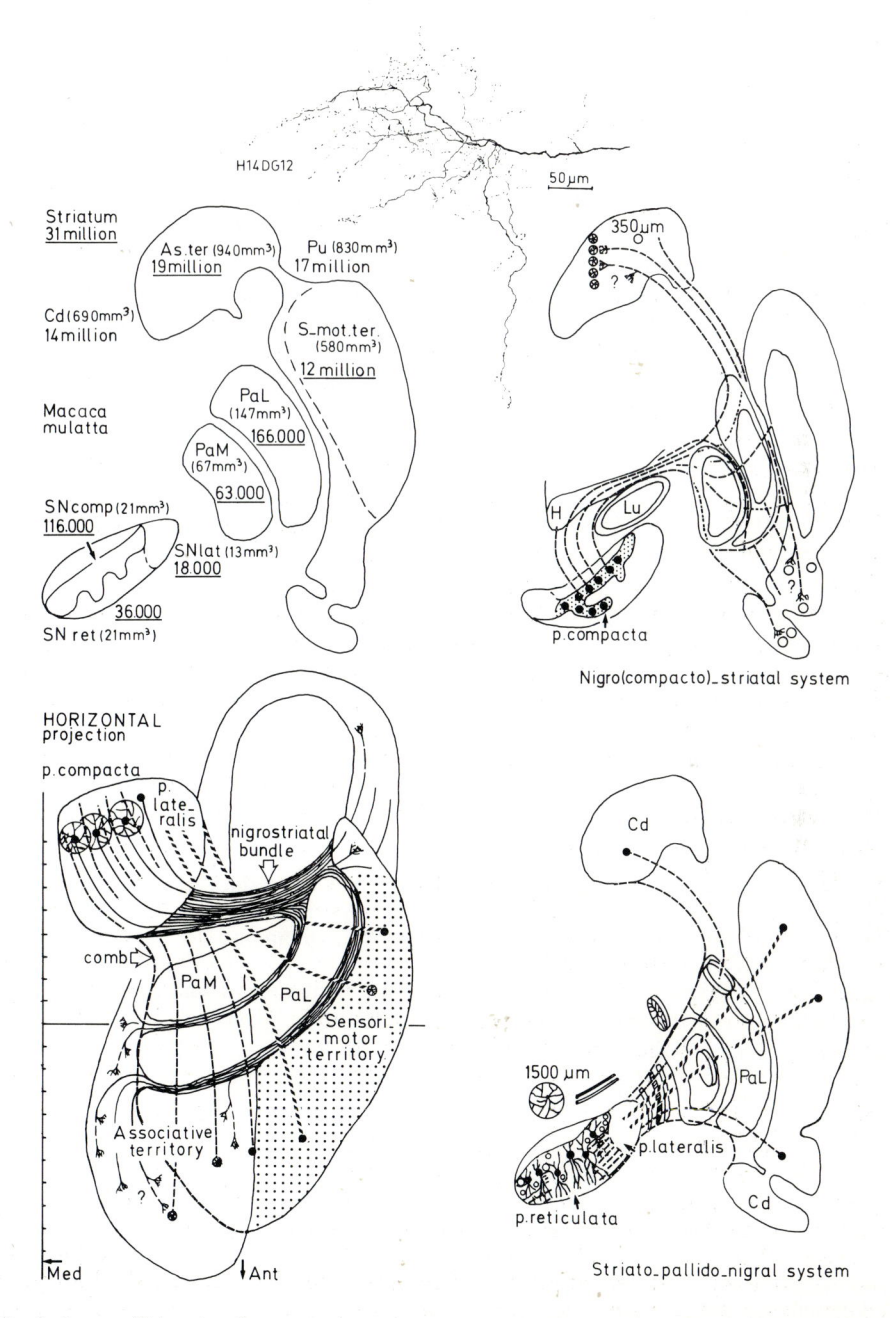

Fig. 2. *Striato-pallido-nigral connections in macaques.* Top left. The striato-pallido-nigral complex. The total number of neurons (underlined) and the volume (in brackets) of each element are indicated. Top right: Transverse representation of the nigro-striatal connection. This system is likely to include branched axons. The top-most drawing shows a terminal axonal arborization found in the putamen which could originate in the substantia nigra. Bottom left: Horizontal representation of the nigro-striatal (full lines) and striato-pallido-nigral (dashed lines) connections emphasizing their different courses. Bottom right: Transverse representation of the striato-pallido-nigral connection. Pallidal discs and neurons of the pars compacta are represented at scale.

References

1. Percheron, G., Yelnik, J. & François, C. (1984): The primate striato-pallido-nigral system. An integrative system for cortical information. In *The basal ganglia: structure and function*, eds J. S. McKenzie, R. E. Kemm & L. N. Wilcock, pp 87–105. New York: Plenum Press.
2. Percheron, G., Yelnik, J. & François, C. (1984): A Golgi analysis of the primate globus pallidus. III. Spatial organization of the striato-pallidal complex. *J. Comp. Neurol.* **227**, 214–227.
3. Percheron, G., François, C. & Yelnik, J. (1987): Spatial organization and information processing in the core of the basal ganglia. In *The basal ganglia II. Structure and function—current concepts*, eds M. B. Carpenter & A. Jayaraman, pp 205–226. New York: Plenum Press.
4. Percheron, G., Yelnik, J. & François, C. (1986): Systems of coordinates for stereotactic surgery and cerebral cartography: advantages of ventricular systems in monkeys. *J. Neurosci. Methods* **17**, 69–88.
5. Percheron, G., François, C. & Yelnik, J. (1986): Instruments and techniques for the stereotactic surgery based on the CA-CP ventricular system of coordinates in monkeys. *J. Neurosci. Methods* **17**, 89–99.
6. Abercrombie, M. (1946): Estimation of nuclear population from microtome sections. *Anat. Rec.* **94**, 239–247.
7. François, C., Percheron, G. & Yelnik, J. (1985): An histological atlas of the substantia nigra of the macaque (Macaca mulatta) in ventricular coordinates. *Brain Res. Bull.* **14**, 349–367.
8. Arsenault, M.-Y., Parent, A., Séguéla, P. & Descarries, L. (1988): Distribution and morphological characteristics of dopamine-immunoreactive neurons in the midbrain of the squirrel monkey (Saïmiri sciureus). *J. Comp. Neurol.* **267**, 489–506.
9. Carpenter, M. B. & Peter, P. (1972): Nigrostriatal and nigrothalamic fibers in the rhesus monkey. *J. Comp. Neurol.* **144**, 93–116.
10. Carpenter, M. B., Nakano, K. & Kim, R. (1975): Nigrothalamic projections in the monkey demonstrated by auto-radiographic technics. *J. Comp. Neurol.* **165**, 401–416.
11. Szabo, J. (1980): Organization of the ascending striatal afferents in monkeys. *J. Comp. Neurol.* **189**, 307–321.
12. Hornykiewicz, O. (1966): Dopamine (3-Hydroxytryptamine) and brain function. *Pharmacol. Rev.* **18**, 925–964.
13. Fields, J. Z., Reisine, T. D. & Yamamura, H. L. (1977): Biochemical demonstration of dopaminergic receptors in rat and human brain using (^{3}H)spiroperidol. *Brain Res.* **136**, 578–584.
14. Beckstead, R. M. (1985): Complementary mosaic distributions of thalamic and nigral axons in the caudate nucleus of the cat: double anterograde labeling combining autoradiography and wheat germ-HRP histochemistry. *Brain Res.* **335**, 153–159.
15. Giguère, M., Marchand, R. & Poirier, L. J. (1984): The nigrostriatal nervous pathways in the brain of the cat. An autoradiographic study. *Adv. Neurol.* **40**, 77–83.
16. Verhaart, W. J. C. (1950): Fiber analysis of the basal ganglia. *J. Comp. Neurol.* **93**, 425–440.
17. François, C., Nguyen-Legros, J. & Percheron, G. (1981): Topographical and cytological localization of iron in rat and monkey brains. *Brain Res.* **215**, 317–322.
18. Féger, J. & Crossman, A. R. (1984): Identification of different subpopulations of neostriatal neurones projecting to globus pallidus or substantia nigra in the monkey: a retrograde fluorescence double-labelling study. *Neurosci. Lett.* **49**, 7–12.
19. Parent, A., Bouchard, H. C. & Smith, Y. (1984): The striatopallidal and striatonigral projections: two distinct fiber systems in primate. *Brain Res.* **303**, 385–390.
20. Penny, G. R., Wilson, C. J. & Kitai, S. T. (1988): Relationship of the axonal and dendritic geometry of spiny projection neurons to the compartmental organization of the neostriatum. *J. Comp. Neurol.* **269**, 275–289.
21. François, C., Percheron, G. & Yelnik, J. (1984): Localization of nigrostriatal, nigrothalamic and nigrotectal neurons in ventricular coordinates in macaques. *Neuroscience* **13**, 61–76.
22. Smith, Y. & Parent, A. (1986): Differential connections of caudate nucleus and putamen in the squirrel monkey (Saïmiri sciureus). *Neuroscience* **18**, 347–371.
23. DiFiglia, M., Pasik, T. & Pasik, P. (1978): A Golgi study of afferent fibers in the neostriatum of monkeys. *Brain Res.* **152**, 341–347.
24. Yelnik, J., François, C., Percheron, G. & Heyner, S. (1987): Golgi study of the primate

substantia nigra. I. Quantitative morphology and typology of nigral neurons. *J. Comp. Neurol.* **265**, 455–472.

25 François, C., Yelnik, J. & Percheron, G. (1987): Golgi study of the primate substantia nigra. II. Spatial organization of dendritic arborizations in relation to the cytoarchitectonic boundaries and to the striatonigral bundle. *J. Comp. Neurol.* **265**, 473–493.

13

HETEROGENEOUS ROLE OF NEOSTRIATAL AND MESOSTRIATAL PATHOLOGY IN DISORDERS OF MOVEMENT: A REVIEW AND NEW FACTS

A. R. Cools, W. Spooren, E. Cuypers, R. Bezemer and R. Jaspers

Research Unit in Psychoneuropharmacology, Department of Pharmacology, University of Nijmegen, P.O. Box 9101, 6500 HB Nijmegen, The Netherlands

Summary

This article reviews data showing that the feline caudate nucleus (CN) contains two functionally, topographically and pharmacologically distinct dopamine receptors, and presents new data showing that oro-facial dyskinesias inherent in stimulation of DA_i receptors within the anterodorsal region of the caudate nucleus are funnelled via the subcommissural part of the globus pallidus (sGP). In part 1, data are reviewed to illustrate that the so-called DA_e and DA_i receptors share several features with D_2 and D_1 receptors, respectively. Moreover, data are reviewed to illustrate that DA_e receptors are especially present in striosomes innervated by A_9 fibres and DA_i receptors in extrastriosomal matrix innervated by A_8 fibres. In part 2, data are reviewed which show that the non-motor (cognitive or motivational) disorders inherent in hypoactivity of DA_e receptors are funnelled via the substantia nigra pars reticulata (SNR) towards the deeper layers of the colliculus superior (dlCS). In part 3, two new sets of experiments are reported. First, it is shown that the sGP is innervated by the caudate nucleus region marked by a predominance of DA_i receptors, but not by the region with a predominance of DA_e receptors. Second, it is shown that the sensori-motor disorders characterized by hyperactivity of DA_i receptors are not funnelled via the substantia nigra towards the dlCS; instead, these disorders can also be elicited from the sGP, ie, the first order output station of the caudate nucleus region marked by DA_i receptors. Finally we discuss the available data which support the previously reported hypothesis that motor and motivational (cognitive) functions of the striatum are carried out by distinct parts of the striatum. We discuss the clinical relevance of the available data.

Functional heterogeneity within the caudate nucleus

Since 1975 the caudate nucleus of cats has been known to be heterogeneous. Studies using unilateral injections of dopamine and related agents have led to the discovery that the caudate nucleus contains two functionally and pharmacologically distinct dopamine-sensitive sites.[1] These studies have given rise to the original concept of two types of dopamine receptors, ie, DA_e and DA_i receptors.[2] Due to the subsequent discovery of two distinct types of dopamine binding sites, the former concept is pushed into the background and replaced by the concept of D_1 and D_2 receptors.[3] Today, it is not yet clear to what degree the pharmacological profiles of DA_e and DA_i receptors differ from those of D_1 and D_2 receptors respectively.[4] Despite this it is useful to recall the following: DA_i and D_1 receptors, as well as DA_e and D_2 receptors share a number of properties[4]: DA_i and D_1 receptors are restricted to nigrostriatal and mesolimbic regions marked by so-called dotted DA fluorescence[2,5]; stimulation of DA_i and D_1 receptors results in oro-facial dyskinesias[1,6]; and DA_i receptors mediate a number of effects which are diametrically opposite to those mediated by DA_e receptors,[7] a phenomenon inherent in D_1 receptors which mediate a great variety of effects that are opposite to those mediated by D_2 receptors.[8] Furthermore, DA_e and D_2 receptors are present in nigrostriatal and mesolimbic regions marked by so-called diffuse DA fluorescence[2,8]; and stimulation of DA_e and D_2 receptors results in characteristic stereotypes.[7,9] Because of the lack of specific ligands, the topographical distribution of DA_e and DA_i receptors could not be mapped in detail. Nevertheless, it is known that the caudate nucleus is marked by subregions in which 90% or more of the tested dopamine-sensitive sites show features typical for either DA_e or DA_i receptors.

Thus, the rostromedial part of the caudate nucleus (Fig. 1: CRM area) contains mainly DA_e receptors, although it is not devoid of DA_i receptors.[1,10] Furthermore, the anterodorsal part of the caudate nucleus (Fig. 1: r-CRM area) contains mainly DA_i receptors.[1,10] And, finally, the remainder of the nucleus contains predominantly DA_i receptors which are diffusely intermingled with DA_e receptors.[1,10] Since the CRM area encompasses a region that is marked by the highest density of striosomes (cf Figs, and[1,11–13]), it is important to recall the features of the latter. Striosomes contain D_2 receptors, ie, receptors sharing several basic features with DA_e receptors (see above).[14]

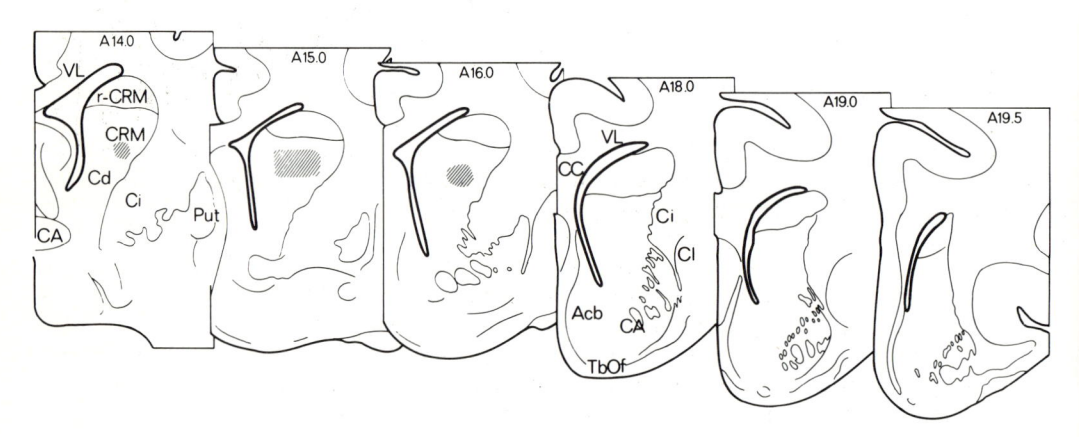

Fig. 1. Semi-diagrammatic outline of the functionally and pharmacologically distinct rostromedial part of the caudate nucleus (CRM area) and anterodorsal part of the caudate nucleus (κ-CRM: open area).

Furthermore, striosomes are primarily innervated by the classical, nigrostriatal A₉ fibres as well as by the prefrontal and insulotemporal cortex and by the basolateral amygdala.[11] From this point of view, it is not amazing that the so-called neostriatal DA_e receptors within the CRM area do not simply transform sensorimotor information (see below). On the other hand, the r-CRM area encompasses a region that is primarily marked by extrastriosomal matrix (cf Figs, in[1,11,12]). The matrix is known to contain D_1 receptors, ie, receptors sharing several features with those of DA_i receptors (see above).[13] Moreover, the r-CRM area is relatively heavily innervated by dopaminergic A₈ fibres (cf Figs in[1,11,12]), as well as by sensory, motor and premotor cortex.[11] Given the latter findings, it is not surprising that the so-called mesolimbic DA_i receptors transform sensorimotor information especially (see below).

CRM area and hierarchically lower order output stations

Today, evidence is available that dopamine within the CRM area allows the organism to switch arbitrarily from one behaviour to another, ie, to switch behaviour without the help of currently available sensory information.[14,15] As long as the spontaneously occurring or experimentally-induced deficit within the CRM area is small, the organism suffers only from a reduced ability to switch complex behaviours, such as social interactions between monkeys and cognitive tasks in man; the ability to switch motor behaviours arbitrarily is still intact.[15–17] In other words, organisms with a small dopamine deficit within the CRM area suffer only from switching disorders that are manifest at the non-motor (cognitive) level. The abnormal output of such a relatively mildly dysfunctioning CRM area is funnelled via the pars reticulata of the substantia nigra towards the deeper layers of the colliculus superior (dlCS).[14,18,19] Whether or not this information is also funnelled via other circuitries such as the striato-pallido-thalamo-cortical circuitry remains to be investigated. Intermediate dopamine deficits within the CRM area result in an additional set of switching disorders. In fact, intermediate dopamine deficits within the CRM area produce motor disorders identical to those typical of a dysfunctioning SNR, ie, motor effects resulting from a reduced ability to switch postures and motor patterns with the help of tonic proprioceptive stimuli.[14,18–22] Moreover, large dopamine deficits within the CRM area lead to motor disorders identical to those typical of a dysfunctioning dlCS, ie, motor effects resulting from a reduced ability to switch motor patterns with the help of tonic exteroceptive stimuli.[14,18–22] These and related findings have led to the conclusion that the latter switching disorders only arise when hierarchically lower order output stations of the CRM area, such as the SNR and dlCS, start to dysfunction as a consequence of the arrival of distorted information sent by the CRM area.[14,18,19]

In summary, deficits from the rostromedial part of the caudate nucleus are funnelled among others via the substantia nigra pars reticulata towards the deeper layers of the superior colliculus.

r-CRM area and its hierarchically lower order output station

By 1975 it had already been found that stimulation of dopamine receptors within the r-CRM area results in oro-facial dyskinesias[1]: cats show random bursts of dyskinetic movements such as sluggish tongue protrusions and rapid tic-like contractions of the facial, eye and ear muscles which are not suppressed by visual or auditory stimuli. These impressive phenomena are specific for the r-CRM area. Neither stimulation of dopamine receptors within the CRM area nor manipulations of the above-mentioned output stations of the CRM area have been found to result in oro-facial dyskinesias.[1,23–25] In order to investigate the pathway along which the oro-facial dyskinesias are achieved, the first order output stations of the r-CRM area were delineated with the help of wheat-germ-agglutinin-conjugated horseradish peroxidase (WGA-HRP) according to previously described procedures.[26] For that purpose, WGA-HRP (0.2–0.3 μl: 5 per cent) was injected either into the CRM area (n = 3) or into the r-CRM area (n = 4) of male cats weighing 3.5–4.0 kg. One of the brain regions which was heavily labelled after r-CRM injections, but not after CRM injections (the subcommissural part of the globus pallidus [sGP; Fig. 2; unpublished data from R. Jaspers, A. R. Cools and H. J. Groenewegen]) was selected for behavioural experiments. Since this area is likely to be innervated by striato-pallidal fibres which, among other substances, release GABA,[27] we chose picrotoxin, a drug that suppresses GABA activity by closing the chloride channels, and the $GABA_a$ agonist muscimol, to study the behavioural effects of local injections into the sGP of freely moving cats. For this purpose, male cats weighing 3.5–4.0 kg (Animal Laboratory, University of Nijmegen) were stereotaxically equipped with cannulas according to previously reported procedures[25] (coordinates[29]: A 15.0; L 5.3; H −3.5; lateral angle: 7°; caudal angle: 5°).

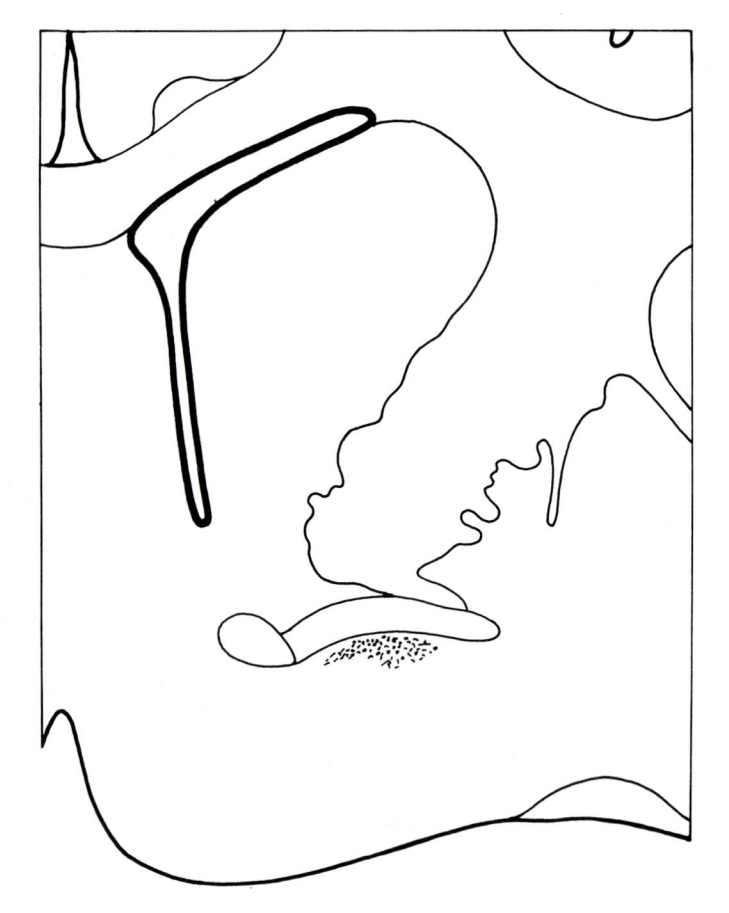

Fig. 2. *Fibre labelling following wheat-germ-agglutin-conjugated horseradish peroxidase in the r-CRM area.* As mentioned in the text, no labelling is found in this subcommissural pallidal region (sGP) following HRP in the CRM area.

Following standard procedures for habituation to the experimental cage (90 × 60 × 60 cm) and injections,[25] cats received bilateral injections (0.5 µl per side) of picrotoxin (Serva), muscimol (Serva), the combination of picrotoxin and muscimol (spaced by an interval of 5 min), and the corresponding control injections (solvent = distilled water). The minimum interval between experiments was 7 days, and a maximum of six injections was given per cat. The drug-induced behaviour, which was stored on videotape with the help of a closed TV circuit, was recorded for a period of 15 min before and 45 min after the injections, and analysed with the help of a standard ethogram. If an animal displayed abnormal behaviour during the pre-injection period, the data of that animal were discarded. Wilcoxon matched-pairs signed-ranks test was used for statistical analysis.

The experiments showed that picrotoxin injections into the sGP elicited full blown oro-facial dyskinesias in a dose-dependent and GABA-specific manner. For the sake of simplicity, only the median values of the frequency of tongue protrusions are given. As shown in Fig. 3, picrotoxin dose-dependently increased the number of tongue protrusions, an effect which was significantly attenuated by muscimol; both the solvent and muscimol alone remained ineffective (Fig. 4). Figure 5 shows the distribution of the most effective and the least effective sites which were traced with standard procedures;[25] despite the limited number of tested sites it appears that the effective sites are restricted to a particular region. The tongue protrusions themselves resulted from both normal and abnormal movements. Whereas normal tongue movements simply consisted of protruding the flat tongue, abnormal tongue movements implied a variety of movements: curling upwards of the lateral sides of the tongue and then protruding the curled tongue via the left or right

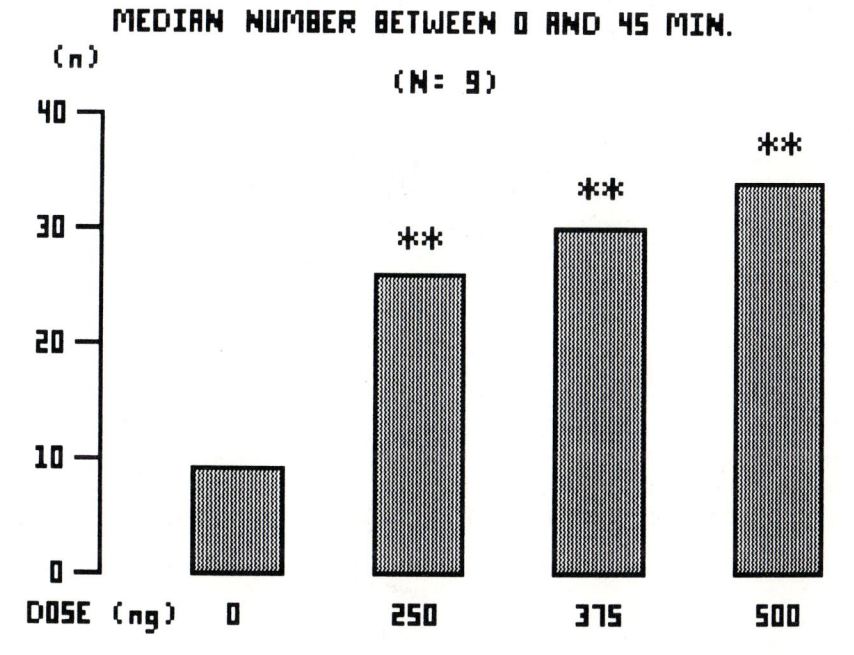

Fig. 3. *Median values of number of tongue protrusions during 45 min following bilateral sGP injections of solvent (left histogram: distilled water) or picrotoxin (250–500 ng/0.5 µl per side) in cats (n = 9). P < 0.01 (picrotoxin vs solvent).*

TONGUE PROTRUSION: GABA-specificity

MEDIAN NUMBER BETWEEN 0 AND 45 MIN.
(n=8)

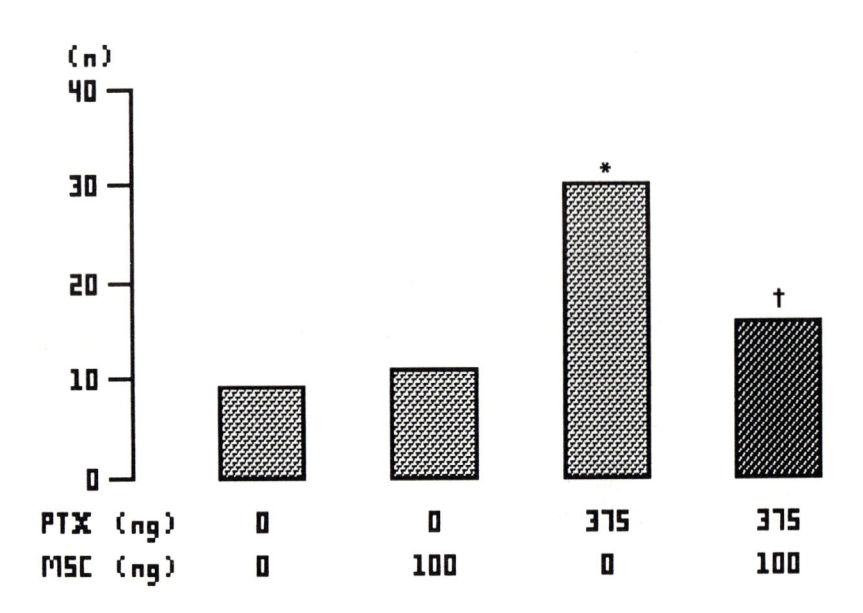

PTX (ng)	0	0	375	375
MSC (ng)	0	100	0	100

Fig. 4. Median values of number of tongue protrusions during 45 min following bilateral sPG injections of 375 ng picrotoxin plus 100 ng muscimol; 375 ng picrotoxin plus solvent of muscimol (distilled water); solvent of picrotoxin (distilled water) plus 100 ng muscimol; and solvent of picrotoxin plus solvent of muscimol (left histogram).* $P < 0.01$ (375 ng plus solvent of muscimol vs solvent of picrotoxin plus solvent of muscimol.† $P < 0.01$ (375 ng picrotoxin plus 100 ng muscimol vs 375 ng picrotoxin plus solvent of muscimol).

corner of the mouth; curling upwards and inwards of the tip of the tongue against the palatum and then protruding it; and pressing the tip of the tongue against the inner side of the cheek and then protruding it. In general, the tongue protrusions, which were at best built-in licking movements directed at objects such as the wall of the cage, were clustered in random bursts of dyskinetic movements. The movements were sometimes sluggish and sometimes rapid and vigorous. The available data strongly suggest that the abnormal output of a dysfunctioning r-CRM area giving rise to oro-facial dyskinesias is funnelled via the sGP. Since the oro-facial dyskinesias elicited from the sGP are far more intense and vigorous than those elicited from the r-CRM area, it is not unlikely that these dyskinesias only arise when hierarchically lower order output stations of the r-CRM area, such as the sGP, start to dysfunction as a consequence of the arrival of distorted information sent by the r-CRM area.

Conclusions

Evidence is now available that experimentally-induced deficits in the basal ganglia elicit disorders of movement only when output stations of the basal ganglia start to

Localisation Tongue protrusion

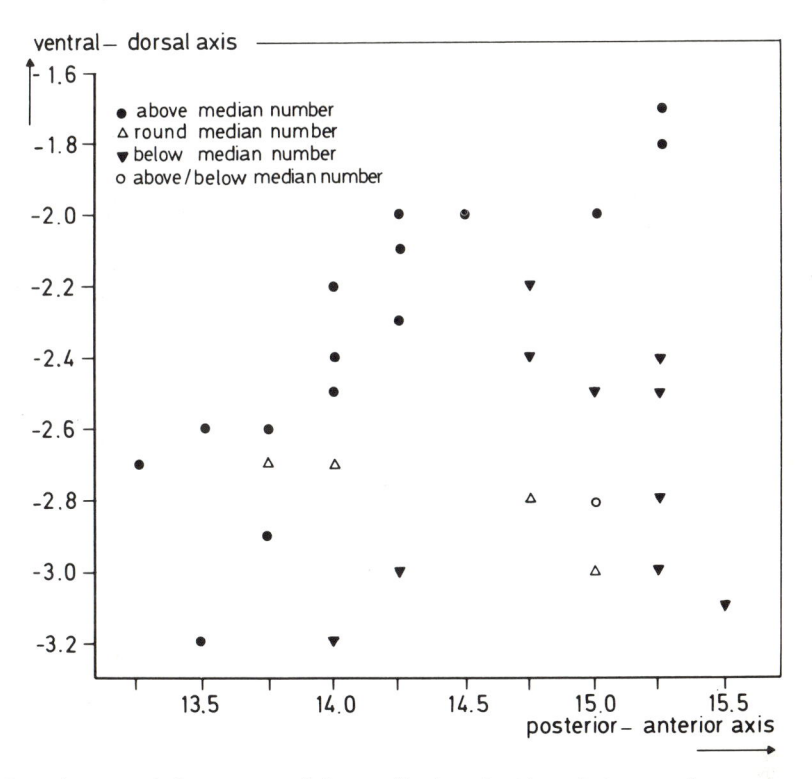

Fig. 5. *Distribution of the most and least effective sites in relation to the number of tongue protrusions during 45 min following bilateral sPG injections in cats (n = 30). The median values were calculated per group of cats having received the same treatment.*

dysfunction.[14,18,19] The basal ganglia are known to have anatomically distinct and interactive input-output channels.[11–13,26,29,30] The present data reveal that the nature of striatally induced disorders of movement varies as a function of the affected output channels. Dopamine hypofunctioning of the CRM area results in disorders such as a reduced ability to arbitrarily switch on-going behaviour (small dopamine deficit), a reduced ability to switch on-going behaviour with the help of tonic proprioceptive stimuli (intermediate dopamine deficit), and a reduced ability to switch on-going behaviour with the help of tonic exteroceptive stimuli (large dopamine deficit), ie, disorders which are funnelled among others via the substantia nigra towards the dlCS. In contrast, dopamine hyperfunctioning of the r-CRM area results in oro-facial dyskinesias, ie, an effect which is certainly not funnelled via the SNR towards the dlCS. Instead, the r-CRM-induced oro-facial dyskinesia is also elicited from a first-order output station of the r-CRM area, the sGP, suggesting that the oro-facial dyskinesia is indeed funnelled via the latter station.

Given the relatively high density of striosomes within the CRM area innervated by nigrostriatal A_9 fibres on the one hand and the relative dominance of extrastriosomal matrix innervated by mesostriatal A_8 fibres within the r-CRM area on the other, it becomes attractive to put together the available pieces of information as follows: dopamine receptors within the CRM area, ie, DA_e receptors sharing several features with D_2 receptors, are postsynaptic receptors belonging to the classical, dopaminergic nigrostriatal A_9 fibres,[7] and are located on cells where information from the prefrontal and insulotemporal cortex and from the basolateral amygdala is integrated in order to allow the organism to switch its on-going behaviour arbitrarily. In contrast, dopamine receptors within the r-CRM area, ie, DA_i sharing several features with D_1 receptors, are postsynaptic receptors belonging to the dopaminergic, mesostriatal A_8 fibres,[7] and are located on cells where information from the sensory, motor and premotor cortex is integrated into a sensorimotor output, disturbance of which results in oro-facial dyskinesias. The present data provide direct evidence in favour of the earlier reported hypothesis that motor and motivational (cognitive) functions of the striatum are carried out by distinct subregions of the striatum.[31-34] As a final comment, switching disorders occur in patients with Parkinson's disease,[18] whereas oro-facial dyskinesias occur in parkinsonian patients treated chronically with levodopa.[23] On the basis of the present data, it is tentatively suggested that parkinsonian symptoms such as a reduced shifting aptitude[17] are funnelled via output stations of the nigro-striatal circuitry, and that levodopa-induced oro-facial dyskinesias are funnelled via output stations of the mesostriatal circuitry. Future research is required to (in)validate the latter hypothesis.

References

1 Cools, A. R., Struyker Boudier, H. A. J. & van Rossum, J. M. (1976): Dopamine receptors: selective agonists and antagonists of functionally distinct types within the feline brain. *Eur. J. Pharmacol.* **37**, 283–293.
2 Cools, A. R. & van Rossum, J. M. (1976): Excitation-mediating and inhibition-mediating dopamine-receptors: a new concept towards a better understanding of electrophysiological, biochemical, pharmacological functional and clinical data. *Psychopharmacology.* **45**, 243–254.
3 Stoof, J. C. & Kebabian, J. W. (1984): Two dopamine receptors: biochemistry, physiology and pharmacology. *Life Sci.* **35**, 2281–2296.
4 Cools, A. R. (1986): Clinical neuropharmacology of the basal ganglia. In *Handbook of clinical neurology*, vol. 5, eds P. J. Vinken, G. Bruyn & H. Klawans, pp 47–63. Amsterdam: Elsevier.
5 Ögren, S. O., Fuxe, K., Ängeby, K. & Köhler, V. C. (1985): The ergolene derivative MPME induces in the rat a behavioural syndrome associated with activation of dopamine D_1 receptors belonging to the dotted type of forebrain dopamine nerve terminals. *Eur. J. Pharmacol.* **106**, 79–89.
6 Rosengarten, H., Schweitzer, J. W. & Friedhoff, A. J. (1983): Induction of oral dyskinesias in naive rats by D_1 stimulation. *Life Sci.* **33**, 2479–2482.
7 Cools, A. R. & van Rossum, J. M. (1980): Multiple receptors for brain dopamine in behavioural regulation: concept of dopamine-e and dopamine-i receptors. *Life Sci.* **27**, 1237–1253.
8 Fuxe, K., Agnati, L. F. Härfstrand, A., Ögren, S. O. & Goldstein, M. (1986): *Recent developments in Parkinson's disease*, eds S. Fahn, C. D. Jenner, & P. Teychenne, pp 17–32. New York: Raven Press.
9 Waddington, J. L. (1986): Behavioural correlates of the action of selective D-1. Dopamine receptor antagonist. *Biochem. Pharmacol.* **35**, 3661–3667.
10 Cools, A. R., Janssen, H. J., Struyker-Boudier, H. A. J. & van Rossum, J. M. (1975). Interaction between antipsychotic drugs and catecholamine receptors. In *Antipsychotic drugs: pharmacodynamics and pharmakinetics*, ed. G. Sedvall, pp 73–87. Oxford: Pergamon Press.
11 Jimenez-Castellanos, J. & Graybiel, A. M. (1987): Subdivisions of the dopamine-containing A8-A9-A10 complex identified by their differential mesostriatal innervation of striosomes and extrastriosomal matrix. *Neuroscience* **23**, 223–242.
12 Graybiel, A. M. (1984): Correspondence between the dopamine islands and striosomes of the mammalian striatum. *Neuroscience* **13**, 1157–1187.
13 Beckstead, R. M., Wooten, G. F. & Trugman, J. M. (1988): Distribution of D_1 and D_2 dopamine receptors in the basal ganglia of the cat determined by quantitative autoradiography, *J. Comp. Neurol.* **268**, 131–145.

14 Cools, A. R., Jaspers, R., Schwarz, M., Sontag, K. H., Vrijmoed-de ries, M. & van den Bercken, J. (1984): Basal ganglia and switching motor programmes. In *The basal ganglia: structure and function*, eds. J. S. McKenzie, R. E. Kemm & L. N. Wilcock, pp 513–544. New York: Plenum Press.
15 Jaspers, R., Schwarz, M., Sontag, K. H. & Cools, A. R. (1984): Caudate nucleus and programming behaviour in cats. Role of dopamine in switching motor pattern. *Behav. Brain Res.* **14**, 17–28.
16 van den Bercken, J. H. L. & Cools, A. R. (1982): Evidence for a role of the caudate nucleus in the sequential organization of behaviour. *Behav. Brain Res.* **4**, 319–337.
17 Cools, A. R., van den Bercken, J. H. L., Horstink, M. W. I., van Spaendonck, K. P. M. & Berger, H. J. C. (1984): Cognitive and motor shifting aptitude disorder in Parkinson's disease. *J. Neurol. Neurosurg. Psychiatry* **47**, 443–453.
18 Gelissen, M. & Cools, A. R. (1988): Effect of increasing doses of intracaudate haloperidol upon motor expressions that require an intact substantia nigra pars reticulata and/or superior solliculus in cats. *Behav. Brain Res.* **27**, 205–214.
19 Jaspers, R. M. A. & Cools, A. R. (1988): Behavioural correlates of a progressive dysfunctioning of the caudate nucleus effects of apomorphine. *Behav. Brain Res.* **27**, 193–204.
20 Gelissen, M. & Cools, A. R. (1986): The interrelationship between superior colliculus and substantia nigra pars reticulata in programming movements of cats. *Behav. Brain Res.* **21**, 85–93.
21 Gelissen, M. & Cools, A. R. (1986): The interrelationship between superior colliculus and substantia nigra pars reticulata in programming movements of cats: a follow-up. *Behav. Brain Res.* **25**, 1–11.
22 Gelissen, M. & Cools, A. R. (1986): Movements of cats on a rotating cylinder: role of the substantia nigra pars reticulata and the deeper layers of the superior colliculus. *Behav. Brain Res.* **25**, 83–96.
23 Cools, A. R. (1983): Mesolimbic system and tardive dyskinesia: new perspectives for therapy. *Mod. Probl. Pharmacopsychiatry.* **21**, 111–123.
24 Cools, A. R., Jaspers, R., Kolasiewicz, W., Sontag, K. H. & Wolfarth, S. (1983): Substantia nigra as a station that not only transmits, but also transforms incoming signals for its behavioural expressions: striatal dopamine and GABA-mediated responses of pars reticulata neurons. *Behav. Brain Res.* **7**, 39–49.
25 Jaspers, R. & Cools, A. R. (1985): GABA-specificity of behaviour responses to picrotoxin injected into the colliculus superior of cats. *Behav. Brain Res.* **18**, 63–69.
26 Haber, S. N., Groenewegen, H. J., Grove, E. A. & Nauta, W. J. H. (1985): Efferent connections of the ventral pallidum: evidence of a dual striato pallidofugal pathway. *J. Comp. Neurol.* **235**, 322–335.
27 Graybiel, A. M. & Ragsdale, C. W. (1979): Fiber connections of the basal ganglia. *Progr. Brain Res.* **51**, 239–283.
28 Snider, R. & Niemer, W. (1964): *A stereotactic atlas of the cat brain.* London: University of Chicago Press.
29 Gerfen, C. R. (1984): Neostriatal mosaic: compartmentalization of corticostriatal input and striatonigral output systems. *Nature* **311**, 461–464.
30 Gerfen, C. R., Herkenham, M. & Thibault, J. (1987): The neostriatal mosaic: II. Patch- and matrix-directed mesostriatal dopaminergic and non-dopaminergic systems. *J. Neurosci.* **7**, 3915–3934.
31 Heimer, L. & Wilson, R. D., (1975): The subcortical projections to the allocortex: similarities in the neural associations of the hippocampus, the piriform cortex and the neocortex. In *Golgi Centennial Symposium*, ed M. Santini, pp 177–93. New York: Raven Press.
32 Nauta, W. J. H., Smith, G. P., Faull, R. L. M. & Domesick, V. B. (1978): Efferent connections and nigral afferents of the nucleus accumbens septi in the rat. *Neuroscience* **3**, 385–401.
33 Kelley, A. E., Domesick, V. B. & Nauta, W. J. H. (1982): The amygdala-striatal projection in the rat, an anatomical study by anterograde and retrograde tracing methods. *Neuroscience* **7**, 615–630.
34 Percheron, G., Yelnik, J. & François, C. (1984): The primate striato-pallido-nigral system: an integrative system for cortical information. In *The basal ganglia: structure and function*, eds J. S. McKenzie, R. E. Kemm & L. N. Wilcock, pp 87–105. New York: Plenum Press.

II

EXPERIMENTAL MODELS OF MOVEMENT DISORDERS

14

THE BASAL GANGLIA MECHANISMS MEDIATING PRIMATE MODELS OF MOVEMENT DISORDERS

M. A. Sambrook, A. R. Crossman, I. Mitchell,
R. G. Robertson, C. E. Clarke and S. Boyce

Experimental Neurology Group, Department of Cell and Structural Biology, University of Manchester, M13 9PT, UK

Summary

The experimental work described indicates that it is now possible to create in the monkey human-like models of movement disorders such as chorea/ballism, dystonia, parkinsonism and levodopa-induced dyskinesia. The specific methods used have offered important insight into the pathophysiology of these disorders and studies of neuronal metabolic activity using 2-deoxyglucose have provided additional information about the neural mechanisms producing them.

Chorea and *ballism* are both associated with reduced activity of the subthalamo-pallidal pathway which in turn is accompanied by a reduction in terminal activity of the pallidal neurons projecting on the ventral anterior and ventral lateral thalamic nuclei. In ballism the underlying pathology usually lies within the subthalamic nucleus, whereas in chorea it is due to neurochemical inhibition of it as a result of increased activity of the GABA-ergic pallido-subthalamic pathway. Experimental models of chorea and ballism induced by manipulation of neuronal activity in the medial and lateral pallidal segments and subthalamic nucleus together with the results of metabolic mapping studies strongly suggest that these disorders are mediated by similar mechanisms which only differ quantitatively.

Metabolic mapping studies in *MPTP-induced parkinsonism* provide virtually a mirror image of chorea and ballism. Neuronal terminal activity is increased in the medial and lateral pallidal segments and the thalamic nuclei to which they project and reduced in the subthalamic nucleus.

These findings appear to confirm that the subthalamo-pallidal pathway is excitatory and evidence is offered to indicate that the transmitter is probably glutamate. It follows that the role of the pallido-thalamic pathway in the mediation of movement disorders needs to be reconsidered in the light of these findings.

The pivotal importance of the subthalamic nucleus in the control of movement is emphasized by these results.

Introduction

The clinical disorders arising from diseases of the basal ganglia are as much perplexing as they are fascinating. Faced with a range of abnormal voluntary and involuntary movements extending from ballism through dystonia to Parkinson's disease, it is attractive where possible to link each type of disorder with pathological changes in a particular region of the basal ganglia. Such an approach has immediate appeal since it offers some degree of rationalization of the structure and function of one of the most complicated areas of the human forebrain to the student of neurology, the practising physician and the neuroscientist who are all attempting to come to terms with it. It does, however, tend to compartmentalize these clinical disorders and at the same time isolate the individual parts of the basal ganglia rather than stressing their interrelationships. Moreover, its weaknesses are apparent upon closer examination. For example, the neuropathology of Parkinson's disease is well described but the mechanism of tremor and the question of whether akinesia and rigidity represent positive or negative phenomena remain unclear. Ballism has become historically linked with damage to the subthalamic nucleus and this has led for many years to a tendency to separate this disorder from chorea and encourage the belief that it results from a release of pallidal activity caused by the destruction of the supposedly inhibitory subthalamopallidal pathway.

Empirical rationalisation is understandable since our ability to investigate Parkinson's disease, chorea, ballism, dystonia and drug-induced dyskinesia *in vivo* is very limited. Computed tomography and magnetic resonance imaging have greatly improved anatomical visualization of the brain but have not led to an immediate increase in our understanding of the functional relationships of the basal ganglia. Positron emission tomography has for the first time provided a non-invasive technique for studying neuronal metabolism and the kinetics of neurotransmitter uptake and receptor binding in man. At present its only limitation in the investigation of movement disorders is one of resolution. Disorders of the gastrointestinal tract, liver and pulmonary system have greatly benefited from the use of biopsy techniques but they cannot be applied to the smaller, unique and relatively inaccessible structures of the basal ganglia.

While these obstacles will not always be a bar to progress they nonetheless increase the attractiveness of creating experimental models of movement disorders. The sophistication of the motor system in man demands that their faithful reproduction can only be achieved in the monkey and not in the rodent or the cat. Such models must of necessity realistically reproduce the disorders seen in man and in turn be developed by specific techniques which can provide important pathophysiological information about their human counterpart. Further, a strictly controlled situation can be created to facilitate cell recording techniques and permit studies of neuronal metabolism, receptor binding and the effect of drug therapy.

Hemiballism

Clinical characteristics and pathology in man

In 1927 J. P. Martin[1] described a form of severe chorea which developed acutely and affected the limbs unilaterally. He was not the first to describe such a condition but his careful analysis of the available literature together with his own experience of it resulted in the recognition of the 'Syndrome of the Body of Luys'. The features of the disorder which made it particularly striking and unique were the mode of onset, the severity and virtually continuous nature of the involuntary movements, and the involvement of the proximal limb and axial muscles which resulted in wild throwing actions of the limbs. Thus was established in the medical literature the term hemiballism which adequately described this particular aspect of the condition. The cases described by Martin and previous authors all had in common partial or complete destruction of the contralateral subthalamic nucleus, although adjacent structures such as the zona incerta, internal capsule, substantia nigra, ansa lenticularis and thalamic fasciculus were sometimes additionally involved. Arteriosclerosis and hypertension appeared to be the main aetiological factors.

Hemiballism has since been described in patients in whom the subthalamic nucleus has been structurally intact, and the condition has been attributed to pathological changes in the striatum, lateral segment of the globus pallidus, thalamus, cerebral cortex and internal capsule.[2,3] It is of course possible that the label of hemiballism has been too loosely applied to forms of involuntary movement which would better be called hemichorea. Equally, these observations might indicate that these regions of the brain have an important influence on subthalamic neurons or the nuclei to which they project, and could provide some insight into their interrelationships.

The clinical and experimental attention that has been paid to hemiballism is totally out of context to its incidence which has been estimated as 1 in 500 000 of the population. The extensive interest in the condition is partly due to its clinical fascination and the unique facility that it has provided for experimental research into movement disorders.

Ablative lesions of the subthalamic nucleus

This established link between the subthalamic nucleus and hemiballism led to the development of one of the most renowned primate models of hyperkinesia. Whittier & Mettler[4] and Carpenter et al.[5] demonstrated that electrocoagulation of the subthalamic nucleus resulted in a disorder for which they used the term 'choreoid hyperkinesia' and which from their description ranged from mild chorea to the 'simian equivalent of ballism'. In the majority of their experiments hyperkinesia was only observed when at least 20 per cent of the nucleus had been destroyed. Where the extent of damage was less the appearance of abnormal movements was associated with damage to the neuronal connections of the nucleus with the pallidum.

These clinical and experimental observations demonstrated that destruction of a significant part of the subthalamic nucleus caused hemiballism but it did not follow that all cases of hemiballism or severe hemichorea were due to pathological changes in the subthalamic nucleus. The experimental data did not directly provide information about the neurotransmitter(s) involved in the mediation of the disorder.

Injections of GABA antagonists into the subthalamic nucleus and medial pallidum

Evidence from electrophysiological and neurotransmitter uptake studies suggest that the subthalamopallidal pathway is inhibitory and utilizes GABA.[6-10] These considerations prompted us to examine the feasibility of replicating ballism in the primate by manipulating neuronal activity in the medial pallidum, using the GABA antagonists picrotoxin and bicuculline methiodide. It was decided that such a technique would require injections of between 2 and 6 μl of the neurotransmitter antagonist into the medial pallidum thereby potentially simulating the effect of a destructive lesion of the subthalamic nucleus. The effect would be temporary and permit repetition at the same or adjacent sites in order to locate the region most closely associated with the production of the movement disorder. These advantages, however, were associated with the not inconsiderable problem of making very small and accurately placed injections in a fully conscious and relatively unrestrained adult monkey to permit observation of the latency and type of movement disorder that might arise.

In conjunction with the University of Manchester Institute of Science and Technology a microinjection pump was developed which could be triggered magnetically.[11] This required the initial stereotaxic implantation of a base plate and guide cannula under general anaesthesia, which was directed towards the brain region to be investigated. The base plate was fixed to the skull by means of screws and acrylic cement. The accuracy of the procedure was improved by prior ventriculography using a radio-opaque contrast medium. Under general anaesthesia the microinjection pump could be located on the base plate and later triggered with the minimum of restraint after the animal had fully recovered consciousness. By attaching injection needles of different lengths to the pump it was then possible to make a series of injections at various predetermined depths within the brain.

Initial micro-injections of picrotoxin were made into the medial pallidum and the lateral tip of the subthalamic nucleus with an obliquely sited cannula that was directed at the lentiform complex.[12] The resulting dyskinesia was a very convincing replica of ballism as seen in man and similar to the most severe form of choreoid hyperkinesia previously produced by ablative lesions of the subthalamic nucleus (by comparison with filmed recordings kindly loaned by Professor M. B. Carpenter).

Involvement of the upper limb typically started with occasional fidgety movements which might easily be ignored if it was not for their repetitive nature. They were small in amplitude, relatively isolated and of short duration. They affected all the major joints of the forelimb and consisted of abduction/adduction and flexion/extension of the shoulder, flexion/extension of the elbow, pronation/supination of the forearm and flexion/extension of the wrist and fingers. As the disorder progressed the movements increased in amplitude, force and frequency and tended to occur in combination. For example, the limb would be stretched out in front of the animal with the forearm pronated and then rapidly withdrawn, internally rotated and extended posteriorly to produce a sweeping motion across the floor of the cage. In its most severe form the movements were continuous and associated with a flailing action of the whole of the upper limb at the shoulder joint.

Mild choreiform movements arising from the hip and ankle joints heralded the onset of dyskinesia in the lower limb. When seated these involved abduction/adduction of the leg at the hip but on standing this was often replaced by internal/external rotation, the heel acting as a pivot. With increasing severity the leg was alternately extended and withdrawn with rapid forceful movements which were interspersed with wide circumductive sweeps of the whole limb.

The latency of hemiballism ranged from 5 to 30 minutes, the shortest latency being associated with the most severe dyskinesia. The duration of the disorder was never greater than 2 to 3 hours and was always associated with complete resolution.

It was not possible from these initial experiments to decide with certainty upon the exact site of action of the GABA antagonist because of the question of diffusion along the track of the injection needle through the internal capsule. A further large series of injections using vertically placed guide cannulae were made at 70 intracerebral sites in the putamen, globus pallidus, subthalamic nucleus, zona incerta, internal capsule, cerebral peduncle and substantia nigra. Subsequent histological verification of the injection sites provided conclusive evidence that hemiballism only occurred after direct injections of picrotoxin or bicuculline into the subthalamic nucleus, while injections directed at the periphery of the nucleus caused mild to severe chorea after a long delay. No effect was observed with injections into the medial pallidal segment unless these were directed along its lateral border, when a mild form of hemichorea was seen.[13]

While the site of action of GABA antagonism was undoubtedly in the subthalamic nucleus, the pharmacological mechanism producing the dyskinesia was unclear. GABA appears to be a transmitter in the subthalamic nucleus asscociated with pallidosubthalamic fibres arising from the lateral pallidal segment and in the absence of a significant number of interneurons it has an inhibitory action upon subthalamic neurons.[14-17] This would infer that hemiballism seen after subthalamic injection of picrotoxin and bicuculline was due to increased activity of these neurons and would contradict the evidence available in man and from ablative experiments in the monkey. Alternatively, GABA antagonism might result in transient neuronal hyperactivity followed by depolarization blockade, thereby mimicking an ablative lesion. While this explanation could resolve the apparent contradiction relating to subthalamic activity it would not account for the lack of discernible effect of GABA blockade in the greater part of the medial pallidal segment. This raised the possibility that the effect of the subthalamopallidal pathway might be mediated by a neurotransmitter other than GABA (see p. 130).

Mechanisms mediating experimental ballism in the primate

It has generally been accepted that ballism is a 'release' phenomenon. The evidence leading to this conclusion has come from anatomical and physiological data and the interpretation of pathological changes and lesion sites both producing and alleviating the disorder in man and the monkey. The relevant observations can be summarized as follows:

(1) The major efferent projections of the subthalamic nucleus are to the globus pallidus and the substantia nigra pars reticulata[18,19] and studies in sub-primates indicate that this is largely by means of axon collaterals.[20,21] These two structures in turn have major projections to the thalamus (ventral anterior, ventral lateral, pars oralis and pars medialis and centromedian nuclei), nucleus tegmenti pedunculopontinus and superior colliculi.[22-25] The importance of the latter brainstem nuclei in the mediation of normal movement and dyskinesia is unclear. The thalamic nuclei project to the cerebral cortex, particularly the premotor cortex the supplementary motor areas.[26]

(2) Secondary lesions can alleviate or modify ballism. Whittier & Mettler[4] and Carpenter *et al.*[5] demonstrated that primary lesions which destroyed the output of the medial pallidal segment in addition to a significant part of the subthalamic nucleus failed to produce dyskinesia. Furthermore, secondary lesions of the medial pallidum or its efferent projection abolished choreoid hyperkinesia produced by a previous subthalamic lesion. Lesions of the globus pallidus have been used in man to reduce the severity of various types of dyskinesia.[27] While these observations are consistent with the hypothesis that medial pallidal activity is released by partial or complete ablation of the subthalamic nucleus it must be noted that secondary lesions of the medial pallidal segment or its efferent projection will probably damage nigrostriatal and pallidosubthalamic fibres as well and thereby significantly influence the primary mechanisms of the dyskinesia. Thalamotomy has been successfully used in the treatment of hyperkinetic movement disorders in man and experimentally in the monkey.[5,27-29] In contrast, lesions of the substantia nigra used for the same purpose have proved ineffective.[30,31]

(3) The inhibitory nature of the subthalamopallidal pathway has been suggested by extracellular and intracellular recording studies which have demonstrated inhibition of pallidal and entopeduncular neurons following subthalamic stimulation and have implicated GABA as the putative neurotransmitter.[6-10]

Metabolic mapping studies using the 2-deoxyglucose (2-DG) uptake technique developed by Sokoloff *et al.*[32] have been used to interpret the neural mechanisms mediating the dyskinesia resulting from unilateral injections of GABA antagonists into the subthalamic nucleus.[33] [^{3}H]2-DG was administered during the period when ballism was most marked. Autoradiographic interpretation of the results using the uninjected side for comparison demonstrated that there was a substantial reduction (20 per cent) in 2-DG uptake by the injected subthalamic nucleus and the ipsilateral medial pallidal segment (Fig. 1). This finding is consistent with a reduction in activity of the subthalamopallidal pathway and suggests that injections of GABA antagonists into the subthalamic nucleus result in depolarization blockade of subthalamic neurons. Further support for this conclusion was obtained from one animal where the subthalamic nucleus was only partially involved by the injection. The uptake of 2-DG was reduced only in the caudal and dorsal part of the nucleus and this was associated with a regional reduction in isotope uptake in the caudal and ventral part of the globus pallidus. This coincides with the known topographical organization of the subthalamopallidal pathway.[19,23] A small (6 per cent) reduction in 2-DG uptake was demonstrated in the substantia nigra pars reticulata ipsilateral to the injected side. This suggests that the subthalamonigral pathway is of less importance in the expression of the movement disorder than the subthalamopallidal projection and coincides with the failure of nigral lesions to modify dyskinesias both clinically and experimentally.

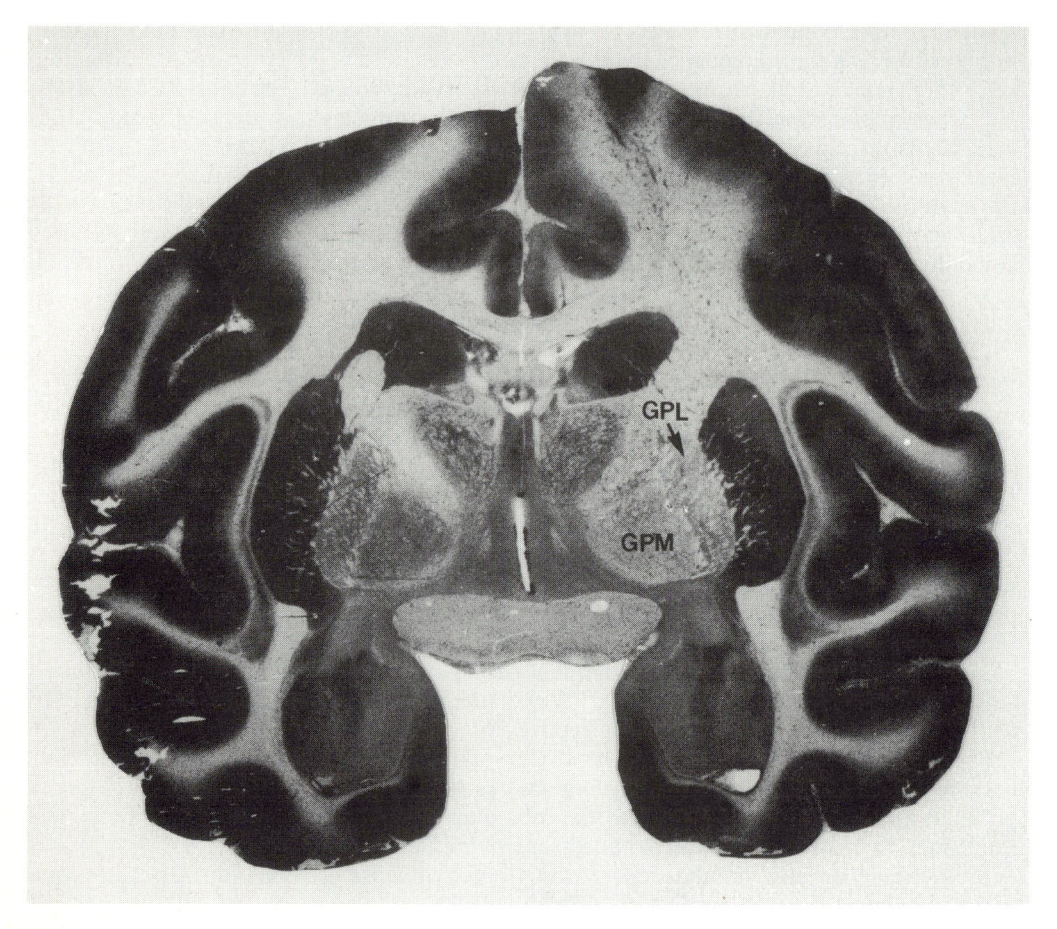

Fig. 1. *A direct reversal print of a 2-deoxyglucose autoradiograph from an animal which received an injection of bicuculline into the right subthalamic nucleus.* This injection resulted in ballism of the contralateral limbs. Note the decreased uptake of 2-deoxyglucose by the medial pallidal segment (GPM) and the lateral pallidal segment (GPL) ipsilateral to the injection.

The above changes were associated with a 13–17 per cent reduction in 2-DG uptake in the ventral anterior and the ventral lateral thalamic nuclei which receive fibres from the medial pallidal segment. This result was quite unexpected since it has been considered that ballism is due to a release of the normal inhibitory influence of the subthalamic nucleus on the globus pallidus producing an increase in the activity of the pallidothalamic pathway. Two explanations can be offered for this finding. First, the subthalamopallidal pathway is excitatory. Kitai & Kita[34] have provided some support for this suggestion by demonstrating that *in vitro* stimulation of subthalamic neurons produces monosynaptic excitatory post-synaptic potentials in the rat substantia nigra. It is known that in the rat single subthalamic neurons project to both the substantia nigra and the globus pallidus and entopeduncular nucleus.[20,21] Moreover, Parent & Smith (this volume, p. 34) have demonstrated immunohistochemically that cell bodies in the subthalamic nucleus of the squirrel monkey do not show immunoreactivity for GABA but react strongly after incubation with an antiserum against glutamate. The second explanation to be considered is that the decreased 2-DG uptake seen in the thalamus is reflective of the metabolic activity of thalamic interneurons and afferents other than those from the globus pallidus which could be masking increased activity in the pallidothalamic pathway.

In summary, hemiballism can be produced in the monkey by micro-injections of the GABA antagonists picrotoxin or bicuculline into the subthalamic nucleus. Metabolic mapping studies confirm that this produces a decrease in subthalamic neuronal activity which is associated with a reduction in subthalamic efferent terminal activity in the globus pallidus and substantia nigra. In turn these abnormal patterns of neuronal activity are transmitted to the ventral anterior and ventral lateral nuclei of the thalamus. The efferent projections of the thalamus to the cerebral cortex are presumably responsible for conveying these changes to the pyramidal system through which they become manifest as a form of dyskinesia, in this instance, hemiballism.

Chorea

Clinical manifestations and pathology

The term chorea is derived from the greek word *choreia*, meaning dance. It was first linked with a condition usually seen in early life and associated with rheumatic heart disease. The disorder was characterized by the development of irregular involuntary movements which when they affected the lower limbs interrupted the normal pattern of walking and created the appearance of a dancing gait known as St. Vitus' dance (Sydenham's chorea). The term however has wider implications and describes sudden, intermittent, unpredictable and short-lived involuntary movements which can arise as a result of various disorders chiefly affecting the basal ganglia. Although they are classically described as unpredictable it is possible in the individual patient to recognize a series of so-called pseudo-purposive actions which are repeated at random. These fragments of normal movement include opening the hand and pronating the forearm, abducting and shrugging the shoulder, turning the head, pursing the lips or retracting the angle of the mouth, raising the eyebrows and flexing the hip. The involuntary movements are more prominent in the distal musculature of the limbs but by no means confined to it. Ballism is probably a quantitative extension of chorea, the movements being more frequent and of greater force and amplitude and as such producing flinging motions of the limbs by reason of their more predominant proximal involvement.

Huntington's chorea is the most classical form of the disorder. George Huntington's treatise of 1872[35] utilized information collected over three generations of medical experience of families afflicted with the condition and demonstrated that it was dominantly inherited and associated with dementia. Davenport & Muncey[36] traced 1000 cases of the condition back to six individuals and claimed that its ancestral source in the USA was three brothers who migrated there from England in the 17th century. As the disease progresses the chorea may be replaced by hypokinesia and rigidity, whereas in its juvenile presentation it is characterized by these features from the onset. The main pathological change in the basal ganglia is degeneration of the medium-sized spiny neurons of the caudate nucleus and putamen which project to the globus pallidus.[37] These neurons use GABA, enkephalin and substance P as their neurotransmitters and the concentrations of these are all significantly reduced[38–40] in contrast to the increased levels of neuropeptide Y and somatostatin which are found in striatal interneurons.[41,42] There is also a reduction in the concentration of the acetylcholine synthesizing enzyme, choline acetyltransferase, whereas the nigrostriatal dopaminergic system is not affected.[38]

Chorea is also a manifestation of other basal ganglia disorders. The term senile chorea is used to denote a form of chorea which appears in later life without a demonstrable familial predisposition. Pathologically the changes in the striatum are similar to those of Huntington's chorea[43] and it is possible either that such patients represent a spontaneous form of the disorder or that a positive family history is not forthcoming. Hemichorea may present acutely as a result of infarction in the putamen[44] and undergo partial or complete resolution over a period of several months. The involuntary movements of drug-induced tardive dyskinesia are predominantly choreiform in nature, involving the bucco-lingual and limb musculature. The suggested mechanism is dopamine supersensitivity[45] induced by long-term neuroleptic therapy, although degeneration of GABAergic striatal projection neurons has also been proposed.[46]

By far the most common form of chorea seen in clinical practice is that associated with the long-term treatment of Parkinson's disease with levodopa. The choreiform movements are not infrequently complicated by dystonia and most classically appear during the 'peak' effect of levodopa or primary dopamine agonist therapy[47] (see p. 139).

Experimental chorea in the primate

Reference has already been made to the production of chorea following microinjections of the GABA antagonists picrotoxin and bicuculline into the periphery of the subthalamic nucleus.[13] In this form it appeared to be part of a spectrum of hyperkinesia ranging from ballism to mild chorea, the severity of the disorder being related to whether injections were made directly into or immediately surrounding the subthalamic nucleus. Whittier & Mettler[4] demonstrated a similar relationship between the extent of damage to the subthalamic nucleus and the severity of the subsequent movement disorder. The only other experimental production of chorea recorded in the primate is that described by Murphey & Dill[48] following injections of the cholinergic agonist carbachol into the putamen or head of the caudate nucleus.

In view of the neuropathological changes occurring in Huntington's chorea it was surprising that injections of GABA antagonists into the medial pallidal segment had only occasionally resulted in any form of hyperkinesia.[13] This raised two important questions about the afferent projections to the medial pallidal segment from the striatum and the subthalamic nucleus. The first has already been considered (p. 129) and relates to whether the subthalamopallidal pathway is mediated by glutamate and not by GABA as has been traditionally accepted. The second question must consider the importance of degeneration of the striato-medial pallidal pathway in the genesis of chorea. Previous injections of bicuculline into a large number of sites performed during the investigation of hemiballism demonstrated that chorea was associated with GABA antagonism more laterally in the lentiform complex.[13] These observations led to a further series of experiments in an attempt to produce chorea from sites other than the subthalamic nucleus.

Experimental chorea in the primate following injections of the glutamate antagonist kynurenic acid into the medial pallidal segment

To test the hypothesis that the subthalamopallidal pathway is excitatory and mediated by the neurotransmitter glutamate, guide cannulae were stereotactically implanted in three cynomologous monkeys and directed towards the medial pallidum using the methodology described above. Injections of the broad spectrum glutamate antagonist kynurenic acid into 20 different sites within this structure resulted in the appearance of dyskinesia ranging from mild hemichorea to hemiballism. The most severe movement disorder with the shortest latency to onset was associated with injections into the ventrolateral part of the medial pallidal segment.[49]

Injections of bicuculline into the same sites again confirmed that GABA antagonism in the medial pallidum was not associated with the production of any discernible dyskinesia. Very mild chorea in the contralateral limbs, however, was seen after injections of the GABA agonist muscimol. The observed dyskinesia was always much less severe than that seen after glutamate antagonism but nonetheless unmistakable in nature.

These observations would appear to conform with the established view that chorea/ballism can arise as a result of reduced activity of subthalamic neurons, but they imply that contrary to previous suggestions this causes a reduction in the activity of medial pallidal neurons because of a decreased release of glutamate from the subthalamopallidal pathway. Interestingly, an increased release of GABA from the striato-medial pallidal pathway would have a similar effect upon medial pallidal neurons, a situation simulated by the injection of muscimol into the medial pallidum. While this might offer a novel mechanism for the development of chorea it would not explain its appearance after destructive or degenerative lesions of the striatum. It would however conform with the facilitation of 'normal' movements through the cortico-striato-pallido-thalamo-cortical circuitry.

Experimental chorea in the primate following injections of bicuculline into the lateral pallidal segment

Experiments were performed on 14 adult monkeys (*Macaca fascicularis*, *Macaca nemestrina*, *Papio papio* or *Papio cynocephalus*) of either sex. Guide cannulae were directed towards the lentiform complex under stereotactic control, again using the same methodology as described above. The GABA antagonist bicuculline methiodide in sterile saline or the vehicle alone was injected on 152 occasions at 121 separate intracerebral sites in the putamen, globus pallidus (lateral and medial segments), substantia innominata, amygdala, anterior commissure, caudate nucleus, corona radiata, internal capsule and optic tract. Injections of bicuculline were associated with the appearance of chorea in 54 of these sites, whereas control injections of saline had no discernible effect.

The abnormal movements observed were typical of chorea, human-like in nature and always contralateral to the injected side. In the lower limb they ranged from occasional alternating flexion/extension of the ankle joint and more distal joints of the foot to more frequent high amplitude flexion/extension of the knee and circumduction of the hip. Initially, the movements might be masked by weight bearing or the animal trapping the affected limb. Dyskinesia in the upper limb was typically heralded by flexion/extension of the fingers and wrist and pronation/supination of the forearm to create a wiping movement. As in the lower limb, the involvement of more proximal joints (flexion/extension of the elbow and circumduction of the shoulder) became apparent as the chorea increased in severity. While mild chorea was usually associated with more distally-sited involuntary movements and severe chorea with both proximal and distal involvement this correlation was not absolute. On some occasions the orofacial musculature was affected, usually in association with generalized hemichorea but sometimes in isolation. It consisted of chewing movements, labial retraction and protrusion and deviation of the tongue away from the injected side.

The striking feature of the dyskinesia was its similarity to that seen after the injection of GABA antagonists into and around the subthalamic nucleus. In its severe form it bore a marked resemblance to hemiballism whereas mild forms of subthalamic-induced dyskinesia were similar to the chorea described above. The same observations were made about the types of dyskinesia seen after injection of kynurenic acid into the medial pallidal segment.

The great majority of sites which were associated with chorea after injection of bicuculline were either in the lateral segment of the globus pallidus or the ventromedial putamen and those sites with the shortest latency (5 min or less) were clustered around the ventral part of the lateral medullary lamina which separates these two structures. The site with the shortest latency of 1 min was in the lateral pallidal segment. Although there was no strict somatotopic correlation between the siting of injections and chorea involving the lower limb, upper limb and orofacial muscles it was possible to make some generalizations. Although lower limb chorea was seen with injections throughout the dorso-ventral extent of the lentiform complex, dyskinesia confined to the upper limb or the orofacial muscles was only observed with injections in the ventral half of the structure. This observation is in keeping with the somatotopic organization of the lentiform complex as demonstrated by microstimulation and electrophysiological recording studies[50] and anatomical tracing experiments.[51]

Neural mechanisms mediating chorea

Classical and human-like chorea has been produced experimentally by injections of the GABA antagonist bicuculline methiodide into specific areas of the lentiform complex of the monkey. Some degree of speculation must remain as to the exact site of action of the drug. It is notable that the site of action with the shortest latency was in the lateral segment of the globus pallidus and that those sites with a latency of 5 min or less were either in the same structure or very close to it in the ventral and medial part of the putamen adjacent to the lateral medullary lamina. Previous studies have failed to demonstrate any form of consistent dyskinesia following GABA blockade in the medial pallidal segment (p. 126) and it would therefore seem probable that the occasional development of chorea with injections of bicuculline into this structure is due to diffusion into the lateral pallidum.

It is attractive to hypothesize that experimental chorea occurs as a result of GABA blockade in the lateral pallidal segment. The best studied form of the disorder in man is Huntington's chorea which is associated with degeneration of striatal neurons projecting on the globus pallidus and substantia nigra. These neurons are inhibitory upon pallidal neurons[52] and utilize GABA as their primary transmitter[53] in association with metenkephalin and substance P. A reduction in GABA release in Huntington's chorea is supported by the finding of increased flunitrazepam binding in the globus pallidus.[54] Pharmacological blockade of striatopallidal GABAergic neurons in the monkey would therefore appear to be the logical experimental model of the disorder in man. This, however, leaves unexplained the mechanism of action of bicuculline in the ventromedial putamen. Two possibilities present themselves; diffusion of the drug into the lateral pallidal segment or a specific pharmacological action of bicuculline in the putamen itself.

The first proposition is supported by the observation that the drug only results in chorea when injected into sites adjacent to the lateral pallidum and it would seem reasonable to accept that diffusion across the lateral medullary lamina could occur. If bicuculline was having an effect within the putamen it might be possible to explain it on the basis of depolarization blockade of putaminopallidal neurons, the probable mechanism of action of the drug in the subthalamic nucleus which produces ballism. If this second and probably less attractive hypothesis were correct it would imply regional heterogeneity within the putamen since injections of bicuculline sited more laterally and dorsally within that structure produced myoclonus.[55]

Pharmacological blockade of the inhibitory transmitter GABA in the lateral pallidal segment would result in an increase in the activity of its major efferent projection to the subthalamic nucleus, which is also inhibitory and mediated by GABA.[14-17] The consequent reduction in subthalamic neuronal activity suggests that common neural mechanisms for the production of chorea and ballism can be inferred. This is in keeping with the effect of infarction of the subthalamic nucleus in man and experimental ablation of it in the monkey. Support for these conclusions comes from studies of 2-DG uptake in animals displaying chorea.[56] These demonstrated a marked increase in the uptake of 2-DG in the subthalamic nucleus contralateral to the hemichorea and ipsilateral to the injected lentiform complex. It is most likely that this is due to increased activity of the terminals of pallidosubthalamic neurons originating in the lateral pallidal segment. Moreover, the increase in 2-DG activity was most apparent in the lateral and dorsal part of the subthalamic nucleus which receives afferents from the ventral portion of the lateral pallidum, the site from which dyskinesia could be most readily elicited. This was confirmed with neuronal tracing studies using horseradish peroxidase, which, when injected into the lateral pallidal sites which produced chorea with the shortest latency, resulted in the anterograde transport of the enzyme to terminal fields within the subthalamic nucleus which corresponded exactly with the area of increased 2-DG uptake.

Deoxyglucose studies also demonstrated a decrease in terminal activity in the medial pallidal segment and ventral lateral and ventral anterior nuclei of the thalamus (Fig. 2). These findings are similar to those seen in subthalamic-induced hemiballism (p. 128) and confirm that both chorea and ballism are mediated by a reduction in subthalamopallidal activity. The reduction in 2-DG uptake in the terminal projection fields of medial pallidal neurons strongly points to an excitatory role for the subthalamopallidal pathway, a conclusion which is supported by the appearance of chorea and ballism after glutamate blockade in the medial pallidal segment produced by injections of kynurenic acid (see p. 131).

In summary, the results of drug-injection studies in the medial pallidum, lentiform complex and the subthalamic nucleus combined with neuronal mapping studies using 2-deoxyglucose indicate that forms of dyskinesia ranging from mild chorea to severe ballism share common neural mechanisms arising from pathophysiological changes in the medial pallidal-subthalamic-lateral pallidal-thalamic pathways. The importance of this basal ganglia circuitry in the mediation of these disorders is also supported by the notable lack of effect of blockade of striatopallidal GABAergic-induced inhibition in the medial pallidal segment. The different clinical manifestations arising from acute infarction of the subthalamic nucleus and progressive degeneration of the striatum can be adequately accounted for by these conclusions. The latter, producing gradual destruction of the large topographically organised striatum would, through its lateral pallidal projection, produce regional inhibition of the subthalamic nucleus and localized involuntary movements, whereas the former would result in a generalized and more severe type of dyskinesia.

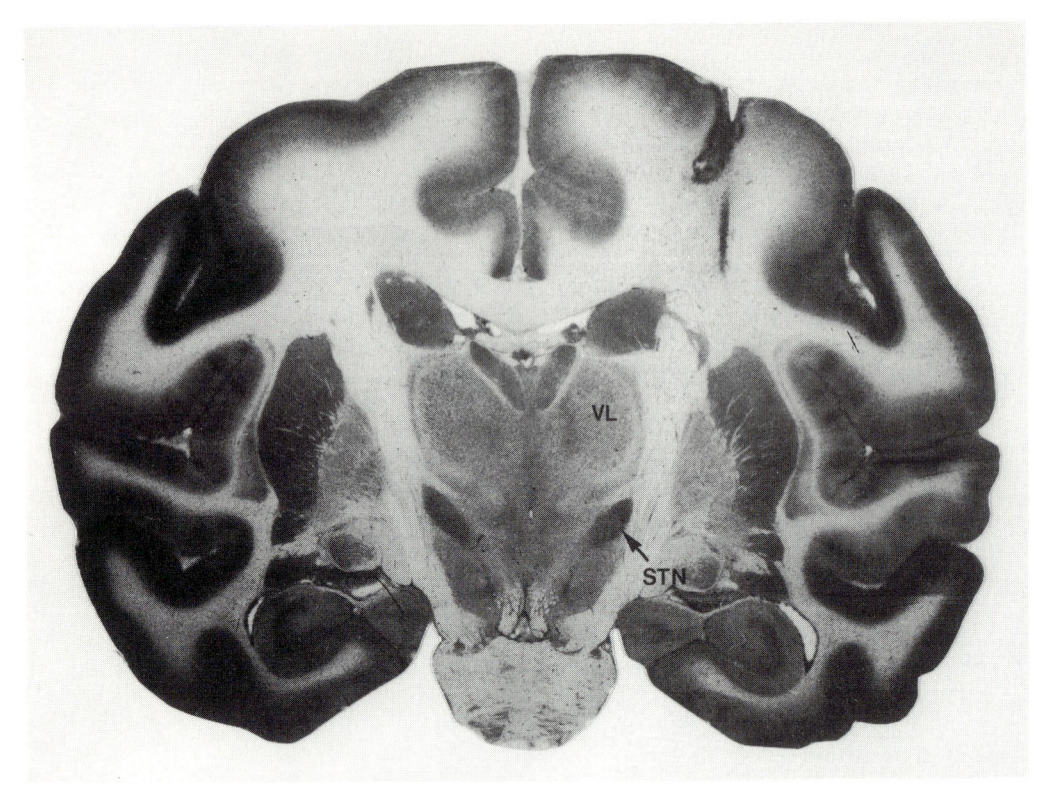

Fig. 2. *A direct reversal print of a 2-deoxyglucose autoradiograph from an animal which received an injection of bicuculline in the right lentiform nucleus.* This injection resulted in choreiform movements of the contralateral limbs. Note the increased labelling of the dorsolateral portion of the subthalamic nucleus (STN) ipsilateral to the injection. VL refers to the ventral lateral nucleus of the thalamus.

Parkinson's disease and levodopa-induced dyskinesia

Clinical characteristics of Parkinson's disease

Clinically, Parkinson's disease is the complete antithesis of chorea and ballism. The clinical entity first described by James Parkinson in 1817 is the most common disease to affect the basal ganglia apart from those disorders induced as a result of drug administration. The prevalence of Parkinson's disease in Europe and the North American continent is approximately 1 in 1000, two and a half times more common than multiple sclerosis. Apart from epilepsy and migraine it is the most common neurological condition with which patients present to their doctor. The necessity for long term follow-up to deal with the primary problem and the complications that arise from treatment ensures its prominence in neurological clinics.

Long-established teaching informs us that the symptoms and signs of Parkinson's disease can be attributed to the classical triad of tremor, hypertonia and hypokinesia. There can be no doubt that the commonest symptom seen in isolation is a coarse tremor affecting one or both upper limbs and sometimes extending into the legs. Initially, it is often unilateral and not infrequently may remain so. The tremor very quickly intrudes into the patient's life since it is most obvious at rest and to a slightly lesser extent with posture, such as supporting a newspaper or a cup and saucer. Like many involuntary movements it is more apparent when the patient is under stress or becomes self-conscious in the presence of an audience, and disappears during sleep. The tremor has a frequency of 3–4 cycles per second and results from alternating flexion and extension of the metacarpophalangeal joints of the fingers and thumb and flexion/extension sometimes combined with adduction/abduction of the wrist. The resultant effect known as pill-rolling is a hallmark of the condition. Tremor in the lower limbs is typically seen as regular flexion and extension of the ankle joint, while involvement of the neck and mandibular muscles produces nodding of the head and rhythmic opening and closing of the mouth. In patients with moderate to severe hypokinesia an action tremor may occur, typically with slowly performed movements of the upper limbs. Although the tremor of Parkinson's disease is often functionally less disabling than that of cerebellar disorders the embarrassment caused by its prominence at rest soon prompts the patient to seek medical attention.

The terms hypokinesia, akinesia and bradykinesia are used to describe the impoverishment and slowness of movements seen in Parkinson's disease. All actions are affected including those related to facial expression, speech, chewing, swallowing, eating, washing and writing. Walking is characterized by small steps often taken in a hurried fashion (festinant gait) with a stooped posture. In addition speech is quiet and monotonous and writing is cramped and tremulous. Balance is impaired with the result that the patient easily falls backwards on standing and tends to stagger sideways with the slightest knock. The initiation of a movement is defective, an example being the tendency to stutter the feet when attempting to walk or the difficulty encountered on starting to write.

Hypertonia is only apparent on examination yet it can give rise to symptoms which can be misleading to both the individual and his doctor. Stiffness and discomfort in the limb and spinal musculature not infrequently leads to the erroneous diagnosis of a rheumatological or orthopaedic condition with unnecessary administration of drugs used for the treatment of rheumatoid arthritis and osteoarthritis or with physiotherapy for backache. Cervical spondylosis and nerve root entrapment may be proposed as the cause of discomfort over the shoulders extending into the arms. To add to the illusion the symptoms are often worse in cold and damp weather. While hypertonia is not confined to any particular group of muscles it is best demonstrated at the wrist and elbow joints. Resistance to passive movement can be detected throughout the full range of flexion and extension in either a constant or a fluctuating manner, very aptly described as lead-pipe or cog-wheel rigidity.

Pathological findings in man

A discussion of the pathological findings demands that the terms Parkinson's disease and parkinsonism should first be clarified. Clinically, Parkinson's disease is a condition typically associated with tremor, hypokinesia and rigidity which classically responds to treatment with a dopamine precursor or agonist. Pathologically, the hallmark of the disorder is degeneration of the pigmented, dopamine-containing cells of the substantia nigra pars compacta associated with the formation of Lewy bodies. Degenerative changes are also found in the ventral tegmental area, locus coeruleus and the dorsal motor nucleus of the vagus nerve.[57] Neurochemically, there is a marked depletion of dopamine in the striatum, nucleus accumbens and parolfactory gyrus, and the concentration of noradrenaline is frequently reduced in those areas receiving projections from the locus coeruleus, namely the striatum and cerebral cortex.[58]

The term parkinsonism is often loosely used to describe patients who have some of the clinical attributes of Parkinson's disease such as bradykinesia and hypokinesia and occasionally hypertonia. Such features can occur in presenile or senile dementia and are probably due to cerebral cortical atrophy involving the motor and premotor areas. Associated degenerative changes in the substantia nigra may also contribute to the clinical picture. Arteriosclerosis is commonly invoked as a cause of parkinsonism but as with so many other disorders linked with this process the association has been overstated. Parkinsonian features are seen in normal pressure hydrocephalus, manganese poisoning, as a result of carbon monoxide inhalation, progressive supranuclear palsy, striatonigral degeneration and olivo-ponto-cerebellar atrophy and are due to more widespread degenerative changes involving the cerebral cortex, striatum, globus pallidus and the cerebellum. The classical features of Parkinson's disease in association with other neurological symptoms occurred after encephalitis lethargica and for several decades after the 1920s provided a significant contribution to the prevalence of parkinsonism.

These observations serve to illustrate the wide spectrum of pathological disorders which may cause parkinsonian symptoms and at the same time highlight the more specific degenerative and neurochemical changes of Parkinson's disease which are the appropriate ones to imitate in attempting to reproduce the condition experimentally.

Experimental parkinsonism in the primate; ventromedial brainstem tegmental and 6-hydroxydopamine lesions

Ablative lesions of the ventromedial brainstem tegmentum in the monkey have consistently failed to reproduce the complete clinical picture of Parkinson's disease. They have however introduced important insight into the mechanism of the various components of the disorder. Experimental lesions confined to the substantia nigra have generally been reported as asymptomatic if unilateral and producing some degree of hypokinesia if bilateral.[59] Tremor, usually described as postural, has occurred in association with hypokinesia only after more extensive lesions involving the ventromedial part of the mesencephalic or upper pontine tegmentum.[60,61] Histological analysis has demonstrated that in addition to retrograde degeneration of the substantia nigra pars compacta the appearance of tremor has necessitated destruction of the rubrospinal and rubrotegmental system and the brachium conjunctivum or severe depletion of striatal dopamine, noradrenaline and 5-hydroxytryptamine.[62] Conversely, animals with lesions of the cerebellum or brainstem-related structures which did not primarily induce tremor, developed tremor after administration of drugs such as harmaline, reserpine, α-methyl-p-tyrosine, phenothiazines and butyrophenones which are known to influence central monoaminergic systems. These findings pointed to a combination of nigral degeneration and involvement of the 'rubro-olivo-cerebello-rubral loop' as being necessary for the development of tremor and also implicated depletion of 5-HT.[63] Rarely was the production of hypokinesia with or without tremor associated with rigidity and in fact in the majority of experiments limb tone was reduced.

The neurotoxin 6-hydroxydopamine which is reasonably selective for dopaminergic neurons has only infrequently been used in primates. In studies performed in the marmoset, injection of the neurotoxin into the nigrostriatal pathway at the level of the caudal hypothalamus induced severe degeneration of the substantia nigra pars compacta and 88–98 per cent depletion of striatal dopamine. The animals developed hypokinesia, torticollis and circling behaviour but no demonstrable tremor or disturbance of muscle tone. Following administration of apomorphine the hypokinesia disappeared and the torticollis and circling was reversed.[64]

Parkinsonism induced in the primate by n-methyl-4-phenyl-1,2,3,6-tetrahydropyridine (MPTP)

The best and clearly the most exciting experimental model of Parkinson's disease came to light purely by chance with the acute development of parkinsonism in a group of drug addicts who were self-administering synthetic narcotics.[65,66] The clinical features of the disorder consisted of severe hypokinesia/bradykinesia, rigidity and rest tremor and were a very realistic replica of Parkinson's disease. The first reported case responded to dopamine precursor therapy but later committed suicide. Marked degeneration of the substantia nigra pars compacta was found at postmortem. It was soon demonstrated that administration of MPTP in the monkey induced a profound parkinsonian state similar to that observed in man.[67] We decided to investigate this MPTP-induced model, examine its histological and neurochemical similarities to idiopathic Parkinson's disease and study the effect of long-term levodopa administration. If the model proved to be an authentic replica of the disorder in man it would also provide information about the neural mechanisms producing it.

Three monkeys (*Macaca fascicularis*) received daily intravenous injections of MPTP over a 6–8 day period culminating in total doses ranging from 2.79–3.85 mg/kg. They became severely parkinsonian over the period of administration of MPTP. They adopted a somersault posture and were virtually akinetic unless disturbed, when movements became temporarily increased in a manner similar to that seen in Parkinson's disease (kinesia paradoxica). Due to their immobility it was possible to approach the animals and demonstrate cog-wheel rigidity by passively flexing and extending the wrist and elbow joints. An intermittent coarse limb and head tremor was observed with an amplitude and rhythm very similar to that seen in man. Its only variation from that seen in Parkinson's disease and MPTP-induced parkinsonism in man was its tendency to be most prominent during attempted movements and with posture, and less marked at rest. It is tempting to speculate that this species variation can be accounted for on the different organization of posture and gait in man and the monkey, the former being a biped which has adapted the upper limbs and hands for skilled movements while the latter remains a quadruped.

All of the clinical features responded well to levodopa therapy, with complete or near-complete resolution for periods of up to several hours after each dose of the drug. This enabled the animals to maintain their food and fluid intake. Fifteen to twenty days after the last dose of MPTP and at least 15 hours after last receiving levodopa the animals were killed by sodium thiopentone overdose. The brain tissue was prepared for histology, neurochemical analysis and autoradiographic assessment of dopamine D-2 receptor binding.

All three acutely MPTP-treated animals had marked cell loss and gliosis of the substantia nigra pars compacta which extended medially and ventrally into the ventral tegmental area. In one animal these changes also involved the locus coeruleus. These areas of damage were quite specific, with nearby cell groups in the midbrain and pons appearing normal. In association with these histological findings there was a 90 per cent or greater reduction in the concentration of dopamine in the caudate nucleus, putamen and nucleus accumbens when compared to the levels estimated in control animals. The concentration of noradrenaline was significantly reduced in the cerebral cortex of all three animals and in the nucleus accumbens of two of them. Dopamine D-2 receptor autoradiography using tritiated spiperone and sulpiride demonstrated an increase in specific binding in the caudate nucleus and putamen ranging from 40 to 180 per cent with the greatest increase in the ventrolateral putamen.[68]

Initial studies of MPTP-induced parkinsonism in the primate reported that the histological changes were confined to the substantia nigra and that the model might therefore be an incomplete replica of Parkinson's disease. The above findings indicate that this is not the case and that the model is clinically, histologically and neurochemically very authentic, thereby enhancing its potential for studies of long-term levodopa therapy and metabolic mapping.

Neural mechanisms mediating MPTP-induced parkinsonism in the primate

In addition to the histological, neurochemical and ligand binding studies described above the opportunity was taken to examine changes in neuronal metabolism in the MPTP-treated monkey using the 2-DG technique of Sokoloff *et al.*[32] Forty-five minutes prior to being killed the animals were injected with 5 mCi of tritiated 2-DG intravenously. At this time they were severely parkinsonian, not having received any levodopa medication for at least 15 hours. Cryostat-cut sections of the brain were exposed to LKB Ultrofilm and the resultant images examined densitometrically. A marked increase in 2-DG uptake was demonstrated in both the medial and lateral pallidal segments and the ventral anterior and ventral lateral thalamic nuclei.[69] Since changes in 2-DG uptake appear to be mainly reflective of nerve terminal rather than neuronal cell body activity[70] these findings have been interpreted as indicating hyperactivity of the afferent projections to these structures, namely the striatopallidal, subthalamopallidal and pallidothalamic pathways. In contrast, 2-DG uptake was reduced in the subthalamic nucleus, implying that pallidosubthalamic activity was decreased. An increase in isotope uptake was also seen in nucleus tegmenti pedunculopontinus, whereas there was no convincing change in the substantia nigra.

Confirmation of these findings was sought in studies of neuronal metabolic mapping in the hemiparkinsonian monkey. Four cynomologous monkeys received over a period of 20 min 0.5 mg/kg of MPTP in 40 ml of heparinized saline by direct infusion into the common carotid artery under general anaesthesia. The external carotid artery was occluded during the course of the infusion. It was necessary to repeat the procedure in two animals in whom clinical signs were absent after the first administration. The monkeys developed a flexed posture of the upper limb contralateral to the infused side which was associated with ipsilateral limb preference and spontaneous circling behaviour. Unilateral degeneration of the substantia nigra pars compacta was subsequently demonstrated histologically. 2-DG autoradiographic studies performed in these animals confirmed most of the changes seen after systemic MPTP treatment (Fig. 3). Increases in terminal activity were seen in the lateral pallidal segment, the thalamus and the nucleus tegmenti pedunculopontinus. The uptake of 2-DG was reduced in the subthalamic nucleus and again remained unchanged in the substantia nigra. The only discrepancy between the unilateral and systemically treated animals was the lack of increased uptake of isotope in the medial pallidal segment of the former, together with an increase in uptake in the ventral striatum which was not apparent in the systemic preparation.

These results suggest that in the parkinsonian monkey the activity of the striatopallidal pathway, particularly that to the lateral pallidal segment, is increased. This causes inhibition of lateral pallidal neurons which predominantly project on the subthalamic nucleus, thus in turn resulting in disinhibition of subthalamic neurons. The resulting increase in activity of the subthalamopallidal pathway is also seen in the pallidothalamic projection, which lends further support to the conclusion that subthalamic neurons are excitatory on the medial pallidal segment.[34] As in chorea and ballism, it is probable that the abnormal neuronal activity resulting from these changes is mediated *via* thalamic efferents to the motor cortex.

These unequivocal results are the mirror image of those previously demonstrated in chorea and ballism and again stress the central importance of the pallidosubthalamic/

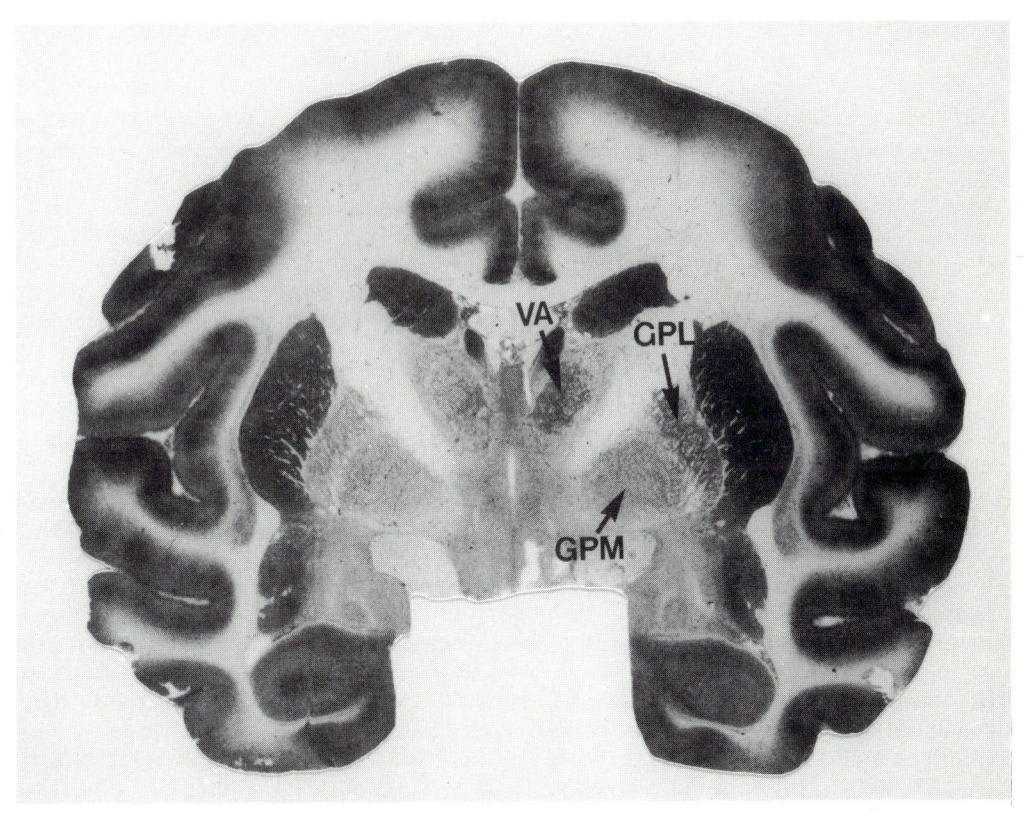

Fig. 3. *A direct reversal print of a 2-deoxyglucose autoradiograph from an animal which received a unilateral injection of MPTP into the right carotid artery.* This procedure produced a hemiparkinsonian condition contralateral to the injection. Note the increased labelling of the lateral pallidal segment (GPL) and ventral anterior nucleus of the thalamus (VA) ipsilateral to the MPTP injection. GPM refers to the medial pallidal segment.

subthalamopallidal circuitry. This in itself tends to support their authenticity while at the same time suggesting a more coherent interpretation of the abnormal neural mechanisms which create disorders of movement. Moreover, the 2-DG findings in the MPTP-treated monkey do not stand in isolation since anatomical and neuronal recording studies provide evidence which correlates with them. For example, Graybiel (this volume, p. 4) stresses the implications of striatal heterogeneity and the subdivisions of motor activity that arise from striatal projections to the pallidum and the substantia nigra. This is in accord with the neuronal metabolic mapping studies described in this section which implicate a greater importance to the striatopallidal projection in the mediation of parkinsonian signs compared to the striatonigral pathway. Furthermore, recordings of neuronal activity in the MPTP-treated monkey confirm that tonic and phasic activity is decreased in the lateral pallidal segment and increased in the medial pallidum.[71]

Levodopa-induced dyskinesia

The majority of patients with Parkinson's disease (as opposed to parkinsonism) initially respond well to dopamine precursor or dopamine agonist therapy. While some undoubtedly have a 'benign' form of the disorder and their symptoms remain satisfactorily controlled over many years the majority develop acute changes in their response to medication (the 'on-off' phenomenon) associated with peak-dose dyskinesia. To extend the duration of action of treatment and attempt to prevent these sudden deteriorations in mobility there is a tendency either to increase the individual doses of the dopaminergic drug or to utilize the same dose more frequently. The almost inevitable consequence of this is the appearance of more severe peak-dose dyskinesia.

Levodopa-induced dyskinesia manifests itself as either choreiform movements of varying severity or dystonia or, as not infrequently occurs, a combination of both. They can affect the axial, facio-bucco-lingual or proximal and distal limb muscles. If the symptoms of Parkinson's disease are predominantly unilateral the dyskinetic features are often most pronounced on the affected side. Despite the potentially disabling nature of this type of dyskinesia, patients often prefer to 'overdose' themselves with treatment to avoid at all costs the risk of becoming immobile. Consequently levodopa-induced dyskinesia is not infrequently one of the most dramatic forms of movement disorder currently seen.

It has been suggested that the gradual development of levodopa-induced dyskinesia and the 'on-off' phenomenon may be related to prolonged levodopa therapy[72,73] rather than progressive nigral degeneration, and the concept of delayed treatment and the wider use of dopamine agonists has been proposed. The MPTP model of Parkinson's disease presents a possible way of investigating this complication of long-term treatment in a controlled situation where the question of disease progression can be excluded. For this purpose six monkeys (*Macaca fascicularis*) received weekly intravenous injections of MPTP over a period of time ranging from several weeks to several months until they developed moderately severe parkinsonism.[74] It was intended that the degree of hypokinesia and rigidity was such that the animals would be able to satisfactorily maintain their nutritional requirements. After completing MPTP administration they were observed over a further period to establish that the physical signs were stable before commencing three of the animals on regular (three times per day) levodopa treatment, given in doses which were just sufficient to reverse their parkinsonian features. The three remaining animals were left untreated but at regular intervals received challenge doses of levodopa to assess their response. A method was developed for observing and quantifying the severity of dyskinesia should it occur.[74]

Two of the chronically treated animals developed a combination of chorea and dystonia which was related to each dose of levodopa. In one animal this first appeared in a very mild form 3 weeks after the onset of therapy whereas in the other it developed after a delay of 7–8 weeks. With continuing medication the severity and duration of the dyskinesia increased and was always related to the peak effect of the dose of levodopa. In the lower limb, chorea took the form of alternating plantar- and dorsiflexion and inversion/eversion movements of the foot, together with flexion/extension of the knee and abduction/adduction of the hip. Choreiform movements in the upper limb affected all joints although they were generally less severe. Bucco-lingual dyskinesia was frequently observed, repeated protrusion and retraction of the tongue being the most common manifestation. Dystonic posturing usually involved the lower limb and consisted of sustained flexion of the hip and knee joints. When the upper limb was affected it was typically extended and internally rotated at the shoulder.

Since this initial study several more animals have received long-term treatment and the above findings have been confirmed. Moreover, more severe forms of dystonia have been observed, sometimes involving the axial muscles and occasionally occurring without chorea (unreported observations). From these observations it has been concluded that chorea and dystonia can occur separately or in combination and that one does not appear to represent a more severe form of levodopa-induced dyskinesia than the other.

Abnormal movements were not observed with challenge doses of levodopa in the untreated group of animals. When taken in conjunction with the progressively severe dyskinesia in the treated group, this suggests that this type of drug-induced dyskinesia is indeed due to a combination of moderately severe to very severe nigrostriatal degeneration and prolonged treatment of the disorder. Langston & Ballard[75] reported a similar form of dyskinesia during the treatment of MPTP-induced parkinsonism seen in those drug addicts who had mistakenly self-administered the compound.

Acknowledgements—the authors wish to acknowledge the financial support of Action Research for the Crippled Child, the Medical Research Council and the Wellcome Trust.

References

1. Martin, J. P. (1927): Hemichorea resulting from a local lesion of the brain. (The syndrome of the body of Luys.) *Brain* **50**, 637–651.
2. Myers, R. (1968): Ballismus. In *Handbook of clinical neurology, Vol. 6, Diseases of the basal ganglia*, eds P. J. Vinken & G. W. Bruyn. Amsterdam: North-Holland.
3. Whittier, J. R. (1947): Ballism and the subthalamic nucleus (nucleus hypothalamicus: corpus Luysi). *Archs. Neurol. Psychiatry.* **58**, 672–692.
4. Whittier, J. R. & Mettler, F. A. (1949): Studies on the subthalamus of the rhesus monkey. I. Anatomy and fiber connections of the subthalamic nucleus of Luys. *J. Comp. Neurol.* **90**, 281–317.
5. Carpenter, M. B., Whittier, J. R. & Mettler, F. A. (1950): Analysis of choreoid hyperkinesia in the rhesus monkey. Surgical and pharmacological analysis of hyperkinesia resulting from lesions in the subthalamic nucleus of Luys. *J. Comp. Neurol.* **92**, 293–332.
6. Yoshida, M., Rabin, A. & Anderson, M. (1971): Two types of monosynaptic inhibition of pallidal neurones produced by stimulation of the diencephalon and substantia nigra. *Brain Res.* **30**, 235–239.
7. Perkins, M. N. & Stone, T. W. (1980): Subthalamic projections to the globus pallidus: an electrophysiological study in the rat. *Exp. Neurol.* **68**, 500–511.
8. Perkins, M. N. & Stone, T. W. (1981): Iontophoretic studies on pallidal neurones and the projection from the subthalamic nucleus. *Q. J. Exp. Physiol.* **66**, 225–236.
9. Hammond, C., Shibazaki, T. & Rouzaire-Dubois, B. (1983): Branched output neurones of the rat subthalamic nucleus: electrophysiological study of the synaptic effects on identified cells of the two main target nuclei, the entopeduncular nucleus and the substantia nigra. *Neuroscience* **9**, 511–520.
10. Rouzaire-Dubois, B., Scarnati, E., Hammond, C., Crossman, A. R. & Shibazaki, T. (1983): Microiontophoretic studies on the nature of the neurotransmitter in the subthalamo-entopeduncular pathway of the rat. *Brain Res.* **271**, 11–20.
11. Needham, G. A., Soden, P. D., Sambrook, M. A. & Crossman, A. R. (1983): A remotely operated pump for intracerebral micro-injection in the primate. *J. Neurosci. Methods* **7**, 281–288.
12. Crossman, A. R., Sambrook, M. A. & Jackson, A. (1980): Experimental hemiballismus in the baboon produced by injection of a gamma-aminobutyric acid antagonist into the basal ganglia. *Neurosci. Lett.* **20**, 369–372.
13. Crossman, A. R., Sambrook, M. A. & Jackson, A. (1984): Experimental hemichorea/hemiballismus in the monkey. Studies on the intracerebral site of action in a drug-induced dyskinesia. *Brain* **107**, 579–596.
14. Fonnum, F., Grofova, I. & Rinvik, E. (1978): Origin and distribution of glutamate decarboxylase in the nucleus subthalamicus of the cat. *Brain Res.* **153**, 370–374.
15. Yelnik, J. & Percheron, G. (1979): Subthalamic neurones in primates: a quantitative and comparative analysis. *Neuroscience* **4**, 1717–1743.
16. Rouzaire-Dubois, B., Hammond, C., Hammon, B. & Feger, J. (1980): Pharmacological blockade of the globus pallidus-induced inhibitory response of subthalamic cells in the rat. *Brain Res.* **200**, 321–329.

17 Vincent, S. R., Kimura, H. & McGeer, E. G. (1982): A histochemical study of GABA-transaminase in the efferents of the pallidum. *Brain Res.* **241**, 162–165.
18 Nauta, H. W. J. & Cole, M. (1978): Efferent projections of the subthalamic nucleus: an autoradiographic study in monkey and cat. *J. Comp. Neurol.* **180**, 1–16.
19 Carpenter, M. B., Batton, R. R., Carleton, S. C. & Keller, J. T. (1981): Interconnections and organisation of pallidal and subthalamic nucleus neurones in the monkey. *J. Comp. Neurol.* **197**, 579–603.
20 Deniau, J. M., Hammond, C., Chevalier, G. & Feger, J. (1978): Evidence for branched subthalamic nucleus projections to substantia nigra, entopeduncular nucleus and globus pallidus. *Neurosci. Lett.* **9**, 117–121.
21 Van Der Kooy, D. & Hattori, T. (1980): Single subthalamic nucleus neurones project to both the globus pallidus and substantia nigra in rat. *J. Comp. Neurol.* **192**, 751–768.
22 Kim, R., Nakano, K., Jayaraman, A. & Carpenter, M. B. (1976): Projections of the globus pallidus and adjacent structures: an autoradiographic study in the monkey. *J. Comp. Neurol.* **169**, 263–290.
23 Carpenter, M. B., Carleton, S. C., Keller, J. T. & Conte, P. (1981): Connections of the subthalamic nucleus in the monkey. *Brain Res.* **224**, 1–29.
24 Nauta, W. J. H. & Mehler, W. R. (1966): Projections of the lentiform nucleus in the monkey. *Brain Res.* **1**, 3–42.
25 Kuo, J. S. & Carpenter, M. B. (1973): Organisation of the pallidothalamic projections in the monkey. *J. Comp. Neurol.* **151**, 201–236.
26 Schnell, G. R. & Strick, P. L. (1984): The origin of thalamic inputs to the arcuate premotor and supplementary motor areas. *J. Neurosci.* **4**, 539–560.
27 Cooper, I. S. (1969): *Involuntary movement disorders*. New York: Hoeber Medical Division, Harper and Row.
28 Martin, J. P. & McCaul, J. R. (1959): Acute hemiballismus treated by ventrolateral thalamotomy. *Brain* **82**, 105–108.
29 Narabayashi, H., Yokochi, F. & Nakajima, Y. (1984): Levodopa-induced dyskinesia and thalamotomy. *J. Neurol. Neurosurg. Psychiatry*, **47**, 831–839.
30 Strominger, N. L. & Carpenter, M. B. (1965): Effects of lesions in the substantia nigra upon subthalamic dyskinesia in the monkey. *Neurology* **15**, 587–594.
31 Spiegel, E. A. & Wycis, H. T. (1952): *Stereoencephalotomy*, Vol. 1. New York: Grune and Stratton.
32 Sokoloff, L., Reivich, M., Kennedy, C., Des Rosiers, M. H., Patlack, C. S., Pettigrew, K. D., Sakurada, O. & Shinohara, M. (1977): The [^{14}C] deoxyglucose method for the measurement of local cerebral glucose utilisation: theory, procedure and normal values in the conscious and anaesthetised albino rat. *J. Neurochem.* **28**, 897–916.
33 Mitchell, I. J., Sambrook, M. A. & Crossman, A. R. (1985): Subcortical changes in the regional uptake of [^{3}H]-2-deoxyglucose in the brain of the monkey during experimental choreiform dyskinesia elicited by injection of a gamma-aminobutyric acid antagonist into the subthalamic nucleus. *Brain* **108**, 421–438.
34 Kitai, S. T. & Kita, H. (1987): Anatomy and physiology of the subthalamic nucleus: A driving force of the basal ganglia. In *The basal ganglia II*, eds M. B. Carpenter & A. Jayaraman. New York: Plenum Press.
35. Huntington, G. (1872): On chorea. *Med. Surg. Reporter* **26**, 317–321.
36 Davenport, C. B. & Muncey, E. B. (1916–17): Huntington's chorea in relation to heredity and eugenics. *Am. J. Insan.* **73**, 195.
37 Vonsattel, J. P., Myers, R. H., Stevens, T. J., Ferrante, R. J., Bird, E. D. & Richardson, E. P. (1985): Neuropathologic classification of Huntington's disease. *J. Neuropath. Exp. Neurol.* **44**, 559–577.
38 Bird, E. D. & Iverson, L. L. (1974): Huntington's chorea. Postmortem measurement of glutamic acid decarboxylase, choline acetyl transferase and dopamine in basal ganglia. *Brain* **97**, 457–472.
39 Gale, J. G., Bird, E. D. & Spokes, E. G. (1978): Human brain substance P distribution in controls and Huntington's chorea. *J. Neurochem.* **30**, 633–634.
40 Emson, P. C., Arregui, A., Clement-Jones, V., Sandberg, B. E. B. & Rossor, M. (1980): Regional distribution of methionine enkephalin and substance P-like immunoreactivity in normal human brain and in Huntington's disease. *Brain Res.* **199**, 147–160.

41. Ferrante, R. J., Kowall, N. W., Beal, M. F., Richardson, E. P. & Martin, J. B. (1985): Selective sparing of a class of striatal neurons in Huntington's disease. *Science* **230**, 561–563.
42. Dawbarn, D., DeQuidt, M. E. & Emson, P. C. (1985): Survival of basal ganglia neuropeptide Y-somatostatin neurons in Huntington's disease. *Brain Res.* **340**, 251–260.
43. Alcock, N. S. (1936): A note on the pathology of senile chorea (non-hereditary). *Brain* **59**, 376.
44. Martin, J. P. (1957): Hemichorea without lesions in the corpus Luysii. *Brain* **80**, 1–10.
45. Tarsy, D. & Baldessarini, R. J. (1977): The pathophysiologic basis of tardive dyskinesia. *Biol. Psychiat.* **12**, 431–450.
46. Fibiger, H. C. & Lloyd, K. G. (1984): Neurobiological substrates of tardive dyskinesia: the GABA hypothesis. *Trends Neurosci.* **7**, 462–464.
47. Marsden, C. D., Parkes, J. D. & Quinn, N. (1982): Fluctuations of disability in Parkinson's disease—clinical aspects. In *Movement disorders*, eds C. D. Marsden & S. Fahn. London: Butterworths.
48. Murphy, D. L. & Dill, R. E. (1972): Chemical stimulation of discrete brain loci as a method of producing dyskinesia models in primates. *Exp. Neurol.* **34**, 244–245.
49. Robertson, R. G., Farmery, S. M., Sambrook, M. A. & Grossman, A. R. (1989): Dyskinesia in the primate following injection of an excitatory amino acid antagonist into the medial segment of the globus pallidus. *Brain Res.* (In Press).
50. Alexander, G. E. & Delong, M. R. (1985): Microstimulation of the primate neostriatum. II. Somatotopic organisation of striatal microexcitable zones and their relation to neuronal response properties. *J. Neurophysiol.* **53**, 1417–1430.
51. Kunzle, H. (1975): Bilateral projections from precentral motor cortex to the putamen and other parts of the basal ganglia. An autoradiographic study in Macaca fascicularis. *Brain Res.* **88**, 195–209.
52. Ohye, C., Le Guyader, C. & Feger, J. (1976): Responses of subthalamic and pallidial neurons to striatal stimulation: an extracellular study on awake monkeys. *Brain Res.* **111**, 241–252.
53. Fonnum, F., Gottesfeld, Z. & Grofova, I. (1978): Distribution of glutamate decarboxylase, choline acetyltransferase and aromatic amino acid decarboxylase in the basal ganglia of normal and operated rats. Evidence for striatopallidal, striatoentopeduncular and striatonigral GABAergic fibres. *Brain Res.* **143**, 125–138.
54. Penny, J. B. & Young, A. B. (1982): Quantitative autoradiography of neurotransmitter receptors in Huntington disease. *Neurology* **32**, 1391–1395.
55. Crossman, A. R., Mitchell, I. J., Sambrook, M. A. & Jackson, A. (1988): Chorea and myoclonus in the monkey induced by GABA-antagonism in the lentiform complex: the site of drug action and a hypothesis of the neural mechanisms of chorea. *Brain* **111**, 1211–1233.
56. Mitchell, I. J., Jackson, A., Sambrook, M. A. & Crossman, A. R. (1985): Common neural mechanisms in experimental chorea and hemiballismus in the monkey. Evidence from 2-deoxyglucose autoradiography. *Brain Res.* **339**, 346–350.
57. Greenfield, J. G. (1958): *Neuropathology*, eds J. G. Greenfield, W. H. McMenemey, A. Meyer & R. M. Norman. London: Edward Arnold.
58. Hornykiewicz, O. (1982): Brain neurotransmitter changes in Parkinson's disease. In *Movement disorders*, eds C. D. Marsden & S. Fahn. London: Butterworths.
59. Carpenter, M. B. & McMasters, R. E. (1964): Lesions of the substantia nigra in the Rhesus monkey. Efferent fiber degeneration and behavioral observations. *Am. J. Anat.* **114**, 293–320.
60. Ward, A. A., McCulloch, W. S. & Magoun, H. W. (1948): Production of an alternating tremor at rest in monkeys. *J. Neurophysiol.* **11**, 317–330.
61. Poirier, L. J. (1960): Experimental and histological study of midbrain dyskinesia. *J. Neurophysiol.* **23**, 534–551.
62. Poirier, L. J., Sourkes, T. L., Bouvier, G., Boucher, R. & Carabin, S. (1966): Striatal amines, experimental tremor and the effect of harmaline in the monkey. *Brain* **89**, 37–52.
63. Poirier, L. J., Pechadre, J. C., Larochelle, L., Dankova, J. & Boucher, R. (1975): Stereotaxic lesions and movement disorders in monkeys. In *Advances in neurology, Vol 10, Primate models of neurological disorders*, eds B. S. Meldrum & C. D. Marsden. New York: Raven Press.
64. Sambrook, M. A., Crossman, A. R. & Slater, P. (1979): Experimental torticollis in the marmoset produced by injection of 6-hydroxydopamine into the ascending nigrostriatal pathway. *Exp. Neurol.* **63**, 583–593.

65 Davis, G. C., Williams, A. C., Markey, S. P., Ebert, M. H., Caine, E. D., Reichert, C. M. & Kopin, I. J. (1979): Chronic parkinsonism secondary to intravenous injection of meperidine analogues. *Psychiatry Res.* **1**, 249–254.
66 Langston, J. W. & Ballard, P. (1984): Parkinsonism induced by 1-methyl-4-phenyl-1,2,3,6-tetrahydropyridine (MPTP): implications for treatment and the pathogenesis of Parkinson's disease. *Can. J. Neurol. Sci.* **11**, 160–165.
67 Burns, R. S., Chiueh, C. C., Markey, S. P., Ebert, M. H., Jacobowitz, D. M. & Kopin, I. J. (1983): A primate model of parkinsonism: selective destruction of dopaminergic neurons in the pars compacta of the substantia nigra by N-methyl-4-phenyl-1,2,3,6-tetrahydropyridine. *Proc. Natl. Acad. Sci. U.S.A.* **80**, 4546–4550.
68 Sambrook, M. A., Clarke, C. E., Robertson, R. G., Mitchell, I. J., Boyce, S., Graham, W. C. & Crossman, A. R. (1987): New parallels between Parkinson's disease and MPTP-induced parkinsonism in the monkey. In *The basal ganglia II*, eds M. B. Carpenter & A. Jayaraman. New York: Plenum press.
69 Crossman, A. R., Mitchell, I. J. & Sambrook, M. A. (1985): Regional brain uptake of 2-deoxyglucose in N-methyl-4-phenyl-1,2,3,6-tetrahydropyridine (MPTP)-induced parkinsonism in the macaque monkey. *Neuropharmacology* **24**, 587–591.
70 Schwartz, W. J., Smith, C. B., Davidsen, L., Savaki, H. & Sokoloff, L. (1979): Metabolic mapping of functional activity in the hypothalamoneurohypophysial system of the rat. *Science* **205**, 723–725.
71 Miller, W. C. & Delong, M. R. (1987): Altered tonic activity of neurons in the globus pallidus and subthalamic nucleus in the primate MPTP model of parkinsonism. In *The basal ganglia II*, eds M. B. Carpenter & A. Jayaraman. New York: Plenum press.
72 Rajput, A. J., Stern, W. & Laverty, W. H. (1984): Chronic low-dose levodopa therapy in Parkinson's disease: an argument for delaying levodopa therapy. *Neurology* **34**, 991—996.
73 Melamed, E. (1986): Initiation of levodopa therapy in parkinsonian patients should be delayed until the advanced stages of the disease. *Arch. Neurol.* **43**, 402–405.
74 Clarke, C. E., Sambrook, M. A., Mitchell, I. J. & Crossman, A. R. (1987): Levodopa-induced dyskinesia and response fluctuations in primates rendered parkinsonian with 1-methyl-4-phenyl-1,2,3,6-tetrahydropyridine (MPTP). *J. Neurol. Sci.* **78**, 273–280.
75 Langston, J. W. & Ballard, P. (1984): Parkinsonism induced by 1-methyl-4-phenyl-1,2,3,6-tetrahydropyridine (MPTP): implications for the treatment and the pathogenesis of Parkinson's disease. *Can. J. Neurol. Sci.* **11**, 160–165.

15

NEURAL MECHANISMS IN THE BASAL GANGLIA RELATED TO THE INITIATION OF MOVEMENTS

Wolfram Schultz*, Ranulfo Romo*, Eugenio Scarnati[†],
Andreas Studer*, Gösta Jonsson[‡] and Erik Sundström[‡]

*Institute of Physiology, University of Fribourg, CH-1700 Fribourg, Switzerland; [†]Laboratory of Human Physiology, School of Medicine, University of L'Aquila, I-67100 L'Aquila, Italy; and [‡]Department of Histology and Neurobiology, Karolinska Institute, S-10401 Stockholm, Sweden

Summary

Different aspects of neural mechanisms related to the initiation of movements were investigated in awake, behaviourally conditioned monkeys. In a reaction time task, animals showed prolonged arm movement reaction times, delayed onset of muscle activity and increased latencies of saccadic eye movements after destruction of nigrostriatal dopamine neurons induced by 1-methyl-4-phenyl-1,2,3,6-tetrahydropyridine (MPTP). These deficits were prevented by pharmacological inhibition of the catecholamine uptake mechanism through which MPTP enters dopamine neurons. Using the same behavioural task, dopamine neurons in unlesioned animals responded with a brief burst of impulses to the signal triggering the arm movement. These responses remained present in the absence of arm movements but disappeared when the same stimuli were used without a behavioural context. In another task, instruction lights served as specific preparatory signals for upcoming movement or no-movement reactions. While dopamine neurons showed an absence of reproducible phasic or tonic responses, many neurons in caudate, putamen and pars reticulata of substantia nigra changed their activity during the instruction period preceding the movement. Similar activations were found in the supplementary motor area of the cerebral cortex which projects to the striatum and receives the bulk of basal ganglia output. Neural activity preceding internally generated movements was investigated during self-initiated arm movements, in the absence of phasic external cues. Only a limited number of dopamine neurons displayed moderately increased activity preceding these movements. In contrast, many neurons in caudate, putamen and supplementary motor area showed pronounced activations up to 3 sec in advance of self-initiated movements. These data suggest that dopamine neurons respond with impulses to external stimuli of immediate behavioural significance, including stimuli used for initiating a movement. Activity more specifically related to different aspects of movement initiation is found in structures of the basal ganglia and cerebral cortex which are directly or indirectly influenced by dopamine neurons.

Introduction

Many deficits arising after destruction of different nuclei of the basal ganglia concern processes linked to the initiation of movements. Parkinsonian akinesia comprises a reduction in movement reactions to external stimuli and a poverty of self-initiated arm and eye movements. These deficits are reproduced in animals with experimental lesions of the nigrostriatal dopamine system.[1–4] Involuntary movements occur after destruction of neurons in the striatum (chorea) or the subthalamic nucleus (ballism). The involvement in the initiation of movements is compatible with the sources of afferent input to the striatum. Heavy projections arise from frontal cortical areas, and from limbic cortical and subcortical structures.[5–10] In many of these areas, neural activity related to the preparation of movements is found.[11–14]

In the present study, we investigated neural correlates of several aspects of movement initiation. We studied neural responses to external stimuli eliciting immediate behavioural reactions (trigger stimuli) or serving to prepare a behavioural reaction to an upcoming trigger stimulus (instructions). We also recorded neural activity during movements initiated by the animal itself without external timing cues (self-initiated movements). Since a major part of this report focuses on the role of dopamine neurons, we shall describe arm and eye movement deficits in a behavioural task arising after destruction of dopamine neurons by 1-methyl-4-phenyl-1,2,3,6-tetrahydropyridine (MPTP). These deficits may help to delineate the scope of akinetic impairments in a reaction time task and serve as comparison when recording the activity of dopamine neurons in unlesioned animals.

Methods

Macaca fascicularis monkeys were seated in a completely enclosed experimental apparatus. They were trained to keep one hand relaxed on a touch-sensitive, immovable key and to reach into a small food box in front of them at eye level when its door opened visibly, audibly, or visibly and audibly (frontal opening 40 × 40 mm). Further details of behavioural tasks will be given, together with presentation of results. Following proficiency in the task, electromyographic (EMG)-electrodes were implanted under general anaesthesia in the extensor digitorum communis and biceps muscles of both arms, together with oculographic electrodes in the canthi of the eyes, and, when used for neural recordings, a microelectrode base on the skull. The activity of further arm, shoulder, dorsum and leg muscles on both sides was monitored through acutely inserted electrodes. All data were collected during the experiment by a laboratory computer which also controlled the behavioural tasks. At the end of neural recordings, animals were perfused with formaldehyde and positions of neurons were reconstructed from the marker lesion.

Some of the monkeys were injected with a sterile solution of MPTP on 5 of 6 consecutive days (0.33–0.36 mg/kg intravenously). In a subgroup, the catecholamine uptake inhibitor nomifensine was administered from 1–2 weeks before until 4 weeks after MPTP administration (4–5 × 0.5–3.0 mg/kg intramuscularly each day). MPTP-treated animals and their controls were sacrificed by exsanguination. The regional levels of monoamines and their metabolites were determined from punches using liquid chromatography with electrochemical detection.

Results

Task performance after treatment with MPTP

MPTP alone. Three monkeys were trained on both sides in a reaction time task and lesioned with MPTP.[3,15,16] In this task, animals released the resting key and reached into the food box in direct reaction to the visible and audible opening of the door of the box. In comparison with control data collected before administration of MPTP in the same animals, both reaction time (from door opening to key release) and movement time (from key release to entering the box) were increased in all three animals by 31–129 per cent and 10–103 per cent, respectively (Fig. 1 left). Although the build-up of EMG activity preceding the arm movement was reduced, the increases in reaction time in this task were predominantly due to a delayed onset of EMG activity following door opening (63–225 per cent increases), while the delay time between EMG onset and arm movement onset only changed unsystematically. In about half of the sessions of 110–130 movements, arm movement and EMG reaction times after MPTP administration showed progressive increases over consecutive trials, the first movements often having normal values. Door opening elicited saccadic eye movements towards the food box regularly preceding the reaching movement of the arm. Latencies of these saccades were increased by 31–90 per

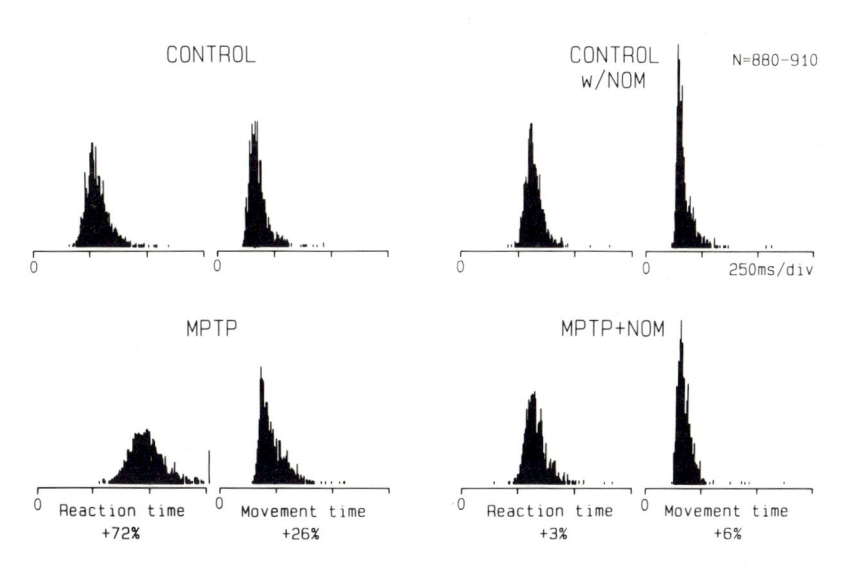

Fig. 1. *Histograms of reaction time and movement time of arm reaching movements during performance of the reaction time task in four different situations.* Left: Control and MPTP: Task performance on one side of one monkey before and after administration of MPTP. Data after MPTP were collected while the animal performed the task without levodopa administration. Right: Control w/NOM and MPTP+NOM: Task performance on one side of another monkey before and after administration of MPTP under nomifensine medication. Data for each histogram were collected in 8 sessions of 110–115 movements. The increases in reaction time and movement time after MPTP administration were prevented by administration of nomifensine.

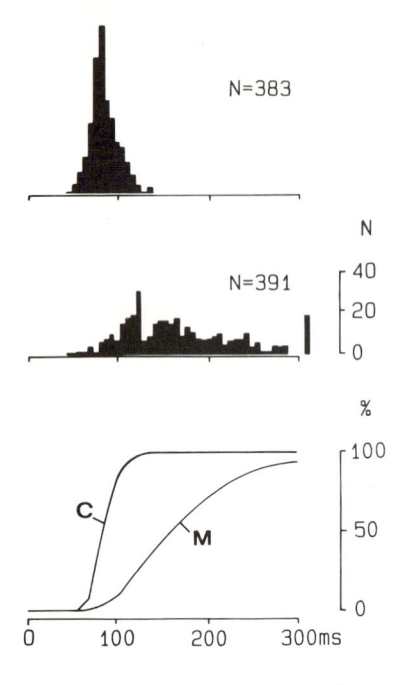

Fig. 2. *Latencies of horizontal saccadic eye movements during performance of the arm reaching reaction time task.* Saccades occurred after opening of the door of the food box and preceded the onset of arm movements. From above downward: Histogram of saccadic latencies before MPTP administration; histogram of saccadic latencies after MPTP administration; cumulative frequency distribution of the same data shown in the histograms above (C = control, M = MPTP-treated). The data were collected from task performance on one side of one monkey and show a median increase of 90 per cent in latency after MPTP. Levodopa (8–22 mg/kg) was administered together with benserazide (8–20 mg/kg) after MPTP treatment to facilitate task performance.

cent after MPTP treatment (Fig. 2). Spontaneous saccades performed in the absence of any task were strongly reduced both in frequency and amplitude.

Dopamine was reduced by 93–99.6 per cent in the caudate and putamen of all three monkeys, and by 40–60 per cent in the prefrontal and anterior cingulate cortex in two of them. The severity of striatal DA depletion and the presence of frontal dopamine depletion corresponded well to the severity of impairments in the task.

Blockade of catecholamine uptake. In contrast to the severe behavioural deficits observed after administration of MPTP alone, two monkeys treated with nomifensine before, during and after MPTP administration showed only minor and inconsistent changes in all parameters of task performance (Fig. 1 right). These results corroborate in a quantitative behavioural task earlier data showing that inhibition of catecholamine uptake is effective in preventing MPTP-induced neurotoxicity in mice[17–19] and monkeys,[20] probably by preventing the toxic metabolite 1-methyl-4-phenylpyridine (MPP^+) from entering dopamine neurons.

Responses of dopamine neurons to trigger stimuli

Using the same reaction time task, we found that the majority of 128 dopamine neurons in the midbrain of two monkeys discharged a short burst of impulses in response to the trigger stimulus (opening of the food box) used for initiating the arm and eye movement.[21] Thus, dopamine neurons in unlesioned animals responded during a period of the task that was prolonged after destruction of dopamine neurons by MPTP (reaction time). Responses remained present when the visual or auditory components of door opening were employed separately.

In order to determine whether responses depended upon an arm movement reaction, a go/no go task was used in which the animal reached into one food box after its door had opened, but refrained from any skeletal movements when the door of a neighbouring, identical box opened in random alternation. More than 100 dopamine neurons in two monkeys typically responded to door opening in both situations but failed to show changes when either one of the doors was opened while the animal was not engaged in any behavioural task (Fig. 3). Inspection of eye movements revealed the presence of stimulus-triggered saccades towards the food box in 50–90 per cent of both go and no go trials, while target-directed eye movements were entirely absent in the control situation. However, responses of dopamine neurons to door opening were equally present in go and no go trials in which saccadic eye movements were absent because the animal already fixated the food box when it opened. These data show that dopamine neurons respond well to external stimuli of immediate behavioural significance that have the capacity to elicit target-directed arm and eye movements. The lack of relationship to individual arm and eye movements suggests that these neurons are related to the behavioural reactivity of the animal but not specifically to the initiation of each arm or eye movement.

Preparation of movements by external signals

In order to investigate preparation processes as factors contributing to the initiation of movements, we trained animals in an instruction-dependent go/no go task. Instruction lights prepared the animal to perform or withhold a movement when the door of a food box opened audibly several seconds later. Thus, the instruction light provided information on how to react, while opening of the food box only signalled the time of reacting.

A total of 150 dopamine neurons in five monkeys was tested in this task([22] and in preparation). Phasic responses to instruction lights were observed in only one animal in

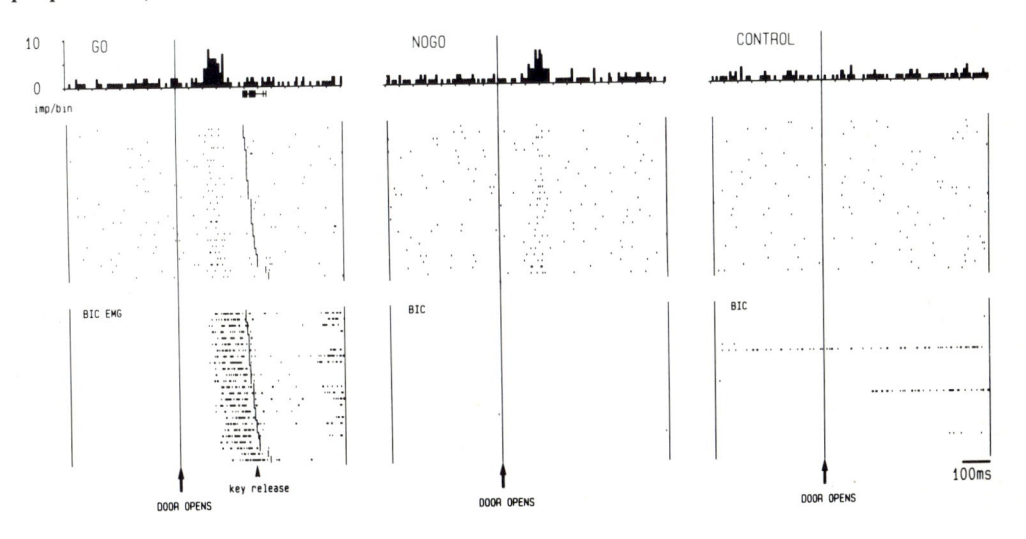

Fig. 3. *Responses of a dopamine neuron in the monkey substantia nigra to contralateral door opening.* Left and middle: Responses in the go/no go task; trials were separated off-line according to go and no go situations (w/arm movement and w/out arm movement, respectively). Right: Lack of response in the control session, using the same door opening stimulus in the absence of any behavioural task. From above downward are shown in each of the three parts: peri-event time histogram of neural impulses summed on the basis of the dot display shown below them; dot display of EMG activity in the biceps brachii muscle (BIC) recorded simultaneously with neural impulses. The distance of each dot to door opening corresponds to their real time interval. Each line of dots represents activity during performance in one trial. The sequence of trials w/arm movements is rearranged according to reaction time, while otherwise the original sequence is preserved downward. Bin width is 5 msec, the time scale of 100 msec comprises 20 bins. Imp/bin = impulses/bin.

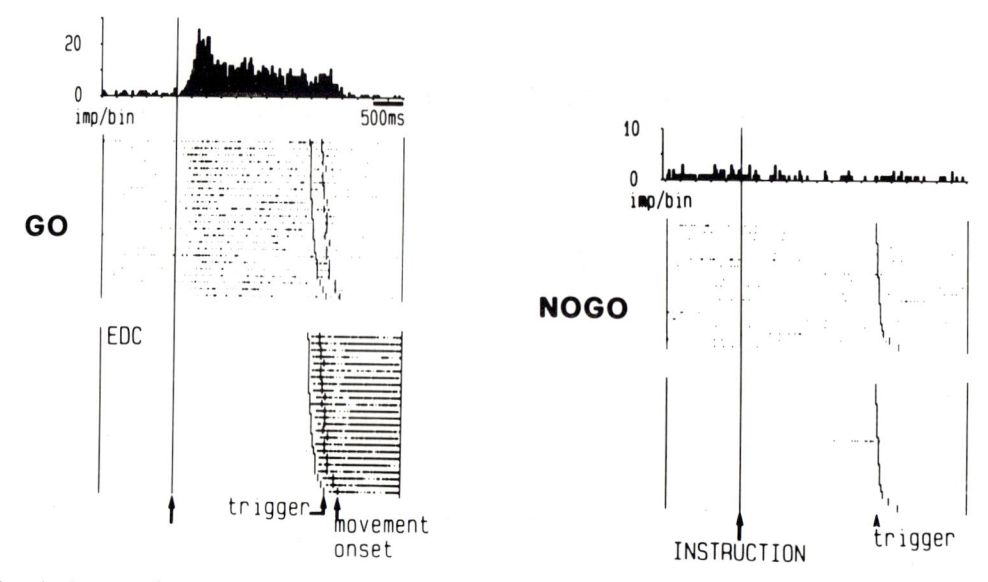

Fig. 4. *Increased activity of a neuron in the monkey caudate nucleus during preparation for movement in the instruction-dependent go/no go task.* Changes were absent during the no-movement instruction (no go). Small vertical bars in dot displays indicate door opening of the food box (trigger) and movement onset. Neural and muscular activity are aligned on instruction light onset. Trials are rank-ordered according to length of intervals between instruction onset and door opening. EDC = dot display of EMG activity in the extensor digitorum communis (go and no go situation). Bin width is 25 msec; the time scale of 500 msec comprises 20 bins. (Reproduced with permission by Springer Verlag from [23]).

which the task was used infrequently (about 300 trials in 8 weeks; 10 of 13 neurons responding). Only two neurons showed a tonic, 50% increase of activity during the instruction light period preceding the no go reaction. Thus, dopamine neurons typically showed an absence of preparatory activity in relation to external signals.

Neurons in both parts of the striatum (caudate and putamen) were activated during the instruction light period. Thus, 20 per cent of 950 neurons in three monkeys were exclusively activated during the movement instruction, 5 per cent only during the no-movement instruction, and 4 per cent in both situations. Neurons responded in similar fractions phasically to light onset, tonically during the entire instruction period (Fig. 4), or with slowly increasing activity prior to door opening ([23] and in preparation). In other studies, preparatory activity in the putamen was related to the direction of the intended arm movement.[24]

The pars reticulata of substantia nigra (SNpr) receives fibres from the striatum and constitutes a major output station of the basal ganglia. Of 117 SNpr neurons recorded in four monkeys, 12 per cent showed tonic decreases or increases in activity during the instruction light period, predominantly in the movement situation.[25] Some of these neurons showed bilaterally symmetrical changes (Fig. 5). Similar instruction-related changes were found following the brief presentation of a stimulus used for a later eye movement (memory-contingent sustained response).[26] These data suggest that the preparatory activity in the striatum may leave the basal ganglia via SNpr, from which it may reach the level of cerebral cortex.

The supplementary motor area in the mesial wall of cortical area 6 projects to both parts of the striatum[7,9] and is a major target of basal ganglia outflow.[27] For this reason, we

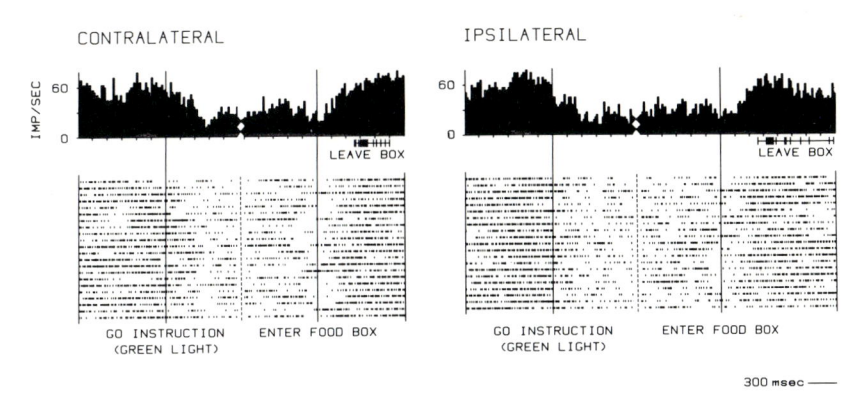

Fig. 5. *Decreased activity of a neuron in the pars reticulata of the monkey substantia nigra during preparation for movement in the instruction-dependent go/no go task.* The decrease is also seen with ipsilateral task performance. Time axes are split at vertical interrupted lines while maintaining the mean time interval between instruction light onset and the moment at which the animal's hand entered the food box. Bin width is 15 msec; the time scale of 300 msec comprises 20 bins. Imp/sec = impulses/second. (Reproduced with permission by the American Physiological Society from [25])

tested 350 of its neurons in this task and found similar responses as in the striatum, albeit at higher frequencies ([28] and in preparation). Thus, 50 per cent of supplementary motor area neurons showed activation during the instruction light period preparing for a movement, while small fractions responded only during the no-movement instruction or in both situations.

Self-initiated arm movements

During waiting periods in the primate chair, monkeys occasionally released the resting key and reached into a food box. These self-initiated movements in the absence of external stimuli were systematically reinforced by food reward as soon as animals were able to remain relaxed for several tens of seconds while their hand rested on the key. The door of the food box was kept open, but a cover in front of the box prevented vision into its interior while permitting access by the hand from below. Intervals between movements varied spontaneously between 5 and 30 sec. Thus self-initiated movements were performed without phasic external cues and with the purpose of obtaining food reward.

Dopamine neurons showed an absence of major changes in activity preceding movement or EMG onset (Fig. 6 left). Only 12 per cent of 104 dopamine neurons in two monkeys displayed moderate (45–128 per cent) increases in discharge rate beginning at 550–1500 msec before movement onset and subsiding up to 600 msec prior to movement, at the time of movement onset, or after the end of reaching. In contrast, the majority of dopamine neurons (84 per cent) showed a burst of activity when the animal's hand touched the food inside the box (Fig. 6 right). The touch response was absent when the bare wire normally holding the food was touched or when the empty food box was manually explored (Fig. 6 lower right). A response of dopamine neurons to touching the food was never found with stimulus-triggered movements employing the same food box, independent of a response to the trigger stimulus. Thus, this somatosensory response appears to be contingent on the behavioural state and the significance of the stimulus.

In both parts of the striatum, 15 per cent of 680 neurons in three monkeys showed increased activity beginning at 700–3000 msec before movement onset ([23] and in preparation). These activations began before the earliest EMG activity and ended before the movement or continued during its execution (Fig. 7). Pre-movement activity only

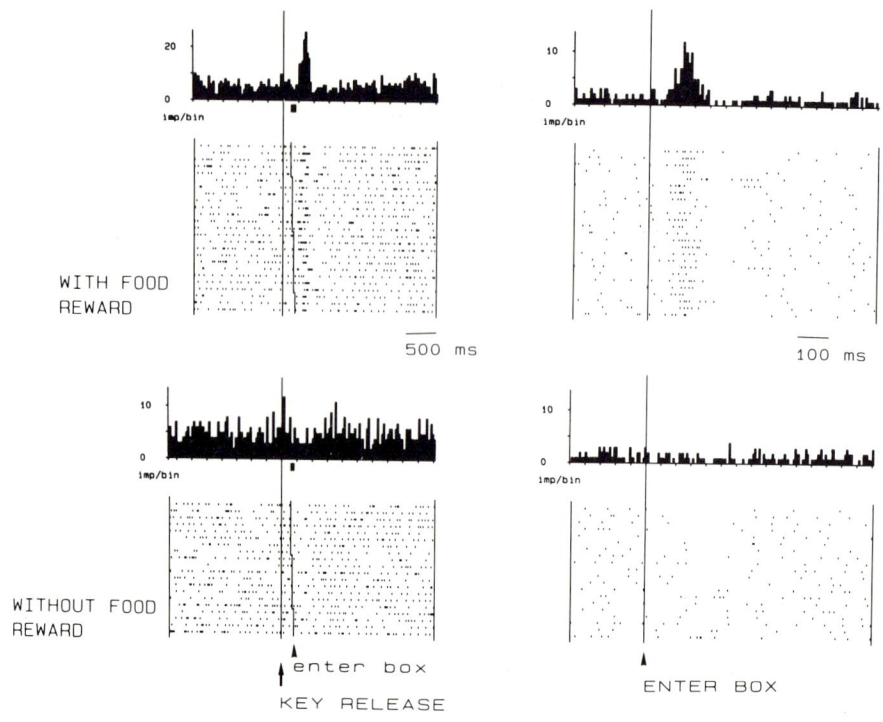

Fig. 6. *Activity of a dopamine neuron of the monkey substantia nigra during contralateral self-initiated arm movements into a food-containing box.* Trials were separated off-line according to the presence (above) or absence (below) of food in the box. The same data are shown with different temporal resolution in left and right parts, referenced to movement onset (key release) and entering the food box, respectively. Left: two histograms and dot displays show an absence of changes before the movement. Right: a brief burst of impulses is seen when the animal's hand touched the food inside the box (above) while active searching the interior of the empty box was not followed by a response (below). Bin width is 25 msec in left and 5 msec in right parts; time scales comprise 20 bins.

occurred when animals performed a self-initiated reaching movement from the well-defined resting position on the key. It was not observed in relation to occasional postural adjustments. Neurons activated before self-initiated movements were found in the lateral caudate and medial putamen.

In the supplementary motor area, 28 per cent of 265 neurons in three monkeys showed similar pre-movement activity as in the striatum ([28] and in preparation). These activations began with progressively increasing intensity at 600–2600 msec before movement onset and reached a maximum before or at the time of EMG onset. Some of these neurons were also activated in advance of ipsilateral movements. Similar pre-movement activations were found with key press movements,[29] suggesting that the presently observed activations were not particularly related to the large amplitude of the reaching movement.

Discussion

The increases in reaction time, EMG reaction time and saccadic latency following MPTP-induced lesions of nigrostriatal dopamine neurons suggest defective mechanisms

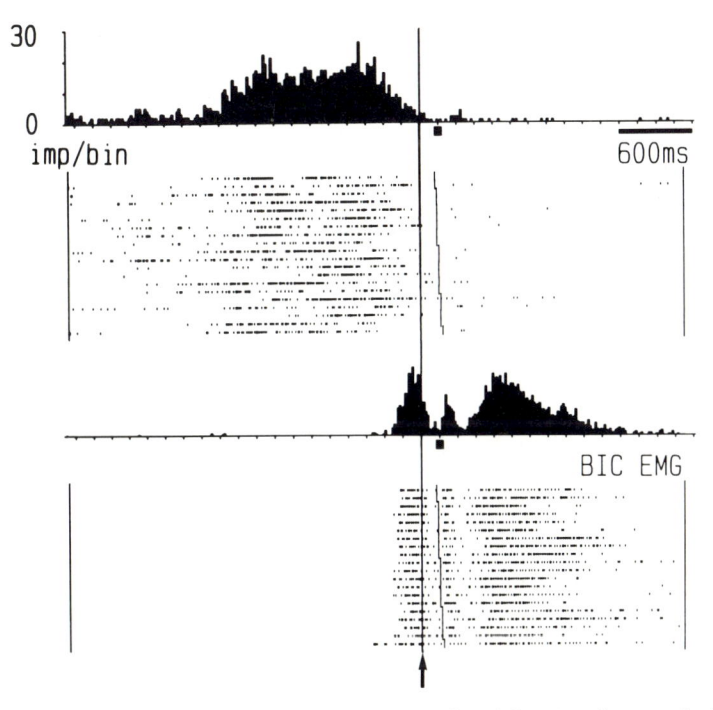

Fig. 7. *Activation of a neuron in the monkey putamen more than 1.5 sec in advance of self-initiated arm reaching movements performed in the absence of phasic external stimuli.* The arrow at the bottom denotes the time of movement onset (key release). Trials are rank-ordered for length of intervals between movement onset (arrow) and entering the food box (small vertical bars below histograms and in dot displays). The peri-event time histogram and dot display of neural impulses are shown above the peri-event time histogram and dot display of EMG activity in the biceps brachii (BIC), recorded simultaneously with neural impulses. Bin width is 15 msec; the time scale of 600 msec comprises 40 bins. (Reproduced with permission by Springer Verlag from [23]).

involved in the initiation of stimulus-triggered arm and eye movements after severe, MPTP-induced depletion of dopamine in the striatum. The initiation of self-initiated movements is also impaired, as shown by impaired spontaneous eye movements. Thus dopamine neurons are necessary for initiating reactions to directly-triggering stimuli and for initiating spontaneous movements.

Dopamine neurons responded well to stimuli triggering a direct movement reaction, which would be compatible with a direct involvement in the initiation of movements. However, detailed analysis of trigger responses and the occurrence of touch responses during movements suggests that dopamine neurons respond in a more general way to external stimuli of immediate behavioural significance. These stimuli also include those used for the initiation of a movement. Thus, impulses of dopamine neurons appear to signal to their target structures the presence of an external stimulus of immediate behavioural significance. Subjects deficient in dopamine neurons would lack this phasic input to striatum and show reduced reactions to external stimuli, including delayed initiation of movements.

Neural impulse activity was investigated in tasks dealing with three aspects of movement initiation: reactions to trigger stimuli, instruction-dependent preparation for behavioural reactions, and self-initiated movements. In these tests, dopamine neurons responded well

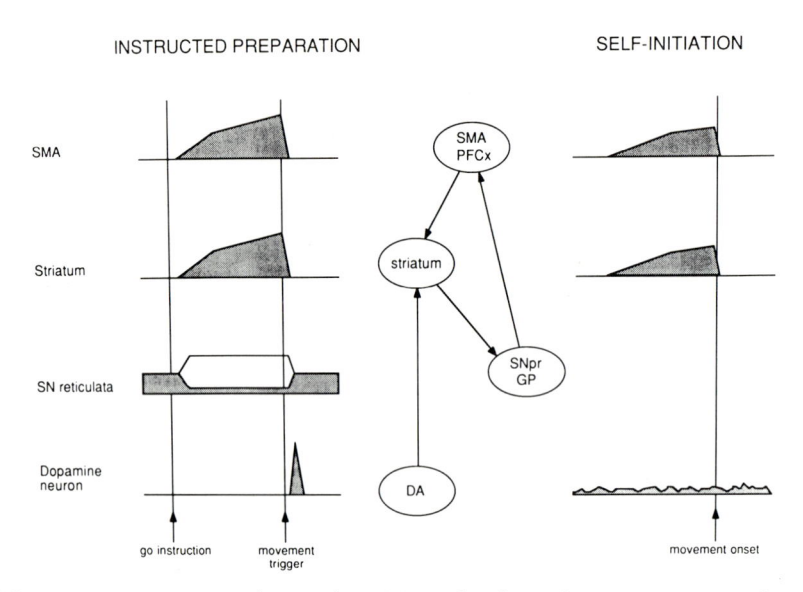

Fig. 8 *Schematic presentation of neural activity related to the preparation and initiation of movements in different regions of the basal ganglia and an associated cortical area, as described in the present report.* Neural activity in the instruction-dependent go/no go tasks is shown to the left, while changes during self-initiated movements are shown to the right. The circuit diagram in the middle depicts the neural loop between the frontal cortex and the basal ganglia and the influence exerted by the ascending dopamine neurons onto this loop. SMA = supplementary motor area, PFCx = prefrontal cortex; SNpr = substantia nigra pars reticulata; GP = globus pallidus; DA = midbrain dopamine neurons.

to trigger stimuli but only showed minor changes in activity preceding self-initiated movements. In contrast, subjects with lesions of dopamine neurons are particularly deficient in self-initiated movements. Also, dopamine neurons showed very little change during instructions serving as preparation for behavioural reactions. Considerable pre-movement activity in both tasks is found in the striatum and the supplementary motor area, structures under direct or indirect influence of dopaminergic neurotransmission (Fig. 8). Thus, although the presence of dopamine in the striatum is essential for self-initiated movements, they apparently do not require major changes in impulse rate of dopamine neurons. It may be speculated that sufficient dopamine for sustaining self-initiated movements is released in the striatum through spontaneous impulses or through presynaptic interactions via glutamatergic afferents from different regions of cerebral cortex[30] occurring at a slower time course.[31]

Acknowledgements—This work was supported by the Swiss National Science Foundation (grants 3.533–0.83, 3.473–0.86, 893.295–0.85), Sandoz Foundation, United Parkinson Foundation, Swedish Medical Research Council (grant 04X-2295), European Science Foundation and Italian National Research Council.

References

1. Burns, R. S., Chiueh, C. C., Markey, S. P., Ebert, M. H., Jacobowitz, D. M. & Kopin, I. J. (1983): A primate model of parkinsonism: Selective destruction of dopaminergic neurons in the pars compacta of the substantia nigra by N-methyl-4-phenyl-1,2,3,6-tetrahydropyridine. *Proc. Natl. Acad. Sci.* **80**, 4546–4550.

2 Poirier, L. J. (1960): Experimental and histological study of midbrain dyskinesias. *J. Neurophysiol.* **23**, 534–551.
3 Schultz, W., Studer, A., Jonsson, G., Sundström, E. & Mefford, I. (1985): Deficits in behavioral initiation and execution processes in monkeys with 1-methyl-4-phenyl-1,2,3,6-tetrahydropyridine-induced parkinsonism. *Neurosci. Lett.* **59**, 225–232.
4 Ungerstedt, U. (1971): Adipsia and aphagia after 6-hydroxydopamine induced degeneration of the nigro-striatal dopamine system. *Acta Physiol. Scand.* **Suppl. 367**, 95–117.
5 Baleydier, C. & Mauguierre, F. (1980): The duality of the cingulate gyrus in monkey. Neuroanatomical study and functional hypotheses. *Brain* **103**, 525–554.
6 Goldman, P. S. & Nauta, W. J. H. (1977): An intricately patterned prefronto-caudate projection in the rhesus monkey. *J. Comp. Neurol.* **171**, 369–386.
7 Kunzle, H. (1978): An autoradiographic analysis of the efferent connections from premotor and adjacent prefrontal regions (areas 6 and 9) in Macaca fascicularis. *Brain Behav. Evol.* **15**, 185–234.
8 Parent, A., Mackey, A. & De Bellefeuille, L. (1983): The subcortical afferents to caudate nucleus and putamen in primate: A fluorescence retrograde double labeling study. *Neuroscience* **10**, 1137–1150.
9 Selemon, L. D. & Goldman-Rakic, P.S. (1985): Longitudinal topography and interdigitation of corticostriatal projections in the rhesus monkey. *J. Neurosci.* **5**, 776–794.
10 Yeterian, E. H. & Van Hoesen, G. W. (1978): Cortico-striate projections in the rhesus monkey: The organization of certain cortico-caudate connections. *Brain Res.* **139**, 43–63.
11 Fuster, J. M. & Alexander, G. E. (1971): Neuron activity related to short-term memory. *Science* **173**, 652–654.
12 Kubota, K. & Niki, H. (1971): Prefrontal cortical unit activity and delayed alternation performance in monkeys. *J. Neurophysiol.* **34**, 337–347.
13 Niki, H. & Watanabe, M. (1976): Cingulate unit activity and delayed response. *Brain Res.* **110**, 381–386.
14 Tanji, J. Taniguchi, K. & Saga, T. (1980): Supplementary motor area: Neuronal responses to motor instructions. *J. Neurophysiol.* **43**, 60–68.
15 Schultz, W., Romo, R., Scarnati, E. Sundström, E., Jonsson, G. & Studer, A. (1989): Saccadic reaction times, eye-arm coordination and spontaneous eye movements in normal and MPTP-treated monkeys. Submitted.
16 Schultz, W., Studer, A., Romo, R., Sundström, E., Jonsson, G. & Scarnati, E. (1989): Deficits in reaction times and movement times as correlates of hypokinesia in monkeys with MPTP-induced striatal dopamine depletion. *J. Neurophysiol.* (In Press)
17 Javitch, J. A., D'Amato, R. J., Strittmatter, S. M. & Snyder, S. H. (1985): Parkinsonism-inducing neurotoxin, N-methyl-4-phenyl-1,2,3,6-tetrahydropyridine: Uptake of the metabolite N-methyl-4-phenylpyridine by dopamine neurons explains selective toxicity. *Proc. Natl. Acad. Sci.* **82**, 2173–2177.
18 Melamed, E., Rosenthal, J. Globus, M., Cohen, O. & Uzzan, A. (1985): Suppression of MPTP-induced dopaminergic neurotoxicity in mice by nomifensine and L-Dopa. *Brain Res.* **342**, 401–404.
19 Sundström, E. & Jonsson, G. (1985): Pharmacological interference with the neurotoxic action of 1-methyl-4-phenyl-1,2,3,6-tetrahydropyridine (MPTP) on central catecholamine neurons in the mouse. *Eur. J. Pharmacol.* **110**, 293–299.
20 Schultz, W., Scarnati, E., Sundström, E., Tsutsumi, T. & Jonsson, G. (1986): The catecholamine uptake blocker nomifensine protects against MPTP-induced parkinsonism in monkeys. *Exp. Brain Res.* **63**, 261–220.
21 Schultz, W. (1986): Responses of midbrain dopamine neurons to behavioral trigger stimuli in the monkey. *J. Neurophysiol.* **56**, 1439–1462.
22 Schultz, W., Ruffieux, A. & Aebischer, P. (1983): The activity of pars compacta neurons of the monkey substantia nigra in relation to motor activation. *Exp. Brain Res.* **51**, 377–387.
23 Schultz, W. & Romo, R. (1988): Neuronal activity in the monkey striatum during the initiation of movements. *Exp. Brain Res.* **71**, 431–436.
24 Alexander, G. I. (1987): Selective neuronal discharge in monkey putamen reflects intended direction of planned limb movements. *Exp. Brain Res.* **67**, 623–634.

25 Schultz, W. (1986): Activity of pars reticulata neurons of monkey substantia nigra in relation to motor, sensory and complex events. *J. Neurophysiol.* **55**, 660–677.
26 Hikosaka, O. & Wurtz, R. H. (1983): Visual and oculomotor functions of monkey substantia nigra pars reticulata. III. Memory-contingent visual and saccade responses. *J. Neurophysiol.* **49**, 1268–1284.
27 Schell, G. R. & Strick, P. L. (1984): The origin of thalamic inputs to the arcuate premotor and supplementary motor areas. *J. Neurosci.* **2**, 539–560.
28 Romo, R. & Schultz, W. (1987): Neuronal activity preceding self-initiated or externally timed arm movements in area 6 of monkey cortex. *Exp. Brain Res.* **67**, 656–662.
29 Okano, K. & Tanji, J. (1987): Neuronal activities in the primate motor fields of the agranular frontal cortex preceding visually triggered and self-paced movement. *Exp. Brain Res.* **66**, 155–166.
30 Romo, R., Chéramy, A., Godeheu, G. & Glowinski, J. (1986): In vivo presynaptic control of dopamine release in the cat caudate nucleus-III. Further evidence for the implication of corticostriatal glutamatergic neurons. *Neuroscience* **19**, 1091–1099.
31 Romo, R. & Schultz, W. (1985): Prolonged changes in dopaminergic terminal excitability and short changes in dopaminergic discharge rate after short peripheral stimulation in monkey. *Neurosci. Lett.* **62**, 335–340.

16

EXCESSIVE AND UNSELECTIVE RESPONSES OF MEDIAL PALLIDAL NEURONS TO BOTH PASSIVE MOVEMENT AND STRIATAL STIMULATION IN MONKEYS WITH MPTP-INDUCED PARKINSONISM

M. Filion, L. Tremblay and P. J. Bédard

Centre de Recherche en Neurobiologie, Université Laval et Hôpital de l'Enfant-Jésus, 1401, 18ᵉ Rue, Québec, Qué, Canada G1J 1Z4

Summary

Parkinson's disease is characterized by the coexistence of negative clinical signs, such as a lack of spontaneous movements, and positive signs, such as muscular rigidity and tremor. This may suggest that the affected nervous structures, the basal ganglia, react to afferent signals simultaneously too little and too much. To elucidate this paradox, extracellular single unit recordings were made in the medial segment of the globus pallidus, an output structure of the basal ganglia, in monkeys with parkinsonism induced by 1-methyl-4-phenyl-1,2,3,6-tetrahydropyridine (MPTP), compared to intact monkeys. Passive movements of limb segments and electrical stimulation of the caudate nucleus and putamen were used to test the reactivity of the neurons. In the intact animals, only some neurons responded to movement about a single contralateral joint. In the parkinsonians, however, many neurons responded to several upper and lower limb joints, bilaterally, and the magnitude of responses was larger. In the parkinsonian compared to intact monkeys, more neurons responded to electrical stimulation of at least one site in the ipsilateral or contralateral striatum. More neurons showed convergent effects of several sites, in particular of both caudate nucleus and putamen. The responses were of longer duration, often including large oscillations. A topological organization of responding neurons, comprising an inhibitory centre and an excitatory periphery, was clearly displayed in the intact animals but blurred in the parkinsonians. Finally, the dopamine agonist apomorphine restored normal responses in the parkinsonians. In conclusion, the medial pallidal neurons of parkinsonian monkeys respond excessively to peripheral and to central signals. This may explain the positive signs of parkinsonism, since the excessive responses are likely to be transmitted to the motor periphery. Simultaneously, the same neurons respond to any signal without selectivity. This may explain the negative signs of parkinsonism, since the most appropriate signals to control behaviour are thus blurred by others.

Introduction

Normal individuals perform spontaneously, and often simultaneously, a large variety of motor behaviours learned from infancy. This capacity is decreased or lost in Parkinson's disease, giving rise to so-called negative clinical signs. Simultaneously, positive signs are also present: muscular rigidity and tremor at rest. Pathologically, the disease is characterized by the degeneration of dopaminergic neurons of the substantia nigra innervating the basal ganglia. Therefore, the negative signs of the disease suggest that the lack of dopamine leaves the basal ganglia unresponsive to peripheral and to central stimuli. Inversely, the positive signs suggest that the same structures are simultaneously excessively reactive. To elucidate this paradox, we tested the reactivity of globus pallidus neurons to peripheral and to central stimuli in parkinsonian compared to intact monkeys.

The nigral dopaminergic neurons that degenerate in Parkinson's disease innervate not only the striatum (caudate nucleus and putamen) but also the globus pallidus and the subthalamic nucleus, as shown recently in the monkey.[1] Therefore, to evaluate the summation of the effects of the lack of dopamine at those different levels of the basal ganglia, one has to examine an output structure of the system, such as the medial or internal segment of the globus pallidus. Indeed, medial pallidal neurons send their axons outside the basal ganglia and directly influence the thalamus and the midbrain. The results of one part of the present study (responses to peripheral stimuli) have been reported in detail elsewhere.[2]

Methods

We have studied five young female cynomolgus monkeys (*Macaca fascicularis*) of about the same weight (2.7–3.3 kg). To render the animals parkinsonian, one or two intravenous injections of 1-methyl-4-phenyl-1,2,3,6-tetrahydropyridine (MPTP) were used in single doses of 0.6 to 1.5 mg/kg. Monkeys A and B were studied both before and after MPTP. Monkeys C and D provided data only in the intact state, since they did not tolerate either the first or the second injection of MPTP. Monkey E had been parkinsonian for 13 months when the electrophysiological studies were begun.

To evaluate the MPTP-induced dopaminergic denervation, we counted the number of nigral neurons of the compacta-type, using Nissl stain and criteria published by Poirier *et al.*[3] from our laboratory. From this reference, there are roughly 62 000 compacta-type neurons on one side of the brain in intact animals. The figure has been corroborated recently, using tyrosine hydroxylase to identify the dopaminergic neurons.[4] We can therefore state that the percentages of decrease of dopaminergic neurons were 86, 99, and 90 in monkeys A, B, and E, respectively.

For extracellular unit recording in the globus pallidus, as already described in detail,[2] the animal sat in a primate chair with the head fixed in the stereotaxic planes by means of a rigid platform, previously anchored to the skull of the animal under general anaesthesia. The animals were free to move body and limbs and rapidly adapted to the painless head restraint. Microelectrodes were lowered vertically on either side of the brain. Medial pallidal neurons were identified by their characteristic irregular but continuous firing at high rates,[5,6] and by the estimated position of the microelectrode tip within the nucleus, which was later verified by histological study.

Passive movements about the main limb joints were simply imposed on the animal by the experimenter. The shoulder, elbow, wrist, hip, knee, and ankle joints were tested systematically and bilaterally. Neurons were judged to respond to stimulation by listening over the audio monitor for variations in the spike train in phase with the imposed movements. The magnitude of responses was graded on a four-point scale: weak, medium, strong and very strong, as judged by two experimenters.

Six bipolar concentric electrodes were used for electrical stimulation of the striatum. They were implanted bilaterally: one in the head of the caudate nucleus, one in the putamen at the same frontal plane, and a third also in the putamen but more caudally. Stimulation was delivered at random intervals between 2.5 and 3.5 secs. It consisted of three pulses of current of 0.1 msec duration and 500 μA amplitude, at 3.3 msec intervals. The responses were studied in the form of peristimulus interval histograms constructed during unit recording. They showed the firing probability at each millisecond for the 500 preceding and the 1000 following the stimulus. Between 30 and 100 responses were added into the histograms, until the baseline preceding stimulation was regular. In a number of cases in parkinsonian animals, the series of histograms showing the responses of the same neuron to stimulation of different sites were repeated during and after the effects of apomorphine: a short-acting (30–45 min) dopamine agonist injected subcutaneously in doses of about 20 μg/kg.

Results

Responses to passive movements

In the intact animals, only eight medial pallidal neurons responded to passive movement, among the 50 neurons tested systematically (Table 1). One of those responded to one upper and one lower limb joint. The seven others responded exclusively to one contralateral joint. In the parkinsonians, 68 neurons were tested and as many as 44 responded at least to one joint. The proportion of the latter neurons responding to more than one joint, to both ipsilateral and contralateral, and to both upper and lower limb joints was always much larger than in the intact animals (Table 1). The effective joints often appeared unrelated. In fact, in many cases they were separated by ineffective joints, ruling out the possibility that the imposed movements were transmitted mechanically from one joint to the next, which could have been facilitated by the parkinsonian rigidity.

Table 1. *Medial pallidal neurons responding to passive movements.* Values are per cent. Numbers of neurons in parentheses.

	Intact		MPTP	
At least one joint	16	(8/50)	65	(44/68)
More than one joint	13	(1/8)	77	(34/44)
Ipsi- and contralateral	0	(0/8)	64	(28/44)
Upper and lower limbs	13	(1/8)	41	(18/44)

MPTP = animals rendered parkinsonian with 1-methyl-4-phenyl-1,2,3,6-tetrahydropyridine.

Finally, the magnitude of responses was larger in parkinsonian than in intact animals; very strong responses were observed only in the parkinsonians.

Responses to electrical stimulation

A total of 64 medial pallidal neurons were tested for responses to striatal stimulation in the intact animals and 80 in the parkinsonians (Table 2). Despite the small number of stimulation sites, as much as 86 per cent of neurons responded to at least one ipsilateral site in the intact animals. Nevertheless, the percentage increased to 96 in the parkinsonians. More strikingly, the proportion of neurons responding to all three ipsilateral sites and that of neurons responding to contralateral sites was about four times larger in the parkinsonians.

Table 2. *Medial pallidal neurons responding to striatal stimulation.* Values are per cent. Numbers of neurons in parentheses.

	Intact		MPTP	
At least one ipsilateral site	86	(55/64)	96	(77/80)
Three ipsilateral sites	7	(4/55)	27	(21/77)
At least one contralateral site	17	(6/36)	80	(47/59)

MPTP = animals rendered parkinsonian with 1-methyl-4-phenyl-1,2,3,6-tetrahydropyridine.

In the intact animals, the great majority of responses began with a decrease in the probability of firing, called early inhibition, followed by an increase, called excitation, and sometimes by a late inhibition and weak oscillations of the probability of firing (Fig. 1A). In a number of cases, the responses began with excitation (Fig. 1B). Very rarely did they begin with late inhibition. In the parkinsonians, however, late inhibition occurred in the great majority of responses, which often began with it. It was pronounced (Fig. 1C) and often accompanied by marked oscillations (Fig. 1D).

In both the intact and parkinsonian monkeys, medial pallidal neurons responding exclusively to caudate stimulation were located in a small dorsomedial zone of the nucleus. Those responding exclusively to stimulation of the putamen were located below, in a larger ventrolateral zone. Neurons responding to both caudate and putamen were located in an intermediate zone. This has been described by Ohye et al.[7] more than ten years ago, and is in accordance with the location of caudatopallidal and putaminopallidal fibres in the monkey.[8,9] The convergence in the intermediate zone is likely to be explained by the long pallidal dendrites, forming large disks at right angles to the incoming striatopallidal fibres.[8] The zone of convergence was larger in the parkinsonians. Superimposed on this topographical organization based on stimulation sites, a topological organization based on response types was disclosed in intact animals. In the centre of the area of influence of a stimulation site (either in caudate or putamen), the pallidal responses always began with the early inhibition. At the periphery of this area, they began with excitation. In the parkinsonians, the topological organization was blurred by late inhibitions and oscillations in both the centre and the periphery.

In a number of cases, to verify the differences between populations of responses in intact and in parkinsonian animals, we studied the responses of the same neuron in parkinsonian animals, before, during and after treatment with the dopamine agonist apomorphine, which transiently abolished the signs of parkinsonism. For example (Fig. 2), in a parkinsonian monkey, the same medial pallidal neuron responded to two ipsilateral sites

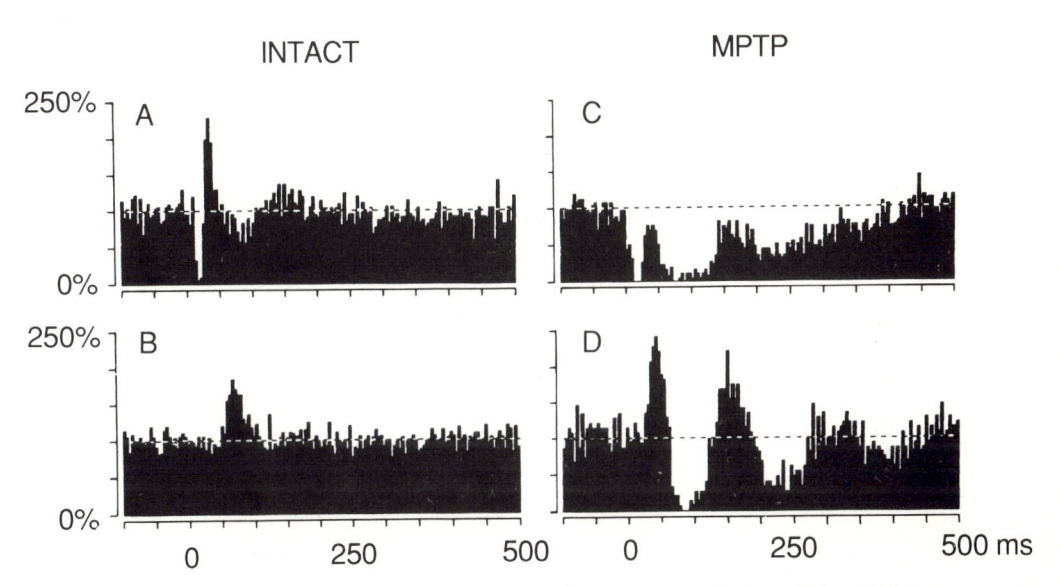

Fig. 1. *Peristimulus interval histograms showing the responses of 4 medial pallidal neurons to striatal stimulation in intact monkeys (A-B) and in monkeys with MPTP-induced parkinsonism (C-D). The bin width is 4 msec. The dashed line (100 per cent) is the average probability of firing during the 500 msec preceding the stimulus, given at time 0.*

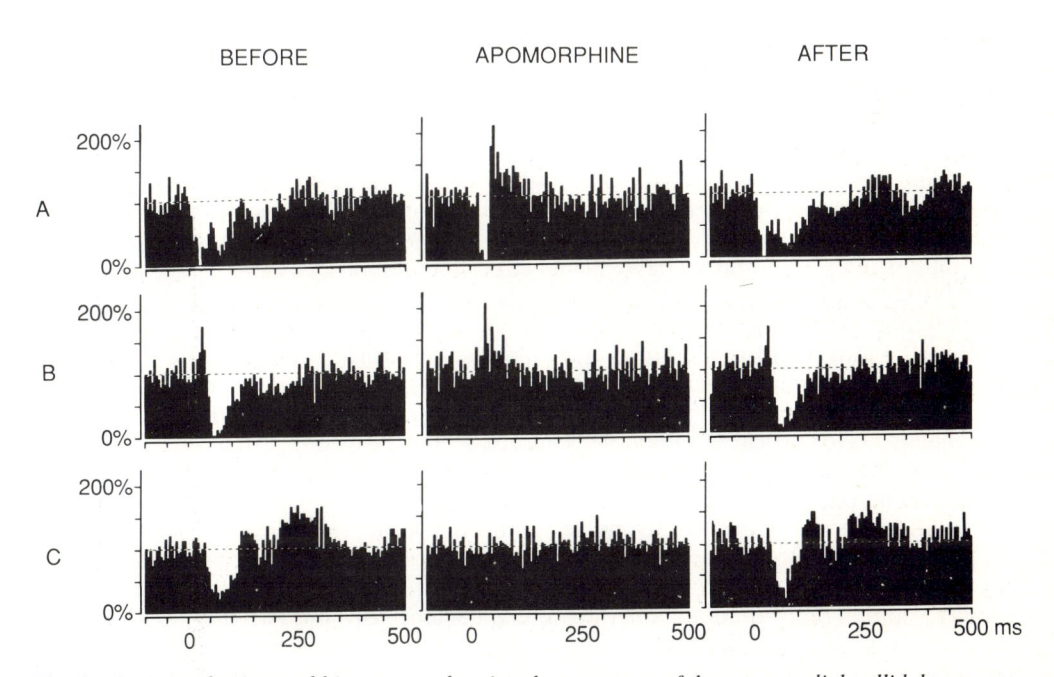

Fig. 2. *Peristimulus interval histograms showing the responses of the same medial pallidal neuron to stimulation of the ipsilateral posterior (A) and anterior (B) and contralateral posterior (C) putamen, before, during and after the effects of apomorphine (20 µg/kg subcutaneously). The bin width is 4 msec. The dashed line (100 per cent) is the average probability of firing during the 500 msec preceding the stimulus, given at time 0.*

(A and B) and to one contralateral site (C), stimulated at the same intensity. All three responses comprised late inhibition. During the effects of apomorphine, one ipsilateral site (A) triggered an early, initial inhibition, which was rapidly curtailed by excitation, a central or focussed response in our topology. The other ipsilateral site (B) triggered a pure excitation, a peripheral response. Finally, the contralateral site was ineffective, as it occurred characteristically in intact animals. About one hour after the injection of apomorphine, the neuron had recovered its large responses to all three sites.

Discussion

In monkeys rendered parkinsonian by MPTP, the responses of medial pallidal neurons to both passive limb movement and electrical stimulation of the striatum are clearly abnormal. There is an increase in both the number of responding neurons and the magnitude of responses. Medial pallidal neurons are therefore more responsive to both peripheral and central stimuli in parkinsonism. However, there is simultaneously a loss in quality of responses. Medial pallidal neurons do not respond exclusively to movement about a single contralateral joint but rather to several, often unrelated joints, bilaterally. They do not respond preferentially to electrical stimulation of restricted sites in the ipsilateral striatum but rather to several sites including the contralateral striatum. Therefore medial pallidal neurons are not only more responsive in parkinsonism but simultaneously less selective towards peripheral and central signals.

The neurotoxin MPTP has been shown to destroy dopaminergic neurons quite specifically in monkeys.[10] Moreover, it has been shown that in MPTP-treated monkeys as in human cases of Parkinson's disease the greatest cell loss occurs in the pars compacta of the substantia nigra (the A9 cell group).[4] These neurons innervate the striatum, the pallidum and the subthalamic nucleus in primates.[1] In our animals, the loss of nigral compacta-type neurons varied between 86 and 99 per cent. This was associated with an increased responsiveness and a decreased selectivity of medial pallidal neurons, which was reversed by the dopamine agonist apomorphine. Therefore we can conclude that it is the lack of dopamine that leaves the striatopallidal system strongly responsive to any signal without selectivity.

Various groups of authors have made experimental observations suggesting that dopamine is associated with control of responsiveness and selectivity. Thus Rolls et al.[11] observed that iontophoretic application of dopamine reduces both the firing rate and the magnitude of movement-related responses of striatal neurons in monkeys. This led them to suggest that dopamine could alter the signal-to-noise ratio or the detectability of signals in the striatum. Similarly, Toan & Schultz[12] have shown that responses of (lateral) pallidal neurons to cortical stimulation in cats are decreased by dopamine-releasing nigral stimulation and, inversely, increased by dopamine antagonists. This led them to suggest that dopamine restricts the flow of information from cortex to pallidum, thus focussing striatopallidal operations on the strongest and probably most significant signals. Finally, Girault et al.,[13] taking into account (1) the inhibitory control exerted by dopamine on corticostriatal excitatory inputs and on excitatory effects of cholinergic striatal interneurons, and (2) the dopaminergic enhancement of intrastriatal GABAergic inhibition (probably effected mainly by the numerous recurrent collaterals of striatal output neurons), suggested that the striatal efferent neurons, in the absence of dopamine, would be activated easily by any excitatory input without selectivity. The results of the present study prove the above hypotheses.

Coming back to the paradox raised at the outset of the present work, parkinsonian akinesia cannot be explained by a lack of responsiveness of the basal ganglia to peripheral and to central signals, which are likely to trigger and organize the spontaneous execution of learned behaviours. On the contrary, our results demonstrate that the striatopallidal system is excessively responsive to these signals in parkinsonism. However, the simultaneous decrease of selectivity may prevent the system from responding exclusively to the most appropriate signals. Indeed, in our parkinsonian compared to intact animals, medial pallidal neurons responded to so many apparently unrelated stimulation sites (especially in the case of peripheral stimulation), that one is led to think that the system was responding not only to significant signals but also to noise. This response to noise is likely to have been transmitted to the motor periphery and to have been responsible not only for the muscular rigidity but also for the scarcity or lack of spontaneous behaviour that characterized our parkinsonian monkeys. Finally, the frequent occurrence of oscillatory responses in our parkinsonian animals suggests that the striatopallidal system can participate in the production of parkinsonian tremor.

The second part of our study sheds light on mechanisms by which the striatopallidal system may control movement and posture. It appears that inhibition is the central signal transmitted from the striatum to groups of pallidal neurons. Excitation is used laterally, probably to focus on only a few neurons and to contrast this inhibitory signal. Excitation is also used centrally, in the focus area, probably to control the duration of the inhibitory signal. Deniau & Chevalier[14] have shown that such a topological organization is not only present in the striato-nigro-thalamic pathway of the rat but is also preserved, although inverted, in the nigro-thalamo-cortical pathway. Knowing that the GABAergic medial pallidal neurons inhibit thalamocortical neurons tonically and thus probably inhibit movement, inhibition of medial pallidal neurons results in disinhibition of thalamocortical neurons and thus probably releases movement. Conversely, the increased thalamocortical inhibition, at the periphery of the disinhibited area, probably results in an increased postural activity. Indeed, injection of GABA agonists into the thalamus results in catalepsy and rigidity, at least in the rat.[15] Thus in intact animals, the responses of medial pallidal neurons to stimulation appear to be organized to focus the release of movement with a peripheral increase in posture. In the present study, those responses were shown to be excessive in number and size, badly focussed and overlapping in parkinsonian animals. Those excessive responses very likely underlie the abnormal firing patterns, bursts of spikes at high frequencies interrupted by pauses, which characterize the spontaneous activity of medial pallidal neurons in monkeys with parkinsonism induced by electrolytic midbrain lesions[6] and by MPTP.[16,17]

Acknowledgements—This study was supported by grant MT-5750 of the Medical Research Council of Canada. L. Tremblay holds a Studentship from the Fonds de la Recherche en Santé du Québec.

References

1 Smith, Y. & Parent, A. (1987): Dopaminergic innervation of pallidum and subthalamic nucleus in primate. *Soc. Neurosci. Abstr.* **13**, 1571.
2 Filion, M., Tremblay, L. & Bédard, P. J. (1988): Abnormal influences of passive limb movement on the activity of globus pallidus neurons in parkinsonian monkeys. *Brain Res.* **444**, 165–176.
3 Poirier, L. J., Giguère, M. & Marchand, R. (1983): Comparative morphology of the substantia nigra and ventral tegmental area in the monkey, cat and rat. *Brain Res. Bull.* **11**, 371–397.
4 German, D. C., Dubach, M., Askari, S., Speciale, S. G. & Bowden, D. M. (1988): 1-Methyl-4-phenyl-1,2,3,6-tetrahydropyridine-induced parkinsonian syndrome in *Macaca fascicularis*: which midbrain dopaminergic neurons are lost? *Neuroscience* **24**, 161–174.
5 DeLong, M. R. (1971): Activity of pallidal neurons during movement. *J. Neurophysiol.* **34**, 414–427.

6 Filion, M. (1979): Effects of interruption of the nigrostriatal pathway and of dopaminergic agents on the spontaneous activity of globus pallidus neurons in the awake monkey. *Brain Res.* **178**, 425–441.
7 Ohye, C., Le Guyader, C. & Féger, J. (1976): Responses of subthalamic and pallidal neurons to striatal stimulation: an extracellular study on awake monkeys. *Brain Res.* **111**, 241–252.
8 Percheron, G., Yelnik, J. & François, C. (1984): A Golgi analysis of the primate globus pallidus. III. Spatial organization of the striato-pallidal complex. *J. Comp. Neurol.* **227**, 214–227.
9 Smith, Y. & Parent, A. (1986): Differential connections of the caudate nucleus and putamen in the squirrel monkey (*Saimiri sciureus*). *Neuroscience* **18**, 347–371.
10 Crossman, A. R., Clarke, C. E., Boyce, S., Robertson, R. G. & Sambrook, M. A. (1987): MPTP-induced parkinsonism in the monkey: Neurochemical pathology, complications of treatment and pathophysiological mechanisms. *Can. J. Neurol. Sci.* **14**, 428–435.
11 Rolls, E. T., Thorpe, S. J., Boytim, M., Szabo, I. & Perret, D. I. (1984): Responses of striatal neurons in the behaving monkey. 3. Effects of iontophoretically applied dopamine on normal responsiveness. *Neuroscience* **12**, 1201–1212.
12 Toan, D. L. & Schultz, W. (1985): Responses of rat pallidum cells to cortex stimulation and effects of altered dopaminergic activity. *Neuroscience* **15**, 683–694.
13 Girault, J. A., Spampinato, U., Glowinski, J. & Besson, M. J. (1986): *In vivo* release of [^{3}H]γ-aminobutyric acid in the rat neostriatum—II. Opposing effects of D1 and D2 dopamine receptor stimulation in the dorsal caudate putamen. *Neuroscience* **19**, 1109–1117.
14 Deniau, J. M. & Chevalier, G. (1985): Disinhibition as a basic process in the expression of striatal functions. II. The striato-nigral influence on thalamocortical cells of the ventromedial thalamic nucleus. *Brain Res.* **334**, 227–233.
15 Klockgether, T., Schwarz, M., Turski, L., Wolfarth, S. & Sontag, K. H. (1985): Rigidity and catalepsy after injections of muscimol into the ventromedial thalamic nucleus: an electromyographic study in the rat. *Exp. Brain Res.* **58**, 559–569.
16 Filion, M., Boucher, R. & Bédard, P. J. (1985): Globus pallidus unit activity in the monkey during the induction of parkinsonism by 1-methyl-4-phenyl-1,2,3,6-tetrahydropyridine (MPTP). *Soc. Neurosci. Abstr.* **11**, 1160.
17 Miller, W. C. & DeLong, M. R. (1987): Altered tonic activity of neurons in the globus pallidus and subthalamic nucleus in the primate MPTP model of parkinsonism. In *The basal ganglia II. Advances in behavioral biology, vol. 32*, ed M. B. Carpenter & A. Jayaraman, pp 415–427. New York: Plenum.

17

GABA/BENZODIAZEPINE RECEPTORS IN THE PRIMATE BASAL GANGLIA FOLLOWING TREATMENT WITH MPTP: EVIDENCE FOR THE DIFFERENTIAL REGULATION OF STRIATAL OUTPUT BY DOPAMINE?

R. G. Robertson, C. E. Clarke, S. Boyce,
M. A. Sambrook and A. R. Crossman

Experimental Neurology Group, Department of Cell and Structural Biology, Stopford Building, University of Manchester, Oxford Road, Manchester M13 9PT, UK

Summary

Gamma-aminobutyric acid (GABA) and benzodiazepine receptors in the basal ganglia of primates treated unilaterally with the neurotoxin 1-methyl-4-phenyl-1,2,3,6-tetrahydropyridine (MPTP) have been studied by quantitative autoradiography.

In unilaterally symptomatic animals with >95 per cent depletion of dopamine in the contralateral striatum there was a consistent increase in the density of GABA and benzodiazepine receptors in the medial segment of the globus pallidus and to a lesser extent in the substantia nigra pars reticulata (SNr). In contrast, the density of GABA and benzodiazepine receptors was decreased in the lateral segment of the globus pallidus.

Two different models are presented to explain these observations. The first suggests that there is a differential regulation of striatal GABAergic neurones by the intact dopamine-containing nigrostriatal system. Interruption of this system leads to increased activity in the population of neurones which project to the lateral globus pallidus, and decreased activity in those innervating the medial globus pallidus and SNr. An alternative explanation relies upon the differential distribution of D1 dopamine receptors in the projection areas of the striatum. In the SNr and medial global pallidus, where D1 dopamine receptors are probably located on the terminals of striatal projections, activation of these receptors may enhance the release of GABA. Depletion of dopamine input to these receptors would lead to a concomitant reduction in dopamine-stimulated GABA release, with ensuing GABA receptor upregulation. In the lateral globus pallidus, which is bereft of D1 dopamine receptors, there would be no such interaction, and hence GABA release and GABA receptor behaviour in this segment would be determined by the effect of dopamine on striatopallidal GABAergic neurons in the striatum alone.

Introduction

The advent of the primate MPTP model of Parkinson's disease has provided considerable insight into the neural mechanisms underlying the motor symptoms of this disease. The 2-deoxyglucose (2-DG) technique and single unit recording studies have been employed to assess the effect of striatal dopamine depletion on the activity of neurons in the primate basal ganglia.[1-3] The results from these procedures suggest that the activity of striatal neurons which project to the lateral globus pallidus is abnormally increased.

The striatal projection neurons which innervate the globus pallidus and the substantia nigra probably utilize GABA as a transmitter.[4-7] In the rat, interruption of the nigrostriatal dopamine projection also increases the apparent activity of striatopallidal neurons,[8] and this is accompanied by down-regulation of pallidal GABA receptors.[9] The present study was carried out to evaluate whether there is a compensatory down-regulation of GABA receptors in the lateral globus pallidus of MPTP-treated primates, which would support the idea that inhibitory GABAergic striatopallidal neurons are abnormally overactive in this model of Parkinson's disease.

Methods

These experiments were based on material from three hemi-parkinsonian cynomolgus monkeys (*Macaca fascicularis*) that had previously received intracarotid injections of MPTP whilst anaesthetized, and were unilaterally symptomatic at the time of sacrifice. This method is covered elsewhere in this volume (Sambrook *et al.*, p. 138). GABA receptors were visualized by autoradiography using [^{3}H]-flunitrazepam ([^{3}H]-FZ) or [^{3}H]-muscimol ([^{3}H]-MUS). Cryostat-cut sections (20 μm) were incubated with either 5 nM [^{3}H]-FZ in 50 mM Tris HCl, pH 7.4, 20°C, or 50 nM [^{3}H]-MUS in 50 mM Tris citrate, pH 7.1, at 4°C. Non-specific binding was defined by excess flunitrazepam (1 μM) and GABA (1 mM) respectively. All sections were then dried in a stream of cold air. Following 3–20 weeks exposure alongside tritium standards with tritium-sensitive film, the autoradiographs were analysed with a microcomputer-based image analysis system.

The levels of dopamine, noradrenaline, 5-HT and their metabolites in samples of brain tissue from the three animals were quantified by high pressure liquid chromatography with electrochemical detection (HPLC-ECD) using a Beckman 112 solvent delivery module and BAS electrochemical detector with LC-4 thin-layer cell. Control and integration were achieved using an IBM PC-AT with Beckman System Gold software and a Beckman 406 analogue interface.

Results

Inspection of Nissl stained sections of the midbrain from the three animals revealed that the unilateral intracarotid injection of MPTP had completely destroyed the neurons in the substantia nigra pars compacta (SNc) on the injected side of the brain. However, in two of the animals there appeared to be a limited amount of damage to the SNc on the

Table 1. *Dopamine levels (pmol/mg protein) in the striata of the unilaterally MPTP-treated primates.* L = treated side, C = non-treated side. Dopamine levels from non-treated animals are also shown for comparison.

	MPTP-treated						Non-treated
	1		2		3		
Side	L	C	L	C	L	C	
Dopamine level	2.9	219	2.8	123	10	19	341 + 68

opposite side of the brain also, which is reflected by the striatal dopamine levels as measured by HPLC-ECD (Table 1).

[^{3}H]-MUS and [^{3}H]-FZ binding was found throughout the primate brain, including the basal ganglia (Figs 1–3).

In all three animals there was a detectable asymmetry (increase with respect to the non-treated side) in the density of [^{3}H]-FZ binding in the striatum and particularly the medial globus pallidus (Table 2, and Fig. 1).

There was also an increase in benzodiazepine receptor labelling in the SNr and the subthalamic nucleus and a decrease in the lateral globus pallidus in two of the animals. There were no detectable asymmetries in these latter structures in the third, where the lesion extended well into the opposite side of the brain. The pattern of GABA receptor changes evinced by [^{3}H]-MUS binding was essentially identical to those defined by [^{3}H]-FZ (Table 1). The asymmetry in the density of binding in the medial globus pallidus was positively correlated with the degree of asymmetry in the level of striatal dopamine.

Discussion

The primate MPTP model of Parkinson's disease has recently been used to investigate the effects of dopamine depletion on the integrative processes of the striatum. 2-DG autoradiography[1,3] and unit recordings[2] have revealed that there is increased synaptic activity and decreased cell activity in the lateral globus pallidus following acute and chronic dopamine depletion with MPTP. Together these observations have been interpreted as suggesting that there is a net increase in the activity of inhibitory striatal neurons projecting to the lateral globus pallidus.

The differential regulation of striatal output?

The results from the present autoradiographic study not only support the contention that there is increased activity in the striatal efferents to the lateral globus pallidus, but in addition indicate that there may be substantial changes in the output from other striatal neurons. In higher mammals, the output from the striatum to the medial and lateral globus pallidus and the SNr seems to be derived from different populations of neurons.[5,10,11] The changes in GABA receptor density encountered in the present experiments suggest that striatal dopamine depletion could be differentially affecting the integrative processes from which the various outputs are derived. Thus the output directed at the lateral globus pallidus appears to increase, whereas the output to the medial globus pallidus and the SNr decreases. This concept was originally proposed on the basis of similar observations in the rat.[9]

However, in terms of basal ganglia output these changes would probably have an additive effect. The output from the lateral globus pallidus, which is also GABAergic and inhibitory, is directed principally at the subthalamic nucleus.[12,13] The results from these experiments

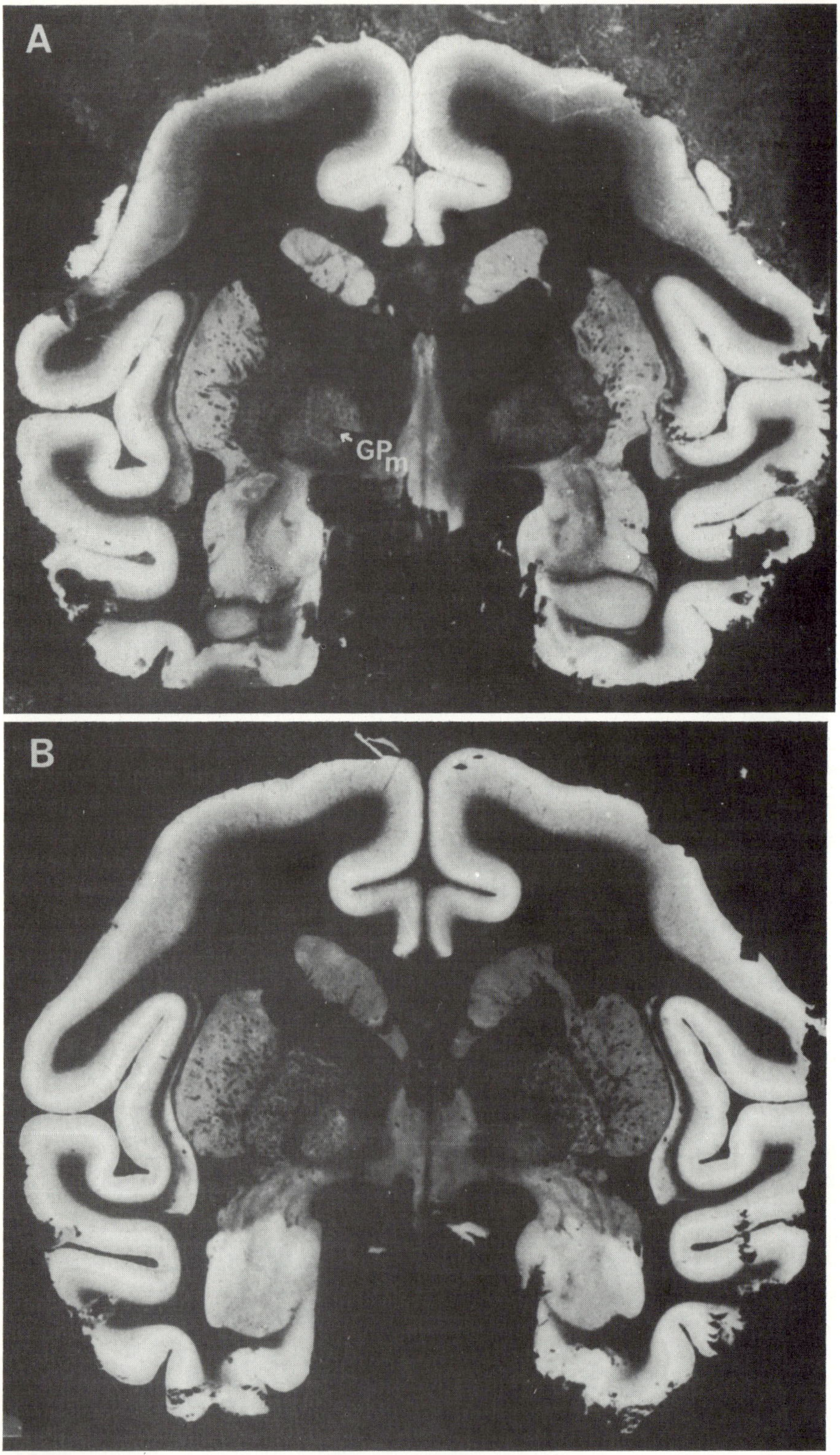
A
GPm
B

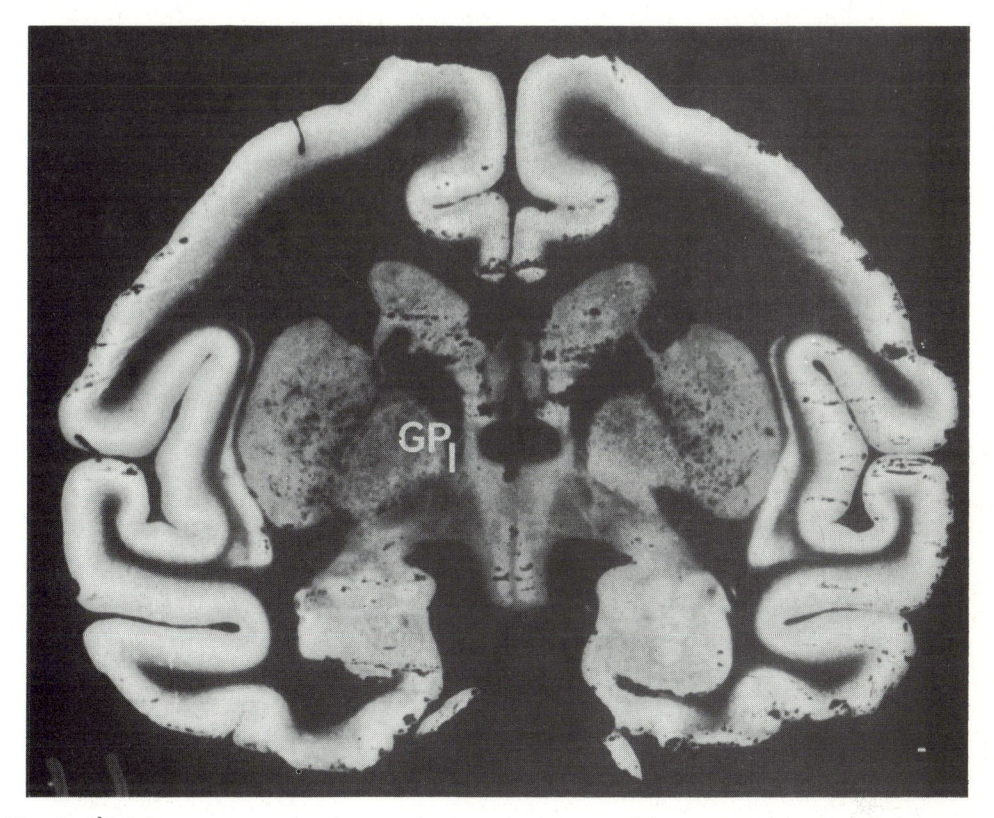

Fig. 2. *[³H]-flunitrazepam binding in the lateral globus pallidus.* Binding is decreased on the treated side of the brain. GPl = lateral segment of the globus pallidus.

and the earlier 2-DG studies suggest that the increased inhibition of the lateral globus pallidus in turn reduces the inhibition of the subthalamic nucleus. The subthalamic nucleus reciprocates the projection from the lateral globus pallidus and also innervates the striatum, medial globus pallidus and SNr.[14] The neurotransmitter utilized by the subthalamic nucleus was originally thought to be GABA also;[15] however, an emerging concensus of opinion favours a model of the basal ganglia with an excitatory subthalamic transmitter.[16-18] In this scheme, the increased inhibition of the lateral globus pallidus would be translated by the subthalamic nucleus into increased excitation of the medial globus pallidus, which, in combination with decreased inhibition directly from the striatum, should lead to an increase in medial globus pallidus activity. This conclusion is endorsed by results from single unit recordings[2] and by the preceding 2-DG experiments.[1]

The differential regulation of striatal efferents by dopamine may be a direct consequence of its physiological influence on these neurones. Although both excitatory

---

Fig. 1. *Positive prints of autoradiographs from the MPTP-treated primates.* A: [³H]-muscimol binding in the striatum and globus pallidus. B: [³H]-flunitrazepam binding in the striatum and globus pallidus. Note increased binding in the medial segment of the globus pallidus (arrow) and the striatum on the treated (left) side of the brain.

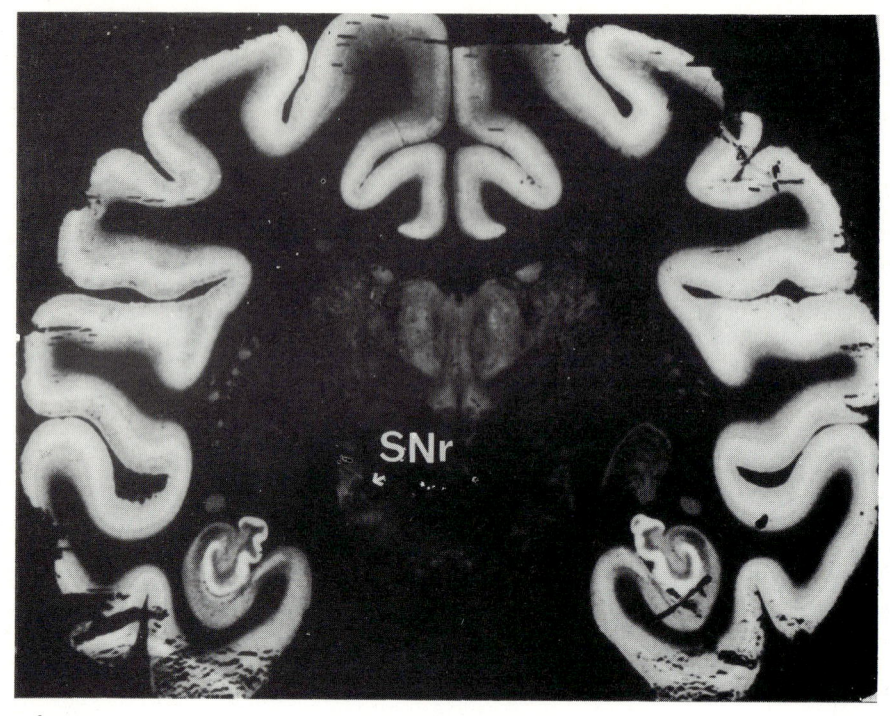

Fig. 3. *[³H]-flunitrazepam binding in the substantia nigra.* SNr = substantia nigra pars reticulata.

Table 2. *Summary of the receptor binding changes in the basal ganglia of the MPTP-treated animals.* Changes in receptor density relative to the non-treated side. Values are based on at least three determinations, or <indicates maximum asymmetry, where the changes are topographically organised. ND = not determined. GPl = lateral segment of globus pallidus; GPm = medial segment of globus pallidus; SNr = substantia nigra pars reticulata; STN = subthalamic nucleus.

		Animal		
Ligand	Structure	1	2	3
[³H]-muscimol	Striatum	+19%	<+10%	+15%
	GPl	−10%	−15%	—
	GPm	<+40%	<+25%	+11%
	SNr	+24%	<+11%	—
	STN	ND	ND	ND
[³H]-flunitrazepam	Striatum	+26%	<+10%	+15%
	GPl	−5%	<−10%	—
	GPm	<+50%	+25%	+17%
	SNr	+23%	+11%	—
	STN	+19%	+14%	—

and inhibitory effects of dopamine on striatal neurons have been observed,[19,20] the responses of striatal neurons to applied dopamine appear to be more uniform than this theory would suggest.[21] Furthermore, in the rat a substantial number of striatal neurons that project to the substantia nigra also possess collateral axons to the globus pallidus.[22]

While this does not entirely rule out the possibility of differential actions amongst the non-collateralized neurons, it may indicate that the basis for these observations lies elsewhere.

D1 dopamine receptors and the presynaptic control of GABA release from striatofugal terminals

An alternative basis for the contrasting changes in GABA receptor density in the medial globus pallidus/SNr and lateral globus pallidus may derive from the differential distribution of dopamine and D1 dopamine receptors in these structures.

There is a well defined dopaminergic innervation of the medial globus pallidus in the primate,[23] which is probably due to collateralization of the nigrostriatal system, and furthermore the nigrostriatal dopamine-containing neurons themselves extend into the SNr.[24] The distribution of dopamine in these structures coincides with the distribution of extrastriatal D1 dopamine receptors, which are particularly abundant in the medial globus pallidus and SNr, but are absent from the lateral globus pallidus in the primate.[25] This pattern of D1 dopamine receptor distribution appears in other species also.[26,27] The function of the D1 dopamine receptors at these sites may include the presynaptic control of GABA release,[28] which would be compatible with their localization on striatofugal terminals.[26] The dopaminergic neurons that innervate these structures are also lost following MPTP treatment, the levels of dopamine and homovanillic acid in the medial globus pallidus being reduced by more than 95 per cent in the MPTP-treated primate (personal observation). In the absence of a functional dopamine input these receptors will not be activated, and GABA release from the striatopallidal terminals may decrease accordingly, giving rise to an upregulation of GABA receptors. In contrast the release of GABA from the terminals of striatal projections to the lateral globus pallidus should only respond to the ebb and flow of activity from the striatum itself.

If there is any substance in this alternative basis for the observed changes in pallidal GABA receptors, then the postulated mechanism based on the differential action of dopamine in the striatum could be rendered redundant and the action of dopamine on striatal projection neurons could be more uniform. Indeed, recent electrophysiological studies suggest that while the predominant effect of dopamine is to inhibit spontaneous activity, it may enhance the effect of both inhibitory and excitatory transmitters at concentrations that have no effect on spontaneous activity.[29] This modulatory action of dopamine may have contributed to the conflicting results that have been encountered in the past.[19,20]

In a functional context, the presence of a second tier of dopamine-mediated signal processing in the medial globus pallidus/SNr may represent a system for the fine tuning of inhibitory signals from the striatum. A closer examination of the functional significance of the pallidal dopaminergic system will be required to pursue this concept.

GABA agonists in PD therapy

Increased benzodiazepine receptor binding has also been revealed post mortem in the medial globus pallidus of patients with Parkinson's disease.[30] In clinical terms, an increase in the density of GABA receptors in the output projections from the basal ganglia could provide a potential target for GABA agonist therapy. Low doses of GABA agonists augment the turning response to apomorphine in unilaterally 6-hydroxydopamine-lesioned rats, and this appears to be due to an action at non-striatal sites.[31] The value of GABA agonist therapy in Parkinson's disease has been investigated, but these studies have not provided conclusive evidence regarding its efficacy.[32,33] The primate MPTP model of Parkinson's disease could provide valuable information regarding the scope for incorporating this class of drugs in the treatment of Parkinson's disease.

Acknowledgement—the authors wish to acknowledge the financial support of the Medical Research Council.

References

1. Crossman, A. R., Clarke, C. E., Boyce, S., Robertson, R. G. & Sambrook, M. A. (1987): MPTP-induced parkinsonism in the monkey: neurochemical pathology, complications of treatment and pathophysiological mechanisms. *Can. J. Neurol.* **14**, 428–435.
2. Miller, W. C. & DeLong, M. R. (1987): Altered tonic activity of neurons in the globus pallidus and subthalamic nucleus in the primate MPTP model of parkinsonism. In *The basal ganglia II. Structure and function—current concepts*, eds M. B. Carpenter & A. Jayaraman, pp 415–427. New York: Plenum.
3. Porrino, L. J., Burns, R. S., Crane, A. M., Palombo, E., Kopin, I. J. & Sokoloff, L. (1987): Changes in local cerebral glucose utilization associated with Parkinson's syndrome induced by 1-methyl-4-phenyl-1,2,3,6-tetrahydropyridine (MPTP) in the primate. *Life Sci.* **40**, 1657–1664.
4. Fisher, R. S., Buchwald, N. A., Hull, C. D. & Levine, M. S. (1986): The GABAergic striatonigral neurons of the cat: demonstration by double peroxidase labeling. *Brain Res.* **398**, 148–156.
5. Smith, Y. & Parent, A. (1986): Differential connections of caudate nucleus and putamen in the squirrel monkey (Saimiri sciureus). *Neuroscience* **18**, 347–371.
6. Smith, Y., Parent, A., Seguela, P. & Descarries, L. (1987): Distribution of GABA-immunoreactive neurons in the basal ganglia of the squirrel monkey (Saimiri sciureus). *J. Comp. Neurol.* **259**, 50–64.
7. Kita, H. & Kitai, S. T. (1988): Glutamate decarboxylase immunoreactive neurons in rat neostriatum: their morphological types and populations. *Brain Res.* **447**, 346–352.
8. Wooten, G. F. & Collins, R. C. (1981): Metabolic effects of unilateral lesion of the substantia nigra. *J. Neuroscience* **1**, 285–291.
9. Pan, H. S., Penney, J. B. & Young, A. B. (1985): Gamma-aminobutyric acid and benzodiazepine receptor changes induced by unilateral 6-hydroxydopamine lesions of the medial forebrain bundle. *J. Neurochem.* **45**, 1396–1404.
10. Beckstead, R. M. & Cruz, C. J. (1986): Striatal axons to the globus pallidus, entopeduncular and substantia nigra come mainly from separate cell populations in cat. *Neuroscience* **19**, 147–158.
11. Feger, J. & Crossman, A. R. (1984): Identification of different subpopulations of neostriatal neurons projecting to globus pallidus or substantia nigra in the monkey: a retrograde fluorescence double labelling study. *Neurosci. Lett.* **49**, 7–12.
12. Kim, R., Nakano, K., Jayaraman, A. & Carpenter, M. B. (1976): Projections of the globus pallidus and adjacent structures: an autoradiographic study in the monkey. *J. Comp. Neurol.* **169**, 263–290.
13. Rouzaire-Dubois, B., Hammond, C., Hammon, B. & Feger, J. (1980): Pharmacological blockade of the globus pallidus-induced inhibitory response of subthalamic cells in the rat. *Brain Res.* **200**, 321–329.
14. Parent, A. & Smith, Y. (1987): Organization of efferent projections of the subthalamic nucleus in the squirrel monkey as revealed by retrograde labeling methods. *Brain Res.* **436**, 296–310.
15. Rouzaire-Dubois, B., Scarnati, E., Hammond, C., Crossman, A. R. & Shibazaki, T. (1983): Microiontophoretic studies on the nature of the neurotransmitter in the subthalamo-entopeduncular pathway of the rat. *Brain Res.* **271**, 11–20.
16. Robertson, R. G., Farmery, S. M., Sambrook, M. A. & Crossman, A. R. (1988): Dyskinesia in the primate following injection of an excitatory amino acid antagonist into the medial segment of the globus pallidus. *Brain Res.* (In Press).
17. Kita, H. & Kitai, S. T. (1987): Efferent projections of the subthalamic nucleus in the rat: light and electron microscopic analysis with the PHA-L method. *J. Comp. Neurol.* **260**, 435–452.

18. Smith, Y. & Parent, A. (1988): Neurons of the subthalamic nucleus in primates display glutamate but not GABA immunoreactivity. *Brain Res.* **453**, 353–356.
19. Kitai, S. T., Sugimori, M. & Kocsis, J. D. (1976): Excitatory nature of dopamine in the nigro-caudate pathway. *Exp. Brain Res.* **24**, 351–363.
20. Gonzales-Vegas, J. A. (1974): Antagonism of dopamine-mediated inhibition in the nigrostriatal pathway: a mode of action of some catatonia-inducing drugs. *Brain Res.* **80**, 219–228.
21. Johnson, S. W., Palmer, M. R. & Freedman, R. (1983): Effects of dopamine on spontaneous and evoked activity of caudate neurons. *Neuropharmacology* **22**, 843–851.
22. Loopuijt, L. D. & Van der Kooy, D. (1985): Organization of the striatum: collateralization of its efferent axons. *Brain Res.* **348**, 86–99.
23. Parent, A. & Smith, Y. (1987): Differential dopamine innervation of the two pallidal segments in the squirrel monkey (Saimiri sciureus). *Brain Res.* **426**, 397–400.
24. Arsenault, M.-Y., Parent, A., Seguela, P. & Descarries, L. (1988): Distribution and morphological characteristics of dopamine-immunoreactive neurons in the midbrain of the squirrel monkey (Saimiri sciueus). *J. Comp. Neurol.* **267**, 489–506.
25. Graham, W. C. & Crossman, A. R. (1987): Autoradiographic localization of dopamine D1 binding sites in areas receiving striatal output. *Eur. J. Pharmacol.* **142**, 479–481.
26. Altar, C. A. & Hauser, K. (1987): Topography of substantia nigra innervation by D1 receptor containing striatal neurons. *Brain Res.* **410**, 1–11.
27. Beckstead, R. M., Wooten, G. F. & Trugman, J. M. (1988): Distribution of D1 and D2 dopamine receptors in the basal ganglia of the cat determined by quantitative autoradiography. *J. Comp. Neurol.* **268**, 131–145.
28. Starr, M. (1987): Opposing roles of dopamine D1 and D2 receptors in nigral gamma-[3H]aminobutyric acid release? *J. Neurochemistry* **49**, 1042–1049.
29. Chiodo, L. A. & Berger, T. W. (1988): Interactions between dopamine and amino acid-induced excitation and inhibition in the striatum. *Brain Res.* **375**, 198–203.
30. Griffiths, P. D. (1988): Alterations in neurotransmitter receptors and iron content in Parkinson's disease and Alzheimer's disease. Ph.D Thesis, Manchester University.
31. Bennett, J. P., Ferrari, M. B. & Cruz, C. J. (1987): GABA-mimetic drugs enhance apomorphine-induced contralateral turning in rats with unilateral nigrostriatal dopamine denervation: implications for the therapy of Parkinson's disease. *Ann. Neurol.* **21**, 41–45.
32. Bergmann, K. J., Limongi, J. C. P., Lowe, Y. H., Mendoza, M. R. & Yahr, M. D. (1984): Potentiation of the "DOPA" effect in Parkinsonism by a direct GABA receptor agonist. *Lancet* i, 559.
33. Bartholini, G., Lloyd, K. G., Worms, P., Constantinidis, J. & Tissot, R. (1979): GABA and GABA-ergic medication: relation to striatal dopamine function and parkinsonism. In *Advances in neurology*, vol. 24, eds L. J. Poirier, T. L. Sourkes & P. J. Bedard, pp 253–257. New York: Raven Press.

18

THE SUPPLEMENTARY MOTOR CORTEX AND INTERNALLY DIRECTED MOVEMENT

D. E. Thaler and R. E. Passingham

*Department of Experimental Psychology, University of Oxford,
South Parks Rd., Oxford OX1 3UD*

Summary

The paper reports a series of behavioural studies of monkeys with bilateral removal of the supplementary motor area (SMA). The spontaneous and unlearned movements of the animals appeared normal. However, they were markedly impaired on a learned task on which they had to raise their arm with no external cue to tell them what to do. When retested after surgery the monkeys with SMA lesions made few attempts at first and their attempts were often inaccurate. It is argued that these animals are poor at retrieving the correct movement on the basis of internal instructions.

Introduction

Early in Parkinson's disease there can be a loss of dopamine in the putamen without a similar loss in the caudate.[1] Unlike the caudate the putamen influences movement via the supplementary motor area (SMA). The pathway is from putamen via ventral pallidum to the ventralateral nucleus, pars oralis, of the thalamus, and thence to the supplementary motor cortex.[2]

One way to study the function of this pathway is to study the effects on behaviour of interrupting it. We have removed the SMA bilaterally in monkeys, including the upper bank of the cingulate sulcus. It would be reasonable to expect that the removal of a somatotopically mapped area might have drastic effects on the animals' repertoire of movements. Movements of each body part can be elicited by microstimulation of the SMA,[3] and the SMA sends a heavy projection to the primary motor cortex.[4]

In fact in the six monkeys with SMA lesions that we have studied there has been no such drastic change in the monkeys' movements. In particular, the monkeys showed no signs of akinesia, nor was there any change in their reaction times or movement times as measured on a lever-pressing task. Before surgery we taught six monkeys to respond to a light by pressing and holding a lever. When the light went off the monkey had to release this lever and then press another lever placed 20 cm above it. After surgery the three monkeys with SMA lesions moved their arm up as fast as the three unoperated control monkeys.[5]

Learned movement

There might be a simple explanation for the absence of an overt effect on movement after the removal of the supplementary motor area. If the SMA plays a role in directing some learned rather than unlearned movements, then mere observation of the animals in their cages would reveal nothing. To see an effect it would be necessary to train the animals on learned motor tasks.

We therefore trained monkeys before surgery to perform a simple movement. (We have followed convention in using the term 'movement' throughout this paper, even though the term 'action' is more strictly appropriate.) To win a peanut they had only to raise their arm so as to interrupt an infra-red beam positioned at arm's length and at roughly shoulder height. Of course, the monkeys were unable to see the beam, and thus they had to learn how to position their arms. Each day the monkeys were given 65 trials. They worked at their own pace, raising their arm, picking up the peanut, and then again raising their arm.

In our first experiment the animals performed in total darkness. In such conditions we could be sure that there would be no visual guides as to the height to which the arm should be raised. We have already reported that when retrained two weeks after surgery three monkeys with bilateral SMA lesions made few successful attempts in the first four days on which they were tested.[5] Figure 1 shows the data for these animals, together with three unoperated control animals.

In a subsequent experiment we further trained the three unoperated control animals. This time the animals performed the task in dim light, and could thus see their arm.

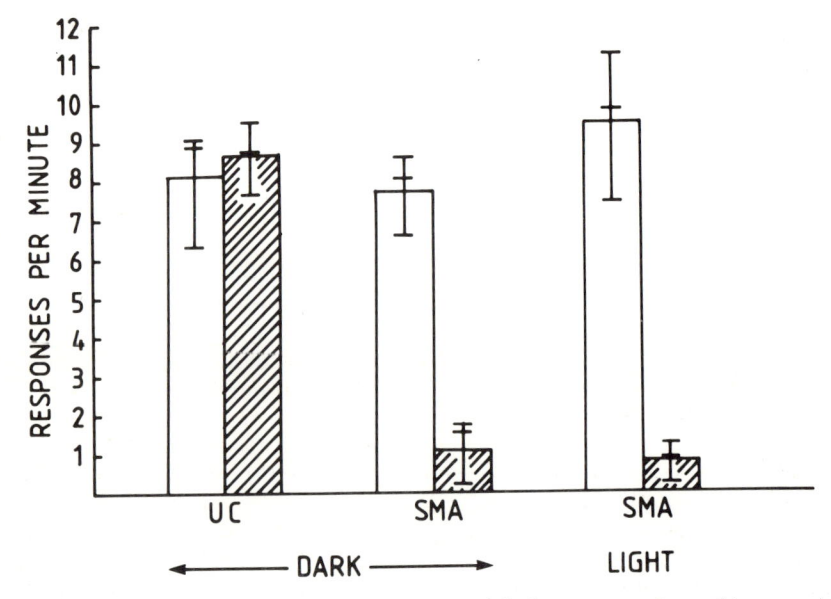

Fig. 1. *Mean responses per minute on the arm raise task before surgery (open histogram) and after (shaded histogram). Bars give data for individual animals. UC = unoperated control, SMA = monkeys with supplementary motor lesions.*

However, care was taken to ensure that there were no visual features of the room at which the animal could aim when raising its arm. The monkeys were retested on the task before surgery and were then tested again, starting two weeks after surgery. As in the previous experiment in which the animals were tested in the dark, the animals tested in the light made few successful attempts in the first four sessions after surgery (Fig. 1).

One possibility is that the monkeys with SMA lesions had trouble in actually executing the movement, that is in raising the arm. There are two reasons for being confident that the animals could in fact execute this movement normally. (1) The first experiment tested the animals for four days in the dark, and then gave them a further session in the light. On each trial in this session a peanut was placed just behind the beam so that if a monkey reached up for the peanut its hand would break the beam. It was remarkable that the monkeys with SMA lesions now reached up to take the peanut at the same rate as the control animals.[5] (2) Furthermore, as already mentioned, the same animals were also trained before and after surgery to release a lower lever and then reach up to another lever above it. The task was designed to measure movement time. The monkeys with SMA lesions were as quick to reach up to the lever as they had been before surgery.[5]

To understand why the monkeys with SMA lesions were poor at raising their arm when there was no visual target it is necessary to analyse their performance in more detail. For the three animals in the second experiment videotapes were taken of the performance of each animal before and after surgery. From this it was possible to count the number of attempts that the animal made; an animal was said to be making an attempt when it moved its arm outside the bars of the cage. In Figs 2 and 3 the number of attempts are plotted along the ordinate and the percentage success of the attempts is plotted on the abscissa. It

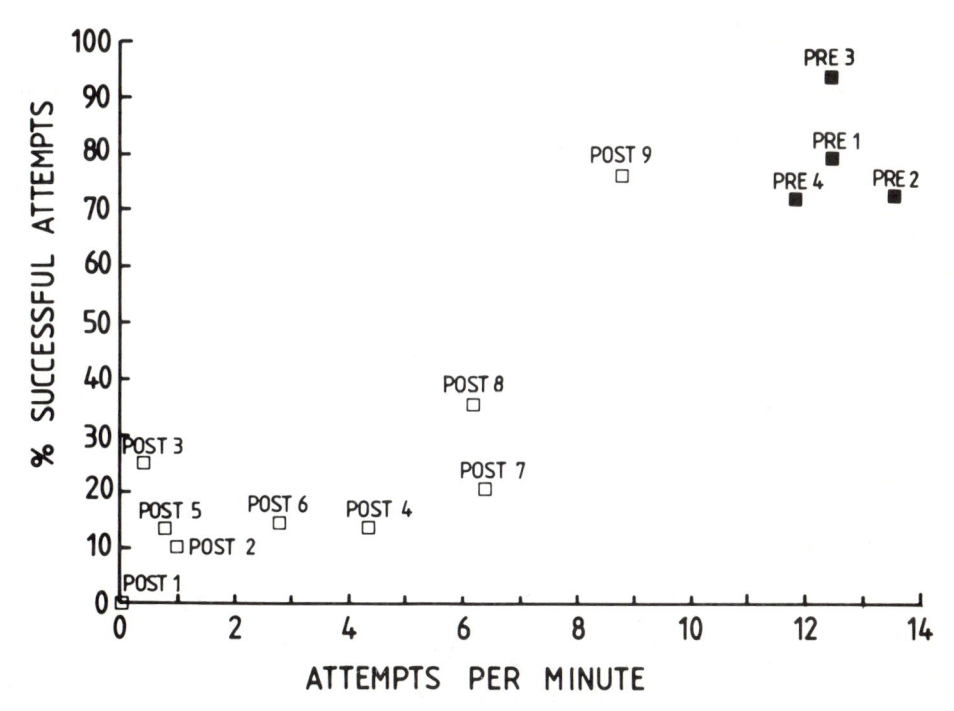

Fig. 2. *Number of attempts and success of attempts on the arm raise task for sessions before and after surgery*. Data for animal S 65. Each point gives the data for a session, and the sessions are numbered and identified as PRE (before surgery) or POST (after surgery).

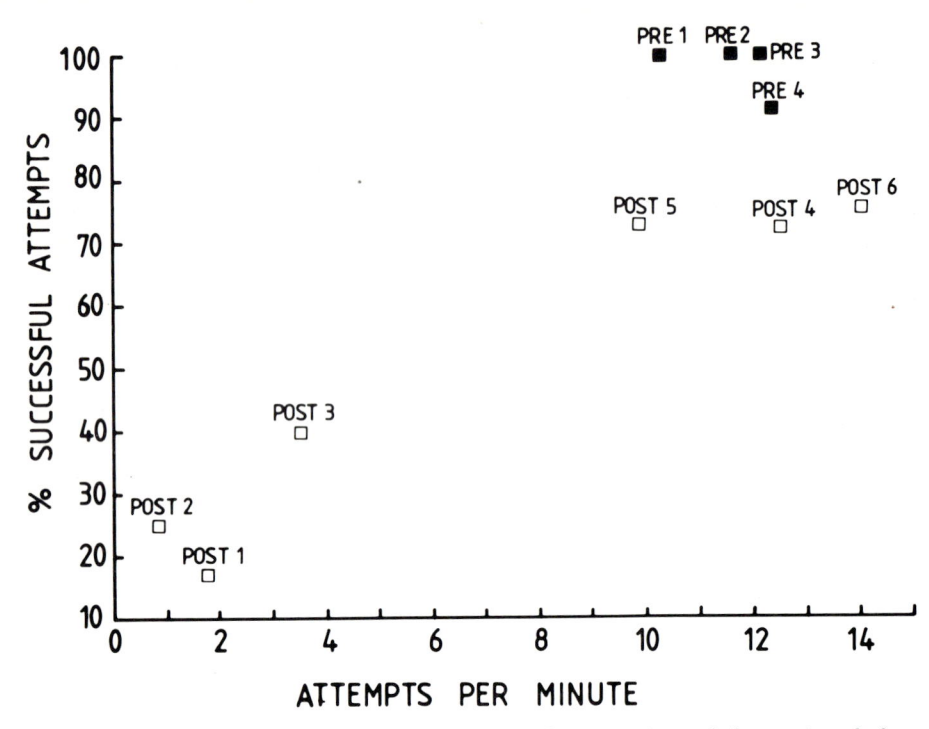

Fig. 3. *Number of attempts and success of attempts on the arm raise task for sessions before and after surgery.* Data for animal S 67. Each point gives the data for a session, and the sessions are numbered and identified as PRE (before sugery) or POST (after surgery).

is evident from these data that in the first post-operative sessions the animals made few attempts. There are two possible explanations. (1) It could be argued that they had some executive difficulty in starting the required movement. The task differs from the lever pressing task described above in that there was no external cue, such as a light, to act as a trigger. (2) It could equally be argued that they made few attempts, not because they knew what to do and could not do it, but rather because they had now forgotten what to do. The suggestion is that they were acting like animals early in training who are uncertain what they are required to do.

It is also evident from Figs 2 and 3 that as post-operative training progressed the animals made more attempts. However, it is clear from the data in Fig. 3 that, even when this animal was making as many attempts as before surgery, the attempts were less accurate. Many of the attempts failed because the arm undershot the required position. Since the animals with SMA lesions were accurate in reaching when there was a peanut for a target, one interpretation is that their difficulty is in locating the target zone when this is specified by information stored on the basis of past learning.

The initiation of movement

It has been common in the literature to discuss these issues in terms of the 'initiation' of movement. This term is unhelpful. It fails to distinguish between the two reasons given above as to why an animal or human subject might fail to perform an adequate movement. In saying that there is a problem in 'initiating' movement it is not made clear whether the trouble is in the triggering of movement or in knowing what movement to make. It is helpful to distinguish between cues that act as triggers to tell the animal when to move and cues that act to give instructions as to what should be done.

On the arm-raise task the monkeys work at their own pace. As pointed out above it could therefore be argued that the monkeys with supplementary motor area lesions may have a problem in triggering their own movements. To find out if this is so we also trained these animals on another task on which they must act without external triggering stimuli to guide them. On each trial the monkey first pressed a button on the left; it had then to wait for between five and eight seconds before operating a joystick. If the monkey moved the joystick within this period it won a peanut, if it did so earlier or later it failed to win a reward. The animals were trained until they reached a criterion level of performance over a block of 500 trials.

After surgery the three monkeys with SMA lesions were as accurate as the unoperated control animals. Figure 4 shows the mean time at which animals in each group responded. The monkeys with SMA lesions were as competent at using an internal time cue to tell them when to respond as were the control animals.

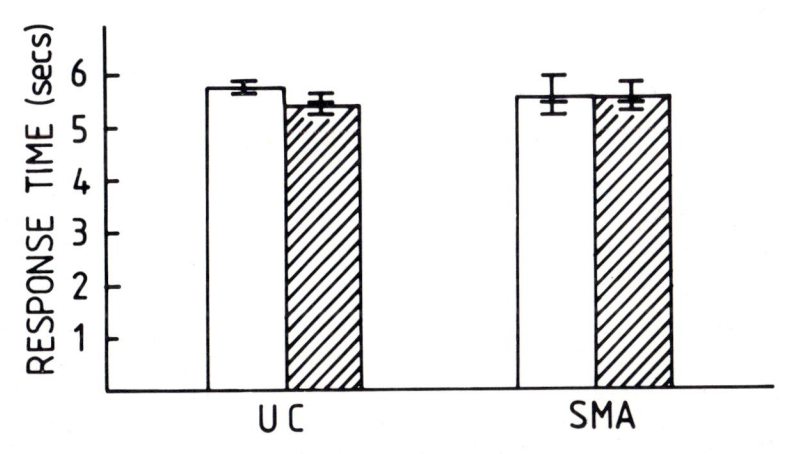

Fig. 4. *Mean times at which the monkeys waited before moving the joystick on the timing task.* Bars give data for individual animals. Data before surgery (open histogram) and after (shaded histogram). UC = unoperated control, SMA = monkeys with supplementary motor lesions.

The timing task is like the arm-raise task in that there is no external triggering stimulus, but it differs in that there is no ambiguity as to what the animal must do: the monkey can see the joystick, and the joystick acts as an external instruction to tell the animal what movement to perform. The situation in the arm-raise task is quite different: there is no cue visible to instruct the animal as to how to act. It is reasonable to conclude that monkeys with SMA lesions are poor on the arm-raise task, not because they are unable to start a movement on their own, but because they are poor at knowing what to do in the absence of an external target to instruct them.

The retrieval of movement

Requiring a monkey to reach into empty space is like asking a subject to turn his eyes into empty space. It is possible to train monkeys to make saccades in the absence of a visual target. This can be done by first specifying the location by presenting a visual target, and then removing the target and requiring the animal to make a saccade to that same position a few seconds later. Hikosaka & Wurtz[6] used such a task to study the influence of the pars reticulata of the substantia nigra on the superior colliculus. When they applied a GABA agonist to the superior colliculi there was an increase in the latency of saccades; but if the target was in memory the saccades also tended to undershoot. Unilateral lesions in the frontal eye fields have a similar effect: the monkeys can make saccades to visual targets, but the same animals are very poor at making saccades to targets in memory.[7] The same specialization can be detected by recording from cells. There are cells in the caudate nucleus[8] and in the substantia nigra pars reticulata[9] that respond particularly when a monkey remembers a target for future eye movements.

The arm-raise task differs from the eye-movement task in two respects. First, when a monkey makes a saccade to a remembered target the instruction is the memory of a visual cue. In the arm-raise task in the dark the target zone is specified only by proprioceptive information about the position of the arm when it intersects the infra-red beam. Second, in the eye-movement task the monkey is instructed on one trial to look here, on another trial there; and it must keep in working memory the position of the current target. On the arm-raise task where the target zone is constant its location is learned by the animal by cumulating information over trials.

In spite of these differences the tasks are similar in two crucial respects. First, the animal has to learn what to do. Whereas a monkey knows how to reach for a peanut and how to look at a visual target it has to be taught to reach up to break a beam or to make a saccade to a location at which a target had previously appeared. Second, in both tasks the animal must make a movement towards empty space. There is nothing in the external environment to tell the animal what to do. The instructions are given not by external cues but by information that has been stored. On both tasks the animal must retrieve the correct movement on the basis of cues that are internal.

The retrieval of a movement is like retrieving a word. The brain must find the appropriate movement given the particular context. A person who tries to think of a word may fail given one cue and yet succeed given another; and in the same way a movement may be available in one context but not in another. In the arm-raise task there are no external cues to prompt retrieval, and the animal must rely on information stored from previous learning trials.

In Parkinson's disease the poverty of spontaneous movement is often described as evidence for a problem in the 'initiation' of movement. It can as easily be viewed as an impairment in the retrieval of movement. It has been shown for the eye movement system that in Parkinson's disease the saccades to visual targets are normal in their latency, peak velocity and accuracy; it is only if the target is in memory that the saccades are inaccurate and fall short (Crawford *et al.*, this volume, p. 317). Similarly for limb movements Flowers[10] has shown that patients with Parkinson's disease are worse at a tracking task if they must act on predictions about the movement of the target that are based on information stored in memory. It is tempting to suggest that in Parkinson's disease the brain is poor at retrieving the correct movement, and that this is especially true when the movement must be retrieved on the basis of learned internal instructions.

Acknowledgements—This work was supported by a grant from the Wellcome Foundation. The senior author was partially supported by an Overseas Research Student Award (ORS 84264).

References

1 Nahmias, C., Garnett, E S., Firnau, G. & Lang, A. (1985): Striatal dopamine distribution in Parkinsonian patients during life. *J. Neurol. Sci.* **69**, 223–230.

2. Alexander, G. E., Delong, M. R. & Strick, P. L. (1986): Parallel organization of functionally segregated circuits linking basal ganglia and cortex. *Annu. Rev. Neurosci.* **9**, 357–382.
3. Mitz, A. R. & Wise, S. P. (1987): The somatotopic organization of the supplementary motor area: intracortical micro-stimulation mapping. *J. Neurosci.* **7**, 1010–1021.
4. Ghosh, S., Brinkman, C. & Porter, R. (1987): A quantitative study of the distribution of neurons projecting to the precentral motor cortex in the monkey (Macaca fascicularis). *J. Comp. Neurol.* **259**, 424–444.
5. Passingham, R. E. (1987): Two cortical systems for directing movement. In *Motor areas of the cerebral cortex*, CIBA symposium 132, p 151. Chichester: Wiley.
6. Hikosaka, O. & Wurtz, R. H. (1985): Modification of saccadic eye movements by GABA-Related substances. I. Effect of muscimol and bicuculline in monkey superior colliculus. *J. Neurophysiol.* **53**, 266–291.
7. Deng, S-Y., Segraves, M. A., Ungerleider, L. G., Mishkin, M. & Goldberg, M. E. (1984): Unilateral frontal eye field lesions degrade saccadic performance in the rhesus monkey. *Soc. Neurosci. Abstr.* **10**, 218.
8. Hikosaka, O. & Sakamoto, M. (1986): Cell activity in monkey caudate nucleus preceding saccadic eye movements. *Exp. Brain Res.* **63**, 659–662.
9. Hikosaka, O. & Wurtz, R. H. (1983): Visual and oculomotor functions of monkey substantia nigra pars reticulata. III. Memory-contingent visual and saccade responses. *J. Neurophysiol.* **49**, 1268–1284.
10. Flowers, K. (1978): Lack of prediction in the motor behaviour of Parkinsonism. *Brain* **101**, 35–52.

19

ANATOMICAL, BEHAVIOURAL AND POSITRON EMISSION TOMOGRAPHY STUDIES OF UNILATERAL EXCITOTOXIC LESIONS OF THE BABOON CAUDATE-PUTAMEN AS A PRIMATE MODEL OF HUNTINGTON'S DISEASE

Ph. Hantraye*, D. Riche†, M. Maziere*, B. Maziere*,
C. Loc'h* and O. Isacson‡

*Service Hospitalier Frédéric Joliot, Commissariat à l'Energie Atomique, Institut de Recherche Fondamentale, Département de Biologie, Orsay, 91406, France; ‡Department of Anatomy, University of Cambridge, Downing Street, Cambridge, CB2 3DY, UK; †Laboratoire de Physiologie Nerveuse équipe de Neuroanatomie Fonctionnelle, Centre National de la Recherche Scientifique, Gif-sur-Yvette, 91198, France

Summary

A primate model of Huntington's disease has been developed in the baboon with the objective of testing therapeutic strategies for pharmacological and neuronal transplantation. Positron emission tomography may also be a valuable tool in determining presymptomatic degeneration of the caudate-putamen in the disease. Our results indicate that an excitotoxic unilateral lesion of caudate-putamen can cause dramatic hyperactivity and dyskinesias in the baboon under apomorphine stimulation. The neuropathological similarity between the excitotoxic lesion in the baboon and features of brain affected by Huntington's disease is also striking.

Introduction

Huntington's disease, an inherited autosomal dominant[1] neurodegenerative disease, is clinically characterized in man by choreiform irregular and involuntary movements of the whole body. Classically, the neuropathology associated with Huntington's disease consists of gross generalized cerebral atrophy involving mostly the caudate-putamen (CP) (80–90 per cent atrophy), the globus pallidus and the cerebral cortex (layers 3,5,6 of Brodmann), while the thalamus and brainstem are not usually affected. The damage to the neostriatum results in severe gliosis and secondary dilatation of the ventricular system.[2,3] The best correlation with the severity of symptoms appears to be with how much atrophy has occurred in the caudate and putamen nuclei, as determined by a lesion grade such as that of Von Sattel et al.[4] To replicate the main neuropathological and clinical features of the disease in the sub-human primate, as a working model for future pharmacological strategies and studies of the effects of neural transplantation, we have made excitotoxic lesions of the CP in the baboon *Papio papio*.[5] Such striatal lesions have been shown previously to be remarkably similar to the neuropathology of Huntington's disease, with behavioural manifestations and deficits in memory and cognitive tests in rodents.[6–9] Since it has also been demonstrated (in rodents) that even a unilateral model of a striatal lesion can reliably be used to test lesion-induced changes in terms of morphology, behaviour, memory and cognition, we decided to develop such an unilateral model in the baboon. Using this model, we found very few spontaneous behavioural abnormalities following subtotal ablations of the CP. However, as has been shown previously in man, administration of dopaminergic receptor agonists can aggravate the symptoms of Huntington's disease patients or even be used in presymptomatic drug testing to exacerbate choreic movements in persons at risk for the disease. Therefore we decided to test the effect of apomorphine administration in asymptomatic baboons suffering from unilateral subtotal lesions of the striatum. Finally, in order to investigate whether positron emission tomography (PET) can be used to diagnose patients at risk for Huntington's disease, [76]Br-bromolisuride PET scans in normal baboons were compared with those performed in three ibotenic-acid-lesioned baboons.

Methods

Ten *Papio papio* and one *Papio anubis* baboons were used. Six animals received unilateral ibotenic acid (IA) injections (350–700 μg) into the right CP, while the remaining five served as controls for behavioural testing and PET studies. Before, and between 2 to 39 weeks after IA lesions, the animals were tested for changes in locomotor activity and motor dyskinesia over a 60 min period, before (spontaneous behaviour) and after injection of different doses of the dopamine agonist drug apomorphine (apomorphine-induced behaviour). All sessions were video-recorded and animals were rated using an index for abnormal movements such as motor dyskinesia and stereotypy. With the exception of two baboons additionally used for PET scanning, lesioned animals were perfused for histological and immunocytochemical analysis, after the behavioural assessment was completed.

Excitotoxic lesions of the right CP were performed (under ketamine-xylazine anaesthesia) during two lesion sessions separated by an average period of 14 days. During the two sessions, IA injections were made under stereotaxic control into the putamen (P) (three injections of 50–100 μg) and the caudate nucleus (four injections of 50–100 μg). Lesion parameters for caudate nucleus were: L:4.5,6; A:28,27; V:15,16; and for putamen: L:12,13; A:27,26,25; V:11,12, from stereotaxic zero. Immediately after surgery, animals received an injection of doxapram chlorhydrate (10 mg/kg intravenously) to counteract the respiratory depressant effect of IA and anaesthetics. Behaviour of the animals was recorded by means of a video camera coupled to a digital clock and a video-recorder. All test sessions (60 min testing, preceded by 60 min habituation) were videotaped to allow subsequent verification of observations and quantification. For apomorphine testing, the video-recording was initiated immediately after the administration of the dopamine agonist compound. Changes in behaviour after unilateral excitotoxic lesions of the striatum were then rated as: (1) changes in locomotor activity and (2) presence of abnormal and dyskinetic movements using a behavioural scale for dyskinesia and involuntary movements (Table 1).

Table 1. *Behavioural scale and categories for dopamine-agonist drug testing.*

Scale	Behaviour
0	sitting—no general locomotion—some mild motor stereotypies such as repetitive and symmetric head movements
1	some locomotion—standing up—motor stereotypies such as repetitive head, face, arm, hand, trunk or leg movements that are mostly asymmetric—tail catatonus—postural asymmetry
2	locomotion—strong motor activation such as general repetitive movements of the trunk and extremities, strong stereotypic jaw movements and biting
3	explosive locomotion such as jumps and ballistic movements of extremities and jerky body movements
4	asymmetric locomotion, stereotypic turning in circles (ipsilateral to the lesioned side)

Locomotor activity

Changes in locomotor activity were measured by visual inspection during the first 40 min of each test and before and after apomorphine administration. These measurements included assessment of: (1) resting time —time spent by the animal sitting or resting on the floor; (2) suspension time—time spent by the animal clung to the cage bars; (3) standing time—time spent in standing up or moving in the cage; (4) number of half clockwise movements—180° turns to the right side; (5) number of half anti-clockwise movements; and (6) net turning—as the number of half clockwise movements minus the number of half anti-clockwise movements.

Dyskinetic movements

Animals were also rated for dyskinetic movements, dystonic postures and irregular and involuntary movements during the first 60 min of the test using the index for dopamine agonist drug testing described in Table 1. The final score (dyskinesia index over a 60 min period) was obtained by adding together the behavioural scores (see scale, Table 1) calculated for each 10 min period of time.

For the PET studies, a PET system (time-of-flight LETI-TTV01, France) equipped with four detector rings and allowing scanning of seven trans-axial 15 mm thick cross-sections, was used. Five sections covered the whole baboon brain with cerebellum and striata being present on the second and the third sections, respectively. During the experiment (3 h duration), the anaesthetized baboon was laying on a bed equipped with a head holder. Data acquisition was started immediately after the administration of the radiotracer. Regions of interest were selected visually on the reconstructed PET images. The radioactivity in each image was corrected for radioactive decay of the radionuclide ([76]Br, $T_{\frac{1}{2}} = 16.2$ h) to the time of administration. [76]Br-bromolisuride was used for the specific *in vivo* labelling of the dopaminergic D2 receptors. Synthesis of the radiotracer was done according to the procedure previously described elsewhere.[10] Changes in radioactive concentrations with time were determined for left and right striata and for cerebellum. Specific binding of the radiotracer in the striata was calculated as the ratio of radioactive concentrations in the left and right striatal regions of interest (total *in vivo* binding) to that present in the cerebellar region of interest (non-specific binding and free concentration of the tracer), according to Maziere *et al.*[10]

Results

Anatomical results

Of the six IA-lesioned baboons analysed for behavioural changes (see below), four were used for histological analysis:

Baboon 1 received a total dose of 700 μg IA in the right CP during one session. As the animal could not sustain its own breathing after the lesion, it had to be artificially ventilated and was sacrificed after one day. Frozen sections (40 μm thick, cresyl-violet-stained) showed damaged areas involving the majority of the caudate nucleus and a large part of the putamen. Considerable oedematous tissue damage was also seen in different cortical areas and in the contralateral caudate nucleus.

Baboon 2 received an effective dose of 350 μg and was sacrificed 6 months after lesion. Frozen sections revealed small lesions in the dorsomedial aspect of the caudate nucleus and in the dorsolateral part of the putamen. Sections tested for acetylcholinesterase (AChE) showed a greatly reduced reaction in the lesioned areas (Fig. 1A). Using a polyclonal antibody against glial fibrillary acidic protein (GFAP), visualized using the PAP method, intense astrocytic gliosis was observed in the lesioned areas (Fig. 1B).

Baboon 3, which received a dose of 350 μg, was sacrificed 5 months later. Paraffin sections showed an enlargement of the lateral ventricle and a small lesion restricted to the most dorsomedial part of the NC (Fig. 1C). The volume of the lesion was approximately 5–10 per cent of the total volume of the structure. Additional minor excitotoxic damage was observed in cortical areas (calloso-marginal gyrus and the depth of the sulcus rectus) (Fig. 1D).

Baboon 4 received 700 μg IA into the right CP and was perfused 1 month later. In this case the excitotoxic damage involved approximately 50–70 per cent of the total CP. The enlargement of the lateral ventricle was substantial. Frozen sections stained for AChE showed reduced reaction in the injected area of the caudate nucleus and a patchy appearance in the rest of the structure. In the putamen the reaction was lowered compared to the contralateral normal putamen. The same phenomenon could be observed in the right globus pallidus (Fig. 2A). With GFAP staining, there was an intense reaction in the lesioned areas with reactive hypertrophied astrocytes observed in the injected putamen (Fig. 2B). With this staining, some reaction was also observed in the globus pallidus, compared to the contralateral intact side (cf[7]).

Behaviour

Two to five days post-lesion, the baboons recovered normal behaviour. Only a few

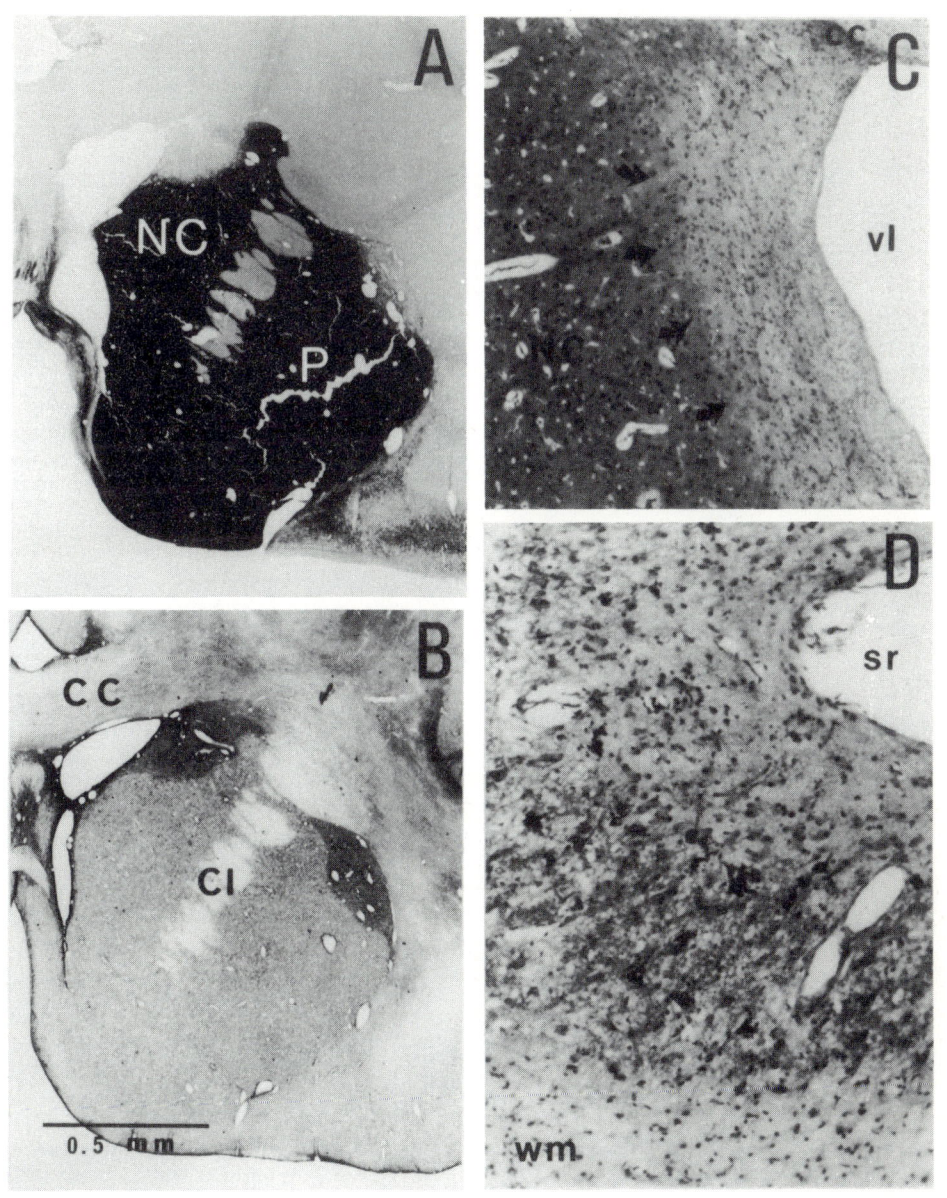

Fig. 1. *Two adjacent frozen sections (40 μm thick) from baboon 4 injected with 700 μg ibotenic acid (IA) into the right CP, showing obvious enlargement of the lateral ventricle (vl) and the shrinkage of the caudate nucleus (NC) on the lesioned side.* (A) Section reacted for acetylcholinesterase. On the right side, the reaction is considerably reduced and takes a patchy appearance in the caudate nucleus (NC). In a large part of the putamen (P), the reaction is also reduced. The globus pallidus (GP), very pale compared to the normal side, seems to be devoid of any reaction. (B) Section reacted for glial fibrillary acidic protein (GFAP) and slightly counterstained with cresyl violet. The reactive glia is difficult to observe in the caudate nucleus at this magnification, but in the putamen, where hypertrophic astrocytes were found, a darker reaction (beneath fibres of the internal capsule) can be seen. Some positive reaction can be observed in the globus pallidus, compared to the normal side.

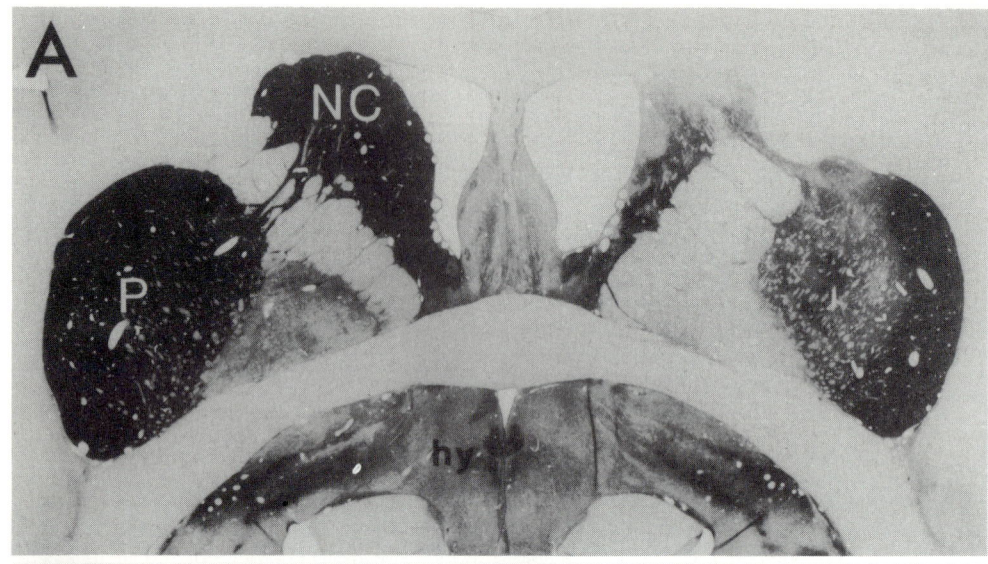

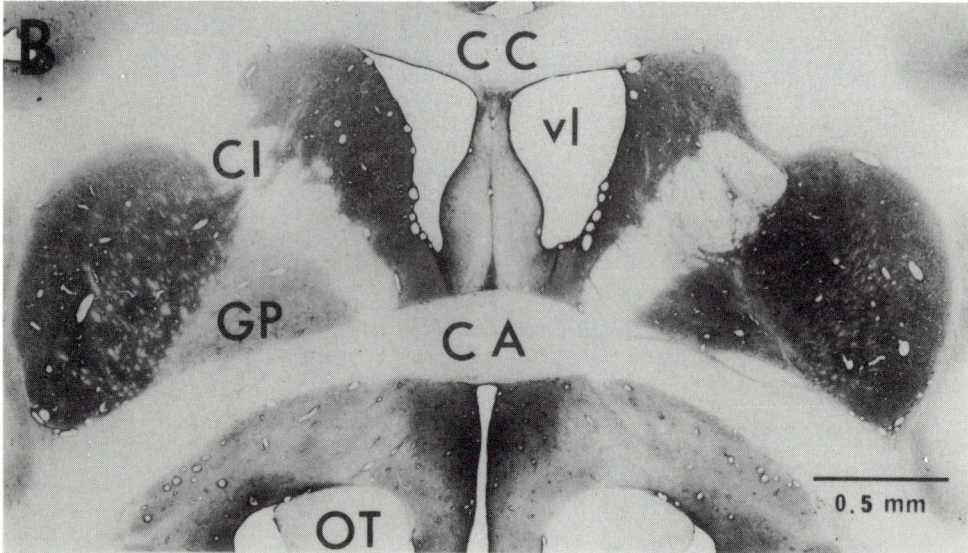

Fig. 2. *Histological appearances after injections of ibotenic acid (IA) into the caudate-putamen (CP)*. (A) Frozen section from baboon 2 injected with 350 μg IA into the right CP, reacted for acetylcholinesterase (60 μg thick). The reaction is very dark and the pale lesioned parts in the dorsal NC and in the dorsolateral part of the P are easily distinguished. (B) Adjacent section reacted for glial fibrillary acidic protein (GFAP) and slightly counterstained with cresyl violet. The lesioned parts of the CP containing reactive astrocytes appear darker than the rest of the structure. (C) Photomicrographs of paraffin section (10 μm thick, cresyl-violet-stained) from baboon 3 showing the lesion involving the dorsomedial aspect of the caudate nucleus. Arrows point to the limit between the lesion (on the right) and normal tissue (on the left). Magnification: ×80. (D) shows at higher magnification a small cortical lesion in the depth of the sulcus rectus (sr). Mostly the deep layers (III, IV, V, VI) are affected. Some dark pyramidal neurons can be observed surrounded by glia. Magnification ×150. Abbreviations: CA, anterior commissure; CC, corpus callosum; CI, internal capsule; GP, globus pallidus; Hy, hypothalamus; NC, nucleus caudatus; OT, optic tract; P, putamen; sr, sulcus rectus; vl, lateral ventricle; wm, white matter.

spontaneous abnormal head movements were seen in lesioned animals. These occasional (but repetitive when occurring) dyskinetic head movements consisted typically of a brisk full turn of the head from the left to the right side.

Changes in locomotor activity. As indicated in the methods section, the behaviour of the animals was quantified in terms of changes in locomotor activity and occurrence of dyskinetic movements. Control animals spontaneously spent about twice the amount of time in the resting state compared to standing up (Fig. 3, open bar, 'spontaneous', standing time divided by resting time). This activity score corresponds roughly to a description of active/inactive states. This ratio was maintained after IA-lesioning (1 to 39 weeks) such that the mean spontaneous activity score afterwards (cross-hatched bars, spontaneous, Fig. 3) was not significantly different from the score prior to the lesion. Following apomorphine injection (0.5 mg/kg dose), the activity score in IA-lesioned baboons was not different compared to control (open bars, apomorphine 0.5 mg/kg, Fig. 3) or spontaneous activity scores performed by the animals either before (open bars, spontaneous, Fig. 3) or after lesioning (cross-hatched bars, spontaneous, Fig. 3). However, there was a dramatic and statistically significant increase in activity following administration of 1 mg/kg apomorphine in the IA-lesioned baboons (cross-hatched bars, apomorphine 1 mg/kg, Fig. 3). There was also a significant decrease in activity score in intact animals at this dose compared to the other test conditions. The direct quantification of rotational behaviour in the baboons is shown in Fig. 4. Normal animals showed no turning behaviour either before (spontaneous) or after administration of 1 mg/kg apomorphine. However, following the IA lesion, two animals showed a stereotypic asymmetric turning behaviour (baboon 5 and baboon 4, in Fig. 4) directed towards the side ipsilateral to the lesion, similar to that observed in rodents following large CP lesions.

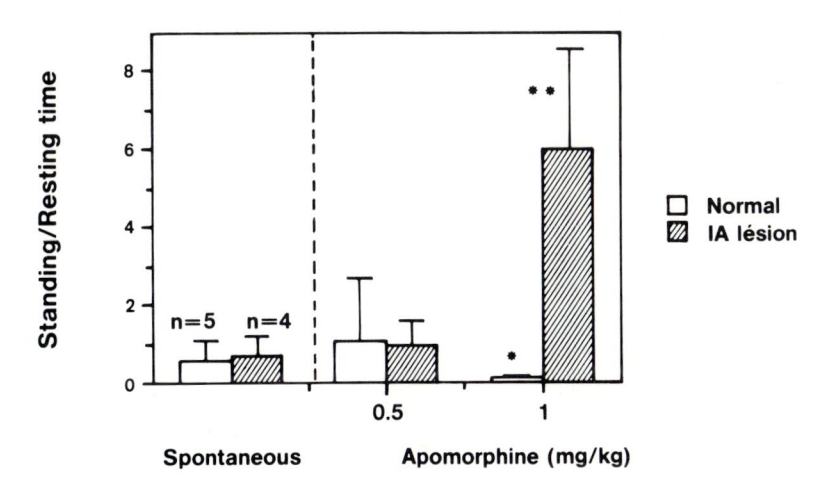

Fig. 3. *Activity score is given as the ratio of the time spent standing divided by time in resting position (mean, SD).* Spontaneous and apomorphine-induced (0.5 and 1 mg/kg) activity scores are shown for normal baboons (n = 5) and IA-lesioned baboons (n = 4). Note the significant increase in the given activity score for the IA-lesioned animals after apomorphine (1 mg/kg) and the significant decrease ($p < 0.05$) in activity scores at 1 mg/kg apomorphine for normal animals.

TURNING BEHAVIOUR

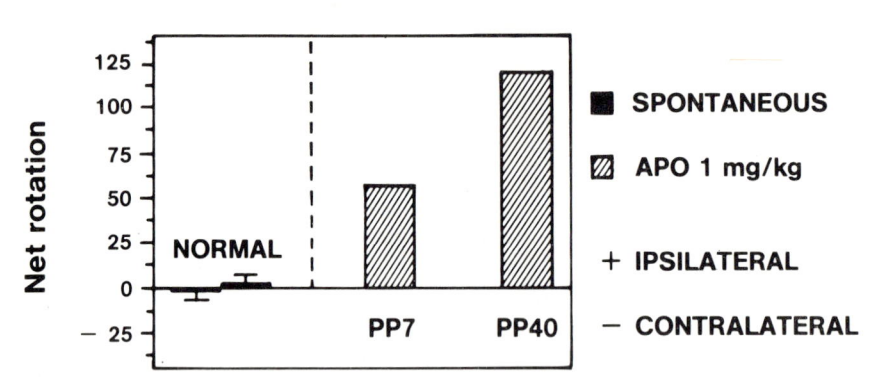

Fig. 4. *Rotational behaviour on apomorphine administration (1 mg/kg)*. Net rotation was calculated as described in the methods section. Normal intact animals (n = 4) showed no asymmetry, while 2 out of 5 IA-lesioned animals (baboons 5 and 4) showed some ipsilateral rotational behaviour.

Apomorphine-induced dyskinesias. The most dramatic features of the behaviours seen on apomorphine administration after IA-lesioning were the various dyskinetic movements observed. Thus, while normal baboons never showed any abnormal movement, a variety of asymmetric stereotypic motor behaviours, explosive movements or asymmetric turning behaviours have been observed with apomorphine treatment in all the IA-lesioned animals. Normal animals responded to 1 mg/kg apomorphine by decreased locomotor activity (see Fig. 3) and repetitive symmetrical head movements (head bobbing). In contrast, the lesioned animals showed repetitive dyskinetic movements of the trunk and limbs as well as the head. Associated with general dyskinesias, there was sometimes stereotypic jaw movements, biting behaviours and also typical dystonic movements or postures. The most pronounced abnormal movement was a stereotypic turning, almost exclusively directed towards the lesioned side (ipsilateral turning). Comparing the severity of the striatal lesions with the dyskinesias observed at 4–8 weeks after lesion, it is clear that animals with the smaller lesions (after 350 μg IA injected in the CP) had the mildest symptoms. As for activity score, the dyskinesias induced by apomorphine in the lesioned animals did not show signs of recovery and persisted for 5–6 months.

Positron emission tomography

[76]Br-bromolisuride PET experiments were performed in six normal baboons and in three different IA-lesioned baboons which received either 350 μg (two animals) or 700 μg (one animal) IA into the right CP. As the IA lesion essentially induced a decrease in the specific binding of the dopamine D2 receptor antagonist in the injected structures (caudate nucleus and putamen), we chose to assess the effects of IA lesions on PET experiments by calculating a left to right ratio (L/R Ratio in Fig. 5). This L/R ratio corresponds to the description of an index of asymmetry between the specific binding of the radiotracer observed in the left (unlesioned) striatum divided by the specific binding observed in the right (IA-lesioned) striatum. Thus, a decrease in the specific binding occurring in the injected structure will correspond to an increase in the L/R ratio. As shown in Fig. 5, no asymmetry was found in normal animals (L/R ratio = 1.01 ± 0.05) demonstrating the good reproducibility of the method. In contrast there was a significant increase in the

**IBOTENIC ACID-LESIONED BABOONS :
POSITRON EMISSION TOMOGRAPHY AND BEHAVIOUR**

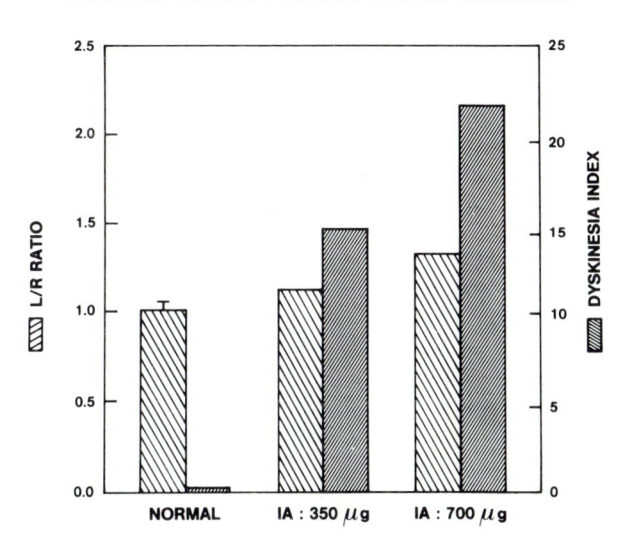

Fig. 5. ^{76}*Br-bromolisuride PET scans in normal and IA-lesioned baboons: relation with abnormal movements.* L/R ratio is given as the ratio of the specific binding of the radiotracer in the unlesioned striatum (left) divided by the specific binding in the IA-lesioned striatum (right). Specific binding of ^{76}Br-bromolisuride was assessed as previously described in the methods section. Dyskinesia scores (from dyskinesia index described in Table 1) after apomorphine injection are given for comparison. Note that normal animals (n = 6) had zero score on the dyskinesia index and an L/R ratio close to 1 (no asymmetry). An increase in the given L/R ratio was noted for all IA-lesioned animals, related to an increase in the dyskinesia scores.

L/R ratio in all IA-lesioned baboons, this effect being more pronounced in the animal with the largest lesion of the CP (L/R = 1.32). These changes (decreases) in the specific binding of ^{76}Br-bromolisuride were observed in IA-lesioned animals under 'spontaneous conditions', ie, without apomorphine injected. These alterations in the specific binding of ^{76}Br-bromolisuride observed *in vivo* by PET in asymptomatic IA-lesioned baboons were compared to the changes in the behaviours observed in the same animals on apomorphine treatment and quantified using the dyskinesia index described in Table 1. As noted from Fig. 5, an alteration in the specific binding of the radiotracer in the right striatum always corresponded to an increase in the dyskinesia index observed on apomorphine testing (1 mg/kg).

Discussion

The excitotoxic lesions of the CP of the baboon presented here produce a neuropathological correlate of Huntington's disease. Although few spontaneous abnormal movements were observed following unilateral lesions, a number of dyskinetic movements and locomotor abnormalities were provoked by administration of a systemic dopamine agonist. Since these drug-induced dyskinesias seemed to correlate well with the size and location of the striatal lesions, we suggest that dyskinesias resulting from impaired striatal function are unmasked by driving the basal ganglia circuitry by dopamine agonist treatment, as was the case for the use of levodopa in a previous prediagnostic test of patients at risk for Huntington's disease. Since we rarely observed spontaneous dyskinesias in the unilaterally lesioned animals (apart from abnormal dyskinetic head movements), while the same animals displayed dramatic dyskinesias on apomorphine administration (1 mg/kg) that were sometimes bilateral, it is necessary to consider the mechanisms underlying these phenomena. Firstly, the excitotoxic CP lesion was only partial and left between 40 and 90 per cent of the remaining CP complex structurally intact. Therefore it is likely that compensatory increase in the output of the remaining CP neurons could maintain almost normal motor control under spontaneous conditions. However, apomorphine administration would drive the basal ganglia circuitry through activation of the contralateral striatum (and associated substantia nigra and pallidal nuclei) and the remaining ipsilateral striatum (such as the nucleus accumbens). This dopaminergic activation would then elicit dyskinesias by overriding the compensatory mechanims of, for example, increased pallidal inhibition on the side ipsilateral to the CP lesion. Recent work in basal ganglia function in the primate also suggests that it is the globus pallidus pars lateralis that renders the system susceptible to chorea and dyskinesias.[11] In the histological analysis of the IA lesion of the CP we observed that even a lesion of only 10–20 per cent of the total CP volume, particularly when the lesion occurred in the dorsal CP, produced an increased locomotor activity (Fig. 3) and dyskinesias (Fig. 5) under apomorphine stimulation. Further, it can be deduced from the histological analysis that the extent or the size of the CP lesion (lesion grade) roughly corresponded to the degree of dyskinesia observed in the behavioural analysis. Interestingly, the most affected parts of the CP complex were always dorsal (even after injection of 700 µg of IA), even though the injections sites were aimed more centrally in the CP (see Fig. 1). This may be compared with previous neuropathological studies of *post mortem* Huntington's disease striata[4] showing a progressive degeneration of the CP complex, starting in the dorsal aspects of the head of the caudate and the putamen. Later in the disease, the entire CP complex apart from the relatively spared ventral nucleus accumbens degenerates.[4] It can therefore be hypothesized that if the disease process occurs by an excitotoxic mechanism, the CP complex could be differentially sensitive to this process in a dorso-lateral and rostro-caudal order. PET experiments in IA-lesioned baboons were performed using ^{76}Br-bromolisuride, a highly specific dopamine D2 receptor antagonist. As the D2 receptors are almost exclusively located on neurons whose soma reside in the CP,[12] the decrease observed in the striatal-specific binding of ^{76}Br-bromolisuride after injection of IA into the CP of the baboon would then reflect a selective loss in neurons intrinsic to this structure. In all the lesioned baboons tested, a decrease in the specific binding of the D2 receptor antagonist was always noted, even in the two animals with small lesions of the CP, indicating that such a loss of intrinsic neurons can be visualized *in vivo* using the PET methodology. Interestingly, these changes in D2 receptor binding were noted in IA-lesioned baboons under 'spontaneous' conditions, ie, in absence of apomorphine, when these animals are essentially asymptomatic (see Results, behavioural experiments). This finding indicates, as has been previously described, that PET[13,14] can be used to detect striatal damage, and more specially suggests that PET scanning, using ^{76}Br-bromolisuride as ligand, could be utilized to detect small striatal lesions, even in presymptomatic patients or patients at risk for Huntington's disease.[14] Work in progress is directed towards systematic studies of the potential of neural replacement by striatal transplants to reverse or alleviate the behavioural syndrome observed in this lesion model.

Acknowledgements—The authors acknowledge the skilful assistance of J. Cayla. Grant support from contract DRET n° 88-053 (M. M.), the Swedish MRC, Royal Academy of Sciences and Fernstrom Foundation (O.I.) is gratefully acknowledged. P. H. is a fellow from the Fondation pour la Recherche Médicale and the Association Claude Bernard.

References

1 Gusella, J. F., Wexler, N. S., Conneally, P. M., Naylor, S. L., Anderson, M. A., Tanzi, R. E., Watkins, P. C., Ottina, K., Wallace, M. R., Sakaguchi, A. Y., Young, A. B., Shoulson, I., Bonilla, E. & Martin, J. B. (1983): A polymorphic DNA marker genetically linked to Huntington's disease. *Nature* **306**, 234–238.
2 Martin, J. B. (1984): Huntington's disease: new approaches to an old problem. *Neurology* **34**, 1059–1072.

3 Sanberg, P. R. & Coyle, J. T. (1984): Scientific approaches to Huntington's disease, *CRC Crit. Rev. Clin. Neurobiol.* **1**, 1–44.
4 Von Sattel, J. P., Myers, R. H., Stevens, T. J., Ferrante, R. J., Bird, E. D. & Richardson, E. P. (1985): Neuropathological classification of Huntington's disease, *J. Neuropathol. Exp. Neurol.* **44**, 559–567.
5 Hantraye, Ph., Riche, D., Maziere, M. & Isacson, O. (1988): A primate model of Huntington's disease: Anatomical and behavioural studies of unilateral excitotoxic lesions of the caudate putamen in the baboon (submitted to *Brain Res.*).
6 Coyle, J. T. & Schwarcz, R. (1976): Lesion of striatal neurons with kainic acid provides a model for Huntington's chorea. *Nature* **263**, 244–246.
7 Isacson, O., Fischer, W., Wictorin, K., Dawbarn, D. & Björklund, A. (1987): Astroglial response in the excitotoxically lesioned neostriatum and its projection areas in the rat. *Neuroscience* **20**, 1043–1056.
8 Beale, M. F., Kowall, N. W., Ellison, D. W., Mazurek, M. F., Swartz, K. J. & Martin, J. B. (1986): Replication of the neurochemical characteristics of Huntington's disease by quinolinic acid. *Nature* **321**, 168–171.
9 Isacson, O., Dunnett, S. B. & Björklund, A. (1986): Graft-induced behavioural recovery in an animal model of Huntington's disease. *Proc. Natl. Acad. Sci. USA* **83**, 2728–2732.
10 Maziere, B., Loc'h, C., Stulzaft, O., Hantraye, P., Ottaviani, M., Comar, D. & Maziere, M. (1986): 76Br-bromolisuride: a new tool for quantitative in vivo imaging of D2 dopamine receptors. *Eur. J. Pharmacol.* **127**, 239–247.
11 Crossman, A. R., Sambrook, M. A. & Jackson, A. (1984): Experimental hemichorea/hemiballismus in the monkey. Studies on the intracerebral site of action in a drug-induced dyskinesia. *Brain* **107**, 579–596.
12 Joyce, J. T. & Marshall, J. F. (1987): Quantitative autoradiography of dopamine D2 sites in rat caudate-putamen: localization to intrinsic neurons and not to neocortical afferents. *Neuroscience* **20**, 773–795.
13 Hagglund, J., Aquilonius, S. M., Eckernas, S. A., Hartvig, P., Lundquist, H., Gullberg, P. & Langstrom, B. (1987): Dopamine receptor properties in Parkinson's disease and Huntington's chorea evaluated by positron emission tomography using 11C-N-methyl spiperone. *Acta Neurol. Scand.* **75**, 87–94.
14 Young, A. B., Penney, J. B., Starosta-Rubinstein, S., Markel, D., Berent, S., Rothley, J., Betley, A. & Hichwa, R. (1987): Normal caudate glucose metabolism in persons at risk for Huntington's disease. *Arch. Neurol.* **44**, 254–257.

20

STRIATAL OUTPUT PATHWAYS INVOLVED IN MECHANISMS OF ROTATION IN RATS

J. S. McKenzie, A. D. Shafton and C. A. Stewart

Department of Physiology, University of Melbourne, Parkville, 3052 Victoria, Australia

Summary

The basal ganglia mechanisms supporting the circling responses to systemic amphetamine or apomorphine in rats with unilateral destruction of the dopaminergic compact substantia nigra have been much debated, the usual assumption being that rotation is directed away from that striatum in which stimulation of dopamine receptors is the stronger. It is inferred that the consequent imbalance of GABAergic striatal outputs to pallidum or reticulate substantia nigra (SNr) mediates the response.

These assumptions have been re-examined by slow microinjection of various drugs into the striatum and its targets in awake, unlesioned, freely-moving hooded male rats. The animals bore guide-cannulae, implanted stereotaxically one week previously under surgical anaesthesia. Rotation and other motor responses were recorded on video tape.

Dopaminergic agents (dopamine, amphetamine, apomorphine) produced no rotation when injected over wide dose ranges into either dorsal striatum or nucleus accumbens on one side, although systemic amphetamine or apomorphine elicited rotation in unilateral 6-hydroxydopamine-lesioned rats. Carbachol in dorsal striatum or nucleus accumbens (0.5 µg/0.5 µl) elicited short latency rotation away from the injected striatum, blocked by atropine. Atropine alone in the striatum failed to induce rotation.

Injection of the GABAergic agonist muscimol into one SNr has been reported to elicit strong contraversive rotation, but in entopeduncular nucleus (internal pallidum) only weak ipsiversive rotation. Injected into the globus pallidus, muscimol elicited similar weak, ipsiversive rotation and head deviation, at shorter latency than in the entopeduncular nucleus. By itself, picrotoxin in the globus pallidus on one side had no motor response, but elicited contraversive rotation on a background of systemic amphetamine.

In the subthalamic nucleus, unilateral muscimol elicited a modest contraversive rotation, while picrotoxin gave complex motor effects.

The results are explained in terms of an interaction of the direct GABAergic inhibitory striato-nigral and indirect facilitatory striato-pallido-subthalamo-nigral pathways in producing striatally-elicited contraversive rotation.

Introduction

Experimentally-induced asymmetry of posture and movement, especially rotation in rats,[2] has long been used as a means of investigating the motor functions of the basal ganglia and their mechanisms.[3,4] Rats with unilateral destruction of the substantia nigra pars compacta (SNc) caused by 6-hydroxydopamine (6-OHDA) do not rotate spontaneously or show resting postural asymmetry (except in the period of recovery from the anaesthetic given during the stereotaxic injection), but will do so in response to tail-pinches or to dosage with dopaminergic agents. They then turn in a direction away from the side on which stimulation of postsynaptic dopamine receptors is thought to be the greater, whether as a result of dopamine release by amphetamine from terminals on the unoperated side, or stimulation of sensitized dopamine receptors by apomorphine on the denervated side.[5]

The dopamine receptors responsible are commonly ascribed to the striatum,[6] normally innervated by the dopaminergic nigrostriatal fibres; possible contributions to the response mechanism from fibres in the pallidum,[7,8] or subthalamus,[7] are seldom considered. It is further proposed that a consequent imbalance of GABAergic striatal outputs to the globus pallidus or reticulate substantia nigra (SNr) mediates the rotation response, which is contraversive to the side of greater GABAergic activity.[9-11]

According to this model, dopaminergic stimulation applied directly into the striatum on one side of a normal unlesioned rat should elicit contraversive rotation. However, in numerous trials we[12] found no sign of rotation in unlesioned male hooded rats following injection of dopamine, apomorphine, or amphetamine, at a range of concentrations and volumes, into either the dorsal striatum or nucleus accumbens, and occasionally into both together (Fig. 1). Solutions of apomorphine or amphetamine that were without effect when given intrastriatally produced rotation responses in the expected directions when injected systematically into rats with unilateral 6-OHDA lesions of SNc, vigorous rotation beginning within 3 min of injection and rising to a peak of 10–14 turns per min in 20 min.[13]

In contrast, unilateral muscarinic stimulation of the dorsal striatum or nucleus accumbens with 0.5 μg carbachol readily elicited contraversive rotation, beginning within seconds and rising to a rate of 6–8 turns per min in about 10 min.[13]

Activation of GABAergic pathways from the striatum to the SNr was presumed to be responsible for this rotation, since injection of the GABA-mimetic muscimol into SNr at low doses (50 ng) also elicited contraversive rotation in the same rats.[13] Involvement of GABAergic projections to the entopeduncular nucleus has been discounted on the basis that muscimol injections elicited only weak, long-latency ipsiversive rotation.[13] Hence striato-entopeduncular GABAergic projections, and by inference the pallido-thalamo-cortical feedback pathway, would not mediate the contraversive rotation response to intrastriatal carbachol. But stimulation of striato-nigral projections, disinhibiting thalamo-cortical and tectospinal projections,[18] remained as likely mediators of the rotation.

The role of the globus pallidus, which in the rat corresponds to the external pallidum projecting to the subthalamic nucleus, was not investigated. Muscimol injection in the globus pallidus would be expected to depress the spontaneous activity of its neurones,[14] and influence SNr discharge indirectly (Fig. 2).

In the present experiments we investigated the effects of manipulating GABAergic transmission in the globus pallidus on one side of unlesioned rats, for comparison with responses to intrastriatal carbachol, and to muscimol in SNr[13] and subthalamic nucleus.

Methods

The experiments were done on unlesioned hooded rats of 250–300 g weight, supplied with

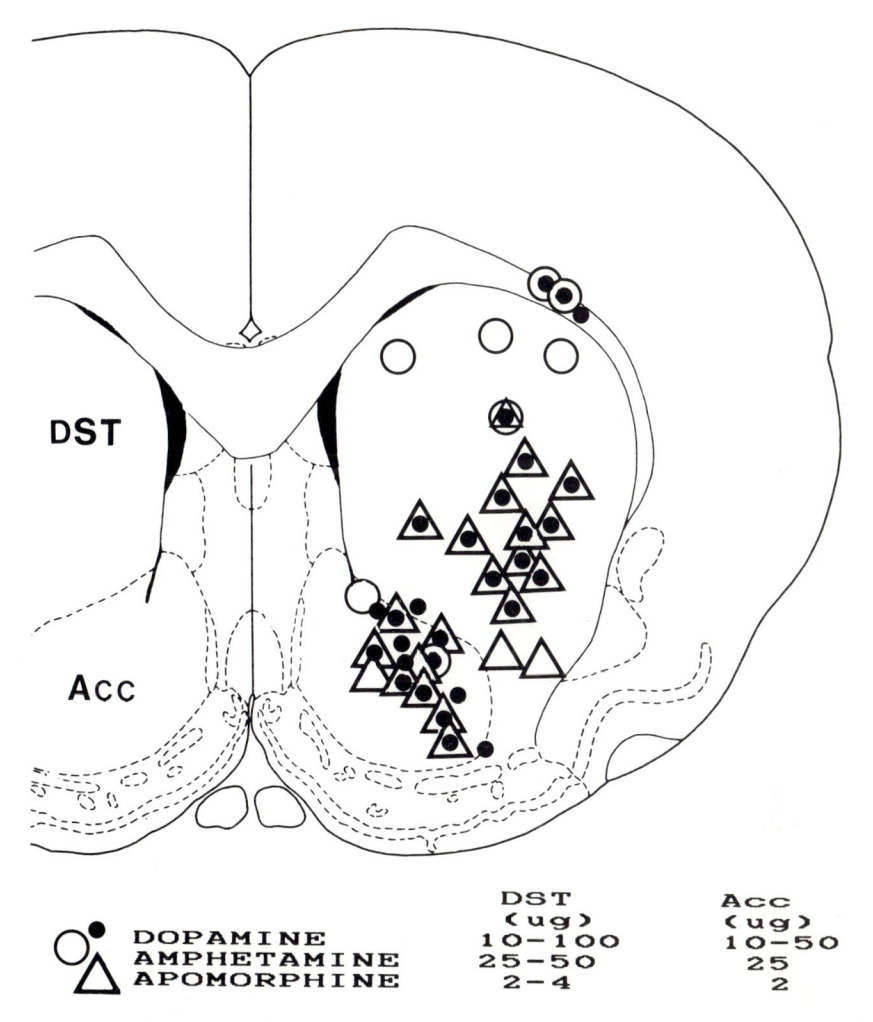

Fig. 1. *Dopamine, amphetamine and apomorphine microinjection centres in dorsal striatum (DST) and nucleus accumbens (ACC) of unlesioned rats.* No rotation over the dose ranges shown.

guide-cannulae terminating 2–3 mm dorsal to targeted structures, fixed to the skull with acrylic cement in a preliminary operation under surgical anaesthesia (sodium amylobarbitone 100 mg/kg intraperitoneally).

The animals were observed and their behaviour videotaped while they moved freely in a field approximately 60 cm × 50 cm. Test solutions were injected from a 0.3 mm needle passing snugly through the guide tube and projecting 2–3 mm beyond it as determined by a stop. During injection, the rat was free to move in the field. Any circling was followed by the experimenter's hand holding the microsyringe, to avoid rotation of the needle in the brain. Injections were made slowly (2–3 min) and the needle subsequently left in place for several minutes more, to minimize mechanical disturbance of brain tissue.

Drugs were dissolved in 0.9 per cent saline at concentrations of 100 ng per μl muscimol (Sigma), 1 μg per μl picrotoxin (Sigma), and 1 μg per μl carbachol (Sigma).

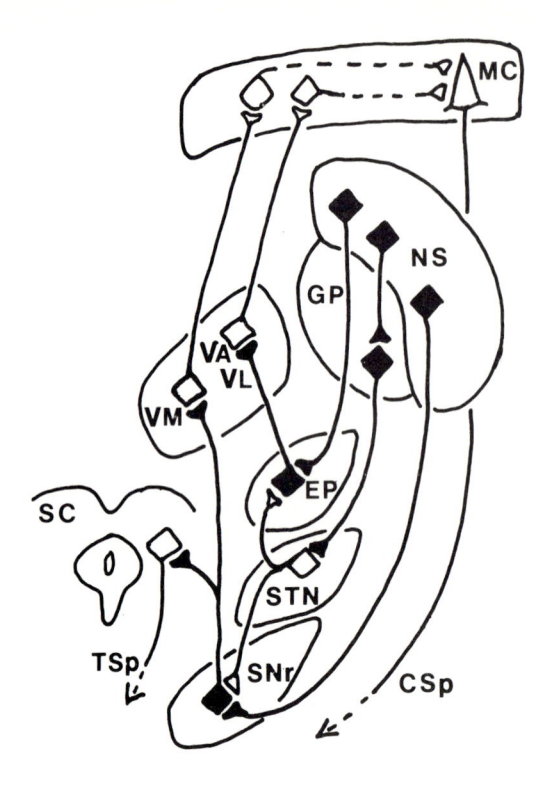

Fig. 2. Basal ganglia pathways potentially involved in contraversive rotation after activation of striatal GABAergic outputs. Filled and open symbols represent inhibitory (GABAergic) and excitatory neurones respectively. Abbreviations: CSp, corticospinal pathways; EP, entopeduncular nucleus; GP, globus pallidus; NS, neostriatum; SC, superior colliculus; SNr, substantia nigra pars reticulata; STN, subthalamic nucleus; TSp, tectospinal pathways; VA, VL, VM thalamic nuclei ventrales anterior, lateralis and medialis.

Motor responses were analysed and rotation rates counted on play-back of the video-taped records. The central points of all injections were defined by the position of the needle tip, as seen in Nissl-stained frozen sections cut in the coronal plane. For the illustrations, these points were transposed to similar positions in standard brain atlas diagrams.[15,16]

Results

Striatum

Atropine (250 ng in 500 nl) injected into either dorsal striatum or nucleus accumbens had no motor effect, either rotational or postural, in normal rats. Nor did it have any effect when so injected after systemic dosage with amphetamine (1.5 mg/kg subcutaneously) had produced hyperkinesia. This negative result suggests that no tonic cholinergic activity is present in the resting striatum, nor is it stimulated by increased dopamine release, at least in relation to rotation mechanisms.

Pallidum

Muscimol injected into the globus pallidus on one side at 30 ng in 300 nl produced weak ipsiversive rotation, beginning approximately 20 seconds after the start of injection. A similar effect was observed following injections into the ventral pallidum. Injections centred in adjacent striatum (Fig. 3) produced either no response, or a similar response to globus pallidus injections but beginning after a long delay (20 min). The ipsiversive rotation was accompanied by head deviation of 45 degrees to the upper trunk in the same direction.

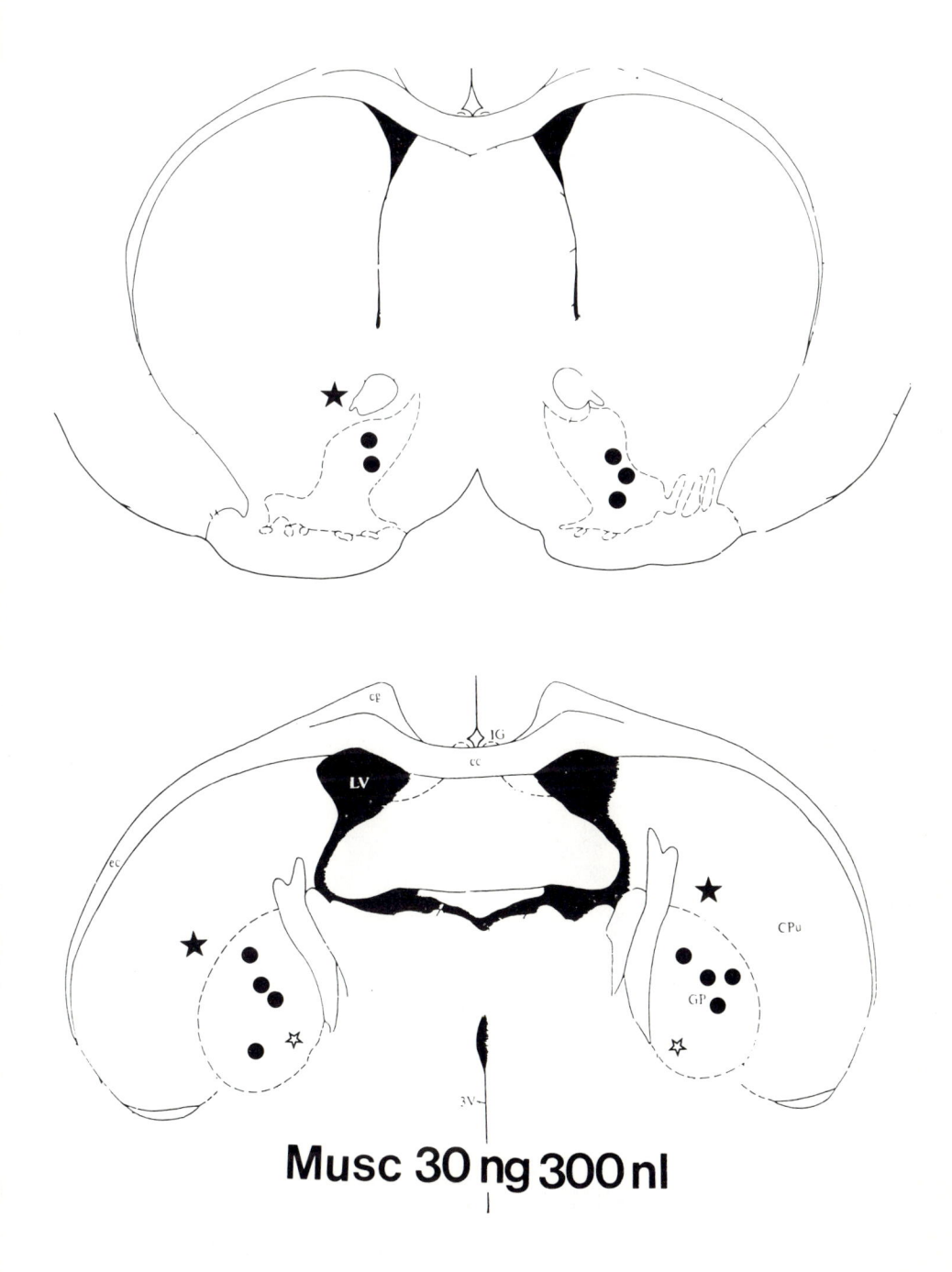

Striatal output pathways involved in mechanisms of rotation in rats

Fig. 3. *Muscimol (musc) microinjection centres in globus pallidus (GP) and ventral pallidum (VP) for ipsiversive rotation.* Filled star = response with longer onset latency and shorter duration. Open star = response initially ipsiversive reversed after 10 min to contraversive.

In two points located ventrally in the globus pallidus (Fig. 3), ipsiversive rotation and head deviation was supplanted after 12 min by a reversal of response direction, ie, contralateral head deviation and contraversive turning up to five per min, lasting about 30 min.

Picrotoxin injected at 300 ng in 300 nl into the globus pallidus on one side elicited no discernible motor response. But if injected 15 min after subcutaneous amphetamine at a dose of 1.5 mg/kg had elicited hypermotility, picrotoxin produced contraversive rotation at a latency less than or equal to 1 min (Figs 4 & 5). Equivalent rotatory responses were elicited if the amphetamine was injected subcutaneously subsequent to a picrotoxin injection into the globus pallidus which by itself produced no response.

Subthalamic nucleus

Muscimol injected into the subthalamic nucleus of one side at 30 ng per 300 nl elicited contraversive rotation of modest intensity and duration (Figs 6 & 7).

Picrotoxin (300 ng per 300 nl) produced a mixed motor response, including contralateral forelimb jerks described as resembling rodent hemiballismus, and ipsiversive trunk torsion, leading into axial rolling.[1]

Discussion

The present results were obtained taking all reasonable technical measures to minimize

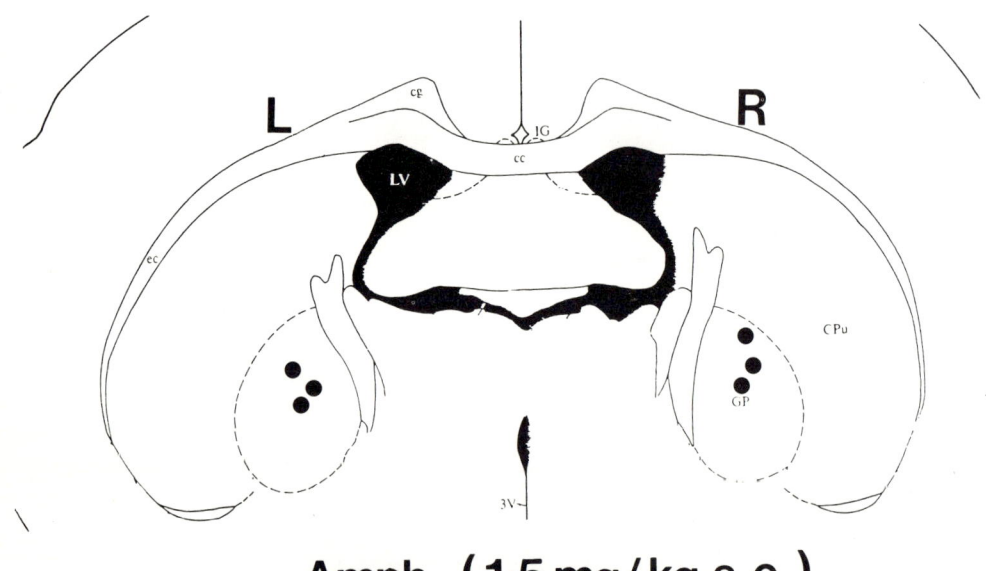

Fig. 4. *Picrotoxin (Picro) microinjection centres in globus pallidus (GP) for picrotoxin (Picro) injected alone, and after subcutaneous amphetamine.*

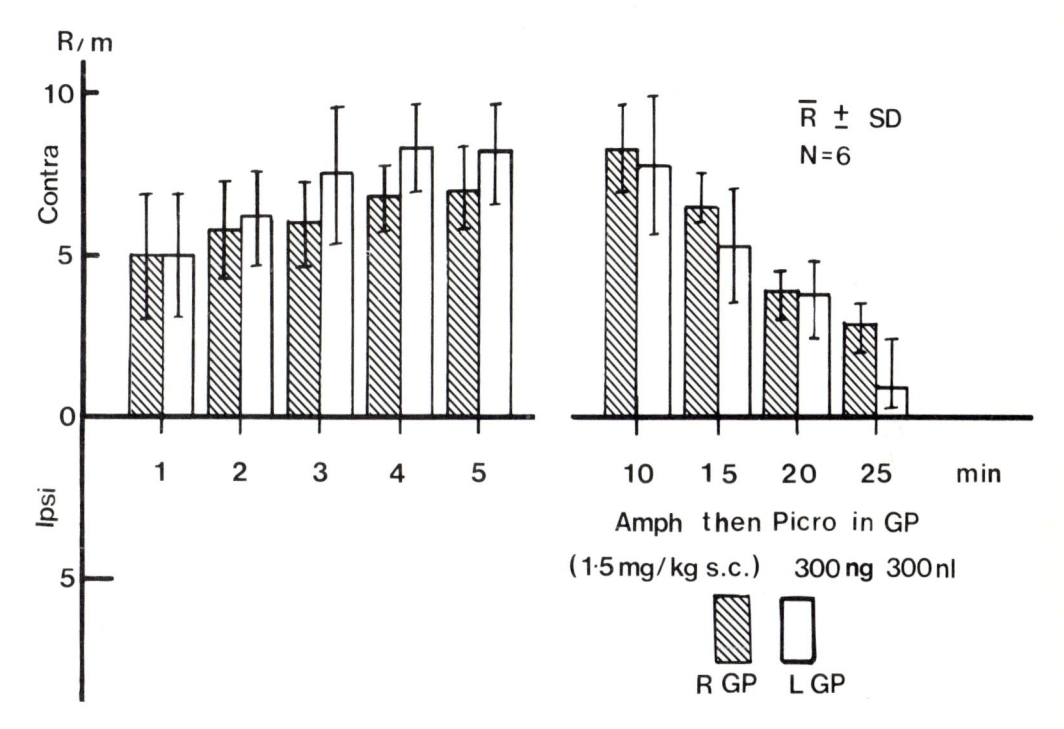

Fig. 5. *Rotation response to picrotoxin (Picro) microinjected in globus pallidus after subcutaneous amphetamine.* Rotations per min shown as mean and SD, separately for injections on right (RGP) and left (LGP) sides, two trials per site.

ambiguity as to the anatomical structures affected by intracerebral microinjections. In addition to the precautions noted above to avoid forceful spread of injected solutions, comparisons between effects (including latency) obtained with needle tips centred in a structure and with tips in neighbouring zones were often valuable.[13] An important example is provided by the different directions of rotation elicited by muscimol in neighbouring entopeduncular and subthalamic nuclei. Such differences in response would not occur if an injection centred in one structure acted only because of spread to its neighbour.

Our results are not consistent with the commonly accepted model, in which asymmetric stimulation of striatal dopamine receptors directly initiates the degree of asymmetric GABAergic output to SNr capable of producing contraversive rotation. On the other hand, direct cholinergic stimulation of the striatum did cause contraversive rotation at short latency. This rotation appears to be the result of an augmentation of striato-nigral GABAergic output. The parallel striato-pallidal GABAergic projections do not appear to be involved, since muscimol in either globus pallidus or entopeduncular nucleus elicited rotation of weak intensity in the inappropriate (ipsiversive) direction.

However, with systemic amphetamine treatment dopaminergic action on the globus pallidus may have been responsible for 'priming' neurons to produce an augmented pallidal discharge when the inhibitory GABAergic striato-pallidal projections were antagonized by picrotoxin (Fig. 8). In this case increased globus pallidus discharge would inhibit subthalamic neurons. Since these neurons are now known to be excitatory to their synaptic targets in globus pallidus, entopeduncular nucleus and SNr[17] (see also

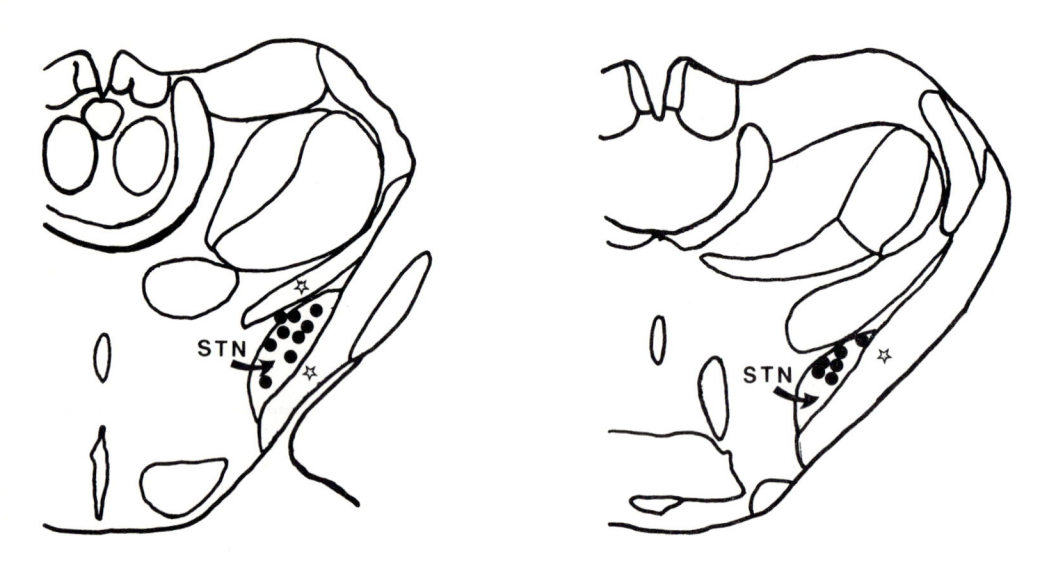

Fig. 6. *Muscimol injection centres in subthalamic nucleus (STN)*. All points within STN gave contraversive rotation (full circles). Neighbouring misplaced points (open stars) gave response in same direction but longer onset latency and shorter duration.

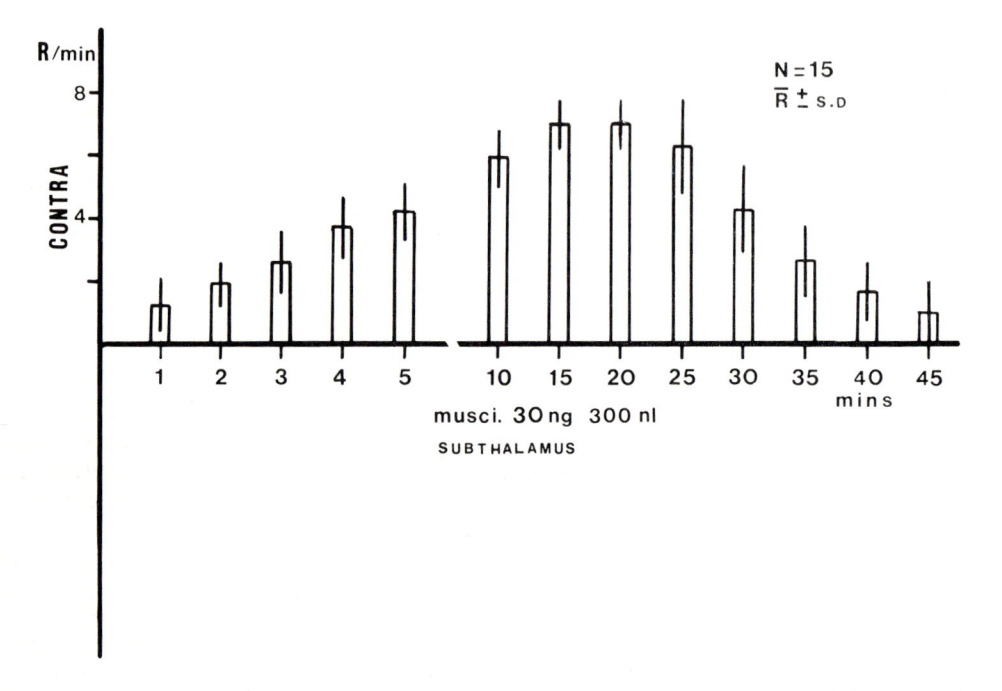

Fig. 7. *Rotation response to muscimol (musci) microinjections centred in subthalamic nucleus.* Rotation per min shown as mean and SD. Time-scale expanded for first five minutes.

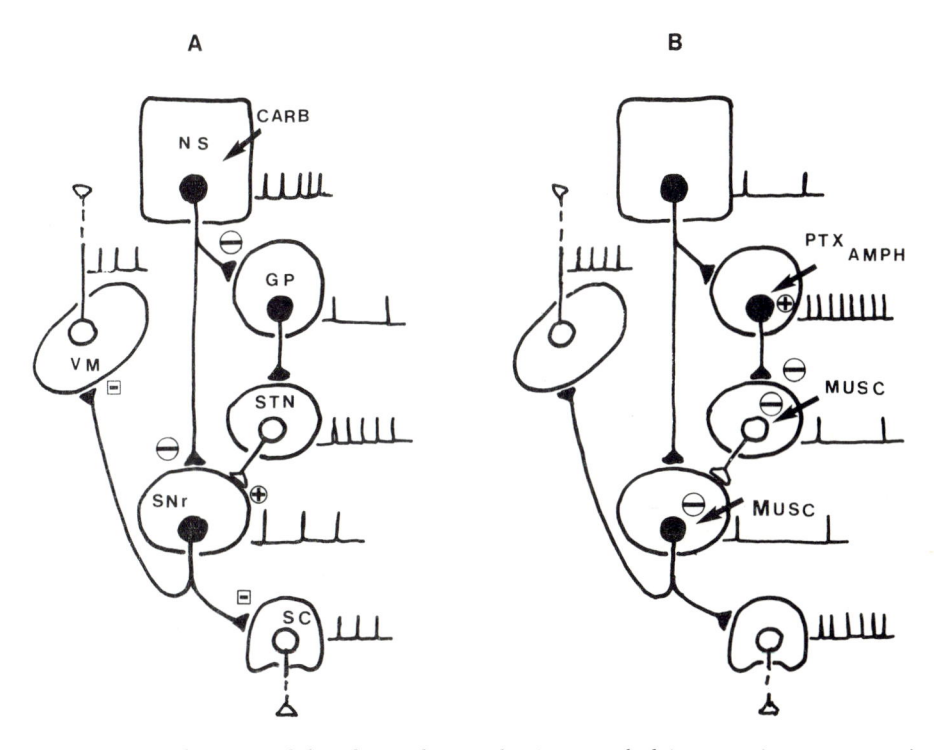

Fig. 8. *Schematic diagram of basal ganglia mechanisms underlying rotation contraversive to microinjection into direct and indirect striato-nigral pathways.* Neural firing rates suggested by sketches beside structures, as labelled in A. Plus and minus signs: facilitation and inhibition resp. Filled and open symbols, and abbreviations, as in Fig. 2. A: Carbachol (carb) in NS stimulates firing of inhibitory outputs to SNr and GP; reduced GP firing disinhibits STN neurons, whose facilitatory action partly opposes direct GABAergic NS-SNr pathway. Balance in favour of latter disinhibits VM and SC outputs (see Fig. 2). B: Facilitation of SNr by STN is reduced by muscimol (musc) injection in STN, or by picrotoxin (PTX) in GP after s.c. AMPH. which increases inhibitory GP discharge; resultant disfacilitation of SNr again facilitates VM and SC outputs.

Robledo *et al.*, this volume, p. 37), depression of their spontaneous firing rate would diminish their tonic facilitation of SNr neurons, thus reinforcing any inhibitory striato-nigral influence activated in parallel, as by intrastriatal carbachol. Nigro-tectal projections have been shown to inhibit tectospinal neurons directly in the intermediate to deep layers of the rat's superior colliculus.[18] If the tonic firing rate of SNr neurons and their GABAergic inhibitory influence on superior colliculus and ventromedial thalamo-cortical cells[19] were thus depressed, it would disinhibit tectospinal and tecto-reticulo-spinal outputs (Figs 1 & 8). Tectospinal facilitation could be expected to elicit head deviation towards the opposite side and generate contraversive postural deviations.[20] The pattern of motor activity in rotation is more complex than such a simplified mechanism suggests, and a concomitant depression of nigrothalamic neurons, disinhibiting ventromedial thalamic projections to frontal cortex,[21] may excite motor areas to drive the limb movements of rotation.[19] This could include contralateral trunk flexion, contributing to the postural deviation typical in rotation. The recent demonstration that subthalamic nucleus outputs are facilitatory to SNr (and other targets) is crucial to the consistent explanation of contraversive rotations elicited by picrotoxin-induced excitation (with amphetamine priming) of the globus pallidus, and by muscimol injections into the subthalamic nucleus, along with the contraversive rotation responses to intrastriatal carbachol or intranigral muscimol (see Fig. 8). The hypothesis that GABAergic striato-nigral pathways are primarily responsible for contraversive rotation thus obtains additional support. In the unilateral 6-OHDA-lesioned rat, dopaminergic stimulation of the globus pallidus may, via the subthalamic nucleus, reinforce effects on the striatum, so as to depress SNr firing strongly on the side subjected to greater dopaminergic action, thus producing rotation in the appropriate sense.

The stimulation of striatal outputs by intrastriatal carbachol would exert two opposing effects on SNr discharge, according to this model. The GABAergic inhibition of SNr would be countered by a disinhibition of subthalamic nucleus neurons, which would tend to facilitate SNr. It is inferred that the direct inhibitory effect outweighs the indirect facilitation, to produce contraversive rotation as described. It is notable, however, that intrastriatal carbachol does not lead to peak rotation rates as high as those elicited by muscimol in SNr,[13] perhaps because of the influence of the globus pallidus-subthalamic nucleus side-loop.

Microinjection of transmitter-mimetics and antagonists into basal ganglia structures provides only a crude model for physiological variations of synaptic operation in these pathways. In the striatum, for instance, even small volumes injected will spread with diminishing concentration, to unknown distances from the centre, with no possibility of any selective action on striosome or matrix output neurons[22] (see also Graybiel, this volume p. 3) as might occur physiologically.

There is little or no possibility of imitating by direct injection the simultaneous action of peptides that may be co-released from GABAergic or independent terminals in striatal targets during normal physiological activity. Detailed anatomical organization of transmitter actions is beyond the reach of the present technique, although evidence is mounting for a complex intermeshing of regional and patchy outputs from the striatal complex to pallidal and nigral targets[22] (see also Young et al., p 20).

Notwithstanding such reservations, microinjection into conscious freely-moving animals can produce organized, directed responses, permitting an analysis of movement patterns induced by more conventional systemic drug administration, especially the familiar rotation in rats. The results suggest that synaptic operations in striatal output pathways are dominated by GABAergic transmission interacting with the excitatory input injected through the subthalamic nucleus, which is presumably driven by cortical input and is modulated by variations in globus pallidus firing-rates. The technique is capable of development towards systematic use of multiple injections, for example to ask whether rotation induced by striatal injection can be halted or reversed by manipulation of GABAergic synapses downstream. In view of the apparent opposition between the direct striato-nigral and indirect striato-pallido-subthalamo-nigral influences (Fig. 8), it would be predicted that altering the balance in favour of the direct route, for example by blocking GABAergic striato-pallidal transmission and thus indirectly disfacilitating subthalamic excitation of SNr, would reinforce the rotation response to intrastriatal carbachol (Fig. 8).

Finally, the technique needs to be combined with unit recording from striatum, globus pallidus, subthalamic nucleus and SNr in freely-moving rats[23] to test directly the mechanisms that have been suggested to explain the above results.

References

1 McKenzie, J. S., Shafton, A. D. & Stewart, C. A. (1986): Experimental hemiballismus in the rat. *Proc. Australian Physiol. Pharmacol. Soc.* **17**, 148P.
2 Pycock, C. J. (1980): Turning behaviour in animals. *Neuroscience* **5**, 461–514.

3 Carpenter, M. B. & Carpenter, C. S. (1955): Relations between the site of dyskinesia and distribution of lesions within the subthalamic nucleus. *J. Comp. Neurol.* **95**, 349–370.
4 Crossman, A. R., Sambrook, M. A. & Jackson, A. (1980): Experimental hemiballismus in the baboon produced by injection of a gamma-aminobutyric acid antagonist into the basal ganglia. *Neurosci. Lett.* **20**, 369–372.
5 Ungerstedt, U. (1971): Postsynaptic supersensitivity after 6-hydroxy-dopamine induced degeneration of the nigro-striatal dopamine system. *Acta Physiol. Scand. Suppl.* **367**, 69–72.
6 Arbuthnott, G. W. & Crow, T. J. (1971): Relation of contraversive turning to unilateral release of dopamine from the nigrostriatal pathway in rats. *Exp. Neurol.* **30**, 484–491.
7 Boyson, S. L., McGonigle, P. & Molinoff, P. B. (1986): Quantitative autoradiographic localization of the D1 and D2 subtypes of dopamine receptors in rat brain. *J. Neurosci.* **6**, 3177–3188.
8 Martres, M.-P., Bouthenet, M.-L., Sales, N., Sokoloff, P. & Schwartz, J.-C. (1985): Widespread distribution of brain dopamine receptors evidenced with (125 I) iodosulpride, a highly selective ligand. *Science* **228**, 752–755.
9 Di Chiara, G. & Morelli, M. (1984): Output pathways mediating basal ganglia function. In *The basal ganglia. Structure and function*, ed J. S. McKenzie, R. E. Kemm & L. N. Wilcock, pp 443–446. New York: Plenum Press.
10 Di Chiara, G., Morelli, M., Porcedu, M. L. & Gessa, G. L. (1978): Evidence that nigral GABA mediates behavioural responses elicited by striatal dopamine receptor stimulation. *Life Sci.* **23**, 2405–2052.
11 Scheel-Kruger, J., Magelund, G. & Oliveras, M. C. (1981): Role of GABA in the striatal output system: globus pallidus, nucleus entopeduncularis, substantia nigra and nucleus subthalamicus. In *GABA and the basal ganglia*, ed G. Di Chiara & G. L. Gessa, pp 165–186. New York: Raven Press.
12 McKenzie, J. S., Shafton, A. D., Mcgrory, S. & Kemm, R. E. (1985): Observations on the role of striatal dopaminergic stimulation in the rotating rat. *Proc. Australian Physiol. Pharmacol. Soc.* **16**, 108.
13 McKenzie, J. S., Shafton, A. D. & Stewart, C. A. (1987): Motor responses to GABA-ergic interference in the rat entopeduncular nucleus in relation to rotation mechanisms. In *The basal ganglia II. Structure and function—current concepts*, ed M. B. Carpenter & A. Jayaraman, pp 327–335. New York: Plenum Press.
14 Everett, P. W., Kemm, R. E. & McKenzie, J. S. (1984): In *The Basal ganglia. Structure and function*, ed J. S. McKenzie, R. E. Kemm & L. N. Wilcock, pp 235–245. New York: Plenum Press.
15 Albe-Fessard, D., Stutinsky, F. & Libouban, S. (1966): *Atlas stereotaxique du diencephale du rat blanc*. Paris: CNRS.
16 Paxinos, G. & Watson, C. (1982): *The rat brain in stereotaxic coordinates*. Sydney: Academic Press.
17 Kitai, S. T. & Kita, H. (1987): Anatomy and physiology of the subthalamic nucleus: a driving force of the basal ganglia. In *The basal ganglia II. Structure and function—current concepts*, ed M. B. Carpenter & A. Jayaraman, pp 357–373. New York: Plenum Press.
18 Chevalier, G., Vacher, S., Deniau, J. M. & Desban, M. (1985): Disinhibition as a basic process in the expression of striatal functions. I. The striato-nigral influence on tecto-spinal/tecto-diencephalic neurones. *Brain Res.* **334**, 215–226.
19 Deniau, J. M. & Chevalier, G. (1985): Disinhibition as a basic process in the expression of striatal functions. II. The striato-nigral influence on thalamo-cortical cells of the ventromedial thalamic nucleus. *Brain Res.* **334**, 227–233.
20 Joseph, J. P. & Boussaoud, D. (1985): Role of the cat substantia nigra pars reticulata in eye and head movements I. Neural activity. *Exp. Brain Res.* **57**, 286–296.
21 Arbuthnott, G. W., Macleod, N. K., Maxwell, D. J. & Wright, A. K. (1987): The detailed morphology of the cortical terminals of the thalamo cortical fibres from the ventromedial nucleus in the rat. In *The basal ganglia II. Structure and function—current concepts*, ed M. B. Carpenter & A. Jayaraman, pp 283–291. New York: Plenum Press.
22 Gerfen, C. R. (1987): The neostriatal mosaic: Compartmental organization of mesostriatal

systems. In *The basal ganglia II. Structure and function—current concepts*, ed M. B. Carpenter & A. Jayaraman, pp 65–80. New York: Plenum Press.

23 McKenzie, J. S., Everett, P. W. & Dally, L. J. (1983): A method for simultaneously recording neural activity and rotation in the rat. *Physiol. Behav.* **30**, 653–657.

21

IPSILATERAL TURNING AFTER LOCAL APPLICATION OF (-)SULPIRIDE INTO THE DORSAL, BUT NOT THE VENTRAL, STRIATUM OF THE RAT

Sven Ahlenius, Viveka Hillegaart,
Christopher J. Fowler and Olle Magnusson

*Department of Neuropharmacology, Astra Research Centre, S-151 85
Södertälje, Sweden*

Summary

The local application of (-)sulpiride, 200–800 ng per side, produced ipsilateral turning in the dorso-lateral neostriatum, but not in the nucleus accumbens, in the rat. Biochemical determinations of local effects by (-)sulpiride on dopamine turnover indicate that there was no diffusion of the injected material from one site to the other. No significant turning was obtained by the local application of 3-(3-hydroxyphenyl)-N-*n*-propylpiperidine, 2.5–40.0 μg per side, or by quinpirole, 0.063–4.0 μg per side. The results obtained by use of (-)sulpiride provide further support for functional subdivisions within the striatum of the rat.

Introduction

The objective of the present series of experiments was to examine possible motor asymmetries following the unilateral application of various dopamine D2-receptor-selective agents into the striatum of normal rats. In order to obtain information on the relative importance of activation *vs* inactivation of dopaminergic neurotransmission, drugs with different degrees of intrinsic activity at the dopamine D2 receptor were used. (-)Sulpiride was chosen as a selective dopamine D2 antagonist[1] and quinpirole and 3-(3-hydroxyphenyl)-N-*n*-propylpiperidine [(-)3-PPP] as selective agonists.[2,3] Of the latter two compounds, quinpirole possesses a much higher intrinsic activity at dopamine D2 receptors than (-)3-PPP.[4,5] The different compounds were injected into either the dorso-lateral neostriatum or into the nucleus accumbens of the ventral striatum in the rat.

The systemic administration of dopamine agonists and antagonists results in biphasic effects on various functional measures[6] presumably due to preferential actions at pre- or post-synaptic receptors in the low and high dose range respectively.[7] Dopamine autoreceptors apparently exist both in the cell body region of the brain stem and in the terminal areas in the forebrain.[7] Thus, in order to enhance the possibility of detecting functional effects by stimulation or blockade of terminal dopamine autoreceptors, a wide range of doses of (-)sulpiride and quinpirole were used. The inclusion of the partial dopamine D2 agonist (-)3-PPP would presumably also be of value in this regard, since this compound has been shown to activate dopamine autoreceptors preferentially in reserpinized as well as in normal rats.[8,9]

Methods

Adult male Sprague-Dawley rats (ALAB Laboratorietjänst, Sollentuna, Sweden) were used. The animal quarters provided controlled conditions of temperature (21°C), relative humidity (55–60 per cent), and light-dark cycle (12 h:12 h, lights on 6 p.m.), and the rats arrived in the laboratory at least 10 days prior to experimental manipulations. Food (E3, Ewos, Södertälje, Sweden) and tap water were available *ad libitum*. Guide cannulae (25 G) were placed on the skull under pentobarbital anaesthesia by means of standard stereotaxic equipment. The guides reached, but did not penetrate, the *dura mater*. Following a post-operative recovery time of one week, injections were made in awake animals by means of 31 G blunt stainless steel needles (1 μl per side, infusion rate 0.67 μl/min). According to Paxinos and Watson,[10] the coordinates were as follows: dorso-lateral neostriatum AP +1.2, L +3.4 and DV +3.6 mm; nucleus accumbens AP + 2.1, L + 1.2 and DV +6.8 mm. Turning behaviour was observed in a plastic cylinder ($\emptyset$ = 250 mm) divided by markings on the floor, in eight segments. These segments were used to record the number of complete 180° turns in 3 min, beginning 10 min after injections started. Dopamine and its acid metabolites dihydroxyphenylacetic acid (DOPAC) and homovanillic acid (HVA) were measured by means of HPLC with electrochemical detection as described by Magnusson *et al.*[11] Striatal dopamine turnover was estimated by calculating the ratio (DOPAC + HVA)/DA. (-)Sulpiride and quinpirole HCl were generously supplied by ICFI (Milan, Italy), and Eli Lilly Co (Indianapolis), respectively. (-)3-PPP was synthesized at the Astra facilities at Södertälje, Sweden.

For each compound and brain site, repeated observations were made on the same group of animals according to a change-over design.[12] There were at least two days between successive injections.

Results and discussion

In the first series of experiments, (-)sulpiride was administered in doses ranging from 50–800 ng per side. When injected into the dorso-lateral striatum, it was found that the 50 ng dose was ineffective, whereas 200–800 ng produced a clear and statistically significant turning towards the ipsilateral side. Corresponding injections into the ventral striatum produced no turning behaviour (Fig. 1). In a following separate experiment on the same animals, the effects of (-)sulpiride, 6.25 and 25 ng per side were examined. The idea was that yet lower doses (below 50 ng) could antagonize dopamine autoreceptors preferentially. However, there were no effects by these doses on turning behaviour.

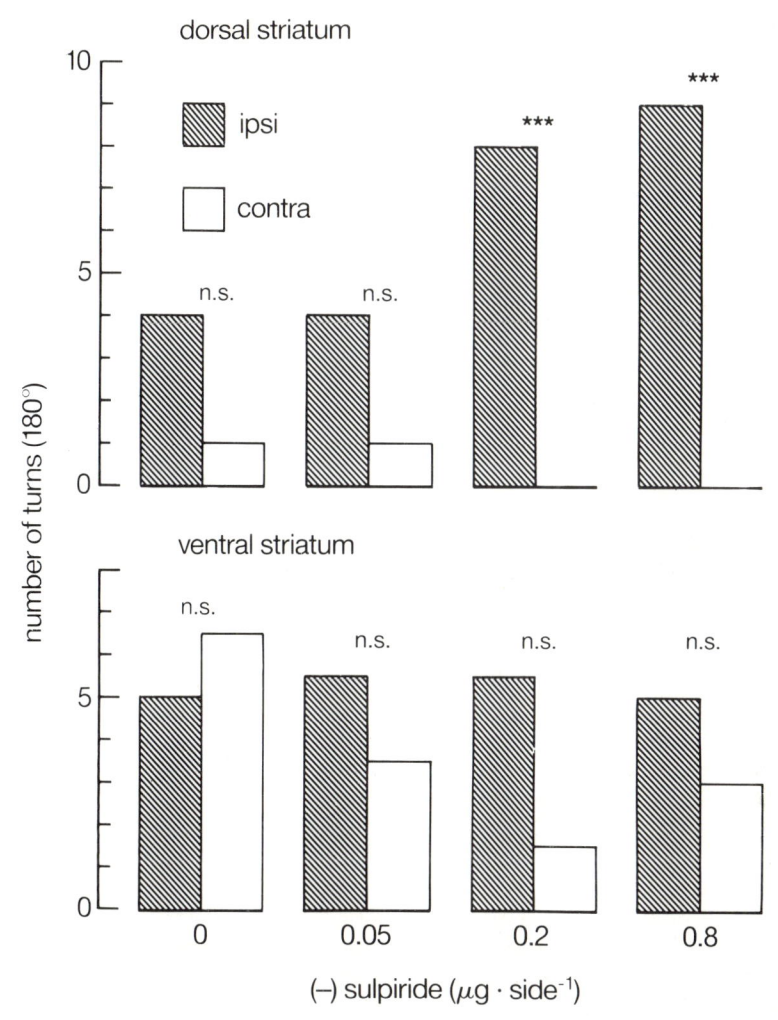

Fig. 1. *Effects of intra-striatal injections of (-)sulpiride on turning behaviour in the rat.* The animals were given a unilateral injection of (-)sulpiride into the dorsal or the ventral striatum 10 min before observations started. The results are presented as medians ($n = 9$ at each dose level), and statistical evaluation was performed by means of the Wilcoxon matched-pairs signed-ranks test.

$^{ns}P > 0.05$ ***$P < 0.01$

The diffusion of (-)sulpiride from the site of injection was estimated by regional dissections and measurements of dopamine, DOPAC and HVA in the striatum. It was found that dopamine turnover was increased in the dorso-lateral striatum, ipsilateral to the injection, but not in the corresponding area contralaterally or in the ventral striatum, ipsi- or contralateral to the injection. After an injection into the ventral striatum dopamine turnover was selectively increased in the same manner at the site of injection (Fig. 2).

This experiment supports the contention that the neostriatum is an important site for asymmetries produced by the administration of dopamine receptor agonists in various

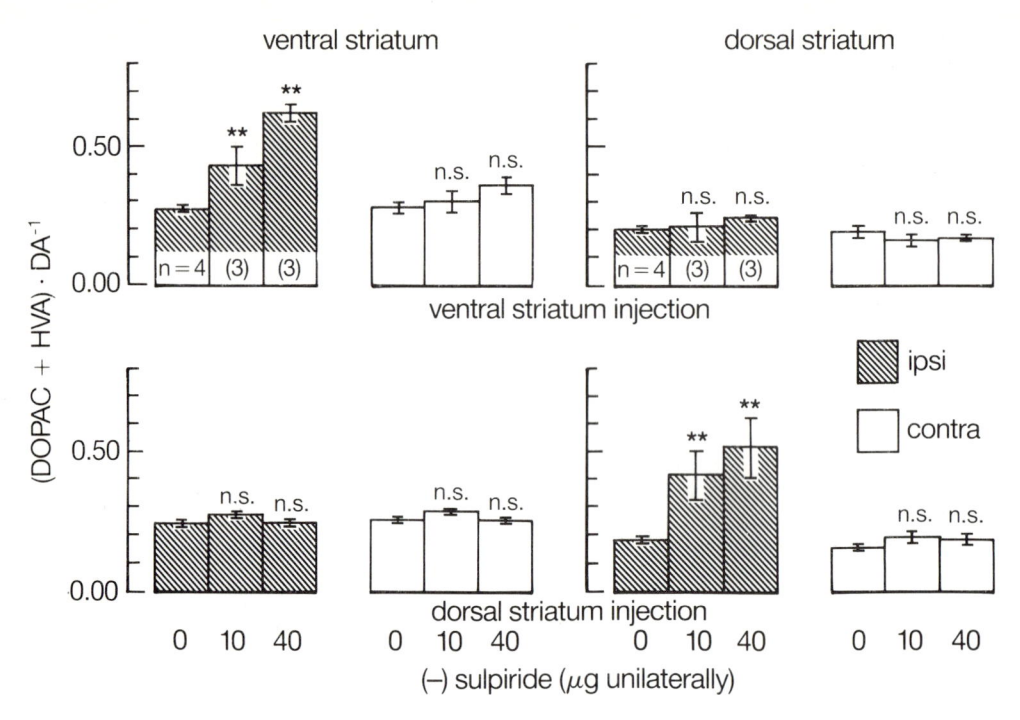

Fig. 2. *Effects of intra-striatal injections of (-)sulpiride on striatal dopamine turnover.* The animals were given a unilateral injection of (-)sulpiride 20 min before decapitation. The results are presented as means. Bars = SD. Statistical evaluation was performed by means of a one-way ANOVA followed by the Dunnett's *t*-test for comparisons with saline injected controls.

$^{ns}P > 0.05$ **$P < 0.01$

animal models of turning. Furthermore, there was no evidence for presynaptically-mediated effects in these experiments. Possibly, the present behavioural recording is not sensitive enough to pick up the functional effects of a presumed preferential blockade of presynaptic dopamine autoreceptors, or that such effects as seen after systemic administration of dopaminergic drugs are mainly due to activation of autoreceptors in the cell body region in the mesencephalon. This latter assumption is reinforced by the fact that the local application of (-)3-PPP into the dorso-lateral aspect of the neostriatum did not produce any asymmetries in doses ranging from 2.5 to 40.0 µg/kg (data not shown).

Finally, the local application of quinpirole, 0.063–4.0 µg per side, into the dorso-lateral neostriatum did not produce any asymmetries (data not shown).

References

1 Trabucchi, M., Longoni, R., Fresia, P. & Spano, P. F. (1975): Sulpiride: A study of the effects on dopamine receptors in rat neostriatum and limbic forebrain. *Life Sci* **17**, 1551–1556.
2 Titus, R. D., Kornfeld, E. C., Jones, N. D., Clemens, J. A., Smalstig, E. B., Fuller, R. W., Hahn, R. A., Hynes, M. D., Mason, N. R., Wong, D. T. & Foreman, M. M. (1983): Resolution and absolute configuration of an ergoline-related dopamine agonist, trans-4, 4a, 5, 6, 7, 8, 8a, 9-octahydro-5-propyl-1H (or2H)-pyrazolo (3,4-g)quinoline. *J. Med. Chem.* **26**, 1112–1116.
3 George, S. R., Watanabe, M. & Seeman, P. (1985): Dopamine D2 receptors in brain and anterior pituitary recognize agonist and antagonist actions of (-)3-PPP. *J. Neural Transm.* **64**, 13–33.

4 Clark, D., Hjorth, S. & Carlsson, A. (1985): (+) and (−)-3-PPP exhibit different intrinsic activity at striatal dopamine autoreceptors controlling dopamine synthesis. *Eur. J. Pharmacol.* **106**, 185–189.
5 Arnt, J. & Perregaard, J. (1987): Synergistic interaction between dopamin D-1 and D-2 receptor agonists: circling behaviour of rats with hemitransection. *Eur. J. Pharmacol.* **143**, 45–53.
6 Ahlenius, S. (1979): An analysis of behavioural effects produced by drug-induced changes of dopaminergic neurotransmission in the brain. *Scand. J. Psychol.* **20**, 59–64.
7 Carlsson, A. (1975): Dopaminergic autoreceptors. In *Chemical tools in catecholamine research*, vol. II, eds O. Almgren, A. Carlsson and J. Engel, pp 219–225. Amsterdam: North-Holland Publishing Co.
8 Hjorth, S., Carlsson, A., Clark, D., Svensson, K., Wikstrom, H., Sanchez, D., Lindberg, P., Hacksell, U., Arvidsson, L.-E., Johansson, A. & Nilsson, J. L. G. (1983): Central dopamine receptor agonist and antagonist actions of the enantiomers of 3-PPP. *Psychopharmacology* **81**, 89–99.
9 Ahlenius, S., Svensson, L., Hillegaart, V. & Thorberg O. (1984): Antagonism by haloperidol of the suppression of exploratory locomotor activity induced by the local application of (-)3-(3-hydroxyphenyl)-N-*n*-propylpiperidine into the nucleus accumbens of the rat. *Experientia* **40**, 858–859.
10 Paxinos, G. & Watson, C. (1986): *The rat brain in stereotaxic coordinates*. London: Academic Press.
11 Magnusson, O., Nilsson, L. B. & Westerlund, D. (1980): Simultaneous determination of dopamine, DOPAC, and homovanillic acid. Direct injection of supernatants from brain tissue homogenates in a liquid chromatography-electrochemical detection system. *J. Chromatogr.* **221**, 237–247.
12 Li, C. C. (1964): *Introduction to experimental statistics*. New York: McGraw-Hill.

22

SUSTAINED-RELEASE 4-PROPYL-9-HYDROXYNAPHTHOXAZINE IN THE TREATMENT OF MPTP-INDUCED PARKINSONISM IN THE PRIMATE

C. E. Clarke, S. Boyce, M. A. Sambrook,
A. R. Crossman and S. M. Stahl*

*Experimental Neurology Group, Department of Cell and Structural Biology, Medical School, University of Manchester, Manchester, M13 9PT; and *Merck Sharp and Dohme Research Laboratories, Neuroscience Research Centre, Terlings Park, Eastwick Road, Harlow Essex, CM20 2QR, UK*

Summary

Three cynomolgus monkeys received intermittent doses of 1-methyl-4-phenyl-1,2,3,6-tetrahydropyridine (MPTP) sufficient to produce a permanent stable parkinsonian syndrome. Nine months after the end of the MPTP regime, animals were challenged with the novel D-2 dopamine agonist 4-propyl-9-hydroxynaphthoxazine (PHNO) prepared in a methylcellulose matrix designed to release the drug over a 12 hr period following oral administration. The preparation produced a dose-dependent anti-parkinsonian effect after a delay of 2.5–7.3 hr which lasted for 1.2–9.7 hr. Combining unformulated PHNO with the sustained release drug resulted in a rapid reversal of parkinsonian features which continued for up to 12 hr. These results indicate that a combined unformulated/sustained release preparation of PHNO could prove to be of great value in the management of Parkinson's disease.

Introduction

The management of Parkinson's disease is complicated by the occurrence of involuntary movements and response fluctuations. These have been attributed to variations in the delivery of levodopa or dopamine agonists to receptors in the striatum.[1] Intravenous levodopa and subcutaneous lisuride infusions overcome many of the pharmacokinetic difficulties of oral treatment and have proved useful in the management of patients with severe 'on-off' fluctuations.[2,3] Clearly, an oral preparation with a pharmacokinetic profile similar to that of parenteral therapy would be of considerable value in such patients.

4-Propyl-9-hydroxynaphthoxazine (PHNO) is a novel D-2 dopamine agonist unrelated to the ergot and morphine derived agents presently in use.[4] It is a highly potent anti-parkinsonian drug in both MPTP-treated non-human primates[5] and in Parkinson's disease in man.[6,7] In view of its short duration of action, a sustained-release formulation (SR-PHNO) has been designed to allow prolonged drug release in the gastro-intestinal tract. Such a preparation may emulate levodopa infusion by providing a continuous supply of dopamine agonist.

The neurotoxin 1-methyl-4-phenyl-1,2,3,6-tetrahydropyridine (MPTP) produces a stable parkinsonian syndrome in primates following repeated intravenous injections.[8] The resulting model may be used to examine the effects of dopaminomimetic drugs.[5,9] In the present study, we have examined the response of MPTP-treated macaques to SR-PHNO.

Methods

Three cynomolgus monkeys received 3.2–4.4 mg/kg MPTP intravenously over 10–12 weeks at 1–2 week intervals. MPTP was discontinued when parkinsonism reached stage IV on the Hoehn and Yahr scale.[10] Two primates received chronic levodopa therapy (75 mg thrice daily as Sinemet-110) which began 1.5 and 7.0 months after the end of MPTP administration. Experiments with SR-PHNO were commenced 9 months after the cessation of MPTP.

SR-PHNO was prepared so as to deliver doses within the therapeutic range[5] for 12 hr. Following an overnight fast, animals were sedated with small doses of ketamine (1.4–1.7 mg/kg), transferred to a primate chair and SR-PHNO (2, 4, 8 or 12 mg) or placebo given. Animals were returned to an observation cage equipped with 3 photo-electric sensors connected to a cumulative counter. Activity counts were recorded at 30 min intervals for 16 hr together with behavioural observations taken from video recordings. Combined experiments with SR-PHNO and a therapeutic dose of unformulated PHNO (0.25 mg/kg) were performed using the same protocol. Additional trials were carried out using the same dose of conventional PHNO without SR-PHNO. Trials were performed in triplicate.

Results

Repeated MPTP administration led to a predictable stepwise decline in motor performance with increasing hypokinesia, bradykinesia, rigidity and both resting and postural tremor. Some improvement occurred for 3 weeks following the termination of MPTP but the animals' condition then remained stable for at least 12 months. Levodopa produced dose-dependent reversal of the parkinsonian syndrome. Animals receiving regular therapy developed peak-dose dyskinesia after just 4–8 weeks treatment.[9]

In placebo trials, the sedative effect of ketamine lasted for 2.0 hr, after which the animals remained active until lights were usually extinguished when they slept. SR-PHNO reversed parkinsonism in all animals in a dose-dependent manner. The optimum therapeutic dose which reversed all parkinsonian features without causing excessive hyperactivity or dyskinesia varied from 1.4–1.7 mg/kg. There was a dose-dependent delay of 2.5–7.3 hr before therapeutic effects were seen. Activity counts returned to control values 10–12 hr post-dose.

Combining a low dose of SR-PHNO (4 mg) with the unformulated drug resulted in two peaks in activity counts (Figure, A). This represented a true biphasic response as seen on videotape recordings of such trials. With larger doses (8 mg), a sustained uniphasic

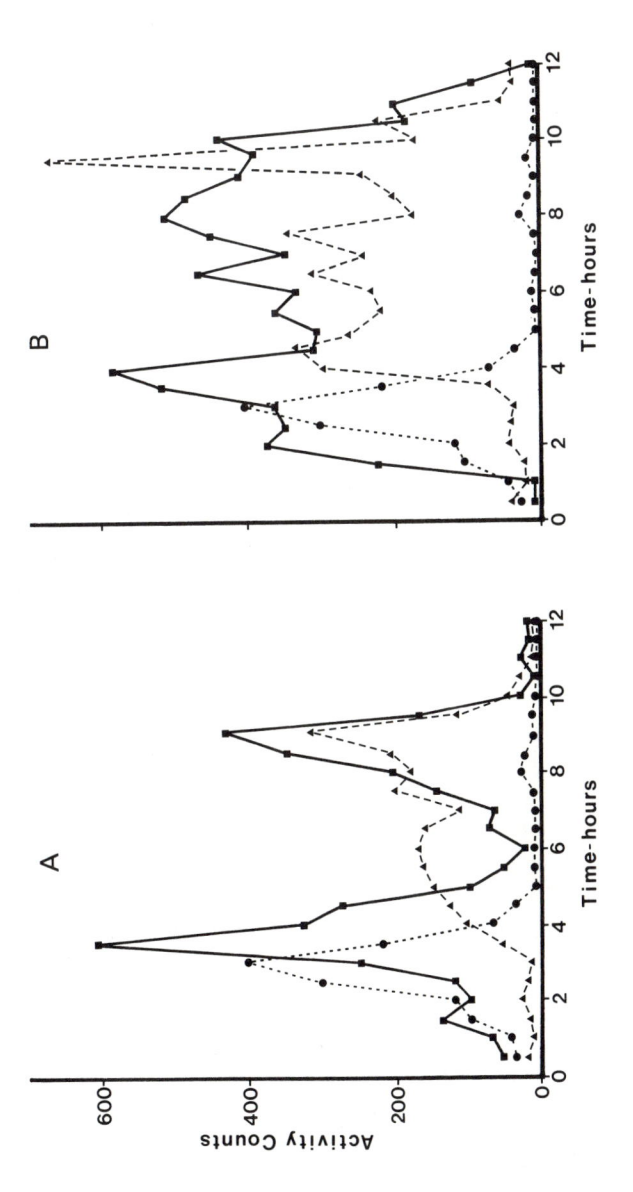

Figure. Effects of PHNO preparations on activity counts summated over 30 min periods in an MPTP-treated primate. Results represent the means of three trials. (A) Responses to unformulated PHNO (1 mg, ●), SR-PHNO (4 mg, ▲) and combined unformulated (1 mg) and SR-PHNO (4 mg, ■). (B) Responses to unformulated PHNO (1 mg, ●), SR-PHNO (8 mg, ▲) and combined unformulated (1 mg) and SR-PHNO (8 mg, ■).

response was seen (Figure, B). Thus, a therapeutic anti-parkinsonian effect was observed within 30 min post-dose which continued for 10–12 hr.

Discussion

The present study demonstrates the value of the MPTP primate model of parkinsonism in the evaluation of novel drug delivery technologies. In this preparation, the methylcellulose matrix delayed and prolonged the anti-parkinsonian effects of PHNO. Combining unformulated and SR-PHNO resulted in a rapid reversal of parkinsonism which lasted approximately 12 hr. Such a combined oral preparation offers more constant dopaminergic stimulation than that currently available with levodopa or other dopamine agonists. It should also benefit from a longer duration of response than recently described sustained-release forms of levodopa.[11] The potential value of such a preparation in the management of Parkinson's disease is considerable, particularly in patients with severe response fluctuations.

Acknowledgements—Supported by grants from Action Research for the Crippled Child and the Medical Research Council. We are grateful to Merck Sharp and Dohme for providing PHNO and Sinemet.

References

1 Fahn, S. (1982): In *Movement disorders*, ed C. D. Marsden & S. Fahn, p. 123. London: Butterworth.
2 Nutt, J. G., Woodward, W. R., Hammerstad, J. P., Carter, J. H. & Anderson, J. L. (1984): The 'on-off' phenomenon in Parkinson's disease. *N. Eng. J. Med.* **310**, 483–8.
3 Obeso, J. A., Luquin, M. R. & Martinez-Lage, J. M. (1986): Lisuride infusion pump: a device for the treatment of the motor fluctuations in Parkinson's disease. *Lancet* **i**, 467–70.
4 Martin, G. E., Williams, M., Pettibone, D. J., Yarbrough, G. G., Clineschmidt, B. V. & Jones, J. H. (1984): Pharmacological profile of a novel potent direct acting dopamine agonist, (+)-4-propyl-9-hydroxynaphthoxazine. *J. Pharmacol. Exp. Ther.* **230**, 569–76.
5 Clarke, C. E., Boyce, S., Sambrook, M. A., Stahl, S. M. & Crossman, A. R. (1988): Behavioural effects of (+)-4-propyl-9-hydroxynaphthoxazine in primates rendered parkinsonian with 1-methyl-4-phenyl-1,2,3,6-tetrahydropyridine. *Arch. Pharmacol.* **338**, 35–38.
6 Stoessl, A. J., Mak, E. & Calne, D. B. (1985): (+)-4-propyl-9-hydroxynaphthoxazine, a new dopaminomimetic, in the treatment of parkinsonism. *Lancet* **ii**, 1330–1.
7 Grandas, F. J., Quinn, N., Critchley, P., Rohan, A., Marsden, C. D. & Stahl, S. M. (1987): Anti-parkinsonian activity of a single oral dose of PHNO. *Movement Disorders* **2**, 47–51.
8 Burns, R. S., Chiueh, C. C., Markey, S. P., Ebert, M. H., Jacobowitz, D. M. & Kopin, I. J. (1983): A primate model of parkinsonism. *Proc. Natl. Acad. Sci.* **80**, 4546–50.
9 Clarke, C. E., Boyce, S., Sambrook, M. A. & Crossman, A. R. (1987): Timing of levodopa therapy: Evidence from MPTP-treated primates. *Lancet* **i**, 625.
10 Hoehn, M. M. & Yahr, M. D. (1967): Parkinsonism: onset, progression and mortality. *Neurology* **17**, 427–42.
11 Juncos, J. L., Fabbrini, G., Mouradian, M. M. & Chase, T. N. (1987): Controlled release levodopa-carbidopa (CR-5) in the management of parkinsonian motor fluctuations. *Arch. Neurol.* **44**, 1010–2.

23

A BEHAVIOURAL MODEL FOR STUDYING DOPAMINERGIC GRAFTS IN THE MARMOSET

L. E. Annett*, S. B. Dunnett*, D. C. Rogers*,
R. M. Ridley[†], H. F. Baker[†], P. Jenner[§]
and C. D. Marsden[‡]

*Department of Experimental Psychology, University of Cambridge, Downing Street, Cambridge, CB2 3EB; [†]Division of Psychiatry, Clinical Research Centre, Watford Road, Harrow, HA1 3UJ; [§]Parkinson's Disease Society Research Centre, Institute of Psychiatry, De Crespigny Park, London SE5 8AF; [‡]Institute of Neurology, Queen Square, London WC1N 3BG, UK

Summary

A series of behavioural tests was used to quantify the effects of unilateral 6-OHDA lesions in marmosets and assess any functional recovery following grafts of embryonic dopaminergic tissue into the striatum. Grafted and lesioned animals rotated *ipsilaterally*, both spontaneously and in response to 0.5 mg/kg amphetamine, during the first two months after surgery. After three months the direction of rotation by the grafted animals changed to become predominantly *contralateral*. The grafts did not produce any consistent changes on any of the other behavioural tests.

Introduction

Transplantation of catecholaminergic tissue may provide a radical new treatment for Parkinson's disease. Autografts of adrenal medulla tissue into the striatum or adjacent lateral ventricle of patients have been used in initial attempts to develop such a treatment.[1,2] While the survival and functional capacities of dopaminergic grafts have been studied extensively in rats,[3,4] there have been only a few reports of the effects of grafts in non-human primates. Adrenal medulla autografts survived when transplanted into the striata of rhesus macaques previously lesioned with 6-hydroxydopamine (6-OHDA), but the behavioural impact of these grafts was limited.[5] Fetal substantia nigra cells transplanted into African green monkeys were reported to reverse the Parkinsonian symptoms induced by the toxin N-methyl-4-phenyl-1,2,3-tetrahydropyridine (MPTP).[6]

The aim of the project described in this report has been to develop a series of behavioural tests for quantifying the effects of unilateral dopamine depletion in a primate, the common marmoset (*callithrix jacchus*), and make a functional assessment of grafts of embryonic dopaminergic tissue. In the first experiment, the duration and stability of the lesion-induced deficits were examined in detail.[7] The lesion, which yielded mean dopamine depletions of 98 per cent throughout the striatum and almost complete loss of cells from the substantia nigra on the lesioned side, produced quantifiable behavioural effects which included a shift in hand preference towards an ipsilateral bias, neglect of contralateral stimuli, reduced activity in a photocell cage, contralateral rotation in response to apomorphine and predominantly ipsilateral spontaneous and amphetamine-induced rotation. Provided the depletion of dopamine was extensive (>98 per cent) the effects generally persisted over the test period of 6 months, although individual animals occasionally showed some recovery on some tests while remaining impaired on others. Over a group of animals the deficits were sufficiently stable to provide a reliable baseline against which the effects could be measured.

Methods

In this pilot graft experiment, we have compared monkeys with nigrostriatal lesions and dopamine-rich grafts against animals with the lesion alone or sham-operated controls. Surgery was carried out under Saffan (Glaxovet Ltd) anaesthesia and aseptic conditions. A total volume of 11 μl of 6-OHDA (4 mg/ml) was injected into five sites distributed across the nigrostriatal bundle. The lesion was made on the side contralateral to the preferred hand as determined pre-operatively in the conveyor belt tests. Sham lesioned animals received injections of saline rather than the toxin.

Fourteen days after the initial lesion half the lesioned animals went on to receive grafts of foetal substantia nigra tissue. Graft tissue was obtained from the ventral mesencephalon of 74 day marmoset embryos (crown-to-rump length 13 mm; Carnegie stage 18–19). A dissociated cell suspension was prepared from the dissected tissue (two embryonic pieces per 30 μl) using standard procedures.[8] Eight sites within the caudate nucleus, putamen and nucleus accumbens on the lesioned side each received injections of 15 μl of the suspension. Six marmosets have received such grafts: two grafted animals, together with their lesion and sham lesion controls, have now been studied over the six month test period. The behavioural data from these animals are presented in this initial report of the experiment.

Behavioural tests were given pre-operatively, after the lesion, and at monthly intervals for 6 months following the graft.

(1.) Hand preference was measured over blocks of 100 trials (50 trials per test day) in which the animals were required to remove cubes of apple from (a) a stationary and (b) a moving conveyor belt on which apple arrived randomly from either direction.

(2.) Spontaneous biases in the home cage were assessed by counting the number of seconds during one minute intervals that the head was turned to the right or left with respect to the body.

(3.) Adhesive labels were placed bilaterally around the feet. The latencies to contact and remove the labels were recorded on six trials.

(4.) Complete rotations, either spontaneous or induced by 0.5 mg/kg amphetamine injected 30 min before the start of the test, were counted over 30 min periods.

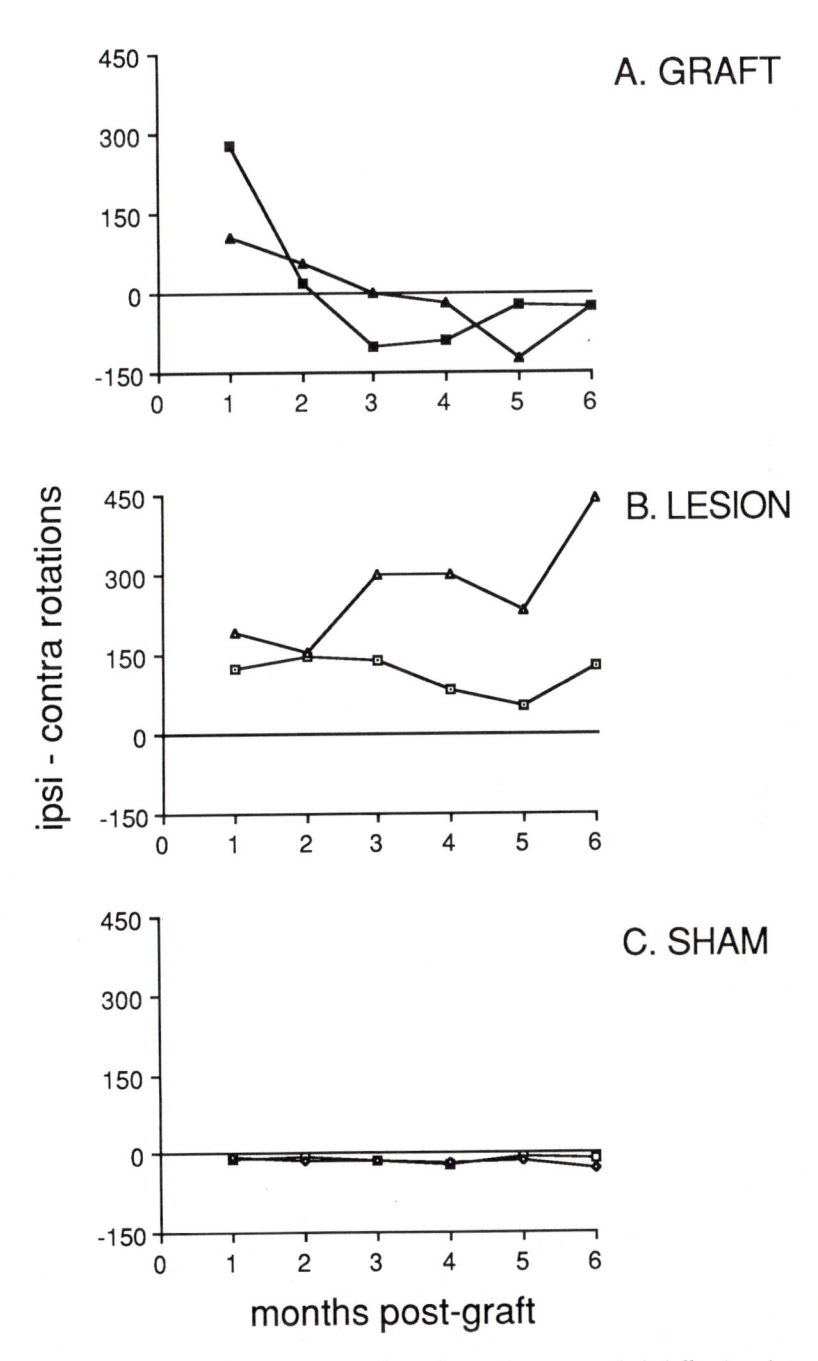

Figure. *Number of ipsilateral minus contralateral rotations recorded following intramuscular injections of 0.5 mg/kg amphetamine.* Individual data from: (A) two grafted; (B) two lesioned; and (C) two sham-lesioned animals.

Results and discussion

During the first 2 months after surgery the grafted and lesioned animals rotated *ipsilaterally*, both spontaneously and in response to 0.5 mg/kg amphetamine. The animals with sham lesions did not rotate. After 3–4 months the direction of rotation by the grafted animals changed to become predominantly *contralateral*. The lesioned animals which had not received grafts continued to rotate *ipsilaterally* (Figure).

In contrast to the changes shown by the grafted animals in the rotation tests, improvements on the other behavioural tasks were less dramatic. The strong ipsilateral hand preference exhibited after the lesion on the stationary conveyor belt trials persisted in both the grafted animals. One of the grafted animals did start to use the contralateral hand 3 months post-graft when retrieving an apple arriving from the ipsilateral direction on the moving conveyor belt. However, the second grafted animal continued to use the ipsilateral hand on all trials. Both animals showed some recovery from the lesion-induced tendency to sit with the head looking over the ipsilateral shoulder, although this recovery only occurred 5 months post-graft and was also seen in one of the lesioned animals. All grafted and lesioned animals continued to contact and remove the adhesive label placed on the ipsilateral foot before that on the contralateral foot. There were, however, some reductions in the latencies taken by the grafted animals to contact the contralateral label. In summary, apart from the changes in the rotation tests, there was no clear evidence of behavioural improvements in the grafted animals which have completed the experiment other than those which may have occurred through spontaneous recovery.

The conclusion that grafts may affect some of the behavioural changes induced by a dopaminergic lesion but leave others unaltered is consistent with the reported effects of grafts in rodents. Thus, while spontaneous and drug-induced rotation, akinesia and sensorimotor neglect can be substantially ameliorated by grafts in rats, other deficits such as the regulation of food and water intake, or skilled use of the contralateral limb, remain.[3,4,9] In primates, information on the effectiveness of grafts over a range of behavioural tests is clearly important given that the predicted extent of behavioural recovery is likely to be an important consideration in the clinical application of neuronal transplantation.

Acknowledgement—Supported by the Parkinson's Disease Society.

References

1 Backlund, E. -O., Granberg, P. -O., Hamberger, B., Knutsson, E., Mårtensson, A., Sedvall, G., Seiger, Å. & Olson, L. (1985): Transplantation of adrenal medullary tissue to striatum in parkinsonism. *J. Neurosurg.* **62**, 169–173.

2 Madrazo, I., Drucker-Colín, R., Díaz, V., Martínez-Mata, J., Torres, C. & Becerril, J. J. (1987): Open microsurgical autograft of adrenal medulla to the right caudate nucleus in two patients with intractable Parkinson's disease. *N. Engl. J. Med.* **316**, 831–834.

3 Dunnett, S. B., Björklund, A., Schmidt, R. H., Stenevi, U. & Iversen, S. D. (1983): Intracerebral grafting of neuronal cell suspensions. IV. Behavioural recovery in rats with unilateral 6-OHDA lesions following implantation of nigral cell suspensions in different brain sites. *Acta Physiol. Scand. Suppl.* **522**, 29–37.

4 Dunnett, S. B., Björklund, A., Schmidt, R. H., Stenevi, U. & Iversen, S. D. (1983): Intracerebral grafting of neuronal cell suspension. V. Behavioural recovery in rats with bilateral 6-OHDA lesions following implantation of nigral cell suspensions. *Acta Physiol. Scand. Suppl.* **522**, 39–47.

5 Morihisa, J. M., Nakamura, R. K., Freed, W. J., Mishkin, M. & Wyatt, R. J. (1987): Transplantation techniques and the survival of adrenal medulla autografts in the primate brain. *Ann. N. Y. Acad. Sci.* **495**, 599–605.
6 Redmond, D. E., Sladek, J. R., Jr, Roth, R. H., Collier, T. J., Elsworth, J. D., Deutch, A. Y. & Haber, S. N. (1986): Fetal neuronal grafts in monkeys given methylphenyltetrahydropyridine. *Lancet* **i**, 1125–1127.
7 Annett, L. E., Rogers, D. C. & Dunnett, S. B. (1988): Unilateral 6-OHDA lesions in marmosets: a primate model of Parkinson's disease: In *Proceedings of an International Conference on the Basal Ganglia*, ed R. H. S. Mindham. Manchester: Manchester University Press. (In Press).
8 Fine, A., Oertel, W. H., Hunt, S. P., Nomoto, M., Chong, P. N., Bond, A., Waters, C., Temlett, J. A., Annett, L. E., Dunnett, S. B., Jenner, P. & Marsden, C. D. (1988): Transplantation of embryonic marmoset dopaminergic neurons to the corpus striatum of marmosets rendered parkinsonian by MPTP. *Prog. Brain Res.* **74**. (In Press)
9 Dunnett, S. B., Whishaw, I. Q., Rogers, D. C. & Jones, G. H. (1987): Dopamine-rich grafts ameliorate whole body motor asymmetry and sensory neglect but not independent limb use in rats with 6-hydroxydopamine lesions. *Brain Res.* **415**, 63–78.

24

COMBINED LEVODOPA AND BROMOCRIPTINE THERAPY FOR PARKINSON'S DISEASE: EVIDENCE SUGGESTING THAT LEVODOPA ACTS AT SITES IN THE SUBSTANTIA NIGRA PARS RETICULATA

H. A. Robertson and G. S. Robertson

*Department of Pharmacology, Faculty of Medicine,
Dalhousie University, Halifax, Nova Scotia, Canada B3H 4H7*

Summary

Levodopa and bromocriptine appear to have at least additive effects in patients. Here we summarize evidence to suggest that the actions of these two drugs are based on activity at the two different dopamine receptors, D1 and D2. We propose that levodopa has important actions on D1 dopamine receptors in the substantia nigra while bromocriptine acts on D2 dopamine receptors in the basal ganglia (caudate-putamen). This idea suggests that the combination of selective D1 and D2 agonists may prove an innovative treatment for Parkinson's disease.

Introduction

Levodopa combined with bromocriptine is an effective treatment for Parkinson's disease and is equal to and, in some patients, probably superior to either agent alone.[1] Several mechanisms have been proposed to explain the effectiveness of combined levodopa and bromocriptine.[2,3] As a result of experiments in which we demonstrated synergistic effects resulting from the combination of selective D1 and D2 agonists,[4] we proposed that the effectiveness of the levodopa/bromocriptine combination might be the consequence of the activation of D1 receptors by dopamine formed from levodopa and the activation of D2 dopamine receptors by bromocriptine.[5] Bromocriptine is a relatively selective D2 agonist. A number of other reports have now confirmed the additive or synergistic effects of D1 and D2 agonists using both behavioural[6,7] and electrophysiological techniques.[8,9]

Paradoxically, while D1 and D2 agonists have synergistic effects *in vivo*, *in vitro* only opposing effects have been observed. For example, although D1 and D2 agonists have synergistic effects *in vivo*, in striatal homogenates D1 and D2 agonists have opposing actions on cyclic AMP levels.[10] D1 agonists produce an increase in cyclic AMP release while D2 selective agonists reduce cyclic AMP release in striatal tissue.[10] These results suggest that the effect of D1/D2 addition may not be expressed solely through interactions at the level of the striatum. To account for this, we have recently extended our hypothesis to include the anatomical sites of action of levodopa and bromocriptine in combination.[11,12]

Recently, the effects of D1 and D2 agonists on neural metabolic activity in rats unilaterally lesioned with 6-hydroxydopamine have been studied using the 2-deoxyglucose (2-DG) method.[13,14] Interestingly, for both levodopa and the D1 selective agonist SKF 38393,[13,14] the principal site of increased metabolic activity is the substantia nigra pars reticulata. It is known that D1 dopamine receptors in the pars reticulata of the substantia nigra are located not on the dopaminergic neurons but on the terminals of GABAergic striatonigral projection neurons.[15] The finding that levodopa and the D1 selective agonist SKF 38393 share the property of stimulating 2-DG uptake in the substantia nigra pars reticulata[13,14] reinforces our contention[5,10,11] that the actions of levodopa are on D1 dopamine receptors. The dendrites of the nigrostriatal pathway are also capable of releasing dopamine[16,17], which may exert an important modulatory action over striatal output by interacting with D1 dopamine receptors in the substantia nigra pars reticulata (SNpR).[16] Dopamine levels in the substantia nigra are also reduced after unilateral infusion of 6-OHDA. Consequently, levodopa may be producing circling in unilaterally lesioned rats by increasing dopamine levels not only in the striatum but also in the substantia nigra.[10,11]

The beneficial effects of the combination of levodopa and bromocriptine in Parkinson's disease may be the result of activation of D1 dopamine receptors in the substantia nigra pars reticulata combined with the activation of D2 dopamine receptors in the striatum. It is presumed that levodopa is converted to dopamine by L-aromatic amino acid decarboxylase (AAAD); the dopamine thus formed then acts at D1 dopamine receptors. As much as 20 per cent of initial AAAD enzyme activity remains in the striatum after loss of dopamine and serotonin neurons;[18] it is possible that similar AAAD activity remains in the substantia nigra after loss of dopaminergic neurons.

To test this idea, we have performed a number of simple experiments. First, we have studied the effects of levodopa on dopamine levels in the substantia nigra and striatum. Secondly, if levodopa does activate D1 dopamine receptors in the substantia nigra pars reticulata, it must first be converted to dopamine by AAAD in the SN. Consequently, blockade of AAAD in the substantia nigra with carbidopa should alter circling behaviour if conversion of levodopa to dopamine has functional importance at this site.

Methods

Studies were carried out in rats unilaterally lesioned with 6-hydroxydopamine. One week later, rats were randomly allocated to a vehicle or levodopa treatment group in which the experimental levodopa condition received carbidopa pretreatment (25 mg/kg, intraperitoneally) followed 1 hr later by a peripheral levodopa injection (25 mg/kg, i.p.). The control group received similar treatment except that the vehicle was administered instead of levodopa. One hour after the levodopa or vehicle injection the animals were killed and the striatum and substantia nigra were rapidly dissected on ice. Dopamine and dihydroxyphenylacetic acid (DOPAC) levels were assessed by high performance liquid chromatography with electrochemical detection. The limit of detection was 25 ng/g tissue (wet weight).

Results and discussion

The peripheral levodopa injection consistently induced contralateral circling in all the animals (230 ± 21 rotations/hr, fig. 2a) for at least a 3 hour period. As expected 6-OHDA injections into the substantia nigra caused a 98 per cent depletion of dopamine in the striatum (Fig. 1a) and a 70 per cent depletion in the substantia nigra (Fig. 1b). Following

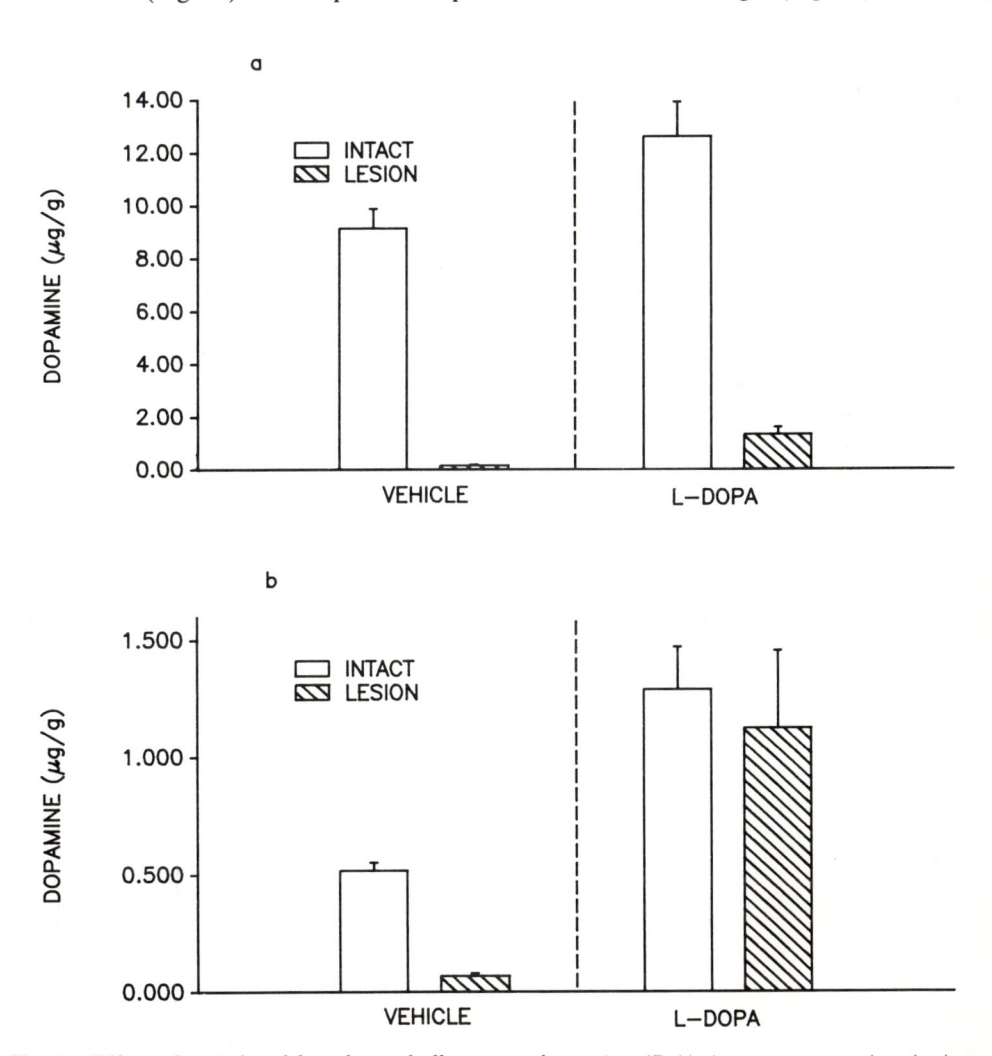

Fig. 1. *Effect of peripheral levodopa challenge on dopamine (DA) tissue concentration (μg/g wet weight) in the striatum and substantia nigra (SN) of the 6-OHDA lesioned rat.* (a) DA tissue concentration in the intact and denervated striatum after vehicle or levodopa in 6-OHDA-treated rats. (b) DA tissue concentration in the intact and 6-OHDA-lesioned SN after vehicle or levodopa. (Reprinted from Robertson, G.S. & Robertson, H. A. *Neurosci. Lett*, 1988, in press)

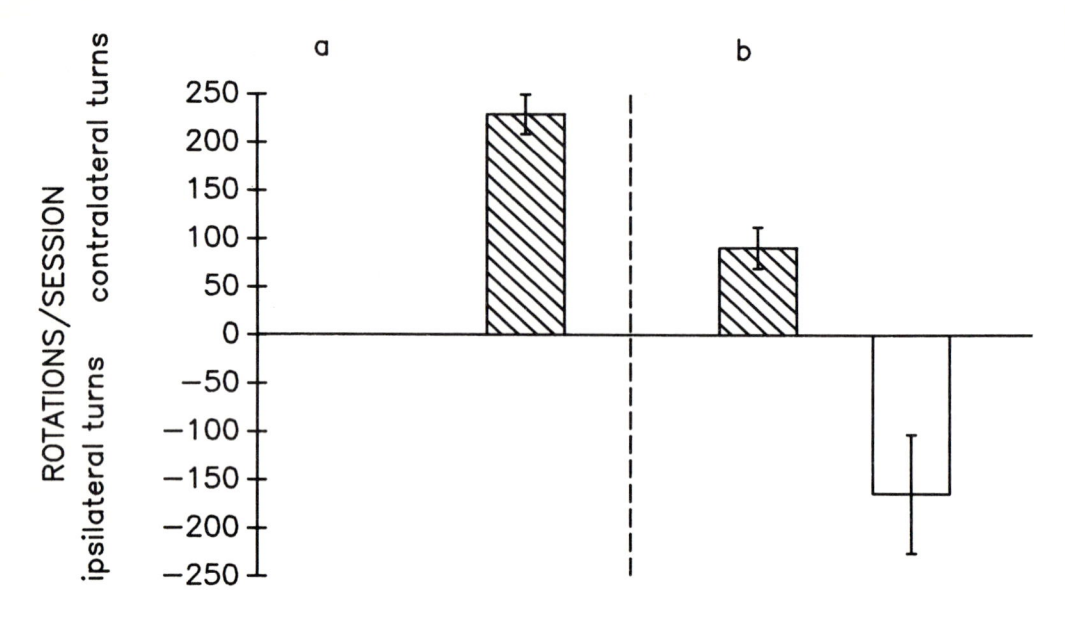

Fig. 2. *Effect of intranigral injection of carbidopa on the magnitude and direction of turning to a peripheral levodopa challenge.* Unilaterally 6-OHDA-treated rats that had been screened behaviourally as described above were implanted with a chronic indwelling cannula in the medial substantia nigra pars reticulata on the lesioned side. (a) Number of rotations in 1 hr to the levodopa treatment alone. (b) Number and direction of turns for a 1.5 hr period to the intranigral carbidopa-peripheral levodopa treatments. Hatched bars represent contralateral turns while the open bar represents ipsilateral rotations after carbidopa injection into the substantia nigra. (Reprinted from Robertson, G. S. & Robertson, H. A. *Neurosci. Lett*, 1988, in press)

levodopa, dopamine levels increase in the striatum on both the intact and the lesioned side after peripheral levodopa (Fig. 1a). The greater increase in dopamine on the lesioned side (150 per cent increase on the intact side compared with a 820 per cent increase on the lesioned side) may be the result of enhanced metabolic activity of the surviving dopaminergic neurons.[19] However, levodopa treatment only partially restores striatal dopamine levels (to about 10 per cent of normal). DOPAC content of the striatum after levodopa parallels the changes seen for dopamine levels in this nucleus after levodopa challenge (data not shown).

In contrast, levodopa was able to restore the dopamine content in the lesioned substantia nigra completely (Fig. 1b). DOPAC levels in the substantia nigra also mirrored the complete recovery seen after levodopa for dopamine levels (data not shown). In order to determine whether the dramatic recovery in dopamine levels in the substantia nigra after levodopa is of functional consequence for the 6-OHDA-lesioned animal, the dopa decarboxylase inhibitor carbidopa was infused directly into the substantia nigra 30 min prior to levodopa challenge. Interestingly, carbidopa pretreatment not only reduced the number of turns contraversive to the lesioned side but also reversed the direction of turning (Fig. 2). Initially, animals turned in the expected contraversive direction, but after approximately 20 min they stopped rotating and then began to rotate in the opposite direction, ie, ipsilaterally (Fig. 2b). Presumably the carbidopa, by blocking dopamine synthesis in the lesioned substantia nigra permitted the intact substantia nigra to become dominant, thus reversing the direction of turning. Circling to levodopa has been shown to continue even after dopamine concentrations in the denervated striatum return to pretreatment levels,[20] indicating that increased dopamine levels in other sites may be able to sustain the circling in its later phase. Consequently, the delay in the ability of carbidopa to reverse the direction of rotation may represent a waning of striatal influence, leaving only nigrally-mediated turning. This nigrally-mediated turning is blocked by carbidopa. The ability of the D1 antagonist SCH 23390 to block the second peak of rotation induced by the mixed D1–D2 agonist apomorphine, but not the inital peak, is also consistent with the suggestion that the D1 receptors in the SNpR may be mediating the later phase of circling to levodopa.[21]

These results are consistent with the idea that the SNpR is an important therapeutic site of action for levodopa in Parkinson's disease and suggest that the search for drugs acting at these sites will lead to improved treatment of the disease.

Acknowledgements—We are grateful for the continued support of the Parkinson Foundation of Canada and the Medical Research Council of Canada.

References

1 Calne, D. B., Teychenne, P., Claveria, L. E., Eastman, R., Greenacre, J. K. & Petrie, A. (1974): Bromocriptine in parkinsonism. *Br. Med. J.* **4**, 442–44.
2 Goldstein, M., Lieberman, A. & Meller, E. (1985): A possible molecular mechanism for the antiparkinson action of bromocriptine in combination with levodopa. *Trends Pharmacol. Sci.* **6**, 436–437.
3 Jackson, D. M. & Jenkins, O. F. (1985): Hypothesis: bromocriptine lacks intrinsic dopamine receptor stimulating properties. *J. Neural. Trans.* **62**, 219–230.
4 Robertson, G. S. & Robertson, H. A. (1986): Synergistic effects of D1 and D2 dopamine agonists on turning behaviour in rats. *Brain Res.* **384**, 387–390.
5 Robertson, H. A. & Robertson, G. S. (1986): The antiparkinson action of bromocriptine in combination with levodopa: a possible role for both D1 and D2 receptors? *Trends Pharmacol. Sci.* **7**, 224–225.
6 Mashurano, M. & Waddington, J. L. (1986): Stereotyped behaviour in response to the selective D2 dopamine receptor agonist Ru 24213 is enhanced by treatment with the selective D1 agonist SKF 38393. *Neuropharmacology* **25**, 947–949.
7 Jackson, D. M. & Hashizume, M. (1986): Bromocriptine induces marked locomotor stimulation in dopamine-depleted mice when D1 receptors are stimulated with SK & F 38393. *Psychopharmacology* **90**, 147–3.
8 Carlson, J. H., Bergstrom, D. A. & Walters, J. R. (1987): Stimulation of both D1 and D2 dopamine receptors appears necessary for full expression of postsynaptic effects of dopamine agonists: a neurophysiological study. *Brain Res.* **400**, 205–218.
9 Weick, B. G. & Walters, J. R. (1987): Effects of D1 and D2 dopamine receptor stimulation on the activity of substantia nigra pars compacta neurons in 6-hydroxydopamine lesioned rats: D1/D2 coactivation induces potentiated responses. *Brain Res.* **405**, 234–246.
10 Stoof, J. C. & Kebabian, J. W. (1981): Opposing roles for D1 and D2 dopamine receptors in efflux of cyclic AMP from rat striatum. *Nature* **294**, 366–368.
11 Robertson, G. S. & Robertson, H. A. (1987): D-1 and D-2 dopamine agonist synergism: separate sites of action? *Trends Pharmacol. Sci.* **8**, 295–299.
12 Robertson, H. A. & Robertson, G. S. (1987): Combined L-Dopa and bromocriptine therapy for Parkinson's Disease: A proposed mechanism of action. *Clin. Neuropharmacol.* **10**, 84–87.
13 Trugman, J. M. & Wooten, G. F. (1986): The effects of L-Dopa on regional cerebral glucose utilization in rats with unilateral lesions of the substantia nigra. *Brain Res.* **379**, 264–274.
14 Trugman, J. M. & Wooten, G. F. (1987): Selective D1 and D2 dopamine agonists differentially alter basal ganglia glucose utilization in rats with unilateral 6-hydroxydopamine substantia nigra lesions. *J. Neurosci.* **7**, 2927–2935.
15 Savasta, M., Dubois, A., Benavides, J. & Scatton, B. (1986): Different neuronal location of [^{H}]SCH 23390 binding sites in pars reticulata and pars compacta of the substantia nigra in the rat. *Neurosci. Lett.* **72**, 265–271.

16 Gauchy, C., Kemel, M. L., Romo, R., Glowiniski, J. & Besson, M. J. (1987): The role of dopamine released from distal and proximal dendrites of nigrostriatal dopaminergic neurons in the control of GABA transmission in the thalamic nucleus ventralis medialis in the cat, *Neuroscience* **22**, 935–946.
17 Reubi, J. -C., Iversen, L. L. & Jessell, T. M. (1977): Dopamine selectively increases H- Gaba release from slices of rat substantia nigra in vitro. *Nature* **268**, 652–654.
18 Melamed, E., Hefti, F., Bitton, V. & Globus, M. (1984): Suppression of L-Dopa-induced circling in rats with nigral lesions by blockade of central dopa-decarboxylase. *Neurology* **34**, 66–70.
19 Hornykiewicz, O. (1974): The mechanisms of action of L-Dopa in Parkinson's disease. *Life Sci.* **15**, 1249–1259.
20 Spencer, S. E & Wooten, G. F. (1984): Pharmacologic effects of L-dopa are not closely linked temporally to striatal dopamine concentration. *Neurology* **34**, 1509–1511.
21 Herrera-Marschitz, M. & Ungerstedt, U. (1985): Effect of the dopamine D-1 antagonist SCH 23390 on rotational behaviour induced by apomorphine and pergolide in 6-hydroxy-dopamine denervated rats. *Eur. J. Pharmacol.* **109**, 49–54.

25

3-PPP ENANTIOMERS SUPPRESS NEUROLEPTIC-INDUCED PERSISTENT ABNORMAL MOVEMENTS IN CEBUS APELLA MONKEYS

David Clark*, Peter LeWitt[†] and Beverly Kovacic[§]

[§]*Department of Neurology, Lafayette Clinic, 951 East Lafayette, Detroit, MI 48207, U.S.A.* [†]*Neuropsychopharmacology Laboratory, Department of Psychology, University of Reading, Earley Gate, Whiteknights, Reading RG26 2AL, U.K.* *Clinical Neuroscience Department, Sinai Hospital of Detroit, 6767 West Outer Drive, Detroit, MI 48235, U.S.A.*

Summary

Effects of the enantiomers of the dopamine agonist 3-PPP were examined in three *Cebus apella* monkeys with persistent abnormal movements induced by prior long-term treatment with fluphenazine enanthate. In two of the monkeys, (−)-3-PPP abolished the abnormal movements with minimal acute motor signs. (+)-3-PPP produced a dose-dependent suppression of the persistent abnormal movements of one of these monkeys, but this was accompanied by the appearance of acute motor signs such as tongue protrusions, hyperkinesia and stereotypy. At the highest dose, there was a clear biphasic effect during the time that persistent abnormal movements were abolished. Acute motor signs were apparent only during an initial phase after injection; during the second phase there were no abnormal movements of any kind. The persistent abnormal movements of a third monkey were not reduced by either enantiomer of 3-PPP. The amelioratory effect produced by these compounds is probably related to their ability to act as dopamine autoreceptor agonists, while the acute motor signs observed with higher doses of (+)-3-PPP are likely to be due to activation of postsynaptic dopamine receptors. The present findings suggest that (−)-3-PPP and drugs with a similar pharmacological profile might be effective as symptomatic treatments for tardive dyskinesia without the liability of inducing acute extrapyramidal dysfunction.

Introduction

Tardive dyskinesia (TD) is a complex syndrome of hyperkinetic involuntary abnormal movements observed in predisposed individuals following prolonged treatment with neuroleptic drugs. The syndrome is thought to be a consequence of an overactivity of striatal dopamine systems in the brain, although it is accepted that other mechanisms or neurotransmitter systems may contribute to the pathophysiology.[1,2] Neuroleptics are the most effective drugs for suppressing symptoms of TD, probably exerting their antidyskinetic effect via blockade of postsynaptic dopamine receptors.[3] However, these drugs are unacceptable as a treatment for TD because they produce the disorder in the first place, and symptoms may re-emerge and worsen with continued use. At present, there is no satisfactory pharmacotherapy for alleviating TD.

One potential strategy for treating TD is based on the principle of auto-regulation of dopamine neuronal function.[4] It is now widely accepted that dopamine receptors located on the presynaptic terminal and somatodendritic regions of dopaminergic neurons are involved in the regulation of synthesis and release of the neurotransmitter, and in the impulse flow of dopaminergic neurons.[5,6] Low doses of classical dopamine agonists preferentially stimulate dopamine autoreceptors leading to a reduction in central dopaminergic function. Several studies have revealed that dopamine agonists such as apomorphine can ameliorate the symptoms of TD, but such beneficial effects have not always been observed.[1,3] At present, it is difficult to judge the value of this strategy, since only a limited number of dopamine agonists have been assessed clinically and these stimulate postsynaptic dopamine receptors in addition to dopamine autoreceptors.

In recent years, a number of more selective dopamine autoreceptor agonists have been developed.[6-8] The most thoroughly studied of these compounds is the dopamine analogue 3-(3-hydroxy-phenyl)-N-n-propylpiperidine (3-PPP) and its enantiomers.[7-11] Racemic 3-PPP was initially described as a very selective dopamine autoreceptor agonist on the basis of *in vivo* biochemical and behavioural findings. Subsequent work has revealed that both enantiomers of this compound are active at dopamine receptors, although they exhibit different pharmacological profiles. (+)-3-PPP acts in a manner similar to classical dopamine agonists, stimulating dopamine autoreceptors in lower doses and also postsynaptic dopamine receptors in the higher dose range. On the other hand, (−)-3-PPP exerts agonist activity at dopamine autoreceptors but acts as an antagonist at normosensitive postsynaptic dopamine receptors. The pharmacological profile of (−)-3-PPP has been considered of particular interest, since this compound reduces behavioural function in laboratory animals considered predictive of antipsychotic activity, but does not induce extra-pyramidal dysfunction. Similar effects have been reported for a transfused analogue of 3-PPP, HW 165, and transdihydrolisuride.[7,8]

The *Cebus apella* species of monkey has been of particular value as an animal model of tardive dyskinesia.[12-29] Long-term treatment of these animals with haloperidol or fluphenazine results in a number of seemingly involuntary movements which persist long after drug withdrawal. Many of these movements resemble the clinical features of tardive dyskinesia and exhibit a similar pharmacological responsiveness. For example, classical dopamine receptor antagonists readily reduce such persistent movements but also induce parkinsonism.[14,18] Interestingly, these abnormal movements could be suppressed by racemic 3-PPP (in two of four monkeys) and its enantiomers (in one tested monkey) without the development of acute extrapyramidal reactions.[20] In the present study, we have evaluated the effects of both (+)- and (−)-3-PPP in three *Cebus apella* monkeys with persistent abnormal movements previously induced by chronic neuroleptic treatment.[16,17,19] A more detailed report of this work has been presented elsewhere.[21]

Methods

Three adult female *Cebus apella* monkeys (Elly, Karman and Ginger) were initially treated with depot intramuscular injections of fluphenazine enanthate (0.1–3.2 mg/kg body weight) every other week for one year. During this period, they displayed a variety of acute neurological signs (eg, parkinsonism and dystonic reactions) similar to those observed in humans receiving this class of drug. Following neuroleptic withdrawal, other abnormal involuntary movements developed and persisted for periods of 2–11 months. Many of these movements resembled the clinical features of TD. Once these persistent movements had remitted, they were restored after withdrawal from a 4 week 'booster' course of fluphenazine. Full details of this initial work have been published elsewhere.[16,17,19]

The present investigation commenced after the monkeys had been drug-free for a period of several months. The following persistent abnormal movements could be easily quantified:

Elly displayed intermittent, stereotyped tic-like head movements; she would throw or swirl her head backward and immediately bring it forward again. This head movement often appeared to be part of, or an extension of, a stereotyped stepping across the cage. However, head and stepping movements also occurred independently of each other.

Karman had a forelimb dyskinesia consisting of spreading and closing of the fingers of the right forepaw, or movement of the forepaws in a manner termed 'handrubbing'. In the absence of humans, this monkey also displayed an intermittent head swirling while standing quadrupedally.

Ginger showed tongue protrusions and repetitive opening and closing of the fingers of the left forepaw.

The behaviour of two of the monkeys (Elly and Karman) in the home cage was assessed from 3 minute videotapes made before or various times after intramuscular injection of (+)-3-PPP, (−)-3-PPP or saline. One investigator (BK) stood near the cage during each taping. Karman was also videotaped for an additional minute with no investigator present. Ginger was taped while she was in a restraining chair to optimize counting of the abnormal movements; each tape consisted of a 2 minute full-view of the monkey followed by a 2 minute close-up of the face. Two of the investigators (BK and DC) counted the abnormal movements at each time interval from the tapes (DC was 'blind' to treatment modality). Karman's finger movements were counted by BK during direct observation, since they could not be reliably counted from the tapes. Motor effects other than alteration of the usual persistent abnormal movements were scored for each monkey on a qualitative scale of 0 to 7 (see Table). The inter-rater agreement for both quantitative and qualitative measures was high (mean Pearson correlation coefficient ± SEM was 0.87 ± 0.04, $P < 0.001$). These methods are described in more detail elsewhere.[21]

Results

Both enantiomers of 3-PPP produced a dose-related suppression of Elly's persistent abnormal movements (head movement and stereotyped stepping) as illustrated in Fig. 1. Low doses (0.5–1.0 mg/kg, intramuscularly) of the drugs were ineffective, while higher doses completely abolished these movements. The amelioratory effects of (−)-3-PPP in Elly were not accompanied by any signs of parkinsonism or other serious acute motor signs. Higher doses of drug (4–8 mg/kg) resulted in a minimal level of checking movements of the head and trembling (see Table). The monkey vomited several times during the initial 30 minutes of these sessions.

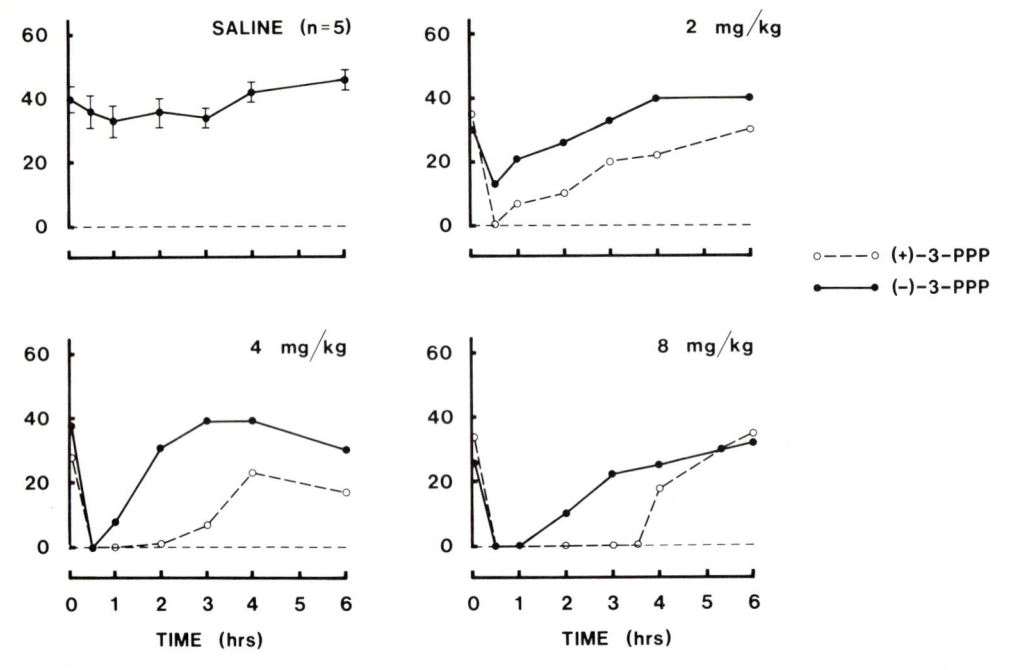

Fig. 1. *Effects of the enantiomers of 3-PPP on Elly's persistent abnormal movements.* Graphs represent the number of counts (per 3 min observation period) of persistent movements (abnormal head movements plus stereotyped stepping movements not accompanied by a head movement) at various time intervals after drug or vehicle injection. Each point shows the average of a count by each of two raters. The saline graph represents the mean ± SEM for five control sessions.

Table. *Acute motor signs of the enantiomers of 3-PPP.* Symptoms were judged as 0-absent; 1-borderline; 2-minimal; 3-mild; 4-moderate; 5-marked; 6-severe; 7-extremely severe.

Monkey	Karman			Elly					Ginger				
3-PPP enantiomer	(−)	(−)	(−)	(−)	(−)	(+)	(+)	(+)	(−)	(−)	(+)	(+)	(+)
mg/kg	6	8	10	4	8	2	4	8[a]	4 chr[d]	8 chr	4 chr	4 hc	8 hc
Trembling		1	1	2	2				3	4	4		
Checking[b]	2	2	3	2		4	6	4				5	
Hyperkinesia[c]							5	3			6		
Tongue protrusions							2	7					
Stereotypy								4					

[a]Effects during phase I of drug reaction. During phase II there were no abnormal movements (see text).
[b]Numerous short quick movements of the head in any direction.
[c]Elly: The animal sat most of the time during phase I displaying almost constant, low magnitude, somewhat stereotyped movements of trunks, legs and feet.
  Ginger: Near constant movement of all body parts in a non-stereotyped fashion.
[d]chr = tested in chair; hc = tested in home cage.

(+)-3-PPP appeared to be more effective than its enantiomeric twin, although it produced significantly more acute motor signs (see Table). The highest dose (8 mg/kg) exerted a clear biphasic effect during the 3.5 hours that the underlying persistent abnormal movements were abolished. During phase I, which lasted about two hours, Elly sat most of the time and displayed tongue protrusions, hyperkinesis, stereotyped movements of the right arm, and checking movements of the head. She appeared tense and was easily startled. Tongue movements during the first 40 minutes of this phase were sustained dystonic movements to one side. Thereafter, many tongue movements were rapid flicks or swirling motions. During phase II, from 2.5–3.5 hours after the drug injection, Elly showed no abnormal movements. She sat calmly and appeared to be unconcerned about the presence of the investigator, which was in contrast to her usual behaviour of standing and then moving about bipedally, always watching the person present. This reduction in general activity, which was also observed with (−)-3-PPP, was not accompanied by any obvious signs of sedation. Details of the acute motor signs observed with other doses of (+)-3-PPP are summarized in the Table. A tendency towards a similar biphasic effect was observed following administration of 4 mg/kg of the drug.

(−)-3-PPP produced a dose-related reduction of Karman's persistent head and forelimb movements at 30 minutes after injection. Higher doses of the drug completely abolished these movements. However, the beneficial effect on finger movements was short-lived; only head movements were still suppressed 1 or 2 hours after drug administration (Fig. 2). The effect of (+)-3-PPP was not assessed in this monkey.

Neither enantiomer of 3-PPP reduced the abnormal tongue and finger movements exhibited by Ginger. When this monkey was first tested in the restraint chair, (+)-3-PPP (4 mg/kg) produced pronounced motor agitation for approximately 2 hours. Finger

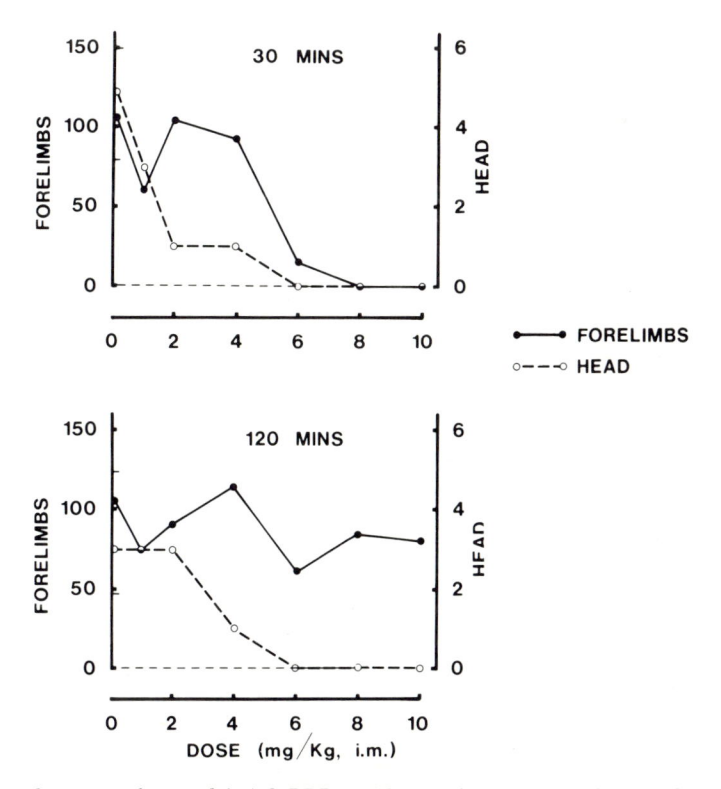

Fig. 2. *Effects of various doses of (−)-3-PPP on Karman's persistent abnormal movements at 30 and 120 min after injection.* Illustrated are the number of abnormal movements of the forelimbs (left ordinate scale) and head (right ordinate scale) during 3 and 1 minute observation periods, respectively. Data for five saline sessions have been averaged (mean ± SEM).

movements and tongue protrusions were increased. However, these effects were not observed when Ginger was subsequently tested with the same dose of drug in the home cage. Only checking movements were induced by 8 mg/kg (+)-3-PPP in this situation. A retest in the restraining chair with 4 mg/kg again resulted in motor agitation, and elevated finger movement and tongue protrusion counts.

Discussion

The present results confirm the observation of Häggstrom and colleagues[20] that the enantiomers of 3-PPP can suppress neuroleptic-induced persistent abnormal movements in *Cebus apella* monkeys. (−)-3-PPP produced beneficial effects in two of the three monkeys, while its enantiomeric twin ameliorated the symptoms displayed by one of two monkeys tested with the drug. The reliability of these results has been examined in one monkey (Elly) by testing two doses of (−)-3-PPP before and after a 9 month period. During this period, the animal received a 4 week 'booster' course of fluphenazine which enhanced the baseline level of persistent abnormal movements. Nonetheless, results obtained with the two doses of (−)-3-PPP before and after the 9 month period were very similar.[21]

The observation that (−)-3-PPP exerted these beneficial effects while producing at worst only minimal acute motor signs (trembling and checking movements of the head) is of particular importance. Although classical dopamine receptor antagonists readily reduce persistent abnormal movements induced in *Cebus apella* monkeys,[14,18] as in humans,[2] this is generally accompanied by pronounced parkinsonism. Such effects were not observed in either the present study or by Häggstrom and colleagues,[20] despite the fact that (−)-3-PPP is known to act as a weak antagonist at normosensitive postsynaptic dopamine receptors.[7,8] Thus it would appear that a reduction of dopamine function produced by this weak postsynaptic action, accompanied by an activation of dopamine autoreceptors, is not sufficient to produce the same marked motor disturbances that follow administration of classical dopamine receptor antagonists. In this context, it is relevant that (−)-3-PPP, in contrast to the former class of drug, does not produce catalepsy or muscular rigidity in normal rodents.[7,8]

Although (+)-3-PPP abolished Elly's underlying persistent abnormal movements, the drug produced a variety of acute motor signs. A clear biphasic effect was observed with the highest dose of drug. Initially, there were acute motor signs, but no persistent abnormal movements. During a second phase, commencing about 2 hours after drug administration, neither acute nor persistent abnormal movements were observed. The initial acute motor signs, which included various forms of tongue protrusion and a generalised hyperkinesia, were very similar to the motor effects observed in this animal following administration of the indirect dopamine agonist d-amphetamine (unpublished observations). Presumably, these stimulatory effects of (+)-3-PPP reflect an activation of postsynaptic dopamine receptors which is in accord with the known pharmacological profile of this compound.[7] It is certainly intriguing that while inducing a stimulation of certain aspects of motor output, (+)-3-PPP still abolishes the underlying persistent abnormal movement. Whether this reflects a pharmacological dissociation between the activation of different receptors linked to different patterns of movement or is simply due to behavioural competition remains to be disclosed.

The lack of acute signs observed during the second phase of Elly's response to 8 mg/kg (+)-3-PPP is likely related to a reduction in brain levels of drug and a loss of the postsynaptic dopamine receptor stimulatory effect. The reduction in persistent abnormal movements could therefore be related to a selective activation of dopamine autoreceptors, similar to that occurring after administration of lower doses of drug. In combination with the (−)-3-PPP data, these findings suggest that the 3-PPP enantiomers reduce persistent abnormal movements by selectively stimulating dopamine autoreceptors and reducing release of the transmitter. However, we cannot exclude an additional role of a weak postsynaptic dopamine receptor antagonist action of (−)-3-PPP.

Although (−)-3-PPP produced beneficial effects in two monkeys, the persistent abnormal movements of a third (Ginger) were not ameliorated. Häggstrom and colleagues[20] also reported that racemic 3-PPP was only effective in reducing the dyskinesias in two of their four monkeys. At present, it is not known why the abnormal movements of some animals are more amenable to certain pharmacological manipulations than are those of others. The present finding cannot simply be attributed to a difference in response topography, since both Karman and Ginger had a finger dyskinesia. Furthermore, Ginger's tongue protrusions were not reduced by doses of (−)-3-PPP which were effective in the monkey with similar symptoms reported by Häggstrom et al.[20]

Several other points relevant to our findings are mentioned briefly. The results obtained with Ginger emphasize the influence of the environment on drug modification of neuroleptic-induced abnormal movements. A dose of 4 mg/kg (+)-3-PPP produced motor agitation when the animal was seated in a restraining chair, but not when free to move in her home cage. Although Ginger was well adapted to the restraining chair, and appeared calm and content during saline control sessions, it is possible that confinement stress might have produced alterations in dopamine systems which combined with drug-induced changes to produce the motor agitation seen after (+)-3-PPP (see [21] for further discussion).

Interestingly, (−)-3-PPP and low doses of (+)-3-PPP produced an apparent calming effect and reduced concern about the presence of the experimenter. The animals were not evidently drowsy, although further studies are required to examine their level of vigilance following administration of these drugs. The previously reported anxiolytic effects of the 3-PPP enantiomers (and low doses of apomorphine)[22] may be of particular relevance to our current observations. However, as we have discussed earlier,[21] it is unlikely that such calming effects underlie the observed antidyskinetic effects of the drugs.

Arnt and colleagues[11] have previously demonstrated that both enantiomers of 3-PPP induce emesis in dogs, probably by virtue of dopamine agonist activity in the emetic trigger zone. (−)-3-PPP induced several vomiting episodes in one or our monkeys; no other instances were observed in our other work or in the study by Häggstrom et al.[20]

The fact that (−)-3-PPP reduced persistent abnormal movements without producing parkinsonism or other extrapyramidal acute signs suggests that this drug, and others with a similar pharmacological profile, might be effective as relatively selective antidyskinetic agents in man. Naturally, their clinical value will also depend on maintenance of such beneficial effects during long-term administration. If such drugs prove to be useful for treating psychotic states,[8,23] their continued use may not produce the extrapyramidal dysfunction which is observed in a significant proportion of patients on current neuroleptic therapy. The results of future clinical trials are eagerly awaited.

Acknowledgements—The present work was carried out at Lafayette Clinic, Detroit and was supported by the State of Michigan. DC is currently supported by the SERC (U.K.).

References

1 Gerlach, J., Casey, D. E. & Korsgaard, S. (1986): Tardive dyskinesia epidemiology, pathophysiology, and pharmacology. In *Movement disorders*, ed N. S. Shah & A. G. Donald, pp 119–147. New York: Plenum Press.

2 Marsden, C. D., Mindham, R. H. S. & Mackay, A. V. P. (1986): Extrapyramidal movement

disorders produced by antipsychotic drugs. In *The psychopharmacology and treatment of schizophrenia*, ed P. B. Bradley & S. R. Hirsch, pp 340–402. New York: Oxford University Press.

3 Jeste, D. V. & Wyatt, R. J. (1982): *Understanding and treating tardive dyskinesia*. New York: The Guilford Press.

4 Carlsson, A. (1975): Dopaminergic autoreceptors. In *Chemical tools in catecholamine research*, vol II, ed O. Almgren, A. Carlsson & J. Engel, pp 219–224. Amsterdam: North-Holland.

5 Roth, R. H. (1979): Dopamine autoreceptors: pharmacology, function and comparison with postsynaptic dopamine receptors. *Community Psychopharmacol.* **3**, 429–445.

6 Wolf, M. E. & Roth, R. H. (1987): Dopamine autoreceptors. In *Dopamine receptors*, ed I. Creese & C. M. Fraser, pp 45–96. New York: Alan R. Liss, Inc.

7 Clark, D., Hjorth, S. & Carlsson, A. (1985): Dopamine receptor agonists: Mechanisms underlying autoreceptor selectivity. I. Review of the evidence. *J. Neural Transm.* **62**, 1–52.

8 Clark, D., Hjorth, S. & Carlsson, A. (1985): Dopamine receptor agonists: Mechanisms underlying autoreceptor selectivity. II. Theoretical considerations. *J. Neural Transm.* **62**, 171–207.

9 Hjorth, S., Carlsson, A., Wikström, H., Lindberg, P., Sanchez, D., Hacksell, U., Arvidsson, L.-E., Svensson, U. & Nilsson, J. L. G. (1981): 3-PPP, a new centrally acting DA-receptor agonist with selectivity for autoreceptors. *Life Sci.* **28**, 1225–1238.

10 Hjorth, S., Carlsson, A., Clark, D., Svensson, K., Wikström, H., Sanchez, D., Lindberg, P., Hacksell, U., Arvidsson, L.-E., Johnansson, A. & Nilsson, J. L. G. (1983): Central dopamine receptor agonist and antagonist actions of the enantiomers of 3-PPP. *Psychopharmacology* **81**, 89–99.

11 Arnt, J., Bøgesø, K. P., Christensen, A. V., Hyttel, J., Larsen, J.-J. & Svendsen, O. (1983): Dopamine receptor agonistic and antagonistic effects of 3-PPP enantiomers. *Psychopharmacology* **81**, 199–207.

12 Gunne, L.-M. & Bárány, S. (1976): Haloperidol-induced tardive dyskinesia in monkeys. *Psychopharmacology* **50**, 237–240.

13 Gunne, L.-M. & Bárány, S. (1979): A monitoring test for the liability of neuroleptic drugs to induce tardive dyskinesia. *Psychopharmacology* **63**, 195–198.

14 Bárány, S. & Gunne, L.-M. (1979): Pharmacological modification of experimental tardive dyskinesia. *Acta Pharmacol. Toxicol.* **45**, 107–111.

15 Bárány, S., Häggstrom, J.-E. & Gunne, L.-M. (1983): Application of a primate model for tardive dyskinesia. *Acta Pharmacol. Toxicol.* **52**, 86–89.

16 Kovacic, B. & Domino, E. F. (1982): A monkey model of tardive dyskinesia (TD): evidence that reversible TD may turn into irreversible TD. *J. Clin. Psychopharmacol.* **2**, 305–306.

17 Kovacic, B. & Domino, E. F. (1984): Fluphenazine-induced acute and tardive dyskinesias in monkeys. *Psychopharmacology* **84**, 310–314.

18 Kovacic, B., Ruffing, D. & Stanley, M. (1986): Effect of neuroleptics and of potential new antipsychotic drugs (MJ 13859-1 and MJ 13980-1) on a monkey model of tardive dyskinesia. *J. Neural. Transm.* **65**, 39–49.

19 Domino, E. F. & Kovacic, B. (1983): Monkey models of tardive dyskinesia. *Mod. Prob. Pharmacopsychiatry* **21**, 21–33.

20 Häggstrom, J.-E., Gunne, L.-M., Carlsson, A. & Wikström, H. (1983): Anti-dyskinetic action of 3-PPP, a selective dopaminergic autoreceptor agonist, in cebus monkeys with persistent neuroleptic-induced dyskinesias. *J. Neural Transm.* **58**, 135–142.

21 Kovacic, B., LeWitt, P. & Clark, D. (1988): Suppression of neuroleptic-induced persistent abnormal movements in cebus apella monkeys by enantiomers of 3-PPP. *J. Neural Transm.* (In Press)

22 Hjorth, S., Carlsson, A. & Engle, J. A. (1987): Anxiolytic-like action of the 3-PPP enantiomers in the Vogel conflict paradigm. *Psychopharmacology* **92**, 371–375.

23 Carlsson, A. (1983): Dopamine receptor agonists: intrinsic activity vs. state of the receptor. *J. Neural Transm.* **62**, 171–207.

26

ALTERATIONS IN THE BINDING OF THE MUSCARINIC LIGAND [3H]-QUINUCLIDINYL BENZILATE (QNB) IN BRAINS FROM PATIENTS WITH PARKINSON'S DISEASE AND IN HEMI-PARKINSONIAN MONKEYS

S. Boyce, P. Griffiths, C. C. Clarke,
M. A. Sambrook and A. R. Crossman

Experimental Neurology Group, Department of Cell and Structural Biology, Stopford Building, University of Manchester, Manchester M13 9PT, UK

Summary

Muscarinic receptor binding was measured using [3H]-quinuclidinyl benzilate ([3H]-QNB) in postmortem brains from six parkinsonian patients and six controls. Specific [3H]-QNB binding was significantly increased by 66 per cent in the medial pallidal segment in parkinsonian brains. A decrease (58 per cent) was found in the putamen but only at the rostral level. In monkeys rendered hemi-parkinsonian following unilateral infusion of MPTP into the right carotid artery, a similar increase (66 per cent) in [3H]-QNB binding was found in the medial pallidal segment in the denervated side. These results suggest that cholinergic muscarinic receptors in the medial pallidal segment become supersensitive in Parkinson's disease and in the hemi-parkinsonian monkey, possibly as a result of reduced activity in the pedunculopontino-pallidal cholinergic pathway.

Introduction

Although striatal dopamine deficiency is the most significant alteration in the parkinsonian brain, many other biochemical abnormalities have been described.

Activity of the acetylcholine synthesizing enzyme, choline acetyltransferase, has been found to be reduced in the putamen and globus pallidus in parkinsonian brains[1,2] but unchanged in the striatum and substantia nigra.[3,4] Reisine and colleagues[2] have also demonstrated that the specific binding of the cholinergic muscarinic ligand [3H]-quinuclidinyl benzilate (QNB) was increased in the putamen but unchanged in the caudate nucleus or the globus pallidus in parkinsonian brains. In this study, we have demonstrated alterations in the distribution of [3H]-QNB binding using *in vitro* autoradiography both in brains from patients with Parkinson's disease and in brains from primates exposed to MPTP.

Methods

Tissue for binding

Post mortem tissue was obtained from six pathologically confirmed cases of Parkinson's disease and six age-matched controls. Sections (20 μm) of striatum and globus pallidus were used for receptor binding.

Three monkeys (*Macaca fascicularis*) were rendered hemi-parkinsonian following an infusion of MPTP (0.5 mg/kg) into the right common carotid artery. Animals were killed by barbiturate overdose and brains immediately frozen in isopentane at −30°C. Tissue was stereotactically blocked and 20 μm sections were thaw-mounted on gelatin-coated slides. Four untreated animals served as controls.

3H-QNB binding

Sections were washed twice in 50 mM sodium phosphate buffer, pH 7.4 for 30 min at room temperature. The sections were incubated at room temperature for 120 min in the buffer containing 1.0 nM (0.125–2 nM for Scatchard experiments) [3H]-QNB (43.6 Ci/nmol). Specific binding was defined as that displaced by 1 μM atropine. Following incubation sections were washed in ice-cold buffer for 2 × 5 min. For Scatchard experiments, striatal sections were wiped from the slide using filter discs and counted in a Packard scintillation counter for 4 min. Sections for autoradiography were air-dried and exposed to tritium-sensitive film for 3 weeks at −20°C.

Results

[3H]-QNB binding

Distribution of cholinergic muscarinic receptors was observed with the use of [3H]-QNB as the radioactive ligand. Specific [3H]-QNB binding (defined using 1 μM atropine) to sections of primate striatum was saturable at high concentrations which from Scatchard analysis showed a single affinity site whose KD and Bmax values were 0.32 nM and 797 fmol per section respectively (Fig. 1). Autoradiograms of [3H]-QNB binding revealed a widespread distribution of muscarinic receptors throughout the basal ganglia. Autoradiograms of non-specific binding, obtained by the incorporation of 1 μM atropine, were homogeneous and did not differ from background.

Parkinson's disease and age-matched controls

In brains from age-matched control patients, specific [3H]-QNB binding was very

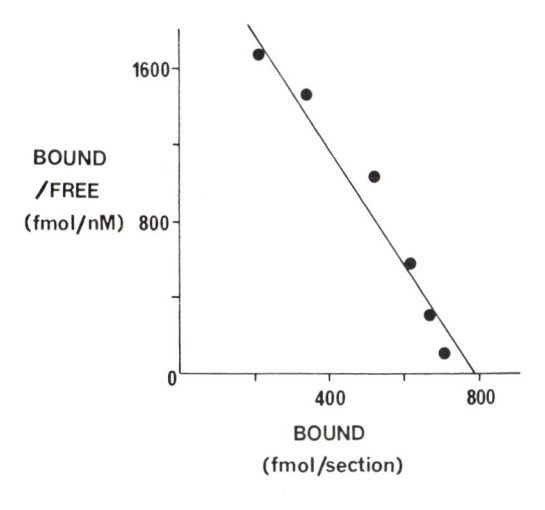

Fig. 1. *Scatchard plot of saturation experiments of [3H]-QNB binding performed on sections of monkey striatum.* Bmax—797 fmol/section KD—0.32 nM.

dense in the caudate nucleus and the putamen, with highest levels in the nucleus accumbens (Fig. 2A, Table 1). There was no consistent rostro-caudal variation in the degree of [3H]-QNB binding in the caudate nucleus or the putamen, although the tail of the caudate showed increased amounts compared to the body at an equivalent level. A lateral to medial variation in the binding was apparent, with higher binding in the lateral region of the striatum. Low binding was found in both segments of the globus pallidus and the substantia nigra, and in the subthalamic nucleus (Table 1).

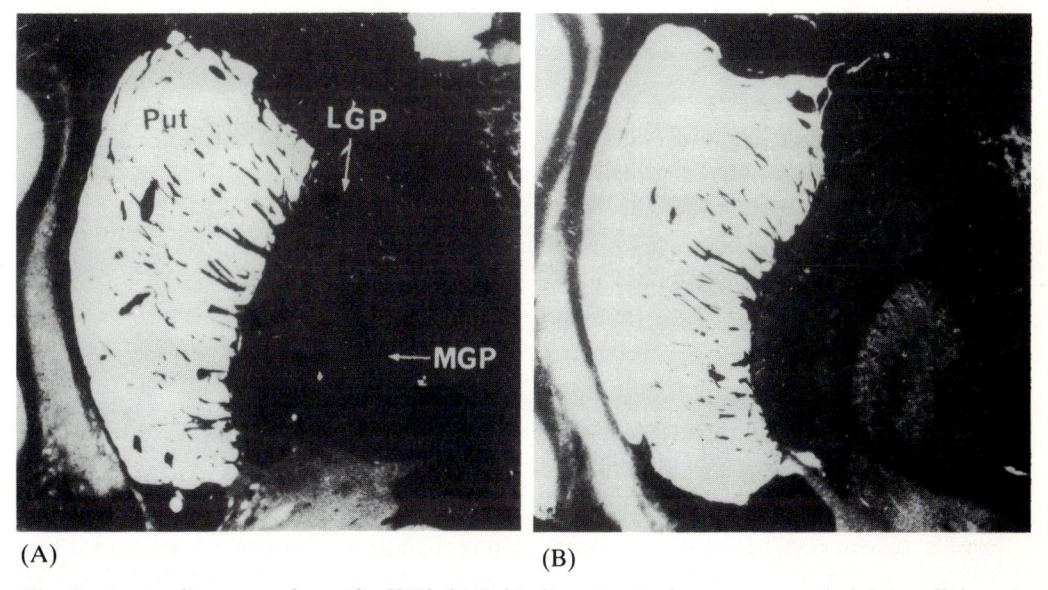

Fig. 2. *Autoradiograms of specific [3H]-QNB binding sites in the putamen and globus pallidus of human brains.* (A) age-matched controls and (B) Parkinson's disease. Abbreviations: LGP = lateral pallidal segment; MGP = medial pallidal segment; Put = putamen.

In parkinsonian brains, no change in [3H]-QNB binding was found at any level of caudate nucleus (Table 1). A decrease (58 per cent) in binding was found in the putamen but only at the rostral level. At more caudal levels of the putamen, the binding showed a

Table 1. *Specific [3H]-QNB binding in the basal ganglia of post mortem tissue from pathologically confirmed cases of Parkinson's disease and age-matched controls. Results are means (SEM). N = 6 in each group.*

Brain region		Specific [3H]-QNB binding (pmol/mg tissue)	
		Control	Parkinson's disease
Caudate nucleus	rostral	348 (23)	283 (57)
	mid	376 (28)	462 (53)
	caudal	331 (34)	435 (53)
Putamen	rostral	366 (32)	210 (20)*
	mid	384 (46)	554 (51)
	caudal	333 (37)	479 (49)
Nucleus accumbens		440 (38)	ND
Globus pallidus	medial	62 (3)	103 (6)**
	lateral	46 (10)	70 (8)
Subthalamic nucleus		23 (7)	ND
Substantia nigra	pars compacta	59 (9)	75 (20)
	pars reticulata	49 (8)	85 (22)

*$P < 0.05$, **$P < 0.01$ compared to values obtained from age-matched controls (Student's t-test). ND = not determined.

tendency to increase in Parkinson's disease. The most significant increase in binding was found in the medial pallidal segment (66 per cent) (Fig. 2B, Table 1).

Hemi-parkinsonian monkeys

Over the week following the final infusion of MPTP, all animals developed a flexed posture of the contralateral upper limb, associated with marked ipsilateral limb preference and spontaneous circling behaviour. Apomorphine (0.05–0.2 mg/kg intramuscularly) produced dose-dependent contralateral rotation which reached a peak 2–3 weeks post-operation. This was associated with dyskinetic movements of the contralateral limbs. Few large cells remained in the substantia nigra pars compacta of the lesioned side but other catecholaminergic cells were intact.

In control monkey brains the distribution of specific [3H]-QNB binding in the basal ganglia showed many regional variations. High binding was found in the striatum (caudate nucleus and putamen), whereas much less binding was found in the globus pallidus, substantia nigra, subthalamic nucleus and thalamus (Fig. 3A, Fig. 4A, Table 2).

Autoradiograms from hemi-parkinsonian monkeys demonstrated a marked increase (66 per cent) in specific binding of [3H]-QNB in the medial pallidal segment on the lesioned side (Fig. 3B). There was a small but non-significant increase (50 per cent) in binding in the substantia nigra pars reticulata on the lesioned side (Fig. 4B, Table 2). In contrast, specific [3H]-QNB binding in the lateral pallidal segment was reduced (38 per cent) in the unlesioned side of the hemi-parkinsonian monkeys compared to the binding in the control monkey brains (Table 2). No asymmetry of binding was observed in the control monkey brains.

Discussion

The results from the present study provide further evidence for the neural mechanisms

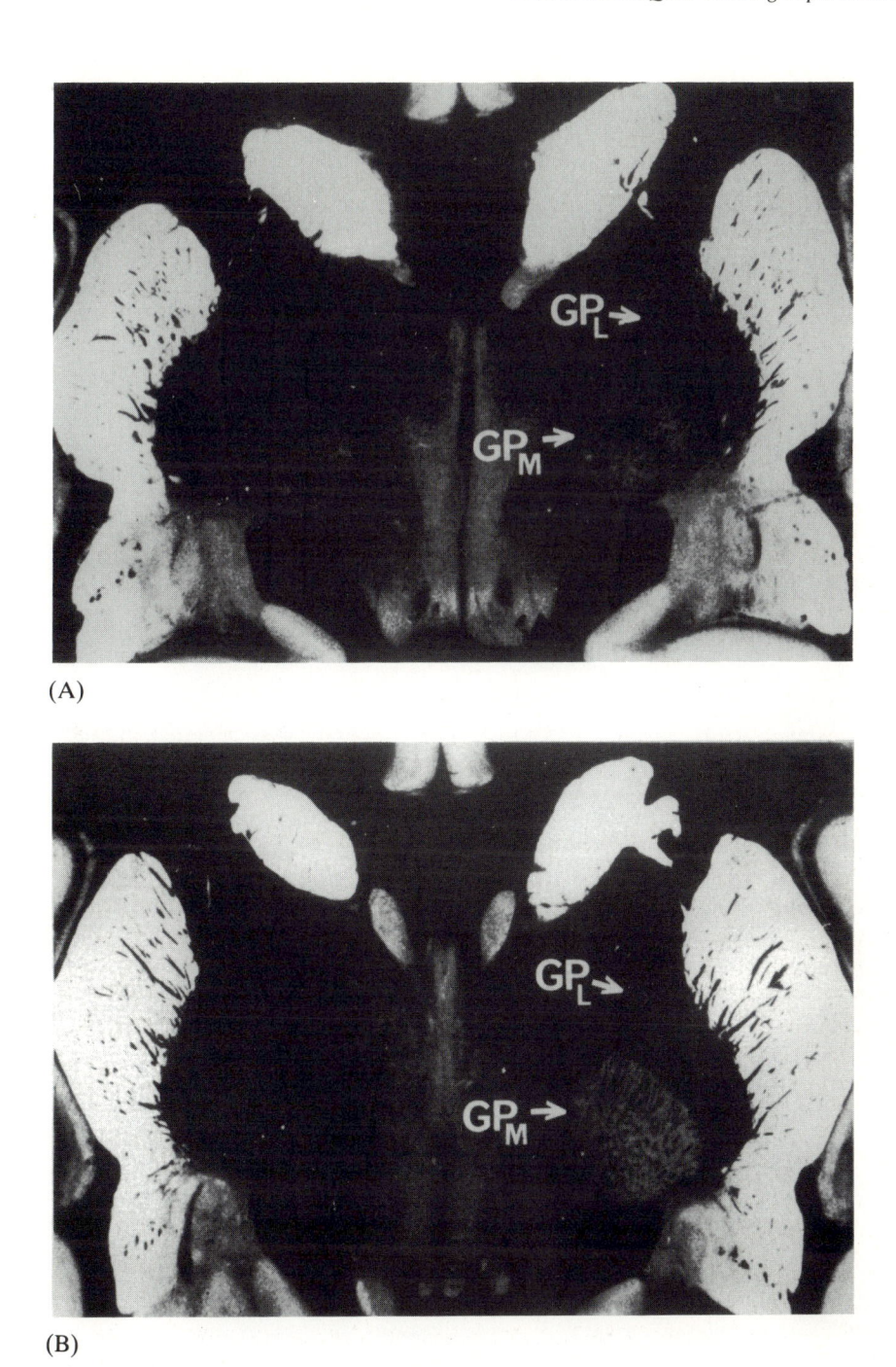

Fig. 3. *Autoradiograms of specific [3H]-QNB binding sites in the basal ganglia of monkey brains.* (A) controls and (B) hemi-parkinsonian monkeys (left – unlesioned; right – lesioned). Abbreviations: GP_L = lateral pallidal segment; GP_M = medial pallidal segment.

(A)

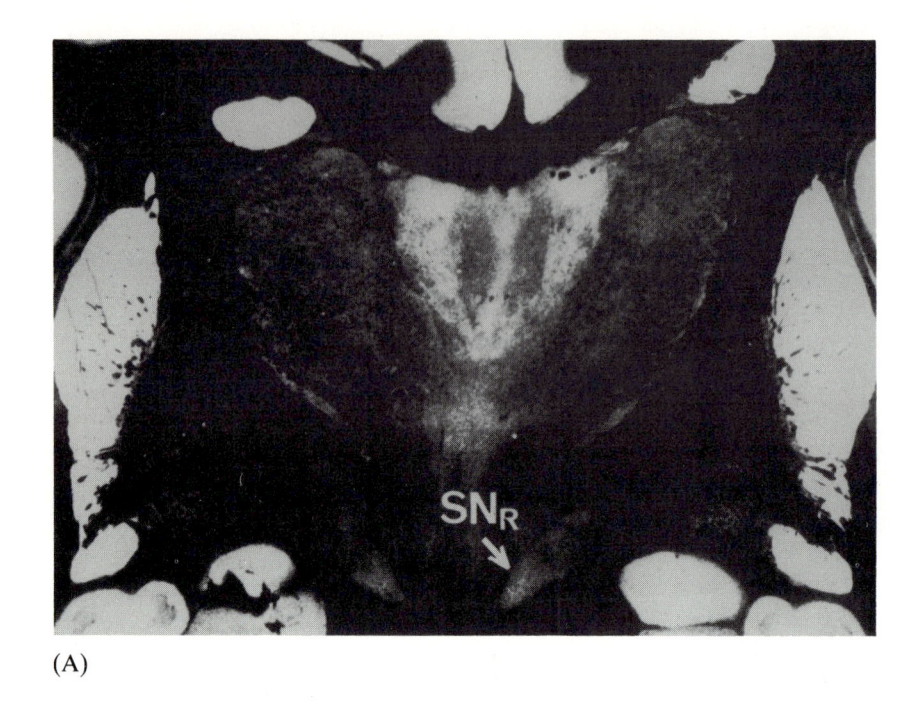

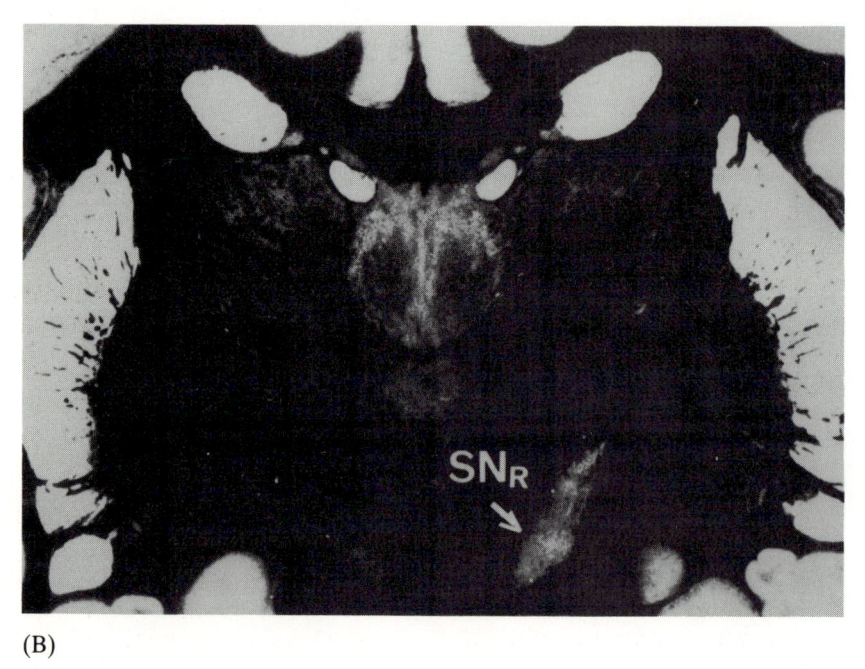

(B)

Fig. 4. *Autoradiograms of specific [3H]-QNB binding sites in the basal ganglia of monkey brains.* (A) controls and (B) hemi-parkinsonian monkeys (left – unlesioned; right – lesioned). Abbreviations: SN_R = substantia nigra pars reticulata.

Table 2. *Specific [3H]-QNB binding in the basal ganglia of hemi-parkinsonian monkeys compared with control monkeys.* Values are means (SEM).

Brain region	Specific [3H]-QNB binding (pmol/mg tissue)			
	Control ($n = 4$)		Hemi-parkinsonian monkeys ($n = 3$)	
	Left	Right	Left	Right
Caudate nucleus	578 (19)	590 (15)	565 (35)	507 (36)
Putamen	522 (25)	522 (31)	481 (28)	525 (31)
Pallidum				
medial	91 (14)	87 (7)	88 (8)	147 (7)**
lateral	53 (4)	54 (6)	34 (1)†	57 (6)*
Subthalamic nucleus	61 (20) ($n = 3$)	51 (7) ($n = 3$)	36 (6)	32 (7)
Substantia nigra pars reticulata	95 (18) ($n = 3$)	91 (25) ($n = 3$)	89 (8)	134 (18)

In the hemi-parkinsonian monkeys *left* refers to the unlesioned side and *right* refers to the lesioned side.
*$P < 0.05$, **$P < 0.01$ compared to the unlesioned side of the hemi-parkinsonian monkeys; †$P < 0.01$ compared to the equivalent side of the control monkeys (Student's t-test).

involved in the production of Parkinson's disease. The major finding was a marked increase in specific [3H]-QNB binding in the medial pallidal segment in both Parkinson's disease and hemi-parkinsonian monkeys. In Parkinson's disease, however, a decrease was also observed in the putamen, but only at the rostral level, while a decrease in binding was found in the lateral segment of the globus pallidus in the unlesioned side of hemi-parkinsonian monkeys. The finding of increased [3H]-QNB binding in the medial pallidal segment may suggest that cholinergic muscarinic receptors become supersensitive in the parkinsonian brain. The major afferent pathways to the medial pallidal segment are from the pedunculopontine nucleus, subthalamic nucleus, putamen and the thalamus. Of these, only the pedunculopontine nucleus is associated with cholinergic function. In support, Beninato & Spencer[5] have shown, using a double-labelling technique utilizing choline acetyltransferase immunocytochemistry combined with retrograde transport of horseradish peroxidase, that the projection from pedunculopontine nucleus to the substantia nigra is cholinergic. Whether the pedunculopontino-pallidal projection is also cholinergic remains to be confirmed. If this pathway is cholinergic, then these results suggest that the pedunculopontino-pallidal cholinergic pathway is underactive in parkinsonism.

Previous studies in this laboratory,[6,7] using the 2-deoxyglucose (2-DG) technique, have demonstrated an increase in the uptake of 2-DG in the VA/VL thalamus, lateral habenula and pedunculopontine nucleus in monkeys rendered hemi-parkinsonian following unilateral injection of MPTP. The increased uptake in these areas is interpreted as abnormal overactivity of cells in the medial pallidal segment which projects to these structures. Since these pathways are thought to be GABAergic, increased release of the inhibitory transmitter upon the pedunculopontine cells would be expected to decrease its level of activity, thus supporting the contention that the pendunculopontino-pallidal pathway is underactive in parkinsonism.

Interestingly, Penney & Young[8] have reported a decrease in muscarinic cholinergic binding in the medial pallidal segment from Huntington's disease brains. This suggests that

243

the pedunculopontino-pallidal pathway is overactive in Huntington's disease and fits in with the decreased 2-DG uptake in the pedunculopontine nucleus in experimental chorea.[9–11]

In a histological study, Jellinger[12] has reported a loss of cells in the pedunculopontine pars compacta in Parkinson's disease which may also contribute to the decrease in the pedunculopontino-pallidal pathway.

In Parkinson's disease, a decrease in [3H]-QNB binding was found in the rostral level of the putamen, although binding tended to increase more caudally. The decrease in binding may reflect overactivity of striatal cholinergic interneurons, as a result of reduced dopamine inhibition following the severe dopamine depletion in Parkinson's disease. Why this should be restricted to the rostral level is unknown. Previous studies have reported an increase in [3H]-QNB binding in the putamen of Parkinson's disease.[2,13] Reisine and colleagues[2] also coupled the increase in binding with a decrease in choline acetyltransferase (ChaT) activity and suggested a possible denervation supersensitivity for acetylcholine in the putamen. The small increase in binding observed in caudal levels of the putamen in the present study seems to be in agreement with previous results. In the two previous studies, however, no increase in binding was reported in the medial pallidal segment, the major finding of this study. One explanation is that Reisine and colleagues[2] did not subdivide the globus pallidus into its medial and lateral segments. Since the lateral pallidal segment was unaltered in this study in Parkinson's disease, this might have masked a possible change in the medial segment. In the case of Kito et al.,[13] it would appear that the exposure time for the autoradiographs may not have been sufficient to allow differences in low binding brain areas (as found in the globus pallidus) to be observed.

In conclusion, these results suggest that cholinergic muscarinic receptors in the medial pallidal segment become supersensitive in Parkinson's disease and in the hemi-parkinsonian monkey, possibly as a result of reduced activity in the pedunculopontine-pallidal cholinergic pathway.

Acknowledgements—Supported by grants from The Medical Research Council and Action Research for the Crippled Child.

References

1 Lloyd, K. G., Moller, H., Heitz, P. & Bartholini, G. (1975): Distribution of choline acetyltransferase and glutamate decarboxylase within the substantia nigra and in other brain regions from control and parkinsonian patients. *J. Neurochem.* **25**, 789–795.

2 Reisine, T. D., Fields, T., Yamamura, H. J., Bird, E. D., Spokes, E., Schreiner, P. S. & Enna, S. J. (1977): Neurotransmitter receptor alterations in Parkinson's disease. *Life Sci.* **21**, 335–344.

3 McGeer, E. G. & McGeer, P. L. (1976): Enzymes associated with the metabolism of catecholamines, acetylcholine and GABA in human controls and patients with Parkinson's disease and Huntington's chorea. *J. Neurochem.* **26**, 65–76.

4 Dubois, B., Ruberg, M., Javoy-Agid, F., Ploska, A. & Agid, Y. (1983): A subcortico-cortical cholinergic system is affected in Parkinson's disease. *Brain Res.* **288**, 213–218.

5 Beninato, M. & Spencer, R. F. (1987): A cholinergic projection to the rat substantia nigra from the pedunculopontine tegmental nucleus. *Brain Res.* **412**, 169–174.

6 Mitchell, I. J., Cross, A. J., Sambrook, M. A. & Crossman, A. R. (1986): Neural mechanisms mediating 1-methyl-4-phenyl-1,2,3,6-tetrahydropyridine-induced parkinsonism in the monkey: relative contributions of the striatopallidal and striatonigral pathways as suggested by 2-deoxyglucose uptake. *Neurosci. Lett.* **63**, 61–65.

7 Crossman, A. R. (1987): Primate models of dyskinesia: The experimental approach to the study of basal ganglia-related involuntary movement disorders. *Neuroscience* **21**, 1–40.

8 Penney, J. B. & Young, A. B. (1982): Quantitative autoradiography of neurotransmitter receptors in Huntington's disease. *Neurology* **32**, 1391–1395.

9 Crossman, A. R., Clarke, C. E., Boyce, S., Robertson, R. G. & Sambrook, M. A. (1987): MPTP-induced parkinsonism in the monkey: Neurochemical pathology, complications of treatment and pathophysiological mechanisms. *Can. J. Neurol. Sci.* **14**, 428–435.
10 Mitchell, I. J., Jackson, A., Sambrook, M. A. & Crossman, A. R. (1985): Common neural mechanisms in experimental chorea and hemiballismus in the monkey. Evidence from 2-deoxyglucose autoradiography. *Brain Res.* **339**, 346–350.
11 Mitchell, I. J., Sambrook, M. A. & Crossman, A. R. (1985): Subcortical changes in regional uptake of [3H]-2-deoxyglucose in the brain of the monkey during experimental choreiform dyskinesia elicited by injection of a gamma-aminobutyric acid antagonist into the subthalamic nucleus. *Brain* **108**, 421–438.
12 Jellinger, K. (1988): The pedunculopontine nucleus in Parkinson's disease, Progressive Supranuclear Palsy and Alzheimer's disease. *J. Neurol. Neurosurg. Psychiatry* **51**, 540–543.
13 Kito, S., Miyoshi, R., Mizuno, K., Nitta, K., Matsubayashi, H., Yamamura, Y. & Tahara, E. (1986): Autoradiographic distributions of neurotransmitter receptor in the human brains of Parkinson's disease and primate models of MPTP-induced parkinsonism. *Adv. Neurol.* **45**, 159–165.

III

CLINICAL ASPECTS

27

THE MEDICAL TREATMENT OF

MOVEMENT DISORDERS

Stanley Fahn

The Neurological Institute of New York, Columbia-Presbyterian Medical Center, New York, NY 10032–3784, USA

Introduction

Movement disorders are a group of neurological dysfunctions in which there is either (1) a paucity of voluntary movement in the absence of weakness or spasticity (referred to as akinesia, bradykinesia or hypokinesia) or (2) an excess of movement referred to as abnormal involuntary movements (also known as dyskinesias or hyperkinesias).

Table 1 lists the various movement disorders. The hypokinetic syndromes are basically parkinsonian states. Gait disorders comprise a heterogeneous group of conditions in which the abnormal shuffling gait—not due to weakness, spasticity, or to another hypokinetic or hyperkinetic disorder listed in Table 1—is the characteristic feature. Some of the entities that can be included in such a definition of 'other' gait disorders are the senile gait disorder,[1-5] fear of falling syndrome, and psychogenic gait disorders.

Pharmacotherapeutic approaches to patients with movement disorders can be divided into two categories: treatment directed at the specific cause of the condition (eg, treating Wilson's disease with copper depleters),[6] and therapy that ameliorates symptoms but does not correct the pathogenesis of the disease (eg, treating Parkinson's disease with dopaminergics). This review will focus predominantly on the latter category, so-called symptomatic therapy, which is the treatment strategy for the overwhelming number of movement disorders.

Non-specific therapy of dykinesias falls into three basic types: (1) physical and behavioural modification techniques, such as sensory biofeedback and other relaxation therapies, including self-hypnosis: (2) pharmacotherapy; and (3) surgical procedures. Only pharmacotherapy is covered in this review. Pharmacotherapy is administered either locally, as drug injections directly into dystonic muscles or muscles in other types of spasm (such as hemifacial spasm), or systemically to produce widespread effects on the body, particularly on the central nervous system (CNS).

Table 1. *List of movement disorders.*

	Section in text
A. *Hypokinesias*	
Parkinson's disease	I, IV, VIII, X
Symptomatic parkinsonism	I, II
Parkinsonism plus	I, II
B. *Hyperkinesias*	
Akathitic movements	III, V
Asynergia/ataxia	VIII
Athetosis	III, X
Ballism	III
Chorea	III, IX, XI
Dysmetria	X
Dystonia	I, VII, X
Hyperekplexias	XIII
Myoclonus	VIII, X
Neuroleptic malignant syndrome	II
Painful legs, moving toes	XIII
Paroxysmal dyskinesias	XIII
Restless legs	XII
Stereotypy	III
Stiff-man syndrome	XIII
Tics	III, IX
Tremor	I, VI, VIII, X

I have chosen to organize treatment strategy not along the lines of different types of abnormal movements (dyskinesias)—for that approach has been recently published[7]—but in relation to the neurotransmitter system which is pharmacologically affected by the drug therapy. This more novel approach should serve to link disorders according to the neurotransmitter system which is apparently involved, either directly or indirectly, in the production of the abnormal involuntary movements.

Of the various neurotransmitter systems that can be manipulated by medications, the dopamine system plays the most prominent role in the pharmacotherapy of movement disorders. There are the parkinsonian states which represent dopamine deficiency and receptor disorders, and there are hyperkinetic disorders, such as the choreas and tardive dyskinesia, that can be listed pharmacologically as conditions of excessive dopamine sensitivity. Other movement disorders treated by systemically manipulating other transmitter systems—such as serotonin, acetylcholine, GABA, and the opioids—are myoclonus, cerebellar tremor, dystonia, stiff-man syndrome, and the restless legs syndrome. Other movement disorders which are treatable, but not by an understandable neurotransmitter modification, are paroxysmal dyskinesias, essential tremor, and hemifacial spasm. All of these will be covered in this review (Table 2). The major criteria for determining whether a disorder is related to a neurotransmitter system are given in Table 3.

Dopamine deficiency disorders (I)

These are shown in Table 4. The most widely recognized dopamine deficiency disorders are the parkinsonian states, manifested by combinations of bradykinesia, rigidity,

Table 2. *Altered neurotransmitter systems producing movement disorders.*

Dopamine deficiency disorders
Dopamine receptor disorders
Excessive dopamine sensitivity
Noradrenaline deficiency disorders
Noradrenaline receptor disorders
Excessive turnover of noradrenaline
Serotonin deficiency disorders
Acetylcholine deficiency disorders
Excessive acetylcholine disorders
GABA deficiency disorders
Opioid deficiency disorder

Table 3. *Criteria for determining whether a neurological syndrome involves a specific neurotransmitter.*

1. Selective increase or decrease of the neurotransmitter, enymes or receptors in CNS
2. Changes in PET scans
3. Changes in CSF concentrations
4. Changes in plasma concentrations
5. Changes in urinary concentrations
6. Effect of drugs
7. Animal models

tremor, and loss of postural reflexes. Striatal dopamine deficiency in patients with Parkinson's disease and postencephalitic parkinsonism was first reported in 1960 (see review by Hornykiewicz[8]). Dopamine depleting drugs, such as reserpine and tetrabenazine, produce a parkinsonian state in animals and humans. The neurotoxin, MPTP, destroys the dopamine nigrostriatal pathway in some animal species, including primates, to produce a parkinsonian disorder that resembles Parkinson's disease.[9,10]

Idiopathic juvenile parkinsonism is a poorly understood disorder. It has been described by some investigators as Parkinson's disease beginning before the age of 40, but many cases of Parkinson's disease begin in their 30s, so this is an unsatisfactory definition. Gershanik & Leist[11] used 35 years as the cut-off since this age is two standard deviations below the mean age at onset of Parkinson's disease. I believe the word 'juvenile' should be defined as beginning before the age of 20, which is in keeping with other disorders, such as juvenile Huntington's disease. Most cases of juvenile parkinsonism are not cases of idiopathic parkinsonism, but are secondary parkinsonism due to Huntington's disease, Wilson's disease, Hallervorden-Spatz disease, ceroid-lipofuscinosis, neuroacanthocytosis, and progressive pallidal atrophy. Few postmortem studies have been performed in idiopathic onset cases. The most recent was the report by Yokuchi et al.,[12] who found immature pars compacta neurons in the substantia nigra which did not contain neuromelanin. This was accompanied by lack of catecholamine

Table 4. *Dopamine deficiency disorders.*

1. Parkinson's disease
2. Postencephalitic parkinsonism
3. Reserpine- & TB-induced parkinsonism
4. MPTP-induced parkinsonism
5. Juvenile parkinsonism
6. Multi-system atrophies
7. Akinetic mutism
8. (?) Dopa-responsive dystonia

It is not certain whether patients with dopa-responsive dystonia actually have reduced levels of dopamine in the striatum. No post-mortem studies have yet been done in this disorder.

synthesizing enzymes. This patient most likely had striatal dopamine deficiency and responded to levodopa therapy, but with severe clinical fluctuations.

Multi-system atrophy (Table 5) is a term to represent some of the parkinson-type syndromes, including various combinations of striatal degeneration, intermediolateral cell loss in the spinal cord giving rise to autonomic dysfunction, cerebellar atrophy and amyotrophy, in addition to nigral degeneration causing parkinsonism. Commonly used names that label various components of multi-system atrophy are striatonigral degeneration, olivopontocerebellar atrophy, and Shy-Drager syndrome. The nigral degeneration is accompanied by striatal dopamine deficiency. Although patients with multi-system atrophy may respond to levodopa therapy initially, when striatal degeneration ensues (with the accompanying loss of the dopamine receptors) they lose their response.

Table 5. *Multi-system atrophies* (± striatum ± cerebellum ± autonomic cell column ± anterior horn cells).

1. Striatonigral degeneration
2. Olivopontocerebellar atrophy
3. Shy-Drager syndrome
4. Parkinsonism & motor neuron disease

Table 6. *Characteristics of DOPA-responsive dystonia.*

1. Onset < 16 years
2. Legs, gait and balance involved
3. Often familial
4. Diurnal fluctuations

A case report of a patient with akinetic mutism who responded to bromocriptine but not to levodopa was published by Ross & Stewart[13]. They speculated that the mesocortical dopamine pathway was involved, but that there was insufficient activity of dopa-decarboxylase in the cortex to generate adequate dopamine from exogenously supplied levodopa. The administration of bromocriptine, however, was effective and allowed the patient to awaken from his comatose state. An analogous case of apathy and compulsion to assume a sleeping position due to a thalamic stroke, and which responded to bromocriptine but not to levodopa, was recently reported.[14] The mechanism for this response is less clear. Bromocriptine was also found to be beneficial in speech fluency, paraphasias, and naming ability in a patient with aphasia.[15]

Another disorder which responds to levodopa, usually in very small doses and without the long-term complications seen in patients with Parkinson's disease, is the entity known as dopa-responsive dystonia[16] (Table 6). Some patients with this disorder present with diurnal fluctuations, where the dystonia is almost absent in the morning and is most severe in the evening,[17] but others present without this type of fluctuation. The age at onset is less than 16 years. Dystonia begins in the legs and trunk; gait is involved, and the condition is often familial. Sometimes signs of parkinsonism are present, such as bradykinesia and loss of postural reflexes. PET scans with fluorodopa have revealed either a reduction of dopamine or normal dopamine in the striatum.[18] It is estimated that about 5 to 10 per cent of childhood onset dystonia may be of the dopa-responsive variant, and therefore a trial of levodopa therapy has been recommended before testing other drugs.[19]

Dopamine receptor disorders (II)

Reduced number of receptors

When striatal neurons degenerate, there is loss of neurotransmitter normally contained within the cells that are lost. Similarly, there is loss of transmitter receptors normally located on those neurons. Thus, movement disorders associated with striatal atrophy with the loss of dopamine receptors on the degenerated cells will often present as a rigid-akinetic syndrome which does not respond to levodopa. Besides the multi-system degenerations described above, other disorders within this category are Huntington's disease of the Westphal variant type, and the parkinsonism associated with hypoparathyroidism.[20]

Blocked receptors

Drugs that block dopamine receptors can produce a number of movement disorder syndromes. Perhaps the easiest to understand is drug-induced parkinsonism in which dopamine receptor blocking drugs, such as the antipsychotics, induce a state of parkinsonism. This is the result of endogeneous dopamine being unable to penetrate the receptor blockade. However, these same drugs produce, due to the blockade of the receptors, a state of supersensitivity of these same receptors. This can lead to the development of tardive dyskinesia, thought to be related to endogenous dopamine penetrating the blockade and producing excessive and abnormal movements via the supersensitive dopamine receptor. Tardive dyskinesias will be discussed in the next section related to excessive dopamine sensitivity states.

In this section, besides mentioning drug-induced parkinsonism, I shall discuss the neuroleptic malignant syndrome. The former should be considered a toxic manifestation of dopamine receptor blocking drugs. If a high enough dose is given, all subjects will develop parkinsonism. It is a result of a severe blockade of the receptors preventing endogenously released dopamine from the nigrostriatal dopaminergic nerve terminals from reaching them, thus producing a parkinsonian syndrome. The symptoms are ameliorated by using antiparkinsonian drugs that are weaker than levodopa, namely anticholinergics and amantadine. Even without treatment, discontinuation of the neuroleptics would eventually result in clinical lessening of the parkinsonian disorder.

The neuroleptic malignant syndrome (NMS) is an idiosyncratic adverse effect of dopamine receptor blocking agents,[21,22] but it has also been reported to occur on discontinuation of levodopa therapy.[23] Thus, the concept is that blockade or desensitization of cerebral dopamine receptors is the pathophysiological mechanism underlying the syndrome.

The clinical features of the syndrome are abrupt onset of a combination of rigidity/dystonia, fever with other autonomic dysfunctions such as diaphoresis and dyspnoea, and an altered mental state including confusion, stupor, or coma. The neuroleptics are administered at therapeutic, not toxic, dosages. There does not seem to be any relationship with the duration of therapy. It can develop soon after the first dose or any time after prolonged treatment. This is a potentially lethal disorder unless treated; up to 25 per cent of cases die.[24]

Treatment of NMS consists of discontinuing the antipsychotic drugs and starting bromocriptine,[25] dantrolene,[26] or a combination of these two drugs.[27] Supportive measures such as cooling blankets, ice packs, alcohol baths, and antipyretic drugs should be provided.[24] Respiratory support, including tracheotomy, may be required in cases with severe dyspnoea.[28]

Excessive dopamine sensitivity (III)

Several hyperkinetic disorders are considered to be associated with excessive dopaminergic sensitivity in that the abnormal movements are reduced with antidopaminergic drugs (Table 7). There are several tardive dyskinesia syndromes distinguished by different motor phenomenology (Table 8) and different pharmacotherapy, suggesting different pathophysiologies. But they have in common their induction by dopamine receptor blocking agents (DRBA). The classical form of tardive dyskinesia is characterized by repetitive oral-lingual-buccal movements resembling chewing movements, often with tongue-popping and repetitive movements of the fingers, toes and trunk. These repetitive movements can be referred to as rhythmical chorea.

The involuntary movements of classical tardive dyskinesia (TD) are as rapid as choreic movements, but their continuous repetitions, in contrast to the flowing and non-repetitive movements of chorea (as in Huntington's disease or Sydenham's chorea), separate these two types of involuntary movements. The movements of classical TD most commonly involve the oral-buccal-lingual regions, although the extremities and trunk can also be affected. The term 'classical' is used to separate this type of dyskinesia from other tardive syndromes secondary to dopamine receptor blocking drugs (Table 8). In this section I shall use the term tardive dyskinesia (TD) to mean classical tardive dyskinesia, also known as oral-buccal-lingual dyskinesia. The nosology of TD requires discussion. because the movements are repetitive, the term stereotypy has been applied to them,[7] but this term is also used for the repetitive complex mannerisms that occur in patients with mental retardation and psychosis. Therefore, the term rhythmical chorea is a reasonable one for classical TD.

Table 7. *Dopamine receptor disorders.*

A. *Reduced number of receptors*
1. Juvenile Huntington's disease
2. Striatonigral degeneration
3. Shy-Drager syndrome
4. Hypoparathyroidism
(5. Huntington's chorea)

B. *Blocked receptors*
1. Drug-induced parkinsonism
2. Neuroleptic malignant syndrome

C. *Supersensitive receptor disorders*
1. Tardive dyskinesia
2. (?) Other tardive syndromes
3. Sydenham's, thyrotoxic and oestrogen-induced choreas
4. Parkinson's disease with dopa-induced dyskinesias
5. (?) Schizophrenia
6. (?) Chorea and ballism
7. (?) Tics/Tourette syndrome

Table. 8. *Tardive dyskinesia syndromes.*

1. Classical TD (rhythmical chorea)
2. Tardive akathisia
3. Tardive dystonia
4. Withdrawal emergent syndrome
5. Tardive chorea
6. Tardive myoclonus
7. Tardive lingual tremor
8. Tardive tics

Treatment of classical tardive dyskinesia

There are a great many problems in the treatment of TD. As with other iatrogenic disorders, a cardinal principle is to eliminate the offending agent. However, in TD, this step usually has two adverse consequences. First, withdrawal of dopamine receptor blockade enhances the dyskinesia. Second, elimination of these drugs may reintroduce the medical condition for which the drug was originally prescribed. For schizophrenic patients, the original disease is usally worse than the tardive dyskinesia. Since it is medically sound to treat the more distressing disorder, in this situation one needs to reintroduce the antipsychotic drug. By increasing the dosage, one can usually suppress the dyskinesia. Of course, by maintaining a patient on these agents, one can never expect to obtain a 'cure' of TD. At best, however, one can keep the symptoms suppressed.

Although many drugs have been reported to reduce the severity of TD, the only ones that dramatically eliminate the dyskinesia and any accompanying akathisia are those that have an antidopaminergic action. The most important ones are of two types: dopamine receptor blockers and dopamine depleters which act on the presynaptic nerve terminal and not at the receptor. Tetrabenazine has a dual action: dopamine depletion and dopamine receptor blockade.[29,30]

Some patients may have only mild psychosis and may not require any antipsychotic drug. Others may have been treated with dopamine receptor blocking agents for reasons other than psychosis, such as for anxiety, nausea, insomnia, tics, and nervousness. In these patients the antipsychotic drug can probably be discontinued. Since there is a good chance that the TD is reversible if caught early, one can watch the patient to see if the symptoms lessen over time. The dyskinesia can be suppressed with high-dosage reserpine. Since this drug does not block dopamine receptors, it does not cause TD and does not prevent an eventual remission. Patients treated with long-term reserpine can eventually have a remission and be off all medication,[31,32] further indicating that reserpine, unlike other neuroleptics, does not cause TD. It should be realized that suppressing symptoms with reserpine merely masks them and does not treat the disease. The physician is 'buying time' by using reserpine, waiting for the natural process of gradual remission to take place.

Treatment of tardive akathisia

The presence of accompanying tardive akathisia is suppressed by these same medications. If drug-induced parkinsonism prevents the use of adequate doses to suppress akathisia, I add an opioid which, in addition to controlling restless legs syndrome, can also suppress akathisia in some patients.[33] The treatment schedule for the opioids is given in the section on the restless legs syndrome.

Treatment of tardive dystonia

Although tardive dystonia[34] is a dystonic disorder and not a rhythmic chorea, it is more practical to discuss its treatment after the discussions of both dystonia and tardive dyskinesia. The two almost equally successful treatment strategies for tardive dystonia are derived from the treatment approaches for idiopathic dystonia on the one hand, and for classical TD on the other.[35] As with TD, it is important to discontinue the offending dopamine receptor blocker if clinically possible. If it is not possible, then this drug is continued at the lowest effective dosage and a dopamine depleter, such as reserpine, is added. If the dopamine receptor blocking drug can be discontinued, one can either treat with reserpine (or tetrabenazine) or with high-dosage anticholinergics. Approximately 50 per cent of patients respond to each of these classes of drugs.[35] If a patient requires continuing use of an antipsychotic drug, I add a dopamine depleter to control the tardive dystonia. If an antipsychotic drug is not required to treat the underlying disease for which such a drug was originally prescribed, one can select either a dopamine depleter or an anticholinergic. Since each class can have its own unpleasant adverse effects, there is little guidance to offer in choosing between them. If one class of drugs does not help, I discontinue it and try the other. Then the combination can be utilized, if necessary. Ultimately, as with TD, one may need to restart the dopamine receptor blocking drug if the clinical trials have failed.

Treatment of chorea and ballism

Chorea refers to involuntary, irregular, purposeless, non-rhythmic, abrupt, rapid, unsustained movements that flow from one body part to another. There are many causes of chorea; the most common is Huntington's disease, which usually has other types of motor problems as well, including clumsiness, dysarthria, and later dystonia. There is also a bradykinetic-rigid form of Huntington's disease known as the Westphal variant (Table 7), which is most common in patients with juvenile onset. Characteristically, although the presence of choreic movements greatly helps in the diagnosis of Huntington's disease, these movements are rarely disabling. Most often progressive cognitive decline, personality changes, psychosis, or affective disorder is the major cause of disability. Therefore it is often unnecessary to use antichoreic drugs, especially since these agents can cause adverse effects, including depression. If chorea is troublesome, antidopaminergic agents can suppress the movements. Because antipsychotic drugs may induce tardive dyskinesia, I prefer to start with the dopamine-depleting drug reserpine, beginning with a dosage of 0.25 mg/day and increasing weekly by a daily dose of 0.25 mg until the severity of chorea is reduced. Apathy, depression, postural hypotension, nasal stuffiness, diarrhoea, and nightmares can occur as adverse effects, requiring discontinuation of the drug. In countries where tetrabenazine is available, this dopamine depleter is begun at a dosage of 25 mg/day and the daily dose increased weekly by 25 mg. Postural hypotension, nasal stuffiness, and nightmares are less common than with reserpine. The antipsychotic drugs, which block dopamine receptors, are also effective antichoreic agents.

The antidopaminergic drugs have been used successfully to suppress choreic movements in more than just Huntington's disease. Sydenham's chorea, chorea gravidarum, and the chorea associated with systemic lupus erythematosus have all been reported to be ameliorated with antipsychotic drugs.[36-39] Non-antidopaminergic agents can sometimes reduce choreic movements. I have personally encountered benefit with clonazepam, and there are reports of effectiveness with valproate and baclofen.[40,41] If choreic movements are mild in patients with Sydenham's chorea, it seems more prudent not to administer an agent that could potentially produce tardive dyskinesia or tardive dystonia. If treatment is necessary, a sedative or mild tranquilizer such as a benzodiazepine may suffice. Corticosteroids may also be effective in patients with Sydenham's chorea.[51] Choreoathetosis is a term applied to choreic movements which also have a slower writhing component to the dyskinesia. This variety of chorea also responds to antidopaminergic drugs.

Ballism refers to very large amplitude choreic movements. Because of the speed of choreic movements, these large amplitude excursions are expressed by flinging and flailing movements when they involve proximal musculature. Ballism is most frequently unilateral and is usually the result of a lesion of the contralateral subthalamic nucleus or multiple small infarcts (lacunes) in the contralateral striatum. In rare instances it occurs bilaterally due to bilateral lacunes in the basal ganglia.

Ballistic movements usually respond to antichoreic agents,[43-46] namely the antidopaminergic drugs mentioned above. It is important to consider the choice of drug for hemiballism in this section. Since vascular hemiballism is usually self-limited, long-term treatment with an antichoreic drug is seldom necessary; a course of 4 to 6 weeks is usually satisfactory. Therefore, one can select a dopamine receptor blocker instead of a dopamine depleter. Although the former can induce tardive dyskinesia, this would be a rare complication with such a short course of therapy. The blockers are rapid in onset of action, and are usually well tolerated in the acute period.

Treatment of tics

It is not clear whether tics are related to abnormalities in dopamine neurotransmission or receptors. The major pieces of evidence implicating such a connection are the amelioration of tics with antidopaminergic agents, the occasional development of tics as a tardive complication to DRBA (Table 8), and the possible decrease of CSF homovanillic acid levels in patients with Tourette syndrome.[47] Tics can be divided into involuntary movements (motor tics), involuntary sounds (phonic tics), and combinations of the two. When phonic tics are present, the designation of Gilles de la Tourette syndrome is commonly applied.

Three categories of medications have been reported to be useful in controlling tics: antidopaminergics, particularly antipsychotic drugs, clonidine and clonazepam. Although the antipsychotics may be the most effective of these, they are also the most dangerous since they can induce persistent TD.[48] Therefore I use them as a last resort. Tics are very common and occur most often in children. If they are mild and do not cause any distress to the child or in the classroom, I prefer not to start any remedial therapy. If the tics become more severe and produce disability (such as social distress), then I begin with clonazepam[49-51] if motor tics are the major problem, and with clonidine if phonic tics are the major symptom. Clonidine was introduced as a treatment for tics by Cohen and his colleagues.[52] Like clonazepam, it does not appear to be as effective as antipsychotics.[53] If either clonazepam or clonidine is ineffective, I try the two together. Finally, if this approach is unsuccessful, antidopaminergics may be necessary.

Noradrenaline deficiency disorders (IV)

Brain noradrenaline (NA) is deficient both in Parkinson's disease, which is associated with cell loss in the locus coeruleus, and in reserpine-induced parkinsonism. However, it is not clear what symptoms occur as a result of such a reduction. Narabayashi et al.[54] suggest that decreased NA is associated with the freezing phenomenon and report improvement of this symptom with threo-dihydroxyphenylserine. However, my personal experience reveals no benefit with this drug. Mayeux et al.[55] found higher CSF levels of the NA metabolite, MHPG, in patients with bradyphrenia.

Noradrenaline receptor disorders (V)

It seems likely that the NA receptor is affected in a way analogous to the dopamine receptor by the administration of antipsychotic drugs, but it is not clear what symptoms may result. Akathisia has been suspected, and acute akathisia has responded to beta-blockers and clonidine. Akathisia (from the Greek, meaning unable to sit still) refers to a feeling of inner restlessness which is relieved by moving about. The typical akathitic patient, when sitting, may stroke his scalp, cross and uncross his legs, rock his trunk, squirm in the chair, and get out of the chair often to pace back and forth. Occasionally, the patient may make repeated moaning sounds. Acute akathisia occurs in the early phases of neuroleptic therapy, worsening as the dosage of medication is increased. It is relieved by discontinuing the neuroleptic. Beta-blockers[56,57] and clonidine[58] are often beneficial in treating acute drug-induced akathisia, supporting the notion that there is an increase of beta-adrenergic activity in brain.

Excessive turnover of noradrenaline (VI)

In the periphery, excessive turnover of NA can result in enhanced physiological tremor, an increase in essential tremor, and an increase of parkinsonian tremor.[59] Thyrotoxic tremor and tremor induced by alcohol, stress, tricyclic antidepressants, and hypoglycaemia are all the result of excess NA turnover in the peripheral tissues. Delirium tremens may be the result of increased NA turnover in both the periphery and in the brain. These conditions can be ameliorated with beta-blockers and clonidine.[60]

Altered noradrenaline in dystonia (VII)

There is speculation that NA may be altered in torsion dystonia. This suspicion is based on several observations. First, plasma NA and its synthesizing enzyme, dopamine-beta-hydroxylase, have been found to be increased in some patients and families with idiopathic dystonia.[61,62] Second, MHPG was found to be altered in lumbar CSF[63] and in ventricular CSF[64,65] in some patients with dystonia. Third, in post-mortem studies, brain NA was found altered in patients with idiopathic torsion dystonia.[66,67] Fourth, in neuroacanthocytosis with symptomatic dystonia, brain striatal NA was found to be increased.[68] Fifth, MSH/ACTH injections affecting the locus coeruleus in rats have produced dystonic posturing.[69] Finally, injections of NA in various brain regions can produce dystonic posturing in rats.[70] These suspicions have not yet been translated into any form of effective therapy for dystonia based on an altered NA hypothesis, however.

Serotonin deficiency disorders (VIII)

Parkinson's disease

Brain serotonin (5-HT) is deficient both in Parkinson's disease, which is associated with cell loss in the locus coeruleus, and in reserpine-induced parkinsonism. The one correlation between such a deficiency and clinical symptoms is the observation by Mayeux and his colleagues[71] that depression in patients with Parkinson's disease correlates with the low levels of CSF 5-hydroxyindoleacetic acid (5-HIAA), the metabolite of 5-HT. Treatment with the serotonin precursor, L-5-hydroxytryptophan (5-HTP), has been beneficial in treating depression in such patients.

Myoclonus

Based on low 5-HIAA levels in CSF and responsiveness to 5-HTP in some patients with myoclonus, a functional deficiency of serotonin has been proposed in some of the myoclonias.[72,73] On the other hand, excessive serotonin from drugs in humans[74] and in animals[75,76] indicates that too little or too much serotonin could be associated with some cases of myoclonus.

Although there are a great many causes of myoclonus,[77] not all have been well studied pharmacologically. The most thoroughly studied type is post-hypoxic action myoclonus, but it appears that drugs helpful in this disorder are also effective in other types of myoclonus.

The principal antimyoclonic drugs are clonazepam, valproate and 5-HTP.[78] Also useful in some patients, but less well studied, are primidone, lisuride,[79] and piracetam.[80] Overall, perhaps the most effective agent is clonazepam, with valproate being next most effective. Both clonazepam and valproate can be effective when given alone, but in some patients they are effective only when given together. If the two fail to be of benefit, I evaluate 5-HTP given together with the peripheral decarboxylase inhibitor, carbidopa, to reduce adverse effects such as diarrhoea, and to potentiate the central serotonergic effect. Lisuride is a direct-acting dopamine receptor agonist but also has serotonin receptor agonist properties. The action of piracetam is unknown, but it appears to have antimyoclonic properties. It should be noted that symptoms of some patients with post-hypoxic myoclonus may be aggravated by 5-HTP.[81]

Some cases of myoclonus may be associated with biotin deficiency, particularly if there is accompanying ataxia and seizures; such cases can respond to treatment with biotin.[82]

Cerebellar ataxia and dysmetria

Based on pharmacotherapeutic responses, Trouillas *et al.*[83] have reported that cerebellar ataxia lessens in severity with 5-HTP treatment. This suggests that increasing serotonergic activity ameliorates cerebellar dysfunction. Since there is widespread distribution of serotonin throughout the brain, the question arises as to which brain region is the critical one for increasing serotonin activity in order to suppress cerebellar symptoms.

Acetylcholine deficiency disorders (IX)

Acetylcholine pathways in brain can conveniently be divided into short intrinsic neurons and long fibre systems. The former group is found in the striatum, nucleus accumbens and cerebral cortex, with the highest concentration of the synthesizing enzyme being in the striatum.[84] The latter group extends from the brainstem and basal forebrain to subcortical and cortical regions. Well recognized pathways include those from the substantia innominata to the cerebral cortex (innominocortical fibres) and those from the septum to the hippocampus. These long fibre systems degenerate in Parkinson's disease, with and without accompanying dementia,[85] as well as in Alzheimer's disease. Such a reduction in cortical acetylcholine probably accounts for the increased sensitivity to anticholinergic drugs in parkinsonian patients, with memory impairment a major limiting adverse effect of these drugs.

Whereas striatal acetylcholine markers are normal in Parkinson's disease, they are reduced in Huntington's disease due to loss of cholinergic neurons in this structure. Unfortunately, this reduction has not been translated into effective therapy for choreic movements or for other clinical features of Huntington's disease.

Another possible cholinergic deficiency disease is Gilles de la Tourette syndrome, because administration of physostigmine, a central and peripheral cholinesterase inhibitor, has been reported to reduce tics.[86] This observation has not been followed up with long-term clinical trials.

Excessive acetylcholine disorders (X)

The concept of excessive acetylcholine disorders derives from pharmacotherapeutic studies in which amelioration of symptoms has come from treatment with anticholinergic drugs.

Parkinsonism

The first class of drugs found to be effective in ameliorating signs of parkinsonism was the anticholinergics. The current explanation is that the normal inhibitory influence from dopaminergic neurons on the postsynaptic cholinergic cells is lost in parkinsonism. By reducing cholinergic activity with anticholinergic drugs, the symptoms lessen. Even today with the far more potent dopaminergic agents, anticholinergics still play an important role, particularly in reducing the severity of tremor.

Torsion dystonia

Based originally on open-label trials,[87] the efficacy of anticholinergic drugs given in high dosages has been substantiated by double-blind investigation[88] and by other open-label trials on large numbers of patients.[89–91] In general, all these studies show that approximately 50 per cent of children and 40 per cent of adults with idiopathic dystonia obtain moderate to dramatic benefit from this class of drugs. Since their introduction for dystonia, high-dosage anticholinergic drugs have become one of the mainstays of non-specific therapy in dystonia. However, as mentioned in the section on dopamine above, there is one subclass of idiopathic torsion that is very responsive to dopaminergics, and a trial of levodopa should be undertaken before beginning anticholinergic therapy. If the response to these drugs is insufficient, other drugs should be tried, including carbamazepine, the benzodiazepines, baclofen, and the antidopaminergics.[91,92] Athetosis associated with cerebral palsy can be considered a variant of dystonia, and can partially respond to high dosage anticholinergics.

Another approach in the treatment of dystonia is to weaken excessively contracting muscles with local administration of botulinum toxin. Botulinum toxin acts presynaptically at peripheral nerve terminals to prevent calcium-dependent release of acetylcholine.[93] Scott et al.[94], after testing the approach in monkeys, were the first to use botulinum toxin in humans. The first focal dystonia so treated was blepharospasm. Since then focal injections have been used to treat spastic dysphonia, oromandibular dystonia, lingual dystonia, torticollis, and other focal dystonias, and also hemifacial spasm.[95–98] For these focal dystonias, botulinum toxin is effective in more than 70 per cent of patients. The most dramatic response is with dystonia of the smallest muscles, the vocal cords. Spastic dysphonia can be completely eliminated with such injections. It should be noted that benefit from botulinum toxin injections lasts approximately three months, so repeated injections are necessary.

Rhythmical myoclonus

Based on pharmacotherapeutic studies, anticholinergics have been found to ameliorate palatal myoclonus and other rhythmical movements, including pendular nystagmus.[99] There are also reports that some patients with non-rhythmic myoclonus, both essential myoclonus and symptomatic myoclonus, respond to anticholinergics.[100,101]

Cerebellar intention tremor

Similarly, cerebellar intention tremor has been reported to respond to high dosage

The medical treatment of movement disorders

anticholinergics.[102] The basis as to why this type of tremor and some of the myoclonias respond to anticholinergics is not understood.

GABA deficiency disorders (XI)

The most consistent decrease of a neurotransmitter in Huntington's disease is that of GABA,[103,104] accompanied by a reduction of its synthesizing enzyme, glutamic acid decarboxylase.[105] This loss is probably a reflection of the loss of GABA-containing neurons in the striatum. Attempts have been made to increase brain GABA levels in HD patients by using inhibitors of GABA-transaminase or to activate GABA receptors with GABA agonists,[106–108] but all such approaches have been ineffective.

Opioid deficiency disorder (XII)

Based on its dramatic response to opioids, the restless legs syndrome has been considered as a possible opioid deficiency state.[109] The term restless legs syndrome refers to more than just the phenomenon of restless legs, where the patient has unpleasant crawling sensations in the legs, particularly when sitting and relaxing in the evening, which then disappear on walking. The complete syndrome consists of several parts, in which one or more may be present in any individual. While the unpleasant dysaesthesias in the legs are the most common symptom, the complete clinical spectrum also includes periodic movements in sleep[110] (previously referred to as nocturnal myoclonus), in which dorsiflexion of the foot and flexion of the knee and thigh occur simultaneously at intervals around 20 seconds, and which can awaken the patient from sleep, as well as other dyskinesias, such as brief myoclonic jerks or more sustained dystonic movements that occur while the patient is awake in the late evening.[111]

A number of drugs have been found to give partial relief from these symptoms, including clonazepam,[112] clonidine,[113] and levodopa.[114,115] I have found opioids to be virtually 100 per cent effective in suppressing symptoms.[109,110] Unknown to us at the time we tried them, the effectiveness of opioids had been reported previously.[116] It is easiest to use non-narcotic prescriptions, such as propoxyphene 65 mg at night or Tylenol 3 capsules at night (each capsule contains 30 mg codeine). In some patients who initially respond to propoxyphene, the response does not last, but increasing the dosage to 130 mg at night or even higher can be effective over a long time. The dramatic response to opioids suggests that the syndrome may be related to an abnormality of the endogenous opiates.

Miscellaneous disorders (XIII)

A number of movement disorders have not been associated with an alteration in neurotransmission, either from biochemical, pharmacological or animal model studies. The treatment of these other conditions are discussed in this section.

Hyperekplexia

Hyperekplexia ('startle disease') is an excessive startle reaction to a sudden, unexpected stimulus. The motor reaction can either be a short or a prolonged complex motor act. This is a rare and poorly understood condition that can be familial or sporadic. Falling is a common symptom. Clonazepam has been reported to ameliorate the condition.[117]

Painful legs, moving toes syndrome

The painful legs, moving toes syndrome (and its analogous disorder, painful arm, moving fingers syndrome) refers to a disorder in which the digits of one foot or hand are in continual flexion-extension with some lateral motion, associated with a deep pain in the ipsilateral leg or forearm.[118] The movements are continual and occur even during sleep, though reduced.[119] In some patients with this disorder, there is evidence for a lesion in the nerve roots or in the peripheral nerves.[119,120] Medications have not been effective for relieving pain, which is the major problem, but an occasional patient may have reduction of the abnormal movements with clonazepam.

Paroxysmal dyskinesias

The paroxysmal dyskinesias represent various types of dyskinetic movements, particularly choreoathetosis and dystonia, that occur 'out of the blue' and then disappear after seconds, minutes, or hours.[121] The patient can remain normal for months between attacks, or there can be several attacks per day.

Paroxysmal kinesigenic choreoathetosis is characteristically triggered by a sudden movement and lasts seconds to a few minutes. Despite its name, the movements can be dystonic as well as choreic. The disorder can be hereditary or symptomatic, and is usually successfully treated with anticonvulsants.

Paroxysmal (non-kinesigenic) dystonia is often familial, is triggered by stress, fatigue, caffeine or alcohol, and can last minutes to hours.[121] It is more difficult to treat than the kinesigenic variety, but often responds to clonazepam or other benzodiazepines,[122] and sometimes to acetazolamide.[123] Most of the cases seen by our Movement Disorder Group have been sporadic and non-familial.[123] The major differential diagnosis is psychogenic paroxysmal dystonia.[123,124]

Stiff-man syndrome

Stiff-man syndrome refers to a rare disorder in which many somatic muscles are continuously contracting isometrically, resembling 'chronic tetanus', in contrast to dystonic movements which produce abnormal twisting movements and postures. The contractions of stiff-man syndrome are usually forceful and painful and most frequently involve the trunk musculature. Benzodiazepines, particularly diazepam[125,126] and clonazepam,[127] are usually effective. Valproate has also been shown to be effective.[127]

References

1. Sudarsky, L. & Ronthal, M. (1983): Gait disorders among elderly patients. A survey study of 50 patients. *Arch. Neurol.* **40**, 740–743.
2. Koller, W. C., Wilson, R. S., Glatt, S. L., Huckman, M. S. & Fox, J. H. (1983): Senile gait: Correlation with computer tomographic scans. *Ann. Neurol.* **13**, 343–344.
3. Adams, R. D. (1984): Aging and human locomotion. In: *Clinical neurology of aging*, ed M. L. Albert, pp 381–403. Oxford, New York: Oxford University Press, 1984.
4. Weiner, W. J., Nora, L. M. & Glantz, R. H. (1984): Elderly inpatients: postural reflex impairment. *Neurology* **34**, 945–947.
5. Sudarsky, L. & Simon, S. (1987): Gait disorder in late-life hydrocephalus. *Arch. Neurol.* **44**, 263–267.
6. Scheinberg, I. H. & Sternlieb, I. (1984): *Wilson's disease*. Philadelphia: W. B. Saunders.
7. Fahn, S. (1987): Drug treatment of hyperkinetic movement disorders. *Semin. Neurol.* **7**, 192–208.

8 Hornykiewicz, O. (1982): Brain neurotransmitter changes in Parkinson's disease. In: *Movement disorders*, ed C. D. Marsden & S. Fahn, pp 41–58. London: Butterworth.
9 Langston, J. W., Ballard, P., Tetrud, J. W. & Irwin, I. (1983): Chronic parkinsonism in humans due to a product of meperidine-analog synthesis. *Science* **219**, 979–980.
10 Langston, J. W., (1987): MPTP: The promise of a new neurotoxin. In: *Movement disorders 2*, ed C. D. Marsden & S. Fahn, pp. 73–90. London: Butterworth.
11 Gershanik, O. S. & Leist, A. (1986): Juvenile onset Parkinson's disease. *Adv. Neurol.* **45**, 213–216.
12 Yokuchi, M., Narabayashi, H., Iizuka, R. & Nagatsu, T. (1984): Juvenile parkinsonism—some clinical, pharmacological and neuropathological aspects. *Adv. Neurol.* **40**, 407–413.
13 Ross, E. D. & Stewart, R. M. (1981): Akinetic mutism from hypothalamic damage: Successful treatment with dopamine agonists. *Neurology* **31**, 1435–1439.
14 Catsman-Berrevoets, C. E. & v Harskamp, F. (1988): Compulsive pre-sleep behavior and apathy due to bilateral thalamic stroke: Response to bromocriptine. *Neurology* **38**, 647–649.
15 Albert, M. L., Bachman, D. L., Morgan, A. & Helm-Estabrooks, N. (1988): Pharmacotherapy for aphasia. *Neurology* **38**, 877–879.
16 Nygaard, T. G., Marsden, C. D. & Duvoisin, R. C. (1988): Dopa-responsive dystonia. *Adv. Neurol.* **50**, 377–384.
17 Segawa, M., Hosaka, A., Miyagawa, F., Nomura, Y. & Imai, H. (1976): Hereditary progressive dystonia with marked diurnal fluctuation. *Adv. Neurol.* **14**, 215–233.
18 Lang, A. E., Garnett, E. S., Firnau, G., Nahmias, C. & Talalla, A. (1988): Positron tomography in dystonia. *Adv. Neurol.* **50**, 249–253.
29 Fahn, S. & Marsden, C. D. (1987): The treatment of dystonia. In: *Movement disorders 2* ed C. D. Marsden & S. Fahn, pp 359–382. London: Butterworth.
20 Muenter, M. D. & Whisnant, J. P. (1968): Basal ganglia calcification, hypoparathyroidism, and extrapyramidal motor manifestations. *Neurology* **18**, 1075–1083.
21 Smego, R. A. & Durack, D. T. (1982): The neuroleptic malignant syndrome. *Arch. Int. Med.* **142**, 1183–1185.
22 Kurlan, R., Hamill, R. & Shoulson, I. (1984): Neuroleptic malignant syndrome. *Clin. Neuropharmacol.* **7**, 109–120.
23 Friedman, J. H., Feinberg, S. S. & Feldman, R. G. (1985): A neuroleptic malignant like syndrome due to levodopa therapy withdrawal. *JAMA* **254**, 2792–2795.
24 Henderson, V. W. & Wooten, G. F. (1981): Neuroleptic malignant syndrome: a pathogenetic role for dopamine receptor blockade. *Neurology* **31**, 132–137.
25 Mueller, P. S., Vester, J. W. & Fermaglich, J. (1983): Neuroleptic malignant syndrome: successful treatment with bromocriptine. *JAMA* **249**, 386–388.
26 Goulon, M., de Rohan-Chabot, P., Elkharrat, D., Gajdos, P., Bismuth, C. & Conso, F. (1983): Beneficial effects of dantrolene in the treatment of neuroleptic malignant syndrome: a report of two cases. *Neurology* **33**, 516–518.
27 Granato, J. E., Stern, B. J., Ringel, A., Karim, A. H., Krumholz, A., Coyle, J. & Adler, S. (1983): Neuroleptic malignant syndrome: successful treatment with dantrolene and bromocriptine. *Ann. Neurol.* **14**, 89–90.
28 Morris, H. H. & McCormick, W. F. (1980): Neuroleptic malignant syndrome. *Arch. Neurol.* **37**, 462–463.
29 Login, I., Cronin, M. & MacLeod, R. (1982): Tetrabenazine has properties of a dopamine receptor antagonist. *Ann. Neurol.* **12**, 257–262.
30 Reches, A., Burke, R. E., Kuhn, C. M., Hassan, M. N., Jackson, V. R. & Fahn, S. (1983): Tetrabenazine, an amine-depleting drug, also blocks dopamine receptors in rat brain. *J. Pharmacol. Exp. Therap.* **225**, 515–521.
31 Fahn, S. (1985): A therapeutic approach to tardive dyskinesia. *J. Clin. Psychiatry* **46**, 19–24.
32 Klawans, H. L. & Tanner, C. M. (1983): The reversibility of 'permanent' tardive dyskinesia. *Neurology* **33**: Suppl. 2, 163.
33 Walters, A., Hening, W., Chokroverty, S. & Fahn, S. (1986): Opioid responsiveness in patients with neuroleptic-induced akathisia. *Movement Disorders* **1**, 119–127.
34 Burke, R. E., Fahn, S., Jankovic, J., Marsden, C. D., Lang, A. E., Gollomp, S. & Ilson, J. (1982): Tardive dystonia: Late-onset and persistent dystonia caused by antipsychotic drugs. *Neurology* **32**, 1335–1346.

35 Kang, U. J., Burke, R. E. & Fahn, S. (1986): Natural history and treatment of tardive dystonia. *Movement Disorders* **1**, 193–208.
36 Heilman, K. M., Kohler, W. C. & LeMaster, P. C. (1971): Haloperidol treatment of chorea associated with systemic lupus erythematosus. *Neurology* **21**, 963–965.
37 Shenker, D. M., Grossman, H. J. & Klawans, H. L. (1973): Treatment of Sydenham's chorea with haloperidol. *Devel. Med. Child. Neurol.* **15**, 19–24.
38 Fermaglich, J., Streib, E. & Auth, T. (1973): Chorea associated with systemic lupus erythematosus. Treatment with haloperidol. *Arch. Neurol.* **28**, 276–277.
39 Patterson, J. F. (1979): Treatment of chorea gravidarum with haloperidol. *South. Med. J.* **72**, 1220–1221.
40 Dhanaraj, M., Radhakrishnan, A. R., Srinivas, K. & Sayeed, Z. A. (1985): Sodium valporate in Sydenham's chorea. *Neurology* **35**, 114–115.
41 Trauner, D. A. (1985): Olivopontocerebellar atrophy with dementia, blindness, and chorea. *Arch. Neurol.* **42**, 757–758.
42 Green, L. N. (1978): Corticosteroids in the treatment of Sydenham's chorea. *Arch. Neurol.* **35**, 53–54.
43 Johnson, W. G. & Fahn, S. (1977): Treatment of vascular hemiballism and hemichorea. *Neurology* **27**, 631–636.
44 Klawans, H. L., Moses, H., Nausieda, P. A., Bergen, D. & Weiner, W. J. (1976): Treatment and prognosis of hemiballismus. *N. Engl. J. Med.* **295**, 1348–1350.
45 Obeso, J. A., Marti-Masso, J. F., Astudillo, W., de la Puente, E. & Carrera, N. (1978): Treatment of hemiballism with reserpine. *Ann. Neurol.* **4**, 581.
46 Koller, W. C., Weiner, W. J., Nausieda, P. A. & Klawans, H. L. (1979): Pharmacology of ballismus. *Clin. Neuropharmacol.* **4**, 157–174.
47 Jankovic, J. (1987): The neurology of tics. In *Movement disorders 2*, ed C. D. Marsden & S. Fahn, pp 383–405. London: Butterworth.
48 Mizrahi, E. M., Holtzman, D. & Tharp, B. (1980): Haloperidol-induced tardive dyskinesia in a child with Gilles de la Tourette's disease. *Arch. Neurol.* **37**, 780.
49 Gonce, M. & Barbeau, A. (1977): Seven cases of Gilles de la Tourette's syndrome: Partial relief with clonazepam: A pilot study. *Can. J. Neurol. Sci.* **4**, 279–283.
50 Kaim, B. (1983): A case of Gilles de la Tourette's syndrome treated with clonazepam. *Brain. Res. Bull.* **11**, 213–214.
51 Truong, D. D., Bressman, S., Shale, H. & Fahn, S. (1988): Clonazepam, haloperidol and clonidine in tic disorders. *South. Med. J.* **81**, 1103–1105.
52 Cohen, D. J., Young, J. G., Nathanson, J. A. & Shaywitz, B. A. (1979): Clonidine in Tourette's syndrome. *Lancet* **ii**, 551–553.
53 Goetz, C. G., Tanner, C. M., Wilson, R. S., Carroll, V. S., Como, P. G. & Shannon, K. M. (1987): Clonidine and Gilles de la Tourette's syndrome: Double-blind study using objective rating methods. *Ann. Neurol.* **21**, 307–310.
54 Narabayashi, H., Kondo, T., Nagatsu, T., Hayashi, A. & Suzuki, T. (1984): DL-Threo-3,4-dihydroxyphenylserine for freezing symptom in parkinsonism. *Adv. Neurol.* **40**, 497–502.
55 Mayeux, R., Stern, Y., Sano, M., Cote, L. & Williams, J. B. W. (1987): Clinical and biochemical correlates of bradyphrenia in Parkinson's disease. *Neurology* **37**, 1130–1134.
56 Zubenko, G. S., Lipinski, J. F., Cohen, B. M. & Barreira, P. J. 1984: Comparison of metoprolol and propranolol in the treatment of akathisia. *Psychiatry Res.* **11**, 143–149.
57 Lipinski, J. F., Zubenko, G. S., Cohen, B. M. & Barreira, P. J. (1984): Propranol in the treatment of neuroleptic-induced akathisia. *Am. J. Psychiatry* **141**, 412–415.
58 Zubenko, G. S., Cohen, B. M., Lipinski, J. F. & Jonas, J. M. (1984): Use of clonidine in treating neuroleptic-induced akathisia. *Psychiatry Res.* **13**, 253–259.
59 Marsden, C. D., Foley, T. H., Owen, D. A. L. & McAllister, R. G. (1967): Peripheral beta-adrenergic receptors concerned with tremor. *Clin. Sci.* **33**, 53–65.
60 Jankovic, J. & Fahn, S. (1980): Physiologic and pathologic tremors. Diagnosis, mechanism, and management. *Ann. Int. Med.* **93**, 460–465.
61 Wooten, G. F., Eldridge, R., Axelrod, J. & Stern, R. S. (1973): Elevated plasma dopamine-beta-hydroxylase activity in autosomal dominant torsion dystonia. *N. Engl. J. Med.* **228**, 284–287.

62 Ziegler, M. G., Lake, C. R., Eldrige, R. & Kopin, I. J. (1976): Plasma norepinephrine and dopamine-beta-hydroxylase in dystonia. *Adv. Neurol.* **14**, 307–315.
63 Riker, D. K., Hurtig, H., Lake, C. R., Copeland, P. & Roth, R. (1982): Open trial of clonidine in dystonia musculorum deformans. *Soc. Neurosci. Abst.* **8**, 563.
64 Wolfson, L. I., Sharpless, N. S., Thal, L. J., Waltz, J. M., & Shapiro, K. (1983): Decreased ventricular fluid norepinephrine metabolite in childhood-onset dystonia. *Neurology* **33**, 369–372.
65 Wolfson, L. I., Sharpless, N. S. & Thal, L. J. (1988): Diminished levels of ventricular fluid norepinephrine metabolite and somatostatin in childhood-onset dystonia. *Adv. Neurol.* **50**, 177–181.
66 Hornykiewicz, O., Kish, S. J., Becker, L. E., Farley, I. & Shannak, K. (1986): Brain neurotransmitters in dystonia musculorum deformans. *N. Engl. J. Med.* **315**, 347–353.
67 Jankovic, J., Svendsen, C. N. & Bird, E. D. (1987): Brain neurotransmitters in dystonia. *N. Engl. J. Med.* **316**, 278–279.
68 de Yebenes, J. G., Brin, M., Mena, M. A., de Felipe, C., Del Rio, R. M., Bazan, E., Martinez, A., Fahn, S., Del Rio, J., Vazquez, A. & Varela de Seijas, E. (1988): Neurochemical findings in neuroacanthocytosis. *Movement disorders* **3**, 300–312.
69 Jacquet, Y. (1988): A dystonia-like syndrome after neuropeptide (MSH/ACTH) stimulation of the rat locus ceruleus. *Adv. Neurol.* **50**, 299–311.
70 de Yebenes, J. G., Russell, N. & Fahn, S. (1988): Intracerebral infusion of norepinephrine produces dystonia in the rat. *Neurology* **38** (Suppl 1), 207.
71 Mayeux, R., Cote, L., Stern, Y. & Williams, J. B. W. (1984): Altered serotonin metabolism in depressed patients with Parkinson's disease. *Neurology* **34**, 642–646.
72 Van Woert, M. H., Rosenbaum, D. & Chung, E. (1986): Biochemistry and therapeutics of posthypoxic myoclonus. *Adv. Neurol.* **43**, 171–181.
73 Chadwick, D., Hallett, M., Jenner, P. & Marsden, C. D. (1986): Treatment of posthypoxic action myoclonus: implications for the pathophysiology of the disorder. *Adv. Neurol.* **43**, 183–190.
74 Lieberman, J. A., Kane, J. M. & Reife, R. (1986): Neuromuscular effects of monoamine oxidase inhibitors. *Adv. Neurol.* **43**, 231–249.
75 Carvey, P., Paulseth, J. E., Goetz, C. G., & Klawans, H. L. (1986): L-5-HTP-induced myoclonic jumping behavior in guinea pigs: An update. *Adv. Neurol.* **43**, 509–517.
76 Wolfson, L. I., Thal, L. J. & Brown, L. L. (1986): Serotonin models of myoclonus in the guinea pig and rat. *Adv. Neurol.* **43**, 519–528.
77 Fahn, S., Marsden, C. D. & Van Woert, M. H. (1986): Definition and clinical classifcation of myoclonus. *Adv. Neurol.* **43**, 1–5.
78 Fahn S. (1986): Posthypoxic action myoclonus: Literature review update. *Adv. Neurol.* **43**, 157–169.
79 Obeso, J. A., Rothwell, J. C., Quinn, N. P., Lang, A. E., Artieda, J. & Marsden, C. D. (1986): Lisuride in the treatment of myoclonus. *Adv. Neurol.* **43**, 191–196.
80 Obeso, J. A., Artieda, J., Luquin, M. R., Vaamonde, J., Martinez-Lage, J. M. (1986): Antimyoclonic action of piracetam. *Clin. Neuropharmacol.* **9**, 59–64.
81 Gimenez-Roldan, S., Mateo, D., Muradas, V., De Yebenes, J. G. (1988): Clinical, biochemical and pharmacological observation in a patient with postasphyxic myoclonus: Association to serotonin hyperactivity. *Clin. Neuropharmacol.* **11**, 151–160.
82 Bressman, S., Fahn, S., Eisenberg, M., Brin, M. & Maltese, W. (1986): Biotin-responsive encephalopathy with myoclonus, ataxia, and seizures. *Adv. Neurol.* **43**, 119–125.
83 Trouillas, P., Brudon, F. & Adeleine, P. (1988): Improvement of cerebellar ataxia with levorotatory form of 5-hydroxytyptophan. A double-blind study with quantified data processing. *Arch. Neurol.* **45**, 1217–1222.
84 Fahn, S. & Cote, L. J., (1968): Regional distribution of choline acetylase in the brain of the Rhesus monkey. *Brain Res.* **7**, 323–325.
85 Agid, Y., Javoy-Agid, F. & Ruberg, M. (1987): Biochemistry of neurotransmitters in Parkinson's disease. In *Movement disorders 2*, ed C. D. Marsden & S. Fahn, pp. 166–230. London: Butterworth.
86 Stahl, S. M. & Berger, P. A. (1981): Physostigmine in Tourette syndrome: evidence for cholinergic underactivity. *Am. J. Psychiatry* **138**, 40–242.

87 Fahn, S. (1983): High dosage anticholinergic therapy in dystonia. *Neurology* **33**, 1255–1261.
88 Burke, R. E., Fahn, S. & Marsden, C. D. (1986): Torsion dystonia: A double-blind, prospective trial of high-dosage trihexyphenidyl. *Neurology* **36**, 160–164.
89 Marsden, C. D., Marion, M.-H. & Quinn, N. (1984): The treatment of severe dystonia in children and adults. *J. Neurol. Neurosurg. Psychiatry* **47**, 1166–1173.
90 Lang, A. E. (1986): High dose anticholinergic therapy in adult dystonia. *Can. J. Neurol. Sci.* **13**, 42–46.
91 Greene, P. E., Shale, H. & Fahn, S.: Analysis of a large series of patients with torsion dystonia treated with high dosages of anticholinergic and other drugs. *Adv. Neurol.* in press.
92 Fahn, S. & Marsden, C. D. (1987): The treatment of dystonia. In *Movement disorders 2*, ed C. D. Marsden & S. Fahn, pp 359–382.
93 Kao, I., Drachman, D. B. & Price, D. L. (1976): Botulinum toxin: mechanism of presynaptic blockade. *Science* **193**, 1256–1258.
94 Scott, A. B., Kennedy, R. A. & Stubbs, M. A. (1985): Botulinum toxin injection as a treatment for blepharospasm. *Arch. Ophthalmol.* **103**, 347–350.
95 Blitzer, A., Brin, M. F., Fahn, S., Lange, D. & Lovelace, R. E. (1986): Botulinum toxin (BOTOX) for the treatment of 'spastic dysphonia' as a part of a trial of toxin injections for the treatment of other cranial dystonias [letter]. *Laryngoscope* **96**, 1300–1301.
96 Tsui, J. K. C., Eisen, A., Stoessl, A. J., Calne, S., & Calne, D. B. (1986): Double-blind study of botulinum toxin in spasmodic torticollis. *Lancet* **ii**, 245–247.
97 Brin, M. F., Fahn, S., Moskowitz, C., Friedman, A., Shale, H. M. et al. (1987): Localized injections of botulinum toxin for the treatment of focal dystonia and hemifacial spasm. *Movement disorders* **2**, 237–254.
98 Jankovic, J. & Orman, J. (1987): Botulinum A toxin for cranial-cervical dysytonia: a double-blind, placebo-controlled study. *Neurology* **37**, 616–623.
99 Jabbari, B., Rosenberg, M., Scherokman, B., Gunderson, C. H., McBurney, J. W. & McClintock, W. (1987): Effectiveness of trihexyphenidyl against pendular nystagmus and palatal myoclonus: Evidence of cholinergic dysfunction. *Movement disorders* **2**, 93–98.
100 Chokroverty, S., Manoch, M. K., Duvoisin, R. C. (1987): A physiologic and pharmacologic study in anticholinergic-responsive essential myoclonus. *Neurology* **37**, 608–615.
101 Sasaki, H., Sudoh, K., Hamada, K., Hamada, T. & Tashiro, K. (1987): Skeletal myoclonus in olivopontocerebellar atrophy: Treatment with trihexyphenidyl. *Neurology* **37**, 1258–1262.
102 Jabbari, B., Gunderson, C. H. & McBurney, J. W. (1983): Improvement of ataxic hemiparesis with trihexyphenidyl. *Neurology* **33**, 1627–1628.
103 Perry, T. L., Hansen, S. & Kloster, M. (1973): Huntington's chorea: deficiency of gamma-aminobutyric acid in brain. *N. Engl. J. Med.* **288**, 337–342.
104 Urquart, N., Perry, T. L., Hansen, S. & Kennedy, J. (1975): GABA content and glutamic acid decarboxylase activity in brain of Huntington's chorea patients and control subjects. *J. Neurochem.* **24**, 1071–1075.
105 Bird, E. D. & Iversen, L. L. (1974): Huntington's chorea: postmortem measurement of glutamic acid decarboxylase, choline acetyltransferase and dopamine in basal ganglia. *Brain* **97**, 457–472.
106 Shoulson, I., Goldblatt, D., Charlton, M. & Joynt, R. J. (1978): Huntington's disease: treatment with muscimol, a GABA-mimetic drug. *Ann. Neurol.* **4**, 279–284.
107 Shoulson, I., Kartzinel, R. & Chase, T. N. (1976): Huntington's disease: treatment with dipropylacetic acid and gamma-aminobutyric acid. *Neurology* **26**, 61–63.
108 Scigliano, G., Giovannini, P., Girotti, F., Grassi, M. P., Caraceni, T. & Schechter, P. J. (1984): Gamma-vinyl GABA treatment of Huntington's disease. *Neurology* **34**, 94–96.
109 Walters, A., Hening, W., Cote, L. & Fahn, S. (1986): Dominantly inherited restless legs with myoclonus and periodic movements of sleep: a syndrome related to the endogenous opiates? *Adv. neurol.* **43**, 309–319.
110 Coleman, R. M., Pollak, C. P. & Weitzman, E. D. (1980): Periodic movements in sleep (nocturnal myoclonus): relation to sleep disorders. *Ann. Neurol.* **8**, 416–421.
111 Hening, W., Walters, A., Kavey, N., Gidro-Frank, S., Cote, L. J., & Fahn, S. (1986): Dyskinesias while awake and periodic movements in sleep in restless legs syndrome: Treatment with opioids. *Neurology* **36**, 1363–1366.

112 Ohanna, N., Peled, R., Rubin, A.-H. E., Zomer, J. & Lavie, P. (1985): Periodic leg movements in sleep: Effect of clonazepam treatment. *Neurology* **35**, 408–411.
113 Handwerker, J. V., & Palmer, R. F. (1985): Clonidine in the treatment of 'restless leg' syndrome. *N. Engl. J. Med.* **313**, 1228–1229.
114 Montplaisir, J., Godbout, R., Poirier, G. & Bedard, M. A. (1986): Restless legs syndrome and periodic movements in sleep: physiopathology and treatment with L-dopa. *Clin. Neuropharmacol.* **9**, 456–463.
115 Akpinar, S. (1987): Restless legs syndrome treatment with dopaminergic drugs. *Clin. Neuropharmacol.* **10**, 69–79.
116 Trzepacz, P. T., Violette, E. J., & Sateia, M. J. (1984): Response to opioids in three patients with restless legs syndrome. *Am. J. Psychiatry* **141**, 993–995.
117 Andemann, F. & Andermann, E. (1986): Excessive startle syndromes: startle disease, jumping, and startle epilepsy. *Adv. Neurol.* **43**, 321–338.
118 Spillane, J. D., Nathan, P. W., Kelly, R. E. & Marsden, C. D. (1971): Painful legs and moving toes. *Brain* **94**, 541–556.
119 Montagna, P., Cirignotta, F., Sacquegna, T., Martinelli, P., Ambrosetto, G. & Lugaresi, E. (1983): 'Painful legs and moving toes' associated with polyneuropathy. *J. Neurol. Neurosurg. Psychiatry* **46**, 399–403.
120 Nathan, P. W. (1978): Painful legs and moving toes: evidence on the site of the lesion. *J. Neurol. Neurosurg. Psychiatry* **41**, 934–939.
121 Lance, J. W. (1977): Familial paroxysmal dystonic choreoathetosis and its differentiation from related syndromes. *Ann. Neurol.* **2**, 285–293.
122 Kurlan, R. & Shoulson, (1983): Familial paroxysmal dystonic choreoathetosis and response to alternate-day oxazepam therapy. *Ann. Neurol.* **13**, 456–457.
123 Bressman, S. B., Fahn, S. & Burke, R. E. (1988): Paroxysmal non-kinesigenic dystonia. *Adv. Neurol.* **50**, 403–413.
124 Fahn, S. & Williams, D. T. (1988): Psychogenic dystonia. *Adv. Neurol.* **50**, 431–455.
125 Howard, F. M. (1963): A new and effective drug in the treatment of the stiff-man syndrome: preliminary report. *Mayo Clin. Proc.* **38**, 203–212.
126 Spehlmann, R. & Norcross, K. (1979): Stiff-man syndrome. *Clin. Neuropharmacol.* **4**, 109–121.
127 Spehlmann, R., Norcross, K., Rasmus, S. C. & Schlageter, N. L. (1981): Improvement of stiff-man syndrome with sodium valproate. *Neurology* **31**, 1162–1163.

CLINICAL ASPECTS

Parkinsons

28

CURRENT TOPICS OF INTEREST IN

PARKINSON'S DISEASE

Erik Ch. Wolters and Donald B. Calne

Belzberg Laboratory of Clinical Neuroscience, Department of Medicine, Division of Neurology, University of British Columbia, Health Sciences Centre Hospital, Vancouver B.C., Canada V6T 1W5

Summary

Parkinson's disease continues to be a rewarding field for those interested in neurobiology and neuropharmacology. There has been recent interest in the relationship between normal nigral neuronal attrition and the loss that occurs in Parkinson's disease. The search for aetiology has also focused on risk factors; they may precede the onset of symptoms by decades. Surgical approaches to the treatment of Parkinson's disease have been directed at the transplantation of dopaminergic cells into the brain. Initial attempts in animals led to encouraging results in certain models of Parkinson's disease. Early enthusiasm for this procedure in human subjects has been followed by a highly critical reappraisal. In pharmacology, attention is currently turning to the role of D1 receptors; could D1 stimulation enhance the response of D2 receptors? A major effort is in progress to develop drugs that act selectively on the D1 system.

Introduction

Normal ageing results in a loss of neurons which is unevenly distributed through the brain and the spinal cord. One of the areas most affected by this attrition is the substantia nigra, which is also the primary site of the pathology of Parkinson's disease. Evidence will be reviewed that suggests that there may be a relationship between ageing and Parkinson's disease, although its aetiology cannot be attributed to ageing alone. Environmental factors indicate the likelihood of an exogenous causal component for Parkinson's disease.

The age-related decline of dopaminergic nigral neurons and the age-related loss of neural plasticity may contribute to the appearance and progression of symptoms. These factors offer a rationale for some new strategies for treating Parkinson's disease: theoretical approaches to reducing the rate of neuronal loss, and the transplantation of dopamine producing cells into the brain. Recent promising reports of synergistic effects of D-1 and D-2 dopamine agonists also prompt further clinical research with D-1 agonists.

Ageing, plasticity and adrenal transplants

Age-related attrition in the central nervous system is a selective process, prominently affecting dopaminergic cells of the substantia nigra,[1,2] cholinergic cells of the basal forebrain, and motor neurons in the spinal cord. With advancing age tyrosine hydroxylase, dopa decarboxylase and dopamine content fall.[1,3,4] Nigral degeneration seems to be more rapidly progressive in the elderly.[3]

The nucleic acid content of neuronal cells is an important determinant of their vulnerability to damage by ageing. Therefore the low concordance rate of Parkinson's disease in identical twins is evidence against the process of normal ageing being the sole cause of Parkinson's disease. A second argument against such a role for ageing is the histological appearance of more active cell disruption in the substantia nigra of parkinsonian brains compared to age-matched controls.[5]

The extent of neuronal plasticity following injury also seems to decline with the ageing process. Substances and processes supporting neuron survival, promoting axonal sprouting and guiding the neurites to their targets, provide the CNS with potential to recover from injury. Neuronotrophic activity is more vigorous in young compared with old rats. Regenerative axonal sprouting after denervation is slower and less extensive in old rats. Experimental depletion of choline acetyltransferase activity in Meynert's nucleus basalis is followed by full recovery in young but not in old rats;[6] ganglioside GM-1 protects young and mature but not old rats from biochemical changes. In this context it is also relevant to mention that 1-methyl-4-phenyl-1,2,3,6-tetrahydropyridine (MPTP) produces sustained dopamine depletion in older mice, but only transient changes in younger animals (using identical doses and the same, intraperitoneal route of administration).[7]

In monkeys 6-hydroxydopamine and MPTP produce nigrostriatal damage and a parkinsonian syndrome and/or rotational behaviour. This syndrome can be reversed by transplantation of fetal nigral tissue or adrenal medulla cells into the neostriatum.

In Sweden, four patients with Parkinson's disease were treated with adrenal medulla transplants, stereotactically implanted in the neostriatum;[8] 10 patients in Mexico had open microsurgical placement of adrenal tissue into a cavity excavated in the caudate nucleus.[9] The Swedish patients did not undergo any worthwhile improvement, whereas several of the Mexican patients were reported to have responded dramatically. Surprisingly, there was claimed to have been bilateral reduction of deficits, implying a mechanism other than simple axonal growth from the unilateral transplant. These results have not been replicated, and many patients have deteriorated after surgery.

Transplantation of adrenal medullary tissue to the neostriatal surface of MPTP-lesioned mice has been reported to induce regeneration of surviving nigrostriatal dopaminergic axons, to re-innervate large areas of the striatum: the transplant may generate a trophic substance. Dense catecholamine-containing neurons, originating from the host, rather than from the grafts, were seen in both the ipsilateral and the contralateral striatum. Diffusion of a trophic substance through the cerebrospinal fluid has been suggested to account for the bilateral effects in the Mexican patients. If so, adrenal medullary transplants are less likely to be beneficial in patients with advanced disease, where the nigrostriatal system is severely damaged, or in elderly patients where the production of trophic substances is likely to be more limited.[6]

Many essential questions in adrenal medullary transplant therapy remain unanswered. Queries concerning the optimal nature of the transplanted tissue, the choice of the site of implantation and the long-term outcome need to be resolved. Human fetal sympathetic neurons secrete twice as much dopamine into culture medium as adrenal chromaffin cells; is this relevant? Can human neuroblastoma cell lines be produced to secrete dopamine and then have their replication controlled? Can dopaminergic tissue be transplanted from animals into humans? Are immunosuppressive drugs required in any of these settings?

Environmental factors and parkinsonism

Parkinsonian syndromes may develop long after a primary subclinical insult. Latency periods ('ageing') of up to several decades have been reported between exposure to infective, traumatic or neurotoxic factors and the appearance of parkinsonian features, for example in the epidemic of encephalitis lethargica, in pugilist's encephalopathy,[10] and in the ALS-Parkinson-dementia complex of Guam (currently argued to be of toxic origin[11,12]). Asymptomatic exposure to MPTP can lead to reduction of striatal fluorodopa accumulation,[13] and delayed onset of symptoms of parkinsonism has been reported. In animals, delayed exacerbation of symptoms has been reported after 6-hydroxydopamine lesions.[14]

Parkinson's disease affects 1.5 per thousand of the European and North American population. The prevalence rises tenfold after the sixth decade of life.[15]

In the pre-levodopa era, DeJong and Burns[16] reported much more rapid progression of Parkinson's disease when symptoms began in late life, but Agid did not confirm this in a recent survey of patients on modern treatment (personal communication). Calne & Lees noted late progression of neurological impairment in patients with post-encephalitic parkinsonism,[17] in accord with a similar natural history of the post-poliomyelitis syndrome. Highly toxic free radicals may play a role in the accelerating neuronal decay of senescence. Antioxidants such as catalase and peroxidase are decreased in the substantia nigra of patients with Parkinson's disease.

Subclinical damage by exposure to a 'slow toxin', or recurrent infections, might impair the life expectation of a group of neurons, which would die collectively after a period of decades. The extensive compensatory activity that takes place may compromise their survival and accelerate their demise. The time interval between exposure to the risk factor and final neuronal death can be construed as an ageing process which has been influenced by a specific environmental event or series of events.[18] Nigral neurons may have been 'sick' for many years before they die.

In contrast to the epidemiological studies in the United States,[15] the prevalence of Parkinson's disease is much less frequent in blacks in South Africa (Natal) as compared with whites.[19] Blacks in Nigeria also show a much lower age-adjusted prevalence ratio of Parkinson's disease than U.S. blacks.[15,20] Prevalence ratios for Parkinson's disease seem to show a north-south gradient: they are lower in regions situated nearer the equator.[15,20,21] Relatively high prevalence ratios are found in rural environments.[15,22,23] Exposure to putative aetiological agents such as pesticides, herbicides, metals (particularly chromium), and pollutants deriving from the forestry industry cannot be linked to this geographical distribution.[20,22] Lower prevalence of parkinsonism among cigarette smokers has been reported,[20,24] and contradicted.

The clinical onset of Parkinson's disease at approximately the same time has recently been noted in the members of six families, with age differences averaging 25 yr between children and parents;[25] another series of six parent-child pairs with age differences at onset averaging about 20 years has been observed.[26] Both reports are in accord with the concept of simultaneous exposure to an environmental risk factor within a family.

D_1 and D_2 receptors

The classification of dopamine receptors into D-1 and D-2 types is now widely accepted. Both receptors may be involved in motor control.[27] Historically, motor effects associated with the clinical features of parkinsonism have been attributed to reduced D-2 receptor activity. Behavioural changes induced by D-1 and D-2 activation in animals are complex and controversial.

In normal rats, treatment with the selective D-1 agonist SKF 38393 induces non-stereotyped abnormal oral movements such as sniffing, grooming, mouth opening, clonic jaw movements, vacuous chewing movements and tongue protrusions, especially in the senescent rat.[28] Selective stimulation of D-2 receptors produces stereotyped behaviour characterized by repetitive sniffing, rearing, licking and gnawing, suppression of spontaneous exploratory activity, yawning and increased locomotor activity. In animals with unilateral nigrostriatal lesions there is a turning response. Stimulation of both D-1 and D-2 receptors by a non-selective dopamine agonist such as apomorphine gives rise to both D-1 and D-2 behaviours; the less pronounced D-1 motor activity, however, is only seen after pretreatment with D-2 antagonists such as sulpiride.[28] A threshold dose of a D-2 agonist such as RU 242113 has been reported to be potentiated by concurrent administration of a D-1 agonist. D-2 dopaminergic activity seems to be regulated, in a facilitatory manner, by D-1 dopaminergic activity.[29,30]

In rats and in humans, ageing causes loss of dopaminergic receptors, especially the D-2 type. Radioligand studies with [^{3}H]spiperone are reported to show a decline in ligand binding with advancing age, amounting to a 46 per cent loss after 50 years.[31] There seems to be no significant difference between normal age-matched subjects and patients with mild to moderate Parkinson's disease. The change in the ratio of D-1 to D-2 receptors in senescence may be relevant to the idiopathic perioral dyskinesias that occur in the elderly.

There is considerable interest in the possibility that D-1 agonists may have clinical potential, but the reported observations cannot be integrated into any coherent picture; there are numerous paradoxes, inconsistencies and controversies. Dopaminergic ergots such as bromocriptine seem more effective in the control of parkinsonian symptoms when they are administered in conjunction with levodopa. This may derive from an effect of bromocriptine in releasing dopamine from nerve endings (in addition to direct D-2 agonism), or alternatively the beneficial interaction may result from increased D-1 receptor tone. One selective D-1 agonist, CY 208-243, has been reported to correct parkinsonian symptoms induced by MPTP in monkeys. Another selective D-1 agonist SKF 38393, however, fails to produce consistent improvement in either MPTP monkeys or patients with Parkinson's disease.[32]

References

1. McGeer, P. L., McGeer, E. & Suzuki, J. S. (1977): Aging and extrapyramidal function. *Arch. Neurol.* **34**, 33–35.
2. Mann, D. M. A. (1984): Dopamine neurones of the vertebrate spine: some aspects of anatomy and pathology. In *The neurobiology of dopamine systems*, eds W. Winlow & R. Markstein, pp 87–103. Manchester: Manchester University Press.
3. Carlsson, A. & Winblad, B. (1976): Influence of age and time interval between death and autopsy on dopamine and 3-methoxytyramine levels in human basal ganglia. *J. Neurol. Transm.* **38**, 271–276.
4. Carlsson, A., Nyberg, P. & Winblad, B. (1984): The influence of age and other factors on concentrations of monoamines in human brain. In *Brain monoamines in normal aging and dementia*, ed P. Nyberg, pp 53–84. Umeo, Sweden: Umeo University.
5. McGeer, P. L. (1988): Measurement of neuronal loss in Parkinson's disease and aging. In

Parkinsonism and aging, ed D. B. Calne. New York: Raven Press (In Press).
6. Cuello, A. C., Stephens, P. H., Maysinger, D., Tagari, P. & Garofalo, L. (1988): In *Neuroplasticity; a new therapeutical in the CNS pathology*, eds R. Masland, A. Portera-Sanchez & G. Toffano. Padua, Italy: Liviana Press (In Press).
7. Ricaurte, G. A., Langston, J. W., Irwin, I., DeLanney, L. E. & Forno, L. S. (1985): The neurotoxic effect of MPTP on dopaminergic cells in the substantia nigra is age-related. *Soc. Neurosci. Abstr.* **11**, 631.
8. Lindvall, O., Backlund, E. O., Farde, L., *et al.* (1987): Transplantation in Parkinson's disease: Two cases of adrenal medullary grafts to the putamen. *Ann. Neurol.* **22**, 457–468.
9. Madrazo, I., Drucker-Colin, R., Diaz, V., *et al.* (1987): Open microsurgical autograft of adrenal medulla to the right caudate nucleus in two patients with intractable Parkinson's disease. *N. Engl. J. Med.* **316**, 831–834.
10. Mawdsley, C. & Ferguson, F. R. (1963): Neurological disease in boxers. *Lancet* **ii**, 795–801.
11. Spencer, P. S. (1987): Guam ALS/Parkinsonism-Dementia: a long-latency neurotoxic disorder caused by "slow toxin(s)" in food? *Can. J. Neurol. Sci.* **14**, 347–357.
12. Garruto, R. M., Gajdusek, D. C. & Chen, K. M. (1980): Amyotrophic lateral sclerosis among Chamorro migrants from Guam. *Ann. Neurol.* **8**, 612–619.
13. Calne, D. B., Langston, J. W., Martin, W. R. W., Stoessl, A. W., Ruth, T. J., Adam, M. J., Pate, B. D. & Schulzer, M. (1985): Positron emission tomography after MPTP: observations relating to the cause of Parkinson's disease. *Nature* **317**, 246–248.
14. Schallert, T. (1988): Aging-dependent emergence of sensorimotor dysfunction in rat recovered from dopamine depletion sustained early in life. In *Central determinants of age-related decline in motor functioning*, ed J. A. Joseph. *Ann. N.Y. Acad. Sci.* (In Press).
15. Schoenberg, B. S. (1987): Epidemiology of movement disorders. In *Movement disorders 2*, eds C. D. Marsden & S. Fahn.
16. De Jong, J.D., Burns, B.D. (1967): Parkinson's disease – a random process *Can. Med. Assoc. J.* **97**, 49–56.
17. Calne, B. & Lees, A. J. (1988): Late progression of post-encephalitic Parkinson's Syndrome. *Can. J. Neurosci.* **15**, 135–138.
18. Wolters, E. Ch. & Calne, D. B. (1988): Is Parkinson's disease related to aging? In *Parkinsonism and aging*, ed D. B. Calne. New York: Raven Press (In Press).
19. Cosnett, J. E. & Bill, P. L. A. (1988): Parkinson's disease in blacks: observations on epidemiology in Natal. *S. Afr. J. Med.* **73**, 281–283.
20. Schoenberg, B. S. (1987): Environmental risk factors for Parkinson's disease: the epidemiologic evidence. *Can. J. Neurol. Sci.* **14**, 407–413.
21. Lux, W. E. & Kurtzke, J. F. (1987): Is Parkinson's disease acquired? Evidence from a geographic comparison with multiple sclerosis. *Neurology* **37**, 467–471.
22. Tanner, C. M., Chen, B., Wang, W. Z., Peng, M. L., Liu, Z. L., Liang, X. L., Kao, L. C., Gilley, D. W. & Schoenberg, B. S. (1987): Environmental factors in the etiology of Parkinson's disease. *Can. J. Neurol. Sci.* **14**, 419–423.
23. Schoenberg, B. S., Anderson, D. W. & Haerer, A. F. (1985): Prevalence of Parkinson's disease in the biracial population of Copiah County, Mississippi. *Neurology* **35**, 841–845.
24. Rajput, A. H., Offord, K. P., Beard, M. & Kurland, L. T. (1987): A case-control study of smoking habits, dementia, and other illnesses in idiopathic Parkinson's disease. *Neurology* **37**, 226–232.
25. Calne, S., Schoenberg, B., Martin, W., Uitti, R. J., Spencer, P. & Calne, D. B. (1987): Familial Parkinson's disease: possible roles of environmental factors. *Can. J. Neurol. Sci.* **14**, 303–305.
26. Quinn, N., Critchley, P. & Marsden, C. D. (1987): Young onset Parkinson's disease. *Movement Disorders* **2**, 73–91.
27. Arnt, J. & Hyttel, J. (1985): Differential involvement of dopamine D-1 and D-2 receptors in the circling behaviour induced by apomorphine, SKF 38393, pergolide and LY 171555 in 6-hydroxy-dopamine lesioned rats. *Psychopharmacology* **85**, 346–352.
28. Clark, D. & White, F. J. (1987): Review: D-1 dopamine receptor—the search for a function. *Synapse* **1**, 347–388.

29 Waddington, J. L. (1986): Behavioural correlates of the action of selective D-1 dopamine receptor antagonists. *Biochem. Pharmacol.* **35**, 3661–3667.
30 Stoof, J. C. & Kebabian, J. W. (1981): Opposing roles for D-1 and D-2 dopamine receptors in efflux of cAMP from rat neostriatum. *Nature* **294**, 366–368.
31 Wong, D. F., Wagner, H. N., Dannals, R. F., Links, J. M., Frost, J. J., Ravert, H. T., Wilson, A. A., Rosenbaum, A. E., Gjedde, A., Douglass, K. H., Petronis, J. D., Folstein, M. F., Toung, J. K. T., Burns, H. D. & Kuhar, M. J. (1984): Effects of age on dopamine and serotonin receptors measured by positron tomography in the living human brain. *Science* **226**, 1393–1396.
32 Barone, P., Bankiewicz, K. S., Corsini, G. U., Kopin, I. J. & Chase, T. N. (1987): Dopaminergic mechanisms in hemiparkinsonian monkeys. *Neurology* **37**, 1592–1595.

29

THE RELATIONSHIP BETWEEN PARKINSONIAN RIGIDITY AND LONG-LATENCY STRETCH REFLEX ACTIVITY STUDIED IN INDIVIDUAL PATIENTS

R. J. Meara and F. W. J. Cody*

*Department of Neurology, Manchester Royal Infirmary, Manchester, M13 9WL and * Department of Physiological Sciences, University of Manchester, Manchester M13 9PT, UK*

Summary

Electromyographic (EMG) reflexes evoked in the voluntarily contracting flexor carpi radialis by forcible extension of the wrist (10 degrees; 100 and 200 degrees per sec) were recorded in rigid parkinsonian patients and in healthy subjects. The reflex responses of the patients, together with clinical assessments of passive and activated rigidity, were measured prior to their routine daily medication (levodopa) and at successive intervals thereafter.

Long-latency (M2) reflexes of the patients, measured in the rigid state before medication, were prolonged and of larger amplitude (normalized for background EMG) than those of age-matched control subjects; short-latency (M1) responses of the patients were within the normal range. The reflex patterns of individual patients showed relatively little change following medication despite substantial improvement in their rigidity and clinical condition. In a large majority of patients no correlation was found between alterations in M2 response amplitudes and corresponding changes in rigidity. Neither did a relationship exist between alterations in M1 or summed M1 and M2 activity and rigidity.

These findings suggest either that enhancement of M2 reflexes in Parkinson's disease is an epiphenomenon of the disease process, which bears little relation to abnormalities of muscle tone, or that a contribution from other essential mechanisms was not revealed by the reflex methodology employed.

Introduction

Rigidity is a major feature of Parkinson's disease, yet its origin is still obscure.[1] Many individuals suffering from this disease exhibit an increased, abnormal resistance in the relaxed state to passively applied displacements of their limbs. This increased resistance, or rigidity, is often readily detected upon clinical examination, by passive flexion and extension movements of the wrist joint.

Rigidity is generally described as an abnormality of muscle tone.[2] Implicit in this concept is the view that rigidity is, at least in part, neurogenic in origin and arises from a disturbance of stretch reflex activity. Clearly several other factors must also be considered in relation to the genesis of rigidity. These include alterations in the mechanical properties of muscle, joints and connective tissues. Nevertheless, the general belief is that the major contribution to rigidity derives from reflexly-mediated muscle contraction. Indeed evidence of reflex abnormality in Parkinson's disease has been demonstrated by studying the segmented stretch reflex activity derived from sudden displacements of actively contracting muscle. Such displacements result not only in a short latency response but also in long-latency activity, the neural pathways of which are uncertain.[3,4] Lee & Tatton[5] studied these responses, called by them the M1 (short) and M2 (long latency) reflexes, in selected, rigid, parkinsonian individuals. Their central finding was that whereas in rigid patients the M1 response was normal, the M2 response was greatly increased. They also felt that the degree of enhancement of the M2 response paralleled the clinical severity of the rigidity present. Some investigators[6] have supported these findings but in several other studies,[7-10] whilst a varying degree of enhancement of the M2 response has been confirmed, no clear, causal, relationship to rigidity has been demonstrated. Furthermore other investigators have either been unable to confirm the presence of any abnormal stretch reflex activity in Parkinson's disease,[11,12] or have reported reduced M1, rather than increased M2 responses.[13]

Allowing for a tendency for the M2 response to be enhanced in Parkinson's disease, a central feature of most reports has been the considerable variation in M2 reflex size between individuals for a similar rigidity grading and in the severity of rigidity for any given reflex size. This type of variation is more striking than the tendency for the M2 reflex size to increase with severity of rigidity in the patient groups studied. In addition, the degree of M2 enhancement has rarely been of the order that was reported in the initial studies by Lee & Tatton.[5] Some of the difficulty in attempting to relate rigidity and reflex size may well reflect the fact that pooled, group data have been used to seek correlation between M2 size and rigidity. A true relationship between M2 and rigidity for an individual could be lost in the pooling process. The behaviour of the M2 reflex in an individual, over periods of time in which rigidity of that individual alters, has not been studied.

We have approached the mechanisms underlying rigidity in Parkinson's disease in two ways. Firstly, we have recorded the EMG patterns generated by sinusoidal movements, passively imposed by the examiner's hand on the wrist joint in controls and in Parkinsonian subjects. These passive movements were identical in magnitude and velocity to those employed in the clinical estimation of rigidity. Secondly, we have studied the M2 as well as the total (M1 + M2) response, generated by servo-controlled ramp and hold displacements of the wrist joint in a group of parkinsonian subjects and similarly-aged controls. The individuals in the parkinsonian group were investigated before their normal medication and at times afterwards, as their clinical condition improved in response to the treatment. Thus, the behaviour of the stretch reflex response of an individual could be investigated from an 'off treatment' rigid state to an 'on treatment' non-rigid condition.

Methods

Subjects

Twenty patients with Parkinson's disease (mean age 62 years, SD 6; 12 male, 8 female) and 19 control subjects (mean age 65 years, SD 9; 8 male, 11 female) were studied. All the patients were taking levodopa, in some instances in addition to other anti-parkinsonian medication. The 20 patients were derived from the study of a larger group of patients and were selected on the basis of their having a clear stable improvement in rigidity after their medication.

Experimental arrangement

Electromyography. Surface electrodes were placed 4 cm apart over the belly of flexor carpi radialis and over the wrist extensor muscle mass. The signals were band-pass filtered (20 Hz–3 kHz) and full wave rectified, before on-line averaging (Medelec DAV 62) with a smoothing time constant of 1 msec.

Rigidity measurement. Rigidity at the wrist joint was assessed clinically by passive flexion and extension movements around the joint. The subject, recumbent, with the forearm fully supported, was asked to relax. A five point scale for rigidity was used: none, a trace, mild, moderate, severe. These were given gradings of 0, 1/2, 1, 2, 3, respectively (see Lakke[14]). This assessment was also made when the subject performed a Jendrassik manoeuvre by clenching the contralateral hand to that under test. This resulted in an estimation of both 'active' and 'passive' rigidity.

Sinusoidal muscle stretch. An accelerometer (Bruel and Kjaer 4332) was strapped to the dorsum of the subject's hand and connected to a charge amplifier (Bruel and Kjaer 2635). Sinusoidal clinically-relevant movements were passively imposed on the wrist joint. A displacement record was obtained by double integration of the output signal of the accelerometer and viewed in conjunction with the rectified surface EMG of the wrist flexors and extensors.

Ramp and hold stretch. The subject sat with the forearm horizontal, supported in a semi-pronated position. The hand grasped a handle which was connected to the arm of a powerful servo-controlled electromagnetic vibrator. The wrist was clamped by vertical bars. An isometric force transducer lay in series with the vibrator arm. The vibrator drove the handle back when activated, thus extending the wrist and stretching the flexor carpi radialis. The displacements were given at 100 and 200 degrees per sec stretch. The subject was asked to maintain a 20 per cent maximum flexion contraction against the handle throughout the handle movement, but not to react to the displacement in any other way. The stretch resulted in a wrist rotation of 10 degrees and lasted 400 msec. Thirty two displacements at each of the two velocities of stretch were presented randomly to provide EMG data for averaging and analysis of stretch reflex activity. A more detailed account of the experimental method for the ramp and hold stretch is given in Cody *et al.*[10]

Subjects were first seen and assessed clinically having been off all treatment for at least 12 hours. The stretch reflexes were obtained as above. The normal medication was then given. Measurement of the stretch reflexes and further clinical estimations of rigidity were performed at 30 minute intervals until a clear and stable improvement in rigidity developed. This occurred on average approximately 1 hour after the medication had been given. The cycle was repeated to obtain six or more sets of stretch reflexes and related rigidity estimations for each individual in the study.

Stretch reflex measurement. The area of EMG activity in the periods for the M1 and M2 response were measured by the use of a graphics tablet and computer. These activities were expressed as a mean area per unit time. Activities between 20 and 40 msec and between 50 and 90 msec were taken to represent the M1 and M2 responses respectively (see Cody *et al.*[10]). For the total response, M1 + M2, all the reflex activity from 20 to 90 msec was measured. The pre-existing background activity was measured as the activity, again expressed as an area per unit time, in the 40 msec period up to the onset of the M1 response. The M1, M2 and total reflex responses were obtained after subtraction of the background and then normalized by division with this same background value (see Rothwell *et al.*[8]). Further reference in the text to stretch reflex values will refer to normalized results unless otherwise stated.

Statistical analysis

In view of the ordinal scale for rigidity the non-parametric Spearman rank correlation coefficient was used in all correlative procedures. Similarly the Mann-Whitney U test was employed as an alternative to the t-test.

Results

EMG patterns evoked by sinusoidal wrist displacements

The rectified surface EMG resulting from passively-applied, approximately sinusoidal movements at the wrist, in a relaxed parkinsonian subject, is shown in Fig. 1. The movements applied by the examiner were identical to those used to determine rigidity at the wrist clinically. The patient exhibited grade 2 rigidity on wrist flexion with additional cog-wheel bursts on wrist extension. The EMG activity is related in both sets of muscles to the stretching phase and as such could generate forces perceived as rigidity by the examiner making the movements. Additionally the phase of the EMG activity is consistent with its generation by muscle stretch. In relaxed control subjects stretch-related EMG responses could also be generated, but they were often inconsistent and of much smaller amplitude than in the parkinsonian group.

EMG patterns evoked by ramp and hold displacements

Control subjects. Wrist displacements, at both 100 and 200 degrees per sec, generated segmented, rectified surface-recorded EMG activity from flexor carpi radialis. This consisted of early, short latency M1 and long-latency M2 responses, as previously described by Cody *et al.*[10] A typical series of six responses from a control subject, recorded every 30 min from time zero to the end of the experiment 150 min later is shown in Fig. 2. In all 19 control subjects the reflex pattern was broadly similar and was readily reproducible over the experimental period. This reproducibility was also seen in control subjects studied on several occasions as part of other experiments. In the control group of individuals little variation was seen in the background levels, or in the M1, M2, or total M1 + M2 reflex responses over the six trials. No significant trend in background level with time (Spearman rank correlation coefficient) was detected in any of the control subjects.

Parkinsonian subjects. A comparable series of responses from a parkinsonian subject, J. S., is shown in Fig. 3. In this figure in addition to the time, the related rigidity grading is

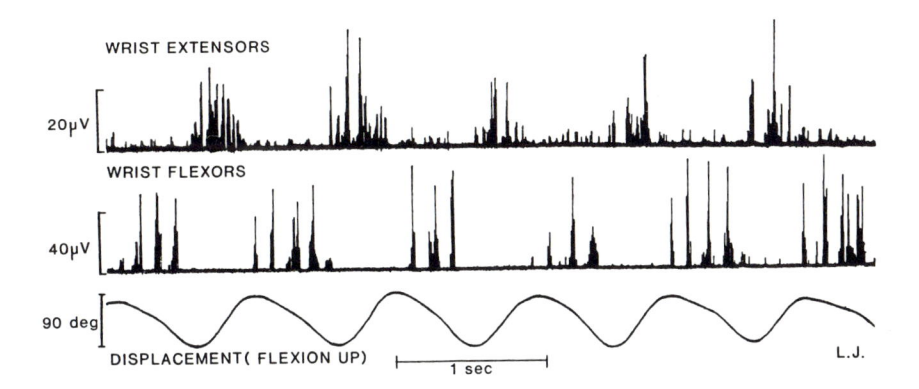

Fig. 1. *Surface rectified EMG activity recorded in a parkinsonian subject from flexor carpi radialis and the wrist extensor muscle mass.* The wrist is passively displaced in an approximately sinusoidal fashion by an examiner, in flexion and extension, with the subject relaxed. The patient exhibited grade 2 (moderate) rigidity on wrist movements with additional cog-wheel bursts on wrist extension.

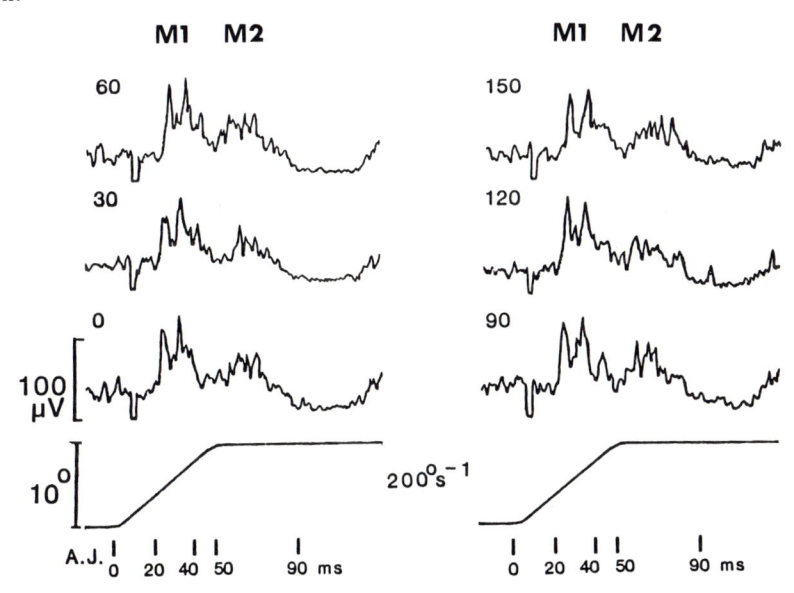

Fig. 2. *A typical series of surface recorded, rectified responses from flexor carpi radialis, upon ramp and hold displacements in a control subject at 200 degrees per sec.* The waveform of the displacement is given in the lower traces; 32 displacements were averaged to give each of the 6 responses from time 0 to 150 min, shown to the left-hand side of each average. The short square wave at the start of each response gives the zero EMG level. Measurement intervals of the M1 (20–40 msec) and M2 (50–90 msec) components of the stretch reflex response are indicated.

given for each of the six responses. In all 20 patients a qualitatively similar reflex pattern to responses of the control subjects was seen. However, as can be appreciated from comparison of Figs 2 and 3, quantitative differences exist. The major difference that can be seen between the patient and control subjects' responses is the greatly enhanced EMG activity occurring over the period of the M2 response in the parkinsonian individual J. S.

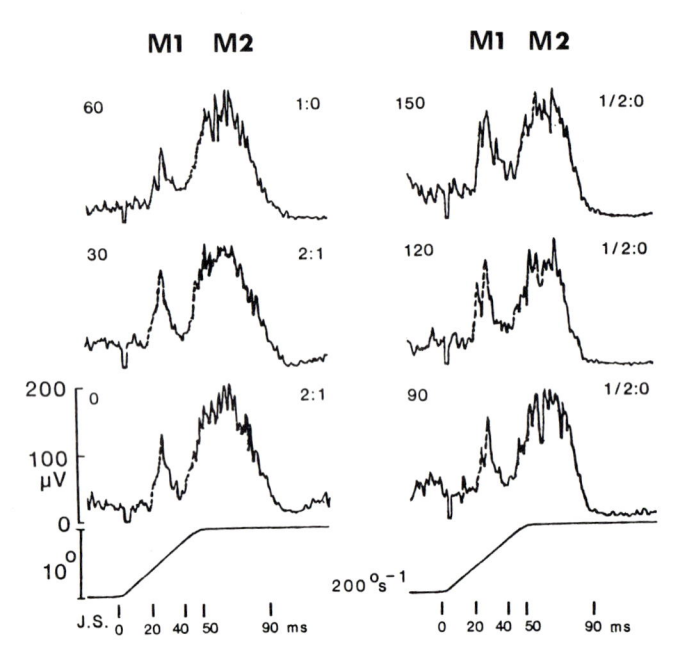

Fig. 3. *A series of surface-recorded rectified EMG responses is shown from flexor carpi radialis in a parkinsonian subject J. S. at 200 degrees per sec stretch.* The time of the responses from 0 min (pre-treatment) to 150 min (post-treatment) is given to the left of each average. To the right the rigidity grading is given (active rigidity: passive rigidity) on a five point scale 0, 1/2, 1, 2, 3, reflecting absent, a trace, mild, moderate, and severe rigidity.

Analysis of the size of the reflex responses in the two groups revealed that at 200 degrees per sec stretch the M2 reflex response was significantly increased in the patients compared to the control subjects (Mann-Whitney U test $P < 0.005$). The M1 response showed no amplitude differences between the two groups. The finding of an enhanced M2 response is consistent with other reports,[5-10] in which a variety of muscles were studied. The background levels in the individual patients showed more variation than in the control subjects, as did the normalized reflex values. However, there was again no trend between background values and time throughout the six trials in the patient group (Spearman rank correlation coefficient) with the exception of two patients.

The behaviour of this enhanced M2 response in relation to rigidity is also illustrated in the responses of J. S. in Fig. 3. The pattern of the reflex responses in the face of widely differing rigidity grades in J. S. remained remarkably similar. The large M2 response showed no alteration when the rigidity improved after medication. The lack of any obvious relationship between rigidity and the M2 response was present at both velocities of stretch as can be seen from Fig. 4. The responses of a further patient, R. G., at both velocities of stretch are also shown in Fig. 4. In this individual the M2 response was less pronounced compared to a prominent M1 reflex, especially at the faster velocity of stretch. In R. G. again, no alteration in the reflex patterns occurred despite the total absence of rigidity to clinical testing by the end of the experiment at 150 min. These two individuals demonstrate the range of reflex responsiveness for the M1 and M2 components that can be associated with similar grades of rigidity in the patient group. This was reflected equally potently in the range of normalized reflex values (M1, M2 and summed M1 + M2) between patients which were found for any rigidity grade. In

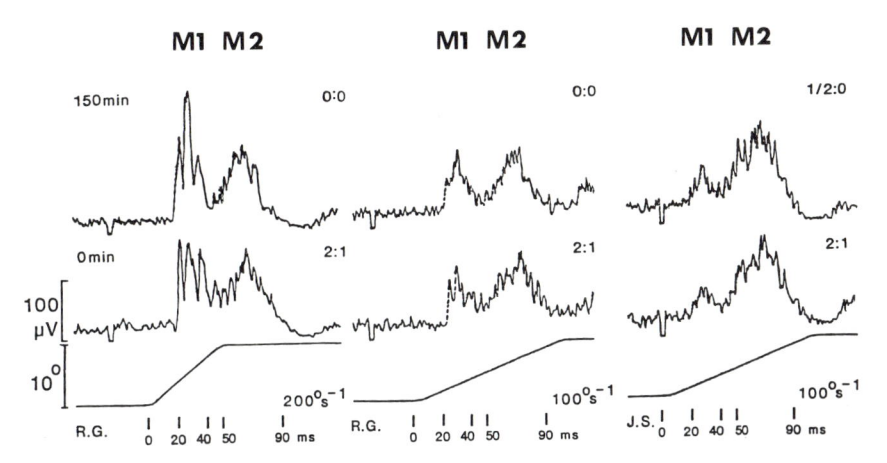

Fig. 4. *Surface recorded rectified EMG responses from flexor carpi radialis are shown from two parkinsonian patients at time zero (lower traces) and 150 min (upper traces). To the right a pair of averaged responses are seen from J. S. (the same individual as in Fig. 3), but at 100 degrees per sec stretch. To the left two pairs of averaged responses are shown at both velocities of stretch for a further subject, R. G. The rigidity grades are given to the right of each trace (active rigidity: passive rigidity; for scale see Fig. 3 and Methods).*

addition, the stretch reflexes in both patients, at the two velocities of stretch, demonstrate the relatively independent behaviour of the M1 and M2 components. Such behaviour was a feature of all individuals in the study, both patient and control (see Cody et al.[10]).

The relationship between rigidity and the M2 response in a further individual, J. A., is illustrated graphically in Fig. 5. A sharp decline in rigidity occurred after the levodopa but no parallel change occurred in the M2 reflex response. The relationships demonstrated in Fig. 5 were typical of the group as a whole.

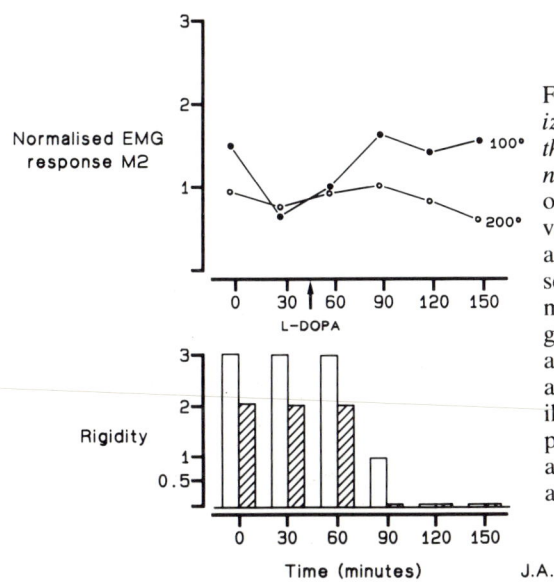

Fig. 5. *The relationship between the normalized M2 reflex and the rigidity grading throughout the experiment in J. A., a parkinsonian subject. The upper panel shows a graph of the M2 reflex size with time, at the two velocities of stretch. The levodopa was given at the time indicated by the arrow between the second and third recording periods. A normalized response of 1 indicates a reflex value greater than the background EMG value by an amount equal to that same background activity (see Methods). The lower histogram illustrates the rigidity grading at each time period corresponding to the M2 values shown above. The columns indicate active (open) and passive (hatched) rigidity grades.*

Statistical analysis of correlation between rigidity and stretch reflexes supported the above impressions. Using the Spearman rank coefficient, no correlation was found between rigidity and the M2 or the total reflex response in 16 out of the 20 patients. In none of the remaining patients did a correlation exist at both velocities of stretch. One subject in whom correlation was found was only studied at the faster velocity of stretch. The variation between M2 values in rigid and non-rigid states for each individual can be seen in Fig. 6. No significant consistent changes in the M2 reflex size in these two extremes of muscle tone was seen. Overall there appeared to be a tendency for a slight decrease in the M2 size in the less rigid state, which occurred after medication towards the end of the experiment. Similar variation in both directions, unrelated to rigidity status, was found between the total reflex values and the two rigidity states. Analysis of control values, averaging the first two and last two results, showed similar but less pronounced variations for the stretch reflex variables.

Discussion

The major new finding of the investigation was that in individual parkinsonian patients no systematic correlation existed between changes in the amplitude of their long-latency (M2) stretch reflexes and alterations in their clinically-assessed rigidity following levodopa medication. Thus the rigidity shown by these patients cannot be uniquely ascribed to an abnormality of M2 stretch reflex activity. Nevertheless, there was clear evidence that M2 responses are, on average, enhanced in patients with Parkinson's disease in comparison with healthy subjects, as a result of accentuation of normal long-latency reflex behaviour.

Enhancement of M2 responses in Parkinson's disease

In common with some,[5-10] but not all[13] recent workers who have studied a variety of muscles of both upper and lower limbs, we found that the later, M2, components of the stretch reflex of flexor carpi radialis were enhanced in Parkinson's disease, whilst amplitudes of the early, M1, responses fell within the normal range. Considerable

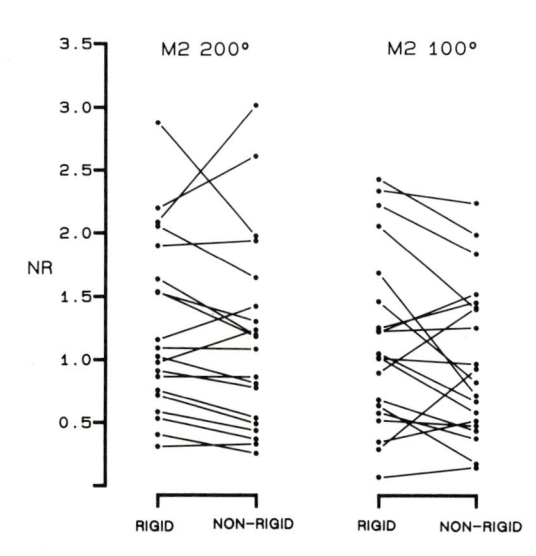

Fig. 6. The normalized M2 reflex size is shown for each indidivual in the patient group when the rigidity is most and least severe, at both velocities of stretch. The two points joined by a line represent an individual's M2 reflex size under the two extremes of rigidity detected in the experimental period. If for a given individual more than one M2 response was recorded at either rigidity extreme, an average for the M2 value was calculated.

overlap existed, however, between the M2 amplitudes (normalized for background EMG levels) of the parkinsonian and control individuals, as has previously been noted in recent studies on the flexor carpi radialis[10] and other muscles.[8,9] These findings allow two main inferences to be drawn. Firstly, enhancement of M2 responses cannot readily be attributed to exaggeration of short-latency reflex action; the M2 response must rather be mediated by essentially separate mechanisms. Secondly, the augmented M2 responses of many patients arise from an amplification of normally operating reflex processes rather than the opening up of novel circuitry.

Further evidence of increased potency of M2 reflex pathways in Parkinson's disease was provided by the observation that M2 responses, albeit of modest size, could often be evoked in the relaxed muscle of those patients showing particularly pronounced long-latency responses during voluntary contraction; the presence of such overt responses was rare in control subjects in the relaxed state. There was, however, no indication even amongst those patients whose long-latency responses were the most prominent, that M2 reflex excitatory mechanisms were saturated in the manner proposed by Rothwell et al.[8] Instead, our finding that the M2 responses of patients were, on average, prolonged compared to the normal, suggests that an active inhibitory mechanism, which usually contributes to termination of the excitatory reflex response, may be reduced in Parkinson's disease.[10]

The present data do not shed any new light upon the contentious issues of the afferent origin and central neural pathways mediating M2 reflexes (for discussion see Cody et al.[10]). It may be noted, however, that there existed a weak trend for the M2 responses of patients to decline following levodopa therapy. Thus dopaminergic systems seem likely to be implicated either directly, as part of the basic reflex circuitry, or more probably indirectly by regulating the excitability of these neural elements.

Relation between stretch reflex activity and rigidity

A range of related observations forcefully argue against there being any straightforward relationship between parkinsonian rigidity and the phasic stretch reflex responses presently studied. The stretch reflex pattern of individual patients, including its M1 and M2 components, usually remained remarkably stable throughout a lengthy recording session, despite the substantial changes in rigidity which regularly occurred after medication. Consequently, any consistent correlation between the degree of rigidity and the overall reflex pattern (or its constituent M1 and M2 components) was absent. Additionally, equivalent grades of rigidity were often accompanied in different patients by widely varying reflex patterns, whilst those with comparable reflex responsiveness could show marked disparities in tone. Equally, amongst the sample of healthy subjects having normal muscle tone, considerable quantitative differences in stretch reflex behaviour was evident.

Our conclusions that rigidity does not arise solely from exaggeration of M2 reflexes (or overall reflex, ie, summed M1 and M2 activity) contrast with those of some early investigators.[5,6] These early reports were, however, based upon rather small and highly selected groups of patients. It seems, therefore, that the present findings, derived from the investigation of individual patients with Parkinson's disease, provide independent support for several recent studies in which the matter was re-examined using pooled data from large samples of patients.[8-10]

Whilst the present results strongly suggest that excitatory reflex mechanisms directly analogous to those mediating M1 and M2 responses are not responsible for rigidity, they cannot be taken as definitive proof against stretch reflex activity playing a part. The major alternative possibility is that rigidity arises principally from non-neurogenic factors, such as altered mechanics of the muscles, joints or tendons (Dietz et al.[15]). This seems highly improbable, considering both the rapidity of clinical change in rigidity after medication and the lack of any hypothetical mechanism whereby levodopa could have such an effect on the muscle and connective tissues. It should also be noted that passive sinusoidal manipulation of the wrist of rigid patients, identical to that applied in clinical examination, generated bursts of EMG activity in wrist flexors and extensors appropriately timed for the generation of rigidity. The response to standard clinical testing may, for example, depend critically upon the precise intensity, temporal profile and receptor origin of sensory discharge, or upon the pre-existing level of excitability of reflex circuitry. If so, these elements may not have been adequately duplicated by the present experimental techniques employed to elicit M1 and M2 reflexes. Further investigations are needed to study these possibilities, which are designed to reproduce clinical procedures more exactly in regard to the type of mechanical stimulation and the patient's background contraction and 'volitional set'.

Acknowledgements—We wish to thank Drs R. G. Lascelles and D. Neary for allowing us to study patients under their care. This work was supported by grants from the North West Regional Health Authority and the Parkinson's Disease Society.

References

1 Denny-Brown, D. (1968): Clinical symptomatology of diseases of the basal ganglia. In *Handbook of neurology*, vol 6, ed P. J. Vinken & G. W. Bruyn, pp 133–172. Amsterdam: North Holland Publishing Company.
2 Rushworth, G. (1960): Spasticity and rigidity: an experimental study and review. *J. Neurol. Neurosurg. Psychiatry* **23**, 99–118.
3 Hammond, P. H. (1956): The influence of prior instruction to the subject on an apparently involuntary neuro-muscular response. *J. Physiol. (Lond)* **132**, 17–18P.
4 Marsden, C. D., Merton, P. A. & Morton, H. B. (1972): Servo action in human voluntary movement. *Nature* **238**, 140–143.
5 Lee, R. G. & Tatton, W. G. (1975): Motor responses to sudden limb displacements in primates with specific CNS lesions and in human patients with motor system disorders. *Can. J. Neurol. Sci.* **2**, 285–293.
6 Mortimer, J. A. & Webster, D. D. (1979): Evidence for a quantitative association between EMG stretch responses and Parkinsonian rigidity. *Brain Res.* **162**, 169–173.
7 Chan, C. W. Y., Kearney, R. E. & Melville Jones, G. (1979): Tibialis anterior response to sudden ankle displacements in normal and parkinsonian subjects. *Brain Res.* **173**, 303–314.
8 Rothwell, J. C., Obeso, J. A., Traub, M. M. & Marsden, C. D. (1983): The behaviour of the long-latency stretch reflex in patients with Parkinson's disease. *J. Neurol. Neurosurg. Psychiatry* **46**, 35–44.
9 Beradelli, A., Sabra, A. F. & Hallett, M. (1983): Physiological mechanisms of rigidity in Parkinson's disease. *J. Neurol. Neurosurg. Psychiatry* **46**, 45–53.
10 Cody, F. W. J., MacDermott, N., Matthews, P. B. C. & Richardson, H. C. (1986): Observations on the genesis of the stretch reflex in Parkinson's disease. *Brain* **109**, 229–249.
11 Evarts, E. V., Teravainen, H. T., Beuchart, D. E. & Calne, D. B. (1979): The pathophysiology of motor performance in Parkinson's disease. In *Dopaminergic ergot derivatives and motor functions*, ed D. B. Calne & K. Fuxe, pp 45–59. London: Pergamon.
12 Dufresne, J. R., Soechting, J. F. & Tolosa, E. S. (1981): Myotactic reflexes and the on-off effect in patients with Parkinson's disease. *J. Neurol. Neurosurg. Psychiatry* **44**, 315–322.
13 Noth, J., Schurmann, M., Podoll, K. & Schwarz, M. (1988): Reconsideration of the concept of enhanced static fusimotor drive in rigidity in patients with Parkinson's disease. *Neurosci. Lett.* **84**, 239–243.
14 Lakke, J. P. W. F. (1981): Classification of the extrapyramidal disorders. *J. Neurol. Sci.* **51**, 311–327.
15 Dietz, V., Quintern, J. & Berger, W. (1981): Electrophysiological studies of gait in spasticity and rigidity. Evidence that altered mechanical properties of muscle contribute to hypertonia. *Brain* **104**, 431–449.

30

CORTICAL LEWY BODY DISEASE:

A PATHOLOGICAL SUBSTRATE FOR DEMENTIA IN

PARKINSON'S DISEASE

Graham Lennox[*,†], James Lowe[†], Jane Byrne[§], Gavin Reynolds[†]
and Richard Godwin-Austen[*]

*Departments of [*]Neurology, [†]Pathology and [§]Health Care of the Elderly,
Queen's Medical Centre, Nottingham NG7 2UH, UK*

Summary

The powerful new neuropathological technique of anti-ubiquitin immunocytochemistry has enabled the first systematic survey of the clinical and pathological features of diffuse or cortical Lewy body disease. Fifteen cases were identified amongst the 216 brains referred to this institution for neuropathological assessment during a single year, suggesting that diffuse Lewy body disease is not rare.

The majority of cases presented with a levodopa-responsive parkinsonian syndrome indistinguishable from idiopathic Parkinson's disease; in time almost all cases developed both a parkinsonian syndrome and progressive dementia.

Quantitative neuropathological studies have shown that the severity of dementia is proportional to cortical Lewy body density, suggesting that the cortical Lewy body is a marker for the pathological process causing the dementia in these cases.

Diffuse Lewy body disease should be considered as a potential pathological substrate for the common and clinically important problem of dementia in Parkinson's disease.

Introduction

Dementia complicates Parkinson's disease in approximately 20 per cent of cases, representing an excess prevalence of some 10–15 per cent over that encountered in the general population of the same age.[1] The pathological basis of the complication remains uncertain; the most widely cited explanation, that the dementia is due to coexistent Alzheimer's disease, has recently been questioned by a series of pathological studies showing that most demented Parkinsonians have no post-mortem evidence of Alzheimer's disease.

Diffuse Lewy body disease offers an alternative explanation. The Lewy body is an eosinophilic inclusion body which is characteristically found within brain stem neurons in Parkinson's disease. In diffuse Lewy body disease the brain stem pathology is identical, but in addition similar Lewy bodies are found throughout the cerebral cortex. With conventional staining techniques the cortical Lewy bodies are, however, camouflaged by their surroundings and are less clearly circumscribed, making the diagnosis and quantification of diffuse Lewy body disease a difficult and time-consuming task.

These practical difficulties may account for the two main problems with the hypothesis that diffuse Lewy body disease is a significant cause of dementia in Parkinson's disease: first, that diffuse Lewy body disease is apparently rare, with only 50 cases reported in the world literature prior to 1988; and second, that most of these case reports describe a syndrome presenting with dementia, and with parkinsonism occurring later or not at all. However, there has been no previous systematic survey of diffuse Lewy body disease to allow a more balanced view of its prevalence and clinical features. In an effort to provide this perspective, we describe the findings of the first such survey.

Anti-ubiquitin immunocytochemistry

This survey has been facilitated by the development of the new technique of anti-ubiquitin immunocytochemistry. Ubiquitin is a small protein which is found throughout the natural world in a highly conserved form.[4] It is produced within cells in response to a wide variety of stresses, including heat shock, nutritional deprivation, toxin exposure and viral infection. Its primary function is thought to be in conjugating with abnormal proteins, thus targeting them for degradation by the powerful extralysosomal proteolytic system. We have recently shown immunocytochemically that ubiquitin is a component of both brainstem and cortical Lewy bodies.[5] This observation has important theoretical implications for the understanding of the molecular pathogenesis of the Lewy body which are beyond the scope of this paper, but from a purely practical point of view ubiquitin immunocytochemistry allows sensitive and reliable detection and quantification of cortical Lewy bodies.

Methods

All 216 brains referred from within the Nottingham Health District (population 616 000) during the year April 1985–March 1986 were examined. Diffuse Lewy body disease was diagnosed where conventional haematoxylin and eosin stains revealed classical brainstem Lewy bodies in association with cortical Lewy bodies in both limbic and neocortical regions.

All the cases identified had been under the care of the Department of Health Care of the Elderly and most had therefore undergone a prospective clinical evaluation as part of a continuing study of dementia in old age; assessment of clinical features was based on this evaluation, supplemented where necessary by a retrospective examination of the hospital case notes. A retrospective assessment of the severity of dementia was made on a five point scale (normal-mild-moderate-severe-very severe) based on the descriptions of Strub & Black.[6]

Quantitative assessment of cortical Lewy body density was carried out using ubiquitin immunocytochemistry (as previously described[15]) in standardized areas of temporal, parietal, frontal, insular, anterior cingulate and parahippocampal cortex. Large areas of cortical ribbon were marked in ink on slide coverslips, counted using an eyepiece graticule, and then measured by projection and computerized planimetry. Neurofibrillary tangle and neuritic plaque density were measured using thioflavine-S and modified Plamgren's stains in the same fashion in the above areas and the hippocampus.

Clinical and neuropathological assessments were made blind with respect to each other.

Results and discussion

Fifteen cases of diffuse Lewy body disease were identified from this unselected series of 216 brains, suggesting that the disease is not rare. All 15 came from within a subgroup of 57 cases of dementia, parkinsonism or both. There was no geographical or occupational clustering to suggest a local environmental cause.

Although six cases (40 per cent) presented with dementia as has previously been described, the remaining cases presented with symptoms and signs which were indistinguishable from those of idiopathic Parkinson's disease, either alone (six cases; 40 per cent) or in association with cognitive impairment (three cases; 20 per cent). As the disease progressed, the majority of cases developed both a parkinsonian syndrome and progressive dementia. The parkinsonian syndrome encompassed all of the major and minor features of Parkinson's disease. Thirteen cases showed three or more of the cardinal features of Parkinson's disease (ie, tremor, rigidity, bradykinesia, gait disturbance and flexed postural deformity); 12 of these cases received levodopa, which in all 12 produced definite improvement in motor but not cognitive disability. Intellectual impairment was mild in one case but moderate to very severe in the remaining 14. These cases showed 'cortical' features, such as dysphasia, dyspraxia and agnosia. In 12 cases the degree of cognitive impairment fluctuated markedly from day to day (leading to an erroneous clinical diagnosis of multi-infarct dementia in some cases).

Quantitative studies showed that the severity of dementia was strongly correlated with the cortical Lewy body density in each individual cortical region and with the mean cortical Lewy body density for all six regions, suggesting that the cortical Lewy body is at least a reliable marker for the pathological process causing the cognitive impairment in these cases, if not the actual cause itself. No such correlation was found between dementia severity and neurofibrillary tangle density, and indeed many of the most severely affected cases had no neurofibrillary tangles, suggesting that Alzheimer's disease cannot account for the dementia in these cases.

In conclusion, diffuse Lewy body disease is not rare; its presentation ranges from dementia with a subsequent parkinsonian syndrome to a parkinsonian syndrome with subsequent dementia. The latter mode of presentation is much commoner than has been appreciated hitherto and is indistinguishable in its clinical features (including levodopa response) from idiopathic Parkinson's disease. Diffuse Lewy body disease should therefore be considered as a potential pathological substrate of the common clinical problem of dementia in Parkinson's disease. It remains to be determined whether a deeper understanding of the molecular mechanism of Lewy body formation as revealed by studies of the ubiquitin system will afford any new diagnostic or therapeutic approaches to this increasingly important problem.

Acknowledgements—These studies were supported by the Parkinson's Disease Society (UK) and the Stanhope Trust. The authors thank Prof. R. J. Mayer and Dr. M. Landon for providing anti-ubiquitin antibody, and Mr. D. McGuire and Mr. K. Morrell for technical assistance.

References

1 Brown, R. G. & Marsden, C. D. (1984): How common is dementia in Parkinson's disease? *Lancet*

ii, 1262–1265.
2 Ball, M. J. (1984): The morphological basis of dementia in Parkinson's disease. *Can. J. Neurol. Sci.* **11**, 180–184.
3 Yoshimura, M. (1983): Cortical changes in parkinsonian brain: a contribution to the delineation of "diffuse Lewy body disease". *J. Neurol.* **229**, 17–32.
4 Finley, D. & Varshavsky, A. (1985): The ubiquitin system: functions and mechanisms. *Trends Biochem.* **10**, 343–347.
5 Lowe, J. S., Blanchard, A., Morrell, K. *et al.* (1988): Ubiquitin is a common factor in intermediate filament inclusion bodies of diverse type in man. *J. Pathol.* **155**, 9–15.
6 Strub, R. I. & Black, F. W. (1981): *Organic brain syndromes*, pp 119–164. Philadelphia: F. A. Davis.

31

IRON LEVELS AND TRANSFERRIN BINDING SITES IN THE POST-MORTEM BRAINS OF PARKINSONIAN PATIENTS AND AGE-MATCHED CONTROLS

P. D. Griffiths, M. A. Sambrook and A. R. Crossman

Experimental Neurology Group, Department of Cell and Structural Biology, University of Manchester, Oxford Road, Manchester, UK

Summary

In this paper we describe alterations of iron content in various regions of the basal ganglia in Parkinson's disease when compared to age-matched controls. In addition we describe a method for localizing transferrin receptors in the human central nervous system. The results are discussed in relation to a current theory of basal ganglia function.

Introduction

Abnormalities of the storage of iron in the brains of parkinsonian subjects have been reported from many sources and using many techniques.[1-3] It is of interest to pursue this topic for three reasons. (1) New imaging methods, particularly nuclear magnetic resonance (NMR), have been able to give an indication of the iron concentration in brain areas *in vivo*. It would appear that many neuropathological conditions causing movement disorders are associated with changes in iron levels in various extrapyramidal nuclei[2] including Parkinson's disease.[2,4] (2) Some authorities have suggested that both 'normal' ageing and some specific neuronal losses may be due to free radical damage. Iron is a catalyst for the production of the highly destructive hydroxyl radical[5] and changes in iron content in areas of cell loss may reflect the action of free radicals. (3) Iron is known to be involved in the monoamine synthetic and degradative pathways[6] and so may influence the level of dopamine. There is also evidence that iron may influence the post-receptor function of dopamine activity[6] and may modulate GABAergic transmitter function.[7]

This study aims to quantify accurately the iron levels in cortical and sub-cortical regions, using absorption atom spectrophotometry. In addition we investigate a possible route by which iron may enter the CNS, by autoradiographically demonstrating the existence of binding sites for the iron-carrying protein, transferrin, in the human brain.

Methods

Dissected post-mortem tissue from eight brain regions in six cases of Parkinson's disease and six age-matched controls was obtained from the Cambridge brain bank. A 50 mg aliquot of each sample was homogenized in 0.5 ml of de-ionized water using a glass tube and pestle which had been soaked in 5 M HNO_3 overnight to remove any traces of iron from the glass. Duplicate 100 µl samples were added to 200 µl of 5 M HNO_3 and allowed to reflux in a boiling water bath for 4 h until the solution was clear, when the volume was made up to 2 ml by the addition of further de-ionised water. A model 357 aa/ae spectrophotometer (Instrumentation Laboratory) was used, with the following settings: flame, oxygen/acetylene; hollow cathode current, 8 mA; bandpass, 0.3 mm; monochrome wavelength, 248.3 nm. The machine was calibrated with standard solutions of 2.5 and 5.0 µg/ml. Readings were taken after the third 3 sec integration.

Transferrin autoradiography

Sections of 20 µm were taken from snap-frozen brains on a Bright cryostat at $-20°C$. These sections were thaw mounted onto subbed glass slides and stored until use (within three days) at $-70°C$.

Transferrin autoradiography was carried out using the technique described by Hill et al.[8] Briefly, the dried sections were pre-incubated for 10 min in Tris HCl (pH 7.4) before a 4 h incubation at room temperature in 1 nM ^{125}I-transferrin. The 50 mM Tris HCl pH 7.4 buffer also contained 0.1 per cent bovine serum albumin, 30 µg/ml phenylmethyl-sulphonyl fluoride, 40 µM iron (III) ammonium sulphate and 0.1 per cent aprotinin. A parallel incubation included 10 µM cold transferrin to evaluate non-specific binding. The slides were washed for 5 min in cold buffer and 10 sec in cold distilled water and, when dry, exposed to tritium-sensitive Hyperfilm (Amersham). After 10 days the films were developed in Kodak D19.

Results and discussion

Iron concentrations in control and parkinsonian tissue are presented in the table. Representative pictures of the distribution of transferrin binding sites in the control human brain are shown in the figure. Non-specific binding accounted for approximately 20 per cent of the total (pictures not shown). Preliminary evaluation has failed to show any significant changes in the parkinsonian tissue.

Athough formal quantification of the density of transferrin binding sites was not attempted, it was possible to produce a ranking of binding density in various anatomical areas:

Table. *Regional iron concentrations in µg/g tissue. Results are means (SD).*

	Frontal BA 10	Parietal BA 39	Temporal BA 21	Putamen	Caudate	LGP	MGP	SNPR
Control (n = 6)	41.8 (8.2)	30.2 (9.3)	50.1 (8.5)	119.8 (11.6)	99.6 (6.6)	207.0 (9.7)	163.8 (18.3)	139.8 (13.1)
PD (n = 6)	51.4 (9.4)	42.7 (10.0)	49.3 (17.7)	184.5 (9.9)	107.7 (13.4)	295.0** (12.5)	113.7* (10.0)	280.9** (21.6)

PD = Parkinson's disease; LGP = lateral globus pallidus; MGP = medial globus pallidus; SNPR = substantia nigra pars reticulata.
**$P < 0.01$, *$P < 0.05$ vs control (Student's t-test).

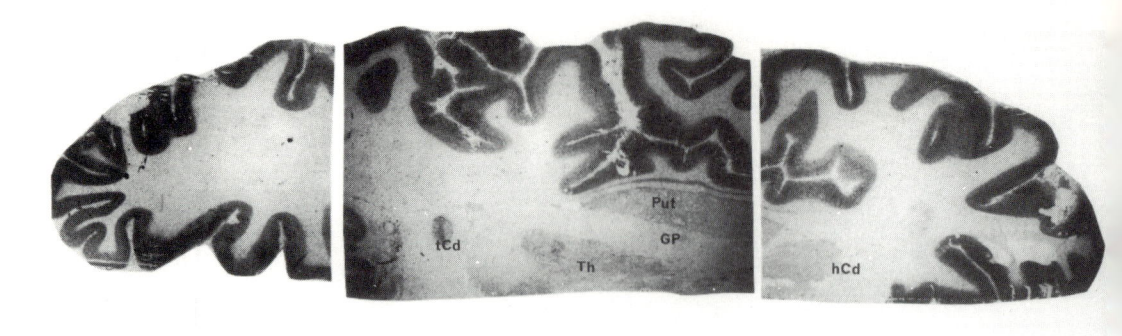

Figure. *Distribution of transferrin binding sites in horizontal section of Control human brain, as revealed by ^{121}I-transferrin autoradiography.* GP = globus pallidus; hCd head of caudate; Put = putamen; tCd = tail of caudate; Th = thalamus.

High density	*Medium density*	*Low density*
Putamen	Thalamus	Globus pallidus
Caudate	Substantia inominata	Substantia nigra
Neocortex	Cerebellar cortex	Deep cerebellar nuclei
Pontine nuclei		

These data are in agreement with Hill's rodent results,[8] and the areas with the highest amounts of iron notably tend to have the lowest transferrin binding. Furthermore, the areas that have high iron concentrations have received a prominent GABA projection from an area of high transferrin binding. This led Hill to propose that iron may be transported neuronally in GABAergic cells.

The finding of increased iron in the substantia nigra in parkinsonian brains is in keeping with many other reports[1,3,4] and has usually been considered secondary to neuronal destruction by gliosis or to a disruption of the blood-brain barrier. The changes in the globus pallidus cannot be accounted for in this way. Most studies previously undertaken have not distinguished between the two pallidal segments and have reported the iron levels to be unchanged in Parkinson's disease. This study suggests that the iron content of the two segments changes in diametrically opposing directions, ie, increased in the lateral portion and decreased in the medial portion. One possible explanation for this is that if iron is neuronally transported the amount deposited at the distal end could be a function of the neuron's activity. Penney & Young[9] have suggested that dopamine affects the two sub-populations of striatal neurons in different ways. The postulated outcome of dopamine depletion, as in Parkinson's disease, is that the inhibitory pathway to the lateral segment is overactive while the inhibitory pathway to the medial segment is hypoactive. Changes in the GABA/benzodiazepine receptors in rats with nigro-striatal lesions,[10] MPTP-treated monkeys (Robertson *et al.*, this volume, p. 167) and parkinsonian humans (personal observations) would appear to corroborate this. In this situation, differences in the iron content of the two pallidal segments would be expected, if the iron transport in a neuronal pathway is related to neuronal activity.

Acknowledgement—These studies were supported by the North West Regional Health Authority

References

1. Hallgren, B. & Sourander, P. (1958): The effect of age on non-haemin iron in the human brain. *J. Neurochem.* **3**, 41–51.
2. Rutledge, J. N., Hilal, S. K., Silver, J. A., Defendini, R. & Fahn, S. (1987): Study of movement disorders and brain iron by MR. *Am. J. Radiol.* **149**, 365–379.
3. Dexter, D. T., Wells, F. R., Agid, F., Agid, Y., Lees, A. J., Jenner, T. & Marsden, C. D. (1987): Increased nigral iron content in post mortem parkinsonian brain. *Lancet* **ii**, 1219–1220.
4. Duguid, J. R., De La Paz, R. & DeGroot, J. (1986): MRI of the midbrain in Parkinson's Disease. *Ann Neurol.* **20**, 744–747.
5. Halliwell, B. & Gutteridge, J. M. C. (1985): Oxygen radicals and the nervous system. *TINS* Jan 1985, 22–26.
6. Youdim, M. B. H., Green, A.. R., Bloomfield, M. R., Mitchell, B. D., Heal, D. J. & Grahame-Smith, D. G. (1980): The effects of iron deficiency on brain biogenic monoamine biochemistry and function in rats. *Neuropharmacology* **19**, 259–267.
7. Hill, J. M. (1984): Pallidal and nigral iron concentration reduced by gamma-vinyl GABA (abstr.). *Soc. Neurosci.* **10**, 974.
8. Hill, J. M., Ruff, M. R., Weber, R. J. & Pert, C. B. (1985): Transferrin receptors in the rat brain. *Proc. Natl. Acad. Sci. (U.S.A)* **82**, 4553–4557.
9. Penney, J. B. & Young, A. B. (1986): Striatal inhomogeneities and basal ganglia function. *Movement disorders*, **1**, 3–15.
10. Pan, H. S., Penney, J. B. & Young, A. B. (1985): GABA and benzodiazepine receptor changes induced unilateral 6-hydroxydopamine lesions of the medial forebrain bundle. *J. Neurochem.* **45**, 1936.

32

A 9 MONTH FOLLOW-UP STUDY OF COGNITIVE IMPAIRMENT IN IDIOPATHIC PARKINSON'S DISEASE

J. L. Hulley, R. J. Smith[†], C. A. Cruickshank, F. Harrop,
R. H. S. Mindham and A. G. Oswald

Department of Psychiatry, University of Leeds, 15 Hyde Terrace, Leeds LS2 9LT; and [†]Applied Psychobiology Research Unit, University of Bradford, 1 Claremont, Bradford, W. Yorks, UK

Summary

Fifty patients with idiopathic Parkinson's disease completed the same battery of neurological, psychiatric and neuropsychological tests 9 months after initial assessment. Repeated measures analysis of variance indicated no significant deterioration on any of these scales, which included measures of disease progression, functional disability, mood disturbance, global intellectual function and global memory. These results suggest that the evolution of cognitive decline may proceed slowly.

Introduction

When James Parkinson (1817)[1] first described the disease that later was named after him, he specifically stated that 'the senses and intellect are uninjured'. Subsequently, many reports have questioned this observation, and there have been reports of cognitive impairment in Parkinson's disease varying from minor disturbances in memory or intellectual function to dementia.[2] A more recent study by the present authors[3] further supports this high incidence of a wide spectrum of cognitive impairment in the disease.

At present, little is known about the evolution of such impairment. Consequently, the present study was designed to determine whether a large group of patients with Parkinson's disease show evidence of a deterioration in cognitive function over a period of time. The present report concerns changes observed over an interval of 9 months.

Methods

Patients attending local neurology clinics and diagnosed as suffering from idiopathic Parkinson's disease were referred to the study. Patients were then seen by members of the research team and their suitability for inclusion to the study was judged according to the following eligibility criteria:

(i) At least two of the three major features of Parkinson's disease, ie, rigidity, bradykinesia and tremor;
(ii) Insidious onset and progression of symptoms;
(iii) None of the following: (a) history of strokes, transient ischaemic attacks, hypertension, syphilis, encephalitis, epilepsy, brain tumour, alcoholism, diabetes mellitus, head injury resulting in loss of consciousness; (b) evidence of physical illness associated with chronic confusional states; (c) other chronic disabling disease; (d) surgery within the last 6 months; or (e) major tranquillisers within the last 3 months.

In addition, information collected routinely included the following: family history of Parkinson's disease or dementia, past personal and family psychiatric history, drugs administered currently, within 3 months, and life-long. The study was non-interventional and therefore with the exception of the above criteria patients continued to take their usual medication.

Procedure

Neurological, psychiatric and psychological assessment was undertaken on all patients. The assessment was undertaken in subjects' homes if they preferred, and took between 90 and 120 min although patients were given appropriate time to rest. This procedure was repeated after a 9 month period on all patients.

Neurological assessment

The assessment was designed to give a measure of disease severity and to indicate the degree of functional disability and impairment of activity in everyday life. It incorporated (1) Hoehn & Yahr[4] staging for Parkinson's disease; (2) Webster's[5] Parkinson's disease rating scale; (3) Northwestern Universities Disability Scale;[6] and (4) Abnormal Involuntary Movements Scale.[7]

Psychiatric assessment

This was administered to provide information on the relationship between affective illness and neurological and cognitive factors. It incorporated (1) The Montgomery & Asberg[8] Depression Rating Scale, and (2) The Irritability, Depression, Anxiety Scale.[9]

Neuropsychological assessment

The psychometric tests chosen for inclusion in this battery are well established and popular in clinical practice. This was considered to be important, given that a long-term aim of the project was to examine the change in subjects' performance on the same tests over a number of years. In addition, psychometric tests were used in order to distinguish changes in cognition associated with normal ageing from those associated with other factors. The battery consisted of the following psychometric tests: (1) National Adult Reading Test;[10] (2) Wechsler Adult Intelligence Scale;[11] (3) Wechsler Memory Scale;[12] and (4) Graded Naming Test.[13]

Results

The results in 50 patients who had been retested after a 9 month interval were analysed (35 males, age range 41–80 years, mean 64.9 years; 15 females, age range 49–80 years, mean 62.7 years).

Repeated measures analysis of variance was used to compare performance on each of the measures in the method section. Examination of the results indicated a statistically non-significant change on all of these measures.

Discussion

These results, taken in combination with our earlier findings of a wide spectrum of cognitive impairment in these patients, suggest that the evolution of both cognitive decline and functional disability may proceed slowly and therefore not be apparent at a 9 month retest interval using global neurological and neuropsychological measures.

We are continuing to monitor the progression of the disease and the interrelationships with cognitive impairment and functional disability.

References

1. Parkinson, J. (1817): An essay on the shaking palsy. In *Medical Classics* (1938): **2**, 964–997.
2. Pirozzolo, F. J., Hansch, E. C., Mortimer, J. A., Webster, D. D. & Kuskowski, M. A. (1982): Dementia in Parkinson's disease: a neuropsychological analysis. *Brain Cogn.* **1**, 71–83.
3. Smith, R. J., Cruickshank, C. A., Oswald, A. G., Hulley, J. L. & Mindham, R. H. S. (1988): In *Proceedings Of The International Conference On The Basal Ganglia*, Leeds 1987. Eds A. Franks, R. H. S. Mindham, R. J. Smith, E. Spokes & W. Winlow. Manchester: Manchester University Press.
4. Hoehn, M. M. & Yahr, M. D. (1967): Parkinsonism: Onset, progression and mortality. *Neurology* **17**, 427–442.
5. Webster, D. (1968): Critical analysis of the disability in Parkinson's disease. *Modern Treatment* **5**, 257–282.
6. Diamond, G. J. (1983): Evaluating the evaluations: Or how to weigh the scales of Parkinsonian disability. *Neurology* **33**, 1098–99.
7. Guy, W. (1976): In *Aims in ECDU assessment manual*. Ed W. Guy, pp 534–37.
8. Montgomery, S. A. & Asberg, M. (1979): A new depression scale designed to be sensitive to change. *Br. J. Psychiatry* **134**, 382–389.
9. Snaith, R. P., Constantopoulos, A. A., Jardine, M. U. & McGuffin, P. (1978): A clinical scale for the self-assessment of irritability. *Br. J. Psychiatry* **132**, 164–171.
10. Nelson, H. E. (1982): *National adult reading test manual*. Windsor: NFER-Nelson.
11. Wechsler, D. (1958): *Manual for the Wechsler adult intelligence scale*. New York: Psychological Corporation.
12. Wechsler, D. (1945): A standardised memory scale for clinical use. *J. Psychol.* **19**, 87–95.
13. McKenna, P. & Warrington, E. K. (1983): *Graded naming test manual*. Windsor: NFER-Nelson.

33

THE BEREITSCHAFTSPOTENTIAL IN

PARKINSON'S DISEASE

J. P. R. Dick, J. C. Rothwell, B. L. Day, R. Cantello,
O. Buruma, M. Gioux, R. Benecke, A. Berardelli,
P. D. Thompson and C. D. Marsden

University Department of Neurology and Parkinson's Disease Society Research Centre, Institute of Psychiatry and King's College Hospital Medical School, DeCrespigny Park, London SE5 8AF, UK

Summary

Anatomical studies show that pallidal output mainly influences the supplementary motor area (SMA). It has been assumed that the Bereitschaftspotential (BP) reflects activity in the SMA, and initial studies showed an abnormality of the BP in Parkinson's disease. However, difficulties in collecting the data caused the original authors to revise their conclusions. We have shown a drug-induced increase in the early BP and therefore have restudied the whole issue in patients off drug therapy. We found a decrease in the early BP and a compensatory increase in the late BP in Parkinson's disease. We suggest that the decreased early BP reflects impaired activation of a medial thalamo-cortical system of motor control, termed predictive by Goldberg (1985), and that the augmented late negativity, probably most marked dorsolaterally, reflects compensatory overactivity of a lateral 'responsive' system.

Introduction

Primate studies show that a major portion of pallidal output is directed at the non-primary motor areas of frontal cortex, in particular the supplementary motor area (SMA).[1,2] Kornhuber & Deecke[3] suggest that the activity of the SMA may be studied by averaging overlying surface EEG activity during the organization of a self-paced, voluntary movement. They termed this the Bereitschaftspotential (BP).[4] If the main functional target area for pallidal output is the SMA one would anticipate an abnormality of the BP in Parkinson's disease, and initial studies suggested that it was abnormally small.[5,6] However, methodological difficulties caused the original authors to suggest that this apparently smaller BP could have arisen as a result of problems triggering the averager.[7,8] In addition, since the amplitude of the BP is critically dependent on age,[9] the use of young controls may have skewed earlier results. Consequent on improved triggering and the use of older normal subjects for comparison, these original authors found no difference between the BP of normal old subjects and patients with Parkinson's disease.[10] However, since some of their patients were still on drugs when studied, and since the oral administration of levodopa alters the amplitude of the early BP,[11] there may have been a drug-induced increase of the early BP amongst the parkinsonian subjects. We therefore restudied this issue in patients *off* drug therapy.

Methods

Fourteen patients with levodopa-responsive parkinsonism aged 59.0 ± 10 (mean $\pm$ SD) and 12 control subjects aged 58.7 ± 12 years were studied. All patients had long-standing disease (disease duration 11.0 ± 6 years), were regular attenders at a specialist Parkinson's disease clinic and were cognitively intact. They were studied at least 12 h after their last dose of anti-parkinsonian medication at a time when they were profoundly akinetic. EEG potentials preceding self-paced flicks of the index finger were averaged on-line by a Digitimer D200 computer from six scalp electrode positions (C3, C4, Cz, 4 cm anterior to Cz, called here FCz; 3 cm anterior to C3, here called C3A; and 3 cm posterior to C3, here called C3P). Scalp muscle activity and blink artefacts were excluded by a facility which automatically rejected any potential greater than ± 0.1 mV. The retrospective collection of digitized EEG data was triggered by the upstroke of the surface-recorded EMG from extensor indicis and was normalized at each of the six electrode positions by drawing a horizontal regression line (calculated by computer) through the first 32 digital points. This horizontal line served as zero, and point amplitudes were measured, using a $10 \mu V$ calibration signal, at peak BP negativity (N1) and 650 ms before EMG onset. The late lateralized component of the BP (NS',[12] here referred to as the NS2) was calculated by subtracting the NS1 from the peak BP negativity (N1). The BPs were compared by an ANOVA with a grouping factor of patients/normals and a within-subject factor of electrode position. The significance of the F value was further restricted by the conservative correction of Greenhouse & Geisser.[13] BP amplitudes from specific electrode positions were compared between groups using Student's t-test.

Results

The averaged BP traces from the normal subjects are superimposed with those from the patients with Parkinson's disease in the Figure. The amplitude of N1 was not significantly different between patients and controls for any electrode position ($F = 0.03$, df 1.24, $P > 0.05$). There was a significant effect of 'electrode position' ($F = 28.53$, df 4.96, $P < 0.01$) but no interaction between the grouping and the within-subject factors ($F = 1.49$, df 4.96, $P > 0.05$). The amplitude of the early component of the BP (NS1) was smaller than normal in patients with Parkinson's disease ($F = 14.4$, df 1.24, $P < 0.01$). Here, by contrast, there was both a significant effect of 'electrode position' ($F = 24.26$, df 5.120, $P < 0.01$) and a significant interaction of 'group' and 'electrode position' ($F = 8.9$, df 5.120, $P < 0.25$). This means that, although the NS1 was larger in the control subjects for all leads, the distribution of that size change was different. It was more marked over the midline (FCz: $P < 0.02$), Cz: $P < 0.05$) and over the ipsilateral hemisphere (C4: $P < 0.01$); however, it did

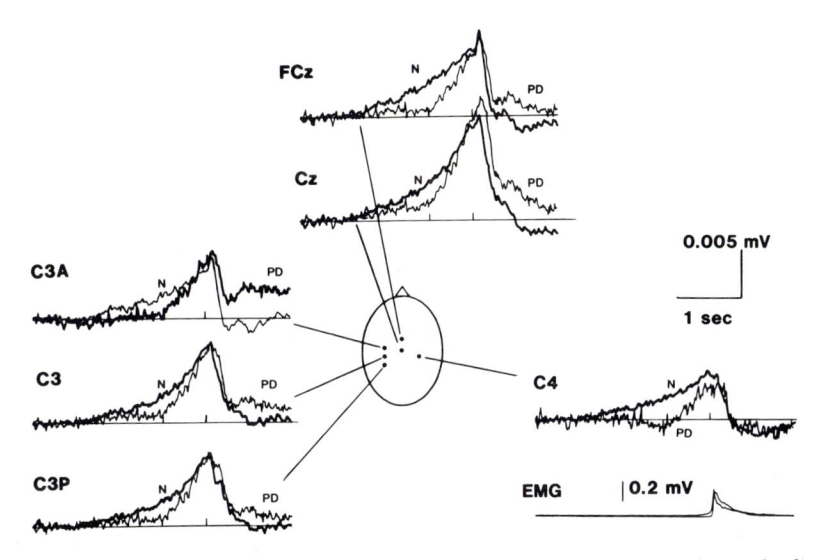

Figure. *Grand average Bereitschaftspotentials (BP) from patients with Parkinson's disease (PD) superimposed on those from age-matched normal subjects (N).* Averaged extensor indicis EMG is shown in the bottom right. Markers are shown at time zero (EMG onset) and at 650 ms before EMG onset. Each subject performed 128 finger movements and the bandpass filters were set 3 dB down at 0.03 and 300 Hz. At all electrode positions the early BP is smaller in patients than in normals but the peak BP is approximately equal.

not reach statistical significance at any individual lead over the contralateral motor cortex (C3A, C3, C3P: $P > 0.05$). The decreased amplitude of the early BP (NS1) was offset by a larger than normal NS2 (F = 9.9, df 1.24, $P < 0.01$) for which there was an effect of 'electrode position' (F = 23.34, df 4.96, $P < 0.01$) but the interaction term failed to reach statistical significance[13] (F = 2.48, df 4.96, $P > 0.05$). There is a suggestion that the NS2 may have been larger in patients with Parkinson's disease over the midline and the contralateral hemisphere anteriorly (Figure).

Discussion

These results show that there is a difference in the BP between age-matched control subjects and patients with Parkinson's disease. This difference comprises a decreased NS1 and an increased NS2. Previous authors have measured only the peak BP and this is unchanged in Parkinson's disease. The one study which has measured the early BP[10] may not have eliminated the effect of drugs.

The origin of the early and late phases of the BP is unresolved. The late component of the BP is lateralized to the hemisphere contralateral to the moving limb and may represent activity in the motor cortex.[6] The early component is not lateralized and may reflect activity in the SMA as it is largest at the vertex (overlying the SMA) for several types of movement (eye, hand, arm and foot).[9,14] The decreased NS1 from midline leads may be due to impaired SMA function and this would be consistent with the hypothesis that SMA function is abnormal in Parkinson's disease. However, there is no definitive proof that the early component of the BP arises in the SMA and it is not entirely clear why there is such an obvious change in the early BP over the ipsilateral motor cortex. This may be a reflection of the unusual callosal connectivity of the motor cortical hand areas,[15] or of the intimate role played by the SMA in the control of bilateral hand movements.[16,17] How might these observations explain the breakdown of movement control in Parkinson's disease? Goldberg[18] has suggested that there are two distinct systems for the control of voluntary movements: a predictive, feedforward mode whereby the subject decides 'internally' the format of a desired movement, and second, a responsive mode whereby the subject responds to environmental cues which themselves determine how a motor response is organized. On the basis of embryological, anatomical and neurophysiological evidence, he suggests these two systems are anatomically distinct; the former involves the SMA and the relevant thalamo-cortical projections and the latter involves the dorsolateral premotor area and a different set of thalamo-cortical projections. Connectivity studies in primates suggest that the major input to SMA is ultimately derived from the pallidum[1,2] whereas the dorsolateral PMA has a significantly greater input from areas of sensory cortex, particularly the visual cortex.[15] It is tempting to suggest that patients with Parkinson's disease rely on the dorsolateral system of motor control as their medial system is defective. This would be consistent with the inordinate dependence of parkinsonian patients on visual information for adequate motor performance[19,20] and permits an interpretation of our BP findings. The impaired early BP may reflect poor cortical activation of the medial predictive system and the augmented late negativity, probably most marked dorsolaterally, reflects compensatory overactivity of the lateral 'responsive' system.

References

1 Jurgens, U. (1984): The efferent and afferent connections of the supplementary motor area. *Brain Res.* **300**, 63–87.
2 Schell, G. R. & Strick, P. L. (1984): The origin of thalamic inputs to the arcuate premotor and supplementary motor areas. *J. Neurosci.* **4**, 539–560.
3 Kornhuber, H. H. & Deecke, L. (1978): An electrical sign of participation of the mesial supplementary motor cortex in human voluntary finger movement. *Brain Res.* **159**, 473–476.
4 Kornhuber, H. H. & Deecke, L. (1965): Hirnpotentialanderungen bei Willkurbewegungen and passiven Bewegungen des Menschen: Bereitschaftspotential und reafferente Potentiale. *Pflugers Arch.* **284**, 1–17.
5 Deecke, L., Englitz, H. G., Kornhuber, H. H. & Schmidt, G. (1977): Cerebral potentials preceding voluntary movements in patients with bilateral or unilateral Parkinsonian akinesia. In *Progress in clinical neurophysiology*, Vol 1, ed J. E. Desmedt, pp 151–163. Basel: Karger.
6 Shibasaki, H., Shima, F. & Kuriowa, Y. (1978): Clinical studies of the movement-related cortical potential (MP) and the relationship between the dentatorubrothalamic pathway and readiness potential (RP). *J. Neurol.* **219**, 15–25.
7 Barrett, G., Shibasaki, H. & Neshige, R. (1985): Technical aspects of recording movement associated premovement potentials. *Electroencephalogr. Clin. Neurophysiol.* **60**, 276–281.
8 Barrett, G., Shibasaki, H. & Neshige, R. (1986a): Cortical potentials preceding voluntary movement: evidence for three periods of preparation in man. *Electroencephalogr. Clin. Neurophysiol.* **63**, 327–339.
9 Deecke, L. (1985): Cerebral potentials related to voluntary actions: parkinsonian and normal subjects. In *Clinical neurophysiology in parkinsonism*, Vol. 1, ed P. J. Delwaide & A. Agnoli, pp 91–105. Amsterdam: Elsevier Publications.
10 Barrett, G., Shibasaki, H. & Neshige, R. (1986b) Cortical potential shifts preceding voluntary movement are normal in parkinsonism. *Electroencephalogr. Clin. Neurophysiol.* **63**, 340–348.
11 Dick, J. P. R., Cantello, R., Buruma, O., Gioux, M., Benecke, R., Day, B. L., Rothwell, J. C., Thompson, P. D. & Marsden, C. D. (1987): The Bereitschaftspotential, L-DOPA and Parkinson's disease. *Electroencephalogr. Clin. Neurophysiol.* **66**, 263–274.
12 Tamas, L. B. & Shibasaki, H. (1985): Cortical potentials associated with movement: a review. *J. Clin. Neurophysiol.* **2**, 157–171.
13 Greenhouse, S. W. & Geisser, S. (1959): On methods in the analysis of profile data. *Psychometrika* **24**, 95–112.

14 Boschert, J., Hink, R. F. & Deecke, L. (1983): Finger movement versus toe movement-related potentials: Further evidence for supplementary motor area (SMA) participation prior to voluntary action. *Exp. Brain Res.* **55**, 73–80.
15 Pandya, D. N. & Vignolo, L. A. (1971): Intra and interhemispheric projections of the pre-central, premotor and arcuate areas in the rhesus monkey. *Brain Res.* **26**, 217–233.
16 Brinkman, C. (1984): Supplementary motor area of the monkey's cerebral cortex: short and long term deficits after unilateral ablation and the effects of subsequent callosal section. *J. Neurosci.* **4**, 918–929.
17 Roland, P. E., Larsen, B., Lassen, N. A. & Skinhoj, E. (1980): Supplementary motor area and other cortical areas in organisation of voluntary movements in man. *J. Neurophysiol.* **43**, 118–136.
18 Goldberg, G. (1985): Supplementary motor area: structure and function: Review and hypotheses. *Brain Behav. Sci.* **8**, 567–616.
19 Martin, J. P. (1967): *The basal ganglia and posture*. London: Pitman.
20 Flowers, K. A. (1976): Visual "closed loop" and "open loop" characteristics of voluntary movement in patients with parkinsonism and intention tremor. *Brain* **99**, 269–310.

34

VIBRATION-INDUCED ILLUSIONS OF MOVEMENT ARE NORMAL IN PARKINSON'S DISEASE: IMPLICATIONS FOR THE MECHANISM OF THE MOVEMENT DISORDER

A. P. Moore

Department of Neurology, Walton Hospital, Rice Lane, Liverpool L9 1AE, UK

Summary

Illusions of elbow movement were generated by vibration of biceps tendons. These illusions represent afferent feedback without a corollary discharge. The velocities of the illusory movements were measured and found to be the same in normal and in bradykinetic limbs. The movement disorder in parkinsonism may be caused by mismatching of afferent and efferent signals with either reduced corollary discharge or exaggeration of afferent feedback. These results provided no support for the latter and thus indirectly support the former.

Introduction

The brain compares sensory with motor signals to monitor the progress of a movement. Although bradykinesia seems to be a motor phenomenon, it may arise from mismatching at a subconscious level of corollary discharges, which are derived from motor commands, and peripheral afferent feedback signals (see Fig. 1). In an earlier experiment, blindfolded patients with asymmetrical bradykinesia slowly flexed and extended both their elbows simultaneously, in active movements, attempting to match the excursion of each movement in the more and in the less bradykinetic arms. They consistently moved the good arm further, even in paradigms where the good arm was tracking its more bradykinetic fellow. This suggested that there is difficulty either in detecting what proportion of a required movement has occurred, or in using this information to modify motor programmes.[1]

A. P. Moore

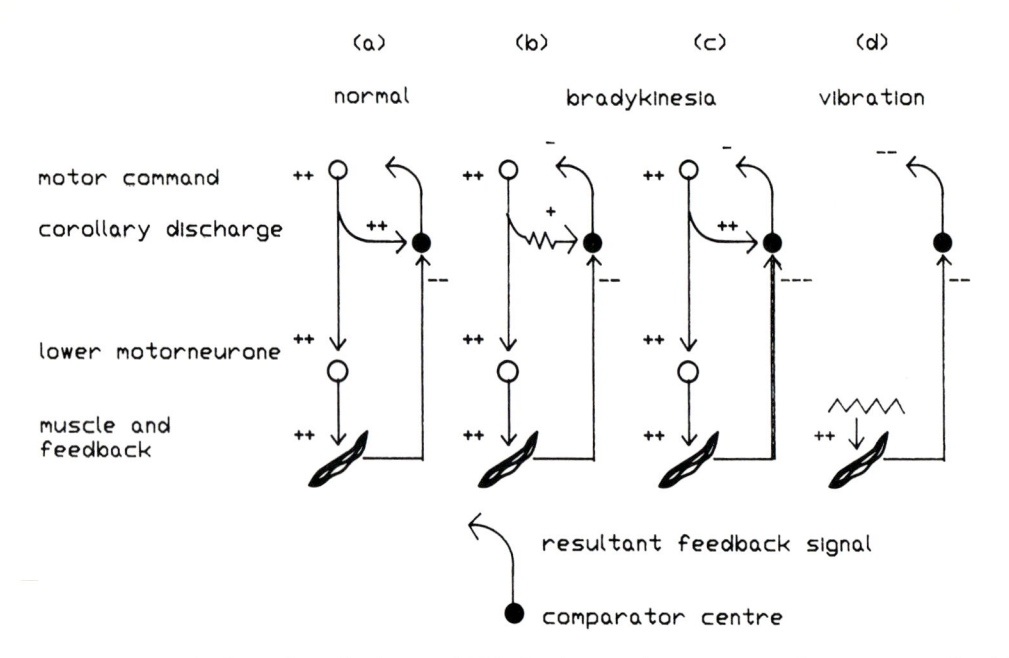

Fig. 1. *Principal of corollary discharges (CD)*. Each stage is not necessarily monosynaptic. (a) Normally the motor command passes unaltered through the system to muscle, simultaneously giving off a CD of equivalent strength. This passes to a comparator which correlates it with returning afferent signals, and the resultant, a kind of error signal, passes back to the motor command and is used to adjust the movement. (b) In bradykinesia, a 'negative' resultant feedback signal from the comparator centre may cause the brain to perceive more effect than was required and provoke reduction of the motor command. Such a signal may be caused by either reduced CD (b) or by exaggerated muscle feedback (c). (d) Muscle tendon vibration generates muscle feedback without a corollary discharge and provokes illusions of passive stretching of the muscle. This allows testing of the afferent arc in isolation.

In the corollary discharges model, these findings would arise if there was a minus signal from the comparator centre. However, the experiment did not distinguish between diminution of corollary discharges (Fig. 1b) or exaggeration of afferent feedback (Fig. 1c), both of which would result in such a minus signal. The present experiment was designed to show whether proprioceptive signals from muscles do have an exaggerated effect on perception of movement in bradykinesia.

Methods

Apparatus

This is illustrated in Fig. 2. The subject's arm rested on a splint which could rotate horizontally with flexion/extension of the elbow. The elbow was at shoulder height and held in front of the subject, with the hand pointing towards an arc of light-emitting diodes (LEDs). A ripple effect was generated electronically on the LEDs and its velocity and direction could be controlled by either the subject or the investigator. The velocities of (1) the ripple and (2) flexion/extension elbow movements could be measured.

LED's

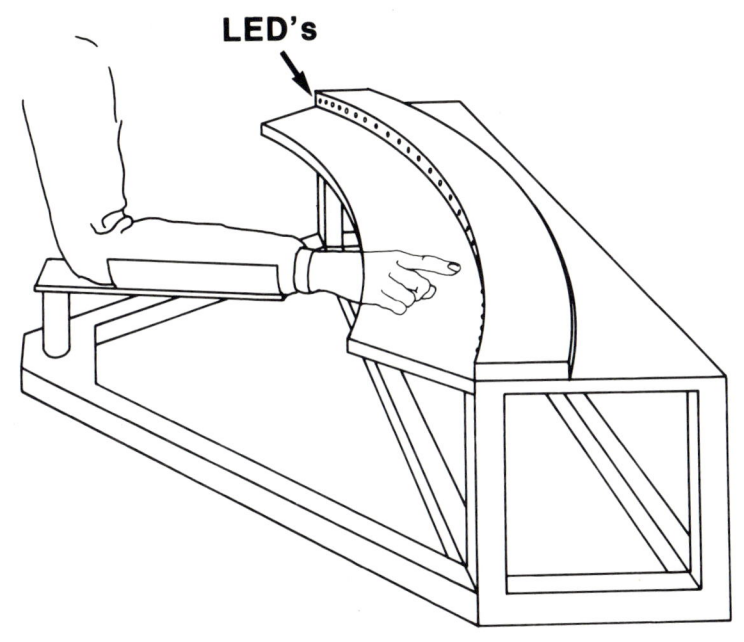

Fig. 2. *The apparatus.*

Procedure

Subjects were trained to match the velocities of the ripple and of arm extension, with a screen blocking sight of the arm. For experiments A and B (Table) recordings were made of (1) ripple and (2) arm velocity so that a regression line could be constructed (Fig. 3). Recordings were then repeated while vibration was applied to the biceps tendon. This generated an additional, illusory, velocity of elbow extension, and the shift of the resulting regression line represents the velocity of this illusion. Illusions were measured in both arms of each subject, and during both active and passive extension of the elbow.

Analysis

Because regression lines were not always parallel, the velocity of the illusion was measured as the area between the two regression lines, bounded by $x = 0$ and $x = 8°s^{-1}$, and expressed in arbitrary units (10 units≃$1°s^{-1}$).

Subjects were chosen to allow two kinds of assessment: (1) seven patients with unilateral bradykinesia, to make intra-individual measurements of illusions developing in normal

Table. *Description of the experiments.*

Experiment A	Experiment B
Perception of velocity of passive arm extension	*Active extension to match ripple velocity*
Investigator extends subject's arm	Investigator sets ripple velocity
Subject sets ripple velocity to match	Subject actively extends arm to match ripple

Vibration Induced Illusion of Movement (VIIM)

B : active arm extension to match ripple velocity

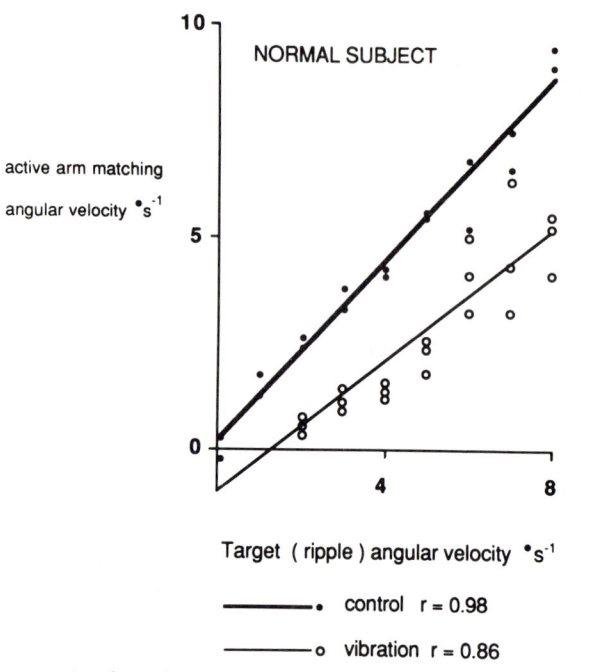

Fig. 3. *Typical regression lines from experiment B; those from experiment A were similar.* The shift between the two lines represents the velocity of the illusory movement.

and bradykinetic limbs; and (2) six normal age-matched subjects, for inter-individual comparisons.

Results and conclusions

The results are shown in Fig. 4A and B. In each panel 'a' shows the mean velocity of illusory movements developing in normal subjects, 'b' and 'c' show those in the more and the less bradykinetic limbs of parkinsonian subjects. There was no statistically significant difference between any of these, ie, no difference was found between the velocities of vibration-induced illusions of movement in normal and in parkinsonian limbs. Such illusions represent resultant feedback from a comparator centre (Fig. 1d) derived from muscle feedback without a corollary discharge. This finding thus provides no support for the notion that afferent feedback is exaggerated in bradykinesia (Fig. 1c) and indirectly supports the idea that corollary discharges may be decreased (Fig. 1b).

However, muscle vibration stimulates only muscle spindle primary endings, and it remains possible that in bradykinesia, spindle secondary endings generate signals whose influence is exaggerated and which provoke a 'minus' resultant from the comparator centre. Signals from secondary endings may be the source of long-latency reflexes, which are increased in Parkinson's disease; neither spindle secondaries nor long-latency reflexes are provoked by vibration.[2]

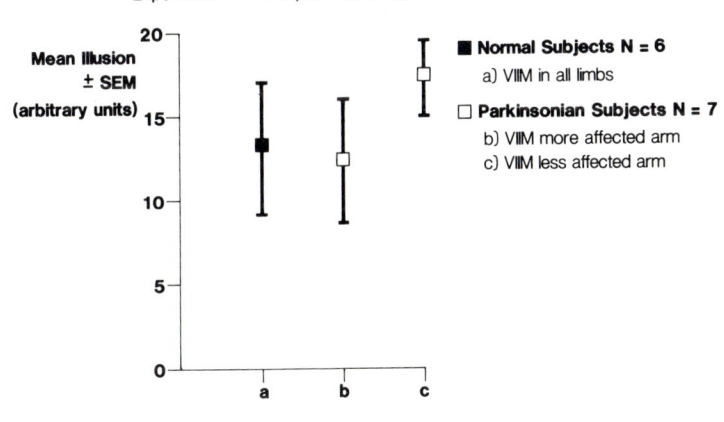

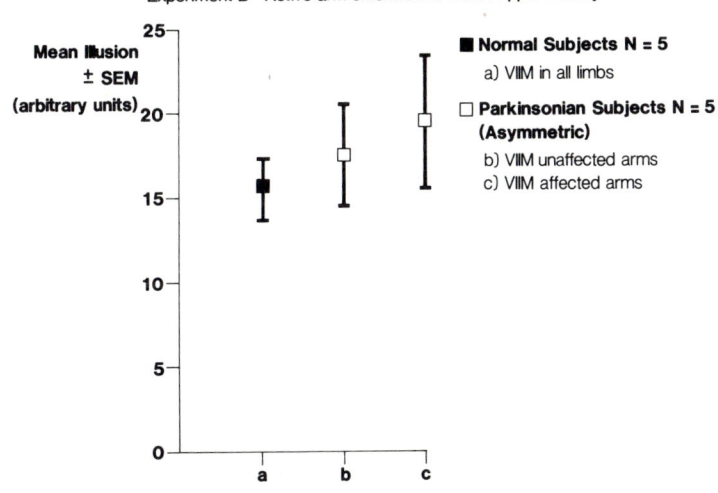

Fig. 4. *Results for experiment A (upper panel) and B (lower panel). See text for explanation.*

References

1 Moore, A. P. (1987): Impaired sensorimotor integration in parkinsonism and dyskinesia: a role for corollary discharges? *J. Neurol. Neurosurg. Psychiatry* **50**, 544–552.
2 Matthews, P. B. C. (1984): Evidence from the use of vibration that the human long-latency stretch reflex depends upon spindle secondary afferents. *J. Physiol.* **348**, 383–415.

35

THE SACCADIC DYSMETRIA IN PARKINSON'S DISEASE IS STIMULUS-DEPENDENT

T. J. Crawford, L. Henderson* and C. Kennard

*The Department of Neurology, The London Hospital, Whitechapel, London E1 1BB; and *The Department of Psychology, Hatfield Polytechnic, Hatfield, Herts, UK*

Summary

Seven parkinsonian patients were compared with seven matched controls in various saccade eliciting paradigms. Eye movements directly elicited by a novel peripheral target appeared unimpaired, whereas predictive saccades and saccades to a remembered target location were hypometric and multi-stepping.

Introduction

Despite the obvious somatomotor abnormalities in Parkinson's disease, saccadic eye movements seem to have been relatively spared. However research on non-human primates has increasingly stressed that variation in the experimental paradigm used to elicit saccades may result in the involvement of different neural centres.[1] In particular, Hikosaka & Wurtz[2,3] have found neurons in the basal ganglia which modulate their activity prior to the initiation of saccades to the locus of remembered targets but not saccades directly elicited to novel targets.

We have therefore employed a variety of paradigms to elicit saccades in parkinsonian patients in an attempt to understand further the role of the basal ganglia in the control of saccades. In addition to saccades to novel and to 'remembered' targets, we have investigated saccades to predictably alternating targets since it has been reported that parkinsonian patients fail to respond predictably in a manual task.[4]

Methods

Seven patients with idiopathic Parkinson's disease (mean age 61 years, range 52–68) were investigated. They had mild to moderate disability (Hoehn & Yahr I-III) and were taking dopamimetic therapy at the time of these studies. They were compared to seven normal subjects (mean age 63 years, range 53–72). Eye movements were recorded using the infra-red reflection technique. The stimuli used were light-emitting diodes (LEDs) controlled by a microcomputer.

The latency, peak-velocity, duration and accuracy of the primary saccade and the final eye position (FEP) were quantified from the chart records, using a digitizing tablet.

Target paradigms

The target paradigms were as follows:
(a) *Random* (RAN). On each trial a central fixation LED was presented. Simultaneous with the offset of this light, a randomly selected target LED appeared, displaced between 3.75 and 15 degrees.
(b) *Overlap* (OLP). This differed from the RAN condition only in that the fixation LED was not extinguished immediately the target LED was presented. In both RAN and OLP, subjects were required to make a saccade quickly and accurately to the peripheral target as soon as it appeared.
(c) *Remembered* (REM). The fixation light appeared. After a delay and with the fixation light still on, the randomly-selected peripheral target was briefly flashed, following which only the central fixation was again visible. The central LED was then turned off and at the same time a brief auditory tone was generated. This was the signal to make a saccade to the previously flashed target which was, of course, no longer visible.
These paradigms are illustrated in Fig. 1.

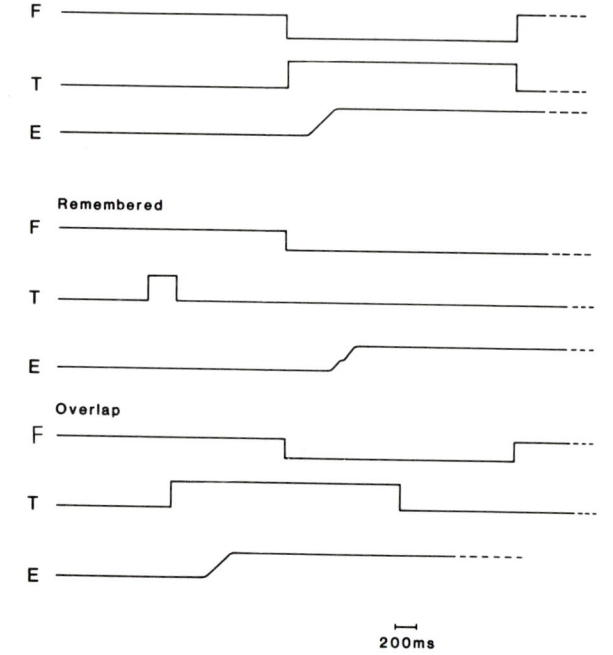

Fig. 1. *Diagram of the RAN, REM and OLP experimental paradigms, showing the fixation (F) stimulus, peripheral target (T) stimulus and an illustrative eye movement (E).*

(d) *Predictive* (PRED). The target alternated between two fixed positions (+ and −11.25 degrees) at a fixed (2 sec) interval. A brief tone accompanied target onsets. Blocks of trials with the visual target present (1 and 3) alternated with blocks (2 and 4) in which only the auditory timing cue was available. Subjects were asked to continue making saccades to the target locations, even when the targets ceased to be visible.

Results

Latency

Although there was a significant increase in latency in the REM compared with the RAN and OLP conditions this was similar for both patients and controls. In the REM task about 30 per cent of saccades were made in both groups soon after the onset of the peripheral target rather than waiting for the offset of the fixation target. These saccades were not included in the subsequent analyses.

In the PRED task (Fig. 2) there was no difference in latency between the two groups in blocks 2, 3 and 4. All the data points in the blocks reveal negative latencies indicating anticipation of target onset. In block 1 it can be seen that there was a difference between the two groups. Whereas the controls rapidly started anticipating within 5–6 trials, the Parkinson's disease patients, while displaying a mean latency which is too low to be attributable to their consistently awaiting the target step before responding, nevertheless stopped short of the unequivocally negative latencies that prevail in later blocks.

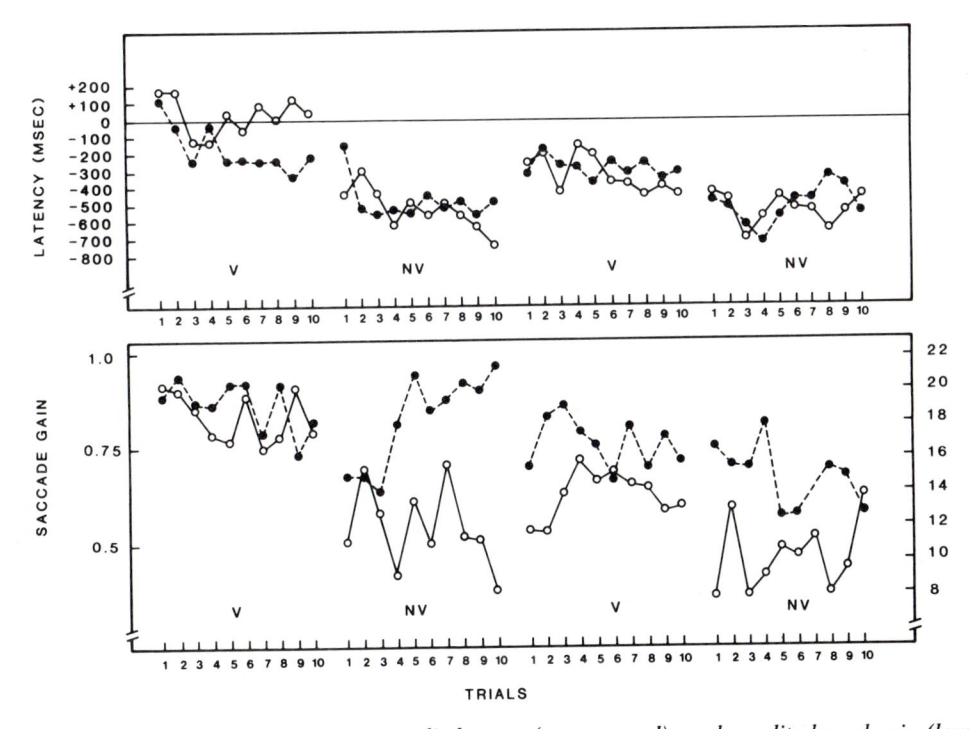

Fig. 2. Trial by trial graph of mean saccadic latency (upper panel), and amplitude and gain (lower panel) for both groups in the predictive task. ● = normals, ○ = PDs. V = visual target present, NV = visual target not present.

Velocity

No clear difference in the main sequence velocity/amplitude was observed between the two groups. Three subjects from the control group and four subjects from the Parkinson's disease group showed REM saccades which were of reduced peak velocity compared to RAN saccades, but the remaining subjects showed no difference.

Primary saccade accuracy

The accuracy was derived by measuring the distance of the primary saccade end point from the target position and expressing this as a function of the target amplitude. Thus a score of unity indicated a perfectly on-target saccade while a score of 0.5 showed that the error was half that of the original target amplitude. Examination of primary saccade accuracy showed no difference between the parkinsonian subjects and controls in the RAN task. However, in the REM task there was a highly significant deterioration in the saccadic accuracy in the Parkinson's disease group but not in the controls (Fig. 3). Since no such deterioration was evident in the OLP task, this effect cannot be due to a spatial averaging of the fixation point and target, as this simultaneous presentation obtained for both REM and OLP tasks (cf 'centre of gravity effect', see[5]).

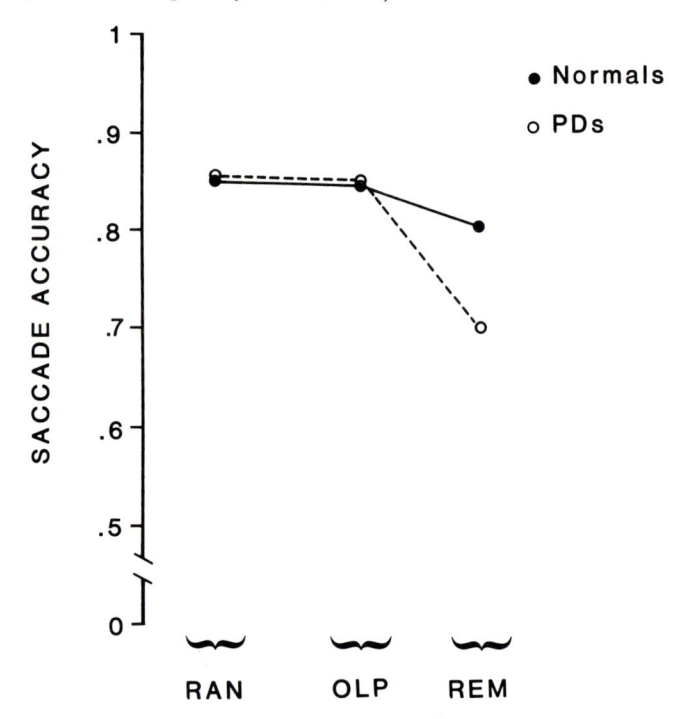

Fig. 3. Mean saccadic accuracy for both groups in the RA (random), OLP (overlap) and REM (remembered) target paradigms.

In the PRED task, when the groups showed equally anticipatory latencies (Fig. 2, Blocks 2–4), the parkinsonian group was markedly more hypometric. The groups did not differ in accuracy during the first block of trials.

Final eye position (FEP)

In neither condition which revealed a deficit in accuracy in parkinsonian subjects (REM and PRED) did the groups differ in FEP, which lay close to the target location (Fig. 4). This shows that the undershoot of the primary saccade found in the parkinsonian group cannot be attributed to an impairment of spatial memory.

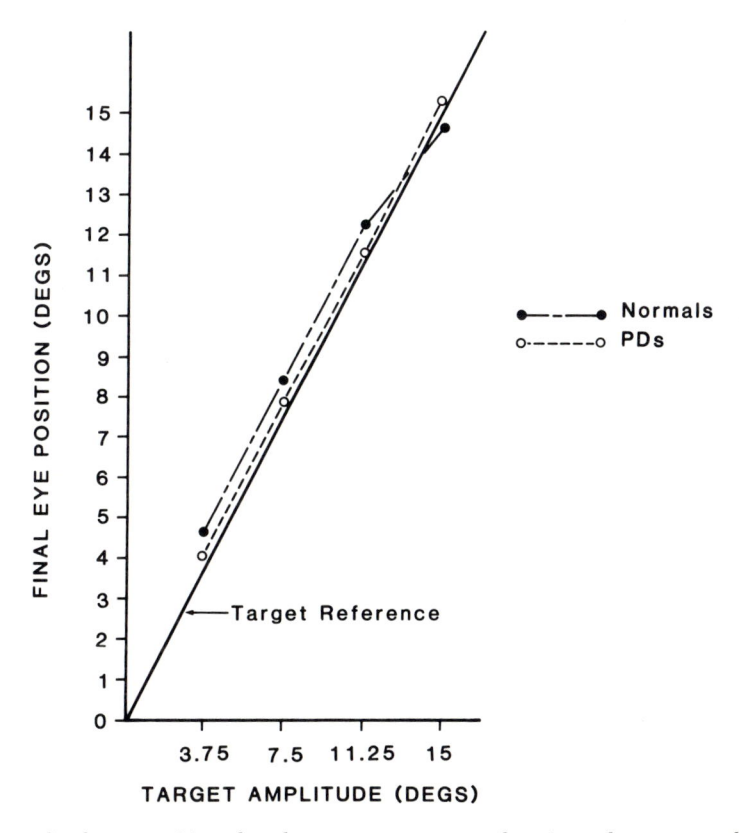

Fig. 4. Average final eye position for the two groups as a function of target amplitude in the remembered target paradigm.

Discussion

The saccade-eliciting paradigms which proved to be most revealing of parkinsonian impairment were the REM and the PRED tasks. In both of these, accuracy was the impaired parameter, with parkinsonian performance typically consisting of a hypometric primary saccade as the first component in a train of miniature saccades. Neither latency nor velocity distinguished our relatively mildly impaired patients from controls.

What the REM and PRED task seem to have in common is that the peripheral target does not serve as the signal immediately summoning the saccade. It is likely that such a stimulus is a necessary condition for the subject to utilize a neural pathway that is dedicated to involuntary or reflex saccades. Since the parkinsonian impairment was only detectable when such an eliciting stimulus was *not* available, we conclude that saccades which are not directly elicited by a novel target rely on an alternative control circuit involving basal ganglia structures.

In view of the specificity of this deficit, at least in mildly afflicted patients, parkinsonian saccades may provide us with a promising means of investigating the properties of this alternative saccadic control pathway. With regard to the suggestion that parkinsonian patients are unable to enagage in predictive as opposed to reactive responding, our data show that they can indeed be induced to move predictively, but at a cost in accuracy. This suggests that their normal reluctance to anticipate may be an adaptation to a deficit in the execution of predictive responses.

Acknowledgement—This research was supported by the Medical Research Council.

References

1 Kennard, C. (1986): Higher control mechanisms of saccadic eye movements. *Trans. Ophthalmol. Soc.* **105**, 705–708.
2 Hikosaka, O. & Wurtz, R. H. (1983): Visual and oculomotor functions of monkey substantia nigra pars reticulata. III. Memory-contingent visual and saccadic responses. *J. Neurophysiol.* **49**, 1268–1284.
3 Hikosaka, O. & Wurtz, R. H. (1985): Modification of saccadic eye movements by GABA-related substances. II. Effects of muscimol in monkey substantia nigra pars reticulata. *J. Neurophysiol.* **53**, 292–308.
4 Flowers, K. (1978): Lack of prediction in the motor behaviour of Parkinsonism. *Brain* **101**, 35–52.
5 Findlay, J. M. (1982): Global visual processing for saccadic eye movements. *Vision Res.* **22**, 1033–1045.

36

ROLE OF GAIT ANALYSIS IN THE ASSESSMENT

OF PARKINSONISM IN OLD AGE

A. L. Leeman, J. Hughes, S. G. Bowes, C. J. A. O'Neill,
C. Weller, P. Clark, A. A. Deshmukh, P. W. Nicholson,
S. M. Dobbs and R. J. Dobbs

*Divisions of Clinical Sciences, Rheumatology and
Bioengineering, Northwick Park Hospital and Clinical Research Centre,
(CRC), Watford Road, Harrow, Middlesex, HA1 3UJ, UK*

Summary

In geriatric practice the benefits accruing from anti-parkinsonian agents, although vital for the maintenance of independence, may be small, variable and documented only by subjective reports. Falls may result from irregularity of gait, striking the ground with the forefoot rather than the heel, and poor posture. There is a need to shift the emphasis from arbitrary and often unrealistic expectations of benefit from therapy to the controlled objective demonstration of response. We have adopted a method of measurement of distance/time parameters of gait suitable for use in the clinic, and have investigated two methods of determining which part of the foot makes contact with the ground first: pedobarography, and video recordings analysed using a slow playback facility. Analysis of double support time during a short walk allowed a short-term response to levodopa to be detected in a group of 14 patients with no overt fluctuations in clinical state in relation to medication. We were unable to detect any relationship between an index of the normality of foot strike and the distance/time parameters of gait. More abnormal foot strikes had been detected by the pedobarography than by our analyses of the video recordings, but the difference in the index did not reach statistical significance: video recordings produce a readily available means of analysis of foot strike, but one which may be subject to error and fatigue on the part of the observer.

Introduction

Bradykinesia and loss of balance are major features of parkinsonism in old age, whilst tremor, asymmetrical features and fluctuations in control may be less prominent. Short steps and hesitancy are easily recognizable features of the parkinsonian gait but, in old people, changes in the pattern of gait in relation to a maintenance dose of medication may not be obvious clinically. Normally the heel strikes the ground before the forefoot: in parkinsonism, the forefoot may strike the ground together with heel, or before it, or ground contact be made only by forefoot and toes. The latter two modes of contact themselves produce instability, and, particularly if associated with an irregular gait and/or abnormal posture, add to the risk of falls. Measurement of distance/time parameters of gait and of the distribution of pressure as the foot makes contact with the ground (pedobarography) might be useful in investigating response to therapy.

Gait analysis, using the gait assessment trolley designed at CRC,[1] is easy to perform and not time-consuming. A graphical record of gait is produced, from which asymmetry, irregularity and any major changes in distance/time parameters are immediately apparent. A computerized recording system allows rapid quantification of the gait parameters and facilitates data storage. Most objective methods of gait analysis are laboratory-based and impose test conditions, such as special lighting, walkways, footwear or garments which may affect performance and preclude their use in aged patients. The trolley is suitable for use in the clinic or on the ward. Patients wear ordinary clothing, and use a walking aid or personal assistance if necessary. The computerized pedobarography system used[2] affords similar freedoms, except that the pressure sensitive area is incorporated into a fixed walkway.

We have studied the response of distance/time parameters of gait and of the nature of foot strike to omission, or not, of a morning dose of levodopa during maintenance therapy in 14 patients aged over 65 years, with no overt fluctuation in clinical state in relation to medication. The relationship of nature of foot strike to distance/time measurements and other patient characteristics, was investigated. Video recording is, of course, widely available as a method of assessing foot strike: we have compared such an assessment with the pedobarographic findings.

Methods

Gait assessment trolley

A cord, clipped to the heels of the patient's shoes, passes round a shaft encoder, mounted on a lightweight trolley. Walking simultaneously transfers a length of cord from behind one foot to behind the other, rotates the encoder and tows the trolley along. The length of cord transferred represents the distance moved and the direction of rotation of the encoder indicates which foot has moved. A battery-powered infra-red transmitter sends the encoded information to a receiver, connected to a chart recorder or to the computerized recording system.

Gait on a given occasion (Fig. 1) is represented by a single plot of distance against time, upward and downward deflections being proportional to distances moved by left and right foot respectively.

Gait traces from two Parkinsonian patients are shown in Figs 2 and 3, the arrows indicate the timing of commands to begin walking. The trace in Fig. 2 appears normal, that in Fig. 3 shows a short-stepped, irregular gait with prolonged double support times and marked initial hesitancy.

Video recording

A video camera, two metres from the patient and at foot level, recorded movement of the lower half of the body as the patient walked past. This allowed a global assessment of gait to be made. A slow playback facility was used when the recordings were reassessed to determine the nature of foot strike.

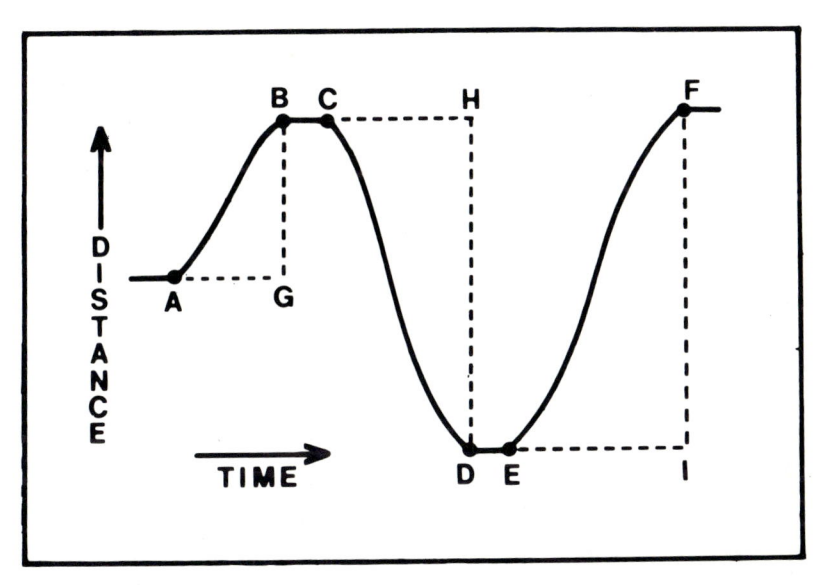

Fig. 1. *Annotated diagram representing the graphical record obtained using the gait assessment trolley. Points A, C and E correspond to left foot, right foot and left foot being lifted off the ground, and B, D and F, the foot striking the ground. A left step of length BG is followed by a right swing, HD, and then a left, IF. BC and DE are double support times.*

Pedobarography

The equipment uses a simple optical principle. A plate of glass is lit from two opposite edges. Light travels through the glass by total internal reflection. Where pressure is applied to a plastic sheet on top of the glass, the conditions necessary for total internal reflection are destroyed. Light escapes, the amount being proportional to the pressure applied.

The computer is programmed to plot pressure against time for defined areas of interest. These are delineated on a display of the distribution of the highest pressures recorded from the time a foot first makes contact with the ground to when it is lifted off. In this case the areas of interest were heel and forefoot.

A simple index of foot strike was calculated both for pedobarograph and video recordings:

$$\frac{\text{(number of heel strikes)} + \text{(number of simultaneous heel and forefoot strikes/2)}}{\text{Total number of steps studied}}$$

An index of one is normal, whereas an index of zero implies the initial strike is always with the forefoot.

Patients

Fourteen patients (aged 65 to 88 years), in whom a clinical response to levodopa therapy had been documented in the past, were studied. Each had been established on an anti-parkinsonian regimen of Sinemet Plus (Merck, Sharp and Dohme Ltd.) alone. They were allocated to receive randomly a tablet of Sinemet Plus or an identical placebo at 10.00 h, with the alternative treatment at least three days later. The treatments were then repeated, after the same minimal interval had elapsed. Measurement of distance/time parameters of gait were carried out immediately before and at 2, 4 and 6 h after the 10.00 h doses on all 4 days. Treatments were repeated a second time with simultaneous pedobarography and video recording 2 h after. No food was taken for 1.5 h before or after a 10.00 h treatment. No routine doses of Sinemet Plus were given after the 22.00 h dose on the night before, until 16.00 h on the treatment day, placebo tablets being substituted where appropriate.

Results and discussion

The global assessment by video recording confirmed that there was no overt difference in gait 2 h after active and placebo treatments. As regards the distance/time parameters of gait, analysis of variance showed no significant difference between treatments with respect to speed and cadence. The two gait parameters, double support time and swing length, analysed for each cycle of the entire walk (to a maximum distance of six metres), showed significant differences between placebo treatments ($P<0.001$ and $P<0.004$, respectively). However, there was a highly significant ($P<0.0005$) interaction between nature and order of treatments and their repetition, with respect to swing length. Thus, although swing length was too labile to serve as a reliable index of treatment effect, the analysis of the double support times during a short walk allowed a short-term response to be detected in a group of patients with no overt fluctuation in clinical state in relation to medication. Foot strike, as assessed by pedobarography, was more abnormal on placebo than on active treatment in nine of the 14 patients. A marginally significant ($P<0.05$) difference in the foot strike index was detected on active treatment: abnormalities of foot strike in Parkinson's disease may be susceptible to drug therapy. Further analysis is in progress to determine whether the magnitude of the effect was determined by the plasma concentrations of levodopa and of its metabolite, 3-0-methyldopa, or influenced by the mean arterial blood pressure.

More abnormal foot strikes were detected using pedobarography than using video recording but the difference [mean (SD) difference in index = 0.1 (0.2)] did not reach significance ($P > 0.1$). There was no relationship between age, severity of Parkinson's disease (Webster's rating scale), duration of treatment with levodopa or the distance/time measurements and the index of foot strike as measured by pedobarography (Spearman's rank correlation test, $P>0.05$ in each case). Thus pedobarography revealed abnormalities of foot strike which were not evident clinically nor predictable from other observations. Indeed, the patient whose apparently normal gait trace is shown in Fig. 2 had the most abnormal foot strike index (0.08) in the study. Determination of the nature of foot strike provides a useful tool for objective evaluation prior to physiotherapy and for assessing progress.

The above study illustrates the usefulness of gait analysis in distinguishing drug-responsive from non-responsive parkinsonism. It may be useful in detecting small and/or transient responses: these may be critical for that patient's daily activities. It may also be useful in distinguishing reversible drug-induced parkinsonism from the idiopathic disease by documenting recovery following withdrawal of the suspected agent. Where gait may be influenced by more than one pathology, changes produced by treatment, whether pharmacological, surgical or by physiotherapy, can be quantified. Both osteoarthritis of the right hip and Parkinson's disease more severe on the left could produce the changes shown in Fig. 4. In the investigation of falls in old age, gait analysis might increase the yield of patients with a treatable cause.

Acknowledgements—Messrs J. Baker and M. Tate, Division of Bioengineering, Clinical Research Centre, co-operated in producing the gait assessment trolley. We are grateful to Professor L.

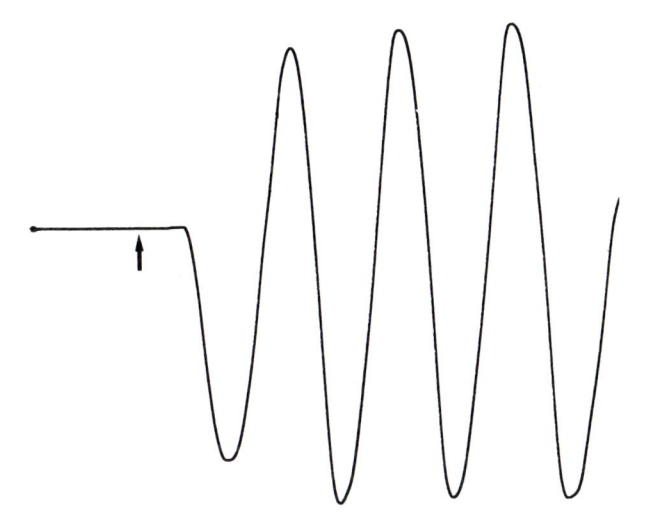

Fig. 2. *Apparently normal gait trace from a parkinsonian patient.*

Fig. 3. *Grossly abnormal gait trace from a parkinsonian patient.*

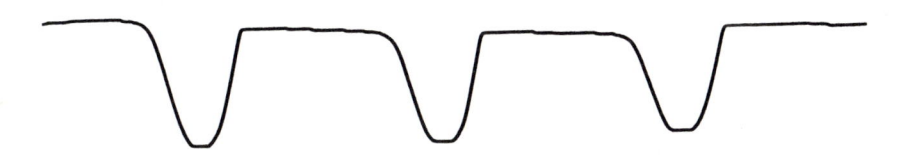

Fig. 4. *Grossly abnormal trace from a patient with osteoarthritis of the right hip.*

Klenerman for his interest and advice, and for affording Mrs Hughes time to carry out the pedobarography. The work was supported by Merck, Sharpe and Dohme Ltd., who supplied the tablets. Mrs Leeman was a PhD student funded by a grant from London University.

References
1 Klenerman, L. & Weller, C. (1987): In *Gait analysis and medical photogrammetry*, pp 63–64. Oxford: Oxford Orthopaedic Engineering Centre.
2 Duckworth, T., Betts, R. P., Franks, C. I. & Burke, J. (1982): The measurement of pressures under the foot. *Foot Ankle* **3**, 130–141.

CLINICAL ASPECTS

Chorea, dystonia and myoclonus

37

RECEPTOR AUTORADIOGRAPHIC STUDIES IN NEURODEGENERATIVE DISORDERS OF THE BASAL GANGLIA

Jeffrey N. Joyce[*], Nedra Lexow[*], Bethany Neal[*], Howard Hurtig[†], John Q. Trojanowski[§] and Andrew Winokur[*]

[*]*Departments of Pharmacology and Psychiatry, University of Pennsylvania School of Medicine; Departments of* [†]*Neurology, Graduate Hospital and The University of Pennsylvania School of Medicine, and* [§]*Pathology and Laboratory Medicine (Neuropathology), The University of Pennsylvania School of Medicine, Philadelphia, Pennsylvania, USA*

Summary

The technique of quantitative autoradiography was used to examine the effects of Huntington's disease and schizophrenia on the organization of striatal dopamine D1 and D2 receptors. In addition, a single autopsy case of Parkinson's disease who received an adrenal medullary autograft, but died of causes unrelated to the surgery 4 months later, was also processed for autoradiography. While the striatum of Huntington's disease cases showed a reduction in the density of D1 ([^{3}H]SCH 23390) and D2 ([^{3}H]spiroperidol) receptors, the patterning of D2 receptor loss did not match that of the D1 receptor loss, the loss of D1 receptors being far greater than the loss of D2 receptors. While there was a dorsal-ventral gradient of effect on both receptor subtypes, the effects of Huntington's disease on D2 receptors in the ventral putamen and nucleus accumbens septi (NAS) were minimal. There appeared to be a relative preservation of [^{3}H]mazindol labelling of dopamine terminals in the striatum of the Huntington's disease cases. In the schizophrenic patients, our autoradiographic studies confirmed previous reports of an elevation of D2 receptor density in the striata in many cases. However, the increase was far greater in the NAS (2–3 fold) and ventral putamen than more dorsally in the striatum. The density of D1 receptors and DA terminals labelled with [^{3}H]mazindol in the striatum of schizophrenics was not significantly different from that of control cases. Thus, in both HD and schizophrenia, the ratio of D2/D1 receptors is altered in favour of the D2 population, particularly in the NAS and ventral putamen. Alteration of the D2/D1 ratio in those 'limbic' and 'motor' zones, respectively, of the striatum may play a role in the clinical symptoms of these two disorders. The Parkinson's case showed a substantial loss of [^{3}H]mazindol binding in the dorsal PUT and caudate nucleus, the 'motor' region of the striatum. The density of both D1 and D2 receptors was down-regulated on the side of the transplant, particularly in the NAS and medial caudate nucleus. There was little evidence of a modulation of dopamine receptors within the 'motor' part of the striatum suggesting that the transplant did not improve dopamine utilization in that region.

Introduction

Over the last 15 years a considerable amount of research has been published describing the compartmental organization of the mammalian striatum. The patterning of the cholinergic enzyme acetylcholinesterase (AChE) shows a dense staining throughout the striatum. However, within a darker matrix are zones of low activity (AChE-poor) which are aligned in serial sections through the rostral-caudal axis of the striatum.[1] The distribution of many neurotransmitters, afferent projections, and cell bodies of striatal efferents obey this organization.[2-5] An important consequence of this organization is that 'motor' and non-motor (eg, limbic) zones of the striatum can be delineated as channels of information processing. We have shown that the pre- and postsynaptic components of the dopamine system also appear to obey this compartmental organization. The dopamine D2 receptor subtype is preferentially enriched in density within the 'motor' region of the striatum of the rat,[6] cat,[7] non-human primate[8] and human.[9] The distribution of the D1 receptor subtype is more homogeneous and shows little evidence for a lateral-to-medial gradient.[7,10] We have observed that the topography of D1 receptors in the cat striatum shows distinct patches that are densest in the 'limbic' zone and tend to avoid D2-rich regions.[11] The distribution of tyrosine-hydroxylase-like immunoreactive terminals is also denser in the matrix or 'motor' component of the striatum.[12,13] In the striatum of several species, we have observed that the patterning of [^{3}H]mazindol sites also conforms to the patch/matrix organization, with denser binding in the matrix component,[14,15] suggesting that [^{3}H]mazindol is a useful marker for dopamine terminal density.

While the delineation of anatomical compartments of the striatum has progressed significantly, evidence that these compartments are functionally important has been more difficult to show. One approach is to examine whether disorders of the nervous system that clearly involve the basal ganglia alter the neurochemical organization of the striatum. Huntington's disease is a useful model in which to initiate studies on the neurochemical pathology of the basal ganglia. First, Huntington's disease has a distinct, well-characterized pathology affecting discrete populations of striatal neurons.[16] Secondly, hyperactivity of dopamine systems has been implicated in both Huntington's disease and schizophrenia.[17] Finally, Huntington's disease is characterized by both 'psychotic' and motor disturbances, and can be initially confused with schizophrenia.[18] Therefore, comparisons with a disorder less clearly demonstrating a basal ganglia neurochemical pathology, such as schizophrenia, can be made. In many respects, Parkinson's disease shows the exact opposite clinical picture. Movement is significantly reduced and the neuropathology involves a loss of dopamine from the striatum. Consequently, alterations in dopamine receptor systems should be very different from those of Huntington's disease and schizophrenia.

Studies have been initiated which examine striatal dopamine receptor changes in striatum of patients who have died with Huntington's disease, and compare those changes with tissue derived post-mortem from schizophrenics and age-matched controls. In addition, autopsy findings on a case of Parkinson's disease who had received an adrenal medullary autograft into the head of the caudate nucleus on the most affected side and died 4 months later of unrelated causes has also been studied. In this paper, we shall present findings suggesting that alterations in the dopamine systems within these striatal subregions plays an important role in the aetiology of the clinical symptoms.[19,20]

Methods

Coronal slabs of whole brain hemispheres at the level of the anterior striatum from patients who had died with a diagnosis of Huntington's disease (grades 3 and 4; 66 yr age, male and female) or schizophrenia (mean age 65, male and female) were obtained from the Brain Tissue Resource Center of McLean Hospital (E. D. Bird, director). Brain tissue from age-matched controls was obtained at autopsy (post-mortem interval less than 20 h) from the Hospital of the University of Pennsylvania. A case with a history of Parkinson's disease (12 years) had received a chromaffin cell autograft to the rostral right caudate nucleus and survived for 4 months with minimal improvement of symptoms. He died 2 weeks after becoming quadriplegic from a cervical epidural abscess. At autopsy (10 h after death; Hospital of the University of Pennsylvania) tissue sections were taken for immunocytochemical demonstration of surviving clumps of chromagranin A positive cells. For autoradiographic experiments the brains were sectioned at 20–30 μm in a cryostat at $-15°$C, thaw-mounted onto gelatin subbed slides, dried (at $0°$C) under reduced pressure, and then stored at $-80°$C until used for experiments. One hour prior to incubation, slide-mounted tissue sections were brought to $0°$C, and just prior to incubation they were brought to $22°$C (except for [^{3}H]mazindol binding). The tissue sections were then processed for autoradiographic studies of dopamine D1 ([^{3}H]SCH 23390)[15] and D2 ([^{3}H]spiroperidol)[9] receptors, and dopamine uptake sites ([^{3}H]mazindol).[15] Adjacent sections were processed for AChE histochemistry. After the incubation procedures, the tissue sections were rapidly rinsed in double distilled H_2O at $0°$C, and then dried on a hot plate at $55°$C after aspiration of excess fluid. The tissue and tritium-containing plastic standards (ARC) were opposed to tritium-sensitive ultrofilm (LKB Produktor) for the appropriate period of time. The film was developed in D-19 (Kodak). Analysis of the autoradiographs was aided by a computer-based image analysis system.

Results

As reported previously,[9] the patterning of D2 receptors in the control striatum was related to the patch/matrix organization, as visualized in adjacent sections stained for AChE. The matrix was enriched in D2 receptors, as compared to the patch (striosomal) region. In the striatum of Huntington's disease cases, the overall density of D2 receptors was reduced by about 30 per cent (Fig. 1D), but the effect was not homogeneous. The loss was far more significant dorsally than ventrally, with the density of D2 receptors in the ventral putamen and nucleus accumbens septi (NAS) not significantly different from control cases. In addition, the patch/matrix pattern was still visible, but the area of the D2 receptor-dense matrix (and AChE-rich matrix) was reduced significantly. Consequently, there was greater 'survival' of the D2-rich regions in the ventral striatum. The control striatum also showed a patchy distribution of D1 receptors, with examples of concordance and discordance with the topography of D2 receptors. The Huntington's disease striata showed a profound loss of D1 sites (Fig. 1E) throughout the striatum (60–70 per cent reduction). The loss was greatest in the dorsal striatum and least in the NAS

(40–50 per cent loss), where the patchy organization was still apparent. The dopamine uptake site, localized presynaptically on dopamine terminals, can be visualized with [^{3}H]mazindol. In the striatum of control cases, the patterning of [^{3}H]mazindol sites also conformed to the patch/matrix organization, with the denser binding in the matrix component (Fig. 1C). The distribution of dopamine-immunoreactive terminals was also denser in the matrix component,[12,13] suggesting that [^{3}H]mazindol is a useful marker for dopamine terminals. Unlike the homogeneous effects of Huntington's disease on dopamine receptors, the effects on dopamine terminals labelled with [^{3}H]mazindol were more heterogeneous. Some cases showed significant loss of binding, with the matrix being reduced in area without a reduction of the patch component. Other cases showed an intact matrix patterning in the caudate nucleus and dorsal putamen, but loss of binding in the NAS and ventral putamen. Finally, other cases were unaffected in the density of sites, evidencing levels similar to control levels.

While several laboratories have reported an increased number of dopamine D2 receptors in schizophrenia,[21] it was only recently reported that an actual decrease in D1 receptors might occur in this neuropsychiatric disease. Such an imbalance in the ratio of D1 to D2 receptors was hypothesized to be an important factor in this disease.[22] To examine this hypothesis further, autoradiographic studies with striatal tissue derived post-mortem from cases diagnosed as schizophrenic were conducted. Significant increases in D2 receptor density were apparent (Fig. 1G), the ventral putamen and NAS exhibiting a two- to three-fold increase in receptor density. No change in D1 receptor density (Fig. 1H) was apparent. A slight reduction in the density of dopamine uptake sites, particularly in the matrix component, was observed.

The parkinsonian case, having received an adrenal medulla transplant, exhibited significant loss of [^{3}H]mazindol binding to dopamine uptake sites in both the left and right (operated) striatum. On the unoperated side, the loss of [^{3}H]mazindol binding was not homogeneous, being greatest in the dorsal caudate nucleus and putamen and least in the medial and ventral striatum (Fig. 2A). There were differences in the density and patterning of binding for [^{3}H]mazindol between the unoperated and operated side for the striatum. Even for sections nearest the transplant, the right striatum showed lower levels of binding than the left striatum, with the densest binding located medially in the central caudate nucleus (Fig. 2D), and somewhat lesser binding more ventrally in the NAS. As compared to the control cases, the left (unoperated) striatum of this case exhibited a small increase of D2 receptor density in the dorsal putamen (18 per cent) but less in other regions of striatum (6–8 per cent). In sections nearest the transplant, the operated side of this case showed a reduction in the density of D2 receptors, as compared to the unoperated side (Fig. 2B, D), the decrease being greatest in the ventral striatum (21 per cent) and least dorsally (5–10 per cent). The left side also showed an enhanced density of D1 receptors, as compared to controls (41–52 per cent), and the transplant side showed a pronounced reduction in D1 receptors (24–34 per cent). The ventral striatum exhibited the greatest reduction in D1 receptors and the dorsal striatum the least (Fig. 2C, E).

Discussion

Recent studies of Huntington's disease have revealed an heterogeneous loss of neurons from the striatum, with a preservation of the aspiny interneurons and a considerable depletion of the spiny output neurons.[23] Consequently, the 'striosomal' or patch/matrix organization of the AChE (cholinergic) and NADPH-diaphorase (somatostatin) staining patterns of the striatum is preserved in Huntington's disease.[23,24] In addition, there is a

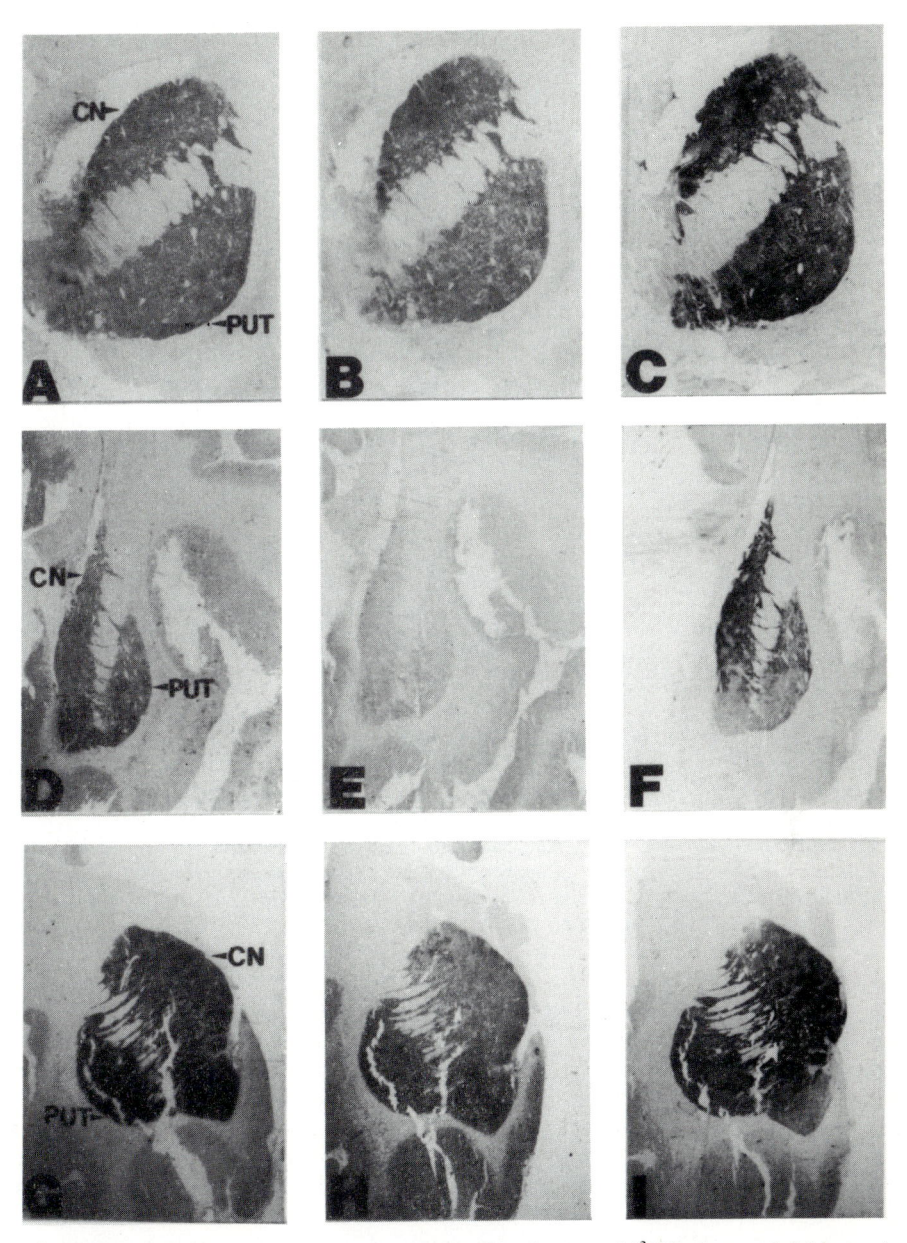

Fig. 1. *Photomicrographs of the autoradiographic distribution of [³H]spiroperidol (dopamine D2 receptors), [³H]SCH 23390 (dopamine D1 receptors) and [³H]mazindol binding (dopamine uptake sites) in representative control, Huntingdon's disease (HD) and schizophrenic cases. D2 receptor binding in striatum of the control, HD and schizophrenic cases (A), (D), (G). D1 receptor binding in striatum of the same control, HD and schizophrenic cases (B), (E), (H). [³H]mazindol dopamine uptake site density in control, HD and schizophrenic cases (C), (F), (I). Abbreviations used: CN, caudate nucleus; PUT, putamen. Printed with permission of Synapse.[19]*

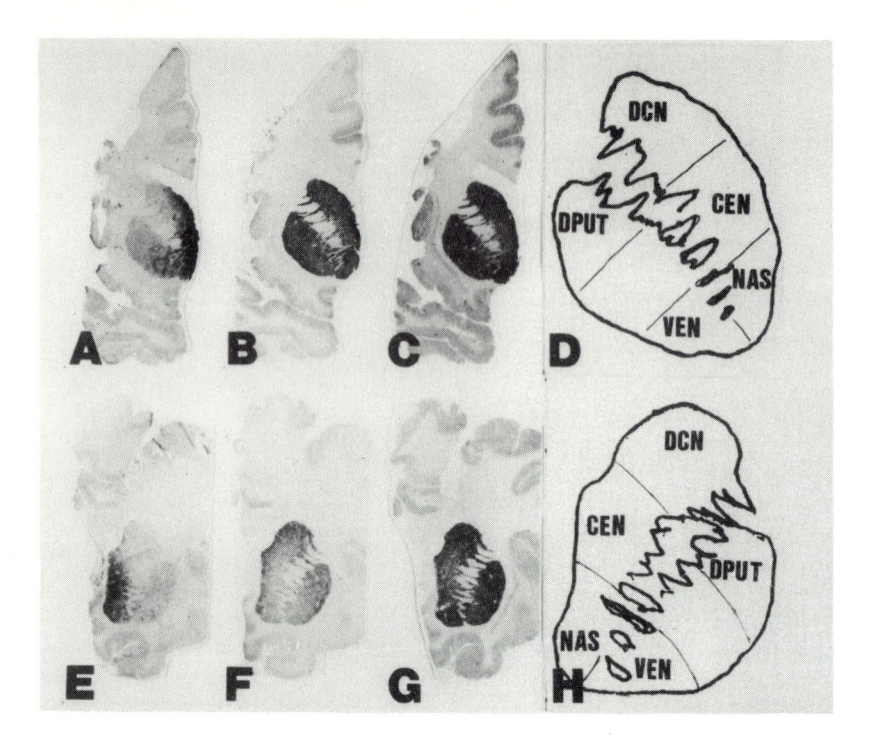

Fig. 2. *Photomicrographs of the autoradiographic distribution of [^{3}H]mazindol binding (dopamine uptake sites), [^{3}H]SCH 23390 (dopamine D1 receptors), and [^{3}H]spiroperidol (dopamine D2 receptors) in representative sections from the unoperated (A, B, C) and operated (E, F, G) striatum of a Parkinson's case having received an adrenal medullary autotransplant into the right caudate nucleus.* [^{3}H]mazindol dopamine uptake site density is shown in (A) and (E). D1 receptor binding in striatum is shown in (B) and (F). D2 receptor binding in striatum is shown in (C) and (G). Note that the density of D1 and D2 sites is less on the operated side, particularly in the nucleus accumbens septi (NAS) and medial portion of the central caudate nucleus (CEN). Abbreviations used: DCN, dorsal caudate nucleus; CEN, central caudate nucleus; NAS, nucleus accumbens septi; DPUT, dorsal putamen; VEN, ventral putamen.

dorsal-ventral gradient of the effects of the disease, such that the ventral putamen and NAS are affected to a lesser extent than the dorsal putamen and caudate nucleus. In Huntington's disease it has been reported that there is a relative sparing of the dopamine input,[17] but a significant decline in D2 and D1 receptor density.[25,26] The results of our studies indicate that D1 receptor loss is far more significant than the D2 receptor loss. Since the neurons selectively affected and spared in Huntington's disease possess different dopamine receptors (Fig. 3A), their topographic loss in Huntington's disease striatum probably reflects the more significant loss of medium-sized spiny output neurons (Fig. 3C). Thus, the D1 receptors are located on the spiny output neurons and are affected by Huntington's disease far more than the D2 receptors located on the aspiny interneurons. Huntington's disease cases also showed a significant sparing of the [^{3}H]mazindol labelling of dopamine uptake sites, suggesting that dopamine input to the D2 receptor-rich matrix is relatively intact in Huntington's disease. In combination with the more selective loss of D1 receptors, this would result in an imbalance of dopaminergic effects in both the 'motor' and 'limbic' zones of the striatum (Fig. 3B). The D2/D1

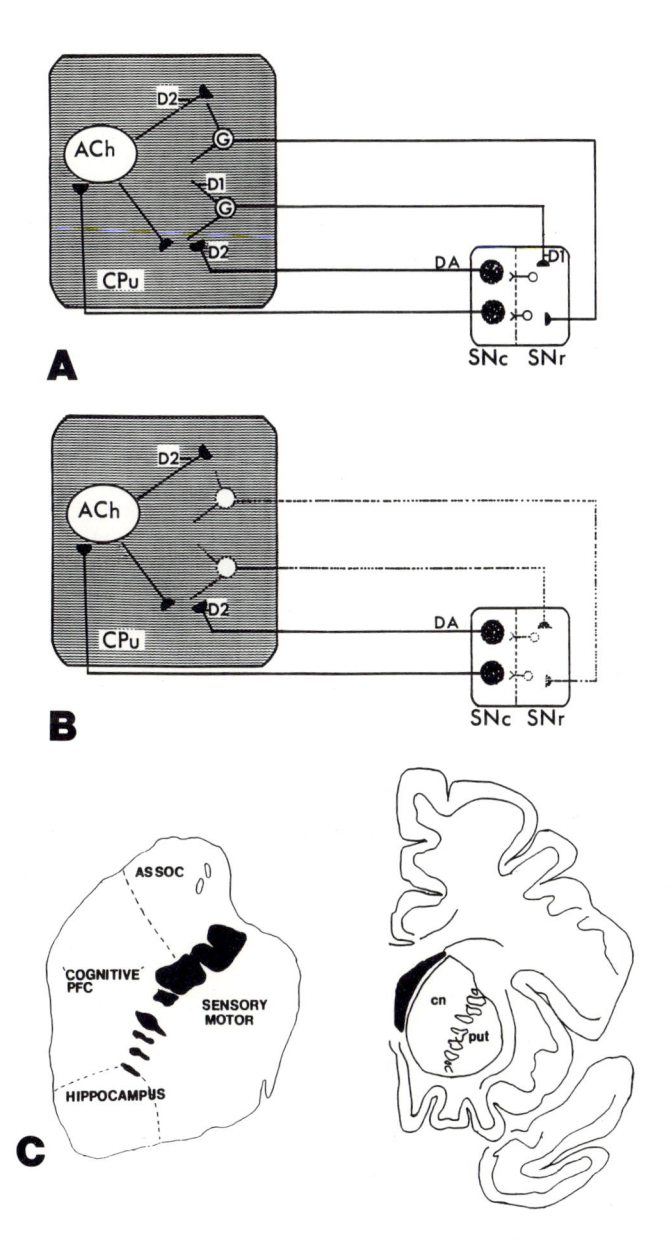

Fig. 3. Schematic drawing of striatum depicting localization of dopamine receptor subtypes to intrinsic neurons and to afferents of substantia nigra (A), (B) and functional compartmentalization of the human striatum (C). The diagram of a normal (A) and Huntington disease (B) striatum depicts the specificity of cell loss (spiny neurons) and cell sparing (aspiny neurons) in this disease. Not shown are cortical afferents, since dopamine receptors are not located there.[6] Accordingly, the more selective loss of the medium-sized spiny efferent neurons would result in a more pronounced loss of D1 than D2 receptors. The diagram of a human striatum (C) depicts the functional compartments of the striatum.[5,30] Abbreviations: ACh, acetylcholine neurons representing the aspiny class of striatal interneurons; G, GABA neurons representing the spiny class of striatal efferent neurons; CPu, caudate and putamen; SNc, substantia nigra pars compacta; SNr, substantia nigra pars reticulata.

imbalance may partially underly the clinical symptoms of Huntington's disease. While the pathology must be very different for the schizophrenia cases, the pronounced increase in D2 receptor density would alter the D2/D1 receptor ratio in a similar manner. Based on the Huntington's disease model, this work suggests that a disturbance in the dopamine D2 receptor population may be reflective of an on-going pathology of the aspiny classes of neurons in this brain region.

The Parkinson's case, having received an adrenal medulla transplant, exhibited significant loss of [^{3}H]mazindol binding in both the left and right (transplant) striatum. This has been observed previously in an MPTP-treated primate[8] and is consistent with the significant loss of pigmented cells in the substantia nigra of this case. The loss of binding was not homogeneous on the unoperated side, being greatest in the dorsal caudate nucleus and putamen and least in the medial caudate nucleus and NAS. Similar results have been reported for a larger population of parkinsonian patients,[27] where the loss of dopamine was greatest in dorsal caudate nucleus and putamen. These data further substantiate the use of this label as an index of dopamine terminal integrity.

In rat[28] and non-human primate models of Parkinson's disease, there is an increase in D2 receptor density in the lateral striatum following dopamine denervation of the striatum. Following a transplant of embryonic substantia nigra into the denervated striatum of the rat, behavioural recovery is correlated with down-regulation of D2 receptors.[29] When tissue sections nearest the transplant were examined for changes in D1 and D2 receptor density by autoradiography, we showed that both receptor sites were decreased in density, as compared to the unoperated side. Inspection of Fig. 2 suggests that the reduction of D2 and D1 binding on the transplant side was greatest in the region of striatum exhibiting the most [^{3}H]mazindol binding (medial caudate nucleus and NAS), indicating that dopamine utilization was greatest in this region. It is worth noting that the dorsal caudate nucleus and putamen, the 'motor' part of the transplant striatum,[30] showed the least increase in [^{3}H]mazindol binding and the least reduction in dopamine receptor density as compared to the left side, consistent with the modest improvement of parkinsonian symptoms in this individual. It may be important that the transplant be placed into the dorsal putamen in order for dopamine utilization to be sufficiently enhanced in that region for clinical improvement to be observed.

Acknowledgements—This research was supported by grants from the Scottish Rite Schizophrenia Research Program, N.M.J., U.S.A. and American Federation for Aging Research to JNJ; and by Research Scientist Award MH00044, BRSG 2-S07-RR-05415-26 and RO1 NS19597 to AW.

References

1 Graybiel, A. M. & Ragsdale, C. W. (1978): Histochemically distinct compartments in the striatum of human, monkey, and cat demonstrated by acetylcholinesterase staining. *Proc. Natl. Acad. Sci. USA*, **75**, 5723–5726.
2 Gerfen, C. R. (1984): The neostriatal mosaic: compartmentalization of corticostriatal input and striatonigral output systems. *Nature* **311**, 461–464.
3 Gerfen, C. R. (1985): The neostriatal mosaic. I. Compartmental organization of projections from the striatum to the substantia nigra in the rat. *J. Comp. Neurol.* **236**, 454–476.
4 Gerfen, C. R., Herkenham, M. & Thibault, J. (1987): The neostriatal mosaic: II. Patch- and matrix-directed mesostriatal dopaminergic and non-dopaminergic systems. *J. Neurosci.* **7**, 3915–3934.
5 Graybiel, A. M. & Ragsdale, W. J. R. (1983): Biochemical anatomy of the striatum. In *Chemical neuroanatomy*, ed P. C. Emson, pp 427–504. New York: Raven Press.
6 Joyce, J. N. & Marshall, J. F. (1987): Quantitative autoradiography of dopamine D2 sites in rat caudate-putamen: localization to intrinsic neurons and not to neocortical afferents. *Neuroscience* **20**, 773–795.

7. Beckstead, R. M., Wooten, G. F. & Trugman, J. M. (1988): Distribution of D1 and D2 dopamine receptors in the basal ganglia of the cat determined by quantitative autoradiography. *J. Comp. Neurol.* **268**, 131–145.
8. Joyce, J. N., Marshall, J. F., Bankiewicz, K. S., Koplin, I. J. & Jacobowitz, D. M. (1986): Hemiparkinsonism in a monkey after unilateral internal carotid artery infusion of 1-methyl-4-phenyl-1,2,3,6-tetrahydropyridine (MPTP) is associated with regional ipsilateral changes in striatal dopamine D-2 receptor density. *Brain Res.* **382**, 360–364.
9. Joyce, J. N., Sapp, D. W. & Marshall, J. F. (1986): Human striatal dopamine receptors are organized in patches. *Proc. Natl. Acad. Sci. U.S.A.* **83**, 8002–8006.
10. Ritchfield, E. K., Young, A. B. & Penney, J. B. (1987): Comparative distribution of dopamine D-1 and D-2 receptors in the basal ganglia of turtles, pigeons, rats, cats and monkeys. *J. Comp. Neurol.* **262**, 446–463.
11. Neal, B. S., Bauer, M. S. & Joyce, J. N. (1988): CNS receptor topography in three strains of rat and the domestic cat. *Soc. Neurosci. Abstr.* **14**, 777.
12. Ferrante, R. J. & Kowall, N. W. (1987): Tyrosine hydroxylase-like immunoreactivity is distributed in the matrix compartment of normal human brain and Huntington's disease striatum. *Brain Res.* **416**, 141–146.
13. Graybiel, A. M., Hirsch, E. C. & Agid, Y. A. (1987): Differences in tyrosine hydroxylase-like immunoreactivity characterize the mesostriatal innervation of striosomes and extrastriosomal matrix at maturity. *Proc. Natl. Acad. Sci. USA*, **84**, 303–307.
14. Sapp, D. W., Joyce, J. N. & Marshall, J. F. (1986): Comparison of dopamine uptake sites with dopamine D-1 and D-2 receptors in rat striatum of defatted tissue. *Soc. Neurosci. Abstr.* **12**, 142.
15. Joyce, J. N., Lowenstein, P. R., Coyle, J. T. & Marshall, J. F. (1986): Striosomal organization of the human striatum: relationship between pre- and post-synaptic elements of the dopaminergic and cholinergic systems. *Soc. Neurosci. Abstr.* **12**, 809.
16. Vonsattel, J. P., Myers, R. H., Stevens, T. J., Ferrante, R. J., Bird, E. D. & Richardson, E. P. (1985): Neuropathological classification of Huntington's disease. *J. Neuropathol. Exp. Neurol.* **44**, 559–577.
17. Sanberg, P. R. & Coyle, J. T. (1984): Scientific approaches to Huntington's disease. *CRC Crit. Rev. Clin. Neurobiol.* **1**, 1–44.
18. Van Putten, T. & Menkes, J. H. (1973): Huntington's disease masquerading as chronic schizophrenia. *Dis. Nerv. Syst.* **34**, 54–56.
19. Joyce, J. N., Lexow, N., Bird, E. & Winokur, A. (1988): Organization of dopamine D1 and D2 receptors in human striatum: receptor autoradiographic studies in Huntington's disease and schizophrenia. *Synapse* **2**, 546–557.
20. Huritg, H., Joyce, J. N., Sladek, J. R. & Trojanowski, J. Q. (1988): Post mortem analysis of adrenal medulla to caudate autograft in a patient with Parkinson's disease. *Ann. Neurol.* (In Press).
21. Seeman, P., Bzowej, N. H., Guan, H. C., Bergeron, C., Reynolds, G. P., Bird, E. D., Riederer, P., Jellinger, K. & Tourtellotte, W. W. (1987): Human brain D1 and D2 dopamine receptors in schizophrenia, Alzheimer's, Parkinson's and Huntington's Diseases. *Neuropsychopharmacology* **1**, 5–15.
22. Hess, E. J., Braca, H. S., Kleinman, J. E. & Creese, I. (1987): Dopamine receptor subtype imbalance in schizophrenia. *Life Sci.* **40**, 1487–1498.
23. Kowall, N. W., Ferrante, R. J. & J. B. Martin (1987): Patterns of cell loss in Huntington's disease. *TINS* **10**, 24–29.
24. Feigenbaum, L. A., Graybiel, A. M., Vonsattel, J. P., Richardson, E. P. & Bird, E. D. (1986): Striosomal markers in the striatum in Huntington's Disease. *Soc. Neurosci. Abstr.* **12**, 1328.
25. Reisine, T. D., Fields, J. Z., Stern, L. Z., Johnson, P. C., Bird, E. D. & Yamamura, H. I. (1977): Alterations in dopaminergic receptors in Huntington's disease. *Life Sci.* **21**, 1123.
26. Bzowej, N. H. & Seeman, P. (1986): Dopamine D1 and D2 receptors in Huntington's chorea. *Soc. Neurosci. Abstr.* **12**, 1248.
27. Kish, S. J., Shannak, K. & Hornykiewicz, O. (1988): Uneven pattern of dopamine loss in the striatum of patients with idiopathic Parkinson's disease. *N. Engl. J. Med.* **318**, 876–880.
28. Savasta, M., Dubois, A., Feuerstein, C., Manier, M. & Scatton, B. (1987): Denervation

supersensitivity of striatal D2 dopamine receptors is restricted to the ventro- and dorsolateral regions of the striatum. *Brain Res.* **74**, 180–186.
29 Freed, W. J., Ko, G. N., Niehoff, D. L., Kuhar, M. J., Hoffer, B. J., Olson, L., Cannon-Spoor, H. E., Morihisa, J. M. & Wyatt, R. J. (1983): Normalization of spiroperidol binding in the denervated rat striatum by homologous grafts of substantia nigra. *Science* **222**, 937–939.
30 Alexander, G. E., DeLong, M. R. & Strick, P. L. (1986): Parallel organization of functionally segregated circuits linking basal ganglia and cortex. *Annu. Rev. Neurosci.* **9.** 357–381.

38

INCREASE IN DIAZEPAM BINDING INHIBITOR

(51–70) IN HUNTINGTON'S DISEASE

J. A. Ball, P. W. J. Burnet and S. R. Bloom

Department of Medicine, Royal Postgraduate Medical School, Hammersmith Hospital, Du Cane Road, London W12 0HS, UK

Summary

In Huntington's disease, reduction in striatal GABA is one of the most striking abnormalities and alterations in benzodiazepine receptors, which are allosterically linked to the $GABA_A$ receptor, have also been reported. Diazepam binding inhibitor (DBI), recently isolated from rat and human brain, has been proposed as an endogenous ligand at the benzodiazepine receptor. The content of DBI-like immunoreactivity (51–70) [DBI-IR (51–70)] has therefore been compared in control post-mortem human brains and in Huntington's disease brains. DBI-IR (51–70) was significantly increased in the putamen, caudate, globus pallidus and nucleus accumbens of Huntington brains ($P <$ 0.001). Gel filtration chromatography showed similar elution profiles of the peptide in both control and Huntington's disease extracts, thus providing no evidence for a change in the nature of the peptide itself.

Introduction

Diazepam binding inhibitor (DBI) is a neuropeptide recently isolated from rat and human brain that displaces ligands bound to the benzodiazepine and beta-carboline recognition site on the gamma-amino-butyric acid $(GABA)_A$ receptor.[1,2] Its amino acid sequence has been determined from tryptic peptide fragments and cDNA probes.[3] When injected intraventricularly DBI causes a proconflict response in rats,[1] and in primary cultures of mouse spinal cord neurones DBI shortens the duration of the Cl^- channel opening induced by GABA.[4] It has therefore been suggested that DBI may be an endogenous ligand or the precursor of a family of endogenous ligands at the benzodiazepine receptor involved in the allosteric modulation of the $GABA_A$ receptor. A fragment of human DBI, DBI (51–70), has similar properties to DBI. Reduction in striatal GABA is one of the most pronounced neurotransmitter alterations in Huntington's disease.[5] Alterations in benzodiazepine receptors have also been reported[6] and may contribute to the mood and motor abnormalities seen in Huntington's disease. The present study was therefore designed to investigate the content of DBI-like immunoreactivity (51–70)[DBI-IR (51–70)] in control and Huntington's disease brains by radioimmunoassay.

Method

Control brains were obtained at post-mortem from the Cambridge Brain Bank from 11 adults who had died without neurological or psychiatric disease (9 male, 2 female, mean age 63 years, range 51–58 years, mean autopsy delay 31 h, range 3–66 h) and from 9 patients with Huntington's disease (6 male, 3 female, mean age 61 years, range 40–79 years, mean autopsy delay 48h, range 24–72 h). The diagnosis of Huntington's disease was based on characteristic signs, symptoms, clinical course, a positive family history and characteristic neuropathological changes. Five Huntington's disease patients had received tetrabenazine and benzodiazepines, two received benzodiazepines alone and three were on no medication. The collection, storage and dissection of brains was as previously described.[7] Tissues were extracted by boiling in 0.5 M acetic acid for 10 min. Aliquots of diluted supernatants were assayed in duplicate. The DBI(51–70) antibody was raised against DBI(51–70), the synthetic 20 amino acid fragment of human DBI (Peninsula), conjugated by glutaraldehyde to bovine serum albumin (BSA) and was used in a final dilution of 1:14 000. There was no cross-reactivity with other neuropeptides. DBI(51–70) fragment was labelled with ^{125}I Bolton Hunter reagent and purified by reverse phase high performance liquid chromatography (HPLC). Assays were performed in a total volume of 0.7 ml of assay buffer (0.06 M phosphate buffer, pH 7.4, 10 mM EDTA, 0.3 per cent BSA). Bound and free peptide were separated by charcoal adsorption of the free fraction. The intra-assay coefficient of variation was 3 per cent. The assay standard was synthetic DBI(51–70) of which 5 fmol per assay tube could be detected with 95 per cent confidence. DBI(51–70) immunoreactivity in both Huntington's disease and control extracts was characterized on a 1.4 × 90 cm column of Sephadex G-50 superfine (Pharmacia) and the elution coefficients were expressed as Kav.

Results

There was no correlation between age, sex, post-mortem delay and DBI(51–70) content in either the control group or in Huntington's disease. The Table shows that in Huntington's disease there was a significant increase of DBI-IR (51–70) in the putamen and caudate (50 per cent), globus pallidus lateral (90 per cent) and medial (70 per cent), $P < 0.001$, and in the nucleus accumbens (40 per cent), $P < 0.005$, compared to the control group (two tailed t-test, unpaired). An increased content of DBI-IR (51–70) was also found in the substantia nigra pars reticulata and pars compacta although this trend did not reach statistical significance. No change in DBI(51–70) content was found in the other areas studied.

The gel chromatography elution profiles of DBI-IR (51–70) in extracts from the putamen and globus pallidus from both control and Huntington's disease brains were similar (Figs 1 and 2), with a single peak Kav value of 0.22, eluting before the synthetic standard, which has a Kav of 0.52. This peak, of larger molecular weight than DBI(51–70), is likely to correspond to the total DBI peptide. Column recoveries were 70–105 per cent (n = 6).

Table. *Regional distribution of DBI-IR(51–70) in control and Huntington's disease brain.* Values (pmol/g wet weight) are means ± SEM. Number of samples in parentheses.

	DBI-IR(51–70)	
Area of brain	Control	Huntington's disease
Caudate	132 ± 10 (11)	199 ± 10 (9)
Putamen	138 ± 8 (11)	**230 ± 15 (9)
Globus pallidus		
lateral	150 ± 20 (11)	**287 ± 12 (9)
medial	157 ± 7 (11)	**258 ± 15 (9)
Subsantia nigra		
pars compacta	247 ± 17 (6)	283 ± 30 (5)
pars reticulata	193 ± 25 (5)	265 ± 30 (5)
Nucleus accumbens	146 ± 12 (11)	*206 ± 10 (9)
Brodmann areas		
4	158 ± 7 (11)	158 ± 10 (9)
10	146 ± 4 (11)	142 ± 9 (9)
21	150 ± 12 (11)	193 ± 12 (9)
Amygdala	282 ± 33 (11)	256 ± 17 (9)
Hippocampus	273 ± 9 (11)	247 ± 12 (9)
Hypothalamus	263 ± 17 (4)	223 ± 17 (4)

**$P < 0.001$, *$P < 0.005$ vs control (Students t-test, two tailed, unpaired)

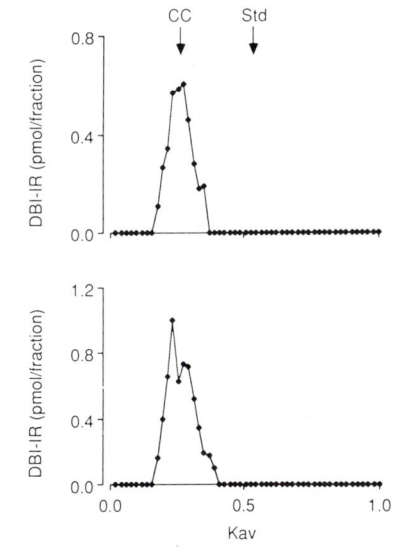

Fig. 1. *Gel chromatographic profile of DBI-IR(51–70) of extracted control globus pallidus (lateral), upper panel, and Huntington's disease globus pallidus (lateral), lower panel. Arrows indicate the elution positions of cytochrome C (CC) and DBI(51–70) fragment standard (Std).*

Discussion

The significant increase in DBI-IR (51–70) in the striatum, globus pallidus and nucleus accumbens is unlikely to reflect medication as there was no difference in DBI(51–70) in the Huntington's disease group between those who were on medication and those who were not. A change in the nature of the peptide is unlikely to be the explanation, since gel chromatographic profiles are similar. Interpretations of the increase depend on the

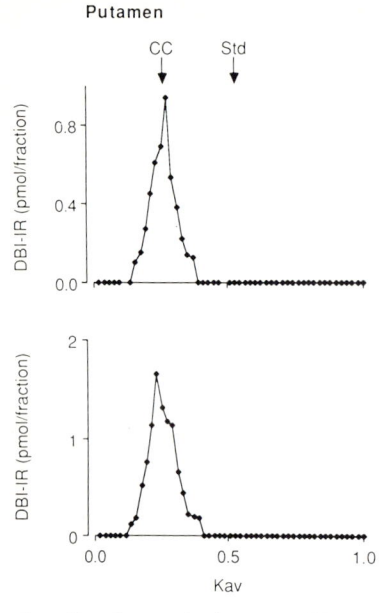

Fig. 2. *Gel chromatographic profile of DBI-IR(51–70) of extracted control putamen, upper panel, and Huntington's disease putamen, lower panel.* Arrows indicate the elution positions of cytochrome C (CC) and DBI(51–70) fragment standard (Std).

localization of the peptide. DBI is co-localized with GABA in some neurons.[8] Therefore whereas a decrease in neurotransmitters such as GABA, enkephalins and substance P may be due to degeneration of specific vulnerable neurons, and an increase in other peptides such as somatostatin and neuropeptide Y to the selective sparing of a subgroup of neurons,[9] to explain both the decrease in GABA and the increase in DBI-IR (51–70) in the same region we would have to propose that the majority of DBI(51–70) is *not* co-localized with GABA in these areas. Alternatively the increase in DBI-IR (51–70) may be secondary to or an adaptive response to changes either in GABA concentration, receptor number or affinity, or in benzodiazepine receptor number or affinity, or to structural changes in the GABA$_A$ receptor complex. However, no simple relationship can be seen (possibly because of the heterogeneity of benzodiazepine receptors): the density and affinity of [^{3}H] flunitrazepam benzodiazepine receptors are reduced in the striatum, where DBI(51–70) content is increased, but increased in the globus pallidus, where DBI(51–70) content is also increased.

Alternatively the gliosis seen in Huntington's disease, although controversial, could explain the increased DBI(51–70) content. The peripheral type benzodiazepine receptor is found in glial cells and is significantly increased in the putamen in Huntington's disease.[10] DBI is also found in peripheral tissues rich in peripheral benzodiazepine receptors[11] and in glial cells and displaces [^{3}H]-PK11195 binding from astrocytes.[12]

This is the first association of a change in DBI(51–70) with a neurological condition and may be related to the pathology of the disease, although possible mechanisms remain speculative. This finding of increased DBI(51–70)-IR in Huntington's disease poses further questions about the role of DBI in the human nervous system.

Acknowledgements—We are most grateful to Professor Paykel and Dr C. Wischik (Brain Tissue Bank, Cambridge, UK) for providing human brain tissue. J. A. Ball is in receipt of a MRC Training Fellowship.

References

1 Ferrero, P., Santi, M. R., Conti-Tronconi, B., Costa, E. & Guidotti, A. (1986): Study of an

octadecaneuropeptide derived from diazepam binding inhibitor (DBI): Biological activity and presence in rat brain. *Proc. Nat. Acad. Sci. USA* **83**, 827–831.
2. Ferrero, P., Costa, E., Conti-Tronconi, B. & Guidotti, A. (1986): A diazepam binding inhibitor (DBI)-like neuropeptide is detected in human brain. *Brain Res.* **399**, 136–142.
3. Gray, P. W., Glaister, D., Seeburg, P. H., Guidotti, A. & Costa, E. (1986): Cloning and expression of cDNA for human diazepam binding inhibitor, a natural ligand of an allosteric regulatory site of the gamma-aminobutyric acid type A receptor. *Proc. Natl. Acad. Sci. USA* **83**, 7547–7551.
4. Bormann, J., Ferrero, P., Guidotti, A. & Costa, E. (1985): Neuropeptide modulation of GABA receptor Cl^- channels. *Regul. Pept.* Suppl. **4**, 33–38.
5. Perry, T. L., Hansen, S. & Kloster, M. (1973): Huntington's chorea: deficiency of gamma-aminobutyric acid in brain. *N. Engl. J. Med.* **288**, 337–342.
6. Whitehouse, P. J., Trifiletti, R. R., Jones, B. E., Folstein, S., Price, D. L., Snyder, S. H. & Kuhar, M. J. (1985): Neurotransmitter receptor alterations in Huntington's disease: autoradiographic and homogenate studies with special reference to benzodiazepine receptor complexes. *Ann. Neurol.* **18**, 202–210.
7. Spokes, E. G. S. (1979): An analysis of factors influencing measurements of dopamine, noradrenaline, glutamate decarboxylase, and choline acetylase in human post-mortem brain tissue. *Brain* **102**, 333–341.
8. Costa, E., Alho, H., Santi, M. R., Ferrero, P. & Guidotti, A. (1986): Co-transmission at GABAergic synapses. *Prog. Brain Res.* **68**, 343–354.
9. Ferrante, R. J., Kowall, N. W., Beal, M. F., Martin, J. B., Richardson, E. P., Bird, E. D. & Martin, J. B. (1985): Selective sparing of a class of striatal neurons in Huntington's disease. *Science* **230**, 561–563.
10. Shoemaker, H., Morelli, M., Deshmukh, P. & Yamamura, H. I. (1982): [^{3}H] RO 5–4864 benzodiazepine binding in the kainate lesioned striatum and Huntington's diseased basal ganglia. *Brain Res.* **248**, 396–401.
11. Ball, J. A., Burnet, P. W. J., Fountain, B. A., Ghatei, M. A. & Bloom, S. R. (1986): Octadecaneuropeptide, benzodiazepine ligand-like immunoreactivity in rat central nervous system, plasma and peripheral tissues. *Neurosci. Lett.* **72**, 183–188.
12. Guidotti, A., Santi, M. R., Berkovich, A., Ferrarese, C. & Costa, E. (1986): Structure-activity relationship of peptide fragments derived from DBI (Diazepam Binding Inhibitor), a putative endogenous ligand of benzodiazepine recognition sites. *Clin. Neuropharmacol.* Suppl. **94**, 217–219.

39

TRYPTOPHAN METABOLISM AND QUINOLINIC ACID IN THE BRAIN IN HUNTINGTON'S DISEASE

S. J. Pearson and G. P. Reynolds

Department of Pathology, University of Nottingham Medical School, Queen's Medical Centre, Nottingham NG7 2UH, UK

Summary

Concentrations of tryptophan, the tryptophan metabolites 5-hydroxytryptamine (5HT) and 5-hydroxyindoleacetic acid (5HIAA), and the tryptophan-derived neurotoxin quinolinic acid (QA) were studied in post-mortem brain tissue from patients with Huntington's disease and control subjects. Tryptophan and QA were unchanged in Huntington's disease, providing no evidence for a general disorder of tryptophan metabolism, or for an aetiological role of QA in the disease. However, concentrations of 5HT and 5HIAA were found to be substantially increased in many regions of the Huntington's disease brain.

Introduction

While there have been substantial advances in our understanding of the molecular genetics of Huntington's disease, nothing is known of the factors responsible for the neuronal degeneration in this disorder. There are several hypotheses involving the production of a neurotoxin (or a toxic concentration of a neuroactive compound) by some aberrant metabolic process. Neurotoxic agents were found to cause axon-sparing lesions when injected into the rat striatum, which resembled the cell losses found in Huntington's disease. It was suggested that glutamate had a neurotoxic role, but it has since been shown to cause only negligible neuronal degeneration. We have previously demonstrated an overall loss of glutamate in most regions of the brain in Huntington's disease,[1] which provides evidence against it having a neurotoxic role in the aetiology of the disease. Quinolinic acid (QA), a tryptophan metabolite, has recently provided an animal model which shows a more selective cell loss than previous models.[2] Although there is some evidence disputing this selectivity,[3] it has been suggested that an abnormal increase in brain concentrations of QA may be the aetiological basis of the disease. QA is not elevated in blood or urine in Huntington's disease,[4,5] although peripheral levels are unlikely to affect or reflect brain concentrations, since it does not cross the blood-brain barrier. Furthermore, QA must be understood in a wider context, as it is an intermediate in the kynurenine pathway following tryptophan metabolism. Kynurenic acid, another intermediate, is known to block the neurotoxic effects of QA,[6] thus further study of this pathway may prove interesting.

Here we present the results of our studies into aspects of tryptophan metabolism in the brain in Huntington's disease. This particularly involved an investigation of QA concentrations in two brain regions taken post-mortem from patients with Huntington's disease and control subjects. In addition the concentrations of the tryptophan-derived neurotransmitter 5HT, its major metabolite 5HIAA, and tryptophan itself were determined in Huntington brain tissue.

Methods

The study was performed on post-mortem brain tissue from neuropathologically-confirmed cases of Huntington's disease and matched controls with no history of neuropsychiatric disease, supplied by the Cambridge Brain Bank. 5HT, 5HIAA and tryptophan concentrations were determined using an established high performance liquid chromatography (HPLC) method for monoamines.[1] This involved sample homogenization in perchloric acid before separation on the HPLC system, which comprised a Spherisorb ODS-2 5 μm column with a pH 3.6 phosphate-acetate buffer. Electrochemical detection was used for quantification.

QA was measured in the putamen and the frontal cortex using a modification[7] of a previous method.[8] Briefly this involved an extraction process and derivatization before injection into a gas chromatograph. A mass spectrometer was used for detection.

Statistical comparisons were made by t-test after logarithmic transformation of the data, and correlations were measured using Kendall's rank correlation.

Results and discussion

5HT and 5HIAA concentrations were found to be substantially increased in many areas of the brain in Huntington's disease. The results in Fig. 1 extend our previous findings[1] to include further areas. The increases may just reflect the tissue atrophy, but in the cortex, at least, the increased 5HIAA/5HT ratio suggests increased serotonergic activity and/or an abnormality in tryptophan metabolism. However, tryptophan levels in the striatum remain unchanged in Huntington's disease (16472 ± 5204) as compared with the control group (18043 ± 3369): values are means (ng/g tissue/ ± SD, n = 6 in each case).

We have shown[7] there to be no significant difference apparent in QA concentrations between the two groups, in either the putamen or the frontal cortex, as seen in Fig. 2. No significant correlation was found with age, sex, or post-mortem delay, nor within the Huntington's disease group with duration of disease. These results provide no support for the hypothesis that increased QA is responsible for the neuronal degeneration of Huntington's disease. However the possibility of neurotoxic effects due to previous transient increases in QA cannot be excluded. The close correlation between the results for the cortex and for the putamen, as seen in Fig. 3, indicates QA concentrations to be consistent within each brain; however there is wide variation in brain QA between individual cases. The factor(s) responsible for this variation must be understood before

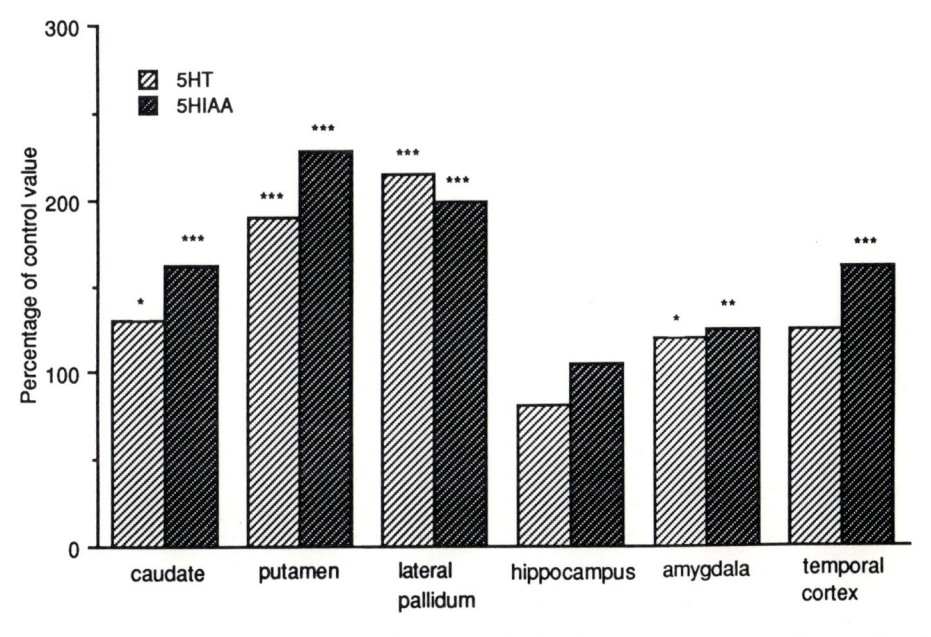

Fig. 1. *5HT and 5HIAA in Huntington's disease brain tissue as percentage of control values.* Huntington's disease n = 46; control n = 27 (including data from Reynolds & Pearson[1]). *p < 0.05; **p < 0.01; ***p < 0.001.

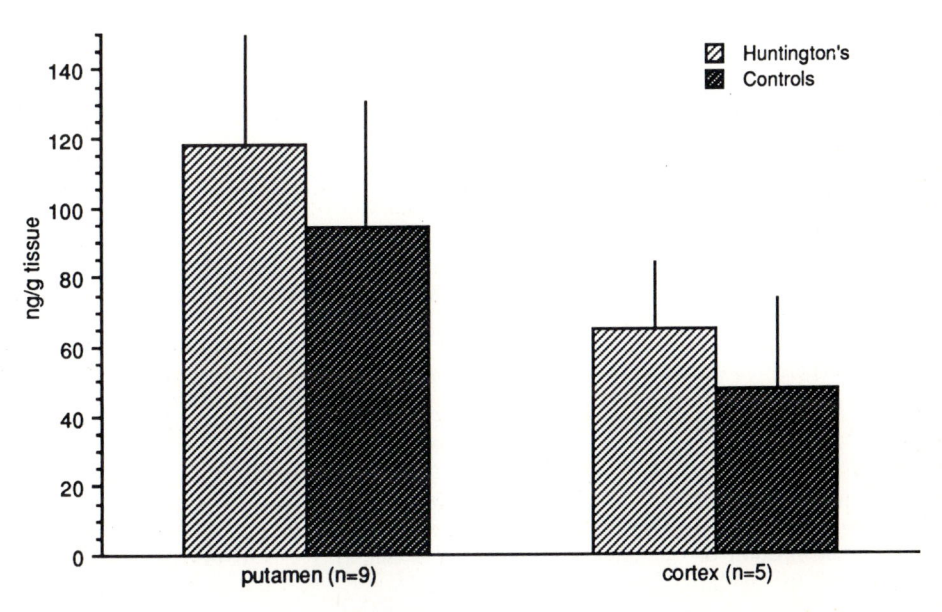

Fig. 2. *Quinolinic acid in Huntington's disease brain.* Mean values. Bars = SEM.

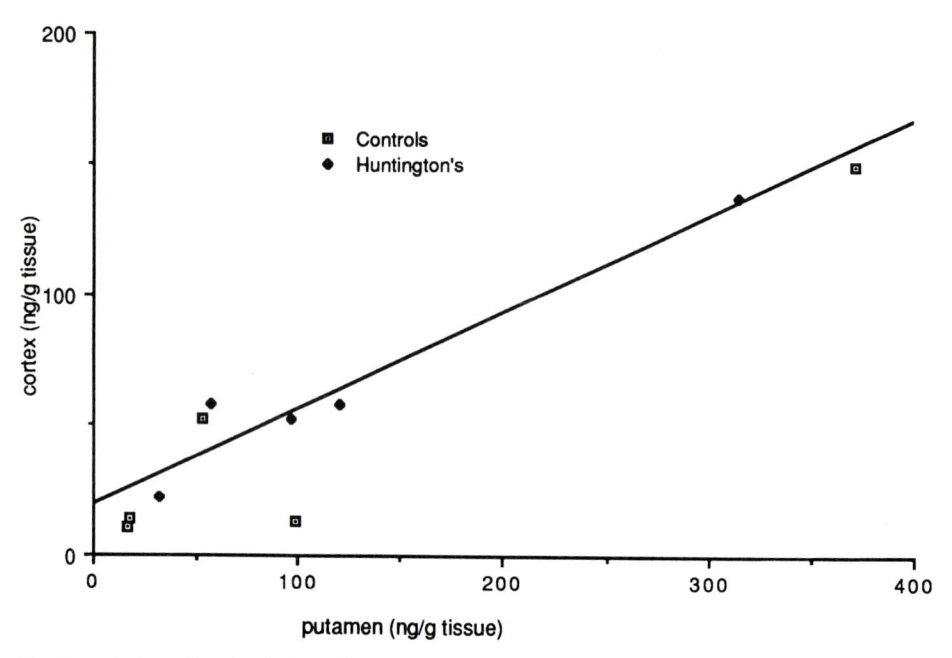

Fig. 3. *Correlation of quinolinic acid concentrations between brain regions.*

we can reach definitive conclusions regarding the role of QA in the aetiology of Huntington's disease.

Acknowledgement—This research was supported by the Association to Combat Huntington's Chorea.

References
1. Reynolds, G. P. & Pearson, S. J. (1987): Decreased glutamic acid and increased 5-hydroxytryptamine in Huntington's disease brain. *Neurosci. Lett.* **78**, 233–238.
2. Beal, M. F., Kowall, N. W., Ellison, D. W., Mazurek, M. F., Swartz, K. J. & Martin, J. B. (1986): Replication of the neurochemical characteristics of Huntington's disease. *Nature* **321**, 168–171.
3. Davies, S W. & Roberts, P. J. (1987): No evidence for preservation of somatostatin-containing neurons after intrastriatal injection of quinolinic acid. *Nature* **327**, 326–329.
4. Heyes, M. P., Garnett, E. S. & Brown, R. R. (1985): Normal excretion of quinolinic acid. *Life Sci.* **37**, 1811–1816.
5. Perry, T. L., Yong, V. W., Hansen, S., Kim, S. U., Kurlan, R. & Shoulson, I. (1987): A tissue culture evidence for a circulating neurotoxin in Huntington's chorea. *J. Neurol. Sci.* **78**, 139–150.
6. Foster, A. C., Vezzani, A., French, E. D. & Schwarcz, R. (1984): Kynurenic acid blocks neurotoxicity and seizures induced in rats by the related brain metabolite quinolinic acid. *Neurosci. Lett.* **48**, 273–278.
7. Reynolds, G. P., Pearson, S. J., Halket, J. & Sandler, M. (1988): Brain quinolinic acid in Huntington's disease. *J. Neurochem.* **50**, 1959–1960.
8. Wolfensberger, M., Amsler, U., Cuenod, M., Foster, A. C., Whetsell, W. O. & Schwarcz, R. (1983): Identification of quinolinic acid in rat and human brain tissue. *Neurosci. Lett.* **41**, 247–252.

40

CHOREA–ACANTHOCYTOSIS
(THE LEVINE-CRITCHLEY SYNDROME): AN UPDATE

E. M. R. Critchley

Department of Neurology, Royal Preston Hosiptal, Preston, Lancs, UK

Introduction

There are two major forms of neuro-acanthocytosis, namely the Bassen-Kornzweig syndrome[1] of abetalipoproteinaemia, retinitis pigmentosa and ataxia of the Friedreich type, and the normolipoproteinaemic form, since renamed chorea-acanthocytosis. Transient forms have been described[2,3] and Mars et al.[4] have described familial hypobetalipoproteinaemia with demyelination and acanthocytic cells *in vitro*.

The earliest example of chorea-acanthocytosis was probably that of a patient with Gilles de la Tourette syndrome and tongue biting described by Striner[5] in 1927. The first family was the Goode family of New England but many of the early reports of this family were misleading: Kuo & Bassett[6] stated that they had hypobetalipoproteinaemia, and Rovito & Pirone[7] entitled their report 'Acanthocytosis associated with schizophrenia'. The clinical features of this condition only became apparent after the papers of Estes et al.[8] and Levine et al.[9] The syndrome as a neurological disorder without abetalipoproteinaemia was first presented in a comprehensive manner by Critchley et al.[10,11] in their description of the Stevens family of Kentucky. The essential clinical features outlined have been substantiated by many additional case reports and post-mortem studies over the past 20 years.

Coexistent amyotrophy

Several other unusual manifestations of the syndrome have been described; thus Hardie & Marsden have three young males who presented with dystonia and acanthocytosis (to be published). However, the most striking additional feature has been that of amyotrophy in conjunction with chorea-acanthocytosis.[12–16] In order to see whether amyotrophy is an essential feature of the condition which had been previously overlooked, the two original families seen personally – the Stevens family[10,11] and the Simpson family of Lancashire[17] – have been re-examined with respect to their muscular status. In fact careful examination of these early patients, and of many others since, fails to reveal evidence of neurogenic atrophy or significant elevation of creatinine kinase. In the Stevens family, neuromuscular abnormalities were suspected since generalized weakness and fatiguability antedated the clinical presentation by 6–8 years, and of three members of the family who had died before the proband presented to the University of Kentucky Medical Center, two had had wasting and weight loss:

Z.S. died aged 31 after an illness beginning with seizures aged 25. Although she never actually lost consciousness she bit her tongue and cheek, had involuntary limb movements, dropped things and was forgetful. In the last two years of her life she lost weight from 150 lb to 90 lb, became emaciated and bedfast and had violent limb movements.

V.S.McK. died aged 26. Her illness began 2 years earlier after the birth of her child, who remains healthy. It started with tongue, lip and cheek biting. She had involuntary limb movements with 'drawing' and finger snapping. During the last six months of her illness she was bedfast and lost weight from 160 lb to 90 lb.

By contrast, J.S. (the proband), aged 29, his sisters E.S.T., aged 35, and E.L.S., who died aged 26, remained obese with absent reflexes but no evidence of muscle weakness or wasting. The proband was extensively examined at the University of Kentucky Medical Center and at the National Institutes of Health, Bethesda, Md. The creatinine kinase was 2.24 IU, muscle and nerve biopsies were normal and nerve conduction studies and electromyography, performed independently by Professor McQuillen and Dr King Engel were normal. Similar investigations on P.Si.[17] were also normal and electrophysiological studies were later confirmed in Professor Gilliatt's department at the National Hospital for Nervous Diseases, Queen Square, London. Her creatinine kinase levels were raised to 10 IU (normal 1.5 IU). Thus apart from slightly raised creatinine kinase, the neuromuscular investigations were negative.

Some neuromuscular involvement was described in the Goode family,[9] with features simulating Charcot-Marie-Tooth disease or limb girdle atrophy, and in the older patients described by Aminoff,[18,19] but the laboratory findings were mild and did not suggest amyotrophy.

Phenotypic variation

Phenotypic variation occurs throughout the neuro-acanthocytic syndromes. Within the Stevens family, from an inbred white community of Appalachian Kentucky, the fact that the niece of the proband had Friedreich's ataxia, deafness and a few acanthocytes could have occurred by chance. She was extensively investigated for abetalipoproteinaemia but the lipid levels were within the low normal range. A possible link case between the neuro-acanthocytic syndromes is Singer's patient[20] with abetalipoproteinaemia, who subsequently developed involuntary movements.[21] Abnormalities linked with the syndrome of chorea-acanthocytosis include Hallervorden-Spatz disease[22] and parkinsonism.[15] There have been yet further case reports of these associations.

Acanthocytes

In both families studied personally the affected members had between 30 and 40 per cent acanthocytosis in the peripheral blood. In the Goode family,[8] three patients had more than 10 per cent and six others had between 1.2 and 6.2 per cent. There are several unpublished reports of phenotypically-similar patients without evidence of acanthocytosis. The nature of the acanthocytic cells remains an enigma. Although there have been many detailed studies of the properties of the acanthocytic membranes there has been little advance on the paper of Betts et al.[23] showing increases in membrane fluidity induced at much lower concentrations of ADP than are normally required.

A few patients with chorea-acanthocytosis exhibit mild haemolysis.[16] Haemolysis is a feature of the acanthocytes of the McLeod syndrome which can be associated with a raised creatinine kinase, a definite but benign myopathy[24] and chorea-acanthocytosis. Whereas the mode of inheritance of chorea-acanthocytosis is primarily as an autosomal recessive gene, that of the McLeod syndrome is linked to the Kell blood group as an X-linked recessive with the genetic locus near that of Duchenne dystrophy on the short arm of the X chromosome.

Conclusions

The syndrome of chorea-acanthocytosis represents a major group of the neuro-acanthocytic disorders with both genetic and phenotypic variation. Inheritance is mostly as an autosomal recessive gene; that of the McLeod syndrome is related to the Kell blood group system with a distinctive genetic locus. The common neurological manifestation is a tic disorder. This is the primary clinical feature, though admittedly with some less obvious choreic manifestations. The association with amyotrophy is not invariable and may represent a spectrum of involvement determined by the presence of a linked gene. An equally definite but uncommon association is seen with Hallervorden-Spatz disease and phenotypic variation may account for the presence of dystonia, ataxia or parkinsonism. The percentage of acanthocytes present in the peripheral blood varies widely and does not appear to be causally related to the presence of neurological manifestations.

References

1 Bassen, F. A. & Kornzweig, A. L. (1950): Malformation of the erythrocytes in a case of atypical retinitis pigmentosa. *Blood* **5**, 381.
2 Gracey, M., Wilson, R. G. & Petersen, M. (1972): Transient acanthocytosis and hypobetalipoproteinaemia. *Austr. N.Z. J. Med.* **4**, 397–401.
3 Critchley, E. M. R. (1974): Acanthocytosis. *DM Thesis*. University of Oxford.
4 Mars, H., Lewis, L. A., Robertson, H. L., Butkus, A. & Williams, G. H. (1969): Familial hypo-β-lipoproteinaemia. *Am. J. Med.* **46**, 886–900.
5 Striner, E. (1927): Untersuchungen uber die postchoreatischen Motilitatss-sstorungen, insbesondere die Beziehungen der Chorea minor sum Tic. *Monatsschr. Psychiatr. Neurol.* **66**, 71–124.
6 Kuo, P. T. & Bassett, D. R. (1962): Blood and tissue lipids in a family with hypobetalipoproteinaemia. *Circulation* **22**, 660.
7 Rovito, D. A. & Pirone, F. J. (1963): Acanthocytes associated with schizophrenia. *Am. J. Psychiatry* **120**, 182–185.
8 Estes, J. W., Morley, T. J., Levine, I. M. & Emerson, C. P. (1967): A new hereditary acanthocytic syndrome. *Am. J. Med.* **42**, 865–881.
9 Levine, I. M., Estes, J. W. & Looney, J. M. (1968): Hereditary neurological disease with acanthocytosis. *Arch. Neurol.* **19**, 403–409.
10 Critchley, E. M. R., Clark, D. B. & Wikler, A. (1967): An adult form of acanthocytosis. *Trans. Am. Neurol. Assoc.* **92**, 132–137.
11 Critchley, E. M. R., Clark, D. B. & Wikler, A. (1968): Acanthocytosis and neurological disorder without abetalipoproteinaemia. *Arch. Neurol.* **18**, 134–140.
12 Kito, S., Hoga, E. Hiroshiga, Y., Matsumoto, N. & Miwa, S. (1980): A pedigree of amyotrophic chorea with acanthocytes. *Arch. Neurol.* **37**, 514–517.

13 Ohnishi, A., Sato, Y., Nagarat, T., Sakai, T., Iwashita, H., Kuriowa, Y., Nakamura, T. & Shida, K. (1981): Neurogenic muscular atrophy and low density of large myelinated fibres of sural nerve in chorea-acanthocytosis. *J. Neurol. Neurosurg. Psychiatry* **44**, 645–648.
14 Gross, K. B., Skrivanck, J. A., Carlson, K. C. & Kaufman, D. M. (1985): Familial amyotrophic chorea with acanthocytosis. *Arch. Neurol.* **42**, 753–756.
15 Spitz, M. C., Jankovic, J. & Killian, J. M. (1985): Familial tic disorder, parkinsonism, motor neuron disease and acanthocytosis: a new syndrome. *Neurology* **35**, 366–370.
16 Spencer, S. E., Walker, F. O. & Moore, S. A. (1987): Chorea amyotrophy with chronic haemolytic anaemia. *Neurology* **37**, 645–649.
17 Critchley, E. M. R., Betts, J. J., Nicholson, J. T. & Weatherall, D. J. (1970): Acanthocytosis, normolipoproteinaemia and multiple tics. *Postgrad. Med. J.* **46**, 698–701.
18 Aminoff, M. J. (1972): Acanthocytosis and neurological disease. *Brain* **95**, 749–760.
19 Lantos, P. L. & Aminoff, M. J. (1972): Fine structural changes in the sural nerve of patients with acanthocytosis. *Acta Neuropathol.* **22**, 257–263.
20 Singer, K., Fisher, B. & Perlstein, M. A. (1952): Acanthocytosis, a genetic erythrocytic malformation. *Blood* **7**, 577–591.
21 Jampell, R. S. & Falls, H. F. (1958): Atypical retinitis pigmentosa, acanthocytosis and heredodegenerative neuromuscular disease. *Arch. Opthalmol.* **59**, 818–820.
22 Swisher, C. N., Menkes, J. H., Cancilla, P. A. & Dodge, P. R. (1972): Coexistence of Hallervorden-Spatz disease with acanthocytosis. *Trans. Am. Neurol. Assoc.* **97**, 212–216.
23 Betts, J. J., Nicholson, J. T. & Critchley, E. M. R. (1970): Acanthocytosis with normolipoproteinaemia: biophysical aspects. *Postgrad. Med. J.* **46**, 702–707.
24 Swash, M., Schwartz, M. J., Carter, N. D., Heath, R., Leak, M. & Rogers, K. L. (1983): Benign X-linked myopathy with acanthocytosis (McLeod syndrome) *Brain* **106**, 717–733.

41

REFLEX RESPONSES AND MOVEMENT VELOCITY INDUCED BY HEAD ROTATION IN SPASMODIC TORTICOLLIS

N. Bathien, P. Rondont*, D. Bazalgette, and M. Zattara*

*Laboratoire de Physiologie, Fac. Méd. St-Antoine 27, rue Chaligny, 75571 Paris Cedex 12; and *Service de Neurologie, Centre R. Garcin 2 Bis B, rue d'Alésia, 75674 Paris Cedex 14, France*

Summary

To determine which muscles are involved in the spasm and disability in movement in spasmodic torticollis, we have investigated 41 patients and 10 control subjects. EMG activity from sternocleidomastoid and splenius muscles and kinematic features of head movement were recorded.

During passive head rotations, shortening reaction (Westphal phenomenon) of dystonic muscles was excessive and exhibited a tonic pattern of EMG activity. Stretch reflex was normal except in the severe stages of torticollis.

During active head rotations (rapid self-paced movement), EMG activity from agonist dystonic muscle was prolonged and the co-contraction activity from antagonist muscle was only recorded in the severe stages of torticollis. Velocity of movement towards the dystonic side was significantly reduced. This phenomenon was exaggerated in standing position as tested by the sitting/standing ratio.

Neck muscles were involved in the pattern of postural adjustment associated with the voluntary flexion of the upper limb. During the advanced stages of torticollis where the dystonic head posture was fixed by spasms (stages, 4,5) changes in postural activity were recorded in neck and lower limbs muscles.

Introduction

Head posture in spasmodic torticollis (ST) is maintained when the forces exerted by the agonist and antagonist muscle groups are in opposition. This implies that when force is applied, the head is displaced by an amount proportional to both the external force and the muscle tension.[1]

In this study, to determine the dystonic muscles and the disability in movement performance, neck muscle activity was investigated during passive and active head rotations. The postural activity associated with a voluntary movement of the upper limb was studied in a special section.

Patients and methods

The study was performed on 10 healthy subjects and 41 patients with essential spasmodic torticollis. Their clinical features are summarized in Table 1. They were classified from clinical examination into stages rated from 0 (no dystonia present) to 5 (extreme pulling with fixed posture, uncorrected by voluntary movement and an artificially applied antagonistic force) (Table 2).[2]

Table 1. *Distribution of patients according to the clinical stages.*

	\multicolumn{5}{c}{Clinical stages}
	0	1	2	3	4–5
Number	10	10	10	12	9
Age (years)	32.8	39.7	52.4	38.5	53.3
range	21–67	28–55	32–67	24–70	42–67
Sex	7M/3F	4M/6F	6M/4F	8M/4F	4M/5F
Duration of disease (months)	—	36	25.2	25.7	37
range	—	12–48	6–42	12–48	12–72

Table 2. *Clinical stages of essential spasmodic torticollis.*

0 = No dystonia present
1 = Occasional pulling
2 = Ocasional pulling with some prolonged spasms
3 = Prolonged spasms corrected by voluntary movements
4 = Fixed posture causing by spasms, corrected by 'geste antagonist'.
5 = Definite dystonic posture.

Head movement in terms of position was measured with a precision multi-turn potentiometer fixed on top of a helmet type device which did not hinder head movement in any way. The goniometer output was differentiated to provide a voltage proportional to angular velocity.

Electromyographic (EMG) activity was recorded using surface electrodes placed over the motor point of sternocleidomastoid (SCM) and splenius (Spl) muscles for head movements and over the anterior deltoid (D) muscle for upper limb flexion. The magnitude activity was rated from 1 to 5 according to the pattern of EMG activity during the moving and the contracted phases of movement (Fig. 1). These estimations were correlated with an integrated EMG. For the samples in Fig. 1 they were respectively : grade 1 = 1.5 mV.sec, grade 2 = 8.9 mV.sec, grade 3 = 37.3 mV.sec, grade 4 = 66.5 mV.sec, grade 5 = 86.4 mV.sec.

Head rotations were made from neutral position to dystonic side and opposite side. Active movements (head rotations or upper limb elevations) were fast, self-controlled

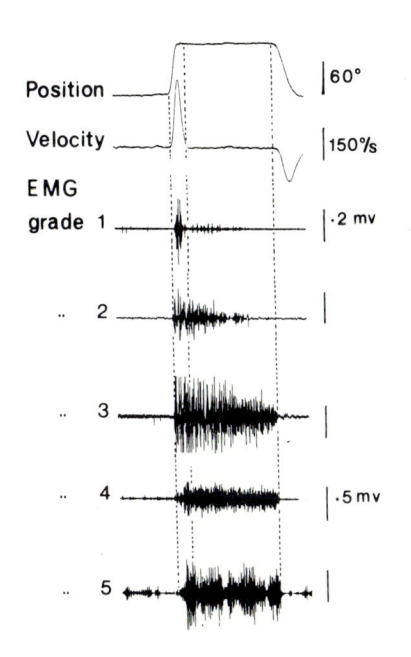

Fig. 1. *Estimation of response amplitude (EMG scale) induced by head rotation according to recorded EMG activity during the moving and contracted phase of movement.*

movements. Subjects were urged to perform 'as fast as possible'. The movements were recorded in both sitting and standing postures.

Results

Shortening reactions and stretch reflexes of neck muscles induced by passive head rotations

Passive head rotation induces a shortening movement from ipsilateral Spl and contralateral SCM muscles, and a stretching of their antagonists. The data collected from 10 healthy subjects and 41 patients with essential spasmodic torticollis (ST) are summarized in Fig. 2. Of the muscles analysed, EMG activity from SCM muscle was chosen for convenience. Control subjects (stage 0) exhibited no activity or a phasic EMG activity during passive shortening of the SCM muscle. The amplitude of the shortening reaction of all patients with ST was higher. The EMG pattern was tonic. Shortening reactions of contralateral SCM muscle were abnormal only in the severe stages (stages 3,4–5) of ST (Fig. 2A).

In the same patients, a tonic stretch reflex activity was recorded from dystonic SCM muscle and its antagonist in the most severe case of ST (stage 4–5).

EMG activity of neck muscles induced by active head rotations

Fast limb movements in man are characterized by a bi- or triphasic pattern of activation in agonist and antagonist muscles. This may be recorded even in patients with complete limb deafferentation.[3] The same pattern was found in the neck muscles during fast self-spaced head rotations (Fig. 3).

In patients with torticollis, we confirmed that prolonged, excessive activity is present during voluntary movement in agonist dystonic muscle (Fig. 3A).

A co-contraction with excessive antagonist muscle activity appeared more frequently in the advanced stages of torticollis. This indicates that antagonist muscle tone is abnormal.

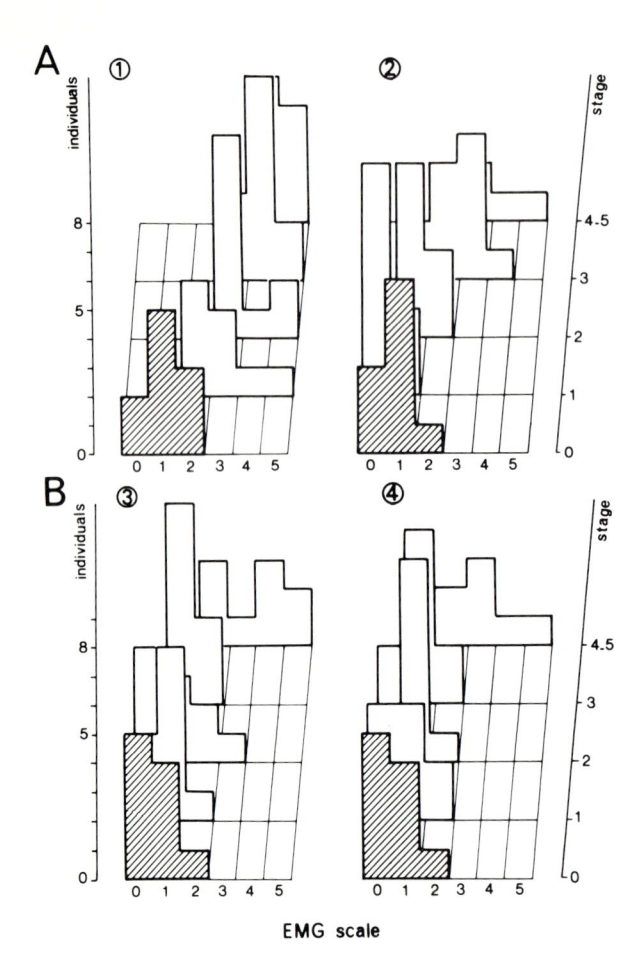

Fig. 2. *Passive head rotation: histograms of response amplitude (EMG scale) from dystonic muscle (1 & 3) and contralateral muscle (2 & 4) of control subjects and patients with different stages of torticollis. The shaded figures are recorded from healthy subjects (stage 0). In this case, EMG activity was recorded from sternocleidomastoid muscle. (A) Shortening reaction: amplitude of response from dystonic muscles is increased and exhibits a tonic pattern of EMG activity. (B) Stretch reflex: the tonic pattern of EMG activity is recorded only in the severe stages of torticollis (stage 4–5).*

The phenomenon was confirmed by head rotation towards the opposite side (Fig. 3B). In this condition, the EMG bursts of antagonist SCM of dystonic muscle fixed by spasms (stages 3, 4–5) were prolonged and exhibited a tonic pattern.

Kinematic properties of active head rotations

Patients with ST in clinical stage 1 to 3 could make voluntary head rotations. The peak velocities of rapid self-paced movements are presented in Fig. 4. The velocity of head rotation towards the dystonic side was significantly reduced. Its mean value determined from patients with stage 2 and 3 ST (n = 20) was 207.2 ± 13.3°/sec (mean ± SEM) as opposed to 325.0 ± 7.1°/sec for rotation towards the opposite side. There was no change in velocity for movements recorded from control subjects (stage 0). The correlation between movement velocity and the clinical stages of torticollis was only significant for rotation from the neutral towards the dystonic side (Fig. 4)

The postural effect on torticollis was studied by comparison of head movements performed in sitting and standing position. In control subjects (stage 0), the velocity of head rotations performed in a standing position was faster, as was recorded for movements towards the normal side of torticollis patients. The phenomenon was reversed for movements towards the dystonic side. They were slower and the sitting-standing ratio of

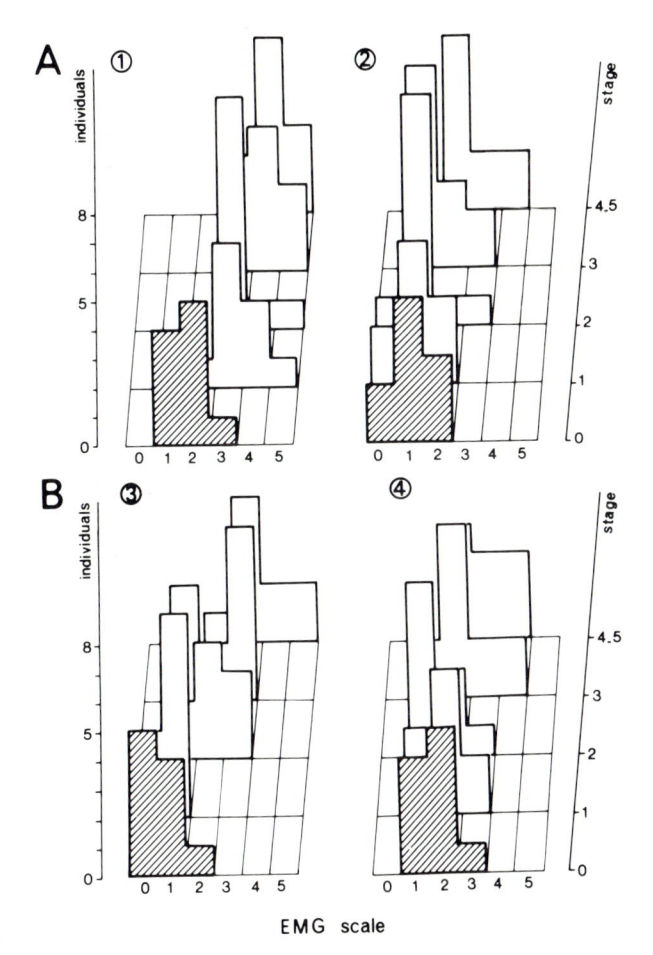

Fig. 3. *Active head rotation: histograms of response amplitude (EMG scale) from dystonic muscle (1 & 3) and contralateral muscle (2 & 4) of subjects and patients with different stages of torticollis. Shaded histograms are from healthy subjects (stage 0). EMG activity was recorded from sternocleidomastoid muscle. (A) Rotation towards the dystonic side: dystonic muscles are the agonists for the movement. (B) Rotation towards the opposite side: dystonic muscles are the antagonists for the movement.*

movement velocity was significantly greater than 1.0. The correlation between this ratio and the clinical stages was significantly positive ($r = 0.806$, $df = 40$, $P < 0.01$).

Neck muscles in posturo-kinetic organization during the early phase of voluntary upper limb movement

It was shown in erect subjects that prior to (and during) a voluntary movement of the upper limb there was a sequence of changes in EMG activity of lower limb, pelvis and trunk muscles.[4-6]

These postural adjustments were organized according to specific patterns. They appeared to counteract the imbalance caused by the forthcoming voluntary movement.

It was confirmed that, in control subjects (n = 5), the earliest changes in EMG activity induced by unilateral upper limb elevations (UF) occurred in the biceps femoris of the ipsilateral side (Fig. 5 – stage 0). These changes preceded activity in deltoid muscle by as much as 54.0 ± 5.8 msec (mean ± SEM). Meanwhile, the first postural activity recorded from neck muscles appeared after the onset of deltoid activity. This occurred in the two sternocleidomastoid muscles and induced no change in head position. During bilateral upper limb elevation (BF), the postural pattern recorded from SCM and biceps femoris appeared to be an integration of the UF movements. EMG activity from SCM increased in

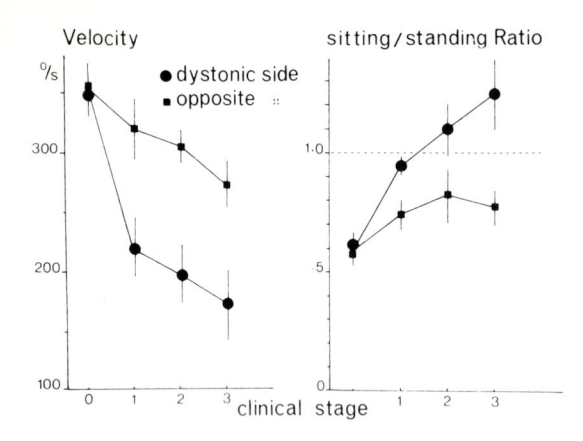

Fig. 4. *Movement velocity and effect of posture in relation to clinical stages.* Peak velocity of active head rotation from the neutral to dystonic opposite sides and its sitting/standing ratio are represented with mean ± 2 SEM values. The correlation is only significant for movement towards the dystonic side (velocity : $r = -0.777$, $df = 40$, $P < 0.01$; sitting/standing ratio : $r = -0.806$, $df = 40$, $P > 0.01$).

amplitude but the timing remained the same. The anticipatory component of postural EMG activity from biceps femoris decreased significantly from UF to BF condition.

Patients with spasmodic torticollis exhibited an abnormal posture of the head induced by dystonic activities from neck muscles. In patients with clinical stage 1, there was only occasional pulling of the head (Table 2). The postural activities recorded from SCM and biceps femoris associated with upper limb movement were similar to healthy subjects (Fig. 5, stage 1).

In patients with clinical stages 4 and 5, the change in head position was more definite and the abnormal posture was fixed by prolonged spasms from neck muscles. We recorded another pattern of postural adjustment. The tonic EMG activity from SCM exhibited systematically a decrease in its pattern prior to the onset of deltoid activity induced by the raising movement of the upper limb. The SCM silence was terminated by a rebound of

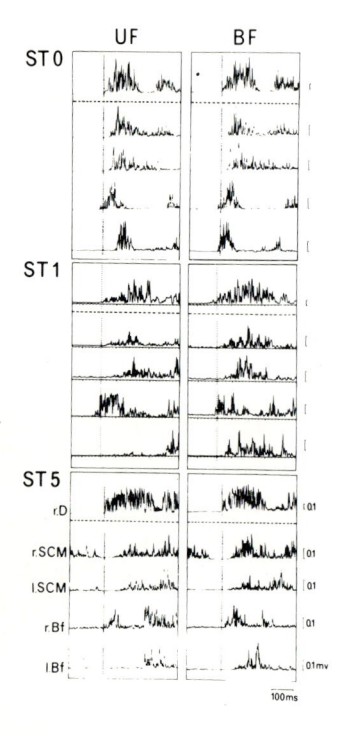

Fig. 5. *Postural activity of neck muscles associated with voluntary upper limb movements in patients with spasmodic torticollis.* ST0 = control subject; ST1 = clinical stage 1; ST5 = clinical stage 5. EMG activity was recorded from : D, anterior portion of deltoid; Bf, biceps femoris; SCM, sternocleidomastoid muscle; r, right side and l, left side. Voluntary movements were UF, unilateral upper limb flexion and BF, bilateral upper limb flexion. Note the changes in postural activity in Bf and SCM muscles when the dystonic head posture is fixed (ST5).

EMG activity. In the ipsilateral biceps femoris, the postural activity started after the onset of deltoid activity, in UF and BF conditions (Fig. 5 – stage 5).

These data indicate that neck muscles are involved in postured activities associated with upper limb movements. A change in their pattern provokes a reorganization of the postural activity at a distal level.

Discussion

In their EMG studies of dystonia, Hoefer & Putnam,[7] Herz & Glaser,[8] Yanagisawa & Goto[9] and Rothwell et al.[10] all observed a tonic, non-reciprocal pattern of activity in agonist and antagonist muscles during any voluntary or postural contraction. Stretch reflexes were not enhanced but frequently an excessive shortening reaction (Westphal phenomenon) was observed. We have confirmed all of these observations in a group of 41 patients with spasmodic torticollis. We pointed out a correlation between these physiological abnormalities and the clinical stages of this kind of dystonia.

In patients with spasmodic torticollis, we observed that an increased shortening reaction from dystonic muscle was recorded in all stages, while the stretch reflex was abnormal only in the severe stages (stages 4, 5). During active head rotations, EMG activity from agonist dystonic muscle was prolonged and co-contraction activity from antagonist muscle was only recorded in the advanced stages of the disease.

Functionally, velocity of movement to the dystonic side was significantly reduced and the postural effect on torticollis can be tested by its sitting/standing ratio.

The major result of our investigation of head movement in spasmodic torticollis was the finding that shortening reaction was the best feature to localize the muscles involved in dystonic spasms, and velocity of active head rotation indicated the disability caused by the disease.

References

1. Bizzi, E., Chapple, W. & Hogan, N. (1982): Mechanical properties of muscles. Implications for motor control. *TINS* **5**, 395–398.
2. Rondot, P., Bathien, N. & Ziegler, M. (1988): *Les mouvements anormaux*, p 208. Paris: Masson.
3. Hallett, M., Shahani, B. T. & Young, R. (1975): EMG analysis of stereotyped voluntary movements in man. *J. Neurol. Neurosurg. Psychiatry* **38**, 1154–1162.
4. Belenkii, Y. Y., Gurfinkel, V. & Paltsev, Y. I. (1967): Elements of control of voluntary movements. *Biofizika* **12**, 135–141.
5. Marsden, C. D., Merton, P. A. & Morton, H. B. (1978): Anticipatory postural responses in the human subject. *J. Physiol. (Lond.)* **275**, 47P–48P.
6. Bouisset, S. & Zattara, M. (1981): A sequence of postural movements precedes voluntary movement. *Neurosci. Lett.* **22**, 263–270.
7. Hoefer, P. F. A. & Putnam, T. J. (1940): Action potentials of muscles in athetosis and Sydenham chorea. *Arch. Neurol. Psychiatry* **44**, 517–531.
8. Herz, E. & Glaser, G. H. (1949): Spasmodic torticollis II. Clinical evaluation. *Arch. Neurol. Psychiatry* **61** 227–239.
9. Yanagisawa, N. & Goto, A. (1971): Dystonia musculorum deformans. Analysis of electro-myography. *J. Neurol. Sci.* **A3**, 39–65.
10. Rothwell, J. C., Obeso, J. A., Day, B. L. & Marsden, C. D. (1983): Pathophysiology of dystonia. In: *Motor control mechanism in health and disease*, ed J. E. Desmedt, pp 851–863. New York: Raven Press.

42

OROFACIAL DYSKINESIA: D-1/D-2 DOPAMINE RECEPTORS IN RODENTS, AND FAMILIAL/OBSTETRIC CORRELATES OF TARDIVE DYSKINESIA IN SCHIZOPHRENIA

John L. Waddington, Angela M. Murray,
Eadbhard O'Callaghan* and Conall Larkin*

*Department of Clinical Pharmacology, Royal College of Surgeons in Ireland, St. Stephen's Green, Dublin 2; and *Cluain Mhuire Family Centre, Newtownpark Avenue, Blackrock, Co. Dublin, Republic of Ireland*

Summary

The problem of disorders of orofacial movement was addressed using a multidisciplinary approach. In rats, acute perioral dyskinesia was most readily induced by stimulation of D-1 dopamine receptors during concurrent attenuation of tonic activity through D-2 receptors, suggesting an oppositional D-1:D-2 interaction in the expression of this behaviour. In schizophrenic patients, the emergence of tardive orofacial dyskinesia during long-term neuroleptic treatment was associated with poor cognitive function, a family history of schizophrenia and an absence of a history of obstetric complications, suggesting an intimate relationship with features of the illness for which the treatment was prescribed. It is argued that such animal studies can provide much useful information on the interaction between D-1 and D-2 receptors in the regulation of orofacial movement, but may not reveal the pathophysiological substrate of tardive dyskinesia.

Introduction

Disorders of orofacial (buccal-lingual-masticatory) movement can occur in a number of clinical situations, including long-term treatment with neuroleptic drugs (tardive dyskinesia), levodopa therapy for Parkinson's disease (levodopa dyskinesia), and in Huntington's chorea and other neurodegenerative brain disorders. However, though abnormalities in dopamine-mediated extrapyramidal motor function have been widely considered in relation to each of these disorders, their overlapping phenomenology does not necessarily indicate a common pathophysiological mechanism. Our studies seek to address two complementary issues: (1) what pharmacological manipulations of dopaminergic function produce orofacial dyskinesia in animals? and (2) what factors distinguish schizophrenic patients who show tardive orofacial dyskinesia during long-term neuroleptic (dopamine antagonist) therapy from those who do not?

Animal studies

There has been a debate on whether tardive orofacial dyskinesia seen in clinical neuroleptic-treated populations can be reproduced in animals given such drugs for a substantial period of their adult life.[1,2] Additionally, it has remained contentious whether those behaviours which have been noted to emerge in such circumstances have any basis in the degree of supersensitivity of brain dopamine receptors which occurs as an adaptive response to their long-term blockade.[3] An alternative strategy is to identify drug challenges/combinations which might induce such a syndrome acutely, and then investigate its phenomenological and pharmacological similarity to the situation which occurs with long-term neuroleptic treatment. It has been reported that acute, selective stimulation of D-1 dopamine receptors in rodents with SK & F 38393 can induce perioral dyskinesia.[4] In our own studies, we have not found this to be a reliable response but have noted it to become more prominent in aged animals, which have a reduced number of D-2 but not D-1 receptors (ie, increased D-1:D-2 ratio).[5] As part of continuing work to characterize what appear to be functional interactions between D-1 and D-2 receptor systems in the regulation of behaviour,[6] we describe selective dopaminergic manipulations resulting in the expression of orofacial dyskinesia.

Methods

Young adult male Sprague-Dawley rats were challenged subcutaneously with the new high potency selective D-1 agonist SK&F 77434,[7] the high potency selective D-2 agonist LY 163502,[8] or their vehicle; this followed 30 min pretreatments with the selective D-1 antagonist *R*-SK&F 83566,[9] the selective D-2 antagonist *R*-piquindone,[9] or their vehicle. Over a 1 h period they were observed using a rapid time-sampling behavioural check-list technique, as previously described,[10] which generates 'counts' for each individual element of behaviour evident.

Results

The D-1 agonist SK&F 77434 induced episodes of non-stereotyped sniffing, and a prominent grooming response that is described elsewhere;[11] at no dose between 0.03 and 3.75 mg/kg did it induce perioral movements. Following pretreatment with the selective D-1 antagonist *R*-SK&F 83566, this sniffing response was blocked (as was grooming). Conversely, after pretreatment with the selective D-2 antagonist *R*-piquindone, these responses were also attenuated, but vacuous chewing was additionally 'released'; this behaviour consisted of masticatory jaw movements which were not directed onto any physical material, and their manifestation was enantioselective for pretreatment with *R*-but not *S*-piquindone (Table 1).

The D-2 agonist LY 163502 also induced episodes of non-stereotyped sniffing, with some increase in locomotion that is described elsewhere;[11] at no dose between 0.003 and 10.0 mg/kg did it induce vacuous chewing or any other atypical behaviour. Following

Table 1. Effects of selective D-2 and D-1 antagonists on the induction of behaviours by the D-1 agonist SK&F 77434 and the D-2 agonist LY 163502. Results are means (SEM), n = 8.

Drug	Dose (mg/kg)	Sniffing	Vacuous chewing	Jerking
SK&F 77434	0.75	14.8(2.9)	1.2(0.5)	0(0)
+S-piquindone	0.75	16.1(3.0)	1.0(0.4)	0(0)
+R-piquindone	0.03	14.4(2.0)	1.1(0.5)	0(0)
	0.15	15.5(2.4)	3.1(0.8)	0(0)
	0.75	5.5(2.0)*	7.8(2.9)*	0(0)
LY 163502	0.05	25.4(1.9)	2.0(0.7)	0.1(0.1)
+S-SK&F 83566	0.75	22.9(2.0)	2.6(0.8)	0.2(0.2)
+R-SK&F 83566	0.03	17.4(2.0)*	3.0(0.7)	0.5(0.4)
	0.15	5.6(1.5)*	2.0(0.6)	3.5(1.0)*
	0.75	2.6(0.9)*	1.0(0.3)	4.6(1.1)*

*$p < 0.05$ vs control

pretreatment with *R*-piquindone, this sniffing response was blocked (as was locomotion). Conversely, after pretreatment with *R*-SK&F 83566, these responses were also attenuated, but myoclonic jerking was additionally 'released'; this behaviour consisted of brief, episodic jerking movements of the limbs or of the whole body, and their manifestation was enantioselective for pretreatment with *R*- but not *S*-SK&F 83566 (Table 1).

Discussion

In the initial report on the induction of perioral dyskinesia by the D-1 agonist SK&F 38393, it was noted that a similar effect was induced by the D-2 antagonists sulpiride and spiperone;[4] this effect of SK&F 38393 was potentiated by pretreatment with spiperone and attenuated by treatment with the D-2 agonist quinpirole. These initial observations were made before the availability of the first selective D-1 antagonists, SCH 23390 and *R*-SK&F 83566, but the authors were subsequently able to show that such responses to SK&F 38393 were indeed blocked by a D-1 antagonist.[12]

We did not find SK&F 38393 to induce such a perioral syndrome readily, but it was much more reliably induced in aged rats having a D-1:D-2 receptor ratio higher than that of their more typical young adult counterparts through selective loss of D-2 receptors.[5] Similarly, perioral dyskinesia induced by SK&F 38393 was potentiated in a strain of rat having a reduced density of D-2 but not of D-1 receptors.[12] Induction of perioral dyskinesia by SK&F 38393 has been noted by others,[13] who have also reported it to be inhibited by quinpirole. In the studies reported here, we find the new high potency selective D-1 agonist SK&F 77434, like 38393, to have little activity in inducing perioral dyskinesia when given as sole treatment, but to induce such behaviour readily when tonic activity through D-2 receptors is blocked by pretreatment with *R*-piquindone. No such behaviour was induced by the selective D-1 agonist given as sole treatment or after pretreatment with either D-1 or D-2 antagonists. However, a syndrome of myoclonic jerking behaviour became apparent when D-2 receptors were stimulated and tonic activity through D-1 receptors blocked by pretreatment with *R*-SK&F 83566.

We conclude that perioral dyskinesia is most readily induced by D-1 receptor stimulation during concurrent attenuation of D-2 dopaminergic tone. Thus, there appears to be an inverse/oppositional interaction between D-1 and D-2 systems in the initiation and expression of this atypical behaviour, which may have a parallel in the inverse/oppositional D-1:D-2 interactions evident in relation to the regulation of adenylate cyclase activity.[6] Such an inverse/oppositional interaction also appears evident in relation to atypical myoclonic jerking behaviour. This direction of functional interaction between D-1 and D-2 receptor systems is clearly opposite to that regulating typical dopaminergic behaviours such as sniffing; here, reduction of D-2 tone attenuates the expression of D-1 agonist-induced sniffing, and *vice versa*, consistent with a co-operative/synergistic D-1:D-2 interaction in their regulation.[6] We have recently reviewed behavioural, neurochemical and neurophysiological correlates of what appear to be at least two distinct forms of D-1:D-2 interaction which can be evident in relation to the regulation of particular elements/composites of behaviour.[6,11]

How are we to relate the profile of acute D-1:D-2 interactions regulating perioral dyskinesia in animals to clinical situations such as tardive orofacial dyskinesia? These opposing interactions have been offered as an acute animal model of tardive dyskinesia, but would require evidence of increased D-1 and reduced D-2 dopaminergic activity in persons so affected. However, the most recent studies continue to suggest that D-2 density is increased (most likely reflecting their neuroleptic history) and D-1 density unaltered or even reduced in post-mortem brains of schizophrenic patients.[14] Additionally, comparison of D-1 and D-2 receptor characteristics in the brains of schizophrenic patients rated in life for the presence or absence of dyskinesia fails to reveal any systematic differences.[15] This raises a final problem for such putative acute animal models of tardive dyskinesia. The clinical disorder is a highly variable one, affecting only a proportion of patients receiving long-term neuroleptic treatment, yet the acute animal phenomena are often highly consistent. This suggests that such animal studies can provide much useful information on the interaction between D-1 and D-2 receptors in the regulation of orofacial movement, but may not reveal the pathophysiological substrate of tardive dyskinesia.

Clinical studies

Much effort has been directed towards identifying vulnerability factors which distinguish patients who show the emergence of typical orofacial dyskinesia. Neither the duration/vigour of neuroleptic treatment, nor dopamine receptor characteristics in post-mortem brain tissue, reliably distinguish schizophrenic patients with and without dyskinesia. Recently, there has been renewed interest in the older hypothesis that patients with organic brain dysfunction might be at particular risk for tardive dyskinesia. Thus an expanding body of evidence indicates that schizophrenic patients with tardive dyskinesia are characterized by greater cognitive dysfunction, suggesting some association with abnormalities in cerebral morphology.[16] Older patients with tardive dyskinesia show an excess of developmental reflexes which is consistent not only with cerebral degeneration, but also with a failure to develop normal cerebral structure and function.[17] To address these issues further we have studied obstetric complications, known to be over-represented in schizophrenia,[18,19] and family history of psychiatric disorder, as two potential antecedents of such processes.

Methods

Forty-five outpatients attending a depot neuroleptic clinic and satisfying DSM-III criteria for schizophrenia consented to participation in the study. They were assessed using the Abnormal Involuntary Movement Scale, and evaluated neuropsychologically using Trail Making Tests A & B. Classical buccal-lingual-masticatory dyskinesia was considered present if there were at least mild but clearly abnormal involuntary movements of one or more orofacial regions. Their biological mothers were interviewed for the obstetric history of each patient, which was evaluated using the Obstetric Complications (OC) Scale of Lewis & Murray;[19] OCs were considered present (OC$^+$) if there was at least one 'definite' complication. Additionally, a family tree was constructed for each patient, for the identification of psychiatric disorders in relatives by the Family History Method.

Results

It was possible to validate maternal recollections of obstetric history by reference to maternity hospital records in 17 of 45 cases. Among these, there was complete concordance for the absence (n = 10) or presence (n = 7) of at least one 'definite' OC when the Scale was applied to each source of information (Kappa = 1.0, Z = 4.12, $P < 0.001$). On the basis of maternal interviews, 15 of the 45 patients had a history of OCs. Those with OCs were less likely to have a family history of psychiatric disorder using both narrow (schizophrenia in a first degree relative: 14 of 30 OC$^-$ patients vs 2/15 OC$^+$, $P = 0.065$) and broad (schizophrenia, affective disorder or completed suicide in a first or second degree relative: 24/30 OC$^-$ patients vs 6/15 OC$^+$, $P < 0.02$) criteria; they also showed a younger age at onset of their illness (20.6 ± 4.8 SD vs 24.0 ± 5.5 years, $P < 0.05$).

Those patients with and without tardive orofacial dyskinesia were of indistinguishable age, sex distribution and age at first illness. Those with orofacial dyskinesia were less likely to have had a history of OCs, and were more likely to have a family history of schizophrenia in a first degree relative (Table 2). They showed poorer performance on neuropsychological testing, particularly in Trailmaking Test B, and, curiously, had significantly more siblings than their counterparts without orofacial dyskinesia.

Table 2. *Characteristics of schizophrenic patients with (TD$^+$) and without (TD$^-$) tardive orofacial dyskinesia. Results are means (SEM).*

Variable	TD$^-$	TD$^+$
Number (male/female)	33(21 M, 12 F)	12(8 M, 4 F)
Age	31.1(1.3)	35.7(1.5)
Age at first illness	22.3(1.0)	24.4(1.1)
Obstetric complications	15/33	0/12*
Family history	8/33	8/12
Number of siblings	4.1(0.4)	6.0(0.9)*
Birth order	2.8(0.4)	3.9(0.7)
Trail Making Test A	45.8(2.4)^a	63.6(9.8)*
Trail Making Test B	101.4(7.3)^a	173.5(20.2)**

*$P < 0.05$, **$P < 0.001$ vs TD$^-$. ^{a} one patient did not complete neuropsychological testing, ∴ n = 32.

Discussion

A genetic component to the aetiology of schizophrenia is widely accepted,[20] and there is a body of evidence that schizophrenic patients are more likely to have a history of OCs than patients with other psychiatric disorders or normal subjects. It is presumed that OCs result in some form of brain dysfunction, and cerebral anoxia is the most widely considered pathophysiological process.[18,19] Our finding that OCs are more common in patients without a family history of psychiatric disorder appears consistent with both 'stress-diathesis' and 'organic phenocopy' hypotheses for gene-environment relationships.[18] OCs appear associated with a younger age at onset of diagnostic symptoms, suggesting that early cerebral dysfunction may be a precipitating factor within various formulations of a neurodevelopmental model for schizophrenia.[21,22]

Some schizophrenic patients are known to show abnormalities in cerebral structure,[16] and it has been argued that they may be most evident in patients with a history of OCs in the absence of a family history of psychiatric disorder.[19,22] We here find again that schizophrenic patients with tardive orofacial dyskinesia are characterized by poorer cognitive function.[16] Therefore, if such cognitive impairment reflects structural abnormalities, patients with tardive dyskinesia might be expected to have a greater likelihood of a history of OCs. Our results are entirely opposite to the predictions of such an analysis; patients with tardive dyskinesia were less likely to have a history of OCs and more likely to have a family history of schizophrenia. This suggests that a strong genetic loading for schizophrenia carries with it a raised vulnerability to this movement disorder.

Regarding genetic aspects of tardive dyskinesia, concordance for its presence or absence has been noted in each of eight sibling or mother-son pairs with a variety of neuroleptic-treated disorders.[23] Similarly, there is a report of concordance for tardive dyskinesia in each of two schizophrenic brothers, one with marked and the other with mild cognitive impairment.[24] However, one group has reported a reduced likelihood of a family history of schizophrenia in patients with tardive dyskinesia,[25] and another has found a greater likelihood of a family history of affective disorder in such patients.[26] Our findings of a greater likelihood of a family history of schizophrenia and of poor cognitive function in patients with tardive dyskinesia is complemented by previous reports that patients with a family history of schizophrenia have poorer cognitive function than do sporadic (non-familial) cases.[27]

If we assume that poor cognitive function in schizophrenia is related in some way to structural brain abnormalities, there appears to be some element of paradox in relation to the above issues: on the one hand, there may be some association between poor cognitive function and family history of schizophrenia; on the other hand, there may be some association between abnormal cerebral structure and non-familial schizophrenia. The answer may reside in how robust these various putative associations prove to be, and in the nature of the relationship between cognitive dysfunction and abnormalities in cerebral morphology; this now appears far more complex than originally envisaged.[28] A more consistent finding is the association between orofacial dyskinesia and cognitive deficit, which is evident not only in schizophrenia but also in bipolar affective disorder.[17] Within schizophrenia, the present report indicates that status in relation to an obstetric complications-family history dichotomy may be an additional, and presumably neurodevelopmental, element in vulnerability to tardive dyskinesia during subsequent long-term neuroleptic treatment.

Conclusion

Clearly, the extrapyramidal motor system plays an important role in orofacial movements, and dopaminergic function is an important regulator of this system. Our animal studies readily confirm this, and further indicate that D-1 and D-2 receptor systems may interact critically to determine orofacial function. However, there is an absence of direct evidence for, and some weight of evidence against, any simple dopaminergic receptor supersensitivity/hyperfunction hypothesis for the pathophysiology of tardive orofacial dyskinesia. Pharmacological effects on dopaminergic neurons can influence orofacial movements, but this need not mean that dysfunction of such neurons is the basis of this movement disorder. Rather, our clinical data suggest further that aspects of the disorder for which treatment is given, rather than of the treatment itself, are critical determinants of vulnerability to tardive orofacial dyskinesia. At least some component of such vulnerability appears to antecede neuroleptic treatment and may imply a neurodevelopmental perspective to this disorder.

Acknowledgements—This work was supported by the Health Research Board, the St. John of God Order, and the Royal College of Surgeons in Ireland. We thank Lilly, Roche, and Smith Kline & French for experimental agents, Drs S. W. Lewis & R. M. Murray for making their Obstetric Complications Scale available to us, and Drs J. Strong and M. Darling, Masters of the National Maternity and Rotunda Hospitals, Dublin.

References

1 Rupniak, N. M. J., Jenner, P. & Marsden, C. D. (1986): Acute dystonia induced by neuroleptic drugs. *Psychopharmacology* **88**, 403–419.
2 Waddington, J. L. & Molloy, A. G. (1987): The status of late-onset vacuous chewing/perioral movements during long term neuroleptic treatment in rodents: tardive dyskinesia or dystonia? *Psychopharmacology* **91**, 136–137.
3 Waddington, J. L., Cross, A. J., Gamble, S. J. & Bourne, R. C. (1983): Spontaneous orofacial dyskinesia and dopaminergic function in rats after six months of neuroleptic treatment. *Science* **220**, 530–532.
4 Rosengarten, H., Schweitzer, J. W. & Friedhoff, A. J. (1983): Induction of oral dyskinesias in naive rats by D-1 stimulation. *Life Sci.* **33**, 2479–2482.
5 Molloy, A. G., O'Boyle, K. M. & Waddington, J. L. (1986): The D-1 dopamine receptor and ageing. In *The neurobiology of dopamine systems*, eds W. Winlow & R. Markstein, pp 104–107. Manchester: Manchester University Press.
6 Waddington, J. L. & O'Boyle, K. M. (1987): The D-1 dopamine receptor and the search for its functional role: from neurochemistry to behaviour. *Reviews in the Neurosciences* **1**, 157–184.
7 Murray, A. M. & Waddington, J. L. (1988): Functional distinction between SK&F 77434 and LY 163502, new putative D-1 and D-2 dopamine receptor agonists. *Irish J. Med. Sci.* **157**, 17.
8 Bymaster, F. P., Reid, L. R., Nichols, C. L., Kornfeld, E. C. & Wong, D. T. (1986): Elevation of acetylcholine levels in striatum of rat brain by LY 163502. *Life Sci.* **38**, 317–322.
9 O'Boyle, K. M. & Waddington, J. L. (1984): Identification of the enantiomers of SK&F 83566 as specific and stereoselective antagonists at the striatal D-1 dopamine receptor: comparisons with the D-2 enantioselectivity of Ro 22–1319. *Eur. J. Pharmacol.* **106**, 219–220.
10 Molloy, A. G. & Waddington, J. L. (1987): Assessment of grooming and other behavioural responses to the D-1 dopamine receptor agonist SK&F 38393 and its R- and S-enantiomers in the intact adult rat. *Psychopharmacology* **92**, 164–168.
11 Waddington, J. L., Murray, A. M. & O'Boyle, K. M. (1988): New selective D-1 and D-2 dopamine receptor agonists as further probes for behavioural interactions between D-1 and D-2 dopamine systems. In *Pharmacology and functional regulation of dopaminergic neurons*, eds P. Beart, G. Woodruff & D. Jackson, pp. 117–123 London: MacMillan Press.
12 Rosengarten, H., Schweitzer, J. W. & Friedhoff, A. J. (1986): Selective dopamine D-2 receptor reduction enhances a D-1 mediated oral dyskinesia in rats. *Life Sci.* **39**, 29–35.
13 Johansson, P., Levin, E., Gunne, L. M. & Ellison, G. (1987): Opposite effects of a D-1 and D-2 agonist on oral movements in rats. *Eur. J. Pharmacol.* **134**, 83–88.
14 Waddington, J. L (1988): Therapeutic potential of selective D-1 dopamine receptor agonists and antagonists in psychiatry and neurology. *Gen. Pharmacol.* **19**, 55–60.
15 Waddington, J. L. (1985): Further anomalies in the dopamine receptor supersensitivity hypothesis of tardive dyskinesia. *Trends Neurosci.* **8**, 200.
16 Waddington, J. L. (1987): Tardive dyskinesia in schizophrenia and other disorders: associations with ageing, cognitive dysfunction and structural brain pathology in relation to neuroleptic exposure. *Hum. Psychopharmacol.* **2**, 11–22.

17 Youssef, H. A. & Waddington, J. L. (1988): Primitive (developmental) reflexes and diffuse cerebral dysfunction in schizophrenia and bipolar affective disorder: over-representation in patients with tardive dyskinesia. *Biol. Psychiatry* **23**, 791–796.
18 McNeil, T. F. & Kaij, L. (1978): Obstetric factors in the development of schizophrenia: complications in the birth of preschizophrenics and in reproduction by schizophrenic parents. In *The nature of schizophrenia*, eds L. C. Wynne, R. L. Cromwell & S. Matthysse, pp 401–429. New York: John Wiley & Sons.
19 Lewis, S. W., Owen, M. J. & Murray, R. M. (1988): Obstetric complications and schizophrenia: methodology and mechanisms. In *Schizophrenia: scientific progress*, eds S. C. Schulz & C. A. Tamminga. New York: Oxford University Press (in press).
20 Gottesman, I. I. & Shields, J (1982): *Schizophrenia: the epigenetic puzzle*. Cambridge: Cambridge University Press.
21 Weinberger, D. R. (1987): Implications of normal brain development for the pathogenesis of schizophrenia. *Arch. Gen. Psychiatry* **44**, 660–669.
22 Murray, R. M. & Lewis, S. W. (1987): Is schizophrenia a neurodevelopmental disorder? *Br. Med. J.* **295**, 681–682.
23 Yassa, R. & Ananth, J. (1981): Familial tardive dyskinesia. *Am. J. Psychiatry* **138**, 1618–1619.
24 Weinhold, P., Wegner, J. T. & Kane, J. M. (1981): Familial occurrence of tardive dyskinesia. *J. Clin. Psychiatry* **42**, 165–166.
25 Bartels, M., Mann, K. & Friedrich, W. (1985): Tardive dyskinesia: marked predominance of non-genetic schizophrenia. *Biol. Psychiatry* **20**, 101–103.
26 Wegner, J. T., Catalano, F., Gibralter, J. & Kane, J. M. (1985): Schizophrenics with tardive dyskinesia. *Arch. Gen. Psychiatry* **42**, 860–865.
27 Walker, E. & Shaye, J. (1982): Familial schizophrenia: a predictor of neuromotor and attentional abnormalities in schizophrenia. *Arch. Gen. Psychiatry* **39**, 1153–1156.
28 Zec, R. F. & Weinberger, D. R. (1986): Relationship between CT scan findings and neuropsychological performance in chronic schizophrenia. *Psychiatr. Clin. N. Am.* **9**, 49–61.

43

DOPA-RESPONSIVE DYSTONIA: THE SPECTRUM OF CLINICAL MANIFESTATIONS IN A FAMILY

Torbjoern G. Nygaard, David Gardner-Medwin*
and C. David Marsden[†]

*Neurological Institute of New York, Columbia University College of Physicians and Surgeons, 710 West 168th Street, New York, NY 10032, USA; *Regional Neurological Centre, Newcastle General Hospital, Westgate Road, Newcastle-upon-Tyne, NE4 6BE, UK; and [†]University Department of Neurology, Institute of Neurology, Queen Square, London, WC1N 3BG, UK*

Summary

We examined 25 members in a family affected with dopa-responsive dystonia (DRD). We found a fully penetrant autosomal dominant, pattern of inheritance. Symptomatic expression varied widely, from childhood-onset generalized dystonia to late-onset parkinsonism without dystonia. We suggest that an abnormality of muscle tone is the minimum expression of this disorder.

Introduction

DRD has been characterized as a distinct subset of idiopathic dystonia.[1] It is considered an autosomal dominant disease with reduced penetrance. Members of an affected family ("Family D" in the series of Deonna[2]) were examined by one of us (TGN) in a standardized manner[3] to better characterize the disorder.

The affected family

Family history

The first generation (Figure; I-1,2) was felt to be unaffected, although little is known about this couple. II-4 had prominent tremor from at least her 30s and suffered from 'Parkinson's disease' for over 20 years prior to death at age 74. II-6 had a 'turned out' left foot from childhood and suffered from 'back problems' in later years; he died at age 76 without apparent parkinsonism. II-8 had a 'turned out' foot from childhood; little is known of his health prior to death at age 60. III-3 was 'lame' from childhood and developed tremor at age 50. Family claimed he was 'like his mother', although not as severely affected; he died at age 63.

Examined affected members

III-6 is 53-year-old man who had been free of complaints until age 35 when he noted 'slowing down' of walking and general physical abilities. After age 45, he began stumbling and suffered several unexpected falls. Some tasks took twice as long to accomplish and extreme exertion caused muscle cramps, often persisting several days. Examination revealed increased tone on 'activation' (motor activity in the contralateral limb), decreased right arm swing, and 4–5 step recovery from a pull.

III-10 is a 44-year-old who became 'pigeon-toed' and 'stumbly' at age 4. In her teens, she experienced left leg 'cramping' following exertion. At age 17, she was carried home once after both legs 'stiffened up'. She remained asymptomatic until recently when she began to experience daily back and leg aches, with 'limping' and easy stumbling following fatigue. Examination revealed left equinovarus, slowed movements in the left extremities, and moderate generalized rigidity. Levodopa gave total relief of symptoms, but caused 'depression'. She returned to her prior status following medication withdrawal.

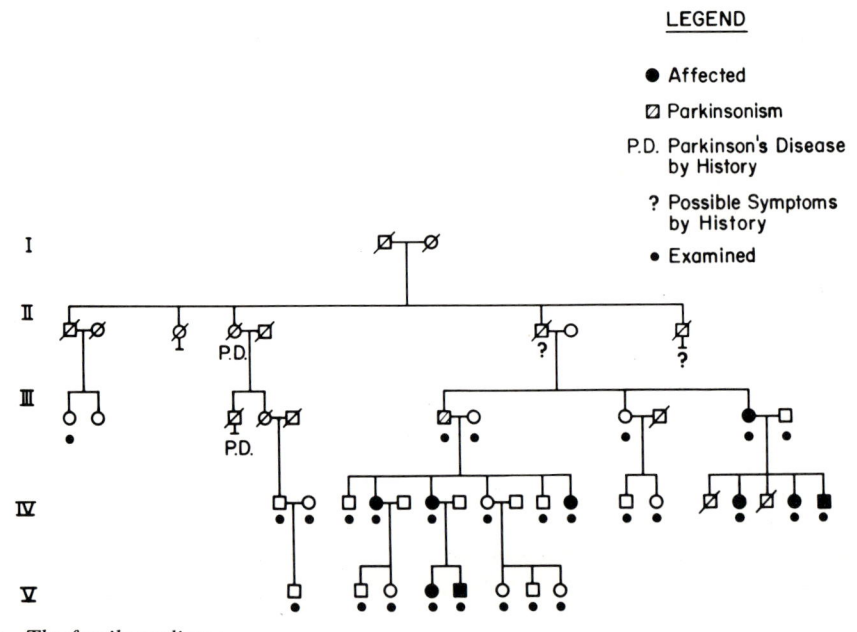

Figure. *The family pedigree.*

IV-4 is a 30-year-old woman who became 'pigeon-toed' at age 5 ('similar to her cousins'), but offered no current complaints. Examination revealed clumsy movement of the left foot, moderate generalized rigidity, and brisk reflexes in the legs.

IV-6 is a 28-year-old woman who was also 'pigeon-toed' as a child but was without current complaint. Examination revealed a right head tilt, dystonic hand posturing when the arms were held in the 'wing' position, increased grip force and adduction of the arm when writing with the right (dominant) hand, right-sided rigidity, and gait with 'in-toeing' and diminished arm swing on the right side.

IV-11 is a 20-year-old woman who developed inturning of the left foot with shoe scuffing beginning at age 13. Examination revealed impaired rapid movements with mild equinovarus on the left and axial and left-sided rigidity.

IV-15 is a 23-year-old woman who developed 'toe-walking' and imbalance at age 4. Initially, she was normal in the morning with worsening in the afternoon, but this diurnal variation soon ceased. Manual difficulties and micrographia appeared at age 8. Retropulsion occurred on standing. A wheelchair was necessary to attend school. Examination at age 13 revealed generalized dystonic posturing, rigidity and bradykinesia. Levodopa gave dramatic benefit. Chorea occurred at 125 mg, *t.i.d.*, but disappeared following dose reduction. Dose-related 'depression' with unexplained crying limited later increases. Examination at age 22, on 125 mg levodopa *t.i.d.* (in combination with a dopa-decarboxylase inhibitor), revealed no dystonia or functional abnormality.

IV-17 is a 17-year-old woman who developed 'toe-walking' at age 3. This was present throughout the day, though worsened with fatigue. The arms were affected the next year and gait disability progressed; a wheelchair was needed for school attendance. Examination at age 7 revealed generalized dystonic posturing, rigidity and bradykinesia. Levodopa gave remarkable benefit. She won a school cross country race at 13. Examination at age 17, on 50 mg levodopa *t.i.d.* with dopa-decarboxylase inhibitor, revealed only mild tone abnormalities but no functional deficit.

IV-18 is a 15-year-old boy who developed 'toe-walking at age 3, with subsequent balance difficulties and a tendency to 'drag' the right leg. His speech and arms were soon affected. Symptoms were worst in the morning. Examination at age 4½ showed dystonia affecting legs more than arms, bradykinesia, generalized rigidity and postural instability. Levodopa gave good effect. Examination at age 15, on 62.5 mg levodopa *q.i.d.* with dopa-decarboxylase inhibitor, was functionally normal with only minor tone abnormalities and slowed foot tapping.

V-4 is a 7-year-old girl without symptomatic complaints. Examination revealed mild dystonic movements in the right arm, slowed hand movements which activated dystonic movements in the feet, slowed foot tapping, generalized rigidity, and left equinovarus on walking.

V-5 is a 3½-year-old boy who developed 'toe-walking' with abnormal arm posturing at age 18 months. No functional difficulties were apparent. Examination revealed intermittent spontaneous equinovarus posturing, slowed limb movements with easy fatiguing, and abnormal gait with equinovarus and abduction of the arms.

Discussion

The clinical expression of disease in the affected members we examined manifested in early childhood. The lone exception was III-6, in whom mild, relatively non-progressive, parkinsonism appeared in the fourth decade. Whether the dystonic signs apparent in the youngest affected members (V-4 and 5) will progress to overt symptomatic involvement or follow a 'benign' course is unknown. The early appearance of signs or symptoms in older individuals did not predict their later course.

The mildest apparent manifestation of disease in affected members is increased muscle tone – with 'activation' or at rest. More overt parkinsonism (bradykinesia, postural instability and rest tremor), as appeared in II-4 and III-3, may be the later expression in affected members who do not present with childhood dystonia. The absence of wearing off or 'on-off' effect and lack of significant change in levodopa dose requirement over 10 years in the three treated individuals is consistent with their classification as being affected with DRD,[4] and would be unexpected in juvenile parkinsonism.[5]

DRD appears to have autosomal dominant expression with full penetrance in this family. Careful clinical examination of other affected families and genetic linkage studies will hopefully expand our understanding of the manifestations of this disease.

Acknowledgement—This work was supported in part by the Dystonia Medical Research Foundation.

References

1 Nygaard, T. G., Marsden, C. D. & Duvoisin, R. C. (1988): Dopa-responsive dystonia. *Adv. Neurol.* **50**, 377–384.
2 Deonna, T. (1986): Dopa-sensitive progressive dystonia of childhood with fluctuations of symptoms – Segawa's syndrome and possible variants. *Neuropediatrics* **17**, 81–85.
3 Burke, R. E., Fahn, S., Marsden, C. D., Bressman, S. B., Moskowitz, C. & Friedman, J. (1985): Validity and reliability of a rating scale for the primary torsion dystonias. *Neurology* **35**, 73–77.
4 Nygaard, T. G. & Marsden, C. D. (1988): Dopa-responsive dystonia: long–term treatment response and prognosis. *Neurology* (Suppl. 1) **38**, 130.
5 Quinn, N., Critchley, P. & Marsden, C. D. (1987): Young onset Parkinson's disease. *Movement Disorders* **2**, 73–91.

44

AN EFFECT OF UNILATERAL FRONTOPARIETAL LESIONS ON IPSILATERAL FINGER STABILITY IN MAN

J. D. Cole, H. I. Philip and E. M. Sedgwick

Wessex Neurological Centre, Southampton General Hospital, Southampton, SO9 4XY, UK.

Summary

A novel technique for the assessment of stability and tremor in the fingers has been used in patients with unilateral frontoparietal lesions. The task involved attempting to keep the index fingers still on a typewriter key connected to a strain gauge. The force required was 0.78 N with the movement allowed 0.1 mm. Visual feedback of force was obtained on a milliammeter. Performance of a task requiring constant force output is only achieved by small perturbations or tremors. Comparison of the amplitudes of this tremor ipsilateral and contralateral to cortical lesions with minimal pyramidal signs showed that the ipsilateral side was significantly less stable than either the contralateral side in these lesions or the performance of normal controls. In more severely affected patients with larger frontoparietal lesions there was an additional peak of tremor seen at 6–7 Hz ipsilateral to the cerebral lesion.

Method

Motor control of the index fingers has been assessed under isometric conditions by placing the finger on a typewriter key connected to a strain gauge and asking the subject to maintain a constant force for about approximately 90 seconds. Visual feedback of that force was obtained from the dial of a milliammeter which had a maximum phase lag of 0.7 s for full scale deflection of the meter and 0.2 s for half scale deflection. The force required was 0.78 N and the movement allowed 0.1 mm. The task could only be performed with small perturbations or tremor. This was recorded directly on an XY plotter and on tape for subsequent analysis, involving the construction of amplitude density histograms of tremor frequencies derived by a fast Fourier transform (FFT) of 24 s of typical record.

Two groups of patients with unilateral fronto-parietal lesions were assessed. The first group (n = 15) had presented with transient pyramidal or cortical sensory problems.

xamination showed either no clinical signs or mild pyramidal weakness (no more than MRC grade 4), or minimal asymmetries in sensation. The second group of patients had the more established signs of spasticity, weakness and reduction in sensation. All patients had been admitted to the Wessex Neurological Centre, examined by a consultant and had undergone a CT brain scan. Diagnoses were of transient ischaemic attacks, stroke or tumour.

Results

In group 1 the effect of the frontoparietal lesion was to reduce the amount of tremor and therefore improve stability on the side contralateral to the lesion, see Fig. 1. However, when compared with normal controls the difference was found to be a statistically significant decrease in stability ipsilateral to the lesion, with the mean tremor amplitudes ipsilaterally (IP) 8.6 g, contralaterally (CP) 4.1 g *versus* controls (n = 54) (C) 5.0 g: (IP vs CP $P > 0.001$, C vs IP $P > 0.001$, Student's t-test).

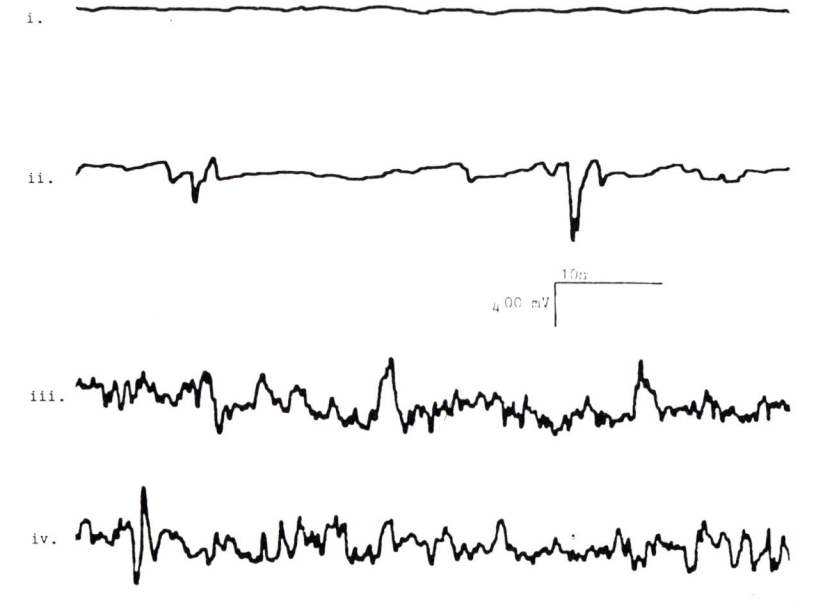

Fig. 1 *XY plot of finger stability in a patient with a left hemi-paresis.* Sensitivity 25 g/V. i. left index eyes shut; ii. left index eyes open; iii. right index eyes shut; iv. right index eyes open.

In 13 out of 22 patients in group 2, with the more established signs of spasticity, reduction in power to MRC grades 3 to 4 and reduction in sensation, an additional tremor peak was found at 6–7 Hz ipsilateral to the cortical lesion, see Fig. 2. This tremor was not apparent clinically and was found in most patients examined with mature classical stroke causing hemiplegia. Although on CT scan some of the lesions were shown to have produced midline shift of subcortical structures this was not so in several cases with stroke. This difference in tremor at 6–7 Hz was statistically significant when comparing ipsilateral and contralateral hands and when compared with normal subjects. (IP 4.68 g, CP 1.6 g, C 1.8 g; IP vs CP $P > 0.001$).

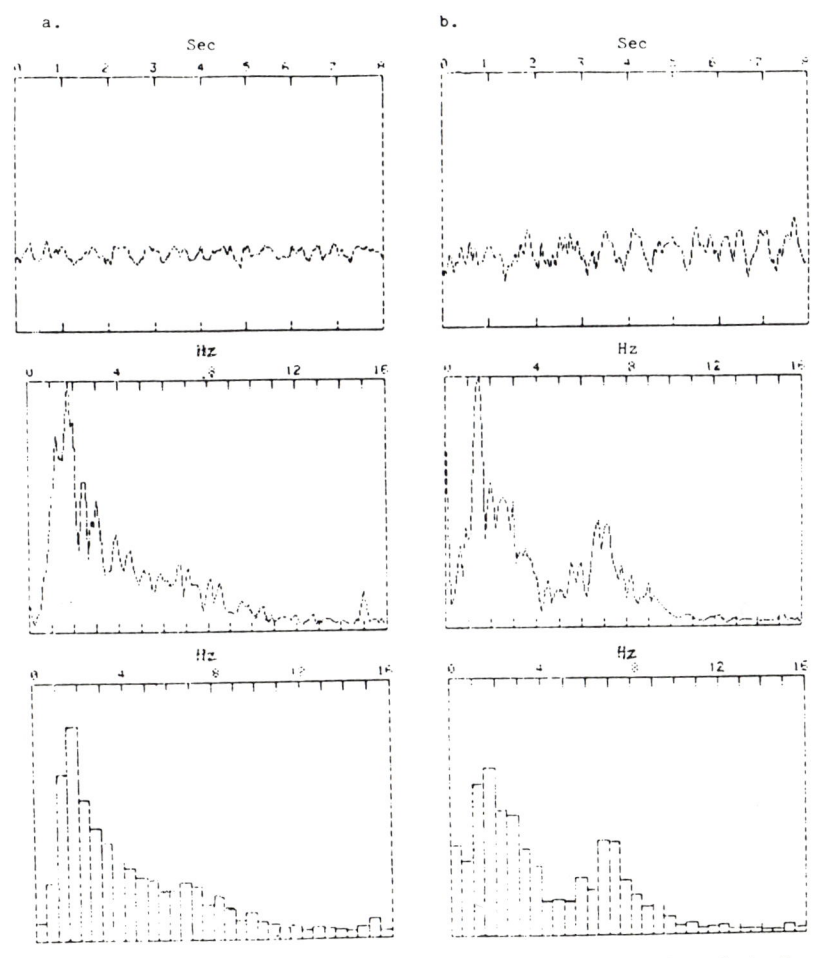

Fig. 2. *Fast Fourier transform (FFT) in a patient with a left hemiplegia to show the ipsilateral tremor peak.* Uppermost box shows XY plot of stability; middle: FFT on a linear-linear scale, abscissa 0–16 Hz; and bottom: histogram of FFT; a. contralateral to lesion; b. ipsilateral to lesion.

Discussion

Brodal[1] noticed a defect in writing with his right hand following a right hemisphere stroke and concluded there must be ipsilateral effects on motor control following unilateral frontoparietal lesions. This has been confirmed with neurophysiological testing by Colebatch et al.[2] Brodal suggested that this ipsilateral effect might be explained by the organization of cerebro-cerebellar pathways, since each cerebellar hemisphere projects to both sides of the spinal cord. Alternatively Cowan et al.[3] have demonstrated the existence of a direct ipsilateral corticospinal pathway whose physiological function has not been revealed.

It is important to realize that the present ipsilateral effect was seen for isometric holding tasks only. The same patients had contralateral deficits for fast finger movements as would be expected with pyramidal loss. It would appear that the motor cortex of one hemisphere has effects not only on contralateral finger movements but also on the maintenance of finger posture ipsilaterally.

References

1 Brodal, A. (1973): Self-observations and neuro-anatomical considerations after a stroke. *Brain* **96**, 675–694.
2 Colebatch, J. G., Gandevia, S. C. & Spira, P. J. (1986): Voluntary muscle strength in hemiparesis: Distribution of weakness at the elbow. *J. Neurol. Neurosurg. Psychiatry* **49**, 1019–1024.
3 Cowan, J. M. A., Day, B. L., Marsden, C. D. & Rothwell, J. C. (1983): Evidence of an ipsilateral corticospinal pathway to forearm muscles in man. *J. Physiol.* **343**, 114P–115P.

45

CLINICAL AND ELECTROPHYSIOLOGICAL OBSERVATIONS IN POST-ANOXIC MYOCLONUS

P. D. Thompson, A. Maertens de Noordhout, B. L. Day
J. C. Rothwell, W. Van der Kamp and C. D. Marsden

MRC Human Movement and Balance Unit and University Department of Clinical Neurology, Institute of Neurology, The National Hospital for Nervous Diseases, Queen Square, London WC1N 3BG, UK

Summary

The clinical and electrophysiological features of nine patients with post-anoxic myoclonus are presented. In seven of these patients the myoclonus occurred purely on action and was predominantly generalised. The myoclonic jerks could be confined to the limb being voluntarily activated but more often were generalised. They were preceded by generalised runs of cortical spike waves which were of maximal amplitude over the vertex and the cortex contralateral to the activated limb. These cortical waves were time-locked to each following jerk, consistent with a cortical origin of the myoclonus. There was no enlargement of the secondary component of the cortical somatosensory evoked potential. The bilaterally synchronous nature of the myoclonic jerks and the time-locked generalised cortical spike waves preceding the jerks suggest that *both* cerebral hemispheres were synchronously activated, perhaps by a subcortical discharge. We suggest that this pattern might be referred to as subcortical-cortical myoclonus. It appears to be distinct from cortical reflex myoclonus and reticular reflex myoclonus, both of which have been described previously in post-anoxic myoclonus. Examples of each of these types was observed in the remaining two patients.

Introduction

The syndrome of action myoclonus following cerebral anoxia described by Lance & Adams in 1963[1] is one of the commonest forms of myoclonus encountered in clinical practice. The muscle jerks characteristic of this syndrome are disabling and affect gait, speech and fine finger movements.[2] Cortical reflex myoclonus (defined by a rostro-caudal pattern of muscle activation, enlargement of the secondary component of the cortical somatosensory response to peripheral nerve stimulation, and a focal or lateralized cortical spike preceding the myoclonic jerks[3-5]) and reticular reflex myoclonus (with a reversed [upward] pattern of cranial muscle activation and normal cortical responses to somatosensory stimulation[6]), or a combination of both,[6] have been described in post-anoxic myoclonus. In this paper we describe some further electrophysiological findings in this condition, and illustrate another mechanism responsible for the action myoclonus.

Clinical features

Pure action myoclonus is the most striking feature of this condition. When completely relaxed, spontaneous or stimulus-sensitive reflex myoclonus is not usually seen, but the slightest attempt to move or adjust posture may be accompanied by a flurry of myoclonic jerks, especially if the stimulus applied carries an element of surprise. Visual menace and loud noises may also precipitate generalized myoclonic jerks in some patients. A single large myoclonic jerk may throw the seated patient off balance and any subsequent voluntary movement initiated to compensate for this would itself be accompanied by action myoclonus, giving the impression of a crescendo of myoclonic jerks.

The myoclonic jerks themselves may be due either to brief shock-like contractions of muscles (positive myoclonus), or to brief loss of contraction in postural muscles (negative myoclonus or asterixis). The former cause the limbs and other body parts to be thrown away from their intended action. The latter leads to sudden lapses of antigravity posture such, for example, as the knees buckling when standing.

A further clinical feature of note is that action myoclonus may be most troublesome to the patient, and most obvious to the observer, at the onset of movement or when changing from one movement to another. Once the required task is under way, there may be relatively few myoclonic jerks. This depends on the complexity of the task; the more skill required, for example manipulating a small object with the fingers, the more obvious the myoclonus. Many of these observations were emphasised by Lance & Adams[1] in their original description.

Clinical features in nine patients with post-anoxic action myoclonus are summarized in Table 1.

Electroencephalography

The EEG may be normal at rest, but with attempts to move, generalized, often bilaterally synchronous, spike and polyspike and wave discharges may appear (Fig. 1). A striking feature in some patients is the presence of repetitive spike discharges in the central head regions culminating in a slow wave. A slightly different pattern of central fast activity is also seen in some cases (Fig. 2), similar to the movement-related fast activity described in action myoclonus.[7,8] Such activity may also be prominent at the onset of movement. Movements of the eyes, hands or feet can all produce this pattern of activity, with a similar distribution in each case (Fig. 1).

EMG patterns

The EMG features of action myoclonus comprise discrete bursts of muscle action potentials of short duration [15–40 msec] occurring repetitively at high frequencies [16–25 Hz], followed by a silent period which corresponds to the observed lapse in limb posture [Fig. 2]. The order of muscle activation is usually from proximal to distal. In cases where the sternomastoid muscle is activated first in a generalized jerk, followed by spread to other cranial and limb muscles, a reticular origin of the myoclonus has been

Table 1. *Clinical features of 9 patients with post-anoxic action myoclonus.*

Case	Sex	Age	Illness	Duration of symptoms* (months)	Seizures	Other signs	Drugs**	Myoclonus action	Myoclonus spontaneous	stimulus-sensitive
1	M	21	asthma	24	+	—	Cl, V	+	—	—
2	F	27	drowning	96	+	—	P, Cl	+	—	—
3	F	17	asthma	12	+	—	V, Cl, Ca	+	—	—
4	F	47	asthma	2	—	—	V, Cl	+	—	—
5	F	68	asthma	4	—	transient R. hemiparesis	V	+	—	—
6	M	68	asthma	5	+	—	Cl, V, P	+	—	—
7	F	68	cardiac arrest	12	—	—	V, Cl	+	—	—
8	M	50	trauma[†]	2	—	dysphasia	Cl	+	—	—
9	M	34	asthma	18	—	—	V	+	—	—

*Duration of symptoms at time of study; [†]Parietal haematoma; **Cl = clonazepam; V = valproate; P = primidone; Ca = carbamazepine.

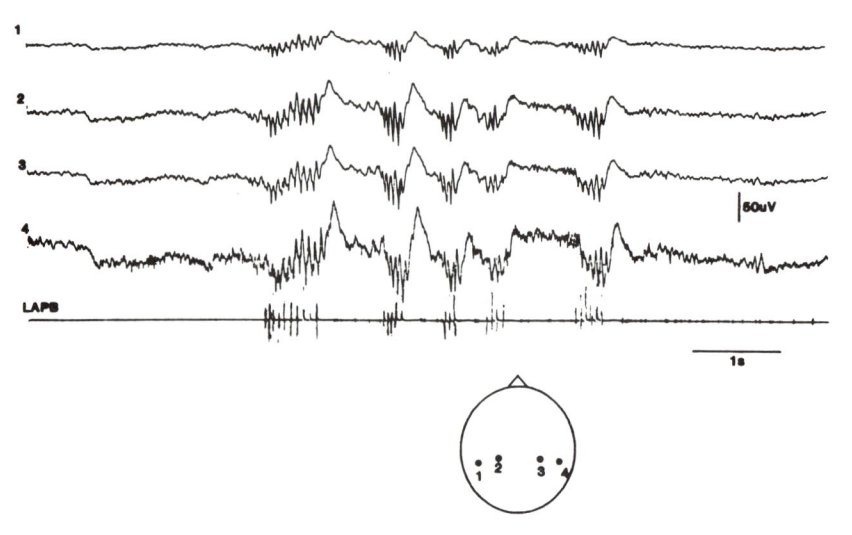

Fig. 1. *Simultaneous electroencephalographic (EEG) recordings from central head regions (referred to linked earlobe electrodes) and electromyographic (EMG) recording from left abductor pollicis brevis (LAPB).* Note that with intended activation of the left hand, short trains of myoclonic jerks occur and are accompanied by polyspike and wave discharges in the EEG, which are generalized but of slightly greater amplitude over the right cerebral hemisphere.

suggested.[5] However it is not always possible to record cranial myoclonic jerks at the same time as the limb myoclonus to examine this timing relationship.

The action myoclonus may be confined to the muscle being activated. However, at the onset of a movement, or when changing the movement strategy, a generalized myoclonic jerk is frequently seen. In these generalized jerks, homologous muscle groups in both limbs tend to be activated synchronously.

The EMG findings in post-anoxic myoclonus are summarized in Table 2.

Table 2. *Summary of EMG findings.*

Short duration bursts (20–40 msec)

Salvos of myoclonic jerks at 16–20 Hz.

Rostro-caudal order of activation in 3 of 4 patients in whom myoclonus could be studied in the cranial muscles.

In the fourth case (case 8) the sternomastoid muscle was the first cranial muscle to contract during a generalized myoclonic jerk suggesting reticular 'reflex' myoclonus.

Unilateral or bilaterally synchronous myoclonus

Silent period (duration 50–200 msec) following myoclonic jerks corresponding to observed lapses in limb posture.

EEG-EMG relationships

The cerebral potentials accompanying myoclonus are often clearly visible in the EEG and can be large enough to detect on single trials (Fig. 2). The lapses in limb posture (asterixis) that are a characteristic feature of action myoclonus are due to EMG silence, which corresponds to slow waves in the EEG (Figs 1,2).

Back-averaging the EEG activity prior to a myoclonic jerk has revealed different patterns. In some patients, a time-locked cortical potential has been recorded as a lateralized event over the contralateral hemisphere, suggesting a cortical origin for the myoclonus. Action- or even stimulus-sensitive myoclonus may have such electrophysiological appearances.[3,9] Other authors have failed to identify a cortical potential preceding

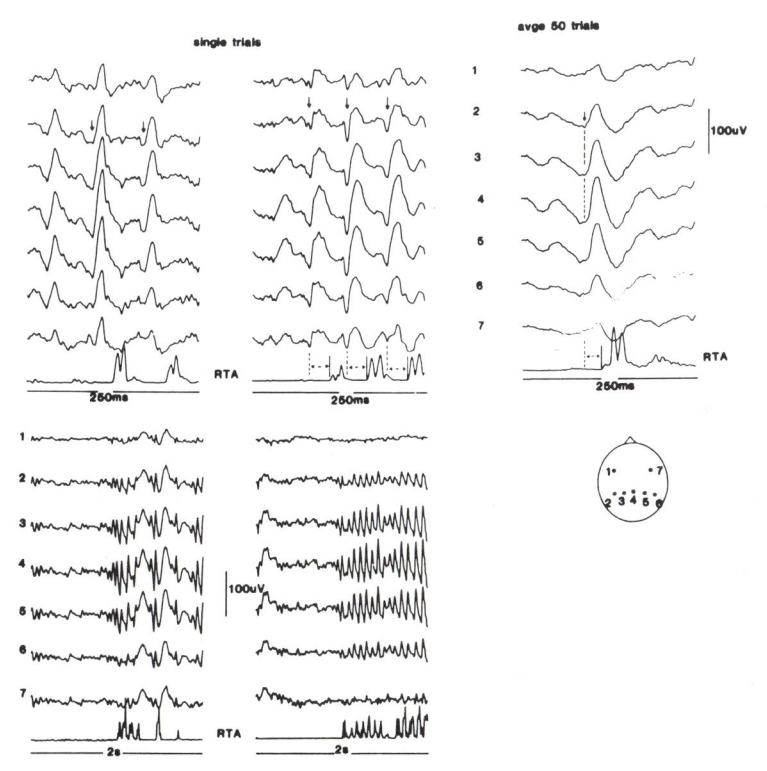

Fig. 2. *Simultaneous EEG recordings from various scalp locations (referred to linked mastoid electrodes) and rectified EMG recording from right tibialis anterior (RTA). The lower two panels show the activities recorded over a period of 2 sec. In the right lower panel the trains of myoclonic jerks in RTA are accompanied by runs of cortical spike waves at high frequency (14–16 Hz). In the left lower panel, the trains of myoclonic jerks are interrupted by EMG silence (which results in the observed lapse in limb posture) and corresponds to the occurrence of a cerebral slow wave ending the spike discharges. In the upper panels, the relationship beween these EEG and EMG discharges is examined in more detail over a period of 250 msec. The left two panels show single trials and the right panel illustrates the average of 50 consecutive trials. All trials shown were collected on a back-averaging program which was triggered by the RTA jerk in the middle of the sweep. It can be seen that each myoclonic jerk is preceded by a cortical spike wave which is generalized, but of maximal amplitude at the vertex. The definition of this wave is not as clear after the average of 50 trials due to some jitter in the latency to onset of the myoclonic jerk after each cortical spike discharge.*

myoclonus when many trials are averaged, even though such cortical discharges are evident on single trials. It has been suggested that this form of myoclonus is due to discharges within the reticular systems and that the cortex and limb muscles are independently activated by the subcortical generator.

More recently we have observed a further pattern which suggests that the cerebral hemispheres are bilaterally and synchronously activated to produce a generalized cortical spike wave, which then recruits a myoclonic jerk in limb muscles at a latency consistent with conduction in large diameter corticospinal fibres. This pattern was observed in seven of nine patients with post-anoxic myoclonus recently studied. The major difference between this pattern and that seen in cortical reflex myoclonus was in the scalp topography of the back-averaged spike waves. The EEG potentials preceded bilaterally synchronous myoclonic jerks, and were generalized with maximal amplitude at the vertex (Fig. 1). These findings, coupled with the interval between the spike and the myoclonic jerk, suggested that the cortex discharge was causally related to the myoclonic jerk. On rare occasions when the myoclonic jerks were confined to one limb the EEG spike discharges also were generalized, but their amplitude was greatest at the vertex and over the hemisphere contralateral to the activated limb.

Somatosensory evoked potentials

Cortical somatosensory evoked potentials (SEP) to peripheral nerve stimulation are often normal in post-anoxic myoclonus. However, in some patients an enlarged secondary component of the cortical SEP may be seen. Such patients exhibit cortical reflex myoclonus with lateralized cortical spikes preceding each myoclonic jerk. These patients may exhibit stimulus-sensitive cortical reflex myoclonus. However, the degree of sensitivity to cutaneous stimuli or muscle stretch is often difficult to judge clinically in the presence of severe action myoclonus, and the majority of cases that we have encountered do not exhibit stimulus-sensitivity when examined electrophysiologically even though clinical examination suggested reflex myoclonus. The findings are summarized in Table 3.

Table 3. *Sumary of somatosensory evoked potentials (SEP) and EEG findings.*

Case	SEP	C-reflex* (latency, msec)	EEG	Bkav
1.	N	—	polyspike/ spike & wave	generalized positive wave maximal amplitude contra-lateral to unilateral jerk
2.	N	52	"	"
3.	N	46	"	"
4.	N	90(TA)	"	"
5.	N	51	"	"
6.	N	55	"	"
7.	N	—	"	"
8.	N	—	"	"
9.	enlarged P1-N2	48	"	lateralized cortical spike

*C-reflex in ABP after stimulation median nerve at wrist except Case 4 (TA), where obtained after posterior tibial N stimulation.

Discussion

This brief summary of the clinical and electrophysiological features of post-hypoxic action myoclonus indicates that, in spite of the rather stereotyped appearance of the myoclonus, there are at least three possible mechanisms that may generate it. Cortical and reticular reflex mechanisms are widely recognized[3-6,9] but a third type also appears to be common.

This form of myoclonus is characterized by (1) striking action myoclonus without cutaneous stimulus sensitivity; (2) generalized myoclonus with bilaterally synchronous activation of comparable muscle groups; (3) a rostro-caudal pattern of muscle activation also suggesting a cortical origin for the myoclonic jerks; (4) normal cortical somatosensory evoked potentials, and (5) a generalized cortical spike wave preceding muscle jerks by latencies consistent with conduction from the cerebral cortex to spinal cord.

The distribution of the cortical wave preceding this type of myoclonus differed from that recorded in patients with cortical reflex myoclonus. The spike discharge tended to be generalized with maximal amplitude over the vertex and the hemisphere contralateral to the jerking limbs. It was as if voluntary activation of a muscle accentuated or 'focused' this generalized wave over the hemisphere appropriate to that particular movement. In contrast, the cortical potentials preceding cortical reflex myoclonus are strictly focal and lateralized.[3]

It is suggested that these cortical potentials, and the bilaterally synchronous myoclonic jerks, arise from bilateral simultaneous activation of the cerebral hemispheres by a subcortical discharge. In contrast to reticular reflex myoclonus, cranial myoclonus was not prominent and the interval between the cortical wave and muscle jerks was compatible with conduction from the hemisphere rather than the brain stem. This form of myoclonus, which might be called subcortico-cortical, therefore appears to be distinct from cortical and reticular reflex myoclonus.

References

1 Lance, J. W. & Adams, R. D. (1963): The syndrome of intention or action myoclonus as a sequel to hypoxic encephalopathy. *Brain* **86**, 111–136.
2 Fahn, S. (1979): Post-hypoxic action myoclonus: review of the literature and report of two new cases with response to valproate and oestrogen. *Adv. Neurol.* **26**, 49–84.
3 Hallet, M., Chadwick, D. & Marsden, C. D. (1979): Cortical reflex myoclonus. *Neurology* **29**, 1107–1125.
4 Kakigi, R. & Shibasaki, H. (1987): Generator mechanisms of giant somatosensory evoked potentials in cortical reflex myoclonus. *Brain* **110**, 1359–1373.
5 Young, R. R. & Shahani, B. T. (1979): Clinical neurophysiological aspects of post-hypoxic intention myoclonus. *Adv. Neurol.* **26**, 85–105.
6 Hallett, M., Chadwick, D., Adam, J. & Marsden, C. D. (1977): Reticular reflex myoclonus: a physiological type of human post-hypoxic myoclonus. *J. Neurol. Neurosurg. Psychiatry* **40**, 253–264.
7 Kelly, J. J., Sharbrough, F. W. & Westmoreland, B. F. (1978): Movement activated central fast rhythms: An EEG finding in action myoclonus. *Neurology* **28**, 1037–1040.
8 Witte, O. W., Niedermeyer, G., Arendt, G. & Freund, H. J. (1985): Post-hypoxic action (intention) myoclonus: a clinico-electroencephalographic study. *J. Neurol.* **235**, 214–218.
9 Marsden, C. D., Hallett, M. & Fahn, S. (1982): The nosology and pathophysiology of myoclonus. In *Movement disorders*, eds S. Fahn & C. D. Marsden, pp 196–248. London: Butterworth.

CLINICAL ASPECTS

Surgical treatment

46

LESSONS FROM SURGICAL TREATMENT OF MOVEMENT DISORDERS

H. Narabayashi

Juntendo University and Neurological Clinic, 5–12–8 Naka-Meguro, Meguro-ku, Tokyo 153, Japan

Summary

Analysis of neuronal activity within the thalamus recorded through microelectrodes during human stereotaxic surgery has enabled us to interpret some types of involuntary movement. Rigidity and levodopa-induced dyskinesia in parkinsonism depend on the pallidothalamic projection and tremor on the VIM nucleus of the thalamus. Careful observation of changes in these symptoms during surgical procedures and also in the postoperative long-term course have given us the important opportunity of reconsidering the nature of so-called akinesia and the reason for progression of Parkinson's disease.

Introduction

After initial trials by Meyer, Bucy and others in the 1930s aiming to control abnormal involuntary movements by neurosurgical means, the technique of stereotaxic surgery was introduced by Spiegel & Wycis and several other groups over the world in the late 1940s.[1] Localized surgical lesions in the depth of the brain were found to produce alleviation of abnormal movements such as tremor, rigidity, chorea, hemiballism and others without producing noticeable side-effects. This also raised the possibility of analysing the intracerebral mechanism of involuntary movements and basal ganglia disorders, which will be described.

Technical aspects

Since 1950, the stereotaxic technique of targeting a specific structure in the brain by needle insertion has depended mainly on radiological measurement, referring to the detailed configuration of the ventricular system and using the brain atlas. It is still the most important morphological basis of the technique and in cases of thalamic surgery, the radiological reference remains the detailed outline of the third ventricle.

Introduction of microelectrode recording of unitary activity from the deep structures of the human brain by Albe-Fessard et al in 1963[2] added the firm basis of identifying the targeted structures physiologically. The physiological information obtained through the technique is the delicate change in the neural noise, which is the sum of the electrical activities of neurons and fibres around the microelectrode tip of 5–10µ in size. The behaviour of unitary neuronal or fibre discharges is specific to each structure impaled along the microelectrode track. These findings and analyses have been reported in detail elsewhere.[3,4]

Identification of VIM

Localization of the ventral intermediate nucleus (VIM), which lies posterior to the ventrolateral nucleus (VL) and anterior to the posterior nucleus (VP), is roughly estimated by radiological measurement but its precise identification can only be done neurophysiologically. VIM usually presents a higher noise level, with spikes of larger amplitude than other neighbouring subnuclei, since it contains neurons of the largest size when compared with the dorsal nucleus or other ventrolaterally-lying subnuclei.[5] VIM is also characterized by its receptive field for proprioceptive sensory afferents. Many of the unitary activities in the ventral part of VIM respond to peripheral stimuli such as muscle stretching or joint movement but not to tactile stimuli. These proprioceptive neurons are organized in a delicate somatotopic fashion similar to the tactile neurons in the ape.

When tremor exists in some part of the contralateral extremities, rhythmic discharges synchronous with the tremulous movement are observed in the corresponding neuronal area. Fig. 1 demonstrates the rhythmic bursts of neuronal discharges within the VIM which are synchronized with the tremor discharges in the contralateral forearm flexor muscle. Subthreshold electrical stimulation of a peripheral nerve, such as the median nerve, produces evoked potentials in the corresponding VIM neurons with a latency of 11–12 msec.[6]

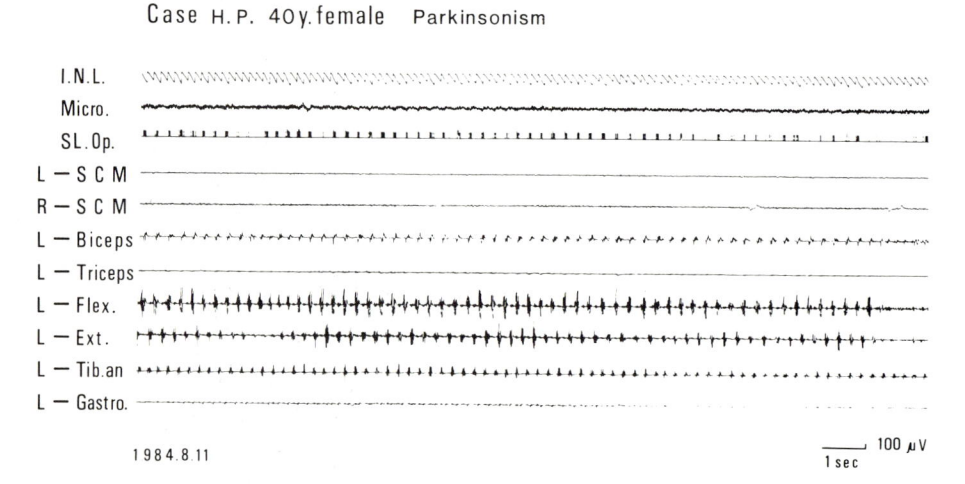

Fig. 1. *Regular rhythmic burst discharges of the right sided VIM unit in a 40-year-old female with parkinsonism.* I.N.L.: integrated neuronal noise; Micro.: original recording; SL.Op.: sliced discharge. Other tracings are EMG of the contralateral (L) side of the body.

When the precise configuration of VIM is obtained, location and delineation of the neighbouring structures such as VL, VP or the centromedian nucleus (CM) is easily calculated.

Analysis of rigidity and tremor

Tremor is completely and immediately alleviated by a selective VIM lesion and rigidity is similarly improved by a VL lesion. High frequency electrical stimulation (routinely 60 Hz, 0.2–0.3 mA) of VIM inhibits tremor and of VL increases tonic stretch reflexes in rigidity. These observations indicate that these two symptoms are dependent on separate structures although located closely to each other, ie, rigidity on VL and tremor on VIM. Rigidity may be mediated by pallidothalamic fibres which project to VL and the ventralis anterior nucleus (VA) but not to VIM. The author has previously described how a pallidal lesion has a sustained effect on rigidity but not on tremor.[7] VIM receives ample projection from the cerebellar deep nuclei and from the periphery, the latter being proprioceptive in nature.

The pallidothalamic pathway is known to be the main exit of the extrapyramidal system. Therefore, when the striatum is involved in dopamine deficiency, the globus pallidus and its efferent projection to VL are considered to produce rigidity. Levodopa-induced dyskinesia is also completely alleviated by the same lesion used for rigidity, which suggests that the same anatomical pathway is responsible for these two symptoms under different pharmacological situations.[8] On the other hand, tremor is assumed to be a symptom more closely related, structurally, to VIM and functionally, to pathophysiology involving the midbrain and cerebellar systems (Fig. 2).[9,10]

Akinesia

Akinesia is a term used vaguely by clinicians to describe poverty or lack of movement, slowness and loss of dexterity and even other types of difficulty with movement.[11] With complete alleviation of rigidity and tremor in the contralateral extremities within a few seconds of placing electrocoagulation lesions in the base of the thalamus as described, voluntary skilled movements of the arm and leg return immediately, in most cases within a few seconds. The most common experience routinely and impressively encountered on the operating table is the recovery of finger separation, supination-pronation and flexion-extention of the forearm and rotation of the shoulder. Therefore, part of akinesia or, at least, hypokinesia or bradykinesia may be ascribed to the secondary difficulty created by rigidity. In cases of hemiparkinsonism, such improvement after a unilateral thalamic lesion is enough to improve and sometimes normalize the general body movements and locomotion.

However, truncal movement in moderately affected bilateral cases, especially in terms of locomotion, is not always normalized by unilateral surgery. It has usually been advised that bilateral surgical intervention should be avoided in classical Parkinson's disease cases. This has limited surgical treatment. However, in carefully selected patients, younger than fifty years of age at the time of surgery, bilateral thalamotomy using the microelectrode technique and producing minimum-sized lesions, can safely be performed without producing any somatic or psychic side-effects. The interval between surgery on the two sides must of more than one year. Such bilateral procedures eliminate almost all akinetic or hypokinetic symptoms with alleviation of rigidity. As a result, the dose of levodopa can be reduced, usually to about half of the preoperative dose or even less. A few satisfactorily improved patients are able to carry on a normal medicine-free social life and daily

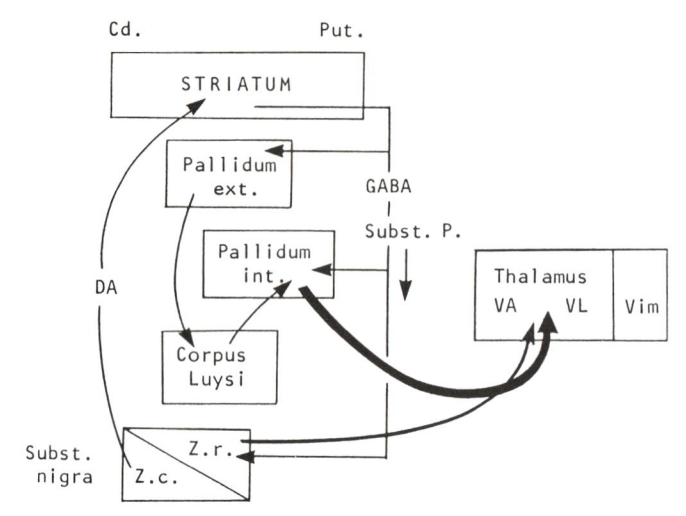

Fig. 2. *Functional and anatomical schema in generation of rigidity, levodopa-induced dyskinesia and tremor from the results of stereotaxic thalamotomy using microelectrodes.*

activities, including jobs such as office worker, farmer or attorney. However, in most of the classical Parkinson's disease cases akinesia, ie, poverty or loss of movement or difficulty in initiating movement, often still remains after surgery, though the symptoms are usually benefited by postoperative levodopa administration.[12,13]

Discrepancies in observations between the (few) bilaterally operated younger patients and older patients can give us an idea as to whether primary akinesia has the same anatomical basis as rigidity. Hughes *et al.* described earlier that the effect of levodopa was the same on the operated and non-operated sides.[14] This suggests that primary akinesia was not changed by surgery and responded only to levodopa. This is also the author's observation. Therefore, akinesia might not be due to nigrostriatal dopamine deficiency. Since primary akinesia responds well to levodopa, the author considers that the ventral striatum is likely to play a role under the influence of the limbic system.

Progression of the disease process

Parkinson's disease has been known as a condition presenting a slow but steady course of progression without spontaneous recovery. This is most adequately expressed in the progression of the disease from Hoehn-Yahr grade I to V. It is generally hypothesized that such progression is due to increasing deterioration of dopamine metabolism in the nigrostriatum, presumably with secondary changes in other neurotransmitters. In reviewing the long-term course of well treated cases of relatively younger onset, which includes not only juvenile parkinsonism (JP) described by Yokochi[15] and Narabayashi *et al.*[16] but also those cases starting before the age of 50, it is generally agreed that these patients are greatly improved or almost normalized for ten to fifteen years or longer. Without adequate treatment, rigidity and akinesia would have progressed, resulting in a bedridden state. It is interpreted that these younger patients have a single pathogenesis mainly caused by nigrostriatal dopamine deficiency. If rigidity, secondary hypokinesia and/or tremor are adequately treated either pharmacologically by a combination of levodopa and a dopamine agonist or by precise bilateral surgery using the sophisticated microelectrode technique, no significant progression occurs. The Table presents details of

Lessons from surgical treatment of movement disorders

Table. Details of the cases of juvenile parkinsonism (JP) who have received bilateral surgical treatment.

Case	Age at onset	Age at 1st surgery	Main symptoms	Preoperative dosage of DIC	Surgery 1st	Surgery 2nd	Follow-up observations in Nov. 1984	DIC dosage at survey	Evaluation
1(m)	33	39	JP & dyskinesia	4T	L ('77)	R ('82)	working in pharmaceutical laboratory, no dyskinesia, up–down++	4T	A
2(m)	45	48	JP(?) & dyskinesia	3T	L ('78)	R ('81)	working as an accountant, no dyskinesia	2T	A
3(m)	25	32	JP & slight dyskinesia	5T	R ('79)	L ('81)	nearly normal working in a small business company, sometimes travelling abroad	3T	A"
4(f)	41	50	JP(?)	3T	R ('81)	L ('82)	normal housewife's work	?	A
5(f)	40	45	JP & slight dyskinesia	levodopa 2.5 g	L ('72)	R ('77)	housewife, normally working in grocery and travelling	0	A"
6(f)	42	50	tremor & JP (?)	levodopa 1.0–2.0 g	L ('72)	R ('78)	no tremor, independent ADL, hypochondriac at home	—	B
7(m)	43	48	JP (?)	levodopa 2.0 g	R ('72)	L ('79)	half working as manager at self-owned food shop, no dyskinesia but with moderate up-down	—	B
8(m)	39	45	JP & moderate dyskinesia	3T	L ('69)	R ('81)	teaching as university professor, but with slight dyskinesia; freezing started, which is being controlled by L-threo-DOPS	2T	B
9(f)	42	45	JP (?)	?	R ('73 at other hosp.)	L ('82)	independent ADL, active in housewife's work	—	B
10(m)	29	34	JP & dyskinesia	4T	L ('75)	R ('82)	leisure at home, sometimes playing baseball, no dyskinesia	4T	A"
11(f)	33	44	JP & dyskinesia	5T	L ('76)	R ('82)	retired journalist, at home no dyskinesia	3T	A

DIC = dopa and decarboxylase inhibitor compound; A = almost normal life; B = home independence, but some limitation; ADL = activity in daily life

389

all our cases of juvenile parkinsonism who have received bilateral operative treatment and have been followed up with regard to daily and social activities for 5–10 years postoperatively. There are 11 cases in all, eight of whom are leading an almost normal life in jobs, with fewer drugs than preoperatively. The remaining three are living independently at home and carrying out all normal domestic tasks.

On the other hand, in cases of classical Parkinson's disease with steady progression of symptoms to grade III and IV (Hoehn & Yahr), symptoms such as difficulty in postural control and walking, freezing of gait and deterioration of emotional and psychic function progress, finally ending in stage V. These later symptoms do not usually respond to levodopa therapy but are often somewhat improved by L-threo-3,4-dihydroxyphenylserine (L-threo-DOPS), which is the precursor of noradrenaline.[17,18]

To sum up (see also [19]), Parkinson's disease is considered to be a condition presenting with progressively worsening metabolism of both dopamine and noradrenaline, the latter becoming affected much later in the disease. By contrast, juvenile parkinsonism or cases of earlier onset are due to a selective disturbance of dopamine metabolism, which is also progressive in nature. Juvenile parkinsonism shows less tendency to impairment of noradrenaline metabolism and may fail to progress if delicately and effectively treated.

References

1 Spiegel, E. A. & Wycis, H. T. (1962): *Stereoencephalotomy, Part II. Clinical and physiological applications*, p 504. New York: Grune & Stratton.
2 Albe-Fessard, D., Arfel, G. & Guiot, G. (1963): Activités électriques caractéristiques de quelques structures cérébrales chez l'homme. *Ann. Chir.* **17**, 1185–1214.
3 Ohye, Ch. (1982): Depth microelectrode studies. In *Stereotaxy of the human brain*, ed G. Schaltenbrand & A. E. Walker, 2nd edn, pp 372–389. Stuttgart, New York: Thieme Verlag.
4 Narabayashi, H. (1986): Tremor: its generating mechanism and treatment. In *Handbook of clinical neurology*, ed P. J. Vinken, G. W. Bruyn & H. L. Klawans, Vol. 5(49), pp 597–607. Amsterdam: Elsevier Science Publishers.
5 Ohye, Ch., Saito, Y., Fukamachi, A. & Narabayashi, H. (1974): An analysis of the spontaneous rhythmic and non-rhythmic burst discharges in the human thalamus. *J. Neurol. Sci.* **22**, 245–259.
6 Ohye, Ch. & Narabayashi, H. (1979): Physiological study of presumed ventralis intermedius neurons in the human thalamus. *J. Neurosurg.* **50**, 290–297.
7 Narabayashi, H., Okuma, T. & Shikiba, S. (1956): Procaine oil blocking of the globus pallidus. *Arch. Neurol. Psychiatry* **75**, 30–48.
8 Narabayashi, H., Yokochi, F. & Nakajima, Y. (1984): Levodopa-induced dyskinesia and thalamotomy. *J. Neurol. Neurosurg. Psychiatry* **47**, 831–839.
9 Narabayashi, H. (1987): Two groups of extrapyramidal involuntary movements. In *The basal ganglia II*, ed M. B. Carpenter & A. Jayaraman, pp 465–473. New York: Plenum.
10 Narabayashi, H. (1987): Analysis of extrapyramidal motor symptoms for stereoencephalotomy. In *Clinical aspects of sensory motor integration*, ed A. Struppler & A. Weindl, pp 240–248. Springer-Verlag.
11 Narabayashi, H. (1980): Clinical analysis of akinesia. *J. Neural Transm.* (Suppl.) **16**, 129–136.
12 Narabayashi, H. (1989): Surgical treatment in the era of levodopa and other pharmacological treatment. In *Parkinson's disease*, ed G. Stern. London: Chapman & Hall Ltd.
13 Narabayashi, H. (1985): Akinesia in parkinsonism. Pharmacological and physiological analysis. In *Electromyography and evoked potentials*, ed A. Struppler & A. Weindl, pp 30–34. Berlin, Heidelberg: Springer-Verlag.
14 Hughes, R. C., Polgar, J. G., Weightman, D. & Walton, J. N. (1974): L-dopa in parkinsonism and the influence of previous thalamotomy. *Br. Med. J.* **i**, 7–13.
15 Yokochi, M. (1979): Juvenile parkinsonism. Part 1: Clinical aspects. Part 2: Pharmacokinetic study. *Adv. Neurol. Sci. (Tokyo)* **23**, 1048–1059, 1060–1073 (in Japanese).

16 Narabayashi, H. Yokochi, M., Iizuka, R. & Nagatsu, T. (1986): Juvenile parkinsonism. In *Handbook of clinical neurology*, ed P. J. Vinken, G. W. Bruyn & H. L. Klawans. Vol. **5**(49), pp 153–165. Amsterdam: Elsevier Science Publishers.
17 Narabayashi, H., Kondo, T., Yokochi, F. & Nagatsu, T. (1986): Clinical effects of L-threo-3,4-dihydroxyphenylserine in cases of parkinsonism and pure akinesia. In *Advances in neurology*, ed M. D. Yahr & R. J. Bergmann, Vol. **45**, pp 593–602. New York: Raven Press.
18 Narabayashi, H. (1987): Similarity and dissimilarity of MPTP models to Parkinson's disease: Importance of juvenile parkinsonism. *Eur. Neurol.* **26**(Suppl. 1), 24–29.
19 Narabayashi, H. (1988): Lessons from stereotaxic surgery using microelectrode techniques in understanding parkinsonism. *Mount Sinai J. Med.* **55**, 50–57.

47

PHYSIOLOGICALLY IDENTIFIED, SELECTIVE VENTROINTERMEDIUS THALAMOTOMY AMELIORATES VARIOUS KINDS OF TREMOR AND OTHER DISORDERS OF MOVEMENT RELATED TO TREMOR

T. Shibazaki, T. Hirai, M. Hirato, Y. Kawashima
M. Matsumura and C. Ohye

*Deparment of Neurosurgery, Gunma University School of Medicine,
3–39, Showa-machi, Maebashi, Gunma, Japan*

Summary

We have developed and now almost established a stereotaxic surgical method to ameliorate various kinds of tremor. So far the results are satisfactory. From our experience of microelectrode recording, we consider the mechanisms of tremor.

Introduction

After the introduction of levodopa, the role of surgical treatment in Parkinson's disease has decreased. However, thalamotomy still has an important place in the management of the condition and we have developed and refined the technology for stereotaxically ameliorating parkinsonian tremor and other types of abnormal tremulous movements.[1–4] Here we summarize our experience on selective ventrointermedius (VIM) thalamotomy using microelectode recording techniques, and we discuss the mechanisms of tremor.

Materials and methods

Patient population

Since 1981, 112 selective VIM stereotaxic thalamotomies have been performed on 93 patients with disorders of movement related to tremor, including Parkinson's disease.

Forty-two patients had Parkinson's disease, 34 had essential tremor (ET), four had post-traumatic tremor (PTT), 11 had tremor after stroke and two had cerebral palsy. The patients comprised 36 women and 57 men, whose ages ranged from 14 to 79 years. There were 80 left unilateral thalamotomies and 28 right unilateral thalamotomies. Those patients who underwent a stereotaxic operation had a preoperative 'stereotaxic' CT scan from which macroscopic anatomical information about the planned electrode trajectory was obtained.[5]

Tremor analysis

Rest and postural tremor was measured with surface EMG and a piezoresistive accelerometer taped to the dorsum of the affected hand. The hand acceleration autospectra provided an accurate measure of mean squared tremor amplitude as distributed over frequency. In some cases, a method for the solution of certain non-linear problems in least squares was used to determine certain parameters of the spectra.

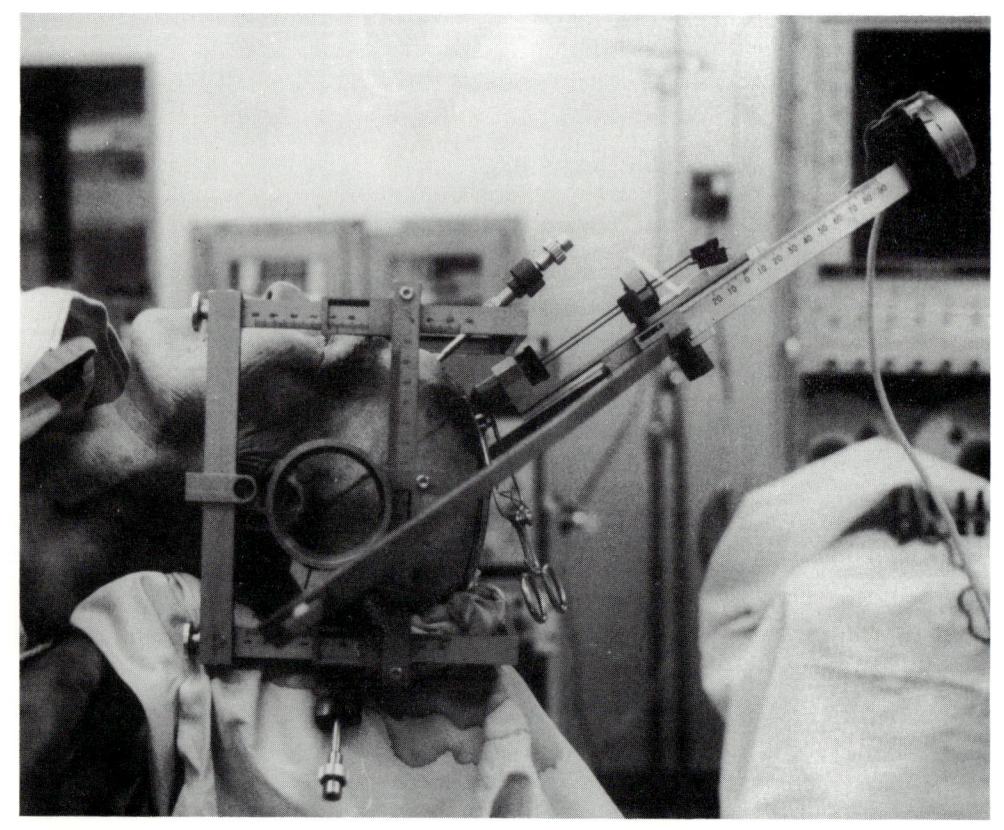

Fig. 1. *Close-up view of the patient's head; the micromanipulator to which a pair of microelectrodes is fixed is controlled by a computer.* Notice that the angle of the electrodes is adjusted to be the same as that of the stereotaxic CT scan by a line on the patient's scalp.

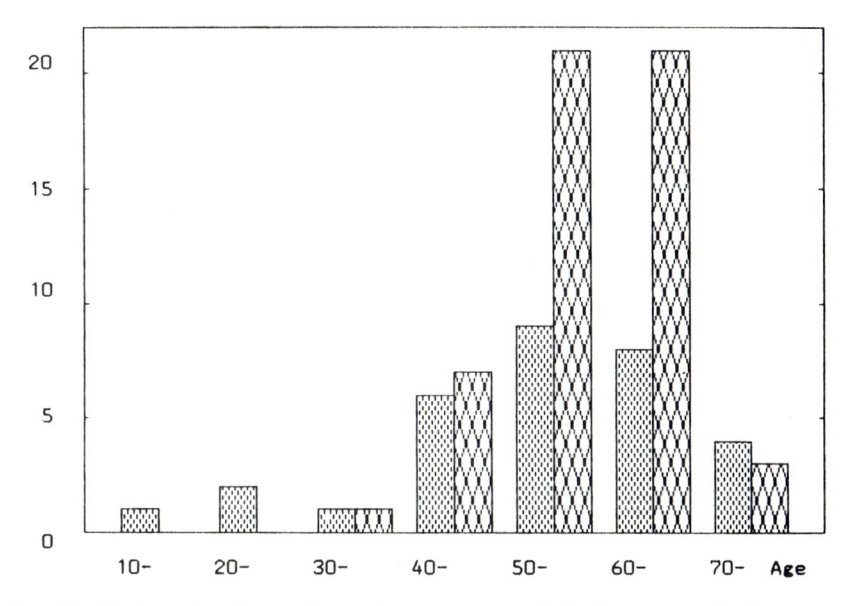

Fig. 2. *Age distribution of patients who underwent stereotaxic thalamotomy.* Ordinate scale shows number of operations: left-hand column, essential tremor; right, Parkinson's disease.

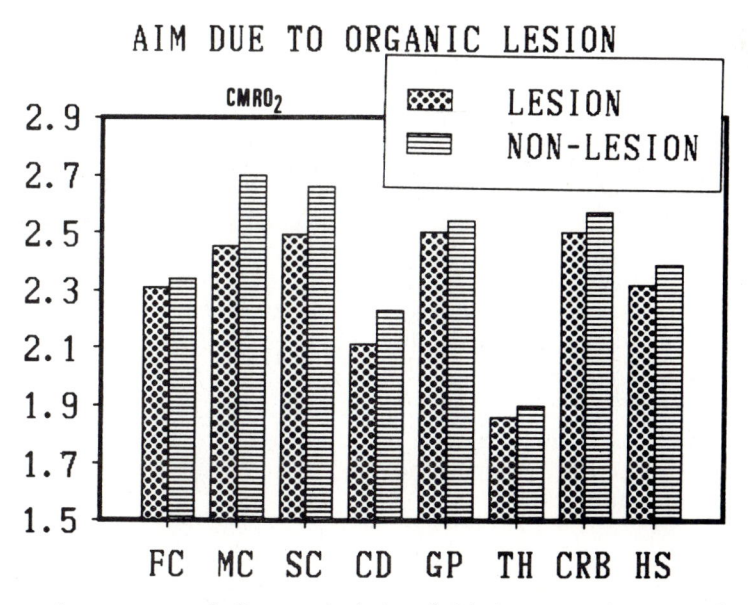

Fig. 3. *Decrease in oxygen metabolism on the lesioned side in cases with tremor after stroke.* The decrease was most marked in the motor (MC) and the sensory cortex (SC) ($P = 0.05$). FC: frontal cortex, CD: caudate nucleus, GP: globus pallidus, TH: thalamus, CRB: cerebellum, HS: cerebral hemisphere.

Positron emission scans (PET)

With the introduction of PET to Gunma University hospital in 1983, patients with parkinsonian tremor or other types of tremulous involuntary movement were studied with this technique prior to stereotaxic thalamotomy.

PET was performed using Hitachi PCT-H-1 tomography. The spatial resolution of this scanner is 8 mm × 8 mm full width half maximum (FWHM), with a slice thickness of 16 mm FWHM. Regional blood flow (rCBF), oxygen extract ratio (rOEF), and cerebral metabolic rate of oxygen (rCMRO$_2$) were measured with the steady-state inhalation technique of cyclotron generated ^{15}O. Regions of interest for each structure, ie, the thalamus, the basal ganglia, and the sensory and motor cortex, were determined from the PET image superimposed with the corresponding CT image, which was taken just before PET study. In some cases, after the initial scanning procedure, the patients were instructed to maintain the forearm in a certain position or to do mental arithmetic. When tremor appeared the scanning procedure was once again made. Comparisons between left and right sides, lesion side and non-lesion side, and 'rest' and tremor periods were made using Student's t-test.

Operative technique

Stereotaxic thalamotomy is performed with the patient in the supine position under local anaesthesia so that involuntary movements can be monitored during the surgery. After fixation of Leksell's stereotaxic frame to the skull, a burr hole is opened for ventricular tapping. Selective third ventriculography with a small amount of water-soluble contrast medium and air makes it possible to delineate the anterior and posterior commissures without causing nausea or vomiting. The posterior commissure and intercommisural line are the basis for calculation of the tentative target point, at the lower border of the VIM nucleus. The point and the trajectory route determined from the ventriculography and CT images may be digitized and stereotaxic coordinates easily calculated. Then a pair of microelectrodes (bipolar concentric type, outer diameter 0.4 mm, tip 10 μm, electrical impedance at 1 KHz 10 Kohm) are introduced from the prefrontal area to the lower border of the VIM nucleus. The electrode picks up not only a single spike discharge but also background neural activities, with which the subcortical structures can be clearly delineated. The pulsemotor-driven micromanipulator (minimum step, 1 μm) facilitates the isolation of unit spikes from the background activity. The VIM zone is delineated by its characteristic high background activity and/or kinesthetic response. Then a small restricted RF thermocoagulation within this defined VIM zone is made after confirmation of the position of the electrode tip on x-ray.

Recently, we have used a computer system for surgical planning, data acquisition, interactive data manipulation and calculation during the stereotaxic procedure.

Postoperative evaluation

Follow-up neurological, radiological and neurophysiological evaluations are made one week after the operation and at adequate intervals thereafter. The follow-up period has ranged from 3 months to 7 years.

Results and discussion

Parkinson's disease

The severity of tremor in patients for surgery was greater than that seen in patients controlled by medication. They exhibited not only typical rest tremor but also postural tremor. In other words, tremor did not disappear during movement in advanced cases. EMG activity showed a typical reciprocal-alternating pattern with, in most cases, a single spectral peak at 4.5 to 6.5 Hz.

Essential tremor

From spectral analysis, there were two types of essential tremor. That which responded to propanolol exhibited a single spectral peak at 5 to 7 Hz. The other type seen in nervous younger patients showed higher (8 to 12 Hz) and more complex peaks, ie, more than two with low amplitude.

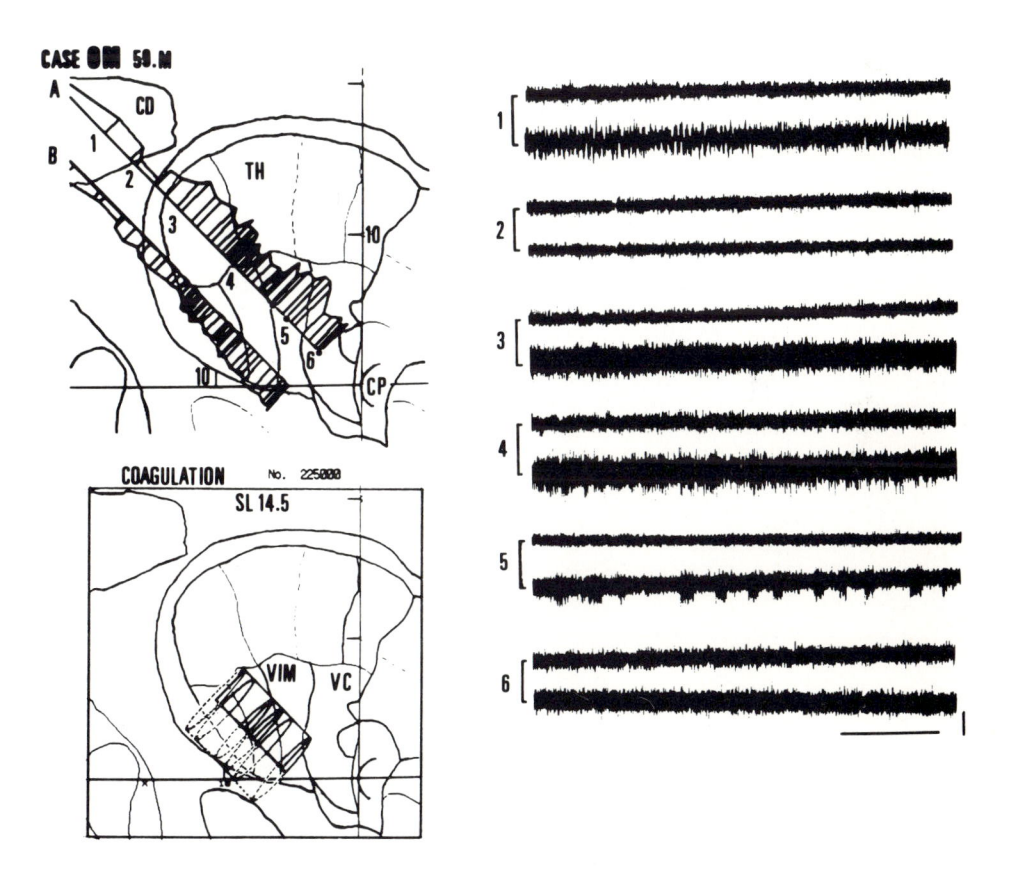

Fig. 4. *Traces recorded during operation and operative data in an illustrative case.* Left upper: operation data from a 59-year-old male with Parkinson's disease. The values of neural activity are plotted along two tracks inserted parallel to the sagittal plane. The superimposed map shows the corresponding profile of the human thalamus. Left lower: Small coagulation lesions were made in the ventral thalamus including VIM. Right: Examples recorded from corresponding points (shown by 1 to 6). Each pair of traces is a simultaneous recording from a pair of electrodes. Note the rhythmic burst discharges recorded in the VIM (lower trace of 5). Calibration 1 sec/100 μV. CP: commissure posterior.

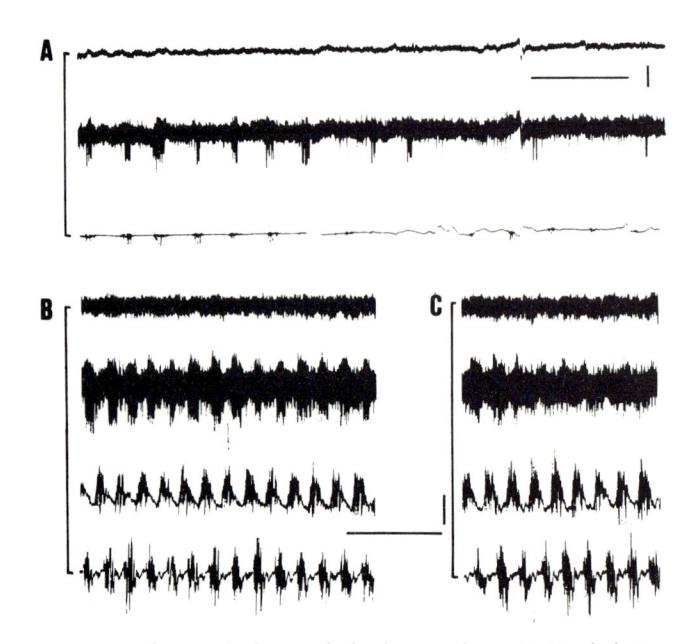

Fig. 5. *Intraoperative recordings of electrical discharges from VIM.* (A) Tremor time-locked rhythmic discharge recorded in the VIM (middle trace). In this case, rhythmic burst disappeared when peripheral tremor EMG (lower trace) stopped. (B) Another tremor time-locked unit in Parkinsonian tremor. It is related to contraction of the forearm extensor (bottom). (C) Multi-unit discharge recorded in the VIM was not related to peripheral tremor. Calibration: (A) 1 sec/100 μV; (B,C) 1.5 sec/100 μV.

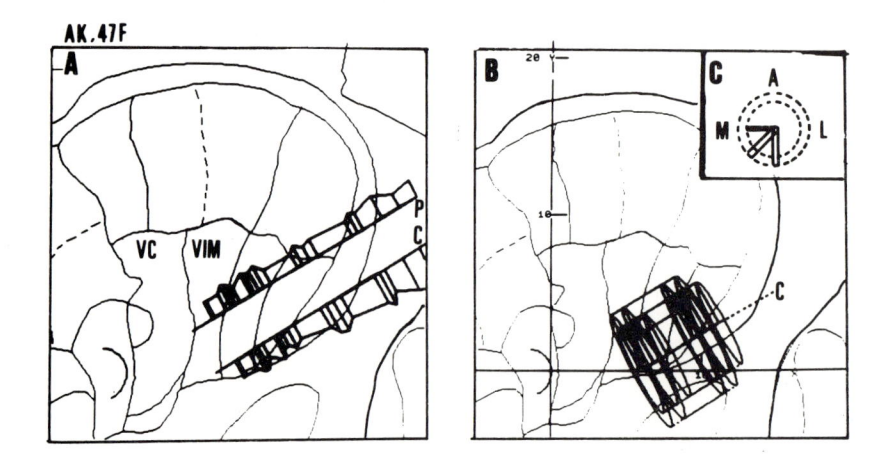

Fig. 6. *Operation data obtained in a case with tremor after stroke (47-year-old female, pontine haemorrhage).* (A) The figure is drawn in the same manner as Figure 4. The coagulation lesion is indicated in lateral view. (B) Corresponding standard atlas is superimposed in simplified form. (C) Extent of the lesions is shown as areas around imaginary cylinders of 3/4 mm radius in overview. A: anterior, C: centre of the cylinder, L: lateral, M: medial.

Post-traumatic tremor and tremor after stroke

Cases with an organic lesion had a lower spectral peak (2.4 to 3.5 Hz) and showed irregular ataxic shaking of the extremities. EMG studies revealed extreme fluctuations in amplitude.

Oxygen metabolism

Asymmetry was present in the motor and sensory cortex in cases of tremor after stroke. The rCMRO$_2$ contralateral to the symptomatic limbs was lower than on the other side. The hypometabolism seen on the lesioned side affected the motor and sensory cortex. Similar observations were reported in cases with thalamic stroke, in whom abnormal involuntary movements were not seen.[7] Most of the parkinsonian patients had bilateral symptoms to a greater or lesser degree and the rCMRO$_2$ tended to decrease in the basal ganglia and the frontal cortex. When compared with the 'resting state', no definite change was noted in any of the structures during trembling.

Depth microelectrode recording

In the course of lowering the electrode array, continuous monitoring of neural activity gave helpful information which enabled delineation of the subcortical structures, ie, white matter (low amplitude with sporadic positive spikes), the caudate nucleus (fast oscillation of 30 Hz with wide spikes) and ventral thalamus (high neural activity with spikes of extremely high amplitude).[8] In cases with tremor after stroke, the general basal activity was much lower than that in Parkinson's disease.[4] Neurons responding to deep or kinesthetic stimuli (compression of the muscle or passive movement of joint) were encountered in this high activity zone. Grouped spike discharges, time-locked to the tremor in the contralateral limb, were frequently observed in cases with spontaneous tremor. There was a somatotopic representation of kinesthetic neurons in the VIM nucleus, with the lower limb area being dorsolateral, the upper limb ventromedial, and the face most medial. Kinesthetic neurons were distributed separately from tactile neurons, which were found more caudally. Electrical stimulation to the median nerve provoked activation in 21 kinesthetic neurons identified, with a latency of about 13 msec. Susceptible VIM neurons were commonly observed in cases with Parkinson's disease and essential tremor. However, in cases with tremor after stroke, the general basal activity was much lower and sensory neurons were less frequently encountered. Moreover, slow-rhythmic discharge related to abnormal ocular movement was recorded in three cases with stoke. The difference might be due to morphological deformity and to the possible reorganization that took place after the stroke in the structures connected to the particular thalamic nucleus.[4]

Results of treatment

The location of the site for destruction was accurately defined by the technique described above. That is to say, the location and the extent of coagulation included tremor-synchronous kinesthetic neurons and avoided tactile neurons. Moreover, care was taken not to injure the internal capsule, which was identified with CT scan or MRI. Temperature-monitored coagulation was performed between two electrodes with 4 mm bare tips separated by a 3 mm gap. The volume of lesions, which was confirmed histologically in one patient, was about 20 mm^3 including the dimensions of the electrodes. In parkinsonian and essential tremor, satisfactory results were obtained with a small coagulation of about

40–60 mm³ without any detectable neurological deficits. Patients with essential tremor became free from medication such as propranolol. The volume of coagulation for essential tremor was almost identical with that for parkinsonian tremor. Parkinsonian patients, however, who pre-operatively had more or less 'midline' symptoms with speech and gait disturbance, required antiparkinsonian drugs postoperatively. In certain cases, the thalamotomy allowed a reduction in the dose of medication, and this might help to prevent the adverse effects of long term treatment.[9] The improvement in tremor was maintained in the majority of cases (95 per cent). In contrast, in cases with coarse tremor after stroke where kinesthetic neurons were encountered less frequently, retracking was necessary to identify the VIM nucleus physiologically. In these cases effective lesions were larger (mean 90 mm³) in comparison with those found effective in parkinsonian and essential tremor cases ($P = 0.05$). This experience has led us to treat other kinds of movement disorders in which an element of tremor is involved. So far, the results are satisfactory.

Tremor mechanisms

Morphological studies revealed that the VIM, located between the ventralis lateralis (VL) and the ventralis caudalis (VC), is the cell-sparse zone in which large neurons (500–900 μm²) and medium neurons (200–400 μm²) are distributed sparsely.[10] It is still uncertain which type of neuron receives kinesthetic input. It is likely that interruption of short-latency kinaesthetic inflow to the VIM may play an important role in tremor alleviation.[11] However, other sources projecting to the VIM such as cerebellum should be considered. It is noteworthy that destruction of a small, confined area in the thalamus abolishes tremor or tremor-like involuntary movement regardless of their aetiology. From our experiences in stereotaxic thalamotomy for tremor, VIM seems to be the 'key nucleus' in the tremor mediating circuits.[12] The technique and method of selective VIM thalamotomy is now established but many problems still remain unsolved.

References

1 Ohye, C. (1986): Role des noyaux thalamiques dans l'hypertonie et le tremblement de la maladie parkinson. *Rev. Neurol.* **142**, 362–267.
2 Ohye, C., Miyazaki, M., Hirai, T., Shibazaki, T. & Nagaseki, Y. (1983): Stereotactic selective thalamotomy for the treatment of tremor type cerebral palsy in adolescence. *Child's Brain* **10**, 157–167.
3 Ohye, C., Miyazaki, M., Hirai, T., Shibazaki, T., Nakajima, H. & Nagaseki, Y. (1982): Primary writing tremor treated by stereotactic selective thalamotomy. *J. Neurol. Neurosurg. Psychiatry* **45**, 988–997.
4 Ohye, C. Shibazaki, T, Hirai, T, Kawashima, Y, Hirato, M. & Matsushima, M. (1985): Plastic change of thalamic organization in patients with tremor after stroke. *Appl. Neurophysiol.* **48**, 288–292.
5 Ohye, C., Kawashima, Y. & Hirato, M. (1984): Stereotactic CT scan for the direct aid of stereotactic thalamotomy and biopsy. *Acta Neurochir.* **71**, 55–68.
6 Elble, R. J. (1986): Physiologic and essential tremor. *Neurology* **36**, 225–231.
7 Baron, J. C., D'Antona, R., Pantano, P., Serdaru, M., Samson, M. & Bousser, M. G. (1986): Effects of thalamic stroke on energy metabolism of the cerebral cortex. *Brain* **109**, 1243–1259.
8 Ohye, C. (1982): Depth microelectrode studies; In *Stereotaxy of the human brain*, 2nd edn, ed G. Schaltenbrand & A. E. Walker, pp 372–389. Stuttgart: G. Thieme Verlag.
9 Narabayashi, H. (1982): The future of stereotaxy. In *Stereotaxy of the human brain*, 2nd edn, ed G. Schaltenbrand & A. E. Walker, pp 686–689. Stuttgart: G. Thieme Verlag.
10 Hirai, T., Miyazaki, M., Nakajima, H., Shibazaki, T. & Ohye C. (1983): The correlation between tremor characteristics and predicted volume of effective lesion in stereotaxic Vim thalamotomy. *Brain* **106**, 1001–1018.

11 Narabayashi, H. (1982): Tremor Mechanisms. In *Stereotaxy of the human brain*, 2nd edn, ed G. Schaltenbrand & A. E. Walker, pp 510–514. Stuttgart: G. Thieme Verlag.
12 Ohye, C. (1987): Neural circuits involved in parkinsonian motor disturbance studied in monkeys. *Eur. Neurol.* **26**(suppl.1), 41–46.

48

CT-GUIDED THALAMOTOMY IN THE TREATMENT OF MOVEMENT DISORDERS

Tipu Zahed Aziz and Michael John Torrens

Department of Neurosurgery, Frenchay Hospital, Bristol BS16 1LE, UK

Summary

CT-guided thalamotomy has been used in the Frenchay Hospital since 1985 in the treatment of movement disorders. This technique avoids intraventricular contrast injections and therefore simplifies the placement of thalamic lesions, decreases patient morbidity and shortens inpatient stay. Our experience with this technique is presented.

Introduction

The introduction of high resolution computed tomography (CT) scanners with the ability to perform multiplanar reformatted images has been one of the major recent advances in modern stereotaxic neurosurgery. It is now possible to identify intracranial structures with a degree of accuracy which obviates the need for intraventricular contrast injections.[1-3]

CT-guided placement of thalamic lesions using the Leksell system has been used in the treatment of movement disorders at the Frenchay Hospital, Bristol, since 1985. The simplicity and accuracy of the procedure and the fact that patients tolerate it so well shortens inpatient stay and decreases morbidity. The experience between 1985 and 1988 with this technique in the treatment of 13 patients with movement disorders is presented.

Patients and methods

Thirteen patients who were unresponsive to medical therapy were treated by thalamotomy. They included 10 cases of tremor (parkinsonism – 4, multiple sclerosis – 3, post-traumatic – 3), one case of Gilles de la Tourette syndrome and two cases of torsion dystonia.

The patients are given a short general anaesthetic, using propofol, because inserting the ear bars of the Leksell frame, the drilling of the holes to fix it to the skull and performing a

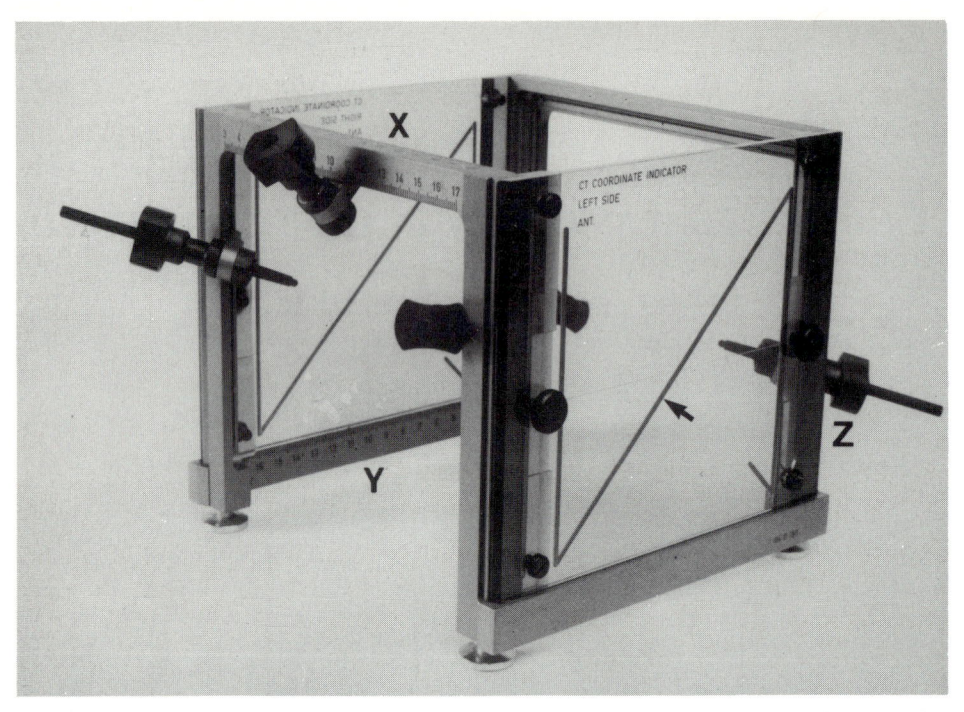

Fig. 1. *The rectangular component of the Leksell stereotaxic frame with the carbon fibres which fix it to the skull* in situ *and the X, Y and Z axes labelled*. The acrylic plate containing the radio-opaque oblique Z fiducial is arrowed.

burr hole may be uncomfortable even with local anaesthetic. Involuntary patient movement is also eliminated. If the patient has a very severe tremor at rest the general anaesthetic is continued while the patient is scanned.

A frontal burr hole is made on the side of the thalamotomy, the dura opened widely, the pia incised and then the scalp is closed, the surface being marked with the most appropriate point of entry into the incision. The Leksell stereotaxic frame is then fixed to the skull with four metal drills, the aim being to place it with the horizontal plane of the frame approximately parallel to the intercommissural line. The frame is made of an alloy to minimize interference on CT. The steel drills are then replaced with carbon fibre rods. Acrylic plates containing radio-opaque fiducials are put onto the sides of the frame. The patient is transferred to the GE8800 CT-scanner. Fourteen horizontal slices at a magnification of 1.4 are performed, starting just above the level of the posterior clinoid processes. Slices are 1.5 mm in depth on a medium body format. Reformatting of these slices provides a mid-sagittal reconstruction of the 3rd ventricle. Accurate identification of the anterior and posterior commissures is possible and usually these will lie on the same or adjacent slices. If not, then the slice on which the mid-point of the intercommissural line is to be found is identified and the position of the anterior and posterior commissures is transferred to this plane using the scanner software.

Before identifying the mid-commissural point the horizontal slices are moved so that the centre of the stereotaxic frame corresponds to the centre of the scanner grid system. The mid-point of the intercommissural line in the centre of 3rd ventricle can conveniently be

Fig. 2. *The fully assembled Leksell stereotaxic frame which is so designed that when the X, Y and Z co-ordinates have been set, the tip of the fully inserted electrode will lie at the centre of a sphere of which the electrode-carrying arc is part of the circumference.*

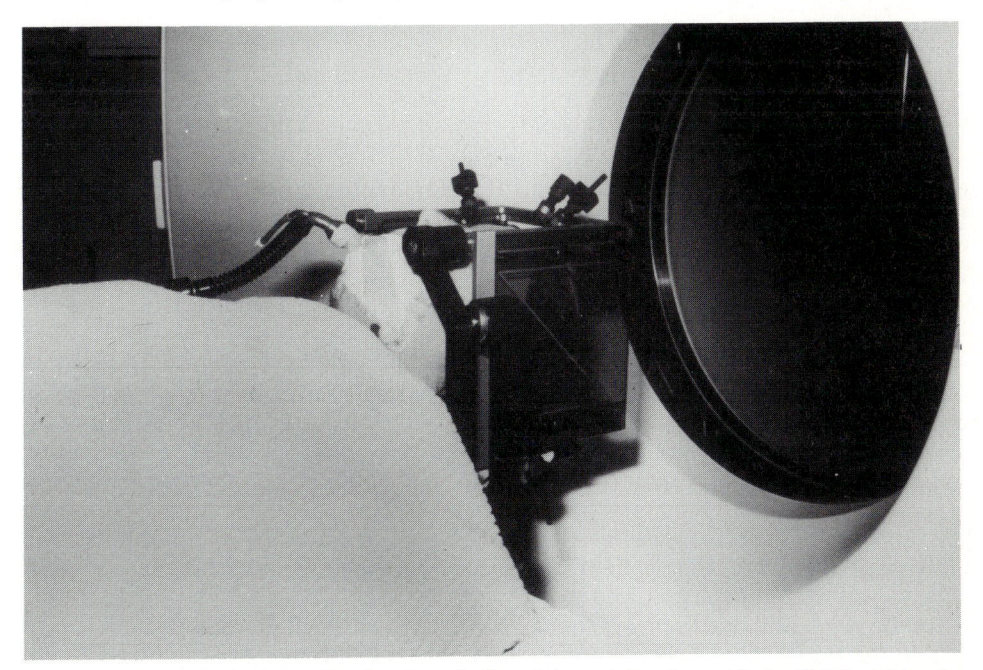

Fig. 3. *A patient with the frame fixed to her skull and the acrylic plate with the Z fiducial in place, about to be scanned.* The general anaesthetic has been continued in this case because of a severe tremor at rest which would have made scanning difficult.

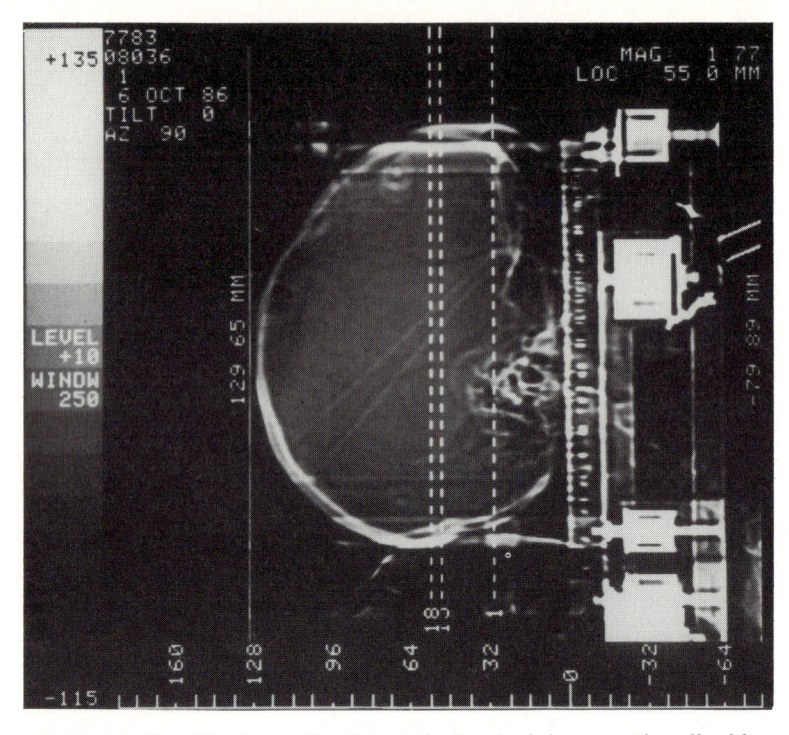

Fig. 4. *A typical scout film.* The lower line lies at the level of the posterior clinoid processes and the upper line at approximately the level of the roof of the third ventricle. The patient is scanned between these two levels.

found by joining the anterior and posterior commissural points with a line containing one step which will be exactly at the mid-point. The cursor can then be placed at this point and the scanner software is used to determine the exact co-ordinates of the point in millimetres from the centre of the scanner grid. This means that the X (lateral) and Y (AP) co-ordinates of the mid-commissural point can be transferred directly to the Leksell frame without the need for any additional calculation except adding a factor of 10.

The vertical (Z) co-ordinate is calculated from the position at which the oblique fiducial is cut in the slice in question. This measurement is obtained by using the scanner software to measure the distance between the oblique fiducial and the vertical marker at the back of the acrylic plate, adding a constant factor of 4, and transferring this to the Z axis of the Leksell frame.

Having calculated the co-ordinates of the mid-commissural point the co-ordinates of any target related to the intercommissural line can be found by simple addition or subtraction. The usual target for thalamotomy is 13 mm lateral, 3 mm posterior and 2 mm above the mid-commissural point. The patient is returned to the theatre and the frame assembled to guide the electrode to the required point.

The electrode is passed without further anaesthetic through the closed wound and burr hole to the target where, after appropriate stimulation studies to attempt to block the tremor (100 Hz) and exclude a capsular motor response (2 Hz) have been performed, a temperature-controlled radiofrequency lesion can be created.

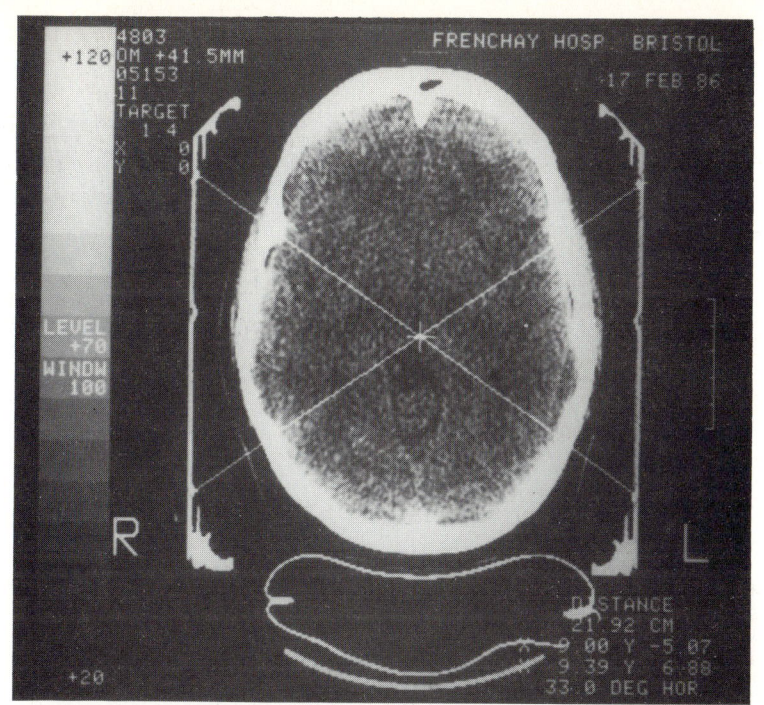

Fig. 5. *Prior to identifying the mid-commissural point the horizontal slices are moved so that the centre of the stereotaxic frame as illustrated is shifted to correspond to the centre of the scanner's grid system.*

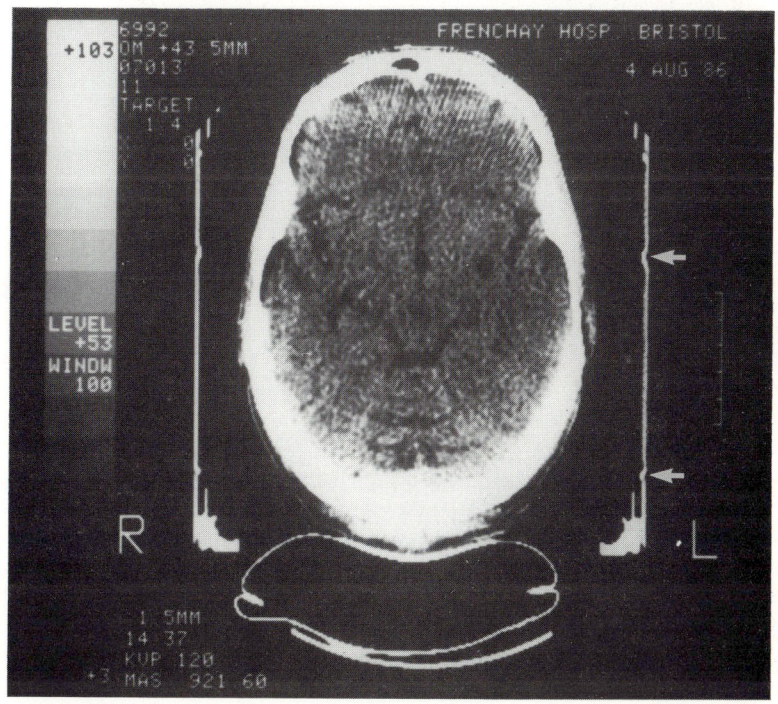

Fig. 6. *A typical horizontal slice of the head with the frame attached.* The upper arrow marks the radio-opaque Z fiducial cut in the plane of the section and the lower arrow, the posterior vertical marker. The distance between these two, from which the Z co-ordinate is calculated, is measured using the scanner software (see text).

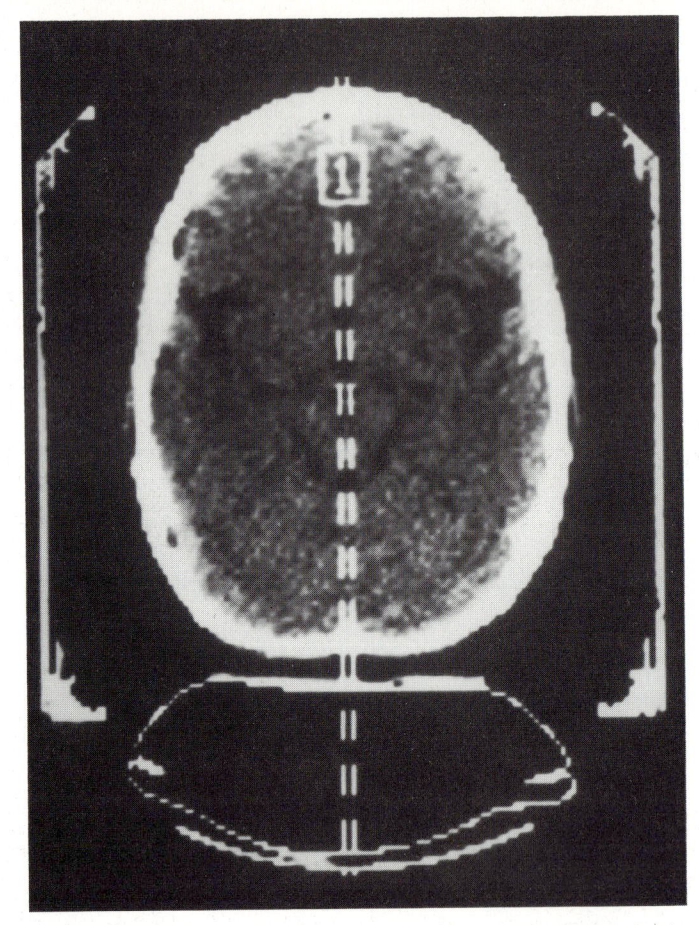

Fig. 7. *A horizontal slice with the mid-saggital plane passing through the third ventricle marked. The computer software is then used to obtain a vertical reformatted image in this plane.*

Results and discussion

In all patients with tremor, regardless of aetiology, the tremor was abolished or very significantly reduced. The constant athetoid movements, explosive expletives and jerks in the patient with Gilles de la Tourette syndrome were significantly relieved. Of the two patients with dystonia, one relapsed after an initial improvement and in the second the relief of dystonia was accompanied by an increase in rigidity.

The results are neither better nor worse than thalamotomy performed using intraventricular contrast medium but they are achieved without the complication of headache or reaction to the contrast. In fact, the patients who underwent a unilateral procedure had no significant complaints other than those related to the lesion itself, such as a mild transient hemiparesis. Patients who were not dependent on institutional care and could be discharged home had an average stay of 7.5 days after intraventricular contrast injection and thalamotomy and 6.6 days after CT-guided thalamotomy. This is a significant saving in time and perhaps inpatient stay could be reduced further as greater experience is obtained.

CT-guided thalamotomy in the treatment of movement disorders

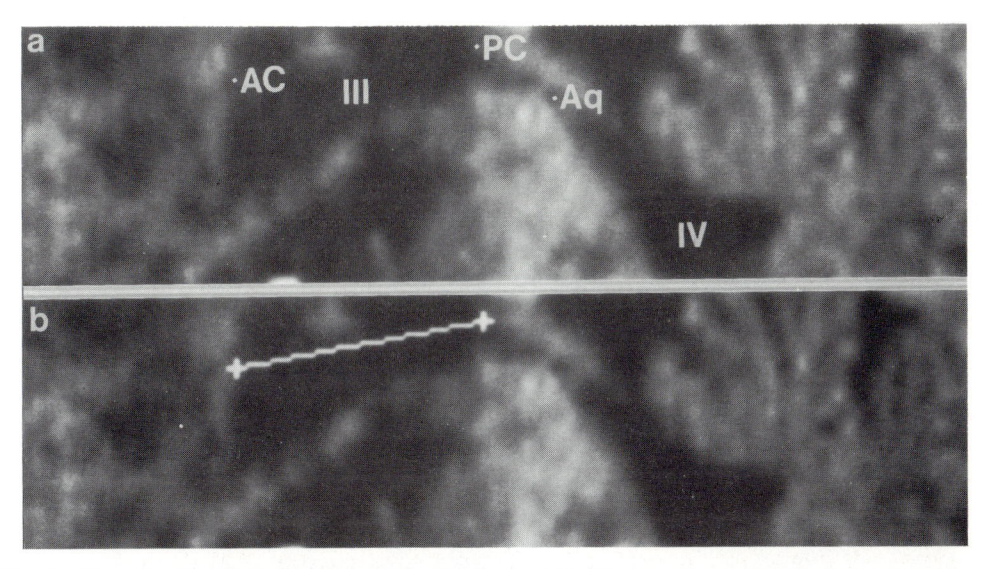

Fig. 8. *The reformatted image through the third ventricle.* The anterior and posterior commissure (AC and PC), the cerebral aqueduct (Aq), third and fourth ventricles (III and IV) are easily identified (8a). From a line joining AC and PC (b) the mid-commissural point is identified and the horizontal slice containing this can be selected.

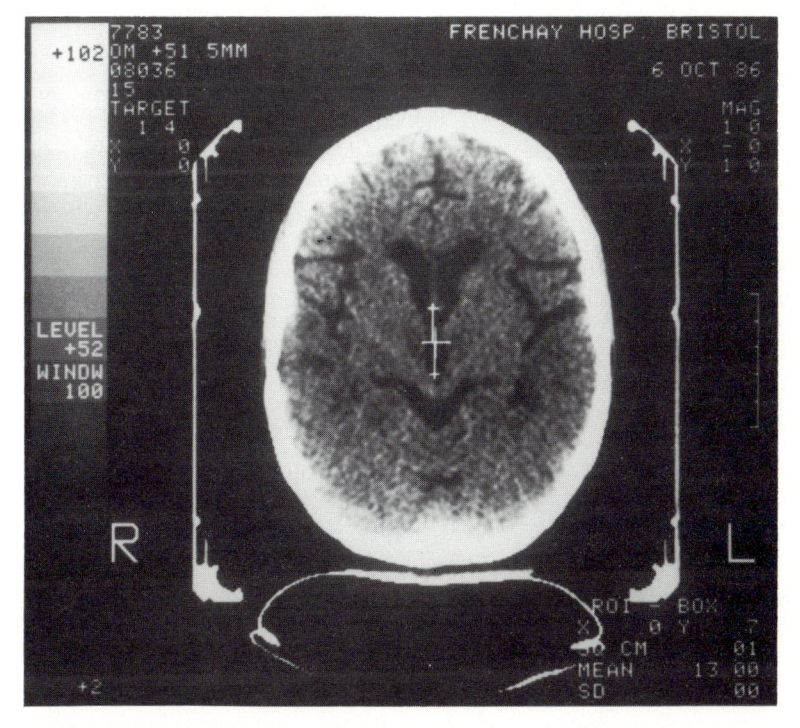

Fig. 9. *The horizontal slice in which the AC and PC have been identified; these are joined by a line with one step which lies exactly at the mid-point.* The cursor is positioned here and the scanner software calculates the co-ordinates of this point.

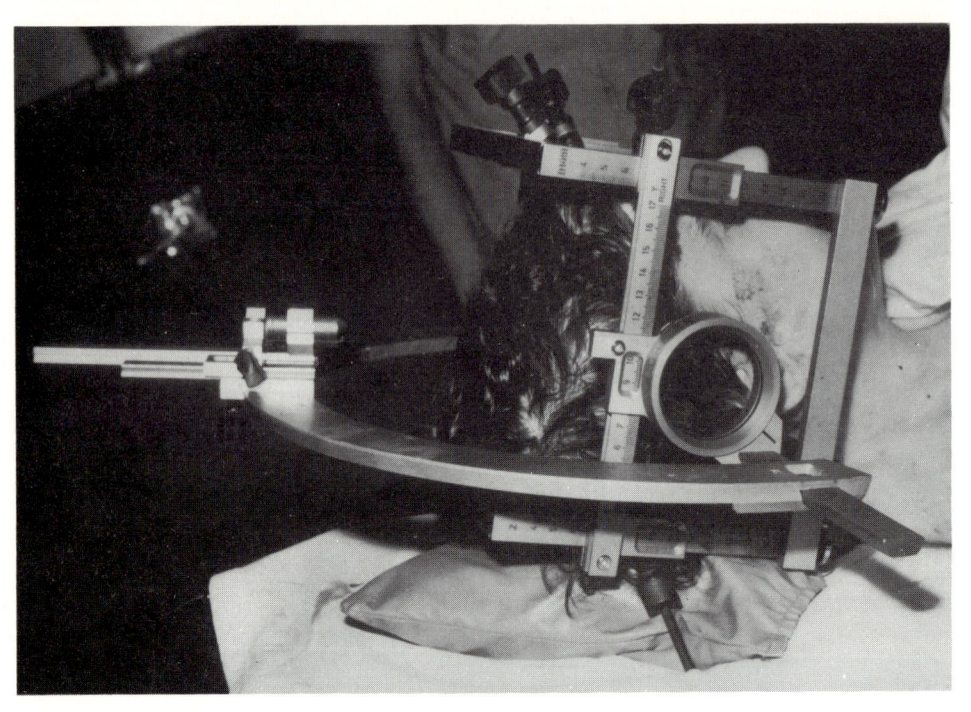

Fig. 10 *A patient with the fully assembled Leksell frame in position about to undergo thalamotomy.*

Using the technique described a resolution of 0.6 mm on reformatted images is obtained[2] and it is possible to visualize the internal capsule and the lateral limits of the thalamus, but not the intra-thalamic nuclei.[4] It is therefore still necessary to calculate our target co-ordinates from the mid-commissural point. Other workers have compared CT-guided thalamotomies with those using intraventricular contrast and have found that variations in target selection for each co-ordinate were no greater than 0.5 mm.[1,2]

Since the Leksell frame and CT-scanners are a widely available combination, CT-guided thalamotomy should be considered for treating patients far more commonly than at present, particularly those with intention tremor.

Recently some workers have used nuclear magnetic resonance for calculating co-ordinates in stereotaxic surgery[5,6] but as yet this is not such a widely available technique and an increase in accuracy sufficient to justify its use has not been demonstrated.

In conclusion we believe that CT-guided thalamotomy using the Leksell stereotaxic system provides the advantages of simplicity, accuracy, widely available technology, and a shorter inpatient stay.

Acknowledgement—To Mrs S. Normanton for her great help in continuously typing our revisions of the manuscript.

References

1 Laitinen, L. V. (1985): CT-Guided ablative stereotaxis without ventriculography. *Appl. Neurophysiol.* **48**, 18–21.
2 Latchaw, R. E., Dade Lunsford, L. & Kennedy, W. H. (1985): Reformatted imaging to define

the intercommissural line for CT-guided stereotaxic functional neurosurgery. *AJNR* **6**, 429–433.
3 Dade Lunsford, L. & Martinez, A. J. (1984): Stereotactic exploration of the brain in the era of computed tomography. *Surg. Neurol.* **22**, 222–230.
4 Burchiel, K. J., Ojemann, G. A. & Bolender, N. (1980): Localisation of stereotaxic centers by computerized tomographic scanning. *J. Neurosurg.* **53**, 861–863.
5 Leksell, L., Leksell, D. & Schwebel, J. (1985): Stereotaxis and nuclear magnetic resonance. *J. Neurol. Neurosurg. Psychiatry* **48**, 14–19.
6 Uematsu, S., Rosenbaum, A. E., *et al.*, al. (1987). Magnetic resonance planned thalamotomy followed by X-ray/CT guided thalamotomy. *Acta. Neurochir.* (Suppl) **39**, 21–24.

49

CHRONIC VIM-THALAMIC STIMULATION IN

MOVEMENT DISORDERS

Alim Louis Benabid, Pierre Pollak*,
Alain Louveau, Marc Hommel*, Jean Perret*
and Jacques De Rougemont

*Service de Neurochirurgie, Hôpital A. Michallon; and *Clinique Neurologique, C.H.R.U. de Grenoble, BP 217 X, 38043 Grenoble Cedex, France.*

Summary

During neurosurgical stereotaxic thalamotomy procedures, it has been shown that acute high frequency (over 100 Hz) stimulation of the ventral intermediate nucleus (VIM) is capable of suppressing tremor and improving dystonia. Subsequently, chronic VIM stimulation was performed in seven patients (three of them having previously undergone contralateral thalamotomy) with the intention of improving the benefit/risk ratio of classical thalamotomy. A coarse mixed tremor was suppressed in three parkinsonian patients and greatly improved in another without any notable adverse effects. In contrast, improvement seen in three other patients with abnormal involuntary movements was only maintained for 1 to 6 months. These preliminary results are encouraging but further evaluation is needed as well as technological improvement and adaptation of the commercial deep brain stimulators presently available.

Introduction

Stereotaxic ventral intermediate nucleus (VIM) thalamotomy can improve various kinds of drug-resistant movement disorders including rest and postural tremor,[1] action tremor and dystonia.[2] However, tremor or abnormal involuntary movements (AIMs) may recur in some patients and the early and late morbidity is not negligible. Furthermore bilateral thalamotomy is known to induce unacceptable adverse effects such as dysarthria in a high proportion of patients.

During the neurosurgical procedures related to thalamotomy, electrical stimulation is one of the neurophysiological means used to control the location of the electrode in the target. According to previous reports,[3] AIMS can be modified by electrical stimulation and in our experience such movements, especially tremor, can be suppressed or greatly improved in a reversible manner if high frequency ($\geq$ 100 Hz) stimulation is applied. We thought that this favourable effect could be maintained in the long term by chronic thalamic stimulation, thus offering a better benefit/risk ratio than classical thalamotomy, more particularly if a bilateral operation is considered.

Patients and methods

The clinical characteristics of the seven patients are shown in the Table. Each patient was placed in a Talairach stereotaxic frame and iopamiron ventriculography was performed. The VIM target was drawn according to Guiot's method.[4] Under local anaesthesia, a Radionics electrode was introduced into the thalamic VIM nucleus and its location was checked by X-ray and by stimulation, which induced paraesthesia in the hand at 50 Hz and blocked tremor or improved AIMs at 100 Hz. After removing the first electrode, a chronic stimulating electrode (Medtronic QUAD or DBS) was implanted in the same location. If necessary, the same procedure was performed in the contralateral hemisphere. This electrode was initially connected to a percutaneous extension for test stimulation during the postoperative period. If the external stimulation was judged satisfactory, a permanent stimulator was implanted (Medtronic SE4 or ITREL).

Results

Tests during surgery

In all patients, at low frequency (50 Hz; 0.5 msec), paraesthesia was usually induced in the contralateral hand at about 0.5 volt. At high frequency (100 Hz; 0.5 msec; 1 to 2 volts), paraesthesia was still present but the tremor was blocked instantly and reappeared immediately after the end of the stimulation. During the blockade, voluntary movements

Table. *Clinical characteristics of patients treated with chronic thalamic stimulation.*

Sex	Age	Motor Symptoms	Aetiology	Previous thalamotomy	Chronic thalamic stimulation
F	66	Mixed tremor	Parkinson's disease	Left	Right
M	64	Mixed tremor	Idiopathic	Right	Left
M	44	Mixed tremor	Parkinson's disease		Left
F	55	Mixed tremor	Parkinson's disease		Right
M	31	Cerebellar tremor	Multiple sclerosis	Left (early recurrence)	Left
F	23	Generalized myoclonic dystonia	Post-anoxic		Right and left
F	43	Segmental dystonia	Idiopathic		Left

were normally performed and the drawing of a spiral was greatly improved. For the three patients with AIMs, the improvement was clear but less impressive.

Chronic VIM stimulation

During the test period, the most effective stimulation frequency was about 200 Hz. This could not be achieved with the ITREL type implantable stimulator, the maximal frequency of which was 130 Hz. This calls for technical improvements. The new DBS Medtronic electrode appears to be more suitable than the QUAD electrode.

A coarse mixed tremor was suppressed in three parkinsonian patients and greatly improved in another. These favourable results in patients with tremor have lasted up to 15 months. Tremor reappears whenever the stimulation is stopped. In contrast, improvement was significant in patients with AIMS only during 1 to 6 months.

Tolerable paraesthesia occurred in three patients, but disappeared in two patients within 2 months.

Discussion

Chronic VIM-thalamic stimulation is suggested as a possible alternative to classical thalamotomy in the treatment of tremors, especially when a bilateral operation is considered.[5] The main advantage of this technique is based on the reversibility of the possible adverse effects.

Thalamic stimulation may not be recommended as a routine procedure for the treatment of AIMs,[6] but evidence is accumulating that this method is safe, has no serious side-effects and may provide improvement in some cases.

Technical developments such as pacemakers operating in the 100–300 Hz range would improve these preliminary but encouraging results.

References

1 Ohye, C., Hirai, T., Miyazaki, M., Shibazaki, T. & Nakajima, H. (1982): VIM thalamotomy for the treatment of various kinds of tremor. *Appl. Neurophysiol.* **45**, 275–280.
2 Andrew, J., Fowler, C. J. & Harrison, M. J. G. (1983): Stereotaxic thalamotomy in 55 cases of dystonia. *Brain* **106**, 981–1000.
3 Andy, P. J. (1983): Thalamic stimulation for control of movement disorders. *Appl. Neurophysiol.* **46**, 107–111.
4 Taren, J., Guiot, G., Derome, P. & Trigot, J. C. (1968): Hazards of stereotaxic thalamectomy. *J. Neurosurg.* **29**, 173–182.
5 Benabid, A. L., Pollak, P., Louveau, A., Henry, S. & De Rougemont, J. (1988): Combined (thalamotomy and stimulation) stereotactic surgery of the VIM thalamic nucleus for bilateral Parkinson disease. *Appl. Neurophysiol*. (In Press).
6 Marsden, C. D. & Fahn, S. (1982): Surgical approaches to the dyskinesias: afterword. In *Movement disorders*, eds C. D. Marsden & S. Fahn, pp 345–347. London: Butterworth Scientific.

CLINICAL ASPECTS

Imaging studies

50

THE INTEGRITY OF THE DOPAMINERGIC SYSTEM IN MULTIPLE SYSTEM ATROPHY AND PURE AUTONOMIC FAILURE STUDIED WITH PET

D. J. Brooks*[†], E. P. Salmon*, R. Bannister[†],
C. Mathias[†] and R. S. J. Frackowiak*[†]

*MRC Cyclotron Unit, Hammersmith Hospital, Du Cane Road,
London W12 0HS; and [†]Institute of Neurology, National Hospital for
Nervous Diseases, Queen Square, London WC1N 3BG, UK

Summary

Using ^{18}F-dopa, ^{11}C-nomifensine, and positron emission tomography (PET), the striatal dopamine storage capacity and integrity of the dopamine re-uptake system has been measured in seven patients with multiple system atrophy (MSA), and four patients with pure autonomic failure (PAF). The MSA subjects showed a parallel fall-out in striatal F-dopa uptake and ^{11}C-nomifensine binding compared to controls, the putamen being worse affected than the caudate. There was a correlation between locomotor disability and fall-off of putamen, but not caudate, dopamine storage capacity. Two of the four patients with pure autonomic failure had subnormal levels of putamen F-dopa uptake, and one of these two had reduced putamen ^{11}C-nomifensine binding. It is concluded that rigidity in MSA correlates with putamen dysfunction, and that patients with pure autonomic failure may have sub-clinical impairment of their dopaminergic system.

Introduction

Patients with autonomic failure in the absence of a peripheral neuropathy may have additional symptoms and signs of extrapyramidal dysfunction, as in Parkinson's disease and multiple system atrophy, or may have pure autonomic failure without signs of central nervous system dysfunction. The pathology of MSA is a fall-out of striato-nigral, brainstem nuclear, and cerebellar neurons.[1] The degree of autonomic failure present in MSA correlates with the cell loss from the intermediolateral columns of the cord.[2] MSA is not associated with Lewy body or neurofibrillary tangle formation. Dopamine and noradrenaline levels are reduced in the striatum, substantia nigra, nucleus accumbens, and locus coeruleus.[1]

In Parkinson's disease loss of cells with Lewy body formation is found in the pars compacta of the substantia nigra, and in the locus coeruleus,[3] with consequent low levels of dopamine in both caudate and putamen.[9] If autonomic failure is present Lewy body degeneration of the cells of the intermediolateral columns, dorsal nucleus of the vagus, and sympathetic ganglia also occurs.[4-7]

Few pathological studies have been performed to date on subjects with pure autonomic failure. Cases that have come to autopsy have shown Lewy body disease similar to that of parkinsonian patients with autonomic failure, though relative preservation of nigral cells has been noted.[4,8]

The purpose of this study was to assess the integrity of the dopaminergic system in patients with long standing pure autonomic failure, to determine whether sub-clinical striatal dysfunction is indeed present in these subjects. It was also desired to examine the pattern of striatal hypofunction in MSA to see whether locomotor disability correlated best with impairment of putamen or caudate function.

Methods

Patient selection

Seven patients with multiple system atrophy, age range 41–73 years, were selected for study. All patients had extrapyramidal rigidity, bradykinesia, and abnormal cardiovascular reflexes on formal testing. Varying degrees of cerebellar ataxia, bladder dysfunction and sexual dysfunction, and hypohidrosis were also present. CT scans were either normal, or showed brainstem and cerebellar atrophy. Four subjects were levodopa unresponsive; three subjects had not been given levodopa due to their initial presentation with profound postural hypotension. Clinical disease duration ranged from 3–12 years.

Four patients with pure autonomic failure were also studied, age range 60–66 years. All patients had impaired cardiovascular reflexes, with variable degrees of bladder dysfunction, sexual dysfunction, and hypohidrosis. Clinical disease duration ranged from 7–12 years.

Patient studies were compared with those of six aged-matched normal controls.

PET scanning

Putamen and caudate dopamine storage capacity were measured by following the kinetics of ^{18}F-dopa uptake using positron emission tomography.[10] Integrity of dopamine re-uptake sites was assessed by measuring ^{11}C-nomifensine striatal uptake.[11] PET scans were performed using a CTI ECAT-V scanner which yielded 15 axial tomographic cuts with a resolution of 7 mm.[12]

Results

Figure 1 shows F-dopa incorporation into the striatum of a normal subject and a patient with multiple system atrophy. The control has higher tracer levels in putamen than head of caudate, while the MSA subject shows profound loss of striatal dopamine storage capacity. Figure 2 shows specific/non-specific ^{18}F-dopa uptake against time for the

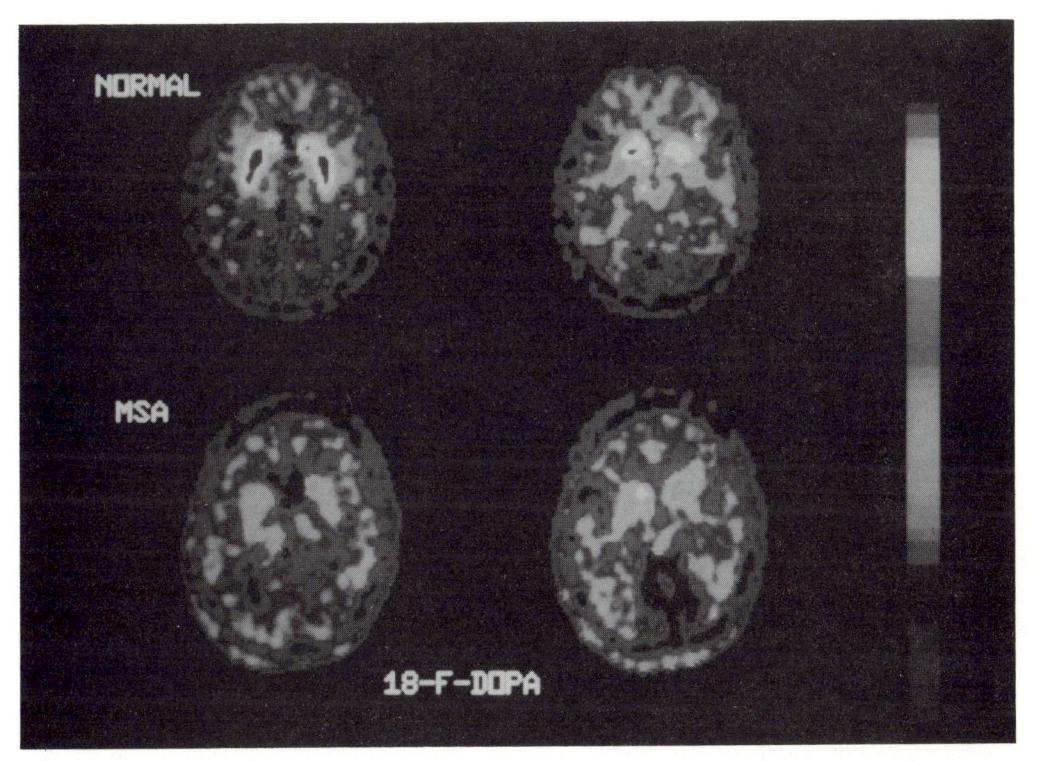

Fig. 1. *PET scans of F-dopa uptake in a normal and an MSA subject at the level of the striatum.*

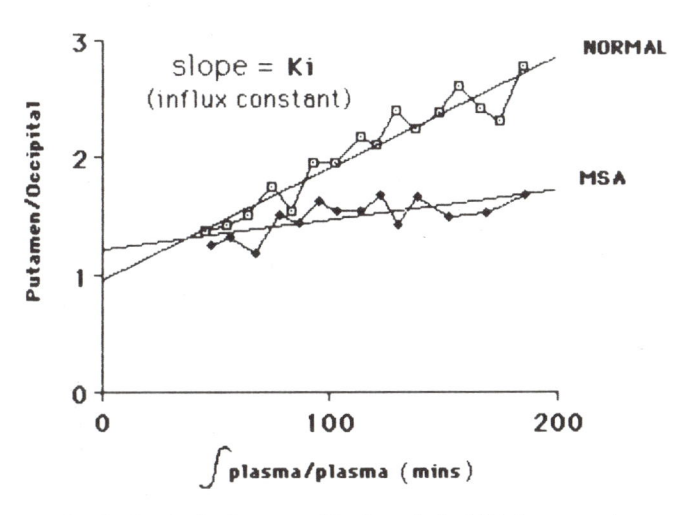

Fig. 2. *Multiple time graphical analysis 18F-dopa uptake.*

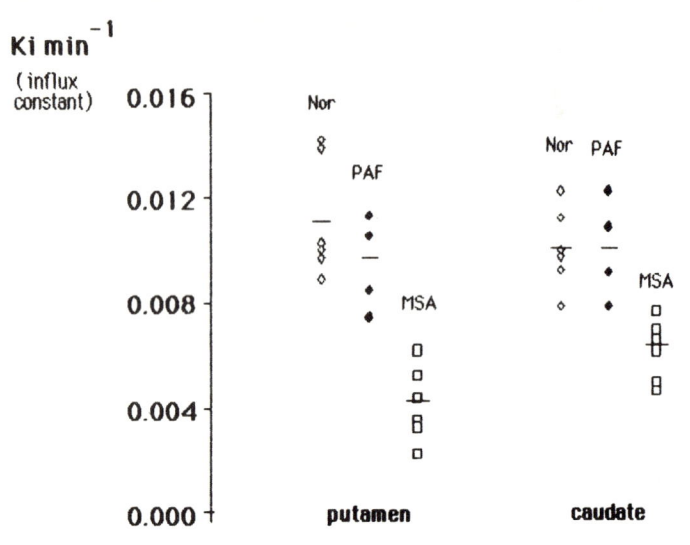

Fig. 3. *18-F-dopa uptake in autonomic failure.*

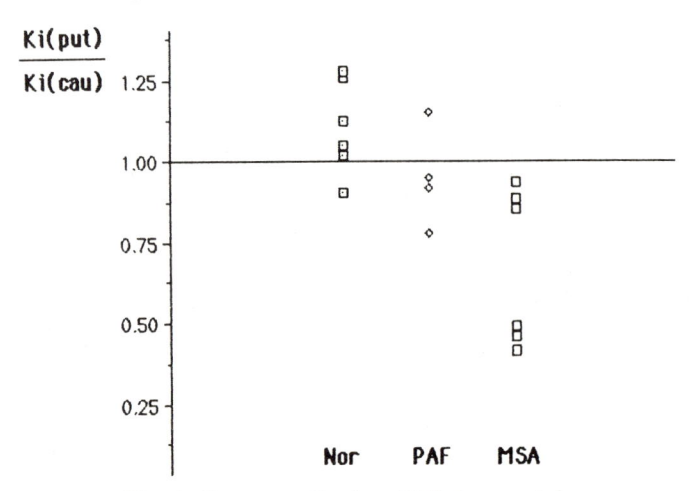

Fig. 4. *Putamen:Caudate 18-F-dopa uptake.*

putamen of normal and MSA subjects, using Patlak analysis.[13] This graphical approach allows tracer influx constants (K_i) to be measured. It can be seen that putamen K_i values are severely depressed for the MSA patients, caudate values being relatively less affected (Fig. 3). Two of the four pure autonomic failure subjects (disease duration 7 and 11 years) also had subnormal putamen ^{18}F-dopa K_i values, though all four PAF caudate K_i values were within the normal range. In five out of six controls, putamen K_i values were higher than caudate. All MSA subjects showed the reverse trend, as did three of the four PAF subjects (Fig. 4). Figure 5 shows that putamen K_i values inversely correlated with the degree of disability of the MSA patients on the Hoehn and Yahr scale. This was not the case for MSA caudate K_i values.

^{11}C-nomifensine (NMF) binding to thalamus and striatum is illustrated in Fig. 6 for a normal subject and an MSA patient. Striatal tracer uptake is severely diminished in the

Multiple system atrophy and pure autonomic failure studied with PET

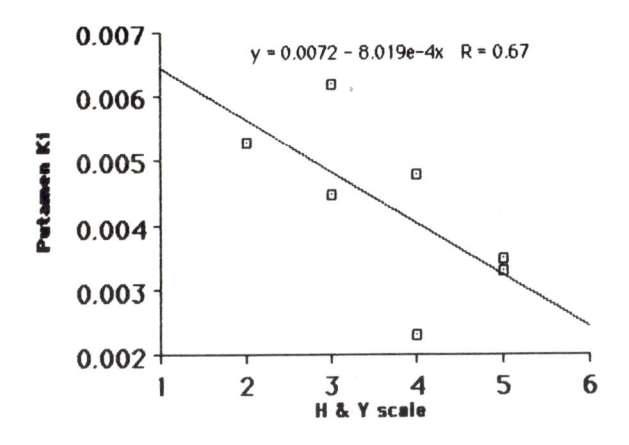

Fig. 5. *MSA F-dopa uptake.*

MSA case. Figure 7 shows the integrated uptake curves for ^{11}C-nomifensine binding to normal putamen and cerebellum. The uptake ratio A/B at 1 hour gives a measure of specific tracer binding to dopamine re-uptake sites. Figure 8 shows that putamen ^{11}C-NMF binding is significantly reduced in MSA, and in one of three PAF subjects.

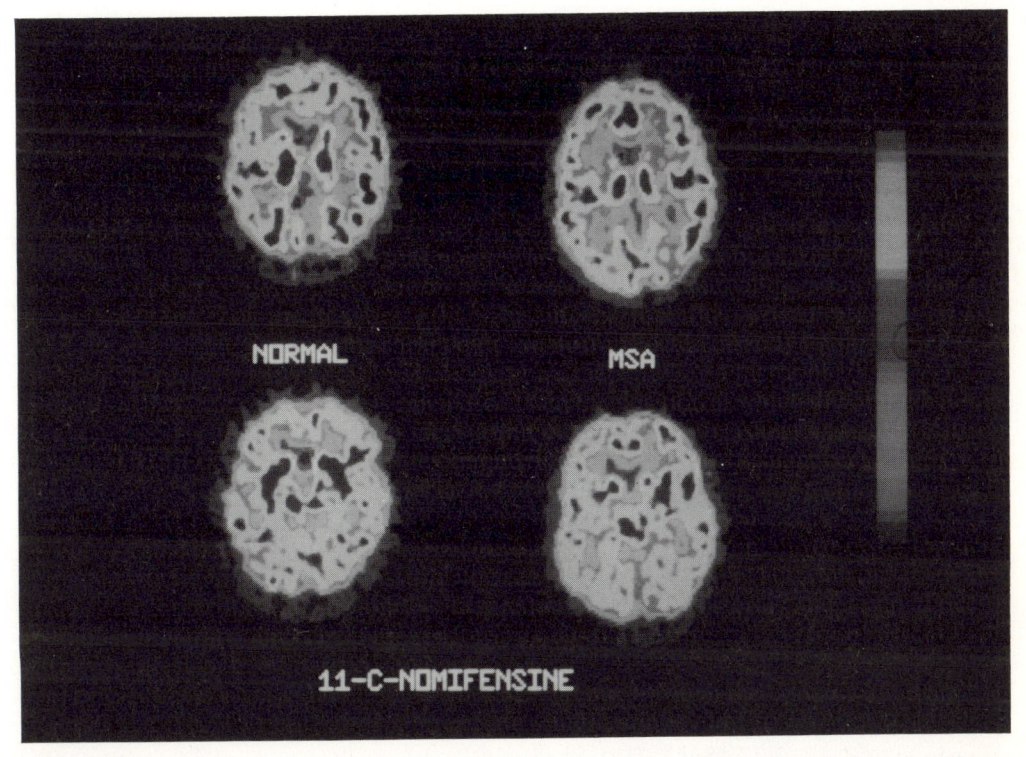

Fig. 6. *PET scans of ^{11}C-nomifensine in a normal and an MSA subject at the level of the thalamus and striatum.*

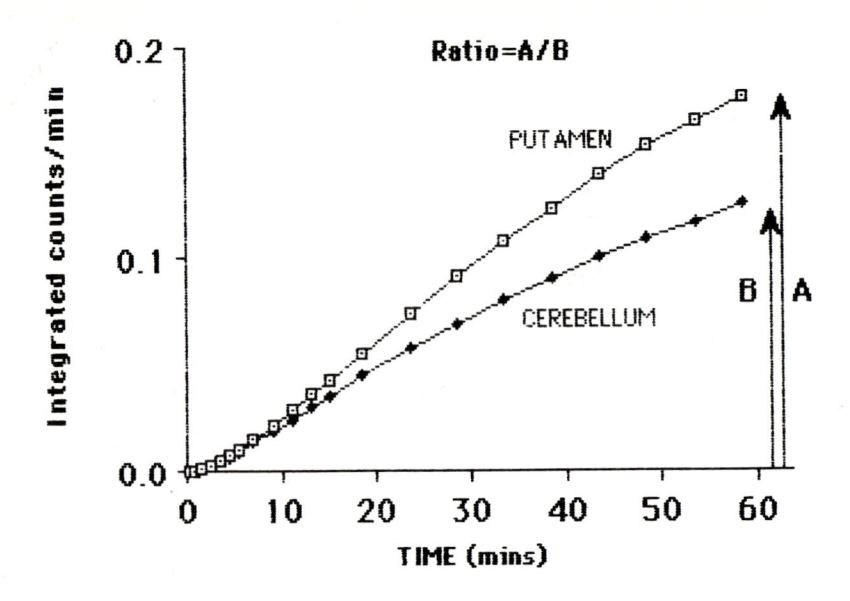

Fig. 7. *Normal integrated ^{11}C-NMF uptake.*

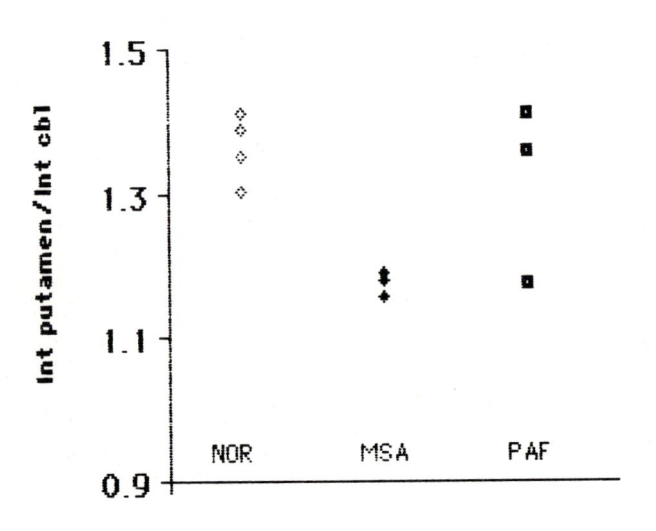

Fig. 8. *^{11}C-nomifensine uptake (putamen).*

Discussion

Our findings suggest that sub-clinical impairment of the integrity of the dopaminergic system can be present in pure autonomic failure. Whether PAF patients with low F-dopa uptake will go on to develop parkinsonism remains to be seen. The MSA subjects showed a parallel fall-out of dopamine storage capacity and dopamine re-uptake sites in both putamen and caudate, suggesting a loss of dopaminergic nerve terminals had occurred. The putamen was worst affected, and putamen fall off of F-dopa uptake correlated well with patient locomotor disability. This was not the case for the caudate nucleus. Primate studies have shown that the motor and sensory cortex have a direct input into the putamen, whereas caudate receives input primarily from association areas.[14] Our results, taken in combination with these primate studies, suggest that the putamen, rather than the caudate, is directly involved with the control of locomotor functions. Whether caudate hypofunction correlates with frontal lobe deficits is currently being evaluated.

References

1. Spokes, E. G. S., Bannister, R. & Oppenheimer, D. R. (1979): Multiple system atrophy with autonomic failure. *J. Neurol. Sci.* **43**, 59–82.
2. Oppenheimer, D. R. (198): Lateral horn cells in progressive autonomic failure. *J. Neurol. Sci.* **46**, 393–404.
3. Den Hartog Jager, W. A. & Bethlem, J. (1960): The distribution of the Lewy bodies in the central and autonomic nervous system in idiopathic paralysis agitans. *J. Neurol. Neurosurg. Psychiatry* **23**, 283–290.
4. Vanderhaeghen, J. J., Perier, O. & Sternon, J. E. (1979): Pathological findings in idiopathic orthostatic hypotension. Its relationship with Parkinson's Disease. *Arch. Neurol.* **22**, 207–214.
5. Schober, R., Langston, J. W. & Forno, L. S. (1975): Idiopathic orthostatic hypotension: biochemical and pathological observations in two cases. *Eur. Neurol.* **13**, 177–188.
6. Rajput, A. H. & Rozdilsky, B. (1976): Dysautonomia in parkinsonism: a clinico-pathological study. *J. Neurol. Neurosurg. Psychiatry* **39**, 1092–1100.
7. Roesmann, U., Van Den Noort, S. & McFarland, D. E. (1971): Idiopathic orthostatic hypotension. *Arch. Neurol.* **24**, 503–510.
8. Johnson, R. H., Lee, G. de J., Oppenheimer, D. R. & Spalding, J. M. K. (1966): Autonomic failure with orthostatic hypotension due to intermediolateral column degeneration. *Q. J. Med.* **35**, 276–292.
9. Javoy-Agid, F., Ruberg, M., Hirsch, E., *et al.* (1986): Recent progress in the neurochemistry of Parkinson's disease. In *Recent developments in Parkinson's disease*, ed S. Fahn *et al.*, pp 67–83. New York: Raven.
10. Leenders, K. L., Palmer, A., Turton, D., *et al.* (1986). Dopa uptake and dopamine receptor binding visualised in the human brain in vivo. In *Recent developments in Parkinson's disease*, ed S. Fahn *et al*, pp 103–113. New York: Raven.
11. Tedroff, J., Aquilonius, S. M., Hartvig, P., *et al.* (1988): Monoamine re-uptake sites in the human brain evaluated in vivo by means of ^{11}C-nomifensine and positron emission tomography: the effects of age and Parkinson's disease. *Acta Neurol. Scand.* **77**, 192–201.
12. Spinks, T. J., Jones, T., Gilardi, M. C. & Heather, J. D. (1988): Physical performance of the latest generation of commercial positron scanners. *IEEE Trans. Nuc. Sci.* (In Press)
13. Patlak, C. S. Blasberg, R. G. & Fenstermacher, J. D. (1983): Graphical evaluation of blood-to-brain transfer constants for multiple-time uptake data. *J. Cereb. Blood Flow Metab.* **3**, 1–7.
14. Alexander, G. D., De Long, M. R. & Strick, P. L. (1986): Parallel organisation of functionally segregated circuits linking basal ganglia and cortex. *Annu. Rev. Neurosci.* **9**, 357–382.

51

SINGLE PHOTON EMISSION TOMOGRAPHY (SPET) IN PROGRESSIVE SUPRANUCLEAR PALSY: A COMPARISON WITH CORTICAL DEMENTIAS

P. J. Goulding, D. Neary, J. S. Snowden,
B. Northen, A. W. I. Burjan*, R. A. Shields*
M. C. Prescott[†] and H. J. Testa[†]

*Departments of Neurology, *Medical Physics and [†]Nuclear Medicine, Manchester Royal Infirmary, Manchester M13 9WL, UK*

Summary

SPET images from patients with progressive supranuclear palsy (PSP) showed reduced uptake in the subcortical regions of the anterior hemispheres and were distinct from those from patients with Alzheimer's disease (AD) and dementia of frontal-lobe type (DFT). The pattern of psychological breakdown in PSP also differed from that demonstrated by those patients. The findings are consistent with the concept of 'subcortical dementia' and suggest that subcortical structures may play an important role in cognition.

Introduction

Progressive supranuclear palsy is a degenerative brain disease which exclusively affects subcortical structures. It is characterized by ophthalmoplegia, pseudobulbar palsy and axial rigidity, and is associated with a progressive decline of mental function.[1] The mental changes in patients with PSP have been referred to as a 'subcortical dementia'[2] and purportedly differ from the 'cortical dementia' of Alzheimer's disease.[3] The concept of subcortical dementia however remains controversial.

This study examines, in patients with PSP, the relationship between pattern of psychological disorder and regions of reduced uptake demonstrated by SPET. Comparisons with AD and DFT[4] permit evaluation of the usefulness of the distinction between cortical and subcortical dementia.

Patients

The study group comprised 14 patients who showed physical findings typical of progressive supranuclear palsy. There was an equal sex incidence. Mean age and length of history were 63 and 5 years respectively. Thirty-five patients with clinically presumed Alzheimer's disease and 21 with a diagnosis of DFT, a form of 'cortical dementia' affecting predominantly the frontal lobes,[4] served as comparison groups. Their age and length of history did not differ from those of PSP patients. The criteria for diagnosis of AD and DFT have been described previously.[4,5]

Methods

Patients had detailed psychological assessment as described elsewhere.[5] SPET imaging was carried out using the radiopharmaceutical ^{99m}Tc-HMPAO. Data were acquired using an IGE 400 A/T rotating gamma camera and a Medical Data Systems A3 computer. Transaxial sections were reconstructed and photographed alongside an anterior planar view, with a horizontal line indicating the level of the section. Images were reported with respect to areas of reduced uptake. All scan reports were performed without knowledge of clinical diagnosis.

Results

Psychological evaluation

In PSP, assessment demonstrated a slowness of response initiation, concreteness of thought, variable amnesia and a difficulty in changing mental set. Performance on tests of abstraction and sequencing, sensitive to frontal lobe function, was impaired. Patients showed an appropriate degree of concern regarding the accuracy of their performance.

The psychological breakdown in PSP was distinct from that in AD. Aphasia and visuospatial disturbance which were characteristic of AD and suggest impaired function of the temporal and parietal cortices did not occur in PSP. Moreover, the severe pervasive amnesia demonstrated by AD patients was not a feature in PSP.

A number of findings were common to PSP and DFT. In both groups, patients showed a concreteness of thought, variable amnesia and impaired performance on 'frontal lobe tests'. However, in contrast to those with PSP, patients with DFT displayed features suggestive of frontal cortical dysfunction. Typically there was a history of progressive personality change and social misconduct, and on mental testing patients were inattentive, disinhibited and distractable and were not concerned by failure.

Neither patients with DFT nor those with AD demonstrated the slowness in initiation of response or difficulty shifting train of thought prominent in patients with PSP.

SPET images

The appearances on the SPET images are presented in Table 1. Scans from patients with PSP were characterized by a selective reduction in uptake in the anterior cerebral hemispheres, contrasting with the reduced posterior hemisphere uptake typical of AD. Though selective reduction in anterior hemisphere uptake occurred also in DFT, the presence of a rim of cortical uptake distinguished images of patients with PSP from those

Table 1. *Regions of reduced uptake.*

	Selective anterior hemisphere reduction	Presence of posterior hemisphere reduction	None
PSP	13	0	1
AD	2	27	6
DFT	16	4*	1

*Three of four had larger anterior regions of reduced uptake.
PSP = progressive supranuclear palsy; AD = Alzheimer's disease; DFT = dementia of frontal-lobe type.

Table 2. *Appearance of selective anterior hemisphere defects.*

	Cortical rim preserved	Cortical rim absent
PSP	10	3
DFT	2	14

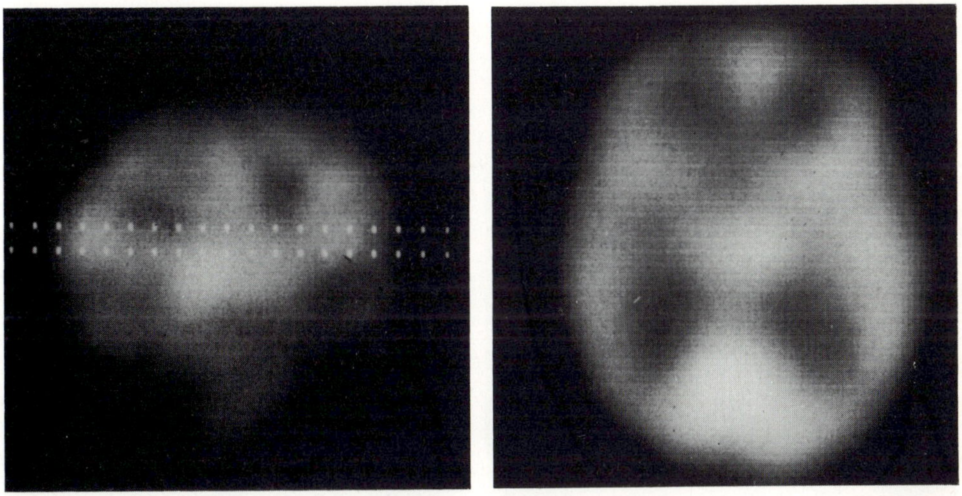

Fig. 1. *Normal control aged 58.* SPET image demonstrates symmetrical uptake in both cerebral hemispheres.

of patients with DFT (Table 2). A scan from a control subject and typical images from the three patient groups are shown in Figs 1–4.

Discussion

Distribution of tracer in PSP was consistent with frontal lobe hypometabolism previously demonstrated by positron emission tomography,[6] though in this study areas of reduced uptake appeared to involve subcortical regions of the anterior hemispheres. SPET findings were in keeping with patients' poor performance on 'frontal lobe tests'. It has been suggested that impaired frontal lobe function in PSP is related to loss of activating afferents from the subcortex.[2]

P. J. Goulding et al.

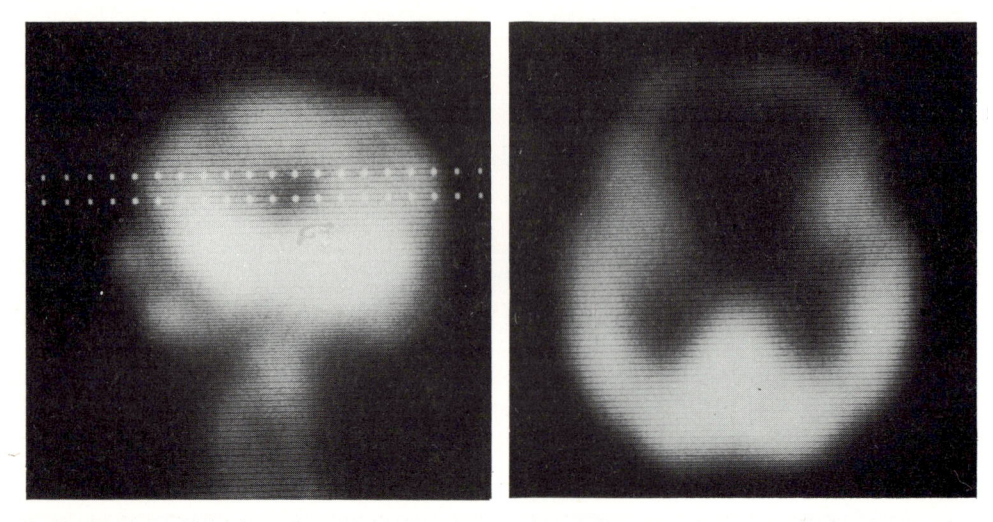

Fig. 2. *64-year-old male with progressive supranuclear palsy.* Psychological evaluation revealed slowing of response initiation and difficulty changing mental set, in the absence of visuospatial disorder or aphasia. There was no history of conduct disorder. SPET image demonstrates a selective reduction of anterior hemisphere uptake with preservation of the cortical rim.

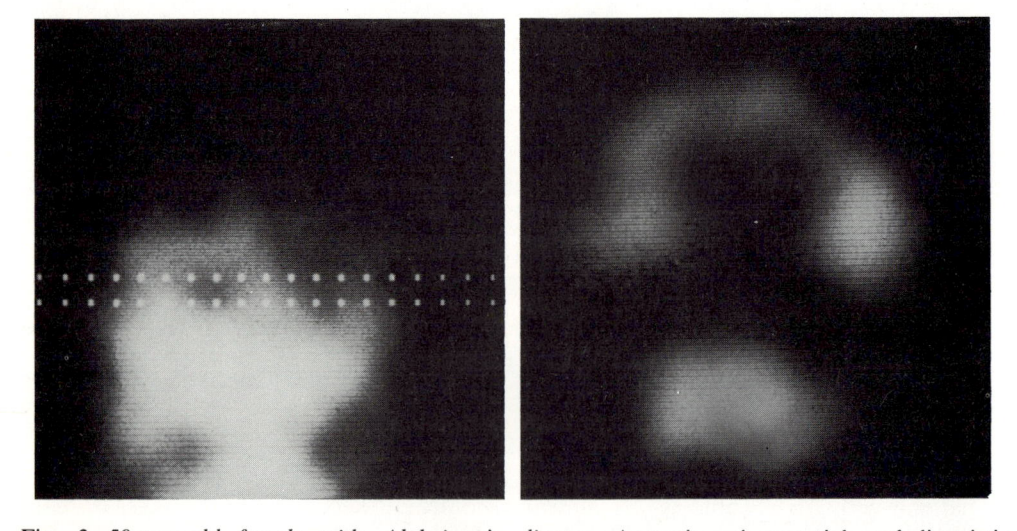

Fig. 3. *59-year-old female with Alzheimer's disease.* Amnesia, visuospatial and linguistic impairment were demonstrated on psychological examination. SPET image shows a symmetrical decrease in uptake in the posterior hemispheres.

As in PSP, patients with DFT showed both psychological and SPET evidence of frontal lobe dysfunction. However, frontal cortical impairment, manifest as conduct disorder, a typical feature of DFT, was not seen in PSP and accorded with preserved anterior cortical uptake on SPET.

Absence of aphasia and visuospatial disturbance in PSP was in keeping with intact posterior hemisphere uptake. By contrast, in AD, where psychological assessment

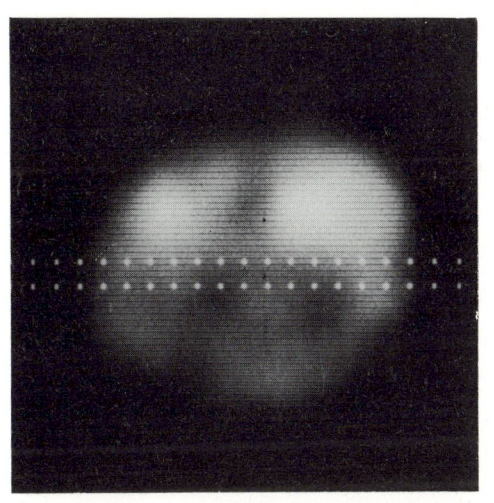

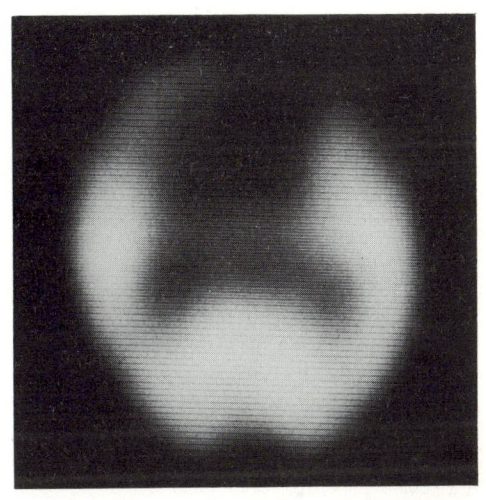

Fig. 4. *This 55-year-old female with dementia of frontal-lobe type displayed disinhibition and social misconduct.* SPET image shows a selective reduction of anterior hemisphere uptake which extends through the cortical rim.

suggested impaired temporoparietal function, posterior hemisphere defects were characteristic.

The pattern of uptake on SPET suggests that anterior subcortical function is reduced in progressive supranuclear palsy. Impaired response initiation and difficulty changing mental set shown by PSP patients may be explained on this basis. These findings are consistent with the concept of 'subcortical dementia'.

Acknowledgement—We thank the North West Regional Health Authority for financial support.

References

1 Kristensen, M. O. (1985): Progressive supranuclear palsy – 20 years later. *Acta Neurol. Scand.* **71**, 177–189.
2 Albert, M. L., Feldman, R. G. & Willis, A. L. (1974): The 'subcortical dementia' of progressive supranuclear palsy. *J. Neurol. Neurosurg. Psychiatry* **37**, 121–130.
3 Cummings, J. L. & Benson, D. F. (1984): Subcortical dementia. Review of an emerging concept. *Arch. Neurol.* **41**, 874–879.
4 Neary, D., Snowden, J. S., Northen, B. & Goulding, P. (1988): Dementia of frontal-lobe type. *J. Neurol. Neurosurg. Psychiatry* **51**, 353–361.
5 Neary, D., Snowden, J. S., Bowen, D. M., Sims, N. R., Mann, D. M. A., Benton, J. S., Northen, B., Yates, P. O. & Davison, A. N. (1986): Neuropsychological syndromes in presenile dementia due to cerebral atrophy. *J. Neurol. Neurosurg. Psychiatry* **49**, 163–174.
6 D'Antona, R., Baron, J. C., Samson, Y., Serdaru, M., Viader, F., Agid, Y. & Cambier, J. (1985): Subcortical dementia. Frontal cortex hypometabolism detected by positron emission tomography in patients with progressive supranuclear palsy. *Brain* **108**, 785–799.

52

A MAGNETIC RESONANCE IMAGING EVALUATION

OF MOVEMENT DISORDERS

Ph. Lebrun-Grandié*[†§], P. Kien*, F. Tison[†],
P. Henry[†], J. M. Caillé*, B. Bioulac[§]

*Service de neuroradiologie, Hôpital Pellegrin, 33076 Bordeaux; [†]Service de Neurologie, Hôpital Pellegrin, 33076 Bordeaux; [§]Laboratoire de Neurophysiologie, Groupe Motricité, UA CNRS 1200, Université de Bordeaux, II 33076 Bordeaux, France

Introduction

Precise morphological information on the central nervous system can be obtained using magnetic resonance imaging (MRI), particularly for the exploration of the sub-cortical and sub-tentorial structures.[1] Because of their magnetic properties, metallic ions can be detected with MRI.[2] It is of particular interest in the exploration of the extrapyramidal structures of the central nervous system. Using high-field MR (1.5 Tesla), different authors have shown the sensitivity of this technique in the analysis of metalloids in the basal ganglia.[1,3] The anatomical basis of movement disorders consists of morphological and structural alterations of the extra-pyramidal system and to explore these disorders MRI is therefore an attractive method.[5–6]

There are metal deposits varying with age in the putamen, pallidum, caudate nucleus, locus niger, and dentate nucleus of the cerebellum. The formation of brain iron is complex. It arises from different metabolic pathways (haemoglobin, ferritin, haemosiderin, cytochromes, neurotransmitters).[1] Iron is a paramagnetic tracer and therefore highlights the basal ganglia. T2-weighted MR images are very similar to anatomical brain sections with Perls stain, which specifically stains ferric iron.[1,3]

Diagnosis of movement disorders is of course based on clinical manifestations.[8] A simplified classification opposes akinetic-rigid syndromes (Parkinson's disease and parkinsonian syndromes) and dyskinesias (choreas and dystonias). Akinetic-rigid syndromes are caused by lesions of the nigro-neostriatal dopaminergic system or of a more complex loop, cortico-ponto-cerebello-dentato-rubro-thalamo-cortical.[9–11] Dystonic and choreic syndromes are caused by lesions of the contralateral caudate nucleus, putamen, pallidum or thalamus altering a cortico-striato-thalamo-cortical loop.[12–15]

Progress in the understanding of movement disorders necessitated better imaging of morphological, structural, biochemical and metabolic changes in the brain. MRI analyses focal atrophies and abnormal deposits in the basal ganglia *in vivo*. Different field strengths, from 0.1 to 1.5 Tesla, have given heterogeneous results in the T2-weighted sequences.[3-5] The example of Wilson's disease is of particular interest: with high-field MR, copper deposits appear to decrease the putaminal signal and increase it on low-field MR.[16,17]

In this study, using 0.5 Tesla MRI, we analysed the morphological alterations and signal changes in the striatum of patients with movement disorders.

Patients and methods

Patients:

We studied 60 patients suffering from movement disorders. There were 23 women and 37 men, their ages were 6 to 79 years (mean 50 years). Diagnoses of extra-pyramidal disorders were made clinically, a biological study being helpful in some cases. The distribution of movement disorders was: Parkinson's disease and parkinsonism (n = 33); Huntington's chorea and symptomatic choreas (n = 13); dystonias and Wilson's disease (n = 14)

Methods

Images were performed with 0.5 Tesla supraconductor Magniscan (CGR Thomson). Sequences were performed in the coronal and transverse plane with a 256 × 256 matrix. In each subject, T1-weighted (SE: 26/500) and T2-weighted (SE: 50/2000, 3 echoes) sequences were used. Anaesthesia was necessary in choreic disorders.

The imaging studies revealed: cortical atrophy, focal atrophy in T1-weighted acquisition and signal changes in extrapyramidal structures in T2-weighted images.

Results

Parkinson's disease

Four women and nine men presented with Parkinson's disease (36 to 65 years old, mean 52 years). Seven of them suffered from juvenile Parkinson's disease, and the others presented with advanced forms. None of them showed specific MR abnormalities. There was a signal decrease in T2-weighted axial images of the locus niger in some of these patients but this is encountered in normal subjects or patients without neurological disease. Moderate diffuse cortical atrophy was encountered in the oldest patients (without clinical signs of dementia).

Parkinsonian syndromes

There were 18 patients with parkinsonian syndromes, aged 19–73 years (mean 46 years).
(1) Two women presented with an akinetic-hypertonic syndrome after several months of treatment with neuroleptics (*toxic parkinsonism*). MRI displayed diffuse cortical atrophy without signal changes in the striatum.
(2) Three men (65–69 years) suffering from *progressive supranuclear palsy* presented a moderate degree of cortical atrophy and focal atrophy of the brainstem (Fig. 1).

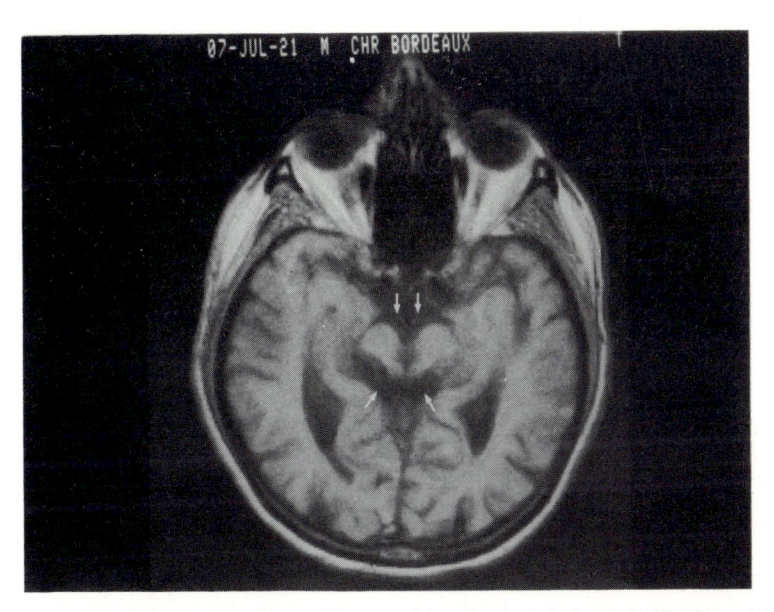

Fig. 1. *Progressive supranuclear palsy in a 65-year-old male.* Axial plane, 0.5T, T1-weighted image (400/12). Cerebral brainstem atrophy with enlargement of cerebrospinal fluid spaces (CSFC) (→).

(3) Two women and four men (19 to 68 years) showed clinical signs and symptoms evoking an idiopathic *olivo-ponto-cerebellar atrophy* (OPCA)(progressive cerebellar syndrome, akinetic-hypertonic syndromes, slowly progressive course, with no family history of movement disorder and no biological, radiological or clinical signs of secondary lesion). In the T1- and T2-weighted MR images, the mid-brain and all the structures of the posterior fossa (cerebellum, cerebral peduncles, pons and bulb) appeared atrophic with enlargement of the cerebrospinal fluid spaces. The cerebral cortex was moderately atrophic.

(4) One women and two men (47 to 73 years) suffering from the *Shy-Drager syndrome* presented a picture of diffuse cortical atrophy with focal atrophy of the posterior fossa, similar to those encountered in OPCA (Fig. 2).

(5) Six patients: four woman and two men (54 to 67 years) presented *unclassified parkinsonian syndromes* (association of an akineto-hypertonic syndrome with other signs: pyramidal syndrome, dysarthria, oesophageal spasms, focal dystonia). Two of them (a 65-year-old woman and a 67-year-old man) presented with moderate diffuse cortical atrophy with no focal abnormality of the extrapyramidal structures. In one 63-year-old women and a 62-year-old man with combined extrapyramidal and pyramidal syndromes, there was a bilateral signal increase on T2-weighted images of the putamen. A 54-year-old woman with probable neuro-axonal dystrophy exhibited an increased signal in both putamen in T2-weighted sequences (Fig. 3). A 50-year-old woman suffering from depression and unilateral akinesia presented with focal abnormalities in contralateral basal ganglia (caudate nucleus, putamen, pallidum, thalamus) and paraventricular leucodystrophy in T1- and T2-weighted images (Fig. 4).

Choreas

Huntington's disease: Four male subjects, aged 6, 25, 32 and 46 years, presented a family history and clinical signs of Huntington's disease. The six-year-old was suffering from a

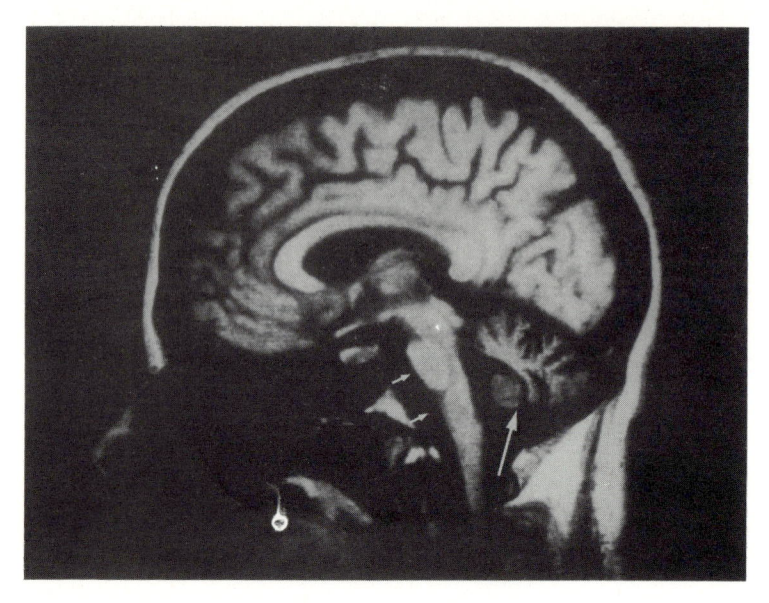

Fig. 2. *Shy-Drager syndrome in a 49-year-old male.* Sagittal plane, 0.5 T, T1-weighted images. Brainstem (→) and cerebellar (⟶) atrophy associated with diffuse cerebral atrophy, enlargement of cerebrospinal fluid spaces.

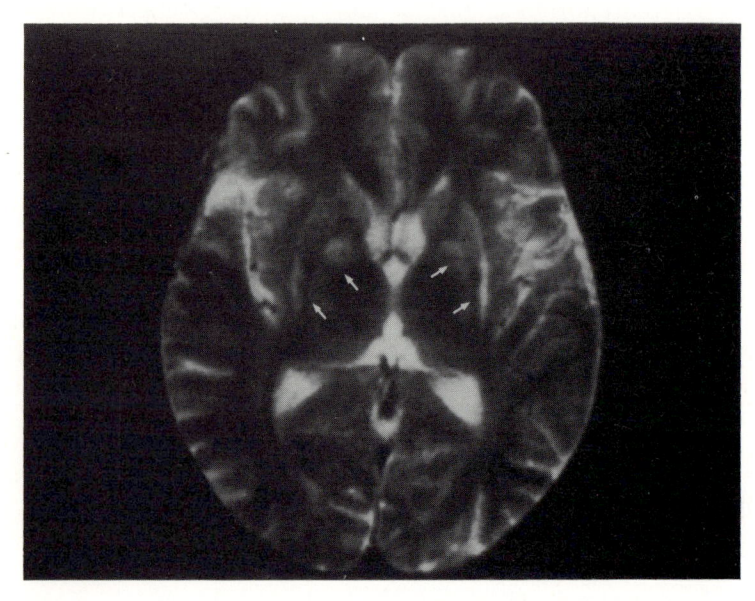

Fig. 3. *Parkinsonian syndrome in a 54-year-old female (akineto–hypertonic syndrome associated with spasms).* Axial plane, 0.5 T, T2-weighted image (2000/60, echo 2). Bilateral increase of signal in the striatum (→).

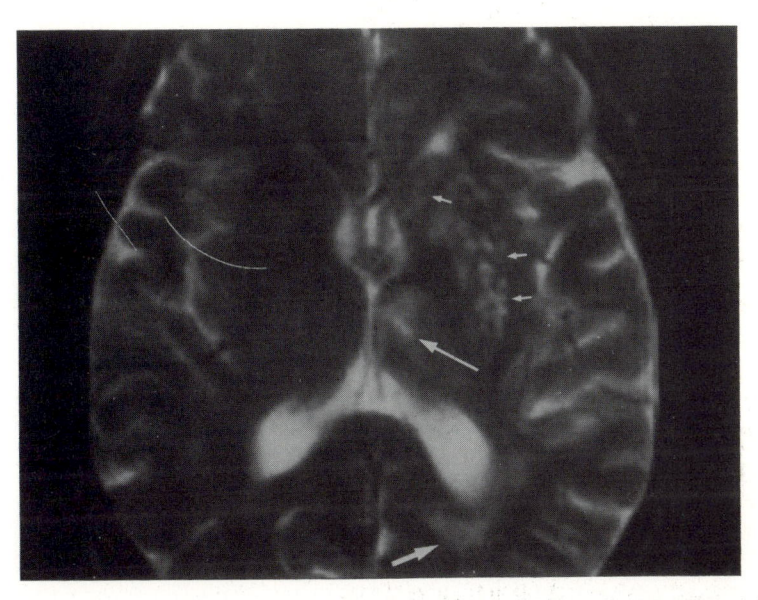

Fig. 4. *Hemiparkinsonism (right) in a 50-year-old female.* Axial planes, 0.5 T, T2-weighted images (2000/60, echo 2). Increased signal in the left caudate nucleus (→), putamen (→), pallidum and thalamus (⟶), associated with unilateral paraventricular leucodystrophy (➙).

rigid form of Huntington's disease with moderate school difficulties (beginning at age 4). The others presented choreic movements with intellectual impairment and their CT scans revealed diffuse cortical atrophy and focal atrophy of the caudate nucleus.

In all these cases, MRI showed more or less a diffuse cortical atrophy, a marked localized atrophy of the caudate nucleus and a lesser atrophy of the putamen. In two cases, the putamen showed an increased signal in T_2-weighted sequences. The degree of localized atrophy seemed to be correlated to the duration and severity of the clinical picture (Fig. 5).

Choreic syndromes: The nine patients presenting pure choreic, myoclonic or combined choreic-dystonic movements were clinically heterogeneous. Two patients presented with hemichorea of sudden onset and vascular lesions were visualized on MRI. In one case (Fig. 6) a lesion in the territory of the posterior choroidal artery was visualized. In the second case, a 79-year-old hypertensive male subject, MRI showed small lesions of the brain stem and hemispheric white matter in T2-weighted sequences.

In two women and three men, aged 24 to 62 years, whose MRIs were normal, the cause of their choreic syndrome was labelled coeliac disease, post-encephalitic tardive dyskinesias and two origin unknown.

Two women (aged 59 and 61 years) presented with progressive hemidyskinesia with onset 1 year before the MRI examination. No biological, familial or toxic cause was recognized. MR images showed a signal increase in the lenticular nucleus in T2-weighted sequences.

Wilson's disease

Three young patients (2 women, aged 15 and 21 years; one man aged 19 years) were suffering from a dyskinetic-dystonic syndrome. The two female subjects presented mental

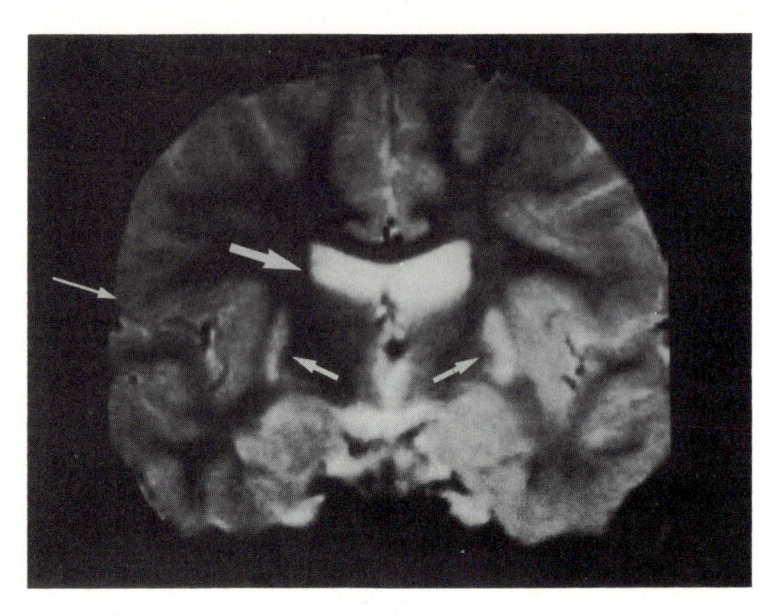

Fig. 5. *Huntington's disease (rigid form) in a 6-year-old male*. Frontal plane, 0.5 T, T2-weighted image (2000/60, echo 2). Bilateral atrophy of the caudate nucleus (→), moderate diffuse cortical atrophy (——→) and bilateral increase of signal in the putamen (→).

impairment, one of them with aphasia and comitiality. Wilson's disease had previously been proven biologically (reduced serum copper and caeruloplasmin, increased urinary copper excretion).

MRI showed bilateral abnormal signals in the putamen on T1- and T2-weighted images, hyposignal in T1, hypersignal in T2. The putamen was heterogeneous and appeared atrophic. In one patient, there were signs of leucoencephalopathy with hypersignal in frontal areas in T2-weighted sequences (Fig. 7).

Dystonias

We studied seven patients presenting with recent localized dystonia with or without associated extrapyramidal rigidity. In one of them, there was a bilateral signal abnormality in the putamen in spite of the unilateral symptomatology. In another patient presenting with a progressive asymmetrical dystonia for the past year, there was a heterogeneous bilateral hypersignal of the pallidum (Fig. 8).

In four cases of generalized dystonia associated with dyskinesia which began in infancy (three of which had presented severe neonatal difficulties), MRI was normal apart from a diffuse cortical atrophy associated with localized atrophies in the cerebellar structures in one of them.

Discussion

In movement disorders, MR imaging shows focal and diffuse morphological changes of the central nervous system and, in some cases, signal abnormalities of the striatum. These findings resemble the histopathological changes but show little correlation with the clinical

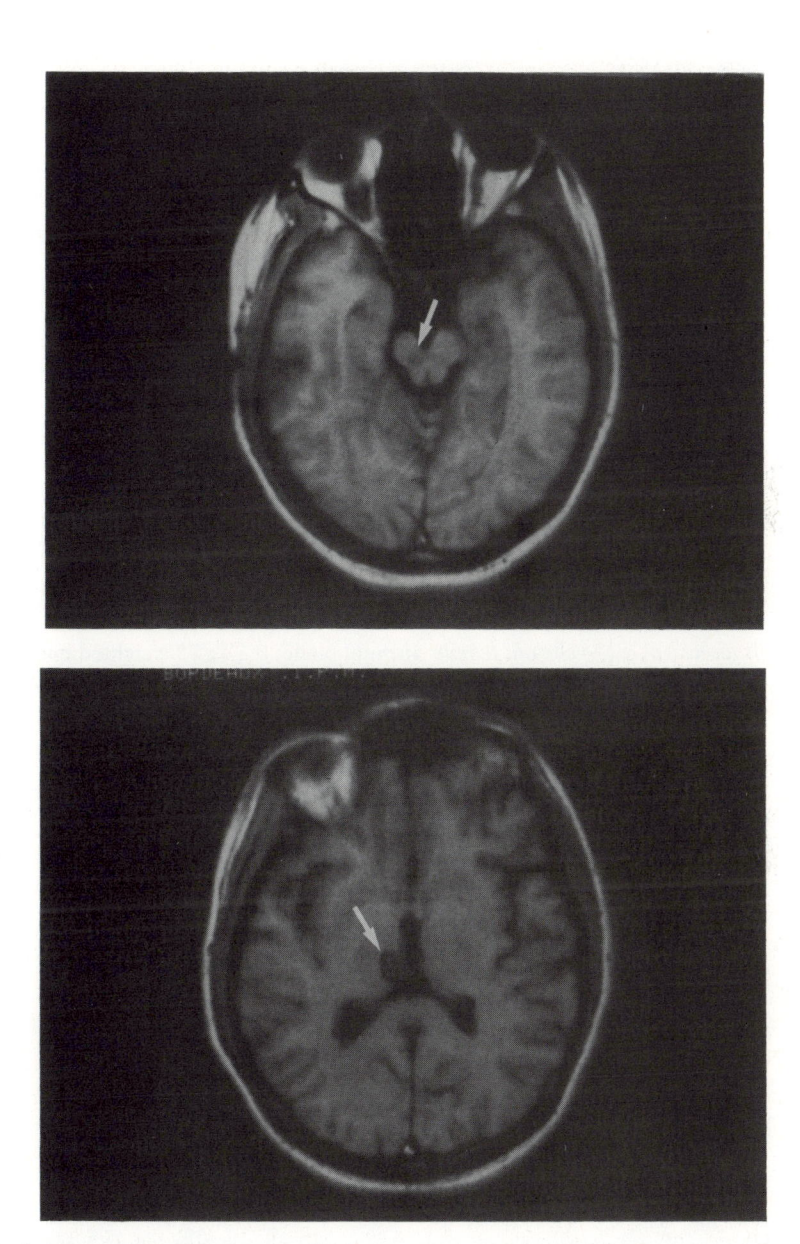

Fig. 6. *Left hemidyskinesia of upper limb in a 27-year-old male (saggital and axial planes).* T1-weighted images. Infarct in the territory of right posterior choroidal artery, with unilateral abnormal signal of (a) medial part of the cerebral peduncle, and (b) subthalamic nucleus and medial thalamic regions.

observations. It has been demonstrated using positron emission tomography that clinical manifestations are caused by biochemical alterations preceding morphological changes.[16] However, an increase or decrease of signal in T2-weighted images demonstrates a structural abnormality, probably caused by an abnormal metal deposit (copper in Wilson's disease, iron in Hallervorden-Spatz syndrome).[3,17–19]

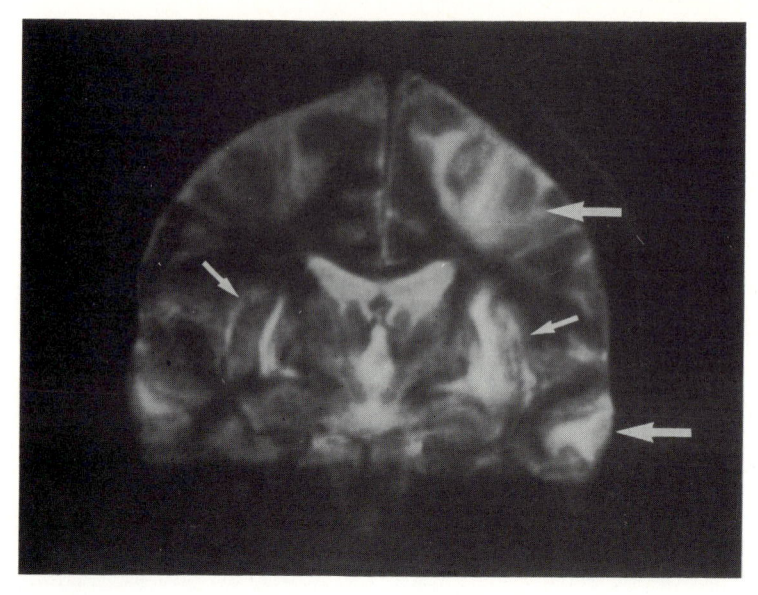

Fig. 7. *Wilson's disease in a 15-year-old female.* Frontal plane, 0.5 T, T2-weighted image (2000/60, echo 2). Bilateral increase of signal in the striatum (→) (putamen and pallidum), leucoencephalopathy (➔).

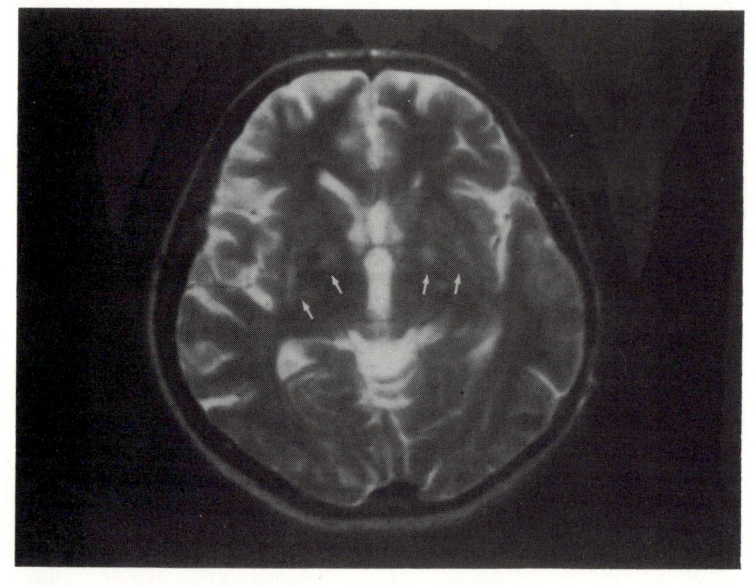

Fig. 8. *Asymmetric dystonic syndrome in a 54-year-old female.* Axial transverse plane, 0.5 T. T2-weighted increase of signal in the striatum, bilaterally (→).

Difficulties in clinical classification and the small number of patients led us to simplify the common classifications to correlate the movement disorders to anatomical lesions.[3] Parkinson's disease is a complex multifactorial degenerative disease,[9] associated with the degeneration of dopaminergic neurons of the locus niger and associated brainstem nuclei, without macroscopic atrophy.[10] This aspect of the extrapyramidal structures is normal in our study, as previously reported.[4] In other reports, focal abnormalities of the locus niger and of the striatum were noted (decrease of the signal in T2-weighted images), but were not convincing.[20-22] With high field strength, Rutledge reported a 'restoration of the signal' in the locus niger, but not differing significantly from normal controls.[3] In our study, we noted no specific signal changes in parkinsonian patients.

In our two patients presenting with toxic parkinsonism (neuroleptic-induced) there were no focal abnormalites.

Multisystem degeneration (supranuclear palsy, OPCA, Shy-Drager syndrome) presented with evident morphological changes, even in early cases, as previously described.[3,5,6,23] MR images in our patients with OPCA and Shy-Drager syndrome are similar, without a signal reduction in the pallidum (except in two cases).

There are often signal changes in the striatum on T2-weighted images suggesting that atypical akinetic-rigid syndromes are caused by a degeneration of the striatum (four of our six cases). These signal changes observed in atypical akinetic-rigid syndromes are helpful in differentiating degenerative diseases (neuroaxonal dystrophy, striato-pallidal degeneration ...) from tumours, multiple sclerosis, and vascular lesions.

Huntington's disease is well-recognized, clinically and radiologically.[3,24,25] We observed in two of our four patients an increase of the signal in the putamen, associated with an atrophic appearance of this structure in T2-weighted images. Signal changes are caused by atrophy of the putamen and probably, in part, by abnormal deposits. With high-field MRI, others described a decreased signal in the striatum.[3]

Symptomatic choreic syndromes are clinically and histopathologically heterogeneous. Choreic disorders of vascular origin due to a lesion in the brainstem give a signal reduction in T1-weighted sequences, and an increase in T2-weighted ones, with a better definition than CT scan. In a few cases with no recognized cause, MRI shows heterogeneities of the striatum of unknown origin (2/6 cases in our study). Aside from the differential diagnosis of tumours, there is some improvement in the exploration of idiopathic choreas using MRI, which can reveal a 'degenerative aspect' of the striatum, an appearance which has no histopathological correlation for the time being.

Wilson's disease is a genopathy and consists of an accumulation of copper in the brain, liver, and cornea. The neuroradiological exploration, with CT-scan,[26,27] and with MRI,[17,18,27] shows abnormalities in the region of the basal ganglia, hypodense on CT-scans, hyperintense on MRI in T2-weighted sequences (low and mild field-strength). There are associated lesions such as cortical atrophy, ventricular dilatation, brainstem atrophy, and leucoencephalopathy. Asymmetrical leucoencephalopathy is an MRI discovery in certain patients (4/24 in Aisen's series[18] and 1/3 in our study). Others found no lesions in white matter.[17,27]

Dystonias are of different origins. Neonatal injuries may produce anatomical changes detected by MRI[3] but without signal changes in the striatum as in our three cases. Secondary dystonias of unknown origin are associated in some cases with other symptoms like rigidity (three cases) with a progressive course. In 3/6 cases, we found increased signal in both putamens. Of three other patients with sudden onset (probable vascular origin), one had lacunar infarction demonstrated with MRI, but not with CT scan. Others have reported increased signal in the striatum closely associated with secondary vascular dystonias.[3]

In conclusion, MRI is a helpful technique in the investigation of movement disorders. The sensitivity in detecting morphological changes of the extrapyramidal system is better than that of CT. Abnormal deposits in the striatum in some pathological states such as degenerative disorders of the basal ganglia or metabolic inherited diseases can be revealed by the MRI signal changes that they induce.

References

1. Drayer, B., Burger, P., Darwin, R., Riederer, S., Herfkens, R. & Johnson, G. A. (1986): Magnetic resonance imaging of brain iron. *AJNR* **7**, 373–380.
2. Bradley, W. G. (1986): Pathophysiologic correlates of signal alterations. In *Magnetic resonance imaging of the central nervous system*, eds M. Brant-Zawadzki & D. Norman, pp 23–42. New York: Raven Press.
3. Rutledge, J. N., Hilal, S. K., Silver, A. J., Defendini, R. & Fahn, S. (1987): Study of movement disorders and brain iron by MR. *AJNR* **8**, 397–411.
4. Lukes, S. A., Aminoff, M. J., Crooks, L., Kaufman, L., Mills, C. & Newton, T. H. (1983): Nuclear magnetic resonance imaging in movement disorders. *Ann. Neurol.* **13**, 690–691.
5. Pastakia, B., Polinsky, R., Di Chiro, G., Simmons, J. T., Brown, R. & Wener L. (1986): Multiple system atrophy (Shy-Drager Syndrome): MR imaging. *Radiology* **159**, 499–502.
6. Drayer, B. P., Olanow, W., Burger, P., Johnson, G. A., Herfkens, R. & Riederer S. (1986): Parkinson plus syndrome: diagnosis using high-field MR imaging of brain iron. *Radiology* **159**, 493–498.
7. Norfray, J. F., Couch, J. R., Elble, R. J., Good, D. C., Manyam, B. V. & Patrick, J. L. (1988): Visualization of brain iron by mid-field MR. *AJNR* **9**, 77–82.
8. Denny-Brown (1975): Clinical symptomatology of disease of basal ganglia. In *Handbook of clinical neurology*, Vol. 6, eds J. P. Vinken & G. W. Bruyn, pp 133–172. Amsterdam: Elsevier.
9. Barbeau, A. (1986): Parkinson's disease: clinical features and etiopathology. In *Handbook of clinical neurology*, vol. 5, eds P. J. Vinken, G. W. Bruyn & H. L. Klawans, pp 87–152. Amsterdam: Elsevier.
10. Jellinger, K. (1986): Overview of morphological changes in Parkinson's disease. *Adv. Neurol.* **45**, 1–15.
11. Gray, F. (1988): Neuropathologie des syndromes parkinsoniens. *Rev. Neurol. (Paris)*, **144**, 229–248.
12. Zeman, W. & Whitlock, C. C. (1968): Symptomatic dystonias. In: *Handbook of neurology*, Vol. 6, eds P. J. Vinken & G. W. Bruyn, pp 544–566. Amsterdam: Elsevier.
13. Marsden, C. D., Obeso, J. A. Zarranz, J. J. & Lang, A. E. (1985): The anatomical basis of symptomatic hemidystonia. *Brain* **108**, 463–483.
14. Bruyn, G. W. & Went, L. N. (1986): Huntington's chorea. In *Handbook of clinical neurology*, vol. 5, eds P. J. Vinken, G. W. Bruyn & H. L. Klawans, pp 267–314. Amsterdam: Elsevier.
15. Pettigrew, L. C. & Jankovic, J. (1985): Hemidystonia: a report of 22 patients and a review of the literature. *J. Neurol. Neurosurg. Psychiatry* **48**, 650–657.
16. Calne, D. B. & Wayne-Martin, W. R. (1986): Chemistry of the basal ganglia. In *Handbook of clinical neurology*, vol. 5, eds P. J. Vinken, G. W. Bruyn & H. L. Klawans. Amsterdam: Elsevier.
17. Lawler, G. A., Pennock, J. M., Steiner, R. E., Jenkins, W. J., Sherlock, S. & Young, I. R. (1983): Nuclear magnetic resonance (NMR) imaging in Wilson disease. *J. Comput. Assist. Tomogr.* **7**, 1–8.
18. Aisen, A. M., Martel, W., Gabrielsen, T. O., Glazer, G. M., Brewer, G., Young, A. B. & Hill, G. (1985): Wilson's disease of the brain: MR imaging. *Radiology* **157**, 137–141.
19. Littrup, P. J. & Gebarski, S. S. (1985): MR Imaging of Hallervorden-Spatz disease. *J. Comput. Assist. Tomogr.* **9**, 491–493.
20. Duguid, J. R., De La Paz, R. & DeGroot, J. (1986): Magnetic resonance imaging of the midbrain in Parkinson's disease. *Ann. Neurol.* **20**, 744–747.
21. Agnoli, A., Galluci, M., Fabbrini, G., Feliciani, M., Ruggieri, S. & Conti. F. (1986): MRI study on Parkinson's disease in relation to the severity of the disease. *Neurology*, vol. 45, pp 103–106. New York: Raven Press.
22. Norfray, J. F., Chiaradonna, N. L., Heiser, W. J., Song, S. H., Manyam, B. V., Devleschoward, A. B. & Eastwood, L. M. (1988): Brain iron in patients with Parkinson disease: MR visualization using gradient modification. *AJNR* **9**, 237–240.
23. Ambrosetto, P., Michelucci, R., Forti, A. & Tassinari, C. A. (1984): CT findings in progressive supranuclear palsy. *J. Comput. Assist. Tomogr.* **8**, 406–409.
24. Stober, T., Wussow, W. & Schimrigk, K. (1984): Bicaudate diameter – the most specific and simple CT parameter in the diagnosis of Huntington's disease. *Neuroradiol.* **26**, 25–28.

25 Simmons, J. T., Pastakia, B., Chase, T. N. & Shults, C. W. (1986): Magnetic resonance imaging in Huntington disease. *AJNR* **7**, 25–28.
26 Williams, F. J. B. & Walshet, M. (1981): Wilson's disease: analysis of the cranial computerized tomographic appearances found in 60 patients and the changes in responses to treatment with chelating agents. *Brain* **104**, 735–752.
27 Metzer, W. S. & Angtuaco, E. (1986): Long-term follow-up Computed Tomography and Magnetic Resonance Imaging findings in hepatolenticular degeneration: Case report and summary of the literature. In *Movement disorders*. Vol. 1, pp 145–149.

53

CEREBRAL GLUCOSE METABOLISM IN PARKINSON'S DISEASE AND THE PD COMPLEX OF GUAM

R. F. Peppard, W. R. W. Martin, M. Guttman,
E. Grochoswki*, J. Okada*, P. L. McGeer[†], G. D. Carr[§],
A. G. Phillips[§], J. C. Steele[‡], J. K. C. Tsui
and D. B. Calne.

*Department of Medicine, *UBC/TRIUMF Program on Positron Emission Tomography, [†]Kinsmen Laboratory of Neurological Research, University of British Columbia, Vancouver, BC, Canada; [§]Department of Psychology, Simon Fraser University, Burnaby, BC, Canada; and [‡]Guam, USA*

Summary

Using positron emission tomography (PET) with ^{18}F-2-fluoro-2-deoxyglucose (FDG), regional cerebral glucose metabolism (LCMR-gl) was assessed in 16 patients with Parkinson's disease (mean age 76.1 years) and eight patients with the parkinsonism-dementia complex of Guam (mean age 58.5 years). Most patients had moderately severe parkinsonism (Hoehn & Yahr stage 3,4 or 5). Mental status ranged from apparently normal to severe dementia. The severity of the parkinsonian motor features was graded by modified Columbia scale. Detailed neuropsychological examination was performed. The results were compared with age-matched groups of normal controls and Alzheimer disease patients (mean age 70.4 years). The pattern of glucose hypometabolism seen in the patients with at least moderately severe intellectual impairment resembled that found in Alzheimer's disease patients: there was a global decrease in glucose metabolism with prominent abnormalities observed in the parietal lobes. LCMR-gl was decreased slightly more in the basal ganglia region and the thalamus in the patients with parkinsonism compared with the Alzheimer disease patients. Hypometabolism in the cortical regions of interest correlated with the severity of mental changes as graded by the Jacobs cognitive capacity screening examination. Parkinson's disease patients with normal neuropsychological testing showed modest widespread glucose hypometabolism. There were no demented patients with Parkinson's disease of Guamanian PD complex who did not have significant widespread cortical hypometabolism. These results suggest the importance of cortical abnormalities in the development of dementia with Parkinson's disease.

Introduction

Although Parkinson's disease is characterized by brainstem pathology and Alzheimer's disease by cortical changes, there has been recent interest in the clinical, morphological and biochemical overlap of these conditions.[1-3] Dementia is the predominant abnormality in Alzheimer's disease, Pick's disease and other cortical neuronal degenerations. Dementia in combination with a movement disorder is seen in degenerative diseases which also involve subcortical structures, such as Huntington's disease, Parkinson's disease, progressive supranuclear palsy, and the parkinsonism-dementia complex of Guam. In these diseases, the relative importance of cortical and subcortical degeneration to the development of dementia is controversial.

In Alzheimer's disease, there is prominent cortical pathology with abundant neurofibrillary tangles and neuritic plaques, neuronal cell loss and decreased somatostatin. Many demented patients with Parkinson's disease have similar changes.[4,5] On the other hand, up to 50 per cent of Alzheimer patients also have subcortical neuronal loss and Lewy bodies affecting the cells of the substantia nigra. Usually these pathological changes are milder than those seen in Parkinson's disease and they are often not associated with a history of clinical parkinsonism.[6]

Subcortical lesions involving the basal forebrain-cortical cholinergic system are believed to play an important role in the development of the cognitive deficits in Alzheimer's disease.[7-13] Cell loss from the nucleus basalis of Meynert has also been described in Parkinson's disease and the parkinsonism-dementia of Guam.[14-16] Dopaminergic underactivity in the mesocortical (substantia nigra-caudate-pallidum-thalamus-cortex) or mesolimbic (ventral tegmental area-ventral striatum-limbic cortex) systems may also contribute to the development of dementia in these disorders.[17] Cell loss from the locus coeruleus and abnormalities of noradrenaline metabolism have been reported in Parkinson's disease and may contribute to the development of dementia.[18]

There has also been interest in the clinical overlap of these diseases. Rigidity and akinesia are often associated with severe intellectual decline in Alzheimer's disease.[6] Moderate to severe dementia is found in up to 35 per cent of patients with Parkinson's disease.[19-21] The determinants of this intellectual deterioration are not yet settled.

The concept of subcortical dementia has been introduced to describe the pattern of mental impairment which occurs in disorders in which the predominant pathology involves subcortical structures.[22] Subcortical dementia is characterized by forgetfulness, slowing of thought processes (bradyphrenia), apathy or depression, impaired ability to manipulate acquired knowledge and absence of aphasia, apraxia or agnosia which are said to be hallmarks of cortical lesions as in Alzheimer's disease.

The pathological features of the parkinsonism-dementia complex of Guam are neuronal loss and marked neurofibrillary change involving the cerebral cortex, the nucleus basalis of Meynert, the basal ganglia, thalamus, locus coeruleus and substantia nigra.[23] Thus both cortical and subcortical degeneration occur and there are clinical and pathological features in common with Alzheimer's and Parkinson's diseases. Understanding of the pathogenesis of this condition may be useful as a model for other neurodegenerative diseases.

Measurement of cortical glucose metabolism with positron emission tomography (PET) provides a method to assess the severity and distribution of cortical pathology *in vivo*. In Alzheimer's disease, LCMR-gl is reduced compared with age-matched controls with the most marked differences occurring in the parietal cortex followed by the temporal and frontal regions. Primary somatosensory and visual cortex, thalamus, basal ganglia and cerebellum are relatively spared. In early dementia there are mild, focal decreases while, in severe dementia, there is more widespread severe hypometabolism.[24-26]

We have studied cerebral glucose metabolism in patients with Parkinson's disease,

Alzheimer's disease and the parkinsonism-dementia complex of Guam. Our aims were to determine the relationship between LCMR-gl and indices of parkinsonism and cognitive impairment, to determine whether cortical LCMR-gl changes occur in the absence of clinical evidence of cognitive impairment, and to compare the pattern of LCMR-Gl in these conditions.

Patients and methods

Cerebral glucose metabolism was studied using PET and ^{18}F-2-fluoro-2-deoxyglucose (FDG) in 16 patients with Parkinson's disease, eight patients with the parkinsonism-dementia complex of Guam, 14 patients with AD and 12 normal subjects.

Assessment of the patients with Parkinson's disease and parkinsonism-dementia complex of Guam included neurological examination with grading of the severity of parkinsonian motor features by modified Columbia scale and a battery of neuropsychological tests. X-ray computerized tomography (CT) or magnetic resonance imaging (MRI) head scans were performed in all patients. In the Parkinson's disease and Guamanian patients, the indices of cognitive function which were used for correlation with the PET scan results were the Jacob's Cognitive Capacity Screening Examination (Jacob's test), the WAIS and the WMS. A score from 0 (normal) to 10 (severe dementia) was devised based on the results from these tests.

Patients with a clinical diagnosis of Parkinson's disease and with intellectual functioning ranging from apparently normal to severe dementia were selected. Patients were included only if their cognitive abnormalities were not attributable to drug toxicity or any cause other than Parkinson's disease. None had acute confusion, hallucinations, psychosis or major depression at the time of assessment.

One patient had mild parkinsonism (Hoehn & Yahr stage 2) and the other 15 had moderate to severe parkinsonism (Hoehn & Yahr stage 3,4 or 5). After detailed neuropsychological assessment, the 16 Parkinson's disease patients were divided into two groups of eight each according to whether their cognitive functioning was considered intact or impaired. The group with intact cognition had a mean age of 61.7 years, mean Columbia score of 23.2 and mean Jacob's score of 27.2. The group with impaired cognition had a mean age of 72.5 years, mean Columbia score of 34.5 and mean Jacob's score of 18.6. In this group, there were three patients with early or isolated intellectual deficits who were still functioning well, two with mild dementia, two with moderate dementia and one with severe dementia.

Guamanian subjects with the parkinsonism-dementia complex were examined and recruited by JS and DBC on Guam and came to Vancouver for full assessment and scanning. The Guamanian group had a mean age of 58.5 years, mean Columbia score of 38 and mean Jacob's score of 17. There were two patients with mild or isolated cognitive impairments, two with mild dementia, and four with moderately severe dementia.

From the Clinic for Alzheimer's disease and Related Disorders at UBC, 14 patients who had been evaluated with full medical, neurological, neuropsychological examination and who had had CT, MRI and PET FDG scans were selected for comparison with the parkinsonian patients. Eleven of these patients met NINCDS-ADRDA criteria[27] for the clinical diagnosis of probable Alzheimer's disease; three had come to autopsy and were classified as definite Alzheimer's. All had Hachinski ischaemic scores of less than 5.[28] Their mean age was 70.2 years. After these diagnostic and age-matching criteria had been met, patients with relatively mild dementia were chosen in order to be as similar as possible to the demented subjects with Parkinson's disease.

Positron emission tomography was performed with the UBC/TRIUMF PETT VI system. LCMR-gl was calculated from the uptake of FDG as described by Phelps and associates.[29] The system gives a seven slice image with centre to centre separation of 14 mm. Two scans are performed after injection of 3–8 milliCuries of FDG. By moving the patient's head axially between these two scans and interleaving the reconstructed images, 14 transverse slices with centre to centre separation of 7 mm were obtained.

Regular regions of interest (ROI) of fixed size and shape were placed along the cortical mantle on each successive slice guided by an atlas of axial tomographic anatomy with adjustments in placement according to the appearance of brain size and variation in head positioning from the orbito-meatal line. For large cortical areas and the cerebellum, the volume weighted mean of the activities of individual ROI from adjacent sites within slices and between consecutive slices was obtained to give a larger sample of activity for these areas. In this way LCMR-gl values were obtained for prefrontal, perirolandic (pericentral), inferior parietal, lateral temporal, medial temporal and medial occipital areas. For smaller, subcortical structures (thalamus, caudate and putamen) LCMR-gl was determined from ROI placed over the appropriate area of maximum activity on the slice which showed maximum activity for that structure. The appearances are shown in Fig. 1.

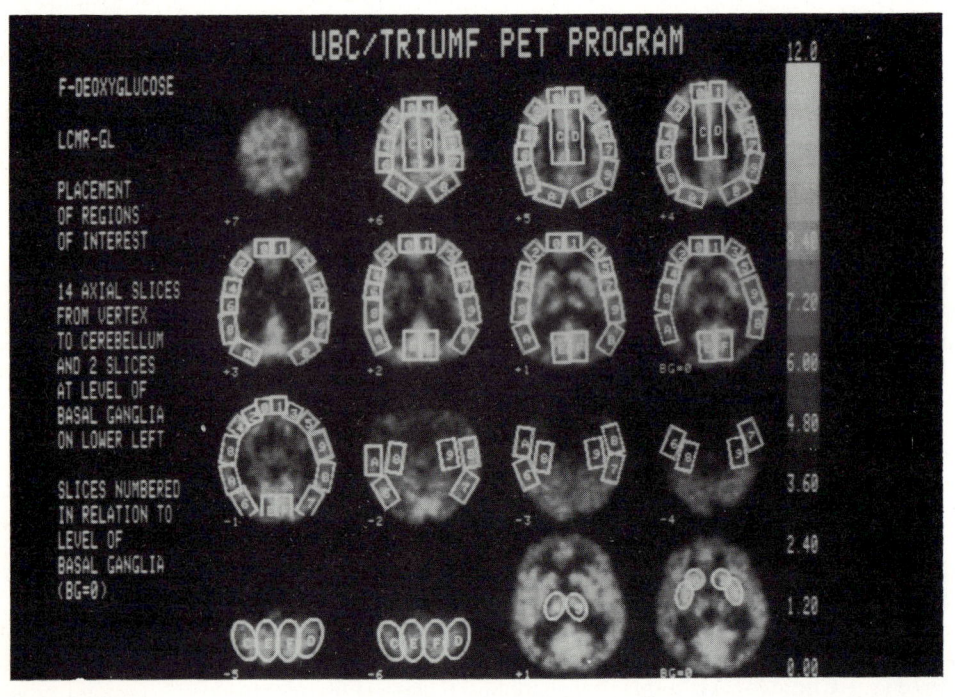

Fig. 1. *Positron emission tomography (PET) scans with ^{18}F-deoxyglucose showing placement of regions of interest.*

Results

LCMR-gl was significantly reduced ($P < 0.005$, Student's t-test) in 10 of 12 cortical regions, caudate and cerebellum in Parkinson's disease with intact cognition *versus* age-matched normals. LCMR-GL in putamen and thalamus was not significantly decreased.

In Parkinson's disease with impaired cognition *versus* age-matched normals, there was a significant decrease ($P < 0.005$) in all cortical regions, and in caudate, left thalamus and cerebellum. Mean activities in the putamen and right thalamus were not significantly decreased.

In the Alzheimer's disease patients compared with age-matched normals, significant decrease ($P < 0.005$) was found in 10 of 12 cortical regions and in the right cerebellar hemisphere. Mean activities in the caudate, putamen and thalamus were not significantly decreased.

The means of activities in all cortical and subcortical ROI were significantly reduced in the group of patients with the Guamanian parkinsonism-dementia complex.

In the 14 patients with Parkinson's disease and 11 with Alzheimer's disease who had CT scans available, cortical atrophy was graded 0 (normal), 1 (mild), 2 (moderate), and 3 (severe). On this scale the mean cortical atrophy in the Parkinson's disease patients was 1.86 and in the Alzheimer's disease patients, 1.91.

Fig. 2. shows the appearances in patients with Alzheimer's disease and Parkinson's disease compared with a normal control.

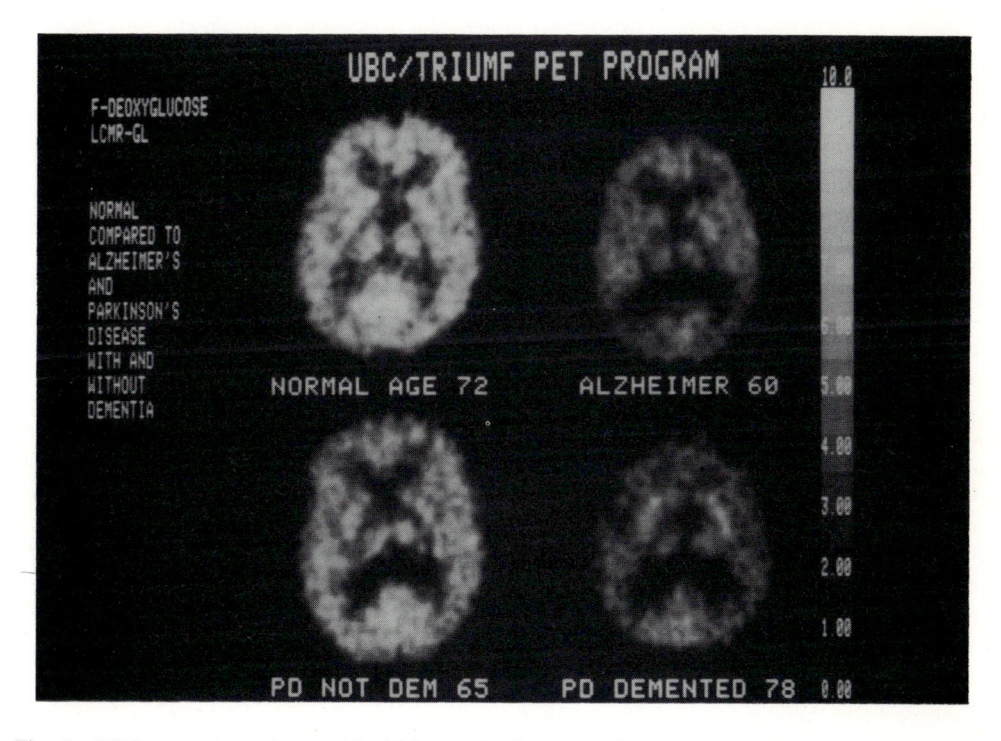

Fig. 2. *PET scans in patients with Alzheimer's disease and Parkinson's disease with and without dementia compared to a normal control.*

Discussion

Though the Alzheimer's and Parkinson's disease groups were approximately matched for age and cortical atrophy, there were difficulties in matching them for the severity of dementia because of problems in determining the relative contributions of cognitive and motor disabilities to decline in social and occupational functioning and neuropsychological test performance. Matching is also made difficult by the heterogeneous course and manifestations of these conditions.[30] Several patients who were in the early stages of intellectual deterioration but were recognized as having Parkinson's disease because of their motor manifestations were difficult to match with patients with Alzheimer's disease because of the diagnostic uncertainty inherent in the early detection of a condition which manifests initially in cognitive functioning only. Moreover the clinical nosology of these diseases is arbitrary, in that one of the exclusion criteria for each is the exclusion of the other diagnosis.[27]

Glucose metabolism in cerebral tissue is probably largely determined by synaptic activity because of the large surface area/volume at these sites which are actively involved in maintaining the electrical gradient across the neuronal membrane. Energy hypometabolism could reflect loss of cortical neurons, the failure of increased dendritic branching, which normally occurs as a compensation for the age-related loss of cortical neurons, or loss of excitatory subcortical influences. Because the spatial resolution of PET does not allow delineation of sulcal patterns or ventricular margins or distinction between white matter and grey matter in the gyri, different components of brain tissue and CSF contribute to the measured activity of a region. Thus cerebral atrophy may lead to apparent reductions in measured metabolic rates.[32] The similar mean global atrophy rates between patients with Parkinson's disease and Alzheimer's disease suggests that metabolic comparisons between these two groups can be made without correction for atrophy.

In Parkinson's disease it has previously been described that global cortical hypometabolism is more severe in demented patients.[33,34] Furthermore, a demented patient with Parkinson's disease with marked parietal hypometabolism resembling that seen in Alzheimer's disease has been reported.[33] We believe our work confirms and extends these previous observations.

Despite the selective nature of the pathological process in Parkinson's disease, we found widespread glucose hypometabolism across the cortical and subcortical regions in patients who were cognitively intact on detailed neuropsychological testing. The cognitively impaired Parkinson's disease group shows more marked hypometabolism in the cortical regions but in the striatum there is little difference between the two Parkinson groups.

The pattern of cortical hypometabolism in parkinsonism resembles that in Alzheimer's disease, but the degree of hypometabolism in the striatum and thalamus relative to the cortical changes was greater in the Parkinson's disease group compared to the Alzheimer patients. The pattern and degree of metabolic abnormality in the parkinsonism-dementia of Guam and the cognitively-impaired Parkinson's disease group were similar for the cerebral cortex and the cerebellum. However, there was more marked hypometabolism in the striatum and thalamus in the Guamanians. These changes suggest the importance of cortical metabolic dysfunction in the dementia associated with Parkinson's disease and the parkinsonism-dementia of Guam.

References

1 Ball, M. J. (1984): The morphological basis of dementia in Parkinson's disease. *Can. J. Neurol. Sci.* **11**, 180–184.
2 Boller, F., Mizutani, T., Roesmann, U. & Gambetti, P. (1980): Parkinson disease, dementia and Alzheimer's disease: clinicopathological correlations. *Ann. Neurol.* **7**, 329–335.
3 Calne, D. B., Eisen, A., McGeer, E. & Spencer, P. (1986): Alzheimer's disease, Parkinson's disease, and motorneurone disease: abiotrophies with similar causal mechanisms? *Lancet* **ii**, 1067–1070.
4 Hakim, A. M. & Mathieson, G. (1979): Dementia in Parkinson disease. *Neurology* **29**, 1209–1214.

5 Alvord, E. C., Forno, L. S., Kusske, J. A., Kauffman, R. J., Rhodes, J. S. & Goetowski, C. R. (1974): The pathology of parkinsonism: a comparison of degenerations in cerebral cortex and brainstem. In Second Canadian-American Conference on Parkinson's disease. Ed. F. McDowell & A. Barbeau. *Advances in Neurology*, vol. 5, pp 175–193. New York: Raven Press.
6 Ditter, S. M. & Mirra, S. S. (1987): Neuropathologic and clinical features of Parkinson's disease in Alzheimer's disease patients. *Neurology* **37**, 754–760.
7 Davies, P. & Maloney, A. J. F. (1976): Selective loss of central cholinergic neurons in Alzheimer's disease. *Lancet* **ii**, 1403.
8 Perry, E. K., Perry, R. H., Blessed, G. & Tomlinson, B. E. (1977): Necropsy evidence of central cholinergic deficits in senile dementia. *Lancet* **i**, 189.
9 Wilcock, G. K., Esiri, M. M., Bowen, D. M. & Smith, C. C. T. (1982): Alzheimer's disease: correlation of cortical CAT activity with the severity of dementia and histological abnormalities. *J. Neurol. Sci.* **57**, 407–417.
10 Whitehouse, P., Price, D. L., Stribble, R. G., Clark, A. W., Coyle, J. T. & DeLong, M. R. (1982): Alzheimer's disease and senile dementia: loss of neurons in the basal forebrain. *Science* **215**, 1237–1239.
11 McGeer, P. L., McGeer, E. G., Suzuki, J., Dolman, C. E. & Nagai, T. (1984): Aging, Alzheimer's disease and the cholinergic system of the basal forebrain. *Neurology* **34**, 741–5.
12 Richter, J. A., Perry, E. K. & Tomlinson, B. E. (1980): Decreased acetylcholine content in Alzheimer's disease. *Life Sci* **26**, 1683–1689.
13 McGeer, E. G., McGeer, P. L., Kamo, H., Tago, H. & Harrop, R. (1986): Cortical metabolism, acetylcholinesterase staining and pathological changes in Alzheimer's disease. *Can. J. Neurol. Sci.* **13**, 511–516.
14 Perry, R. H., Tomlinson, B. E., Candy, J. M., Blessed, G., Foster, J. F., Boxham, C. A. & Perry, E. K. (1983): Cortical cholinergic deficit in mentally impaired parkinsonian patients. *Lancet* **ii**, 789–790.
15 Whitehouse, P. J., Hedreen, J. C., White, C. L. & Price, D. L. (1983): Basal forebrain neurons in the dementia of Parkinson disease. *Ann. Neurol.* **13**, 243–248.
16 Nakano, I. & Hirano, A. (1983): Neuron loss in the nucleus basalis of Meynert in parkinsonism-dementia complex of Guam. *Ann. Neurol.* **13**, 87–91.
17 Javoy-Agid, F. & Agid, Y. (1980): Is the mesocortical dopaminergic system involved in Parkinson's disease? *Neurology* **30**, 1326–1330.
18 Hornykiewicz, O. & Kish, S. J. (1984): Neurochemical basis of dementia in Parkinson's disease. *Can. J. Neurol. Sci.* **11**, Suppl. 1, 185–190.
19 Liebermann, A., Dziatolowski, M., Coopersmith, M., Cerb, M., Goodgold, A., Lorein, J. & Goldstein, M. (1979): Dementia in Parkinson's disease. *Ann. Neurol.* **6**, 355–359.
20 Mayeux, R. & Stern, Y. (1983): Intellectual dysfunction and dementia in Parkinson disease. In *The dementias*, ed R. Mayeux & W. G. Rosen, pp 211–227. New York: Raven Press.
21 Brown, R. G. & Marsden, C. D. (1987): Neuropsychology and cognitive function in Parkinson's disease. In *Movement disorders*, BIMR Neurology vol. 6, eds C. D. Marsden & S. Fahn, pp 99–123. London: Butterworths.
22 Albert, M. L. (1978): Subcortical dementia. In *Alzheimer's disease: senile dementia and related disorders*, eds R. Katzman, R. D. Terry, & K. L. Bick, pp 173–180. New York: Raven Press.
23 Hirano, A., Malamud, N. & Kurland, L. T. (1961): Parkinsonism-dementia complex, an endemic disease on the island of Guam. 1. Pathological features. *Brain* **84**, 662–679.
24 Chase, T. N., Foster, N. L., Fedio, P., Brooks, R., Mansi, L. & Di Chiro, G. (1984): Regional cortical dysfunction in Alzheimer's disease as determined by positron emission tomography. *Ann. Neurol.* **15** (suppl), S170–S174.
25 Duara, R., Grady, C., Haxby, J., Sundaram, M., Cutler, N. R., Heston, L., Moore, A., Schlageter, N., Larson, S. & Rapoport, S. I. (1986): Positron emission tomography in Alzheimer's disease. *Neurology* **36**, 879–887.
26 McGeer, P. L., Kamo, H., Harrop, R., Li, D. K. B., Tuokko, H., McGeer, E. G., Adam, M. J., Amman, W., Beattie, B. L., Calne, D. B., Martin, W. R. W., Pate, B. D., Rogers, J. G., Ruth, T. J., Sayre, C. I. & Stoessl, A. J. (1986): Positron emission tomography in patients with clinically diagnosed Alzheimer's disease. *Can. Med. Assoc. J.* **134**, 597–607.
27 McKhann, G., Drachman, D., Folstein, M., Price, D. & Stadlan, E. (1984): Clinical diagnosis

Department of Health and Human Services Task Force on Alzheimer's disease. *Neurology* **34**, 939–944.
28 Hachinski, V. C., Iliff, L. D., Phil, M., Kilhka, E., Du Boulay, G. H., McAllister, V. L., Marshall, J., Ross Russell, R. W. & Symon, L. (1975): Cerebral blood flow in dementia. *Arch. Neurol.* **32**,632–637.
29 Phelps, M. E., Huang, S. C., Hoffman, E. J., Selin, C., Sokoloff, L. & Kuhl, D. E. (1979): Tomographic measurement of local cerebral glucose metabolic rate in humans with (F-18)2-fluoro-2-deoxyglucose: validation of method. *Ann. Neurol.* **6**, 371–388.
30 Pillon, B., Dubois, B., Lhermitte, F. & Agid, Y. (1986): Heterogeneity of cognitive impairment in progressive supranuclear palsy, Parkinson's disease, and Alzheimer's disease. *Neurology* **36**, 1179–1185.

INDEX

A8 cell group   8, 51
A9 cell group   8, 51, 162
A10 cell group   8, 51
acetylcholine   99, 259
acetylcholinesterase   7, 186, 328
afterhyperpolarization   75
akathisia   257
akathisia, tardive   255
akinesia   135, 146, 162, 175, 387, 446
Alzheimer's disease   259, 287, 427, 446
amfonelic acid   83
amphetamine   83, 196, 218, 134
amygdaloid nucleus   11, 46, 64
apomorphine   136, 159, 160, 171, 184, 196, 230, 240, 274
atropine   198
autonomic failure   419

ballism   124, 146, 256
basal nucleus of Meynert   272, 446
benzodiazepine receptors   167, 337
benztropine   83
bereitschaftspotential   301
bicuculline   38, 125
botulinum toxin   260
bradykinesia   135, 214, 307, 319, 387
[76]Br-bromolisuride   186
butyrophenones   136
bromocriptine   223, 252, 274

calcium binding protein   46
carbachol   130, 196
caudate nucleus   3, 18, 30, 64, 82, 90, 112, 137, 148, 158, 175, 184, 218, 238, 329, 338, 420, 434
cerebral glucose metabolism   445
choline acetyltransferase   7, 46, 130, 238, 272
cholinergic striatal interneurons   4, 18, 162, 330
chorea   129, 146, 183
chorea-acanthocytosis   347
clonazepam   257
clonidine   257
corollary discharges   307
cortex, cerebral   184, 288
cortex, cingulate   148, 175

cortex, motor   59, 90, 303
cortex, prefrontal   90, 148
cortex, premotor   56, 127
cortex, primary motor   60, 175
CY-208243   274

dementia   287, 297
2-deoxyglucose (2-DG)   127, 133, 138, 224, 243
2-deoxyglucose, ^{18}F-2-fluoro- (FDG)   447
diazepam binding inhibitor   337
3,4-dihydroxyphenylacetic acid (DOPAC)   90, 208, 225
dopa, ^{18}F   420
dopamine   46, 75, 81, 90, 112, 136, 137, 148, 162, 166, 175, 196, 272, 328, 419
dopamine autoreceptors   208, 230
dopamine receptors   196, 213, 230, 274
dopamine D1 receptors   9, 77, 112, 171, 224, 273, 328, 360
dopamine D2 receptors   9, 112, 186, 207, 224, 373, 328
dopamine DA_e receptors   112
dopamine DA_i receptors   112
dopamine D1 receptor agonists   224, 360
dopamine D2 receptor agonists   207, 214, 224, 360
dopamine D1 receptor antagonists   224, 360
dopamine D2 receptor antagonists   18, 207, 360
dopaminergic neurons   4, 104, 148, 158, 224, 230, 272
doxapram chlorhydrate   184
dynorphin   11, 20
dyskinesia   7, 127, 184
dyskinesia, levodopa-induced   139, 359, 387
dyskinesia, orofacial   113, 360
dyskinesia, peak-dose   140
dyskinesia, tardive   130, 230, 254, 359
dystonia   23, 24, 124, 185, 231, 367, 403, 413, 438
dystonia, tardive   255

Edinger's comb system   104
electroencephalography   376
electromyography   279, 302, 352, 376, 394,
enkephalin   10, 20, 46, 130
entopeduncular nucleus   20, 95, 97, 129, 196
excitotoxin   184

453

Index

fast-blue fluorescent tracer   30
flunitrazepam ligand binding   132, 166
fluorogold tracer   46
fluphenazine   230
frontal eye fields   180

GABA   114, 125, 130, 163, 166, 180, 261
GABAergic striatal efferents   18, 162, 166, 196, 224, 332
GABA/benzodiazepine receptors   19
GABA-glutaraldehyde-lysyl-protein complex   34
GABA receptors   166, 337
gait analysis   320
ganglioside GM-1   272
Gilles de la Tourette disease   11, 257, 347, 403
glial fibrillary acidic protein   186
globus pallidus   20, 30, 90, 106, 126, 158, 175, 184, 196, 238, 434
globus pallidus, medial   7, 125, 158, 167, 240, 338
globus pallidus, lateral   7, 132, 166, 338
glutamate   35, 78, 343
glutamate, carbodiimide-fixed   35
glutamic acid decarboxylase (GAD)   23

habenula, lateral   41
haloperidol   230
harmaline   136
hemiballismus (hemiballism)   42, 124, 131, 200
hemichorea   125, 131, 438
hemiparkinsonism   138, 166, 238, 387
hippocampus   64
homovanillic acid (HVA)   90, 208
Huntington's disease   10, 17, 129, 132, 183, 243, 256, 328, 337, 343, 359, 436, 446
Huntington's disease, juvenile onset   24, 256
HW-165   230
6-hydroxydopamine (6-OHDA)   136, 171, 196, 217, 224, 272
5-hydroxyindolacetic acid (5-HIAA)   258
3-(3-hydroxyphenyl)-N-n-propylperidine (3-PPP)   207, 230
5-hydroxytryptamine (5-HT)   136, 166, 258, 343
5-hydroxytryptophan (5-HTP)   258
hyperekplexia   261
hyperkinesia   233
hypertonia   135
hypokinesia   135, 214, 387

ibotenic acid   90, 184
internal capsule   106, 126, 410
iron   292, 434

kainic acid   99
kynurenic acid   131, 344

lamina, accessory medullary   33, 104

lamina, external medullary (putamino-pallidal)   33, 132
lamina, internal medullary (interpallidal)   33, 104
lenticular nucleus   29, 131, 438
levodopa   83, 137, 213, 223, 252, 274, 279, 368, 393, 420
levodopa-induced dyskinesia (*see* dyskinesia, levodopa-induced)
Lewey body   135, 288, 419, 446
lisuride   213, 259
locus coeruleus   4, 137, 257, 420, 446
LY-162502   360

M1 (short latency) reflex   278
M2 (long latency) reflex   278
magnetic resonance imaging   438, 447
matrix   4, 20, 45, 104, 111, 328
mazindol   83, 328, 329
median forebrain bundle   82
methylphenidate   83
a-methyl-p-tyrosine   136
1-methyl-4-phenylpyridine (MPP+)   148
1-methyl-4-phenyl-1,2,3,6-tetrahydropyridine (MPTP)   137, 146, 158, 238, 251, 272
MPTP-induced parkinsonism   11, 23, 137, 157, 166, 214, 218, 274, 334
multiple system atrophy   252
muscarinic receptors   8, 238
muscimol   114, 131, 196
muscimol ligand binding   166
myoclonus   258

neuroleptic malignant syndrome   253
neuronal recording   58, 64, 76, 386, 396
neuropeptide Y   130
N-methyl-D-aspartate (NMDA) agonists   21
nomifensine   83, 146
[11]C-nomifensine   400
noradrenaline   136, 137, 166, 257, 390, 420, 446
nuclear yellow fluorescent tracer   30
nucleus accumbens septi   4, 8, 46, 90, 137, 192, 196, 208, 218, 239, 329, 338, 420

olfactory tubercle   4, 9, 90
olivo-ponto-cerebellar atrophy   252

Parkinson's disease   11, 17, 98, 118, 124, 134, 158, 175, 180, 213, 217, 223, 238, 271, 278, 287, 292, 297, 301, 310, 313, 328, 387, 393, 419, 434, 446
parkinsonism   64, 231, 319, 435
parkinsonism, drug induced   251
parkinsonism, juvenile   251
parkinsonism, post-encephalitic   251
parkinsonism-dementia complex of Guam   273, 446
peak-dose dyskinesia (*see* dyskinesia, peak-dose)
pedobarography   319

Index

pedunculopontine nucleus   41, 95, 97, 127, 243
Phaseolus vulgaris-leucoagglutinin (PHA-L)   30, 46
phenothiazines   136
physostigmine   259
picrotoxin   41, 114, 125, 197
piratecam   259
piquindonc   338
positron emission tomography (PET)   184, 396, 420, 446
primidone   259
progressive supranuclear palsy   17, 427, 435, 446
propoxyphene   261
propranolol   397
4-propyl-9-hydroxynaphthoxazine (PHNO)   214
putamen   4, 18, 30, 59, 64, 82, 90, 126, 137, 148, 158, 175, 184, 218, 238, 329, 338, 420, 434

quinolinate   21
quinolinic acid   343
quinpirole   207, 361
quinuclidinyl benzilate (QNB)   238
quisqualate receptors   21
quisqualic acid   91

raphé nucleus   4, 18
reserpine   136, 251
restless legs syndrome   261
reticular formation   98, 104
rigidity   135, 158, 214, 278, 387, 446
RU-242113   274
rubro-olivo-cerebello-rubral loop   136

saccadic eye movements   7, 18, 147, 179, 313
SCH-23390   227, 329, 361
schizophrenia   328
serotonin, (see 5-hydroxytryptamine)
Shy-Drager syndrome   252
single photon emission tomography (SPET)   427
SKF-38393   224, 274, 360
SKF-77434   360
SKF-83566   360
somatostatin   130, 446
somatostatin/neuropeptide Y/NADPH-diaphorase positive interneurons   21, 330
spiperone   137, 274, 361
spiroperidol   329
sterotypy   184
stiff man syndrome   262
striatum   3, 18, 45, 64, 104, 146, 158, 196, 208, 213, 217, 224, 238, 328, 420, 434
striatum, dorsal   90
striatum, ventral   46, 64, 75, 89, 208
striosome   4, 20, 51, 104, 111, 328
substance P   10, 20, 46, 130
substantia nigra   30, 46, 97, 126, 158, 218, 225, 238, 271, 334, 420, 434, 446

substantia nigra, pars compacta   9, 18, 104, 162, 166, 196, 240, 338
substantia nigra, pars reticulata   7, 20, 104, 113, 127, 150, 170, 180, 196, 224, 240, 316
subthalamic nucleus   7, 20, 29, 37, 97, 104, 125, 146, 158, 167, 196, 239
sulpiride   137, 207, 274, 361
superior colliculus   7, 113, 127, 180
supplementary motor area   56, 127, 151, 175, 301
Sydenham's chorea   256
syndrome of the Body of Luys   124

tardive dyskinesia (see dyskinesia, tardive)
tegmentum, ventromedial brainstem   136
tetrabenazine   251
tics   257
tissue autografts, adrenal medulla   217, 272, 328
tissue grafts, dopaminergic   217
tissue grafts, mesencephalic   218
thalamic stimulation   414
thalamotomy   127, 387, 403, 413
thalamus   7, 19, 41, 90, 410, 434
thalamus, centromedian nuclei   127, 387
thalamus, intralaminar nuclei   4, 46, 90
thalamus, midline nuclei   89
thalamus, parafascicular nucleus   89
thalamus, paraventricular nucleus   48
thalamus, ventral anterior nucleus   127, 387
thalamus, ventral intermediate nucleus   386, 393, 413
thalamus, ventral lateral nucleus   127, 175, 386
thalamus, ventral posterior nucleus   386
L-threo-3,4-dihydroxyphenylserine (L-threo-DOPS)   257, 390
tongue protrusions   115, 233
torticollis   136, 351
transdihydrolisuride   230
transferrin binding   292
tremor   386
tremor, essential   394
tremor, in multiple sclerosis   403
tremor, parkinsonian   134, 158, 393, 403, 415
tremor, post-traumatic   394, 403
tremor, postural   214, 403
tryptophan   343
Tylenol   261
tyrosine hydroxylase   9, 158, 272, 328

ubiquitin   288

ventral tegmental area   11, 137

wheat germ agglutinin-horseradish peroxidase conjugate (WGA-HRP)   30, 114, 133
Wilson's disease   17, 438

zona incerta   126

455